Strategic Corporate Social Responsibility

This book is dedicated to:

チャンドラー 泰子
who, every day, embraces the opportunities and navigates
the challenges of globalization.

and to

Chase and Hunter Werther,
who are growing into an increasingly socially responsible world.

Strategic Corporate Social Responsibility

Stakeholders, Globalization, and Sustainable Value Creation

Third Edition

David Chandler
University of Colorado Denver

William B. Werther, Jr.
University of Miami

Los Angeles | London | New Delhi
Singapore | Washington DC

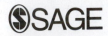

Los Angeles | London | New Delhi
Singapore | Washington DC

FOR INFORMATION:

SAGE Publications, Inc.

2455 Teller Road

Thousand Oaks, California 91320

E-mail: order@sagepub.com

SAGE Publications Ltd.

1 Oliver's Yard

55 City Road

London EC1Y 1SP

United Kingdom

SAGE Publications India Pvt. Ltd.

B 1/I 1 Mohan Cooperative Industrial Area

Mathura Road, New Delhi 110 044

India

SAGE Publications Asia-Pacific Pte. Ltd.

3 Church Street

#10-04 Samsung Hub

Singapore 049483

TABLE OF CONTENTS

LIST OF FIGURES

CSR NEWSLETTERS

The CSR Newsletter is a freely-available resource generated by the authors as a dynamic complement to the text. To sign-up to receive the CSR Newsletter regularly during the fall and spring academic semesters, e-mail author David Chandler at david.chandler@ucdenver.edu.

Chapter 8: Societal Issues and Case-studies

Glossary of Terms

CSR Terms[1]

Consistent definitions, labels, and vocabulary remain elusive and fiercely debated within the field of CSR. As such, the range of competing terminology that is used can be a source of confusion for executives, academics, journalists, and other students of CSR. In our research, for example, we regularly see CSR, as we understand it, referred to in a number of different ways:

- "Corporate responsibility" or "business responsibility"
- "Conscious capitalism" or "sustainable business"
- "Corporate citizenship" or "global business citizenship"
- "Corporate community engagement" or "strategic philanthropy"
- "Sustainability" or "corporate environmental responsibility"
- "Social responsibility" or "corporate social performance" or "corporate social action."

In many cases, writers are using different terms to mean very similar things, yet heated debates can sprout from these semantic subtleties. Rather than engage in this debate, we continue to use the term "corporate social responsibility" due to its widespread diffusion, even though we recognize that different people interpret this term in different ways. In order to clarify some of the confusion and provide a consistent vocabulary with which to read this book, therefore, brief definitions of key CSR concepts are detailed below. These terms are widely discussed in the CSR literature and referred to throughout this book:

CSR—Terminology, Concepts, and Definitions

Accountability: The extent to which a firm attends to the needs and demands of its primary stakeholders (see *Transparency*).

Activism: Actions (e.g., campaigns, boycotts, protest) by individuals, nonprofit organizations, or NGOs designed to further social, political, or environmental goals.

Advocacy advertising: Efforts by firms to communicate their political, social, or business arguments with the intent of positioning themselves favorably in the eyes of the public or other opinion makers to persuade them of the validity of their point of view.

Benefit corporation: A "b-corp" is a firm with a governance structure that expands its fiduciary duty to include the needs and concerns of a broad range of stakeholders beyond shareholders alone. "B Corps are certified by the nonprofit B Lab to meet rigorous standards of social and environmental performance, accountability, and transparency."[2]

Business citizenship: Societal-oriented actions by firms designed to demonstrate their role as constructive members of society.

Business ethics: The application of ethics and ethical theory to business decisions.

Cash mob: A group of residents who use social media to assemble at a given date and time to spend money in support of a local business.

Cause-related marketing: Efforts to gain or retain customers by tying purchases of the firm's goods or services to a benefit provided by the firm to a nonprofit organization or charity. For example, when a proportion of sales are donated to an identified cause.

Civic engagement: Efforts by employees to improve communities in which the firm operates.

Clicktivism: A form of social or environmental protest that is conducted via the Internet—by using mouse clicks (e.g., signing an online petition).

Clicktivists: Social activists who practice clicktivism (see *Clicktivism*).

Coalitions: Collections of firms, stakeholders, or individuals that collaborate to achieve common goals. Should not be confused with cartels, which are illegal.

Community advocacy panels (CAPS): Formal or informal groups of citizens who advise organizations about areas of common interest. Topics range widely, but can be collectively defined as specific areas in which the firm's actions affect the local community.

Conscious capitalism: "[An] emerging form of capitalism that holds the potential for enhancing corporate performance while simultaneously advancing the quality of life for billions of people."[3] Synonymous with *strategic* CSR, it is based on four principles that encourage the development of values-based businesses: Higher purpose, Stakeholder interdependence, Conscious leadership, and Conscious culture (see *Values-based Business*).

Consumer activism: Efforts by customers to have their views represented in company policies and decision making. As such activism becomes more organized, it is more likely referred to as a "consumer movement," which can advocate for more far-reaching changes in consumer rights and laws.

Consumer boycott: Consumers who avoid specific industries, firms, or products based on performance metrics that they value.

Consumer buycott: Consumers who actively seek to support specific industries, firms, or products through their purchase decisions based on performance metrics that they value.[4]

Corporate citizenship: See Business citizenship.

Corporate philanthropy: Contributions by firms that benefit stakeholders and the community, often through financial or in-kind donations to nonprofit organizations.

Corporate responsibility: A term similar in meaning to corporate social responsibility, but preferred by many companies.

Corporate social opportunity: An approach to CSR that focuses on the benefits to firms of pursuing a CSR agenda in an attempt to remove the perception of CSR as a cost to business.[5]

Corporate social performance: The performance benefits to the firm (often measured in traditional financial or accounting metrics) gained from the implementation of its CSR program.

Corporate social responsibility (CSR): A view of the *corporation* and its role in *society* that assumes a *responsibility* among firms to pursue goals in addition to profit maximization and a *responsibility* among a firm's stakeholders to hold the firm accountable for its actions (see *Strategic corporate social responsibility*).

Corporate social responsiveness: Actions taken by a firm to achieve its CSR goals in response to demands made by specific stakeholder groups.

Corporate stakeholder responsibility: A responsibility among a firm's stakeholders to hold the firm accountable for its actions.

Corporate sustainability: Business operations that can be continued over the long term without degrading the ecological environment (see *Sustainability*).

Downcycling: A recycling process that reduces the quality of the recycled material over time (see: *Upcycling*).

Eco-efficiency: An approach to business that is characterized by the need to "do more with less" and popularized by the phrase, "reduce, reuse, recycle."

Ecopreneur: "Environmental and social entrepreneurs [who] lead socially committed, break-through ventures that are driven by environmental, social, and economic goals"[6] (see *Social entrepreneur*).

Enlightened self-interest: The recognition that businesses can operate in a socially conscious manner without forsaking the economic goals that lead to financial success.

Ethics: A guide to moral behavior based on social norms and culturally-embedded definitions of right and wrong.

Externality: "A side-effect or consequence (of an industrial or commercial activity) which affects other parties without this being reflected in the cost of the goods or services involved; a social cost or benefit."[7]

Fair trade: Trade in goods (often internationally) at prices above what market forces would otherwise generate in order to ensure a living wage for the producer and sustainable supply of a valued raw material.

Garbology: The story that can be told by what we throw away.[8]

Glocalization: "[D]ealing with big global problems through myriad small or individual actions."[9]

Greenwash: "Green-wash (green'wash', -wôsh') – verb: the act of misleading consumers regarding the environmental practices of a company or the environmental benefits of a product or service"[10] (see *Pinkwash*).

Human rights: Rights that are an inalienable element of what it means to be human.[11]

Impact investing: A variety of investment vehicles (e.g., mutual funds, low-interest loans, bonds, and ETFs) that seek to maximize social benefits in addition to providing a financial return to investors (see *Social finance*).

Integrated reporting: The publication of a firm's triple bottom line (economic, environmental, and social) performance in a unified document (see *Triple bottom line*).

Islamic finance: An investment philosophy that is guided by the principles of Shariah Law. "Shariah-Compliant funds are prohibited from investing in companies which derives income from the sales of alcohol, pork products, pornography, gambling, military equipment or weapons."[12]

Iron law of social responsibility: The axiom that those who use power in ways society deems to be abusive will eventually lose their ability to continue acting in that way.[13]

Living wage: A level of pay that is designed to meet basic living standards for an employee above subsistence levels. A "living wage," which is socially-defined, is usually set at a higher level than a "minimum wage," which is legally defined.

Moral hazard: To take risk in search of personal benefit where the consequences of that risk are not born by the individual. As such, moral hazard encourages behavior contrary to the spirit of the agreement. During the Financial Crisis, this effect was captured in a phrase used to criticize the financial industry—*privatizing gains and socializing losses.*

Natural Corporate Management (NCM): A business philosophy "based upon genetic, evolutionary, and neuroscience components that underlie and help drive corporate management, including behavior, organizational, and eco-environmental relationships."[14]

Nongovernmental organizations (NGOs): Organizations that pursue social good exclusively, rather than profits or the political goals of government (although many NGO activities are government-funded). For example, an NGO might help feed the poor after a disaster, although this activity may be seen as a governmental task in other societies or under other conditions (see *Nonprofits*).

Nonprofits: Organizations that exist to meet societal needs rather than seek profits for their owners or the political concerns of government. Nonprofits often differ from NGOs by having a domestic, rather than an international, focus.

Philanthropy: A donation made, either by an individual or organization, to a charity or charitable cause.

Pinkwash: "When a company promotes pink-ribboned products and claims to care about breast cancer while also selling products linked to disease or injury"[15] (see *Greenwash*).

Public policy: Government decisions aimed at establishing rules and guidelines for action with the intent of providing benefit (or preventing harm) to society.

Renewable energy: A source of energy that is not carbon-based (e.g., solar, wind, or tidal energies). Also referred to as "alternative energy."

Social entrepreneur: An entrepreneur who seeks to achieve social and environmental goals by utilizing for-profit business practices (see *Ecopreneur*).

Social finance: An approach to finance that emphasizes the social return on investment via a variety of investment criteria (e.g., ethical, faith-based, and environmental) that also seek to secure financial returns for investors (see *Impact investing*).

Social innovation: An approach to business where firms develop new products and services that meet not only the customers' technical needs, but also their broader aspirations as citizens.

Social license: The ability of a for-profit firm to continue to operate due to society's approval of its activities.

Socially Responsible Investing (SRI): A portfolio investment strategy that seeks returns by investing in firms or projects that pursue socially responsible goals.

Stakeholders: "A stakeholder in an organization is (by definition) any group or individual who can affect or is affected by the achievement of the organization's objectives."[16]

Strategic corporate social responsibility: The incorporation of an holistic CSR perspective within a firm's strategic planning and core operations so that the firm is managed in the interests of a broad set of stakeholders to achieve maximum economic and social value over the medium to long term.

Sustainability: "Sustainable development is development that meets the needs of the present without compromising the ability of future generations to meet their own needs."[17]

Sweatshops: Operations that employ children or apply working standards with little, if any, respect for human rights. Conditions are deemed to be unsafe and unfair, often in comparison to minimum legal conditions established in more affluent societies.

Transparency: The extent to which organizational decisions and operating procedures are open or visible to outsiders (see *Accountability*).

Triple bottom line: An evaluation of businesses by comprehensively assessing their financial, environmental, and social performance.

Upcycling: A recycling process that increases the quality of the recycled material over time (see: *Downcycling*).

Values: Beliefs about appropriate goals, actions, and conditions.

Values-based Business: A for-profit firm that is founded on a vision and mission based on social values and the other four principles that define conscious capitalism: Higher purpose, Stakeholder interdependence, Conscious leadership, and Conscious culture (see *Conscious capitalism*).

Whistleblower: An insider who alleges organizational misconduct and communicates those allegations of wrongdoing outside the firm to the media, prosecutors, or others.

STRATEGY TERMS

In addition to the CSR terms that are used throughout this book, there are a number of specialized terms used to describe a firm's strategy or strategic decision making processes. The intersection between CSR and corporate strategy is central to the argument presented in *Strategic CSR*. As such, brief definitions of the key concepts associated with a firm's strategic planning and implementation are detailed below:

Strategy—Terminology, Concepts, and Definitions

Agents: The managers of a firm, whom the owners (the principals) appoint to operate the business on their behalf and to protect their investment (see *Principals*).

Business strategy: The strategy of specific business units within a firm that enable it to differentiate its products from the products of other firms on the basis of low cost or another factor, such as superior technology, in order to create a sustainable, competitive advantage (see *Differentiation* and *Low cost*).[18]

Capabilities: Actions that a firm can do, such as pay its bills, in ways that add value to the production process.

Company (or corporation): A legal organizational form permitted to engage in commercial business. The name *company* comes from a combination of the Latin words *cum* and *panis,* the literal translation of which originally meant "breaking bread together."[19]

Competencies: Actions a firm can do very well.

Competitive advantage: Competencies, resources, or skills that enable the firm to differentiate itself from its competitors and succeed over a sustained period of time.

Core competence (or capability): The processes of the firm that it not only does very well, but is so superior at performing that it is difficult (or at least time consuming) for other firms to match its performance in this area.[20]

Core resource: An asset of the firm that is unique and difficult to replicate.

Corporate governance: The structure and systems that officially allocate power within organizations and manage the relationships between the owners (principals) and managers (agents) of a business.[21]

Corporate strategy: The strategy of the firm. Strategy at this level involves decisions that allow the firm to navigate its competitive environment, identifying the businesses in which the firm will compete and whether to enter into partnerships with other firms via joint ventures, mergers, or acquisitions (see *Business strategy*).

Differentiation: A business strategy used by firms to distinguish their products from the products of other firms on the basis of some component other than price (see *Low cost*).

Fiduciary: A responsibility of one party that is a result of a formal relationship, either legal or ethical, with another party. The responsibility is founded on trust and often involves financial transactions.

Firm: A business (or enterprise or for-profit firm) is an organization that marshals scarce or valuable resources to produce a good or service that it then sells to consumers or other businesses at a price that is greater than the cost of production.

Five forces: A macro-level analysis of the competitive structure of a firm's industry that indicates a firm's potential for profit (see *Industry perspective*).[22]

Globalization: The process, facilitated by rapidly improving communication technologies, transportation, trade, and capital flows, that allows a firm's operations to transcend national boundaries, and facilitates greater interaction among people, societies, cultures, and governments worldwide.

Industry perspective: An external perspective of the firm that identifies the structure of the environment in which the firm operates (in particular, its industry) as the main determinant of competitive advantage (see *Five forces* and *Resources perspective*).

Low cost: A business strategy used by firms to distinguish their products from the products of other firms on the basis of more efficient operations (see *Differentiation*).

Mission: States what the organization is going to do to achieve its vision. It addresses the types of activities the firm seeks to perform (see *Vision*).

Offshoring: Relocating jobs to overseas countries in search of lower labor costs.

Onshoring (or **reshoring**)*:* Returning jobs closer to home in order to create more flexible and responsive supply chains.

Principals: The owners of a firm, the shareholders, and their representatives, the board of directors (see *Agents*).

Resources perspective: An internal perspective of the firm that identifies the resources, capabilities, and core competencies of the firm as the main determinant of a sustainable competitive advantage (see *Industry perspective*).

Strategy: Determines how the organization is going to undertake its mission. It sets forth the ways it will negotiate its competitive environment in order to attain a sustainable advantage.

Strategic planning: The process (often annual) whereby firms create or reformulate plans for future operations.

Supply chain: The linkages formed by relationships among firms that provide a firm with the materials necessary to produce a product (see *Value chain*).

SWOT analysis: A tool used to identify the internal Strengths and Weaknesses of the firm and the external Opportunities and Threats present in the firm's environment. The goal is to match the firm's strengths with its opportunities, while strengthening the weaknesses and avoiding any threats.

Tactics: Day-to-day management decisions made to implement a firm's strategy.

Value chain: An analysis of the linkages within the production process that identifies each value-adding stage in the process. This analysis is possible within a firm or among firms.[23]

Vision: A statement designed to answer why the organization exists. It identifies the needs the firm aspires to solve for others (see *Mission*).

FOREWORD

There are two distinct approaches to CSR taken by companies in the modern world. These are values-based and systems-based approaches.

Values-based companies are extremely rare, but they make the most compelling case studies. They can create laughably simple statements of values – but then make them powerful by absolutely living by them. They develop a powerful 'purpose beyond profit' and that often leads to them doing well in the marketplace.

Although such companies are rare, the delusion that one's own business belongs to this exclusive group is extremely common. All you need is a poster on the CEO's wall that has a list, preferably long and convoluted with ten or more clauses. Because that is, obviously, evidence that you have values.

But companies are expressions of aggregate human behaviour. What distinguishes a corporate identity, much more than a logo or a typeface, is the organisation's ability to have its people behave in consistent ways faced with certain sets of circumstances.

Values-led companies actively recruit people that are a fit with their values. They seek high performers, but will part company with high performers if they have the wrong fit. They get consistent behaviours because the values provide a reference point – at all levels of the company, in all circumstances, at the level of day-to-day decision making.

For the rest, it's the numbers that talk. Senior management can preach values, and ethics, and social responsibility. But the middle managers find that they are judged on the numbers, and so that sets the hierarchy of what's important in a systemic way.

That doesn't make these bad companies. It simply means that they have to achieve consistent behaviours within a much more active, rules-based framework. They may have framed corporate values to which they aspire, but they have to rely on policies and procedures to achieve those consistent behaviours because they have not achieved a strong, commonly understood and wholly embedded corporate culture.

They will also find it difficult, if not impossible, to break out of the logic of their market sector.

Why did so many banks end up following disastrous practices that collectively led to the global financial crisis? Predominantly because, as systems-led companies, they were forced to follow the logic of the system.

As Chuck Prince, formerly of CitiGroup put it, "so long as the music plays you have to keep dancing".

So if the moral compass of the entire business sector is off, individual companies feel powerless to do anything other than follow the trend until society inevitably steps in to apply corrective measures. It happened (and largely still does) with the tobacco companies. It happened with the banks.

It could well be that we will look back at this period in history and see that it also happened with a lot more business sectors – particularly those that had a role in resisting some of the implications of sustainability to the practice of business as usual.

This is why values-based businesses can be so important. Standing against the tide of peer pressure can be a distinctly uncomfortable thing to do. But sometimes it needs to be done. People in business can be largely seen to be following the incentives that the marketplace defines for them. Values-driven businesses are the ones that can challenge perverse incentives and seek to transform their marketplace by so doing.

But because of their rarity, values-driven companies are not enough of a guarantee that businesses can be effectively challenged to meet the demands of a rapidly changing future.

This is why David Chandler and William Werther are right to place the emphasis on the role of external stakeholders in putting pressure on business when the outcomes of business as usual are unacceptable. Although businesses like to imagine themselves as forward-looking, the truth is that it is far more common that they find themselves responding to external pressure.

Stakeholder engagement has been seen as a key part of corporate social responsibility for many years, but for all that, its role is still widely misunderstood.

All too often it has defined CSR as a process whereby different stakeholders – of varying legitimacy – present their wish-lists for companies to consider which they can help to fulfil.

But proper stakeholder engagement is about helping to make the consequences of decisions visible at the point where the decisions are made. And, as the authors point out, not all stakeholders are created equal in terms of their value and importance to the business. Businesses have to prioritise their stakeholders to enable them to inform a smart and strategy approach to CSR.

And not only do businesses have to exercise judgement in terms of which stakeholders are important to their decision making – they also have to analyse and understand the perspective of those stakeholders in a much smarter way than is traditionally the case.

Marketers, utilising such advanced techniques as neuromarketing, have come to understand just how often customers fail to effectively vocalise their true reactions in the face of marketing concepts. They have become considerably more sophisticated in understanding what really drives customer behaviours.

But very little of that sophistication is yet carried over into how companies understand and consider their stakeholders. Even those same customers. They may be profoundly understood in their role as customers – but only as caricatures in their role as citizens and stakeholders.

It is high time that this changed. For many years, the terms of the debate around companies and their social responsibilities have been that of managing the trade-off between the interests of the company and society.

But companies do not stand apart from society – they are an integral part of it. If companies and society have different, conflicting, interests then that is a problem that needs to be resolved.

Because the logic that says that businesses can behave as though they were separate, simply aiming to maximise profits while keeping to the rules of the game as defined by society, is outdated.

Companies are now expected to use the power of the marketplace to help create a more sustainable future. And to be a successful business in that new environment, you have to see CSR as a strategic imperative for your business.

That makes this updated edition a very timely text for our times.

Mallen Baker
Founding Director, Daisywheel Interactive
Contributing Editor, Ethical Corporation

PREFACE

WHY CSR MATTERS

In sitting down to write the third edition of this textbook, one thing we struggled with was its title. In particular, we felt the need to reflect the evolution of the CSR debate and the argument that there is still no clear consensus in the field around the meaning of labels such as *CSR* or *sustainability*, while, at the same time, wanting to protect the brand value that has been established with a title that reaches third edition.

At first glance, this may seem a trivial matter. From our perspective, however, the title speaks to the book's central message. As such, we decided to keep the core, *Strategic CSR*, but alter the sub-title to *Stakeholders, Globalization, and Sustainable Value Creation*. The result, *Strategic CSR: Stakeholders, Globalization, and Sustainable Value Creation* captures what was essential to the arguments advanced in prior editions (that CSR is an integral component of the firm's day-to-day operations and strategic planning), but extends our thesis to talk more comprehensively of CSR as essential to the firm's overall objective (to create value). For all the baggage that accompanies a label like *CSR*, it is its role as a strategic asset that locates it at the core of a firm's operations. While topics like philanthropy exist as components of CSR, they are peripheral. It is operational relevance that focuses the ideas we discuss here. Most importantly, this focus on CSR as central to strategy and operations speaks directly to a firm's ability to create value in a global competitive environment over the medium to long term.

Value creation is the foundation for building a sustainable business model. It speaks to what is core about a firm, across business disciplines. While preconceived notions of *CSR* and *sustainability* may cause some CEOs to pre-judge or reject these ideas, *value creation* is front and center to everything that the firm does and should be constantly in the forefront of the CEO's mind. In order to counter the idea of CSR as a cost to business, it is important to embed supporting arguments in operational and strategic relevance—by striving to meet the needs and demands of key stakeholders, broadly defined, the firm secures the societal license necessary to operate. In the process, CSR moves from perceptions of an optional add-on, to the core of what the firm is and what it does. It is this belief in the existential nature of CSR for organizations that guides the ideas we present in this third edition—ideas that constitute CSR and related issues as central to the business model of the twenty first century firm.

Unfortunately, this argument is not yet widely accepted, by either executives or business school academics. This is partly because, on the surface at least, CSR is more obvious in its absence than its presence. It is difficult to justify investments in harm avoided, even though today's news headlines remind us constantly of the extent of that possible harm. The scale of the Deepwater Horizon oil spill in the Gulf of Mexico in 2010, for example, reminds us of the central role CSR plays in the day-to-day operations of the firm and the very real consequences (both for the firm and for the broader society) when those processes break down. The devastating effects of the Financial Crisis, which began in 2008 with the bankruptcy of Lehman Brothers, linger and continue to define the economic policy of governments worldwide. CSR is not an abstract concept or peripheral set of activities; it resides at the center of firm operations.

As today's society becomes increasingly interconnected, artificial borders between organizations and their stakeholders become less and less meaningful. Firms are constructed of individuals who, together, constitute society. And, as a society, the most important question we face is how to maximize welfare, broadly speaking—How do we build a culture and environment that enables people to pursue their dreams with equal opportunity? For-profit firms, the most efficient organizational form for transforming scarce and valuable resources into the products and services we rely on daily, are central to this effort. Ultimately, as business professors, we endorse the importance of business in advancing social welfare and economic prosperity. That doesn't mean, of course, that we are necessarily satisfied with the status quo. As such, this book is not an excuse for business—it is a proud endorsement of the positive role for-profit firms play in our lives, but also a platform for how that role can be improved. This book is also an endorsement of the profit motive and market economics, but one that argues that competitive forces maximize welfare when embedded in a framework of values. This book is filled with ideas that challenge what we often take for granted, but within the parameters defined by the human condition. In the process, therefore, we advocate for *evolution*, not *revolution*—what is practical and realizable, not what is ideal and out-of-reach. Human character is a significant constraint that should not be ignored and there is a reason why our economic system has evolved the way it has. Nevertheless, this book is a manifesto for change that you, as a future leader of business, can implement today.

The third edition of *Strategic Corporate Social Responsibility: Stakeholders, Globalization, and Sustainable Value Creation*, therefore, is designed as a road-map. It provides a framework that can be taken into the workforce and wider society, and that firms can use to navigate the complex and evolving issue of corporate social responsibility. *Strategic CSR* was written in the hope that you, as a future business leader, will create a more responsive and responsible business culture in which for-profit firms take their rightful place as the solution to society's largest problems. But, we have a lot of work to do. What is clear to us, however, is that CSR is central to the effort. It is not an optional add-on to which we pay lip service in good times and quietly put aside during difficult times. Rather, it is an essential refinement of the market model that has generated such economic prosperity to date. CSR is a business philosophy for firms that seek to maximize growth (and profits) over the medium to long term. It is a strategic imperative that is central to operations. Its main focus is to maximize value-added—the central concern that CEOs face every day. CSR is not one way of doing business among many, it is *the* way of doing business in the globalized, wired world in which we live today. We welcome you to join us as we embark on sculpting a sustainable business model for the twenty first century.

CORPORATE SOCIAL RESPONSIBILITY

Understanding CSR is important because it represents nothing less than an attempt to define the future of our society. CSR, corporate responsibility, corporate citizenship, and sustainability all matter because they influence all aspects of business. And, businesses matter because they create much of the wealth and well-being in society. As such, CSR is increasingly crucial to both business and societal success.

Central to the concept of CSR, therefore, is deciding where companies fit within the social fabric. By addressing business ethics, corporate governance, environmental concerns, and other issues, society creates a dynamic context in which firms operate. The context is *dynamic* because the ideal mix of business goals and societal expectations is constantly evolving. Along the way, complex questions arise: Why does a business exist? Is the goal simply to maximize profits, or do for-profits serve other goals? Who defines the boundaries between private profits and the public good? What obligations do businesses have to the societies in which they operate? Are these *obligations* voluntary, or should they be mandated by law? To whom are companies ultimately accountable—their shareholders, or also to a broader array of stakeholders? Can the interests of firms, owners, and other stakeholders be aligned, or do they conflict inherently?

While businesses are largely responsible for creating wealth and driving progress within society, they do not act alone. Governments are crucial because they set the rules and parameters within which society and businesses operate. In addition, nonprofit or nongovernmental organizations (NGOs) exist to do social good without seeking profit or fulfilling the duties of a government organization—they reach into areas where politics and profit often do not go. Nevertheless, without the innovation that capitalism inspires, social and economic progress declines. Without the great wealth-producing engines of business, the taxes and charity needed to run government and nonprofits fade away, in time reducing our standard of living to some primitive level. A simple thought experiment underscores these points: Look around you and subtract everything that was produced by a business. What is left? Or, another example: What is the difference between the poorest and wealthiest nations? Is it not primarily the creativity and productivity of competitive businesses embedded in a societal-defined context?

CSR Newsletters: IBM

An article in *The Economist*[24] attempts an interesting exercise—to compare the relative influence of IBM and the Carnegie Foundation over the last 100 years. Both organizations were founded in 1911 and, as such, both celebrated their centenary in 2011. *The Economist's* goal is to identify which organization (for-profit or non-profit) has "done more for society" during its lifespan.

Two things become apparent reading the article. First, that it is not a very close contest. While the Carnegie Foundation certainly did some good things early on in its life, it has faded significantly in recent decades. The clinching argument in the article was that:

> IBM, by contrast, is now as influential as it has ever been, with a stock-market value of around $200 billion and nearly 427,000 employees, many of them in the developing world. . . . Its corporate philanthropy has grown steadily, so that its annual grants now exceed those of the Carnegie Corporation.

Second, the article speaks volumes in terms of how far *The Economist* has come regarding CSR that it was willing to even attempt the exercise. *The Economist* of 10 years ago would not have been interested in this question and would have considered the answer a foregone conclusion. Instead, it makes a valiant attempt to compare the two organizations; so much so that the Carnegie Corporation remained in the running longer than it should have. Rather understating the case for IBM (after pointing out many of the errors made by the firm over the years, including its brush with Hitler and the Holocaust), *The Economist* concludes:

Judged on the past 50 years, there is a strong case for saying IBM has had more impact than Carnegie—especially if you count its accidental contribution to philanthropy by incompetently failing to stop Mr. Gates from creating Microsoft. In part this is because its business, the management of information, has unusually large social benefits, and causes relatively few social or environmental costs.

Ultimately, the weight of evidence sits strongly in favor of IBM. The advantage of the for-profit firm is its ability to adapt and re-invent itself, while the Carnegie Foundation has found its enthusiasm slowly wane over time:

Another reason for Carnegie's relative decline may be that 100 years is too old for a philanthropic foundation. The absence of an existential threat may have made it too comfortable. IBM transformed itself under Lou Gerstner when it nearly ran out of cash in the early 1990s, and again more recently under Mr Palmisano when Indian rivals threatened to steal its business. By contrast, it is not clear what, if anything, keeps the people in charge of the Carnegie Corporation awake at night. The passage of time saps a foundation of the unique energy of its founder. Carnegie said of the unknown future leaders of his foundation that "they shall best conform to my wishes by using their own judgment." That much they have done, but he would probably have fared better.

The article is an interesting thought-experiment, but, ultimately, reaffirms that, regarding CSR, while for-profit firms are a big part of the problem, they are also the main hope for a solution.

Businesses produce much of what is good in our society. At the same time, however, they also cause great harm, as pollution, layoffs, industrial accidents, and economic crises amply demonstrate. When these toxic by-products become too onerous to society, nonprofits may emerge to ameliorate the harm; however, their dependence on external funding often limits the effectiveness of these organizations. Alternatively, governments react with regulation to curb the worst excesses of business, but are often slow to act and legislation is not always effective. Only after public consensus is reached does political will tend to follow. Yet a successful alignment of dynamic business self-interest and general social benefit creates optimal outcomes, as when a new lifesaving drug emerges from the profit motive.

Between the great good and terrible harm businesses produce, therefore, lies concern about the proper role of corporations in society, especially as globalization and technological innovation expand the reach and potential of multi-national corporations. Moreover, this concern has gained renewed attention after the high-level accounting and governance scandals that emerged in the early years of the new century, followed by the global economic crisis less than a decade later. As a result, corporate executives face conflict and confusion about societal expectations of their organizations. On the one hand, for example, Milton Friedman, the Nobel Prize–winning economist, argues that:

> Few trends could so thoroughly undermine the very foundations of our free society as the acceptance by corporate officials of a social responsibility other than to make as much money for their stockholders as possible.[25]

On the other hand, however, corporations are increasingly expected to act with a multiple-constituency approach—embracing the needs and concerns of employees, shareholders, lenders, and customers, while assuming responsibility for suppliers (throughout their extended supply chain), communities, and the wider environments in which they operate. Which perspective is *ideal*? Which is *right*? Are the two positions necessarily mutually exclusive? Perhaps, more accurately, what is the best mix of the two that produces a sustainable society that maximizes societal benefit and welfare?

Strategic CSR provides a framework with which readers can explore and debate these questions. This book identifies the key issues of CSR, models them around conceptual frameworks, and provides both the means and resources to investigate this evolving and important topic. Our perspective is the *strategic* outlook of the firm—we look at the organization's interface with its stakeholders in the larger environment. As this complex web of relationships reveals, however, even simple answers are colored by honest debate, wherein reasonable, honorable, and well-intentioned people disagree, sometimes vehemently.

What makes this exploration exciting and worthy of study is that CSR is as topical as this morning's headlines—jobs and job losses, financial bailouts and record profits, corruption and scientific breakthroughs, pollution and technological innovations, and personal greed and corporate charity all spring from the relentless drive for innovation in the pursuit of profit that we call *business*. As such, CSR can only be studied at the cutting edge, where corporate competencies mold the business strategies that enable firms to compete with each other. And, when they compete in the marketplace, CSR offers a sustainable path between unbridled capitalism, with its mixed consequences, and rigidly regulated economies that are plagued with artificial and stifling limitations. CSR helps businesses optimize both the *ends* of profit and the *means* of execution. And, forces are afoot that heighten the importance of optimizing this balance *today,* which makes CSR considerations even more important *tomorrow.*

Still, the question remains: What issues matter under the broad heading of corporate social responsibility? The answer depends on the industry context and the firm's strategy, or *how* it delivers value to its customers. Since industries and strategies vary widely, the appropriate mix of issues will differ from firm-to-firm and also evolve as firms adapt their strategy and execution to their specific business environment. The result? It is impossible to prescribe the exact CSR mix to deal with any particular landscape. Instead, we argue that a strategic lens offers the best perspective through which firms should approach CSR because it is through the strategic reformulation process that organizations adapt to their social, cultural, and competitive context.

Hence, we view *strategic* CSR from a stakeholder perspective that embraces an external environment made up of many constituent groups, all of whom have a stake in the firm's profit-seeking activities. It demonstrates the value to firms of defining CSR in relation to their operational context and then incorporating a CSR perspective into their strategic planning and throughout the organization. The situations change, but the questions remain the same: Who are the primary stakeholders? Which claims are legitimate? What do we say to those stakeholders who will disagree with the decision? What value are we adding and to whom? Is our business sustainable? These and other issues force business thinkers to understand CSR from a stakeholder vantage point that is set against the backdrop of each firm's industry and strategy.

A *stakeholder perspective,* viewed through a strategic lens, conveys the complexity of balancing competing interests in forming company policy, regardless of whether CSR is taught as a standalone elective or as a core component of the business school curriculum across all functional areas. Still, two additional constraints remain:

- How should we cover the broad range of topics that fall under the CSR banner without being encyclopedic?
- How should we organize a book that maximizes learning and interest within a global society that is increasingly online and connected?

What makes *Strategic CSR* a unique tool for this journey is our approach and underlying thesis: Exploration is the best form of learning. We focus on the technological innovation that makes CSR more relevant today than ever before—the Internet. In *Strategic CSR*, you will find scores of issues, case-studies, and websites. Rather than laying out each issue in detail, our sense is that you would prefer the original sources to track down yourself. By seeking out these sources online, it is easier to engage and construct informed opinions. For those who like to form their own opinions, *Strategic CSR* offers a guided tour. It intends first to provoke and then present a roadmap of questions, examples, case-studies, and signposts to guide an online search for solutions and supporting examples. Using this approach, we aim to cover all of Bloom's stages of learning, from Remembering through to Creativity (see Figure I.1). While we cannot cover all aspects of every topic in this volume, we aim to provide a launching pad (via key concepts) along with the means to explore (via additional sources and references).

In our own investigation, we have found that there are no simple answers and few absolutes. Where simple solutions are prescribed, unintended consequences usually arise. Many answers are relative to a specific industry and to the specific situation in which each company finds itself. And, even when answers exist, they inevitably are a result of tradeoffs among competing stakeholder freedoms with few parties emerging completely satisfied. Rather than provide absolute answers, therefore, we seek to stimulate the *best* questions that consider a broad range of

Figure I.1   Bloom's Taxonomy of Learning

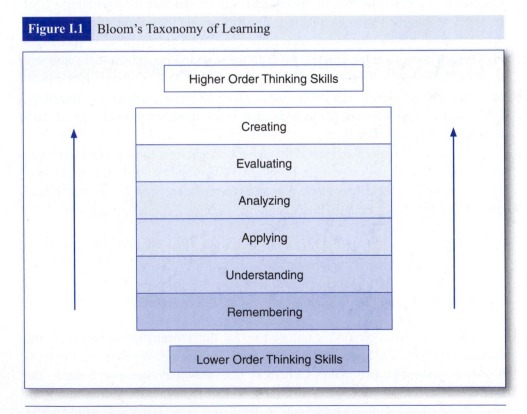

Source: Lorin W. Anderson & David R. Krathwohl, (eds.), *A Taxonomy for Learning, Teaching, and Assessing: A Revision of Bloom's Taxonomy of Educational Objectives*, New York: Longman, 2001.

perspectives, provoke vibrant debate, and encourage further research. As such, this book does not search for solutions to the pressing CSR problems of today. Undoubtedly, such solutions would be generalizations of limited use, quickly outdated by changing societal expectations. Instead, we present a stakeholder perspective as the most effective means of understanding the bigger picture of CSR as a strategic business philosophy. Understanding the issues at hand and the past mistakes made by firms, as well as possessing a structural framework that encourages an holistic perspective, is crucial to avoid repeating these same mistakes in the future.

The journey you are about to undertake will help equip you for a career that is changing at an accelerating rate. CSR is an increasingly important component of this change. Gaining insight into the broad scope of this dynamic topic will increase your understanding and sophistication as a thinker, as a future business leader, and as an informed citizen.

We wish you good luck!

David Chandler &
William B. Werther Jr.
March 2013

Disclaimer

An important feature of this book is its many web-based links. Relying on such resources, however, can be problematic because, due to the nature of the Internet, some of the urls provided will change or disappear over time.[26] We feel this is an occupational hazard of working in such a dynamic subject area and, as such, is a small price to pay for timely information that captures the ever-evolving debate. Nevertheless, it is a concern that we attempt to minimize by presenting a balanced and varied selection of links to many sources and organizations. These citations are not intended as an endorsement of any particular organization or message, but a reflection of the all-encompassing importance of CSR for firms, together with our desire to bring multiple viewpoints to the conversation.

PLAN OF THE BOOK

*S*trategic Corporate Social Responsibility is organized into two distinct parts. Part I highlights the breadth and depth of corporate social responsibility (CSR), while Part II presents a series of practical issues and case-studies, with online resources and questions for further investigation and classroom debate.

Chapters 1 and 2 of Part I lay the foundation for this book by defining CSR and providing a broader understanding of the context from which it emerged. Chapter 1 introduces CSR, providing detail on where this topic has come from and how it has evolved over time. In discussing its evolution, four different arguments for CSR are presented—ethical, moral, rational, and economic. Importantly, this chapter identifies why CSR is a growing concern to students and business leaders. Though firms are economic entities that exist to meet needs in society and further the financial interests of their owners, we argue that the most effective way to achieve this today is by considering the needs and values of a broad range of groups that have a stake in the outcome of the pursuit of profit. These *nonowner* stakeholders are vital because they can affect the success, even the survival, of the business. This is particularly true in light of the globalized environment that corporations operate within today.

Chapter 2 reflects the importance of a stakeholder perspective to the argument we present in *Strategic CSR*. Throughout this century, as business schools worldwide evolve to account for the changing environment in which firms operate, we believe that CSR will occupy an increasingly core component of the curriculum. In addition to being relevant to all core classes, however, CSR finds a natural home within corporate strategy. The ideal vehicle for the integration of CSR and strategy is a multi-stakeholder perspective that enables firms to respond to the dominant trends in society today—globalization and the increasingly free flow of information. In addition to the stakeholder perspective that we integrate throughout the book, therefore, this chapter explains why the traditional strategy perspectives (principally, the resource-based and industry views) are insufficient tools to help firms craft strategies in today's globalized business environment. We outline a stakeholder model that enables firms to identify and prioritize their key stakeholders, allowing them to respond in ways that maximize value, broadly defined.

The focus of much of the CSR debate (and captured by the term 'corporate social *responsibility*') is the assumption that firms have a *responsibility* to pursue goals other than profit maximization. In Chapter 3, we explore this assumption in detail and examine some of the more contentious elements of the CSR debate. In particular, we propose the idea that the CSR community expects too much of firms; that firms *react* better than they *initiate*; and that if, as a society, we decide that firms should act with greater social responsibility, then it is a firm's stakeholders (and their consumers, in particular) that have an equal, if not greater, *responsibility* to demand this behavior from firms. More importantly, they need to demonstrate that they will support such behavior. In order for CSR to be a stakeholder responsibility, however, stakeholders need to care about CSR. The economic argument for CSR presupposes an economic advantage for a company that is a net contributor to society, or at least a belief that there is economic disadvantage for any company that negatively affects key stakeholder groups. Managers, as suggested by advertising campaigns and philanthropic activities, already understand this logic. Although many people say they want responsible companies, however, there are limits to what societies and consumers are willing to pay for this outcome. This willingness to pay for social responsibility is therefore arguable and central to the CSR debate. Without sufficient stakeholder interest in CSR behavior, corporations have less incentive to embrace CSR.

Chapters 4 and 5 conclude Part I of *Strategic CSR* by outlining how firms integrate CSR into day-to-day operations. Chapter 4 places CSR within a competitive context, arguing that CSR fits naturally within the organization's strategic framework. As the firm matches its capabilities with the opportunities in its competitive environment, it pursues its mission in order to move toward its aspirations, or vision. CSR is an integral part of this strategic process because it serves to filter how businesses interact with their environments and implement ideas. While strategy seeks competitive success, CSR acts as a screen that both enables and protects the firm in its pursuit of profit and long-term viability. Planet-wide trends of increased affluence, globalization, the Internet, massive media conglomeration, and branding combine to heighten the strategic importance of CSR today and for the foreseeable future.

Finally, Chapter 5 explores the challenges of integrating CSR into the firm's day-to-day operations and organizational culture. Here, our intent is to identify the factors that strengthen or impede the creation of a strategic CSR orientation at the firm level. Central to this integration process is the commitment of senior management. Strategic direction, mission statements, and core operating practices must all reinforce this commitment to attaining CSR goals. Ultimately, in order to integrate CSR into the firm's strategy and culture, leaders must start an ongoing dialog within the organization and with key stakeholders about the strategic and operational importance of CSR. This chapter provides a framework for implementing CSR firm-wide.

Part II of *Strategic CSR* reflects the range of issues that define CSR in practice, each segmented into one of the three stakeholder groups detailed in Chapter 2: organizational, economic, or societal stakeholders. Chapter 6 contains issues primarily involving organizational stakeholders; Chapter 7, economic stakeholders; and Chapter 8, societal stakeholders. Each issue is illustrated with a firm-centered case-study and supporting sources. Both complementary and competing viewpoints are also available via the websites provided. As such, Part II reveals the unique nature of *Strategic CSR*. We believe that the scope of CSR is a mosaic of issues. Which issues are most important today or tomorrow evolve with changes in society and the competitive environment. Moreover, given individual interests, our approach in Part II is to introduce issues and then provide Internet links to stimulate further in-depth investigation.

Interspersed throughout Parts I and II of the book, we also introduce the reader to the CSR Newsletters that are distributed by the authors as a dynamic complement to the text. Taken from daily news sources, the Newsletters present a value-added library of examples beyond the case-studies and online references provided throughout. These topical themes, together with access to the complete library of Newsletters that are archived on the book's blog (http://strategiccsr-sage.blogspot.com/), capture the breadth of the CSR debate and provide an added dimension to classroom discussion and student investigation into this complex subject.

In addition to the two parts that constitute *Strategic CSR*, the third edition is accompanied by an interactive website (http://www.sagepub.com/strategiccsr/) that enhances the content provided in these pages. Primarily, the website does this by archiving material from the book's prior editions (e.g., issues and case-studies) that was replaced in writing the current edition. Equally important, however, this website provides instructors with secure access to the Instructor's Manual that accompanies this text and other resources of relevant and topical materials that can be used in the classroom. Our goal is for this website to provide an additional online dimension to *Strategic CSR* that aids its use in the classroom.

Finally, much of the value of the book, in terms of background explanation and additional online resources, is embedded in the book's notes and references at the end of each chapter. We encourage readers to investigate these notes and use them as stepping-stones to further online research. Undoubtedly, there is a never-ending supply of information and perspectives on the topical, dynamic subject of CSR. Our goal for these notes is to capture a broad overview then, along with the book's website and blog, provide you with the tools to explore this fascinating topic in more detail.

TEACHING AND ONLINE RESOURCES

Instructor Resources Site

The password-protected Instructor Site at **www.sagepub.com/chandler3e** gives instructors access to a full complement of resources to support and enhance their courses. The following assets are available on the instructor site:

- A test bank with multiple-choice, true/false, and essay questions. The test bank is provided in Word format as well as in our Respondus computerized testing software.
- PowerPoint slides for each chapter, for use in lecture and review. SLides are integrated with the book's distinctive features to provide powerful teaching tools for lecturing in class.
- Faculty Notes are provided to give detailed chapter summaries and outlines for instructors to reference as teaching materials.
- Suggested sample syllabi for semester and quarter classes provide syllbus templates to build the course around the text.
- and more!

Student Study Site

To maximize students' understanding of Strategic Corporate Responsibility and promote critical thinking and active learning, we have provided valuable study aids for students on the Student Study Site. Students can access the free study site at **www.sagepub.com/chandler3e** to learn more.

ACKNOWLEDGMENTS

Though we remain ultimately responsible for the ideas we present in *Strategic Corporate Social Responsibility*, this book is a result of a long journey that has been aided by many friends and colleagues along the way.

Crucial to the book's development has been the support of our colleagues at The Business School at the University of Colorado Denver and the School of Business Administration at the University of Miami. At the University of Colorado Denver, we would like to thank Dean Sueann Ambron, Associate Dean Cliff Young, and Associate Dean J.C. Bosch who are revitalizing the work and mission of the Business School and further establishing its role at the intersection of the business and academic communities in Denver and throughout the Rocky Mountain Region. In addition, Management Division Chair, Ken Bettenheusen and Finance Professor John Byrd, together with the members of the Managing for Sustainability faculty, are ensuring that CSR and sustainability remain at the forefront of the school's work. At the University of Miami, we would particularly like to thank Deans Paul Sugrue, Barbara Kahn, and Eugene Anderson for their support. Likewise, the continued encouragement of Linda Neider, Yadong Luo, Haresh Gurnani, and Jeff Kerr as Chairs of the Management Department during this revision is much appreciated, as is the early support of Rene Sacasas, Chair of the Business Law Department. We would also like to extend our gratitude further to Jeff Kerr and John Mezias, professors of strategic management at UM, who provide constant sources of valued insight and friendship. Without the support of our two business schools, the classroom laboratories where these ideas were tested, and the encouragement of colleagues, *Strategic Corporate Social Responsibility* would not have been possible.

In addition, we express our sincere gratitude to Anita Cava and Ken Goodman, Co-directors of the University of Miami Ethics Programs (http://www.miami.edu/ethics/), for creating the environment that helped germinate many of the ideas that were the foundation for this book. Their tireless progress and innovation, working with key community activists such as Daniella Levine of the Human Services

Coalition of Dade County (http://catalystmiami.org/), are building an environment in Miami where many of the ideas expressed in this book are becoming reality. We would particularly like to thank Anita Cava of the University of Miami's Business Law Department for her central role in making this project possible.

It is important to recognize that *Strategic CSR* is possible, in large part, because of the prior and ongoing work of many leading scholars in the field of CSR. We would particularly like to acknowledge the pioneering work of Archie B. Carroll of the University of Georgia, William C. Frederick of the University of Pittsburgh,[27] Stuart L. Hart of Cornell University, Thomas M. Jones of the University of Washington, Joshua D. Margolis of Harvard Business School, Jim Post of Boston University, C.K. Prahalad of the University of Michigan, and Sandra Waddock of Boston College. Their work, along with the work of many others, has provided the foundation for the field of CSR/Business and Society upon which we are able to build.

Dale Fitzgibbons of Illinois State University was an early and enthusiastic supporter of the book. He has been thinking about CSR and teaching the subject in his classrooms for many years. He has a valuable perspective on many of the ideas we present here and we continue to benefit from his ideas and willingness to share his knowledge.

We are also indebted to the ideas and comments offered by the many reviewers of the second edition who provided valuable guidance as we prepared this edition: Mark A Buchanan, Boise State University; Terrence B. Dalton, University of Akron, College of Business Technology; M. Kenneth Holt, Austin Peay State University; Julie O'Neil, Ph.D., Texas Christian University; Janis Prewitt, Drury University; and LaDawn Schouten Marsters, Boise State University. Where we were on target, they offered encouragement; where the manuscript could be improved, they pushed us to develop our ideas further. This publication is a better product because of their insights and involvement.

Patricia Quinlin, Lisa Cuevas Shaw, Liz Thornton, Katie Guarino, Mayan White, and Gina Fenwick at Sage Publications have been an incredibly supportive and responsive editorial team, ensuring a timely update of this book. In addition, Laura Barrett oversaw the production process that converted our manuscript into this finished book. The vision and professionalism of Michele Sordi, Vice President, Editorial and Brenda Carter, Executive Editorial Director, and all of the team at Sage who were involved, helped make the process of revising this book as painless as possible, while guiding us toward the finish line. It is good to work with an organization that not only invests in CSR, but enacts the values and practices outlined in this book on a day-to-day basis.

Finally, we would like to thank the late Leonard Turkel—mentor, community activist, social entrepreneur, and founding Co-director of the Center for Nonprofit Management at the University of Miami—who ceaselessly finds ways to better both his community and the people around him.

Notes and References

1. For a comprehensive review of the evolution of CSR as an academic discipline see Archie B. Carroll, 'Corporate Social Responsibility: Evolution of a Definitional Construct,' *Business and Society,* Vol. 38, No. 3, September 1999, pp 268–295. Also, traditional textbooks elaborate on these issues, in particular: Anne T. Lawrence & James Weber, *Business and Society: Stakeholders, Ethics, Public Policy*, 13th edition, McGraw-Hill, 2010. Finally, William C. Frederick, *Corporation Be Good! The Story of Corporate Social Responsibility*, Dog Ear Publishing, 2006, offers a comprehensive timeline and discussion about the evolution of CSR.

2. http://www.bcorporation.net/

3. http://www.consciouscapitalism.org/

4. Amy J. Hebard & Wendy S. Cobrda, 'The Corporate Reality of Consumer Perceptions: Bringing the Consumer Perspective to CSR Reporting,' *GreenBiz Reports*, February, 2009, p. 13.

5. See: David Grayson & Adrian Hodges, 'Corporate Social Opportunity! Seven Steps to Make Corporate Social Responsibility Work for your Business,' *Greenleaf Publishing*, July, 2004.

6. 'Making Money and Sustainable Progress with Ecopreneurship,' *Network for Business Sustainability*, March 5, 2012, http://nbs.net/knowledge/making-money-and-sustainable-progress-with-ecopreneurship/

7. Oxford English Dictionary, Second Edition, 1989, http://dictionary.oed.com/cgi/entry/50080908?single=1&query_type=word&queryword=externality&first=1&max_to_show=10

8. See: A. J. Weberman, *My Life in Garbology*, Amazon Digital Services, Inc., 2011 and Edward Humes, *Garbology: Our Dirty Love Affair With Trash*, Avery Publishing, 2012.

9. 'Effluence of affluence,' *The Economist*, January 7, 2012, p. 52.

10. 'The Seven Sins of Greenwashing,' *Terrachoice Environmental Marketing*, 2010, http://sinsofgreenwashing.org/findings/greenwashing-report-2010

11. For a description of these rights, see the United Nation's Universal Declaration of Human Rights (http://www.un.org/en/documents/udhr/index.shtml), which was adopted by the UN General Assembly on December 10, 1948.

12. Investopedia, http://www.investopedia.com/terms/s/shariah-compliant-funds.asp

13. Keith Davis, 'The Case for and Against Business Assumption of Social Responsibilities,' *Academy of Management Journal*, Vol. 16, Issue 2, 1973, pp. 312–322.

14. This concept was developed by William C. Frederick to capture his belief that all business actions are products of natural evolutionary processes. The concept is explained in more detail on Bill's website: http://www.williamcfrederick.com/business%26nature.html and in his book: *Natural Corporate Management: From the Big Bang to Wall Street*, Greenleaf Publishing Ltd., 2012.

15. Center for Media and Democracy. Quoted in: Andrew Adam Newman, 'Good/Corps Aims to Help Business Meet Social Goals,' *The New York Times*, May 13, 2011, pB3.

16. R. Edward Freeman, *Strategic Management: A Stakeholder Approach*, Pitman Publishing, Inc., 1984, p. 46.

17. Bill Baue, 'Brundtland Report celebrates 20th anniversary since coining sustainable development,' *Ethical Corporation Magazine*, June 18, 2007, http://www.ethicalcorp.com/content.asp?ContentID=5175. This definition of *sustainability* was developed by the Brundtland Commission (which got its name from its Chair, Gro Harlem Brundtland, the former Prime Minister of Norway). The Commission was established by the United Nations in 1983 to address growing concerns about the deteriorating condition of the natural environment. See also: http://www.un-documents.net/wced-ocf.htm

18. Michael E. Porter, *Competitive Strategy*, The Free Press, 1980.

19. John Micklethwait & Adrian Wooldridge, 'The Company: A Short History of a Revolutionary Idea,' Modern Library, 2003, p. 8.

20. C.K. Prahalad & Gary Hamel, 'The Core Competence of the Corporation,' *Harvard Business Review*, May-June, 1990, pp. 79–91; Gary Hamel & C.K. Prahalad, *Competing for the Future*, Harvard Business School Press, 1994.

21. Corporate governance has risen to prominence within the CSR field because of high-profile corporate scandals following the Internet bubble around the turn of this century. Much of the legislative response was an attempt to redress the balance of power between management and stockholders, represented by the board of directors. This issue revisits the fundamental conflict between principals (owners) and their agents (managers), an issue that has plagued limited liability joint stock companies since they were established in the UK by the Companies Act of 1862 (see John Micklethwait & Adrian Woolridge, 'The Company: A Short History of a Revolutionary Idea,' Modern Library, 2003, pp. xvi & xviii).

22. Michael E. Porter, 'The Five Competitive Forces That Shape Strategy,' *Harvard Business Review*, January, 2008, pp. 79–93; Michael E. Porter, *Competitive Strategy*, The Free Press, 1980.

23. Michael E. Porter, *Competitive Advantage*, The Free Press, 1985.

24. 'The Centenarians Square Up: IBM v Carnegie Corporation,' *The Economist*, June 11, 2011, pp. 64–66.
25. Milton Friedman, *Capitalism and Freedom*, University of Chicago Press, 1962, p. 133.
26. Attempts to archive the enormous amount of digital information that has been uploaded to the Internet ever since it was launched by Tim Berners-Lee in 1991 (and continues to be uploaded daily), represent an ongoing challenge for humanity. To this end, The Wayback Machine (http://archive.org/web/web.php) seeks to copy every website ever to go online, while the Open Library (http://openlibrary.org/) aims to create a webpage for every book that has ever been published. See also: 'Lost in cyberspace,' *The Economist: The Economist Technology Quarterly*, September 1, 2012, p. 11.
27. See: http://www.williamcfrederick.com/

PART I

STRATEGIC CORPORATE SOCIAL RESPONSIBILITY

Part I of *Strategic Corporate Social Responsibility* (*Strategic CSR*) demonstrates the breadth and depth of corporate social responsibility (CSR).

Chapters 1 and 2 lay the foundation for this book by defining CSR and related concepts, while outlining how this subject area has evolved over time. Chapter 1 provides core definitions, identifies different arguments for CSR (ethical, moral, rational, and economic), and shows why CSR is of growing importance to businesses large and small. Though companies exist to further the financial interests of their owners, they can achieve this most effectively by broadening their perspective and avoiding a narrow focus on the short term. Without an understanding for the broader social context in which it is embedded, a firm can become exploitive, antisocial, and corrupt, losing legitimacy and its ability to pursue the owners' economic goals over the medium to long term.

Chapter 2 reflects the importance of a stakeholder perspective to *Strategic CSR*. All organizations, like organisms, survive or perish depending on how they interact with their environment. Stakeholders, both internal and external, are key elements of a firm's environment. In this chapter, we explore in more detail *who* and *what* stakeholders are, and why their needs and demands should be of primary concern for firms that are looking to succeed. In particular, we focus on not only identifying stakeholders, but constructing models firms can use to prioritize among competing interests. As such, this chapter explains why a multi-stakeholder perspective best enables firms to craft competitive strategies in today's global, wired business environment.

Chapter 3 examines some of the more contentious elements of the CSR debate. Expectations about CSR appear in different ways in different cultures and play out on a firm-by-firm, industry-by-industry basis. Businesses that embrace CSR can be a source of pride, retention, and invigoration for employees and are also more likely to engender the support of external stakeholders. Provocatively, however, this chapter contests the assumption that CSR is solely a corporate responsibility and argues, instead, that stakeholders have an equal, if not greater, responsibility in relation to CSR. If consumers, for example, demonstrate a willingness to pay a price premium for CSR behavior (rather than reporting in surveys that they think firms should be more responsible, but basing their purchase decisions mainly on price), firms will quickly adapt. If consumers are unwilling to pay this premium, however, this chapter asks if it is in society's best interests for firms to bear the burden of producing such products?

Chapters 4 and 5 conclude Part I by outlining how firms integrate CSR into strategic planning and day-to-day operations. Chapter 4 first places CSR in a strategic context. Pursuit of the firm's mission must strike a balance between economic ends and socially acceptable means. Restated, strategy seeks competitive success, whereas CSR acts as a filter that helps ensure profit-directed actions do not harm stakeholders and a firm's viability over the long term. This chapter also analyses in more detail the five driving forces of CSR through the strategy lens.

Finally, Chapter 5 presents a plan to implement CSR, integrating principles and related practices throughout the firm's culture and day-to-day operations. Central to the implementation process is a genuine commitment by senior management. Ultimately, if CSR is to be an integral part of the firm's culture, leaders must initiate an ongoing dialog with key stakeholders (both internal and external) about the strategic and operational importance of CSR.

Chapter 1

WHAT IS CSR?

People create organizations to leverage their collective resources in pursuit of common goals. As organizations pursue these goals, they interact with others inside a larger context called society. Based on their purpose, organizations can be classified as for-profits, governments, or nonprofits. At a minimum, *for-profits* seek gain for their owners; *governments* exist to define the rules and structures of society within which all organizations must operate;[1] and *nonprofits* (sometimes called NGOs—nongovernmental organizations) emerge to do social good when the political will or the profit motive is insufficient to address society's needs.[2] Aggregated across society, each of these different organizations represents a powerful mobilization of resources. In the United States alone, for example, there are currently more than 1.5 million nonprofit organizations working to fill needs not met by either government or the private sector.[3]

Society exists, therefore, as a mix of these different organizational forms. Each performs different roles, but each also depends on the others to provide the complete patchwork of exchange interactions (products and services, financial and social capital, etc.) that constitute a well-functioning society. Whether called corporations, companies, firms, or proprietorships, for example, for-profit businesses interact constantly with government, trade unions, suppliers, NGOs, and other groups in the communities in which they operate, in both positive and negative ways. Each of these groups or actors, therefore, can claim to have a stake in the operations of the firm. Some benefit more, some are involved more directly, and others can be harmed by the firm's actions, but all are connected in some way to what the firm does on a day-to-day basis.

R. Edward Freeman defined these individual actors or groups as a firm's *stakeholders*. His definition reflects the broad reach of for-profit activity in our society and includes all those who are related in some way to the firm's goals:[4]

A Firm's Stakeholders

A stakeholder in an organization is (by definition) any group or individual who can affect or is affected by the achievement of the organization's objectives.[5]

Simply put, a firm's stakeholders include those individuals and groups that have a *stake* in the firm's operations. Such a broad view has not always been the norm, however. Over time, as the impact of business on society has grown, the range of stakeholders whose concerns a company needs to address has fluctuated—from the initial view of the corporation as a legal entity that is granted societal permission to exist by government charter, to a narrower focus on the rights of owners (shareholders), to a broader range of constituents (including employees and customers), and back again towards the end of the 20th century to a disproportionate focus on shareholders. Increasingly, however, companies are again adopting a broader stakeholder outlook, extending their perspective to include constituents such as the communities in which they operate and even the natural environment. Today, companies are more likely to recognize the degree of interdependence between the firm and each of these groups, leaving less room to ignore stakeholders' pressing concerns.

Just because an individual or organization meets this definition of an "interested constituent," however, does not compel a firm (either legally or logically) to comply with every stakeholder demand. Nevertheless, affected parties ignored long enough may take action against the firm, such as a product boycott,[6] or turn to government for redress. In democratic societies, laws (such as antidiscrimination statutes), rulings by government agencies (such as the Internal Revenue Service's tax exempt regulations for nonprofits), and judicial interpretations (such as court rulings on the fiduciary responsibilities[7] of executives and board members) provide a minimal framework for business operations that reflects a rough consensus of the governed. Because government cannot anticipate many issues, the legislative process takes time, and a general consensus is often slow to form, however, regulatory powers often lag behind the need for action. This is particularly so in areas of high complexity and rapid change, such as bioethics or information technology innovation. Thus, we arrive at the discretionary area of decision making that exists between legal sanction and societal expectation that business leaders face on a day-to-day basis, and which generates two questions from which the study of CSR springs:

- What is the relationship between a firm and the societies within which it operates?
- What responsibility does a firm owe society to self-regulate its actions in pursuit of profit?

CSR, therefore, is both critical and controversial. It is *critical* because the for-profit sector is the largest and most innovative part of any free society's economy. Companies intertwine with the broader society in mutually beneficial ways, driving social progress and affluence. In fact, the term *company* comes from a combination of the Latin words *cum* and *panis,* the literal translation of which originally meant "breaking bread together."[8] Today, however, the meaning of a company implies a far greater degree of complexity. Companies create most of the jobs, wealth, and innovations that enable the larger society to prosper. They are the primary delivery system for food, housing, medicines, medical care, and other necessities of life. Without modern day corporations, the jobs, taxes, donations, and other resources that support governments and nonprofits would decline significantly, negatively affecting the wealth and wellbeing of society as a whole. Businesses are the engines of society that propel us toward a better future. An interesting thought experiment: Today, if you wanted to do the most social good in your career, would you enter public service (politics or nonprofits) or would you go into business? Fifty years ago, you would probably have answered "public service." Today, the answer is not so clear.

At the same time, however, CSR remains *controversial.* People who have thought deeply about *Why does a business exist?* or *What is the purpose of business within society?* do not agree on the answers. Do companies have obligations beyond the benefits their economic success already provides? In spite of the rising importance of CSR today for corporate leaders, academics, and bureaucrats alike, many still draw on the views of the Nobel Prize-winning economist Milton Friedman, who argued against CSR because it distracted leaders from economic goals. Friedman believed that the only "social responsibility of business is to increase its profits"[9]—that society benefits most when businesses focus on maximizing their financial success. There are others, however, who look to the views of business leaders such as David Packard, a cofounder of Hewlett-Packard:

I think many people assume, wrongly, that a company exists simply to make money. While this is an important result of a company's existence, we have to go deeper and find the real reasons for our being. As we investigate this, we inevitably conclude that a group of people get together and exist as an institution that we call a company so that they are able to accomplish something collectively that they could not accomplish separately—they make a contribution to society, a phrase which sounds trite but is fundamental.[10]

This book will try and navigate between these competing perspectives to outline a view of CSR that recognizes both its strategic value to firms, while also incorporating the social value such a perspective brings to a firm's many stakeholders.[11] The goal is to present a comprehensive assessment of corporate social responsibility.

CORPORATE SOCIAL RESPONSIBILITY

The entirety of CSR can be discerned from the three words this phrase contains: *corporate, social,* and *responsibility.* CSR covers the relationship between corporations (or other for-profit organizations) and the societies with which they interact. CSR also includes the responsibilities that are inherent on both sides of these relationships. CSR defines society in its widest sense and, on many levels, to include all stakeholder and constituent groups that maintain an ongoing interest in the organization's operations.

CSR[12]

A view of the *corporation* and its role in *society* that assumes a *responsibility* among firms to pursue goals in addition to profit maximization and a *responsibility* among a firm's stakeholders to hold the firm accountable for its actions.

Stakeholder groups range from clearly defined consumers, employees, suppliers, creditors, and regulating authorities, to other more amorphous constituents such as local communities and even the natural environment. For the firm, tradeoffs must be made among these competing interests. Issues of legitimacy and accountability exist, with many nonprofit organizations, for example, claiming expertise and demanding representative status, even when it is unclear exactly how many people support their vision or claims. Ultimately, however, each firm must identify those stakeholders that constitute its operating environment and then prioritize their strategic importance. Increasingly, companies need to incorporate the concerns of stakeholder groups within their strategic outlook or risk losing societal legitimacy. CSR provides a framework that helps firms embrace these decisions and adjust the internal strategic planning process to maximize the long-term viability of the organization.

This framework is broad, however, and definitions regarding the mix of responsibilities and obligations have varied considerably over time. One of the most respected CSR academics, Archie B. Carroll, defined CSR in 1979 in the following way: "The social responsibility of business encompasses the economic, legal, ethical, and discretionary expectations that society has of organizations at a given point in time."[13] Figure 1.1 presents Carroll's conceptual framework in graphical form.

Figure 1.1   The Corporate Social Responsibility Hierarchy

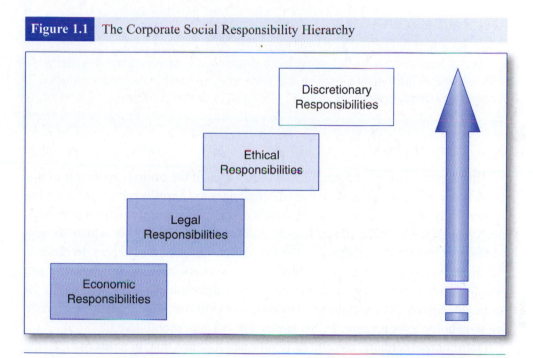

Source: Archie B. Carroll, 'The Pyramid of Corporate Social Responsibility: Toward the Moral Management of Organizational Stakeholders,' *Business Horizons*, July–August, 1991, p. 42.

The Corporate Social Responsibility Hierarchy

Archie Carroll was one of the first academics to make a distinction between different kinds of organizational responsibilities. He referred to this distinction as a firm's "pyramid of corporate social responsibility."[14]

- Fundamentally, a firm's *economic responsibility* is to produce an acceptable return on its owners' investment.

(Continued)

(Continued)

- An important component of pursuing economic gain within a law-based society, however, is a *legal responsibility*—a duty to act within the legal framework drawn up by the government and judiciary.
- Taken one step further, a firm has an *ethical responsibility* to do no harm to its stakeholders and within its operating environment.
- Finally, firms have a *discretionary responsibility*, which represents more pro-active, strategic behaviors that can benefit the firm and society, or both.

As a firm progresses up Carroll's pyramid, so its responsibilities move from being fundamental to becoming more discretionary or voluntary. A socially responsible firm encompasses all four responsibilities within its culture, values, and day-to-day operations.

This useful typology is not rigid, however.[15] One of the central arguments of this book is that what was ethical, or even discretionary in Carroll's model, is becoming increasingly necessary today due to the changing environment within which businesses operate. As such, ethical responsibilities are more likely to equate to economic and legal responsibilities as the foundation for business success. In order to fulfill its fundamental economic obligations to owners in today's globalizing and wired world, a firm should incorporate a broad stakeholder perspective within its strategic outlook. As societal expectations of the firm rise, so the penalties imposed by stakeholders for perceived CSR lapses will become prohibitive.

Definitions, therefore, can and do evolve and it seems that, in terms of CSR, the variance is considerable with at least five dimensions of CSR identified from the many different published definitions: environmental, social, economic, stakeholder, and voluntariness.[16] And, of course, there is not only variance within countries over time, but across countries and cultures:

CSR Definitions Across Cultures

Hong Kong: "The notion of companies looking beyond profits to their role in society is generally termed corporate social responsibility (CSR)....It refers to a company linking itself with ethical values, transparency, employee relations, compliance with legal requirements and overall respect for the communities in which they operate. It goes beyond the occasional community service action, however, as CSR is a corporate philosophy that drives strategic decision-making, partner selection, hiring practices and, ultimately, brand development."[17]

United Kingdom: "CSR is about businesses and other organizations going beyond the legal obligations to manage the impact they have on the environment and society. In particular, this could include how organizations interact with their employees, suppliers, customers and the communities in which they operate, as well as the extent they attempt to protect the environment."[18]

European Union: "[A] process to integrate social, environmental, ethical and human rights concerns into their business operations and core strategy in close collaboration with their stakeholders."[19]

United States: "CSR is about how companies manage the business processes to produce an overall positive impact on society."[20]

Canada: "The rules of modern business are changing. Bare economic success is no longer enough. Firms must still be financially successful, but they must do so in a way that is socially responsible and respectful of the impact of their actions on the natural environment. . . . The traditional logic of the corporation is being challenged along with longstanding frameworks and models of competition. There is a growing awareness that our business practices must be sustainable and our firms must be good corporate citizens."[21]

United Nations: "Corporate Social Responsibility (CSR) can be understood as a management concept and a process that integrates social and environmental concerns in business operations and a company's interactions with the full range of its stakeholders."[22]

CSR, therefore, is a fluid concept. Importantly, it is both a means and an end. It is an integral element of the firm's strategy—the way the firm goes about delivering its products or services to markets (*means*). It is also a way of maintaining the legitimacy of its actions in the larger society by bringing stakeholder concerns to the foreground (*end*). Ultimately, the success of a firm is directly related to its ability to incorporate stakeholder concerns into its business model. CSR provides a means to do this by valuing the interdependent relationships that exist among businesses, their stakeholder groups, the economic system, and the communities within which they exist. The dangers of managing these interdependent relationships ineffectively were apparent to Peter Drucker as far back as 1974:

The business enterprise is a creature of a society and an economy, and society or economy can put any business out of existence overnight. . . . The enterprise exists on sufferance and exists only as long as the society and the economy believe that it does a necessary, useful, and productive job.[23]

As such, CSR covers an uneven blend of different issues that rise and fall in importance from firm-to-firm over time. Recently, ethics and corporate governance, for example, have been of growing societal concern. This is a result of the lack of board oversight and poor executive decision making that led to the accounting-related scandals that were exposed during the first decade of this century, followed shortly thereafter by the Financial Crisis. The corporate response to this heightened concern is apparent by the rapid growth of the Ethics and Compliance Officers Association (ECOA). Figure 1.2 shows that, since its founding in 1992, the ECOA has grown to more than 1,300 members (http://www.theecoa.org/).[24] In addition, the ECOA estimates that, today, approximately 60% of Fortune 500 firms had adopted the Ethics and Compliance Officer position (with an additional 30% having a Compliance Officer), with much of that expansion occurring in the last decade.

CSR, therefore, is a vehicle for discussing the obligations a business has to its immediate society, a way of developing the means to meet these obligations, as well as a tool by which the mutual benefits that result can be identified. Simply put, CSR addresses a company's relationships with its stakeholders and recognizes that these relations are essential to the success of the enterprise. In particular, it recognizes:

Figure 1.2 The Growth in ECOA Membership (1992–2012)

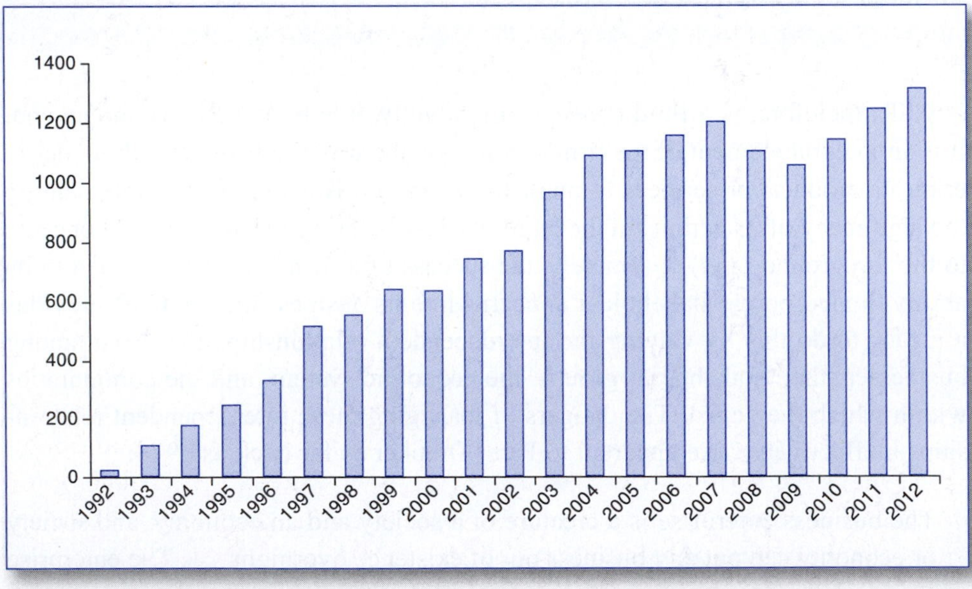

That markets operate successfully only when they were embedded in communities; that trust and cooperation are not antithetic to a market economy, but essential to it; that the driving force of innovation is pluralism and experiment, not greed and monopoly; that corporations acquire legitimacy only from the contribution they make to the societies in which they operate.[25]

CSR, therefore, encompasses the range of economic, legal, ethical, and discretionary actions that affect the economic performance of the firm. A significant part of a firm's fundamental responsibilities is complying with the legal or regulatory requirements that relate to day-to-day operations. To break these regulations is to break the law, which does not constitute socially responsible behavior. Clearly, adhering to the law is an important component of any ethical organization. But, legal compliance is merely a minimum condition of CSR.[26] Rather than focus on firms' legal and regulatory obligations, *Strategic CSR* focuses more on the ethical and discretionary concerns that are less precisely defined and for which there is often no clear societal consensus, but which are essential for firms to accommodate. Firms do this (minimizing competitive risk, while maximizing potential benefit) by fully embracing CSR and incorporating it within the firm's strategic planning process.

STRATEGY AND CSR

Strategy strives to provide the business with a source of sustainable competitive advantage. For any competitive advantage to be sustainable, however, the strategy must be acceptable to the wider environment in which the firm competes. CSR, therefore, is a key element of business strategy. In the words of *The Economist*, it is "just good business."[27] CSR implemented ineffectively—or, worse, completely ignored—may threaten whatever comparative advantage the firm holds within its industry. At the beginning of the twentieth century, for example, Standard Oil pressured industry suppliers to treat its competitors unfairly in the eyes of society. The result was a 1911 U.S. Supreme Court case (221 U.S. 1, 1911) that found the company in breach of the Sherman Antitrust laws, forcing Standard Oil to break into separate companies.[28] Today, activist organizations such as Greenpeace and the Rainforest Action Network (RAN) target corporate actions they deem to be socially irresponsible. The result of these protests and boycotts can be dramatic shifts in corporate policies and damage to the brand, such as Shell's change of course regarding the breakup of the *Brent Spar* oil platform,[29] or Citigroup's adoption of wide-ranging environmental metrics in the criteria it uses to grant loans.

As these examples demonstrate, however, CSR is not only about avoiding potential threats to the brand. There is also great potential for firms that embrace CSR.[30] For example, in part, Citigroup's reaction to RAN's campaign helped encourage the firm to play a leading role in the creation of the Equator Principles.[31] Shell also reinvigorated its business model in the years after Brent Spar. Today, Unilever's adoption of its "sustainable living plan"[32] and GE's commitment to "ecoimagination"[33] demonstrate the competitive advantage that CSR can deliver to firms that embrace CSR as a strategic point of differentiation in the market.

In other words, CSR allows executives to address stakeholder concerns in ways that carry strategic benefit for the firm. CSR is not about saving the whales or ending poverty or other worthwhile goals that are unrelated to a firm's operations and are better left to government or nonprofits. Instead, CSR is about the economic, legal, ethical, and discretionary issues that stakeholders view as directly related to the firm's plans and actions. The solutions to these issues, the overlap where economic and social value intersect, lie at the heart of any successful CSR policy. Michael Porter and Mark Kramer outline this approach in defining "strategic corporate philanthropy," but the same approach can be applied to the wider issue of CSR:

> The acid test of good corporate philanthropy is whether the desired social change is so beneficial to the company that the organization would pursue the change even if no one ever knew about it.[34]

Beyond the desired outcomes, however, are the approaches employed to achieve those changes. Too often, the end (profit maximization and share price growth) has been used to justify the means (operations that ignore the firm's broader stakeholder obligations). A firm that seeks to implement a CSR policy that carries strategic benefits is concerned with both the ends of economic profitability, but, more importantly, is concerned about the means by which those profits are achieved. As such, the connection between these means and ends, the processes by which the firm operates, is central to the concept of *strategic* CSR and something that sets it apart from other areas of social responsibility.

This distinction becomes apparent when discussing an issue such as ethics, which is concerned about the honesty, judgment, and integrity with which various stakeholders are treated. There is no debate—ethical behavior is a prerequisite assumption for strategic CSR. Ethics, however, is not the central focus for strategic CSR, except insofar as constituents are affected or society defines a firm's actions as unethical, thus harming the firm's legitimacy and profit potential. Likewise, other socially important issues exist outside the direct focus of strategic CSR. Concerns over domestic and international income disparity, gender issues, discrimination, human rights, spirituality and workplace religiosity, technological impacts on indigenous populations, and other issues all affect societal well-being. Unless firm operations directly affect stakeholders in these areas, however, the study of these topics might better fall under ethics, public policy, sociology, or developmental economics courses, which are better suited to explore these complex and socially important topics in greater depth.

THE EVOLUTION OF CSR

The call for social responsibility among businesses is not a new concept. Ancient Chinese, Egyptian, and Sumerian writings often delineated rules for commerce to facilitate trade and ensure that the wider public's interests were considered. Ever since, public concern about the interaction between business and society has grown in proportion to the growth of corporate activity:

> Concerns about the excesses of the East India Company were commonly expressed in the seventeenth century. There has been a tradition of benevolent capitalism in the UK for over 150 years. Quakers, such as Barclays and Cadbury, as well as socialists, such as Engels and Morris, experimented with socially responsible and values-based forms of business. And Victorian philanthropy could be said to be responsible for considerable portions of the urban landscape of older town centres today.[35]

Evidence of social activism in attempts to influence organizational behavior also stretches back across the centuries, mirroring the legal and commercial development of companies as they established themselves as the driving force of market-based societies:

> The first large-scale consumer boycott? England in the 1790s over slave-harvested sugar.[36]

What is clear is the effectiveness in these early consumer-led protests, initially in terms of raising public awareness, but soon after in terms of tangible, legislative change:

> Within a few years, more than 300,000 Britons were boycotting sugar, the major product of the British West Indian slave plantations. Nearly 400,000 signed petitions to Parliament demanding an end to the slave trade. . . . In 1792, the House of Commons became the first national legislative body in the world to vote to end the slave trade.[37]

Although wealthy industrialists have long sought to balance the mercantile actions of their firms with personal or corporate philanthropy as a response to social activism or other demands, CSR ultimately is strongest when leaders view their role as stewards of resources owned by others (e.g., shareholders, broader society, the environment). The words of the late Ray Anderson, founder and Chairman of Interface Carpets,[38] are instructive:

> Can any product be made sustainably? . . . One day early in this journey it dawned on me that the way I had been running Interface is the way of the plunderer, plundering something that is not mine; something that belongs to every creature on earth. And I said to myself, my goodness, the day must come when this is illegal, when plundering is not allowed [and] . . . people like me will end up in jail. The largest institution on earth, the wealthiest, most powerful, the most pervasive, the most influential, is the institution of business and industry— the corporation, which also is the current present day instrument of destruction. It must change.[39]

Leaders such as Anderson[40] face a balancing act that addresses the tradeoffs between the owners (shareholders) that employ them, the society that enables their firms to prosper, and the environment that provides them with the raw materials to produce products and services of value. When specific elements of society view leaders and their firms as failing to meet societal needs, activism results. That is equally true of eighteenth century England as it is today.

Current examples of social activism in response to a perceived lack of CSR by organizations are in this morning's newspapers, TV news, and spread online via social media, blogs, and websites. Whether the response is civil disobedience by protestors occupying Wall Street and capital cities around the world to highlight the distorted values of global finance, consumer boycotts of products that are hazardous to health, or NGO-led campaigns to eradicate sweatshops in developing economies contracting for apparel brands, CSR has become an increasingly relevant topic in recent decades in corporate boardrooms, business school classrooms, online, and in family living rooms. It is a subject that has evolved considerably since the beginnings of industrial society and continues to evolve today. Figure 1.3 illustrates the key events that have defined the history and evolution of CSR.

In addition to public relations fiascos that damage a firm's sales and image, the direct financial impact of CSR failures in a litigious society is never far behind. Widespread, long-term industry practices, which were previously considered discretionary or ethical concerns, can be deemed illegal or socially unacceptable under aggressive legal prosecution or novel social activism. Such violations are less likely in firms with a strong commitment to CSR. For example, the uncovering of the

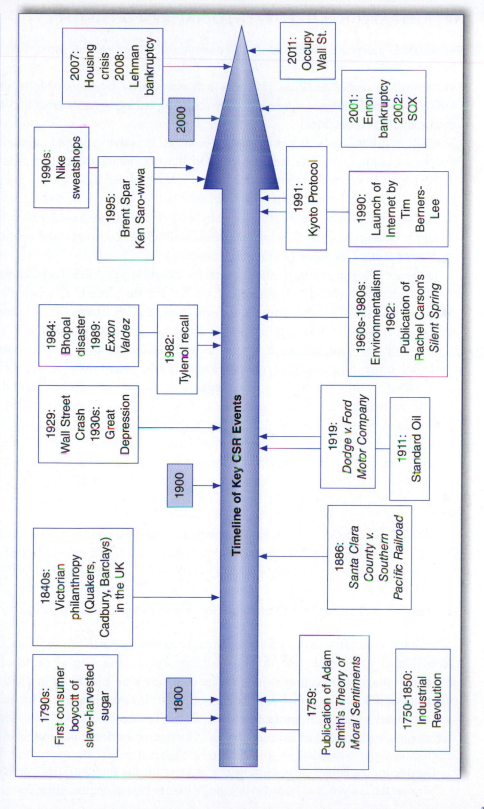

Figure 1.3 The History and Evolution of CSR

Timeline of Key CSR Events

1790s: First consumer boycott of slave-harvested sugar

1800

1840s: Victorian philanthropy (Quakers, Cadbury, Barclays) in the UK

1929: Wall Street Crash 1930s: Great Depression

1984: Bhopal disaster 1989: *Exxon Valdez*

1982: Tylenol recall

1990s: Nike sweatshops

1995: Brent Spar Ken Saro-wiwa

2007: Housing crisis 2008: Lehman bankruptcy

2000

2011: Occupy Wall St.

2001: Enron bankruptcy 2002: SOX

1991: Kyoto Protocol

1990: Launch of Internet by Tim Berners-Lee

1960s–1980s: Environmentalism 1962: Publication of Rachel Carson's *Silent Spring*

1919: *Dodge v. Ford Motor Company*

1911: Standard Oil

1886: *Santa Clara County v. Southern Pacific Railroad*

1759: Publication of Adam Smith's *Theory of Moral Sentiments*

1750–1850: Industrial Revolution

1900

widespread practice of back-dating of employee stock options by firms, first publicized widely by the *Wall Street Journal*,[41] indicates the dangers of assuming that yesterday's accepted business practices will necessarily be acceptable to others today. Businesses operate against an ever-changing background of what is considered socially responsible.

CSR, in other words, is not a stagnant concept. It is dynamic and continues to evolve as cultural expectations change. On the one hand, these ever-changing standards and expectations compound the complexity faced by corporate decision makers. Worse, these standards vary from society to society; even among cultures within a given society. Worse still, they also evolve over time. Faced with a kaleidoscopic background of evolving standards, business executives must consider a variety of factors on the way to implementation.

In the early history of the United States, for example, the Alien Tort Claims Act "was originally intended to reassure Europe that the fledgling U.S. wouldn't harbor pirates or assassins. It permits foreigners to sue in U.S. courts for violations of the law of nations."[42] Today, this 1789 law is being used to try and hold U.S. firms accountable for their actions overseas, as well as the actions of their partners (whether other businesses or governments). Thus, what may be legal, even encouraged, in one country may bring legal repercussions in another. And, this is not just an isolated example. Firms such as Citibank, Coca-Cola, Gap, IBM, J.C. Penny, Levi Strauss, Limited, Pfizer, Shell, Texaco, and Unocal have all faced litigation under this same law, which may extend to hundreds of other national and international firms.[43] Unocal, one of the companies in this list whose case had advanced the furthest in U.S. courts, announced in December 2004, on the eve of having its case heard on appeal, that it would settle for an undisclosed sum:

> Lawsuits filed by 15 villagers from Myanmar . . . said the company 'turned a blind eye' to atrocities allegedly committed by soldiers guarding a natural gas pipeline built by the company and its partners in the 1990s. . . . A joint statement by the two sides said Unocal would pay the plaintiffs an unspecified sum and fund programmes to improve living conditions for people living near the pipeline.[44]

In 2008, in the first major case to be brought to trial under the Alien Tort Claims Act, Texaco was cleared of any responsibility for the shooting to death of two Nigerian villagers protesting on one of the company's oil platforms in 1998. The villagers were killed by police and security officers who were brought in by the firm to diffuse the situation. Importantly, however, the Texaco case sets a precedent for future prosecutions against firms operating in foreign countries to be brought to trial:

> Despite the outcome, . . . the trial was a success for the human rights community because the lawyers succeeded in bringing a case to trial under the Alien Torts law.[45]

In 2012, Shell found itself before the U.S. Supreme Court to argue whether the Ogoni people of Nigeria had standing to sue in U.S. courts under the Alien Tort Claims Act. The Ogoni people accuse Shell of colluding with the Nigerian government to commit human rights abuses in order to protect Shell operations in that country:

> The federal government and judges in two other federal appeals courts . . . have rejected the idea that corporations are immune from liability under the [Alien Tort Claims Act].[46]

Nike, more commonly, reacted to stakeholder criticism of sweatshop conditions in its Asian factories by demanding that its suppliers provide their employees with wages and working conditions that meet the expectations of consumers in developed societies—consumers who might boycott Nike products if they perceive the company to be acting in an unfair or irresponsible manner. Today, Apple faces similar allegations over its controversial relationship with the Taiwanese electronics components supplier, Foxconn (formally, Hon Hai Precision Industry Co., Ltd.). Increasingly, the media and NGO activists will criticize the poor treatment of workers in developing economies by holding corporations to standards found in their home markets, especially the United States and the European Union (EU). The result is increased complexity and risk that can harm economic outcomes when CSR is lacking.

On the other hand, however, the pursuit of economic gain remains an absolute necessity. CSR does not repeal the laws of economics under which for-profit organizations must operate (to society's benefit). The example of Malden Mills, below, demonstrates that, unless a firm is economically viable, even the best of intentions will not enable stakeholders to achieve their goals and maximize social value.

Malden Mills[47]

Aaron Feuerstein, CEO of Malden Mills (founded in 1906, family owned), was an excellent man to work for:

> Here was a CEO with a unionized plant that was strike-free, a boss who saw his workers as a key to his company's success.[48]

In 1995, however, a fire destroyed the firm's main textile plant that was based in Lawrence, Massachusetts, an economically deprived area in the north of the state:

(Continued)

(Continued)

> With an insurance settlement of close to $300 million in hand, Feuerstein could have, for example, moved operations to a country with a lower wage base, or he could have retired. Instead, he rebuilt in Lawrence and continued to pay his employees while the new plant was under construction.[49]

> He met the payroll for idle workers as the company rebuilt, and he was idolized throughout the media.... The national attention to Feuerstein's act brought more than the adulation of business ethics professors—it brought increased demand for his product, Polartec, the lightweight fleece the catalogue industry loves to sell.[50]

In addition to full pay, Feuerstein also continued all his employees on full medical benefits and guaranteed them a job when the factory was ready to restart production:

> Rebuilding in Lawrence would cost over $300 million while keeping 1,400 laid-off workers on full salaries for a period of up to 3 months would cost an additional $20 million. 'I have a responsibility to the worker, both blue-collar and white collar,' Feuerstein later said. 'I have an equal responsibility to the community. It would have been unconscionable to put 3,000 people on the streets [two weeks before Christmas] and deliver a death blow to the cities of Lawrence and Methuen. Maybe on paper our company is [now] worth less to Wall Street, but I can tell you it's [really] worth more.'[51]

But the increased demand for Polartec clothing (http://www.polartec.com/) that Feuerstein's actions generated wasn't enough to offset the debt he had built up waiting for the plant to be rebuilt: $100 million.[52] This situation was compounded by the downturn in the market, as well as cheaper fleece alternatives flooding the market. Malden Mills filed for bankruptcy protection in November 2001.[53]

Profit, therefore, is a necessary, but insufficient justification for business and, by itself, an inaccurate determinant of value added. Just because money *can* be made, does not mean necessarily that it *should* be made. CSR is a valuable filter through which the firm's business decisions should pass. As such, CSR is an important component of a company's operations and strategic perspective. Equally, however, CSR alone it is not enough. It certainly does not replace the need for an effective business model, and no company, whatever the motivation, can or should spend money that it does not have indefinitely.

Which actions should be pursued depend on many factors that are specific to the firm and industry, but also to the society in which the firm is based and the timing of the decision. Manufacturing offshore in a low-cost environment, for example, remains a valid strategic decision, particularly in an increasingly globalizing business world. It is strategic because it can provide competitive advantage for some firms, such as Apple,[54] even while other firms, such as Master Lock[55] and Zara,[56] see strategic value in onshoring operations due to rising costs in China and the advantages of having a shorter, more responsive supply chain:

> Factories used to move to low-wage countries to curb labour costs. But labour costs are growing less and less important: a $499 first-generation iPad included only about $33 of manufacturing labour, of which the final assembly in China accounted for just $8. Offshore production is increasingly moving back to rich countries not because Chinese wages are rising, but because companies now want to be closer to their customers so that they can respond more quickly to changes in demand. And some products are so sophisticated that it helps to have the people who design them and the people who make them in the same place. The Boston Consulting Group reckons that in areas such as transport, computers, fabricated metals and machinery, 10-30% of the goods that America now imports from China could be made at home by 2020, boosting American output by $20 billion-55 billion a year.[57]

Given the economic and social consequences of these decisions, both strategy and CSR considerations are involved. As *The Economist* notes, however, while the intellectual argument is convincing, there is still plenty of room left for improvement in terms of practical implementation:

> Corporate social responsibility, once a do-gooding sideshow, is now seen as mainstream. But as yet too few companies are doing it well.[58]

As societies rethink the balance between societal needs and economic progress, CSR will continue to evolve in importance and complexity. And, although this complexity muddies the wealth-creating waters, an awareness of these evolving expectations holds the potential for increased competitive advantage for those firms that do it well. The examples above indicate that the cultural context within which CSR is perceived and evaluated is crucial.

CULTURE AND CONTEXT

As already discussed, firms operate within the context of broader society. The resulting interaction requires a CSR perspective in order for firms to maintain their societal legitimacy. Yet, societies differ, and so, therefore, does what they consider to be acceptable. Though differences range from the anthropological and sociological, to the historical and demographic, two dimensions consistently influence the visibility of CSR: democracy and economics.

Different societies define the relationship between business and society in different ways. Unique expectations spring from many factors, with wealthy societies having greater resources and, perhaps, more demanding expectations that emerge from the greater options wealth brings. The reasoning is straightforward: In poor democracies, the general social wellbeing is focused on the necessities of life—food, shelter, transportation, education, medicine, social order, jobs, and the like. Governmental or self-imposed CSR restrictions add costs that poor societies can ill afford. As societies advance, however, expectations change and the *general social wellbeing* is redefined. This progression of development is reflected in Maslow's hierarchy of needs:

> At the bottom was what we needed to survive—oxygen, food and water. Above that was the need to be safe. Once we had those, we could turn to the need for love, affection and a feeling of belonging. After that, we could go for esteem and respect. At the top of the hierarchy was self-actualization, or self-fulfillment.[59]

The ongoing evolution of societal expectations causes the acceptable level of response also to shift, as this example of air pollution and public transportation in Chile indicates:

Santiago, Chile

In the 1980s, air pollution in downtown Santiago, Chile, was an important issue, just as it was in Los Angeles, California. The problem, however, was addressed differently in relation to the level of economic development found in these two pollution-retaining basins. Stringent laws went into effect in the Los Angeles basin during the 1980s. At the same time in Chile, necessities (including low-cost transportation) got a higher priority because of widespread poverty. After more than a decade of robust economic growth, however, Chileans eventually used democratic processes to put limitations on the number of cars entering Santiago and required increasingly stringent pollution standards. This shift in priorities reflected their changing societal needs and expectations, along with the growing wealth to afford the new rules and legal actions.

Different expectations among rich and poor societies are a matter of priorities. The need for transportation, for example, evolves into a need for nonpolluting forms of transportation as society becomes more affluent. Though poor societies value clean air just as advanced ones do, there are other competing needs that may take priority—one of which will be the need for low-cost transportation. As a society prospers economically, new expectations compel producers to make vehicles that pollute less—a shift in emphasis. In time, these expectations may evolve from a discretionary to a mandatory (legal) requirement. What was true of transportation in the 1980s is true of issues like recycling today in São Paulo, Brazil[60] and is true of social and political development, in general, throughout South America:

> As Latin Americans become less poor, they want better public services. Latin Americans are demanding more of their democracies, their institutions and governments; they worry about crime almost as much as about economic problems; and fewer of them think that their country is progressing.[61]

This discussion reinforces the idea that it is in any organization's best interest (for-profit, nonprofit, or governmental) to anticipate, reflect, and strive to meet the changing needs of its stakeholders in order to remain successful. In the case of for-profit firms, the primary stakeholder groups are its shareholders, customers, and employees, without whose support the business fails. Other constituents, however, from suppliers to the local community, also matter greatly. Businesses must satisfy the primary groups among these constituents, therefore, if they hope to remain viable over the long term. When the expectations of different stakeholders conflict, CSR enters a gray area and management has to balance competing interests. An important part of that conflict arises from different expectations, which, in turn, reflect different approaches to CSR.

FOUNDATIONS OF CSR

CSR therefore represents an argument for a firm's economic interests, where satisfying stakeholder needs becomes central to retaining societal legitimacy (and, therefore, financial viability). Much debate (and criticism) in the CSR community, however, springs from well-intentioned parties who argue the same *facts* from different perspectives, breaking down along philosophical and ideological lines. Understanding these different perspectives, therefore, is an important component of understanding the breadth and depth of CSR. An introduction to the underlying ethical, moral, rational, and economic arguments for CSR follows.

An Ethical Argument for CSR[62]

The danger of promoting a perspective of CSR that focuses primarily on its strategic value to the firm is that the ethical and moral foundations on which much

CSR debate rests are ignored. The advantage of making the business case for CSR is that it is more convincing to those most skeptical of broadening the firm's responsibilities and more likely to be implemented. In other words, the business case is expedient—it offers the greatest potential gain because it will appeal to the widest possible audience. We recognize, however, that downplaying an ethical or moral component to CSR ignores an intellectual philosophical foundation that many believe is important in order to fully understand CSR.

Core to an argument grounded in ethics is the issue of whether ethical values are subjective or absolute. An ethical argument for CSR states that, rather than being relative constructs (i.e., varying from individual-to-individual and culture-to-culture), ethical values are absolute (i.e., inalienable *rights* that are consistent across cultures and apply to all human beings). Absolute values are easily definable and, as such, exist as a standard against which behavior can be assessed.

Although many discussions around CSR assume an ethical component, the precise relationship between ethics and CSR is often left unspecified. As such, the late Rushworth Kidder poses a fascinating question when he asks: "Can a socially responsible company be unethical?"[63] His answer is that it can. In constructing that answer, he indicates the importance of ethics in relation to the broader concept of CSR.

CSR Newsletters: CSR vs. Ethics

In an article in *Ethics Newsline*,[64] Rushworth Kidder draws an instructive distinction between a socially responsible company and an ethical company. Kidder is not objective (he is writing for the Institute of Global Ethics), but that does not diminish the value of the conversation. In short, Kidder conceptualizes CSR as a subset of the broader idea of ethics:

> Responsibility . . . is one of five distinct core values that define, globally, the idea of ethics. A necessary but not sufficient condition for ethics, it needs to be fleshed out by the other four values: honesty, respect, fairness, and compassion. Ethics requires all five. So can an individual or a corporation have a strong sense of responsibility without necessarily being honest? Yes. The opposite can also arise, where a deeply honest person proves to be irresponsible. These are two big, different ideas.

> Partly, this characteristic of being more than one thing at once reflects the complexity of modern corporations. No firm is either all-good or all-bad and any means of measuring CSR that suggests otherwise is not sufficiently subtle

to be of value. It is Kidder's broader argument, however, that is stimulating. Implicitly, Kidder is taking aim at the superficial nature of much of the work firms refer to as CSR, but he is also questioning the ability of the CSR community to validate that work. This explains why firms like Enron and BP can be heralded by the CSR community as examples of 'best-practice' organizations, only to be later exposed as unethical (non-CSR) firms in reality. Whenever a third party attempts to evaluate a firm, they are liable to some degree of obfuscation or distortion:

> Of course corporate responsibility attracts customers. Of course it is good business. And of course it must be fully ethical. They must not only do the right things (which is CR) but do things right (which is ethics). Increasingly, customers are demanding both. Look for smart CR companies to make this connection quickly and bring the two together.

> *Greenwashing* is a label that is too-easily thrown around, but it speaks to a core problem within CSR—the ability of stakeholders to define and measure what we think of as responsible behavior in a way that allows comparisons across organizations. The answer is easy to conceptualize and difficult to implement. First, we need to find a way to assess accurately those firms that are genuinely conducting business in a way that is qualitatively different to those firms that are simply using CSR to sell more products; then, we need to educate the firm's stakeholders to differentiate among these firms in ways that reward the firms that most constructively contribute to social value, broadly defined. Both steps are essential to ensure sufficient, meaningful change.

Broadly, an ethical argument for CSR rests on one of two philosophical approaches—consequentialist reasoning or categorical reasoning.[65] Consequentialist (or teleological) reasoning locates ethicality in terms of the outcomes caused by an action. This stream of thought is closely aligned with utilitarianism, which was most famously advocated by the eighteenth century English political philosopher, Jeremy Bentham. As such, "an action is considered ethical according to consequentialism when it promotes the good of society, or more specifically, when the action is intended to produce the greatest net benefit (or lowest net cost) to society when compared to all the other alternatives."[66]

In contrast, categorical (or deontological) moral reasoning "is defined as embodying those activities which reflect a consideration of one's duty or obligation."[67] As such, categorical reasoning represents more of a process-orientation, rather than the outcome-oriented focus of consequentialist reasoning. This perspective most closely maps on to the work of Emanuel Kant's categorical imperative, but also includes guiding principles such as religious doctrine and core values such as trustworthiness, honesty, loyalty, accountability, and a broad sense of citizenship (i.e., acting out of a sense of responsibility to the commonweal).

An Ethical Argument for CSR

CSR is an argument of two forms of ethical reasoning—either consequentialist (utilitarian) or categorical (Kantian). Consequentialist ethical reasoning justifies action in terms of the outcomes it generates (the greatest good for the greatest number of people), while categorical ethical reasoning justifies action in terms of the principles by which that action is carried out (the application of core ethical principles, regardless of the outcomes they generate). These two philosophical approaches are codified in the organization and guide practices and policies via the firm's Code of Conduct or Ethics.

In terms of practical application, the two ethical perspectives become realized in social norms—"those standards . . . which have been accepted by the organization, the industry, the profession, or society as necessary for the proper functioning of business" and are codified within the organization in the form of a Code of Conduct or Ethics, which then act as a point of reference in determining "whether a company is acting ethically according to the conventional standard."[68]

Though not always codified into dogma or laws, the cultural heritage, founded on ethical principles, leads to an evolving definition of social justice, human rights, and environmental stewardship, the violation of which is deemed ethically wrong and socially irresponsible. This logic is the foundation for the 'social contract' that is based on societal expectations that bind firms because compliance is directly related to a social license to operate. To violate these implicit ethical boundaries can lead to a loss of legitimacy that threatens the long-term viability of the organization.

A Moral Argument for CSR

Although recognizing that profits are necessary for any business to survive, for-profit organizations are only able to obtain those profits because of the society in which they operate. CSR emerges from this interaction and the interdependent relationship between for-profits and society. It is shaped by individual and societal standards of morality that define contemporary views of human rights and social justice.

Thus, to what extent is a firm obliged to repay the debt it owes society for its continued business success? That is, what moral responsibilities do businesses face in return for the benefits society grants? And also, to what extent does the profits the business generates, the jobs it provides, and the taxes it pays already meet those obligations? As an academic study, CSR represents an organized approach to answering these questions. As an applied discipline, it represents the extent to which businesses need to deliver on their obligations as defined by societal expectations.

A Moral Argument for CSR

CSR is an argument of moral reasoning that reflects the relationship between a company and the principles expected by the wider society within which it operates. It assumes businesses recognize that for-profit entities do not exist in a vacuum and that a large part of their success comes as much from actions that are congruent with societal values and norms as from factors internal to the company.

Charles Handy constructs a compelling argument that businesses have a moral obligation to move beyond the goals of maximizing profit and satisfying shareholders above all other stakeholders:

The purpose of a business . . . is not to make a profit, full stop. It is to make a profit so that the business can do something more or better. That "something" becomes the real justification for the business. . . . It is a moral issue. To mistake the means for the end is to be turned in on oneself, which Saint Augustine called one of the greatest sins. . . . It is salutary to ask about any organization, "If it did not exist, would we invent it?" "Only if it could do something better or more useful than anyone else" would have to be the answer, and profit would be the means to that larger end.[69]

A similar sentiment is expressed in a quote attributed to Peter Drucker who argues there is no moral justification in pursuing profit alone:

Profit for a company is like oxygen for a person. If you don't have enough of it, you're out of the game. But if you think your life is about breathing, you're really missing something.[70]

At one level, the moral argument for CSR reflects a give-and-take approach, based on a meshing of the firm's values and those of society. Society makes business possible and provides it directly or indirectly with what for-profits need to succeed, ranging from educated and healthy workers to a safe and stable physical and legal infrastructure; not to mention a consumer market for their products. Because society's contributions make businesses possible, those businesses have a reciprocal obligation to society to operate in ways that are deemed responsible and beneficial. And, because businesses operate within a social context, society has the right and the power to define expectations for those who operate within its boundaries:

> [Free-market economists] like to portray "wealth-producing" businesses as precarious affairs that bestow their gifts independently of the society in which they trade. The opposite is the case. The intellectual, human and physical infrastructure that creates successful companies, alongside their markets, is a social product and that, in turn, is shaped by the character of that society's public conversation and the capacity to build effective social institutions and processes.[71]

As a result, for many, a focus on money alone is dispiriting—"as vital as profit is, it seems insufficient to give people the fulfillment they crave."[72] In other words, money is a means, rather than an end. It follows from this logic that, to some degree, money is a social good that is accompanied by a moral obligation to return to the collective a percentage of the proceeds of economic gain, which were earned based on advantages conferred by society to the firm. As Adam Smith[73] wrote in *The Wealth of Nations*:

> The subjects of every state ought to contribute towards the support of the government, as nearly as possible, in proportion to their respective abilities; that is, in proportion to the revenue which they respectively enjoy under the protection of the state. The expense of government to the individuals of a great nation is like the expense of management to the joint tenants of a great estate, who are all obligated to contribute in proportion to their respective interests in the state.[74]

At a deeper level, societies rest upon a cultural heritage that grows out of a confluence of religion, mores, and folkways. This heritage gives rise to a belief system that defines the boundaries of socially acceptable behavior by people and organizations. All members of society have a moral responsibility to uphold these *rules* in the interests of the commonweal.

A Rational Argument for CSR

The loss of societal legitimacy can lead to the countervailing power of social activism, restrictive legislation, or other constraints on the firm's freedom to pursue its economic and other interests. Violations of ethical and discretionary standards are not just inappropriate; they also present a rational argument for CSR.

Because societal sanctions (such as laws, fines, prohibitions, boycotts, or social activism) affect the firm's strategic goals, efforts to comply with societal expectations are rational, regardless of ethical or moral reasoning. When compliance with societal expectations is based on highly subjective values, the rational argument rests on sanction avoidance—it may be more cost-effective, for example, to address issues voluntarily, rather than wait for a mandatory requirement based on government or judicial action. Archie Carroll, for example, argues that businesses can wait for the legally mandated requirements and then react to them.[75] This reactive approach may permit for-profit firms to ignore their ethical and moral obligations and concentrate on maximizing profits or other business goals; however, it also inevitably leads to strictures being imposed that not only force mandatory compliance, but often force compliance in ways that the firm may find neither preferable nor efficient. By ignoring the opportunity to influence the debate in the short term through proactive behaviors, an organization is more likely to find its business operations and strategy hampered over the long term. One need only consider the evolution of affirmative action in the United States to see this rationale in action:

Affirmative Action

Prior to the 1960s, businesses could discriminate against current or potential employees on the basis of race, sex, religion, age, national origin, veteran's status, pregnancy, disability, sexual preference, and other non-merit based criteria. Putting aside the moral concerns, doing so was a discretionary right that was legal, if far from ethical. Social activism moved these ethical and discretionary decisions into the arena of public debate and, in time, into legal prohibitions. The result for many businesses that were guilty of past or present discrimination meant affirmative action plans to redress racial or other imbalances in their workforce. Those organizations that lagged quickly found themselves the test case in litigation focused on institutionalizing the new legislation.

As Robert Kennedy said during the civil rights movement to those firms that were reluctant to change:

> If you won't end discriminatory practices because it's the right thing to do; then do it because it's good for business.[76]

We are not suggesting firms should have acted to ensure discrimination remained legal. That would be an ethical and moral lapse that would have involved fighting the evolving societal consensus and risking the societal legitimacy of the firm. Instead, the rational argument advocates self-interest in avoiding the inevitable confrontation. By not adopting a proactive (or at least accommodative) approach to fair treatment, many businesses found their behavior suddenly (and expensively) curtailed through legislation, judicial and agency interpretations, and penalties because of a failure to interpret correctly the evolving social and business environment.

A Rational Argument for CSR

CSR is a rational argument for businesses seeking to maximize their performance by minimizing restrictions on operations. In today's globalized world, where individuals and activist organizations feel empowered to enact change, CSR represents a means of anticipating and reflecting societal concerns to minimize operational and financial constraints on business.

The rational argument for CSR is summarized by the *Iron Law of Social Responsibility*, which states that: In a free society, discretionary abuse of societal responsibilities leads, eventually, to mandated solutions.[77] Restated: In a democratic society, power is taken away from those who abuse it. The history of social and political uprisings—from Cromwell in England, to the American and French Revolutions, to the overthrow of the Shah of Iran or the Communist government of the Soviet Union, to the rise of the Arab Spring—underscores the conclusion that those that abuse power or privilege sow the seeds for their own destruction.

Parallels exist in the business arena. Financial scandals around the turn of this century at Enron, WorldCom, Adelphia, HealthSouth, and other icons of U.S. business caused discretion-limiting laws and rulings, such as the Sarbanes-Oxley legislation of 2002, just as the Financial Crisis that began in 2007/2008 gave rise to the Dodd-Frank Wall Street Reform and Consumer Protection Act that was passed by the U.S. Congress in 2010. Such transgressions result in heightened political oversight that results in previously discretionary and ethical issues moving into the legal arena. Similarly, firms that compensate their CEOs and other executives with financial packages that are perceived to be excessive, especially following poor performance, face unwelcome oversight from regulatory agencies and politicians who have to answer to their own stakeholders (the voting electorate):

> …public corporations are political institutions: They depend on the good will of the public to operate successfully. The absence of that good will leaves them open to attacks from Congress, regulators, ambitious attorneys general, pension

funds, hedge funds, unions, nongovernmental organizations and just about any-one else who wants a say in a corporation's affairs.[78]

By adopting a rational argument for CSR, however, firms seek to interpret changing societal values and stakeholder expectations, and act to avoid future sanctions. Sensing that the tide of public opinion in the U.S. was moving in favor of regulating carbon emissions, for example, firms formed groups to lobby the government for change. The group BICEP (Business for Innovative Climate and Energy Policy)[79] was established by five firms with proactive CSR track records—Levi Strauss, Nike, Starbucks, Sun Microsystems, and Timberland. Perhaps more surprisingly, however, USCAP (United States Climate Action Partnership),[80] which "supports the introduction of carbon limits and trading. . . . was set up by energy companies and industrial manufacturers" who might otherwise have opposed government action in this area.[81] General Motors, for example, became the first U.S. automobile manufacturer to join USCAP, "which seeks economy-wide greenhouse gas emission reductions of 60 to 80 per cent by 2050."[82]

Implementing a rational perspective, these firms realize that it is in their inter-ests to engage with regulators, rather than oppose legislation that they see as inevitable. As James Rogers, CEO of Duke Energy succinctly puts it, "If you're not at the table when these negotiations are going on, you're going to be on the menu."[83] In other words, acting proactively in a socially responsible manner to avoid unwelcome intrusion or help shape prospective legislation is an act of rational business—particularly so in light of the overwhelming anecdotal evidence that discretionary abuses lead to a loss of decision-making freedoms and financial repercussions for for-profit organizations.

An Economic Argument for CSR

Summing the previous three arguments for CSR leads to an economic argument. In addition to avoiding ethical, moral, legal, and other societal sanctions, incorpo-rating CSR into a firm's operations offers a potential point of differentiation and competitive market advantage upon which future success can be built.[84]

An Economic Argument for CSR

CSR is an argument of economic self-interest for business. CSR adds value because it allows companies to reflect the needs and concerns of their various stakeholder groups. By doing so, a company is more likely to retain its societal legitimacy and maximize its financial viability over the medium to long term. Simply put, CSR is a way of matching corporate operations with societal values and expectations that are constantly evolving.

CSR influences all aspects of a business's day-to-day operations. Everything an organization does causes it to interact with one or more of its stakeholder groups. As a result, companies are best served by building positive relationships with as broad an array of key stakeholders as possible. Whether as an employer, producer, buyer, supplier, or as an investment, a firm's attractiveness and success are increasingly linked to its organizational values and culture. Concerning socially responsible investments (SRI), for example, "Funds that invest with a conscience have more than doubled in size over the last 10 years."[85] Even for those who believe that the only purpose of a business is to increase the wealth of the owners, being perceived as socially *irresponsible* risks losing access to an already significant (and growing) segment of investors and their capital:

> At the start of 2010, professionally managed assets following SRI strategies stood at $3.07 trillion, a rise of more than 380 percent from $639 billion in 1995. . . . Over the same period, the broader universe of assets under professional management increased only 260 percent from $7 trillion to $25.2 trillion. During the most recent financial crisis, from 2007 to 2010, the overall universe of professionally managed assets has remained roughly flat while SRI assets . . . have enjoyed healthy growth.[86]

CSR affects operations within a corporation because of the need to consider constituent groups. Each area builds on all the others to create a composite of the corporation in the eyes of its stakeholders. Businesses must satisfy key groups among these constituents if they hope to remain viable over the long term. Importantly, in doing so, the messages that firms send to stakeholders "are not incompatible with pursuing shareholder value. Rather, they give the companies a license to operate in order to pursue it."[87]

Strategic CSR expounds the economic argument in favor of CSR. We believe it is the clearest of the four (ethical, moral, rational, and economic) arguments supporting CSR and emphasizes the importance of CSR for businesses today. The economic argument for CSR operates at the intersection of the economic self-interest of the firm and the broader well-being of society. As such, this perspective offers a plan of action that has as its goal the maximization of value, broadly defined.

An important distinction that helps explain the particular value of this perspective is between an effective *business model* and a broader, more sustainable *model for (all) businesses*. The Body Shop, for example, has implemented a successful *business model* that subscribes to a moral argument for CSR. It is an activist organization that is able to draw on support from the small percentage of the population that is aware and sufficiently responsive to a progressive social agenda and translate it into economic success. In contrast, an economic argument for CSR speaks to a broad *model for businesses* that recognizes the limited application of moral activism and, instead, searches for a minimum standard to which all organizations can subscribe. The result is an approach to business that identifies the strategic benefits of a CSR and stakeholder perspective in a way that sustains the firm and maximizes the total added value of its operations.

FIVE DRIVING FORCES OF CSR

CSR is important, therefore, because it influences all aspects of a company's operations. Consumers want to buy products from companies they trust; suppliers want to form business partnerships with companies they can rely on; employees want to work for companies they respect; large investment funds want to support firms that they perceive to be socially responsible; and nonprofits and NGOs want to work together with companies seeking practical solutions to common goals. Satisfying each of these stakeholder groups (and others) allows companies to maximize their commitment to their shareholders (their ultimate stakeholders), who benefit most when all of these groups' needs are being met.

This is an abstract argument, however. In order for strategic CSR to be convincing, it is necessary to place it within a contemporary context that makes the case for this perspective today. We believe that CSR is increasingly crucial to success because it gives companies a mission and strategy around which multiple constituents can rally. Equally important, however, we believe that there is a confluence of forces that make this argument particularly relevant. The firms most likely to succeed in today's dynamic business environment will be those best able to balance the often conflicting interests of their multiple stakeholders. In particular, CSR as an integral component of strategy is increasingly relevant for businesses due to five identifiable trends—trends that will continue to grow in importance throughout the 21st century.[88]

Affluence

A poor society, in need of work and inward investment, is less likely to enforce strict regulations and penalize organizations that might otherwise take their business and money elsewhere. Consumers in developed societies, on the other hand, can afford to choose the products they buy and, as a consequence, expect more from the companies whose products they buy. This sense has increased in the wake of the corporate scandals at the turn of this century and the current financial crisis, both of which reduced public trust in corporations and the finance industry, in particular, and public confidence in the ability of regulatory agencies to control corporate excess. Affluence matters and leads to changing societal expectations. Firms operating in affluent societies, therefore, face a higher burden to demonstrate they are socially responsible. As a result, increasing affluence on a global basis will continue to push CSR up the agendas of corporations worldwide.

Sustainability

An increase in general affluence and changing societal expectations is enhanced by a growing concern for the environment. When the Alaskan pipeline was built in the 1970s, crews could drive on the hardened permafrost 200 days a year. Today, climate changes leave the permafrost solid for only 100 days each year, while NASA photographs reveal that the Arctic ice cap "has shrunk more than 20 percent" since 1979,[89] a rate of decrease that is accelerating.[90] Increasing raw materials prices, rising mutation rates among amphibian populations, shrinking biodiversity, and other empirical indicators all support what is intuitive—that the Earth has ecological limits. The speed at which we are approaching the earth's limits and the potential consequences of our actions are complicated issues about which experts do not agree. What is not in doubt, however, is that human economic activity is depleting the world's resources and causing dramatic changes to the earth's atmosphere—changes that could become irreversible in the near future. As a result, firms that are perceived to be indifferent to their environmental responsibilities are likely to be criticized and penalized. Examples include court-imposed fines (*Exxon Valdez*),[91] negative publicity (Monsanto's genetically modified foods),[92] or confrontations by activist groups (Friends of the Earth).[93]

Globalization

Increasingly, corporations conduct business in a global environment. Operating in multiple countries and cultures magnifies the complexity of business exponentially. Not only are there more laws and regulations to understand, but many more social norms and cultural subtleties to navigate. In addition, the range of stakeholders to whom multinational firms are held accountable increases, as does the potential for conflict among competing stakeholder demands. While globalization has increased the potential for efficiencies gained from production across borders, it has also increased the potential to be exposed to a global audience if a firm's actions fail to meet the needs and expectations of the local community.

Media

The growing influence of social media makes sure that any CSR lapses by companies are brought rapidly to the attention of the worldwide public, often instantaneously. Scandal is news, and yesterday's eyewitnesses are today armed with pocket-size video cameras and mobile phones that provide all the evidence necessary to convict by video, blog, or instant message. In addition, the Internet fuels communication among activist groups and like-minded individuals, empowering them to spread their message while giving them the means to coordinate collective action. Such technologies are reaching beyond the control of autocratic governments and allowing people to find new ways to mobilize and protest. Thomas Friedman, for example, explains how this communication revolution is affecting the relationship between the government and people of Iran:

> What is fascinating to me is the degree to which in Iran today – and in Lebanon – the more secular forces of moderation have used technologies like Facebook, Flickr, Twitter, blogging and text-messaging as their virtual mosque, as the place they can now gather, mobilize, plan, inform and energize their supporters, outside the grip of the state.[94]

Google is one company that is increasingly finding new ways to apply these new communication technologies:[95]

CSR Newsletters: Google

These two articles in *The Wall Street Journal* and *The New York Times*[96] demonstrate the power of the internet to re-shape the way information is communicated around the globe. This phenomenon will continue to evolve in ways that we have not yet even begun to imagine (at least, those of us who do not work for Google):

> You can Google to get a hotel, find a flight and buy a book. Now you may be able to use Google to avoid the flu.

> The philanthropic arm of the internet search company (http://www.google.org/) has released a new service (http://www.google.org/flutrends/) that will track internet search terms related to the flu nationally (e.g., "cough" or "fever") and use this information to help identify potential outbreaks of the illness:

>> It displays the results on a map of the U.S. and shows a chart of changes in flu activity around the country. The data is meaningful because the Google arm that created Flu Trends found a strong correlation between

(Continued)

(Continued)

the number of Internet searches related to the flu and the number of people reporting flu symptoms.

This information is powerful because of the speed with which it identifies early trends to which government agencies and health providers can then react:

Tests of the new Web tool from Google.org, the company's philanthropic unit, suggest that it may be able to detect regional outbreaks of the flu a week to 10 days before they are reported by the Centers for Disease Control and Prevention.

Firms are just beginning to appreciate the ways in which these communication tools will affect their operations and reputations. What seems apparent, however, is that the affect will be dramatic and that firms that are not transparent and accountable to their stakeholders will suffer as a result.

Brands

All of these trends that are driving the importance of CSR overlap in terms of the importance of a firm's reputation and brand. Brands today are often a focal point of corporate success. Companies try to establish popular brands in consumers' minds because doing so increases their competitive advantage, which then results in higher sales and revenue. In addition, consumers are more likely to pay a premium for a brand they know and trust. Due to growing demands from increasing numbers of stakeholders, however, combined with the increased complexity of business in a global environment and the ability of individuals and the media to spread missteps instantaneously to a global audience; today, more than ever before, a firm's reputation is precarious—hard to establish and easy to lose. Lifestyle brands (which base more of their appeal to consumers on aspirational values), in particular, need to live the ideals they convey to their consumers. As a result, as *Interbrand's* annual brand survey demonstrates,[97] brands are more valuable than ever and firms need to take ever greater steps to protect an investment that is essential to their continued success.

NEXT STEPS

Beyond the five driving forces that locate strategic CSR within its larger context, CSR must also work in practice. It must allow firms to prosper, as well as act as a conduit for stakeholder concerns. But, how are firms supposed to identify key stakeholders and prioritize among their competing interests? Does CSR matter to stakeholders? Are stakeholders willing to enter the debate and impose their views on corporations? Do they share some of the responsibility for shaping corporate actions? And, how should firms begin integrating a CSR perspective into their strategic planning and day-to-day operations?

The importance of the stakeholder model to the arguments presented in *Strategic CSR* will be explored further in Chapter 2. Arguments *against* CSR (and the often unintended implications of progressive CSR applications) exist and will be explored in Chapter 3. Chapter 4 puts CSR into strategic perspective and expands on the growing importance of CSR and its impact on corporate strategy. Issues that influence the implementation of CSR within a strategic decision-making framework provide the basis for Chapter 5, which will conclude Part I of *Strategic CSR*.

QUESTIONS FOR DISCUSSION AND REVIEW

1. Why do firms exist? What value do businesses serve for society?

2. Define *corporate social responsibility*. What arguments in favor of CSR seem most important to you? How is CSR different from *strategic* CSR?

3. Name the four responsibilities of a firm outlined in Archie Carroll's "Pyramid of CSR" model. Illustrate your definitions of each level with corporate examples.

4. Milton Friedman argued that, "Few trends could so thoroughly undermine the very foundations of our free society as the acceptance by corporate officials of a social responsibility other than to make as much money for their stockholders as possible."[98] Give two arguments in support of Friedman's assertion and two against.

5. Define and discuss briefly the ethical, moral, rational, and economic arguments for CSR?

6. What five driving forces make CSR more relevant today?

7. Of these five factors, is there any one that you feel is more important than the others? Defend your choice with examples from your own experiences and knowledge.

STUDENT STUDY SITE

Visit the Student Study Site at **www.sagepub.com/chandler3e** for additional learning tools.

NOTES AND REFERENCES

1. For an idea of the potential for government to work in relation to CSR, including its definition of corporate responsibility, see the UK government's CSR homepage at: http://www.bis.gov.uk/policies/business-sectors/green-economy/sustainable-development/corporate-responsibility

2. It is interesting to speculate where organizations founded by social entrepreneurs fit within this taxonomy. Organizations that seek to meet social goals via business practices are neither for-profit firms as we know them, nor nonprofit organizations. The emergence of Benefit corporations (or b-corps) further confuses traditional definitions of organizational forms. At this stage, we do not think such hybrid organizations are sufficiently well-defined or prevalent to warrant a fourth 'type' of organization, but their evolution is an important component of the CSR landscape. For greater consideration of these organizational forms see Issues: Corporate Governance and Issues: Social Entrepreneurship in Chapter 6.

3. National Center for Charitable Statistics (http://nccs.urban.org/), Number of Nonprofit Organizations in the United States, 1999-2009, http://nccsdataweb.urban.org/PubApps/profile1.php

4. Post, Preston, and Sachs provide an alternative, narrower, definition of a firm's stakeholder that ties the group or actor more directly to the firm's operations: "The stakeholders in a firm are individuals and constituencies that contribute, either voluntarily or involuntarily, to its wealth-creating capacity and activities, and who are therefore its potential beneficiaries and/or risk bearers." In: 'Managing the Extended Enterprise: The New Stakeholder View,' *California Management Review*, Vol. 45, No. 1, Fall 2002, p. 8.

5. R. Edward Freeman, Strategic Management: A Stakeholder Approach, Pitman, 1984, p. 46.

6. Libby Brooks, 'Power to the People,' *The Guardian*, December 20, 2002, http://www.guardian.co.uk/world/2002/dec/20/debtrelief.development

7. The phrase "fiduciary responsibility" is widely used in business, but not widely understood. In its most simple form, it means a responsibility of one party that is a result of a formal relationship with another party. The responsibility is founded on trust and often involves financial transactions. While this responsibility can clearly exist as a result of a legal or contractual relationship, it can also emerge from an ethical relationship, which expands its relevance within a discussion of CSR. The Oxford English Dictionary reports that the origin of the term lies in the late 16th century and comes from the Latin *fiduciarius*, which means 'trust.'

8. John Micklethwait & Adrian Wooldridge, 'The Company: A Short History of a Revolutionary Idea,' Modern Library, 2003, p. 8.

9. Milton Friedman, 'The Social Responsibility of Business is to Increase its Profits,' *The New York Times Magazine*, September 13, 1970.

10. Charles Handy, 'What's a Business For?' *Harvard Business Review,* December 2002, p. 54.

11. Of course, this debate continues today. For one discussion that was hosted by a skeptical source, but includes different perspectives from the Rainforest Action Network to G.E., see 'Corporate Social Responsibility: Good Citizenship of Investor Rip-off?' Big Issues: The Journal Report, *Wall Street Journal*, January 9, 2006, p. R6.

12. For a comprehensive review of the evolution of CSR as an academic discipline see Archie B. Carroll, 'Corporate Social Responsibility: Evolution of a Definitional Construct,' *Business and Society*, Vol. 38, No. 3, September 1999, pp. 268–295 and Herman Aguinis & Ante Glavas, 'What We Know and Don't Know About Corporate Social Responsibility: A Review and Research Agenda,' *Journal of Management*, Vol. 38, No. 4, July, 2012, pp. 932-968. Also, traditional textbooks elaborate on these issues, see: Anne T. Lawrence & James Weber, *Business and Society: Stakeholders, Ethics, Public Policy*, 13th edition, McGraw-Hill, 2010. Finally, William C. Frederick, *Corporation Be Good! The Story of Corporate Social Responsibility*, Dog Ear Publishing, 2006, offers a comprehensive timeline and discussion of the evolution of CSR.

13. Archie B. Carroll, 'A Three-Dimensional Conceptual Model of Corporate Performance,' *Academy of Management Review*, 1979, Vol. 4, No. 4, p. 500.

14. Archie B. Carroll, 'The Pyramid of Corporate Social Responsibility: Toward the Moral Management of Organizational Stakeholders,' *Business Horizons*, July–August, 1991.

15. See Mark S. Schwartz & Archie B. Carroll, 'Corporate Social Responsibility: A Three-domain Approach,' *Business Ethics Quarterly*, Vol. 13, 2003, pp. 503–530 for an update on Carroll's pyramid of CSR. Instead of four levels of responsibility, Schwartz and Carroll divide a firm's responsibilities into three domains—economic, legal, and ethical. These three overlapping domains result in seven "CSR categories," or firm profiles, with the appropriate category determined by the firm's orientation (i.e., the different emphases placed on each domain).

16. See: Alexander Dahlsrud, 'How Corporate Social Responsibility is Defined: An Analysis of 37 Definitions,' *Corporate Social Responsibility and Environmental Management*, 2006. Other researchers have identified "three fundamental lines of CSR inquiry prevalent in the academic literature"—stakeholder driven, performance driven, and motivation driven. See: Kunal Basu & Guido Palazzo, 'Corporate Social Responsibility: A Process Model of Sensemaking,' *Academy of Management Review*, Vol. 33, No. 1, 2008, p. 122.

17. Michael McComb, 'Profit to Be Found in Companies That Care,' *South China Morning Post*, April 14, 2002, p. 5.

18. Ruth Lea, 'Corporate Social Responsibility: IoD Member Opinion Survey,' *The Institute of Directors*, UK, November, 2002, p. 10.

19. 'A renewed EU strategy 2011-14 for Corporate Social Responsibility,' *European Commission*, COM(2011) 681 final, Brussels, 25.10.2011, Clause 3.1, p. 6, http://eur-lex.europa.eu/LexUriServ/LexUriServ.do?uri=COM:2011:0681:FIN:EN:PDF

20. Mallen Baker, 'Corporate social responsibility: What does it mean?' 2012, http://www.mallenbaker.net/csr/definition.php

21. Canadian Center for Corporate Responsibility, 2012, http://www.business.ualberta.ca/en/Programs/ExecutiveEducation/Programs/CSR.aspx

22. 'Introduction to Corporate Social Responsibility,' United Nations Institute for Training and Research, 2012, http://www.unitar.org/event/introduction-corporate-social-responsibility

23. Michael Hiltzik, 'Peter Drucker's revolutionary teachings decades old but still fresh,' *Los Angeles Times*, December 31, 2009, http://articles.latimes.com/2009/dec/31/business/la-fi-hiltzik31-2009dec31

24. In March 2007, the ECOA had 1,388 individual members and approximately 750 organizational members. Individual members are defined by the ECOA as "ethics and compliance professionals."

25. John Kay, 'The left is still searching for a practical philosophy,' *Financial Times*, May 5, 2010, p. 9.

26. It is worth reinforcing the idea that actions that are legally permissible may still be morally or ethically objectionable to certain stakeholder groups. In response, these activists can use obscure treaties and statues (e.g. Alien Tort Claims Act passed in 1789 by the first U.S. Congress) to file lawsuits against firms in order to right actual or perceived wrongs.

27. 'Just Good Business: A Special Report on Corporate Social Responsibility,' *The Economist*, January 19, 2008.

28. See: *Standard Oil Co. of New Jersey v. United States*, (221 U.S. 1, 1911). Ironically, it was the proceeds from stock sales as a result of the breakup of Standard Oil that gave John D. Rockefeller "a cash windfall of unprecedented magnitude" that he then used to begin the Rockefeller Foundation. See: Jonathan Lopez, 'The Splendid Spoils of Standard Oil,' *The Wall Street Journal*, November 20-21, 2010, p. C7.

29. http://archive.greenpeace.org/comms/brent/brent.html. See, also, Alex Kirby, 'Brent Spar's long sage,' *BBC News*, November 25, 1998, http://news.bbc.co.uk/1/hi/sci/tech/218527.stm

30. See: David Grayson & Adrian Hodges, 'Corporate Social Opportunity! Seven Steps to Make Corporate Social Responsibility Work for your Business,' *Greenleaf Publishing*, July, 2004.

31. Marc Gunther, 'The Mosquito in the Tent: A Pesky Environmental Group Called the Rainforest Action Network is Getting Under the Skin of Corporate America,' *Fortune Magazine*, May 31, 2004, http://money.cnn.com/magazines/fortune/fortune_archive/2004/05/31/370717/index.htm. The Equator Principles is "a credit risk management framework for determining, assessing and managing environmental and social risk in [financial] transactions." Equator Principles website, March, 2013, http://www.equator-principles.com/index.php/about-ep

32. See: http://www.unilever.com/sustainable-living/. For more comment on Unilever's approach to CSR, see: http://strategiccsr-sage.blogspot.com/2011/03/strategic-csr-unilever.html

33. See: http://www.ecomagination.com/

34. Michael Porter & Mark Kramer, 'The Competitive Advantage of Corporate Philanthropy,' *Harvard Business Review,* Vol. 80, Issue 12, December 2002, p. 67.

35. Adrian Henriques, 'Ten things you always wanted to know about CSR (but were afraid to ask); Part One: A Brief History of Corporate Social Responsibility (CSR),'

Ethical Corporation Magazine, May 26, 2003, http://www.ethicalcorp.com/content .asp?ContentID=594

36. Michael Arndt, 'An Ode to 'The Money-Spinner,' *BusinessWeek,* March 24, 2003, pp. 22–23; review of 'The Company: A Short History of a Revolutionary Idea,' by John Micklethwait & Adrian Wooldridge, Modern Library, 2003.

37. Adam Hochschild, 'How the British Inspired Dr. King's Dream,' *New York Times,* January 17, 2005, p. A21.

38. For more on Interface's revolutionary approach to environmental stewardship and its zero emissions, zero waste commitments, see: http://www.interfaceflor.com/default .aspx?Section=3&Sub=4

39. http://www.triplepundit.com/pages/ray-anderson-ex.php. Excerpt from an interview with Ray Anderson that appeared in *The Corporation,* http://www.thecorporation.com/

40. For a video update on Interface's progress towards its "Mission Zero" project (http://www.interfaceflor.eu/internet/web.nsf/webpages/528_EN.html) and goal of "leaving zero footprint, by the year 2020," see: http://www.interfaceflor.eu/internet/web.nsf/webpages/58150_EN.html

41. Mark Maremont, 'Authorities Probe Improper Backdating of Options—Practice Allows Executives To Bolster Their Stock Gains; A Highly Beneficial Pattern,' *Wall Street Journal,* 11 November 2005, p. A1, http://www.biz.uiowa.edu/faculty/elie/wsj1 .htm and Charles Forelle and James Bandler, 'The Perfect Payday—Some CEOs reap millions by landing stock options when they are most valuable; Luck — or something else?' *Wall Street Journal,* March 18-19, 2006, p. A1, http://www.biz.uiowa.edu/faculty/elie/wsj2.htm

42. Paul Magnusson, 'Making a Federal Case Out of Overseas Abuses,' *BusinessWeek,* November 25, 2002, p. 78.

43. Paul Magnusson, 'Making a Federal Case Out of Overseas Abuses,' *BusinessWeek,* November 25, 2002, p. 78.

44. Lisa Roner, 'Unocal settles landmark human rights suits,' *Ethical Corporation Magazine,* December 20, 2004, http://www.ethicalcorp.com/content.asp?Content ID=3312

45. Richard C. Paddock, 'Chevron cleared in 1998 shootings at Nigerian oil platform,' *Los Angeles Times,* December 2, 2008, http://articles.latimes.com/2008/dec/02/local/me-chevron2

46. Daniel Fisher, 'Is Shell The Equivalent Of Nazi-Era Firm? Legally, Perhaps' *Forbes Magazine,* February 24, 2012, http://www.forbes.com/sites/danielfisher/2012/02/24/is-shell-the-equivalent-of-nazi-era-firm-legally-perhaps/

47. For additional background information on Malden Mills, see Rebecca Leung, 'The Mensch of Malden Mills,' 60 Minutes, *CBS,* July 6, 2003, http://www.cbsnews.com/stories/2003/07/03/60minutes/main561656.shtml. See also, Gretchen Morgenson, 'GE Capital vs. the Small-Town Folk Hero,' *New York Times,* October 24, 2004, p. BU5.

48. Marianne Jennings, 'Seek Corporate Balance,' *Miami Herald,* September 1, 2002, p. 11L.

49. Roger Martin, 'The Virtue Matrix,' *Harvard Business Review,* March 2002, Vol. 80, No. 3, pp. 68–75.

50. Marianne Jennings, 'Seek Corporate Balance,' *Miami Herald,* September 1, 2002, p. 11L.

51. Manuel G. Velasquez, 'Business Ethics: Concepts and Cases,' 5th edition, Prentice Hall, 2002, pp. 122–123.

52. Mitchell Pacelle, 'Can Mr. Feuerstein Save His Business One Last Time?' *Wall Street Journal,* May 9, 2003, pp. A1 & A6.

53. In spite of emerging from bankruptcy protection in 2004, the firm continued to struggle and filed for bankruptcy again in 2007. Today, the company continues to make its clothing under the brand name Polartec (http://www.polartec.com/).

54. Charles Duhigg & Keith Bradsher, 'How the U.S. Lost Out on iPhone Work,' *The New York Times,* January 21, 2012, http://www.nytimes.com/2012/01/22/business/apple-america-and-a-squeezed-middle-class.html

55. Zachary Roth & Daniel Gross, 'President Obama Touts 'Onshoring': Is Made in America Back?' *The Daily Ticker,* February 15, 2012, http://finance.yahoo.com/blogs/daily-ticker/president-obama-touts-onshoring-made-america-back-221759270.html

56. Frank Worstall, 'Offshoring and Onshoring: It's All a Bit More Complex Than You Think,' *Forbes Magazine*, March 21, 2012, http://www.forbes.com/sites/timworstall/2012/03/21/ofshoring-and-onshoring-its-all-a-bit-more-complex-than-you-think/

57. 'The third industrial revolution,' *The Economist Editorial*, April 21, 2012, p. 15.

58. 'Just Good Business: A Special Report on Corporate Social Responsibility,' *The Economist*, January 19, 2008, p. 3.

59. Michael Skapinker, 'The purpose of business is to win respect,' *Financial Times*, February 23, 2010, p. 9.

60. Dom Phillips, 'Ambitious law seeks São Paulo transformation,' *FT Special Report, Green New Deal: Regional Solutions*, *Financial Times*, September 21, 2009, p. 1.

61. 'The Latinobarómetro poll: The discontents of progress,' *The Economist*, October 29, 2011, p. 48.

62. With sincere thanks to William C. Frederick for pushing us to develop our ideas further on this point. See: http://www.williamcfrederick.com/

63. Rushworth Kidder, 'Why Corporate Social Responsibility Needs Ethics,' *Ethics Newsline*, October 3, 2011, http://www.globalethics.org/newsline/2011/10/03/social-responsibility/

64. Rushworth Kidder, 'Why Corporate Social Responsibility Needs Ethics,' *Ethics Newsline*, October 3, 2011, http://www.globalethics.org/newsline/2011/10/03/social-responsibility/

65. For more information and debate about these different ethical approaches, see Michael Sandel's Harvard University undergraduate course, 'Justice.' A series of videos relaying a semester of classes from the course is online at: http://www.justiceharvard.org/

66. Mark S. Schwartz & Archie B. Carroll, 'Corporate Social Responsibility: A Three-domain Approach,' *Business Ethics Quarterly*, Vol. 13, 2003, p. 512.

67. Mark S. Schwartz & Archie B. Carroll, 'Corporate Social Responsibility: A Three-domain Approach,' *Business Ethics Quarterly*, Vol. 13, 2003, p. 512.

68. Mark S. Schwartz & Archie B. Carroll, 'Corporate Social Responsibility: A Three-domain Approach,' *Business Ethics Quarterly*, Vol. 13, 2003, pp. 511–512.

69. Handy, op. cit.

70. Design Thinking, 'Peter Senge's Necessary Revolution,' *BusinessWeek*, June 11, 2008, http://www.businessweek.com/innovate/content/jun2008/id20080611_566195.htm

71. Will Hutton, 'The Body Politic Lies Bleeding,' *The Observer*, May 13, 2001, http://www.guardian.co.uk/politics/2001/may/13/election2001.uk6

72. Michael Skapinker, 'How to fill the philanthropy-shaped hole,' *Financial Times*, January 27, 2009, p. 13.

73. Adam Smith published *The Wealth of Nations* in 1776, but it is his book, *The Theory of Moral Sentiments* (first published in 1759), that leads many observers to describe Smith as a moral philosopher, rather than an economist. For example, see: James R. Otteson, 'Adam Smith: Moral Philosopher,' The Freeman Ideas on Liberty, Vol. 50, Issue 11, November, 2000, http://www.thefreemanonline.org/features/adam-smith-moral-philosopher/

74. Adam Smith, 'An Inquiry into the Nature and Causes of the Wealth of Nations,' Book V, Chapter 2, Part II (On Taxes), 1776. Quoted in: Sam Fleischacker, 'Adam Smith vs. George Bush on Taxes,' *Los Angeles Times*, January 22, 2001, http://articles.latimes.com/2001/jan/22/local/me-15437

75. Carroll, 1979, op. cit.

76. Eliot Spitzer, 'Strong Law Enforcement is Good for the Economy,' *Wall Street Journal*, April 5, 2005, p. A18.

77. Keith Davis & Robert Blomstrom, *Business and Its Environment*, McGraw-Hill, 1966. See also: Keith Davis, 'The Case for and Against Business Assumption of Social Responsibilities,' *Academy of Management Journal*, Vol. 16, Issue 2, 1973, pp. 312–322.

78. Alan Murray, 'Twelve Angry CEOs—The Ideal Enron Jury,' *Wall Street Journal*, February 15, 2006, p. A2.

79. http://www.ceres.org/bicep

80. http://www.us-cap.org/

81. Jonathan Birchall, 'Business fights for tougher rules on emissions,' *Financial Times*, November 20, 2008, p. 4.

82. John Reed, 'GM joins 'green' coalition in the US,' *Financial Times*, May 9, 2007, p. 18.

83. Suzanne Charlé, 'When Addressing Climate Change Is Good Business,' *strategy+business magazine*, February 20, 2007, p. 1, http://www.strategy-business.com/article/li00014?gko=66a28.

84. Some of the most important research in the business management literature on the relationship between CSR and firm performance is being done by Joshua Margolis of Harvard Business School (see: Joshua Margolis and James Walsh, 'Misery Loves

Companies: Rethinking Social Initiatives by Business,' *Administrative Science Quarterly*, Vol. 48, Issue No. 2, 2003, pp. 268-305; Joshua Margolis, Hillary Elfenbein, and James Walsh, 'Does it Pay to be Good? What a Meta-analysis of CSP and CFP Can (and Cannot) Tell Us,' *Academy of Management Annual Meeting*. Philadelphia, PA, 2007; and Joshua Margolis and Hillary Elfenbein, 'Do Well by Doing Good? Don't Count on It,' *Harvard Business Review*, Vol. 86, Issue No. 1, 2008, pp. 19-20). Margolis' main conclusion from his research is that, while there is little evidence that CSR predicts firm performance, there does seem to be evidence of the reverse relationship—firm performance predicting CSR. In other words, while CSR does not increase profits, higher profits lead to greater CSR. One explanation for this failure to establish a conclusive link between CSR and firm performance is that the tools we currently use to measure CSR are not very good. While data and methods are improving all the time, we are yet to identify a sufficiently comprehensive means of establishing a firm's CSR profile. In the absence of such a measure, continuing to research whether or not such activities have positive (or negative) correlations with firm performance (creating a huge black box in the process) seems difficult to justify. Margolis' response is to call on researchers to move beyond investigating the relationship between CSR and firm performance (or vice-versa) and, instead, focus on understanding how and why firms decide to act in relation to CSR—"understanding the mechanisms that connect CFP to CSP, rather than the reverse."

85. Tara Kalwarski, ' Numbers: Do-good Investments are Holding up Better,' *BusinessWeek*, July 14 & 21, 2008, p. 15.

86. 'Report on Socially Responsible Investing Trends in the United States,' *Social Investment Forum Foundation*, 2010, p. 8, http://ussif.org/resources/research/documents/2010TrendsES.pdf

87. Andrew Likierman, 'Stakeholder dreams and shareholder realities,' Mastering Financial Management, *Financial Times*, June 16, 2006, p. 10.

88. For a more detailed discussion of these trends that are driving the relevance of CSR, see Chapter 4.

89. 'Global Warming Puts the Arctic on Thin Ice,' *Natural Resources Defense Council*, November 22, 2005, http://www.nrdc.org/globalwarming/qthinice.asp

90. 'New NASA Satellite Survey Reveals Dramatic Arctic Sea Ice Thinning,' Jet Propulsion Laboratory, *NASA*, July 7, 2009, http://www.jpl.nasa.gov/news/news.cfm?release=2009-107

91. 'Images From the Exxon Valdez Oil Spill,' National Oceanic and Atmospheric Administration, March 7, 2001, http://response.restoration.noaa.gov/photos/exxon/exxon.html

92. 'Farmers & Consumers Protest at Monsanto's Headquarters in St. Louis,' Organic Consumers Association, August 19, 2000, http://www.organicconsumers.org/corp/monprotest.cfm

93. 'Corporate Campaigns: Case studies: http://www.foe.co.uk/campaigns/economy/case_studies/index.html and Success stories: http://www.foe.co.uk/campaigns/economy/success_stories/index.html

94. Thomas L. Friedman, 'The Virtual Mosque,' *New York Times*, June 17, 2009, p. A21.

95. In addition to tracking flu epidemics, Google is also using its search data to measure inflation using the "Google price index." See: Aki Ito & Alisa Odenheimer, 'Google: Central Banks' New Economic Indicator,' *Bloomberg BusinessWeek*, August 9, 2012, http://www.businessweek.com/articles/2012-08-09/google-central-banks-new-economic-indicator; Christoper Caldwell, 'Government by search engine,' *Financial Times*, October 16/17, 2010, p. 9; and, Robin Harding, 'Google to measure inflation by using web data,' *Financial Times*, October 12, 2010, p. 1.

96. Robert A. Guth, 'Sniffly Surfing: Google Unveils Flu-Bug Tracker,' *Wall Street Journal*, November 12, 2008, p. D1, http://sec.online.wsj.com/article/SB12264430 9498518615.html; Miguel Helft, 'Aches, a Sneeze, a Google Search,' *New York Times*, November 12, 2008, p. A1, http://www.nytimes.com/2008/11/12/technology/internet/12flu.html

97. 'Best Global Brands 2012,' *Interbrand*, http://www.interbrand.com/en/best-global-brands/2012/Best-Global-Brands-2012.aspx

98. Milton Friedman, *Capitalism and Freedom*, University of Chicago Press, 1962, p. 133.

Chapter 2

STRATEGY + CSR: A STAKEHOLDER PERSPECTIVE

All organizations, like organisms, survive or perish depending on how they adapt to their environment. As discussed in Chapter 1, a firm's stakeholders are key elements of its environment. While stakeholders depend on firms to provide the products and services that they demand, companies depend on suppliers, customers, employees, and other stakeholders for the societal legitimacy they need to remain in business. How stakeholders evaluate the firm, therefore, depends not only on *what* the firm does, but also on *how* it does it. Strategy seeks a sustainable competitive advantage. Its success rests on matching the organization's internal competencies with the demands of its external competitive environment. Central to both sides of that equation (the firm's internal capabilities and its external environment) are the firm's internal and external stakeholders.

Before exploring who and what stakeholders are, we consider the different perspectives of corporate strategy. We argue that, while these perspectives contain important insights into a firm's ability to convert resources into a competitive advantage, a stakeholder perspective is better suited for firms trying to navigate the global business environment of the 21st century. A stakeholder perspective enables firms to identify the multiple constituents that are affected by the firm's operations, while also allowing them to prioritize among those stakeholders' often competing demands. By integrating a stakeholder/CSR perspective within strategic planning and day-to-day operations, firms are better prepared to respond effectively to their stakeholders' needs. And, that responsiveness to its environment helps ensure that the company strategy is effective and durable. Conversely in today's increasingly global, interconnected world, if key constituencies are ignored, the firm's strategy risks a lack of support, even active resistance, with potentially negative consequences for firm performance and, eventually, firm survival.

WHAT IS STRATEGY?

Although businesses exist for many reasons, survival depends on success, and *success*, in business, equals profits. At its simplest, these profits are determined by the extent to which the firm's revenues exceed the costs incurred during the value creation process. The firm generates its revenues from its customers, who are satisfied with the value the firm offers through the goods and services produced by its employees.[1] The pursuit of profit, however, is so broad a mandate that it offers little guidance about where to begin or what to do. Instead, insight comes from understanding the need in society that the business seeks to meet. That need, toward which the organization strives, forms the basis of its aspirations or *vision*. Ideally, an organization's vision is an ennobling, articulated statement of what it seeks to do and become. A vision that ignores the larger role that a firm plays in society is likely to be neither noble nor sustainable. Vision statements must appeal to multiple stakeholders, including members of the organization (employees), its direct beneficiaries (shareholders), its economic partners (customers and suppliers), and the larger community in which the organization operates (society, broadly defined). But, to do so, they also must be statements of genuine intent.

From these aspirations, the firm's *mission* identifies what the organization is going to do in order to attain its vision. A food bank, for example, may have a vision of "ending hunger in the community" and a mission to "feed the poor." An automobile company may have a vision of "providing the best personal transportation vehicles to a broad section of society" and a mission of "making affordable, efficient cars." But, here again, the mission must balance both the methods and the results to be considered socially responsible. The vision identifies what the organization is striving toward, while the mission tells us what the organization is going to do to get there. Both these statements are constrained by what the firm's stakeholders and society deem to be acceptable.

A firm's *strategy* explains how the organization intends to achieve its vision and mission. It defines the organization's response to its competitive environment. At the corporate level, a firm's strategy determines which businesses the firm will operate and whether it will enter into partnerships with other firms (via joint ventures, mergers, or acquisitions). Thus, a food bank may have a corporate level strategy of partnering with a government agency to enhance its access and distribution capabilities, whereas an auto firm may have a corporate level strategy of securing multiple brands to gain exposure to multiple market segments and minimize risk. At the level of the business unit, a firm's strategy determines how the unit will differentiate its products from the products of its competitors. Thus, the food bank may have a strategy of using a mobile soup kitchen that can transport the food to where the poor live, whereas the auto firm may have a strategy of producing cars with specific technological advantages over its competitors' products.

A firm's *tactics* are the day-to-day management decisions that implement the strategy. Tactics are the actions people in the organization take every day. As a result, tactics are flexible and can be altered more easily to reflect changes in operational context. Ultimately, however, the purpose of these day-to-day tactical actions is to realize the firm's strategy.

A Firm's Vision, Mission, Strategy, and Tactics

- The *vision* answers why the organization exists. It identifies the needs the firm aspires to solve for others.
- The *mission* states what the organization is going to do to achieve its vision. It addresses the types of activities the firm seeks to perform.
- The *strategy* determines how the organization is going to undertake its mission. It sets forth the ways it will negotiate its competitive environment in order to attain a sustainable advantage.
- The *tactics* are the day-to-day management decisions made to implement the firm's strategy.

Aligning its vision, mission, strategy, and tactics gives direction to the firm and focus to its employees. As important as giving direction of the firm, this chain also informs the organization of what it will *not* do. An accounting firm, for example, will not build airplanes without a major revision of its vision, mission, strategy, and tactics. Ultimately, this set of aspirations and policies gives decision makers a template against which decisions can be made and evaluated. The overall goal is to ensure that the strategy and tactics achieve the firm's guiding vision and mission.

COMPETING STRATEGY PERSPECTIVES

Often, the strategy planning process begins with a SWOT analysis. A SWOT analysis is a tool that allows a firm to identify its internal *Strengths* and *Weaknesses*, while also analyzing the external *Opportunities* and *Threats*. The goal of a firm's strategy, therefore, is to recognize its strengths and align them with the opportunities that are present in the environment, ensuring that the strategy and tactics remain consistent with its vision and mission. Weaknesses are addressed to the extent that they impair the strategy's effectiveness, while threats in the environ-ment are monitored and evaluated for their disruptive potential.

Building on the foundation of the SWOT analysis, *strategy* is traditionally viewed from two competing perspectives—the resources perspective and the industry perspective.[2] Although it is not clear that these perspectives enjoy empir-ical support, they are well established and commonly taught. The two competing perspectives draw on the two sides of the SWOT analysis—the *internal* strengths and weaknesses, and the *external* opportunities and threats. The *resources per-spective* is an internal view of the firm that identifies its unique resources (e.g., highly skilled employees or monopoly access to valuable raw materials) and capa-bilities (e.g., effective research and development or efficient production processes) as the main determinant of a sustainable competitive advantage. Those firms that have the most valuable resources or most innovative capabilities (collectively called *competencies*), will most likely produce the most valued products and ser-vices in the most efficient manner. As a result, these firms are able to build and sustain a competitive advantage over the competition.

An alternative view is the *industry perspective*, which focuses instead on the company's immediate operational context. This external perspective of the firm identifies the structure of the environment in which it operates (in particular, its industry) as the main determinant of its competitive advantage. Success in the market, this perspective argues, is less to do with individual differences among firms and more to do with the competitive structure of the firm's industry. To the extent that an industry is structured favorably (as in the case of an oligopoly or through favorable government regulation), the companies operating in that indus-try will enjoy greater profit potential than those firms that operate in a more con-strained industry environment.

The tensions between these two perspectives form a central theoretical compo-nent of strategy thinking and, as such, merit further elaboration.

THE RESOURCES PERSPECTIVE

The resources perspective is detailed in a 1990 *Harvard Business Review* article[3] by C.K. Prahalad and Gary Hamel, who then expanded on their ideas in a 1994 book.[4] The core idea that Prahalad and Hamel convey is the distinction between a firm that is built around a portfolio of business units and a firm that is built around a portfolio of *core competencies*. While separate business units encourage func-tional replication and inefficiencies, core competencies develop efficient systems that can be applied in multiple settings across business units and throughout the firm. Walmart's core competency of efficient distribution, for example, can be applied at all stages of its retail operations. Equally, Google's core competency of writing sophisticated algorithms that allow the firm to pursue its mission to "organize the world's information,"[5] can be applied to searching for products, images, academic papers, and many other topics. Moreover, core competencies can be built, given the correct set of circumstances. It is a firm's set of core competencies that will differentiate it from its competition and allow it to sustain a competitive advantage:

> In the short run, a company's competitiveness derives from the price/performance attributes of current products. . . . In the long run, competitiveness derives from an ability to build, at lower cost and more speedily than competitors, the core competencies that spawn unanticipated products. The real sources of advantage are to be found in management's ability to consolidate corporatewide technologies and production skills into competencies that empower individual businesses to adapt quickly to changing opportunities.[6]

Prahalad and Hamel apply three tests to define a core competency: It should be applicable in multiple different markets, it should be valued by the consumer, and it should be difficult for a competitor firm to copy. Importantly, the resources perspective argues that, while different firms have valuable resources and different firms have unique capabilities, it is the combination of the two that leads to a core competency and a sustainable competitive advantage. Southwest Airlines, for example, has a valuable resource in its corporate culture and a unique capability in its ticketing and boarding technologies (in particular, its airplane turnaround times). But, it is the combination of culture and technology that delivers the firm's sustained competitive advantage and profitability. As a result:

> [Southwest Airlines' profitability is] a record unmatched by any airline in the world.[7]
>
> As the United States' most successful low-fare, high frequency, point-to-point carrier, yearend financial results for 2011 marked Southwest's 39th consecutive year of profitability.[8]

Limitations of the Resources Perspective

In spite of its intuitive value, there are two main limitations of the resources perspective. First, by focusing primarily on the internal characteristics of the firm, the resources perspective ignores much of the context in which the firm operates. It is highly likely, however, that this context will influence directly the firm's ability to build core competencies. By not including context in the model, therefore, this perspective provides an incomplete description of the processes that generate the phenomenon (core competencies) that it is seeking to explain.

Second, the resources perspective provides a description of the firm that is very deliberate and rational. The suggestion is that firms are quite capable of identifying potential core competencies and then proceed to gather the necessary resources and design the necessary processes to allow them to flourish. Decades of research on organizations, however, tells us that, even if managers are able to act rationally (which is far from clear), there is a whole host of other factors (ranging from political infighting to events beyond managers' control) that intervene to prevent the intended goal from being realized.

The combination of these two limitations suggests that, while valuable, the resources perspective alone provides an incomplete understanding of firm strategy in today's global business environment.

THE INDUSTRY PERSPECTIVE

The industry perspective is grounded theoretically in industrial economics. Its main proponent in the management literature is Michael Porter, whose five forces model is a staple component of corporate strategy. Porter first outlined his ideas in a 1979 *Harvard Business Review* article.[9] He later published two books that expanded on his initial ideas by introducing a distinction between business and corporate level strategies[10] and the value chain.[11] More recently, in a 2008 *Harvard Business Review* article, Porter updated his five forces model to account for changes since the initial publication.[12]

The industry perspective focuses on the firm's operating environment (in particular, its industry structure) as the most important determinant of competitive advantage. There are five competitive forces in Porter's model (adapted in Figure 2.1): suppliers, buyers, new entrants, substitutes, and industry rivalry. These five forces compete for a fixed pool of resources and it is this competition that determines the ability of any individual firm to profit in the industry. As such, Porter envisions competition as a zero-sum game between these five forces and the focal firm. The strength of each force is measured relative to the strength of the focal firm. In other words, to the extent that any of the five forces grows in strength, this occurs to the detriment of the focal firm, which becomes relatively weaker. The application of this model can be illustrated effectively by looking at the competitive structure of two specific examples—the carbonated soft drinks concentrate industry and the passenger airlines industry:

Figure 2.1 Porter's Five Competitive Forces

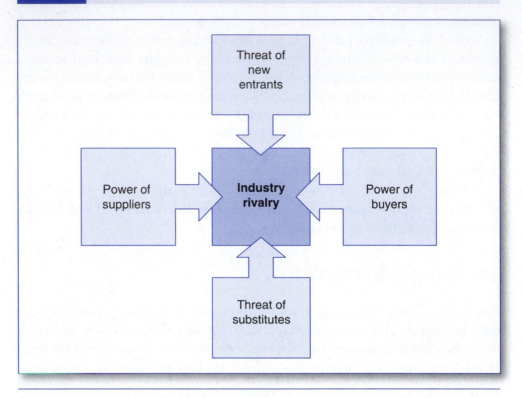

Source: Porter, M. E. (1979, March/April). How competitive forces shape strategy. *Harvard Business Review*, 141.

Porter's Five Forces Model

Examples of two different industries illustrate the value of Porter's model in analyzing a firm's competitive environment:

Carbonated Soft Drinks Concentrate

This industry is dominated by two firms—Coca-Cola and Pepsi:[13]

Power of suppliers: Weak. In this industry, the power of suppliers is weak because the raw materials needed to make the concentrate that Coke and Pepsi sell to their bottlers are cheap and readily available. The recipes are tightly-held trade secrets, but it is hard to imagine the ingredients are much more than water, corn syrup, and flavorings.

Power of buyers: Weak. The buyers in this industry are not the end consumers of the drinks, but the bottlers that Coke and Pepsi have signed up to long term contracts. In recent years, the bottlers have begun to consolidate somewhat, increasing their power relative to their parents, but, structurally, they remain in a relatively weak position.[14]

Threat of new entrants: Low. The barriers to entry in terms of global distribution networks and brand recognition suggest that Coke and Pepsi are not likely to see any serious competitors in this industry.

Threat of substitutes: High. This is the main weakness in the industry. With rising concerns about obesity and the growth in the non-carbonated drinks industry, this is a threat to the products that still drive a large percentage of Coke and Pepsi's profits.

Industry rivalry: Low. Although the end consumer sees Coke and Pepsi competing on advertising and price in supermarkets and other retail outlets, the burden of these costs are borne largely by the bottlers (who sell to these outlets), not the concentrate makers. Coke and Pepsi retain significant control over the price they charge bottlers for the concentrate and each bottler is committed in an exclusive relationship to either Coke or Pepsi.

As a result of this structure, the carbonated soft drinks concentrate industry contains a very favorable competitive structure for Coke and Pepsi. They are well-established competitors in a stable industry.

Passenger Airlines

In contrast to the cola concentrate industry, the airlines industry is populated by a large numbers of firms that are competing furiously:[15]

Power of suppliers: High. There is a great deal of consolidation in the aircraft manufacturing industry, which consists of only two major firms, Boeing and Airbus. As a result, there are not many alternative sources of the airline industry's main input—large airplanes.

Power of buyers: Low. This is one factor that works in the airlines' favor. Buyers (i.e., airline passengers) are diffuse and invariably there are great discrepancies in the amounts of money paid by different passengers for comparable seats on the same flight. The rise in online websites that allow passengers to compare prices, however, has reduced the advantage the airlines hold in this area.

Threat of new entrants: High. In spite of low profits, it is relatively common for new airlines to enter this industry. Virgin America, for example, received

(Continued)

(Continued)

approval to operate a low-cost airline from the U.S. government[16] and there has been a great deal of activity in the Asian market. There is added danger because new airlines are immediately competitive because they do not have the legacy costs (e.g., pension and health benefits) and inefficiencies that diminish profitability for the more established airlines.

Threat of substitutes: Low. In the United States, alternative forms of public travel for long distances (such as train) are not well established. As a result, people have little choice but to purchase the services that many airlines offer today.

Industry rivalry: High. Evidence of the high level of competition among airlines lies in the fact that Southwest Airlines' consistent profitability in the industry is the exception, rather than the norm.[17]

As a result of this competitive structure, the airline industry is unfavorable for the different airlines, who operate in an industry with high demand and few alternatives, but who seem unable to make sustained profits.

Limitations of the Industry Perspective

There are three main limitations inherent with the industry perspective. First, is the presentation of business as a combative pursuit—a zero-sum game of survival. This model teaches firms that their relationship with their different stakeholders is confrontational and that, in order for a firm to survive, it needs to beat its stakeholders in a battle for relative supremacy. In other words, if its customers or suppliers gain an advantage, it is to the detriment of the focal firm.

Second, the industry perspective presents a narrow view of the firm's operating environment. Only five forces are included, which cover only three stakeholders—the firm's buyers, suppliers, and competitors. This picture omits numerous stakeholders that have the potential to alter dramatically a company's competitive environment and profitability—such as the local community, the government, and other stakeholders.[18]

Third, the industry perspective fails to give sufficient recognition to differences in characteristics among companies, which are likely to be predictive of their ability to thrive in a given environment. An holistic model of the firm in its environment that also recognizes the value of the firm's resources and capabilities would provide a more comprehensive tool that firms can use to analyze their operating context (both internal and external conditions) and plan their strategy accordingly.

While the resources and industry perspectives are valuable conceptual tools that provide insight into the actions of businesses, the situations in which they operate, and the potential to build a sustained competitive advantage, therefore, these two perspectives have their limits. Both are narrow in application and exclude factors that intuitively contribute to a firm's strategy and, therefore, its success. As such, they limit attention to the components of the larger context facing the firm. More relevant to the argument presented in *Strategic CSR* is a broader perspective that incorporates the total mix of influences, expectations, and responsibilities firms face in their day-to-day operations and that necessarily shape their strategies in response. As students from Generation Y, or the Millennials (people born from about 1980 to 2000), begin to enter business schools, the curriculum will need to account for their more global goals and interests:

> . . . they like personal attention and are used to getting information how they want it, when they want it. They are strong-willed, passionate, optimistic, and eager to work. And . . . they care deeply about the world and its problems.[19]

These students, who will become the executives of the twenty-first century, require comprehensive tools that allow them to craft strategies that fit a dynamic, globalized business environment. In addition to the two traditional strategy perspectives, therefore, we propose a *stakeholder perspective* as a more complete tool to analyze a firm's operating context and create the most appropriate strategic plan of action.

A STAKEHOLDER PERSPECTIVE[20]

Throughout this century, as businesses worldwide evolve to account for the changing environment in which they operate, CSR will occupy an increasingly core component of the strategic planning process and day-to-day operations of the business. As such, CSR finds a natural home within corporate strategy.[21] The ideal vehicle for the integration of CSR and strategy is a multi-stakeholder perspective that enables firms to respond to the dominant trends in society today—globalization, rapidly evolving communication technologies, and ever-increasing expectations to attend to social goals beyond profit maximization. While definitions of what constitutes a stakeholder may differ in emphasis, with different groups included, they largely agree in terms of sentiment. Here are three foundational definitions:

Definitions of a Stakeholder

Stakeholders in an organization are the individuals and groups who are depending on the firm in order to achieve their personal goals and on whom the firm is depending for its existence.

Eric Rhenman[22]

(Continued)

(Continued)

A stakeholder in an organization is (by definition) any group or individual who can affect or is affected by the achievement of the organization's objectives.

R. Edward Freeman[23]

The stakeholders in a firm are individuals and constituencies that contribute, either voluntarily or involuntarily, to its wealth-creating capacity and activities, and who are therefore its potential beneficiaries and/or risk bearers.

Post, Preston, and Sachs[24]

A stakeholder, therefore, is a group or individual with an interest in the activities of the firm.[25] In Chapter 1, we outlined why it is in firms' best interests to meet the needs and expectations of as broad an array of stakeholders as possible. The model presented in Figure 2.2 provides a framework that firms can use to identify their key stakeholders.

Figure 2.2 divides a firm's stakeholders into three separate groups: organizational stakeholders (internal to the firm) and economic and societal stakeholders (external to the firm). Together, the three kinds of stakeholders form a concentric set of circles with the firm and its organizational stakeholders at the center within a larger circle that signifies the firm's economic stakeholders. Both of these circles sit within the largest outside circle, which represents society and the firm's societal stakeholders. This model of concentric circles is important because some stakeholders exist simultaneously as multiple stakeholder types. A company's employees, for example, are primarily organizational stakeholders. They are also, however, occasional customers of the company, as well as being members of the society in which the business operates. The government that regulates the firm's industry, however, is only a societal stakeholder and has no economic relationship with the company (beyond the taxes it levies), nor is it a formal part of the organization.

The firm's economic stakeholders represent the interface between the organizational and societal stakeholders. A firm's customers are, first and foremost, economic stakeholders of the firm. They are not organizational (internal) stakeholders, but they are part of the society within which the firm operates. They are also one of the primary means by which the firm delivers its product and interacts with its society. Without the economic interface, an organization loses its mechanism of accountability and, therefore, its legitimacy over the long term. This is true regardless of whether the organization is a business, government, or nonprofit.

Figure 2.2 A Stakeholder Model

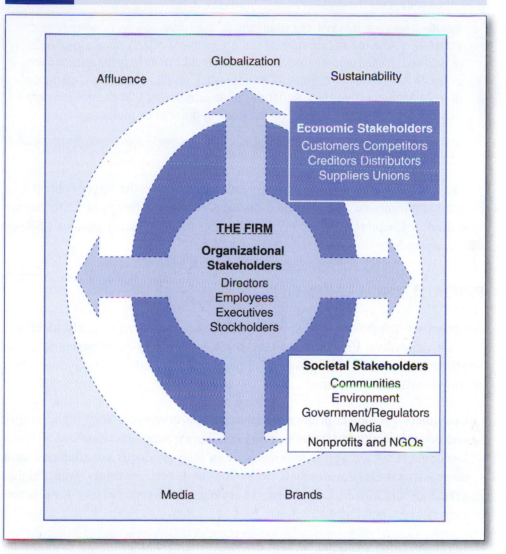

The Environment as a Stakeholder

It is interesting to debate whether the natural environment, as a non-independent actor, should be included as an identifiable stakeholder of the firm. Many argue that it should and that, in fact, the environment has rights that should be protected by law.[26] Others, however, argue that it should not be

(Continued)

> (Continued)
>
> included because it is not the environment itself that speaks or feels or acts; rather, it is how the degradation of the environment affects other stakeholder groups (e.g., NGOs) who then advocate on its behalf. We include the environment in Figure 2.2 as one of the firm's societal stakeholders because of the importance of sustainability within the CSR debate, while recognizing that the environment requires actors to speak and act on its behalf in order to be protected.

The three layers of a firm's stakeholders all sit within the larger context of a business environment that is shaped by the five driving forces of CSR that we identified in Chapter 1 and which, together, enhance the importance of CSR for businesses today.

PRIORITIZING STAKEHOLDERS

An effective stakeholder model, however, must do more than merely identify a firm's stakeholders. Equally important, if the model is to be of practical use in implementation, is the ability to prioritize among these stakeholders because they are notoriously hard to please:

> Customers want lower prices and higher quality; employees want higher wages and better benefits and better working conditions; suppliers want to give fewer discounts and want you to pick up more of their products; communities want more donations; governments want higher taxes; investors want higher dividends and higher stock prices – every one of the stakeholders wants more, they always want more.[27]

In other words, being able to prioritize among stakeholder groups is important because their interests often conflict. As John Mackey, CEO of Whole Foods, states, each stakeholder group "will define the purpose of the business in terms of its own needs and desires, and each perspective is valid and legitimate."[28] As such, it is essential to be able to identify this conflict and, where possible, act to mitigate it, because it represents a potential threat to the organization:

> Some industries – especially energy . . . have long had to contend with well-organized pressure groups. . . . Many of the world's major pharmaceutical companies have been pushed to sell low-cost drugs to developing countries.

Gap and Nike had been attacked for exploiting child labour in the Indian sub-continent. Coca-Cola, Kraft and other food and beverage companies have been accused of contributing to child obesity in the developed world. . . . Companies that do not acknowledge such claims run risks of reputational damage.[29]

The businesses most likely to succeed in today's rapidly evolving global environment will be those best able to adapt to their dynamic environment by balancing the conflicting interests of multiple stakeholders. It can even be argued that the fundamental "job of management is to maintain an equitable and working balance among the claims of the various . . . interest groups" that are directly affected by the firm's operations.[30] Just because an individual or organization merits inclusion in a firm's list of relevant stakeholders, however, does not compel the firm (either legally or logically) to comply with every demand that stakeholder makes. This would be counter-productive as the business would spend all its time addressing these different demands and negotiating among stakeholders with diametrically opposed requests. Integrating a stakeholder perspective into a strategic framework allows firms to respond to stakeholder demands in ways that maximize both economic and social value. A central component of this strategic framework is the ability to prioritize among stakeholders—both in absolute terms, as well as on an issue-by-issue basis.

The concentric circles of organizational, economic, and societal stakeholders presented in Figure 2.2 provide a rough guide to prioritization. By identifying the firm's key stakeholders *within* each category, executives can prioritize the needs and interests of certain groups over others. In addition, we argue that *among* categories, stakeholders decrease in importance to the firm the further they are removed from core operations. Implicit in our model, therefore, is the idea that organizational stakeholders are a firm's most important set of constituent groups. Organizational stakeholders are followed in importance by a firm's economic stakeholders, who provide it with the economic capital to survive. Finally, a firm's societal stakeholders deliver it with the social capital that is central to the firm's legitimacy and long term validity, but are of less immediate importance in terms of the firm's day-to-day operations.

In seeking to prioritize its stakeholders, however, a firm needs to keep two key points in mind: First, no organization can afford to ignore consistently the interests of an important stakeholder, even if that group is less important in the firm's relative hierarchy of stakeholders or relatively removed from the firm's day-to-day operations. A good example of this is the government, which is a societal stakeholder in our model and, therefore, in theory, less important to the firm than an organizational or economic stakeholder. It would not be wise, however, for a firm to ignore repeatedly the government in relation to an important issue that enjoys broad societal support. Given that the government has the power to constrain industries dramatically, it is only rational that firms should adhere to the government's basic needs and requests.[31]

Second, it is vital to remember that the relative importance of stakeholders will inevitably differ from firm-to-firm, from issue-to-issue, and from time-to-time. And, depending on these factors, the change in relative ordering can be dramatic. As such, addressing the fluctuating needs of stakeholders and meeting them wherever possible is essential for firms to survive in today's dynamic business environment. In order to do this, it is important that executives have a framework that will enable them to prioritize stakeholder interests for a given issue and account for those expectations in formulating a strategic response.

Simon Zadek, founder and CEO of AccountAbility[32] has developed a powerful tool that firms can use to evaluate which issues pose the greatest potential opportunity and danger.[33] First, Zadek identified the five stages of learning that organizations go through "when it comes to developing a sense of corporate responsibility"[34]—defensive (to deny responsibility), compliance (to do the minimum required), managerial (to begin integrating CSR into management practices), strategic (to embed CSR within the strategy planning process), and civil (to promote CSR practices industry-wide). Zadek combines these five stages of learning with four stages of intensity "to measure the maturity of societal issues and the public's expectations around the issues"[35]—latent (awareness among activists only), emerging (awareness seeps into the political and media communities), consolidating (much broader awareness is established), and institutionalized (tangible reaction from powerful stakeholders). The range of possible interactions of these different stages is presented in Figure 2.3.

The maximum danger, Zadek argues, is for companies that are in defensive mode when facing an institutionalized issue, as they will be ignoring an issue that poses a potentially significant threat to their business. A firm that continues to deny publicly the existence of climate change, for example, falls into this category. In contrast, those businesses that are promoting industry wide adoption of standard practices in relation to a newly emerging issue face the maximum opportunity. A firm that introduces a standardized process to measure carbon footprints and report the information on product labels in the retail industry, for example, falls into this category. Such a company stands to gain the maximum economic and social value for their effort.

One limitation of this model, however, is that it focuses on the firm's interaction with the particular issue, rather than focusing on the firm's interactions with its various stakeholders, which will vary within stakeholders, but across issues and within issues, but across stakeholders. To address this concern, we have developed a three-dimensional model in Figure 2.4 that allows firms to prioritize stakeholder concerns and determine when to act. The three dimensions of this model are

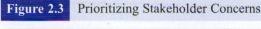

Figure 2.3 Prioritizing Stakeholder Concerns

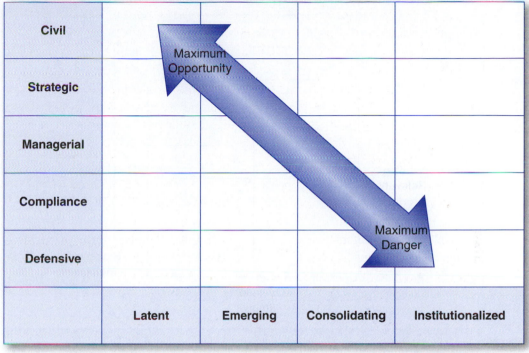

Source: Zadek, S. (2004, December). The path to corporate social responsibility. *Harvard Business Review*, p. 129.

Strategic Relevance, Operational Impact, and *Stakeholder Motivation.* Strategic relevance measures how important the issue is to the firm—in other words, how proximal it is to the firm's core competency or source of competitive advantage. Operational impact measures the extent to which a particular stakeholder group can affect firm operations—in other words, the stakeholder's ability to damage reputation, diminish earnings, or de-motivate employees. Finally, stakeholder motivation measures how important the particular issue is to the stakeholder—in other words, how likely the stakeholder group is to act.

The extent to which a firm should respond to a stakeholder concern with substantial action, therefore, is determined by the interaction of these three dimensions. Importantly, this framework should be embedded within a culture of outreach to stakeholders that allows firms to understand their evolving concerns and assess which issues are more or less important to which stakeholder group. Ultimately, when strategic relevance, operational impact, and stakeholder motivation are all high (the top right shaded box), the firm is compelled to act, and act quickly, in order to protect its self-interest.

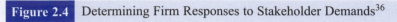

Figure 2.4 Determining Firm Responses to Stakeholder Demands[36]

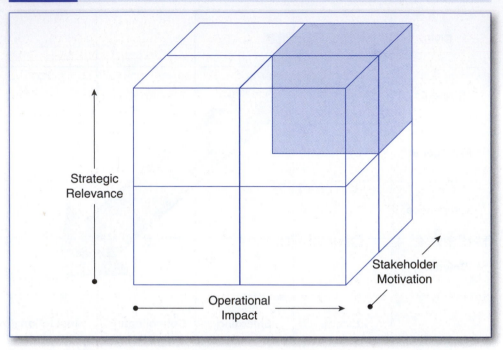

By combining Figure 2.2, Figure 2.3, and Figure 2.4, the firm is armed with a set of tools that empowers executives to analyze their operating environment on an ongoing basis. In order to assess how a firm should act in relation to a particular issue, therefore, it is important that the following four steps are followed:

The Four Steps of Stakeholder Prioritization

1. **Identify** the set of stakeholders that are relevant for this particular issue (Figure 2.2).

2. **Analyze** the nature of the issue to see how it relates to firm operations (Figure 2.3).

3. **Prioritize** among the stakeholders and their competing interests and demands (Figure 2.4).

4. **Act** as quickly as is prudent, attempting to satisfy as many stakeholders, in order of priority, that is feasible.[37]

Utilizing these four steps maximizes the value of a stakeholder perspective for firms. Importantly, this process can be applied to identify stakeholder concerns on either an issue-by-issue basis (i.e., a single issue and multiple stakeholders) or on a stakeholder-by-stakeholder basis (i.e., a single stakeholder and multiple issues), depending on the firm's strategic interests. The matrix in Figure 2.4, for example, can be used to plot either where multiple stakeholders stand on any particular issue, or it can be used to plot where one stakeholder stands in relation to multiple issues. Importantly, this model is also both proactive and reactive. It constitutes a tool that firms can use to either anticipate or respond to stakeholder concerns in relation to both opportunities and threats. In all cases, this process of stakeholder prioritization allows firms to maximize value (economic and social), while avoiding potential harm to operations.

THE INTEGRATION OF STRATEGY AND CSR

That the key proponents of both the resources and industry perspectives implicitly recognize the limitations of their earlier work can be deduced from their more recent publications. In two important respects, both Prahalad and Porter have evolved their positions: First, to integrate both the internal (resources) and external (industry) perspectives, into one comprehensive vision; and, second, to incorporate components of CSR and, implicitly, a broader stakeholder perspective.

Combining the Resources and Industry Perspectives

This evolution of their ideas is apparent in the late Prahalad's most recent work detailing the business opportunity for multi-national firms in serving the estimated four billion people (65% of the world's population) who exist on less than $2,000 per year.[38] This group of people forms the largest and bottom tier of the four-tier pyramid that comprises the world's population—the bottom-of-the-pyramid (BOP).[39] Prahalad views these people as potential consumers who, at present, are largely ignored by multi-national firms that tend, instead, to focus on consumers in developed economy markets:

> It is simply good business strategy to be involved in large, untapped markets that offer new customers, cost-saving opportunities, and access to radical innovation. The business opportunities at the bottom of the pyramid are real, and they are open to any MNC willing to engage and learn.[40]

In Porter's case, the evolution of his ideas is apparent in three *Harvard Business Review* articles that he wrote with Mark Kramer in 2002 ('The Competitive Advantage of Corporate Philanthropy'),[41] 2006 ('Strategy & Society'),[42] and 2011 ('Creating Shared Value'):[43]

> For any company, strategy must go beyond best practices. It is about choosing a unique position—doing things differently from competitors in a way that lowers costs or better serves a particular set of customer needs. These principles apply to a company's relationship to society as readily as to its relationship to its customers and rivals.[44]

Both Prahalad and Porter, therefore, talk more expansively in their recent work and, in the process, come much closer to combining the resources and industry perspectives. Prahalad, in discussing the potential opportunity for firms at the BOP, recognizes that a change in environmental context alters the potential of a fixed set of resources and capabilities. In addition, Porter and Kramer incorporate both "inside-out linkages" (a firm level perspective) and "outside-in linkages" (an environmental level perspective) within one view of the firm and its strategic environment that emphasizes "the interdependence between a company and society."[45]

Integrating CSR

Concerning the integration of CSR into their ideas, there is a strong theme running through all of Prahalad and Porter's most recent work. In addition to identifying new markets for multi-national corporations, Prahalad is clearly also concerned with the social value that the efficient delivery of products and services can provide to the developing world. In addition, Porter writes equally about the potential social and economic value to the strategic decision making process in firms:

> Efforts to find shared value in operating practices and in the social dimensions of competitive context have the potential not only to foster economic and social development but to change the way companies and society think about each other.[46]

CSR Newsletters: Shared Value

In 2011, Michael Porter and Mark Kramer released their latest foray into CSR—'Creating Shared Value.'[47] Ultimately, the argument that Porter and Kramer are building[48] is that firms should identify issues containing both economic and social goals, and then utilize their expertise to generate market-based solutions. In this way, both economic value and social value are maximized. The reaction of the CSR community has been to point out that, while they are very welcome to join the party and can do much to push CSR up the agenda of many unpersuaded CEOs, they are late and somewhat behind the times.[49]

The idea Porter and Kramer present, as we understand it, is similar to Bill Gates and Muhammad Yunus' work on "caring capitalism"—essentially a re-branding of the ideas behind social entrepreneurship. Our criticism of the idea, therefore, is the same—that, while the idea sounds good in theory, in reality, the potential reach of this business model is limited. A good example is Product (RED),[50] which is very successful as a cause-related business, but has fallen short of the game-changing solution its founders were hoping for.

What we argue in *Strategic CSR* is that firms should focus on identifying problems for which there is a clear market-based solution and then deliver that solution in an efficient and socially responsible manner. The idea of CSR as an integrated component of strategy focuses on firms' areas of expertise throughout all aspects of operations, but de-emphasizes actions that stray outside a firm's areas of expertise for which there either may not be a market solution, or the firm is not well-suited to deliver. That is how long-term shareholder value is maximized—by operating in a way that seeks to meet the needs and demands of the firm's stakeholders, broadly defined. In other words, the focus of business remains the same; it is the way you go about it that is different with a *strategic* CSR perspective. Porter and Kramer, however, want to change the focus. As they put it in their introduction:

> The purpose of the corporation must be redefined as creating shared value, not just profit per se.

In some instances, these two perspectives (caring capitalism and strategic CSR) will produce the same behavior, but the motivating force is different and this is important because it will ultimately lead to different outcomes in terms of the success or failure of the venture. For example, Starbucks should not form partnerships with shade-grown coffee farmers in Guatemala because the firm recognizes those farmers face an uncertain future and there is an insufficient welfare net in place to support them if they go out of business (a social goal), but because Starbucks needs to secure a stable supply of high quality coffee beans and supporting these farmers in a sustainable manner is the best way to guarantee that supply (an economic goal). In other words, Starbucks should form stable and lasting partnerships with these key suppliers not because they are seeking to fill a social need; they should do it because these farmers produce a raw material that is essential to their business. As such, Starbucks is incentivized to

(Continued)

(Continued)

protect that raw material in a sustainable way, rather than ruthlessly exploit it. If those Guatemalan farmers are not producing a product that is in demand (i.e., if the business logic is not there), the argument that Starbucks should get involved is difficult to make.

Ultimately, although for-profit firms can help with the first perspective (caring capitalism), they are much better suited to the second perspective (market capitalism). Ideally, it is the role of effective governmental and nonprofit sectors to focus on those areas that the market ignores or cannot solve. In contrast, Porter and Kramer argue that social goals should be considered equally with economic goals and firms should then utilize their market-based skills and expertise to solve that problem—In other words, that they should become less like for-profit firms and more like social entrepreneurs, government agencies, or nonprofit organizations. While well-intentioned, we believe that this is not an effective plan for "how to fix capitalism" and, instead, is a misunderstanding of the value of for-profit firms in our society (and of the role that a CSR perspective brings in maximizing that value). As argued in this article in the *Financial Times*:[51]

In her 2009 book SuperCorp, . . . Rosabeth Moss Kanter warned of the pitfalls for companies that make "social commitments that do not have an economic logic that sustains the enterprise by attracting resources." More companies are learning to reap commercial benefits from strategies that have a wider social value. That's great. But the basic job of coaxing capitalism in the right direction is the same as it always has been: find ways to harness society's needs to companies' self-interest and hope the two stay together.

On the one hand, it is clear that CSR can be thought of as a core competence of the firm. In order to integrate CSR effectively throughout the organization, a firm needs to draw on resources and capabilities that are valuable, rare, difficult to imitate, and non-substitutable.[52] The development of these competencies presents the firm with the potential to differentiate itself from its competitors and build a sustainable competitive advantage.[53] On the other hand, however, CSR is also clearly a means to evaluate a firm's operating environment in terms of its primary stakeholder groups—identifying the structural components of that environment that present the firms with a favorable opportunity to succeed.

An important question remains: How do companies define socially responsible action that is strategic? In their work, both Prahalad and Porter are correct to focus on areas of expertise and relevance to organizations. There is a strong connection between the economic competence of firms and the potential for social progress. This is a central component of the concept of strategic CSR—areas of social concern that extend beyond profit maximization, but, importantly, that are related to the business' core operations. It is to this area of firm activity, located at the intersection of strategy, CSR, and a stakeholder perspective, that we turn next.

STRATEGIC CSR

There are four components that are essential to defining *strategic CSR*: First, that firms incorporate a CSR perspective within their strategic planning process; second, that any actions they take are directly related to core operations; third, that they incorporate a stakeholder perspective; and, fourth, that they shift from a short term perspective to managing the firm's resources and relations with key stakeholders over the medium to long term.

Strategic CSR

The incorporation of a holistic *CSR perspective* within a firm's strategic planning and *core operations* so that the firm is managed in the interests of a broad set of *stakeholders* to achieve maximum economic and social value over the *medium to long term*.

It is the combination of these four pillars that ensures the integration of CSR within the strategic planning and day-to-day operations of the organization.

CSR Perspective

Essential to any definition of strategic CSR is that firms incorporate a CSR perspective within their strategic planning process.

In outlining their ideas on how firms can incorporate a social dimension to their strategic decision making, Porter and Kramer provide a three-tiered framework that forms a guide to how organizations can assess and prioritize the range of social issues with which they are expected to deal.[54] The interaction between firms and issues of concern to the societies in which they operate are divided into three levels of interaction:

- "Generic social issues" (not directly related to a firm's operations)
- "Value chain social impacts" (the extent to which a firm's operations affect society)

- "Social dimensions of competitive context" (the extent to which the environment constrains a firm's operations)

In the case of a retail clothing company that outsources production to low cost environments overseas, for example, the issue of a livable wage (as opposed to a minimum wage) in the U.S. is a *generic social issue*—an issue that is important and something on which the firm might even take a position, but which is not directly relevant to the firm's operations. The issue of a livable wage in a country in which the firm's products are made, however, is a clear example of a *value chain social impact*, an issue in which its operations directly affect the local community. The prospect of legislation on this issue by government represents a *social dimension of competitive context* for the organization, as it has the potential to constrain operations.

Figure 2.5 illustrates how Porter and Kramer use the interactions among social issues, firm operations, and environmental constraints to distinguish between "Responsive CSR" and "Strategic CSR." *Responsive CSR* occurs when the firm proactively becomes involved in a generic social issue that is not related to operations or structures its value chain to avoid any negative social impacts. *Strategic CSR*, however, involves a more proactive integration of a social dimension into the firm's strategic planning. This form of CSR occurs when the organization

Figure 2.5   Porter & Kramer's *Strategy and Society* Model

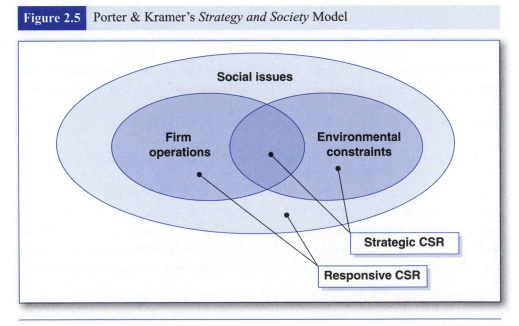

Source: Michael E. Porter & Mark R. Kramer, 'Strategy & Society,' *Harvard Business Review*, December, 2006, p. 89.

seeks actively to benefit society as a consequence of its value chain or influence its competitive context through activities such as "strategic philanthropy."[55] Strategic CSR occurs where there is a direct effect of a firm's operations on society and vice-versa, allowing it to identify which issues and stakeholders it has the ability to influence. Accounting for CSR as an integrated component of the firm's strategic planning process in this way, therefore, constitutes a good example of strategic CSR in action.

Core Operations

A second component of strategic CSR is that any action a firm takes is directly related to its core operations. In short, the same action will differ in terms of whether it can be classified as strategic CSR, depending on the core expertise of the firm and the relevance of the issue to the firm's vision and mission. Consider the following two questions:

- Does it make sense for a large financial firm to donate money to a group researching the effects of climate change because the CEO believes this is an important issue?
- Does it make sense for an oil firm to donate money to the same group because it perceives climate change as a threat to its business model and wants to mitigate that threat by investigating possible alternatives?

The action is the same—the donation of money from a for-profit firm to a non-profit organization that is researching the effects of climate change. It is harder for the company in the first example to justify its actions, however, assuming that its operations are not directly related to the environment and the CEO is not an expert on this issue. It is much easier to see the relevance of climate change to the second company. It is in this firm's strategic interests to understand an area of debate that is likely to influence its operating environment directly in the foreseeable future.[56]

Using a similar logic, it makes a great deal of sense for a computer company like Dell to offer a computer recycling program as part of its product awareness throughout the lifecycle.[57] It makes much less sense, however, for Dell to offer a "Plant a Tree for Me" program as a way for consumers to offset greenhouse gas emissions produced as a result of the production of their new computer.[58] Dell knows about computers and should know how best to recycle them. Less obvious is Dell's expertise in relation to tree planting—What trees to plant, where to plant them, or whether tree planting is an efficient use of the firm's resources or an effective means of combating climate change. Even though Dell outsources much of these responsibilities to its program partners—The Conservation Fund and

CarbonFund.org, it is still not clear how well qualified Dell is to select partners in this area, or how able the firm is to monitor the behavior of those partners.

Stakeholder Perspective

A third component of strategic CSR is that firms incorporate a stakeholder perspective. A barrier to the implementation of a stakeholder perspective, however, is the primary emphasis currently given by many corporations to the interests of its shareholders.

As discussed above, an issue that is rarely raised in relation to a stakeholder model is the issue of prioritization. It is important for an organization to be able to identify its different stakeholders and their different interests and demands, but the difficulty comes when those interests and expectations conflict, which they often do. The most effective means of dealing with stakeholder conflict is prioritization. If a firm has two stakeholder groups whose demands conflict (i.e., the firm is unable to satisfy fully both stakeholders), it makes sense for it to respond more wholeheartedly to the most important of the two, while attempting not to offend the other.

Cynics might point out that this is what firms have been doing all along—it is just that they always give top priority to their shareholders. In reality, however, the choice is not between either a shareholder or stakeholder perspective. A firm's shareholders are one of its organizational stakeholders and, as such, are important to the firm. It is not the case, however, that this automatically ensures their demands are given top priority. Anecdotal evidence suggests that, in fact, some of the most successful businesses are those that have considered other stakeholders to be a higher priority than their shareholders.[59] The basis for this claim rests on the argument that investors do not have the same risk-exposure to the firm's performance as other stakeholders, such as employees:

> The claim of shareholders is solely on the residual income of the company. But, since shareholders can diversify their portfolios with ease, their exposure to the risks generated by an individual company is far less than the exposure of workers with firm-specific knowledge and skills.[60]

Johnson & Johnson is an excellent example of a company that has formally prioritized its stakeholders in its famous Credo.[61] Importantly, the Credo places its customers first and its shareholders (stockholders) last as a "final responsibility." The firm rationalizes that, as long as "we operate according to these principles," with its customers (health practitioners), suppliers and distributors, employees, and communities in which it operates being given a higher priority than its shareholders, then "the stockholders should realize a fair return":[62]

Small wonder then that, when the Tylenol scare hit in the '80s and seven Chicago residents died after ingesting cyanide-laced capsules, J&J managers knew what they had to do—even without consulting with then-CEO James Burke, who was on a plane as the news broke. By the time Burke had landed and caught up with his top managers, they already had called for all Tylenol products to be pulled off shelves and for production of all Tylenol items to be halted.[63]

The recall involved the firm recalling 32 million Tylenol bottles, at a cost of "more than $100 million."[64] The value to Johnson & Johnson's reputation of acting proactively, however, was much greater, increasing trust in the brand and protecting its market competitiveness so that, "Within a year [of the recall], Tylenol had recaptured its 35% market share."[65]

Although not as formalized as Johnson & Johnson, business leaders as diverse as Herb Kelleher and Colleen Barrett at Southwest,[66] Howard Schulz at Starbucks,[67] Sam Walton at Walmart,[68] and Yves Chounard at Patagonia,[69] all recognized that shareholders are best served when stakeholders that are more immediate to operations (in particular, employees) are motivated, loyal, and committed to serving customers. Amazon has a similar "customers first" approach to business.[70] In addition, Costco routinely rejects investors' calls to reduce the pay and benefits they provide to their employees. In spite of their resistance, Costco's share price has greatly outperformed the share price of its main competitor, Walmart, over the last decade.[71]

None of this, of course, is to argue that shareholder interests do not matter, or that they should never be placed above the interests of other stakeholders. Instead, the important point is that shareholders should not automatically be the primary concern of executives in those instances when the consideration of the interests of a broader set of stakeholders will better serve the overall interests of the organization.

Medium to Long Term

The final, and most important, component of strategic CSR is the shift from a short-term perspective when managing the firm's resources and stakeholders relations to a medium- or long-term perspective. If executives alter their horizons from the next quarter or next season to the next decade or beyond, that automatically changes the nature of the decisions they make today. If a CEO is only interested in the next quarter, it is difficult to make the case for CSR. But, if the CEO is concerned with the continued existence of the firm 5, 10, or 20 years from now; priorities shift and, for example, the value of building lasting, trust-based relationships with key stakeholders increases exponentially.

As discussed in this chapter, businesses must satisfy key groups among their various constituents if they hope to remain viable in today's business context. When the expectations of different stakeholders conflict, firms need to be able to balance the competing interests. Not only are these competing interests apparent *among* stakeholders, however, but also *within* stakeholder types. An example of such conflict exists between different classes of investors who might have different definitions of what they consider to be an acceptable level of performance.

The Shareholder Shift—From Investor to Speculator

The evolving role of shareholders has greatly influenced the CSR debate and strengthened the case for adopting a broader stakeholder approach to a business's strategic outlook. In particular, the role of ownership has narrowed considerably over time. Shares today are perceived less and less as a long-term investment in a company and more and more as a stand-alone, short-term investment for personal benefit. A distinction can be drawn, therefore, between *investors*, who seek firms with a share price that reflects sound economic fundamentals (e.g., a reasonable price-earnings ratio, profitability, long-term planning), and *speculators*, who gamble on firms based on whether they think the share price will rise, irrespective of whether it deserves to go up or is valued at a fair price.

This shift or contrast is indicated by the fact that "the average holding period of a stock has fallen from eight years in the 1960s to around five days today"[72] and also be claims from CEOs that, today, "People aren't investing in your company; they're investing in your stock. That's a huge difference."[73] As John Bogle, founder of Vanguard, the mutual fund firm, puts it in his 2012 book, *The Clash of Cultures: Investment vs. Speculation*:

> A culture of short-term speculation has run rampant, . . . superseding the culture of long-term investment that was dominant earlier in the post–World War II era.[74]

This trend was taken to an extreme during the Internet boom at the turn of the century when share trading was driven by speculation and the desire to maximize returns. There was little attempt to establish a company's business worth or potential:

> Amazon's entire float changes hands twice a week. . . . It would take average annual profits of over $1 billion to make sense of Amazon's current $20 billion-odd market value. Yet Amazon's total sales in 1998 were only $600 million. . . . Today's appetite for equities rests

on an erroneous belief that they are a one-way bet: that, in the long run, they always pay higher returns than other assets.[75]

An important driver of this transitory equity trading was the rise of day trading, a phenomenon that emerged in the United States at the height of the Internet boom,[76] but also found its way to other countries such as the UK.[77] Day trading became possible because of the rise in personal Internet access and developing communications technology. It can be defined as speculation, "where investors buy shares with the express intent of selling for a quick profit, often within 24 hours"[78] and presents additional compelling evidence that any link the investor has with the long-term interests of the company in which they are investing has been largely severed.[79]

In short, the democratization of the investor class ("The proportion of households with money invested in the market increased from just over 20% in 1983 to more than 50% by 2001")[80] has combined with the consolidation of the investor class ("Assets in 401(k)s, which mainly invest in mutual funds, soared from $135 billion in 1980 to $12 trillion in 2007")[81] to present Wall Street with a powerful control mechanism over corporate action. And, this trend has been exacerbated massively in recent years by technological innovation that increases the importance of computer-assisted, high-frequency trading. The result is a huge increase in both volume and turnover, an effect that has been termed the "three-million-shares-per-second casino of Wall Street":[82]

Too much money is aimed at short-term speculation – the seeking of quick profit with little concern for the future. The financial system has been wounded by a flood of so-called innovations that merely promote hyper-rapid trading, market timing and shortsighted corporate maneuvering.[83]

In these instances, is it true to say that shareholders actually own the company in which they are investing? When a computer program is triaging miniscule differences in share prices across trading exchanges, holding individual positions for micro-seconds, does that shareholder own a part of the company in the sense that an owner values and protects the item being held? Because of this shift in trading patterns, there is an increasing tendency today to register indifference to the overall health of an organization and seek merely to protect the dollar investment. As *The Economist* notes, this rise in technology is also causing greater stock market volatility and a higher probability of flash crashes:

> . . . high-frequency traders are not making decisions based on a company's future prospects; they are seeking to profit from tiny changes in price. They might as well be trading baseball cards. The liquidity benefits of such

(Continued)

(Continued)

trading are all very well, but that liquidity can evaporate at times of stress. And although high-frequency trading may make markets less volatile in normal times, it may add to the turbulence at the worst possible moment.[84]

This changing nature of investments and the evolving relationship between companies and owners has seen the importance of shareholders rise to a position that is distracting for businesses. Managers now have to concentrate a disproportionate amount of their time on the short-term considerations of quarterly results,[85] dividend levels, and share price in order to keep demanding shareholders happy. By reducing costs today, for example, the firm improves its financial statements, but can also raise longer term risks of operational failure.[86] As such, this short-term perspective often comes at the cost of long-term strategic considerations of the company and its business interests. And, the consequences for not delivering that short-term profit can be severe. As Bill George, the retired CEO of Medtronic, observed,

They want to know why you didn't make the numbers. . . . You tell them, we're investing in our research programs for the long term. But that doesn't fly. . . . When you [miss stated targets] your stock gets inordinately punished. . . . If your earnings are up 15 percent, but they expected 20 percent, then your stock will go down—not 5 percent, but 25 percent. Then you're vulnerable to a takeover.[87]

Many observers see this development as a corruption of the fundamental purpose of the stock market and have begun calling for a transaction tax on financial trades.[88]

Businesses still have a duty to provide a return for investors (it is central to their economic mission), but the idea that shareholders have the best interests of the firm at heart no longer necessarily holds true. In today's business environment, a broader stakeholder perspective provides the stability necessary for managers to chart the best course for the company so that it remains a viable entity over the medium to long term. This is in the interests of a company's investors, rather than those of its speculators.

A focus on short term results, often driven by those investors or other shareholders (such as the firm's executives) who have no interest in the long term health or viability of the organization, can be hugely damaging to the organization and represents a relatively recent development in western capitalism. As Alfred Chandler notes, this was not always the case:

. . . in making administrative decisions, career managers preferred policies that favored the long-term stability and growth of their enterprises to those that maximized current profits.[89]

The development of stock options and other compensation policies designed to solve the principal-agent conflict and align the interests of owners and managers, however, has produced negative consequences.[90] It is the short-term nature of shareholder investments in firms, combined with the financial incentives executives have to develop personal wealth at the expense of the long-term health of the firm, that have distorted the conditions under which executives are forced to make decisions.[91] The focus is less and less on the underlying value of a business and more and more on the perception of value held by the crowd of investors. John Maynard Keynes perceived of this distorting influence of stock exchanges, comparing the process of stock picking to a beauty contest. The object is not to choose the most beautiful face, merely the one that the investor thinks others will find the most beautiful. In other words, for the investor, "It is better . . . to be conventionally wrong than unconventionally right."[92]

It is not a case of choosing those [faces] that, to the best of one's judgment, are really the prettiest, nor even those that average opinion genuinely thinks the prettiest. We have reached the third degree where we devote our intelligences to anticipating what average opinion expects the average opinion to be. And there are some, I believe, who practice the fourth, fifth and higher degrees.[93]

As a result, CEOs are increasingly wary of being over-sensitive to the needs and demands of short term investors. Robert C. Goizueta, Coca-Cola's CEO from 1981 to 1997, for example, preferred the term "share owner" to share holder as it implied a greater ownership stake in the firm.[94] Similarly, Wendelin Wiedeking, the CEO of Porsche from 1993 to 2009, long argued for a broader perspective to strategic planning that shifts executives' attention beyond the short-term demands of investors:

I have never understood shareholder value as it leaves so many things out. Shareholders give their money just once, whereas the employees work every day.[95]

Firms' willingness to pander to short-term shareholder interests is no more obvious than in the value placed on quarterly earnings reports. Such reports sacrifice medium- and long-term decisions and investment strategies in favor of hitting arbitrarily generated numbers. In recent years, companies such as Unilever, Coca-Cola, McDonald's and AT&T have stopped releasing such reports, "stating that they detract from creating a sustainable company for the long term."[96] Sumantra Ghoshal, the late strategy professor at the London Business School, argues that one of the main reasons why this misplaced emphasis on shareholders damages the long term value of the firm is that it does not reflect the relative contributions of different stakeholders to the success of the organization:

> After all, we know that shareholders do not own the company—not in the sense that they own their homes or their cars. They merely own a right to the residual cash flows of the company. . . . They have no ownership rights on the actual assets or businesses of the company, which are owned by the company itself, as a "legal person." . . . Most shareholders can sell their stocks far more easily than most employees can find another job. In every substantive sense, employees of a company carry more risks than do the shareholders. Also, their contributions of knowledge, skills, and entrepreneurship are typically more important than the contributions of capital by shareholders, a pure commodity that is perhaps in excess supply.[97]

CSR Newsletters: The Long Now

The Long Now Foundation (http://longnow.org/) is an organization that focuses on combating the "here and now" culture in which we live and trying to get people to think in terms of the bigger picture and a longer time frame. The organization posts these guidelines for thinking in the longer term:

- *Serve the long view*
- *Foster responsibility*
- *Reward patience*
- *Mind mythic depth*
- *Ally with competition*
- *Take no sides*
- *Leverage longevity*

To reinforce their perspective, all the years on the website are written in terms of 10,000 years, rather than 1,000 years (e.g., 01996 = 1996):

The Long Now Foundation was established in *01996 to creatively foster long-term thinking and responsibility in the framework of the next 10,000 years.

The organization's major project is the 10,000 Year Clock, which was first proposed by the computer scientist, Daniel Hillis:

When I was a child, people used to talk about what would happen by the year 02000. For the next thirty years they kept talking about what would happen by the year 02000, and now no one mentions a future date at all. The future has been shrinking by one year per year for my entire life. I think it is time for us to start a long-term project that gets people thinking past the mental barrier of an ever-shortening future. I would like to propose a large (think Stonehenge) mechanical clock, powered by seasonal temperature changes. It ticks once a year, bongs once a century, and the cuckoo comes out every millennium.

In essence, strategic CSR represents an enlightened approach to management that retains the focus on creating and adding value that is emphasized by a traditional bottom-line business model, but, importantly, also incorporates a commitment to meeting the needs and demands of key stakeholder groups, broadly defined. Equally important, in order to implement strategic CSR in a meaningful way, the focus of the firm has to be on maximizing both economic and social value over the long term and acting in areas in which it has expertise (related to core operations). A short-term focus, driven by quarterly earnings guidelines to investors with little long-term interest in the organization, has little value (and is most likely detrimental)[98] to firms committed to implementing strategic CSR.

This focus on long-term added value, therefore, is the principal difference between a traditional shareholder focused business model and a strategic CSR model integrated throughout operations. This shift in perspective (from short- to long-term) is relatively easy to envision, but much more difficult to implement firm-wide. Nevertheless, this shift alone brings a firm a lot closer to a CSR perspective. Combining this shift with the integration of a stakeholder perspective into the firm's strategic planning process and a focus on activities that are relevant to the firm's core operations re-focuses executives on the implementation of strategic CSR throughout the organization.

CSR is as simple (and as complex) as conducting all aspects of business operations in a responsible manner. Strategic CSR is incorporating this perspective into the strategic planning processes of the firm in ways that maximize social and economic value. The firm retains the societal legitimacy to remain an ongoing entity by seeking to implement its strategic plan and conduct operations while considering the needs and concerns of a broad array of stakeholders. The result is that, rather than profit maximization through a short-term focus, profit optimization emphasizes the importance of striving to meet the needs of stakeholders, broadly defined, over the medium to long term.

NEXT STEPS

Beyond the stakeholder model in this chapter, there are a number of contentious areas of debate within the CSR community. These debates lead to confusion regarding possible best-practice standards and difficulties for firms in implementation. As such, Chapter 3 will explore some of the arguments *against* CSR (and the often unintended implications of progressive CSR applications) that are yet to be resolved.

In the final two chapters of Part I, we will outline how firms integrate CSR into day-to-day operations. Chapter 4 puts CSR into strategic perspective and expands on the growing importance of CSR and its effect on firm strategy. Finally, Chapter 5 discusses the issues that influence the implementation of CSR within a strategic decision-making framework of the firm.

QUESTIONS FOR DISCUSSION AND REVIEW

1. Define each of these terms: vision, mission, strategy, and tactics. What is the relationship among them in relation to a firm's strategy planning process?

2. Outline the Resources perspective. Identify a firm and its core competency—show how it meets the three tests proposed by Prahalad and Hamel that identify it as a source of sustainable competitive advantage for a firm.

3. Outline the Industry perspective. Chose an example industry and conduct an analysis of its competitive structure using Porter's Five Forces model.

4. Using a real-life example, list a firm's stakeholders and use one of the models presented in the chapter to prioritize their importance. What criteria do you think should be used to prioritize competing stakeholder interests?

5. Define strategic CSR in your own words. What are the signs you would look for to indicate that a firm has implemented a strategic CSR perspective?

6. What are the four key components of the definition of strategic CSR? Which of these four do you think will generate the greatest resistance or difficulty for firms?

7. Are shareholders in a firm *investors* or *speculators*? Why?

STUDENT STUDY SITE

Visit the Student Study Site at **www.sagepub.com/chandler3e** for additional learning tools.

NOTES AND REFERENCES

1. Bruce D. Henderson, 'The Origin of Strategy,' *Harvard Business Review,* November-December, 1989, pp. 134-143.

2. An alternative tool to analyze a firm's strategy that emphasizes the importance of a comprehensive approach is the "Strategy Diamond." This approach is detailed in an article by Donald C. Hambrick and James W. Fredrickson: 'Are you sure you have a strategy?' *Academy of Management Executive*, Vol. 19, No. 4, 2005, pp. 51–62. The strategy diamond contains five elements that cover the range of actions taken by firms to achieve their goals: arenas (the areas in which the firm will compete), vehicles (the ways in which the firm will achieve its goals), differentiators (the means by which the firm will differentiate itself from the competition), staging (the speed and order of implementation), and economic logic (the route to profitability). While the strategy diamond draws on existing knowledge, its value lies in combining this knowledge into a comprehensive tool to analyze a firm's strategy—"an integrated overarching concept of how the business will achieve its objectives" (p. 51).

3. C.K. Prahalad & Gary Hamel, 'The Core Competence of the Corporation,' *Harvard Business Review*, May-June, 1990, pp. 79–91.

4. Gary Hamel & C.K. Prahalad, *Competing for the Future*, Harvard Business School Press, 1994.

5. "Google's mission is to organize the world's information and make it universally accessible and useful." http://www.google.com/corporate/

6. C.K. Prahalad & Gary Hamel, 'The Core Competence of the Corporation,' *Harvard Business Review*, May-June, 1990, p. 81.

7. James L. Heskett, 'Southwest Airlines—2002: An Industry Under Siege,' *Harvard Business School Press*, [9-803-133], March 11, 2003, p. 4.

8. 'About the Company,' October, 2012, http://www.southwest.com/html/about-southwest/history/fact-sheet.html

9. Michael E. Porter, 'How Competitive Forces Shape Strategy,' *Harvard Business Review*, March/April, 1979, pp. 137–145.

10. Michael E. Porter, *Competitive Strategy*, The Free Press, 1980.

11. Michael E. Porter, *Competitive Advantage*, The Free Press, 1985.

12. Michael E. Porter, 'The Five Competitive Forces That Shape Strategy,' *Harvard Business Review*, January 2008, pp. 79–93.

13. David B. Yoffie & Renee Kim, 'Cola Wars Continue: Coke and Pepsi in 2010,' *Harvard Business School Press*, [9-711-462], May, 2011.

14. In 2009, both Coke and Pepsi announced moves to begin purchasing their main bottlers. In August, 2009, for example, Pepsi paid $7.8bn to buy its two largest bottlers (Michael J. de la Merced, 'PepsiCo to Pay $7.8 Billion To Buy Its Two Top Bottlers,' *The New York Times*, August 5, 2009, p. B7), while Coke acquired the North American operations of its largest bottler in February, 2010 in a deal valued at "more than $13 billion" (Michael J. de la Merced, 'Coke Confirms Purchase of a Bottling Unit,' *The New York Times*, February 26, 2010, p. B4).

15. James L. Heskett & W. Earl Sasser, Jr., 'Southwest Airlines: In a Different World,' *Harvard Business School Press*, [910419], April 22, 2010. See also: James L. Heskett, 'Southwest Airlines—2002: An Industry Under Siege,' *Harvard Business School Press*, [9-803-133], March 11, 2003.

16. Ben Mutzabaugh & Dan Reed, 'Virgin America gets tentative approval to launch U.S. service,' *USA Today*, March 23, 2007, http://www.usatoday.com/travel/flights/2007-03-20-virgin-america-cleared-fly_N.htm

17. "After breaking even less than two years after its founding in 1971, the airline . . . enjoyed 30 consecutive years of profit beginning in 1973, a record unmatched by any airline in the world." 'Southwest Airlines—2002: An Industry Under Siege,' *Harvard Business School Press*, [9-803-133], 2003, p. 4.

18. To some extent, this issue is addressed in Porter's 2008 update of his original paper ('The Five Competitive Forces That Shape Strategy,' *Harvard Business Review*, January 2008, pp. 79-93.) The original five forces structure remains intact, however, to the exclusion of all other stakeholder relationships.

19. Geoff Gloeckler, 'Here Come the Millennials,' *BusinessWeek*, November 24, 2008, p. 47, http://www.businessweek.com/magazine/content/08_47/b4109046025427.htm

20. Many commentators present a stakeholder perspective as an alternative to a shareholder perspective. We believe that the shareholder value vs. stakeholder value debate is a red herring. Since shareholders are also stakeholders, a shareholder perspective is actually the same thing as a stakeholder perspective, with the line concerning which stakeholders the firm will concern itself with drawn in a different place (Do you draw the line at shareholders only, or include many other stakeholders as well?). Rather than arguing over where to draw the line, the key area for debate is temporal. Attempts to maximize profits over the short term lead to all the problems that people criticize about shareholder value. If a firm seeks to maximize profits/value over the long term, however, many of those problems go away and the importance of building meaningful, lasting relations with a broad range of stakeholders becomes central to the firm's mission. Firms like Unilever understand this distinction and are focusing on encouraging long-term thinking, rather than arguing about whether stakeholders or shareholders (who are stakeholders anyway) should get the most value. The primacy of shareholders emerged out of a belief that U.S. law compelled a fiduciary duty among executives to the shareholder. For an excellent source debunking this myth, see Lynn Stout, *The Shareholder Value Myth: How Putting Shareholders First Harms Investors, Corporations, and the Public*, Berrett-Koehler Publishers, May 7, 2012.

21. For a more complete discussion of the importance of approaching CSR using a strategic lens, see Chapter 4.

22. Eric Rhenman, *Foeretagsdemokrati och foeretagsorganisation*, S.A.F. Norstedt: Företagsekonomiska Forsknings Institutet, Thule, Stockholm, 1964.

23. R. Edward Freeman, Strategic Management: A Stakeholder Approach, Pitman, 1984, p. 46.

24. James E. Post, Lee E. Preston, & Sybille Sachs, 'Managing the Extended Enterprise: The New Stakeholder View,' *California Management Review*, Vol. 45, No.1, Fall 2002, p. 8.

25. The earliest reference to the term *stakeholder* in the management literature that we can find is to "an internal memorandum at the Stanford Research Institute in 1963" (quoted in: R. Edward Freeman & David L. Reed, 'Stockholders and Stakeholders: A New Perspective on Corporate Governance,' *California Management Review*, 1983, p. 89). In addition, Klaus Schwab claims to have "developed the 'stakeholder' theory for business" around 1970 (quoted in Klaus Schwab, 'A breakdown in our values,' *The Guardian*, January 6, 2010, http://www.guardian.co.uk/commentisfree/2010/jan/06/bankers-bonuses-crisis-social-risk)

26. See Rebecca Tuhus-Dubrow, 'US: Sued by the forest,' *The Boston Globe*, July 19, 2009, in CorpWatch, http://www.corpwatch.org/article.php?id=15413

27. John Mackey quoted in: April Fulton, 'Whole Foods Founder John Mackey on Fascism and 'Conscious Capitalism,'' *National Public Radio*, January 16, 2013, http://www.npr.org/blogs/thesalt/2013/01/16/169413848/whole-foods-founder-john-mackey-on-fascism-and-conscious-capitalism

28. John Mackey quoted in: John Bussey, 'Are Companies Responsible for Creating Jobs?' *The Wall Street Journal*, October 28, 2011, p. B1.

29. Andrew Likierman, 'Stakeholder dreams and shareholder realities,' Mastering Financial Management, *Financial Times*, June 16, 2006, p. 10.

30. Hedrick Smith, 'When Capitalists Cared,' *The New York Times*, September 2, 2012, http://www.nytimes.com/2012/09/03/opinion/henry-ford-when-capitalists-cared.html

31. See the discussion around 'A Rational Argument for CSR' in chapter 1.

32. http://www.accountability.org/

33. Simon Zadek, 'The Path to Corporate Responsibility,' *Harvard Business Review*, December, 2004, pp. 125–132.

34. Simon Zadek, 'The Path to Corporate Responsibility,' *Harvard Business Review*, December, 2004, p. 127.

35. Simon Zadek, 'The Path to Corporate Responsibility,' *Harvard Business Review*, December, 2004, p. 128.

36. This model was developed with the assistance of Michael Petschel, University of Colorado Denver MBA student (2010–2012). We thank him for his drive and his ideas.

37. Anne Lawrence suggests that there are four strategies managers can employ to engage stakeholders: "Wage a fight," "Withdraw," "Wait," and "Work it out." See: Anne T. Lawrence, 'Managing Disputes with Nonmarket Stakeholders,' *California Management Review*, Vol. 53, No. 1, Fall, 2010, pp. 90–113.

38. C.K. Prahalad & Allen Hammond, 'Serving the World's Poor, Profitably,' *Harvard Business Review*, September 2002, Vol. 80, No. 9, pp 48–58; C.K. Prahalad, 'The

Fortune at the Bottom of the Pyramid: Eradicating Poverty Through Profits,' *Wharton School Publishing*, 2006.

39. The person most closely associated with continuing Prahalad's work at the bottom of the pyramid is Stuart L. Hart of Cornell University. For an overview of his ideas, in addition to a list of publications, see: http://www.stuartlhart.com/

40. C.K. Prahalad & Allen Hammond, 'Serving the World's Poor, Profitably,' *Harvard Business Review,* September 2002, Vol. 80, No. 9, pp. 48–58.

41. Michael E. Porter & Mark R. Kramer, 'The Competitive Advantage of Corporate Philanthropy,' *Harvard Business Review*, December, 2002, pp. 57–68.

42. Michael E. Porter & Mark R. Kramer, 'Strategy & Society,' *Harvard Business Review*, December, 2006, pp. 78-92.

43. Michael E. Porter & Mark R. Kramer, 'Creating Shared Value,' *Harvard Business Review*, 89: 62-77, 2011

44. Michael E. Porter & Mark R. Kramer, 'Strategy & Society,' *Harvard Business Review*, December, 2006, p. 88.

45. Michael E. Porter & Mark R. Kramer, 'Strategy & Society,' *Harvard Business Review*, December, 2006, p. 84.

46. Michael E. Porter & Mark R. Kramer, 'Strategy & Society,' *Harvard Business Review*, December, 2006, p. 92.

47. Michael E. Porter & Mark R. Kramer, 'How to fix Capitalism—The Big Idea: Creating Shared Value,' *Harvard Business Review*, 89: 62–77, 2011, http://hbr .org/2011/01/the-big-idea-creating-shared-value/. A pdf of the article is available from HBR at: https://archive.harvardbusiness.org/cla/web/pl/product.seam?c=8062&i=806 4&cs=1b64dfac8e4d2ef4da5976b5665c5540

48. This is now Porter & Kramer's third *HBR* CSR article, following on from 'The Competitive Advantage of Corporate Philanthropy' (2002) and 'Strategy & Society: The Link Between Competitive Advantage and Corporate Social Responsibility' (2006).

49. See: http://tobywebb.blogspot.com/2011/01/does-michael-porter-understand.html

50. http://www.joinred.com/

51. Andrew Hill, 'Society and the right kind of capitalism,' *Financial Times*, February 22, 2011, p. 14.

52. For a detailed explanation of the characteristics of Valuable, Rare, Imperfectly imitable, and Non-substitutable resources that lead to a "sustained competitive advantage" for the firm, see Jay Barney, 'Firm Resources and Sustained Competitive Advantage,' *Journal of Management*, Vol.17, No.1, 1991, pp. 99–120.

53. The authors would like to thank Marta White of Georgia State University for introducing this idea to us and allowing us to build on it for inclusion in this chapter of *Strategic CSR*.

54. Michael E. Porter & Mark R. Kramer, 'Strategy & Society,' *Harvard Business Review*, December, 2006, p. 85.

55. Michael E. Porter & Mark R. Kramer, 'The Competitive Advantage of Corporate Philanthropy,' *Harvard Business Review*, December, 2002, pp. 57–68.

56. Notwithstanding this logic, however, at its 2008 AGM, Exxon rejected a shareholder motion that was instigated by the Rockefeller family (politically influential shareholders of the firm) to force Exxon to take the issue of climate change and the search of alternative sources of energy more seriously. "A survey carried out by the UK's Royal Society found that in 2005 ExxonMobil distributed $2.9m to 39 groups that the society said "misrepresented the science of climate change by outright denial of the evidence." In: David Adam, 'Exxon to Cut Funding to Climate Change Denial Groups,' *The Guardian*, May 28, 2008, http://www.guardian.co.uk/environment/2008/may/28/climatechange.fossilfuels. The primary motion proposed that the CEO and Chair positions at Exxon be split to better account for potential shifts in Exxon's operating environment that pose a threat to its core areas of profit generation (oil exploration, refining, and distribution). The motion received 39.5% share of the vote and was reported as a strong rebuke to Exxon's management. See: Stephen Foley, 'Rockefeller's Descendants Tell Exxon to Face the Reality of Climate Change,' *The Independent*, May 1, 2008, http://www.independent.co.uk/news/business/news/818778.html and Andrew Clark, 'Exxon Facing Shareholder Revolt Over Approach to Climate Change,' *The Guardian*, May 19, 2008, http://www.guardian.co.uk/business/2008/may/19/exxonmobil.oil

57. http://www.dell.com/recycling/. See also: 'Dell Will Offer Free Recycling for its Computer Equipment,' *Wall Street Journal*, June 29, 2006, p. D3.

58. http://content.dell.com/us/en/home/d/corp-comm/PlantaTreeforMe.aspx. See also: 'Dell unveils 'plant a tree for me," *Financial Times*, January 10, 2007, p. 17.

59. Jack Welch, former CEO of GE, condemned firms' primary focus on shareholder value, even though he was closely associated with such a focus during his time at GE, in a series of articles: first, in the *Financial Times* (Francesco Guerrera, 'Welch condemns share price focus,' March 12, 2009); and, second, in *BusinessWeek* ('Jack Welch Elaborates: Shareholder Value,' March 16, 2009). In the FT article, Welch said that "On the face of it, shareholder value is the dumbest idea in the world. . . . Your main constituencies are your employees, your customers and your products." In the BW follow-up article, Welch confirmed that "I was asked what I thought of 'shareholder value as a strategy.' My response was that the question on its face was a dumb idea. Shareholder value is an outcome—not a strategy."

60. Martin Wolf, 'Britain's strategic chocolate dilemma,' *Financial Times*, January 29, 2010, p. 9.

61. http://www.jnj.com/connect/about-jnj/jnj-credo/

62. Although J&J's response to the Tylenol crisis remains a best-practice model for crisis management, there is evidence to suggest that the firm has strayed from its core principles in recent years. See: 'Patients versus Profits at Johnson & Johnson: Has the Company Lost its Way?' *Knowledge@Wharton*, February 15, 2012, http://knowledge.wharton.upenn.edu/article.cfm?articleid=2943 and Alex Nussbaum, David Voreacos & Greg Farrell, 'Johnson & Johnson's Quality Catastrophe,' *Bloomberg Businessweek*, March 31, 2011, http://www.businessweek.com/magazine/content/11_15/b4223064555570.htm

63. Heesun Wee, 'Corporate Ethics: Right Makes Might,' *BusinessWeek*, April 11, 2002, http://www.businessweek.com/bwdaily/dnflash/apr2002/nf20020411_6350.htm

64. Jonathan D. Rockoff, 'J&J CEO Amid Tylenol Scare,' *The Wall Street Journal*, October 2, 2012, p. B5.

65. Jonathan D. Rockoff, 'J&J CEO Amid Tylenol Scare,' *The Wall Street Journal*, October 2, 2012, p. B5.

66. James L. Heskett, 'Southwest Airlines—2002: An Industry Under Siege,' *Harvard Business School Press*, [9-803-133], March 11, 2003.

67. 'Starbucks Corporation: Building a Sustainable Supply Chain,' *Stanford Graduate School of Business*, [GS-54], May, 2007.

68. Stephen P. Bradley & Pankaj Ghemwat, 'Wal-Mart Stores, Inc.,' *Harvard Business School Press*, [9-794-024], November 6, 2002.

69. Yvon Chouinard, *Let My People Go Surfing: The Education of a Reluctant Businessman*, Penguin Press, October 6, 2005.

70. Joe Nocera, 'Putting Customers First? What an Amazonian Concept,' *New York Times*, January 5, 2008, p. B1.

71. Steven Greenhouse, 'How Costco Became the Anti-Wal-Mart, *The New York Times*, July 17, 2005, http://www.nytimes.com/2005/07/17/business/yourmoney/17costco.html. See, also: John Helyar, 'COSTCO: The Only Company Wal-Mart Fears,' *Fortune,* November 10, 2003, http://money.cnn.com/magazines/fortune/fortune_archive/2003/11/24/353755/index.htm

72. Sam Ro, 'Stock Market Investors Have Become Absurdly Impatient,' *BusinessInsider.com,* August 7, 2012, http://www.businessinsider.com/stock-investor-holding-period-2012-8

73. Bill George, retired CEO of Medtronic, speaking to Marjorie Kelly, 'Conversations with the Masters,' *Business Ethics,* Spring 2004, pp. 4–5.

74. Quoted in: Jeff Sommer, 'A Mutual Fund Master, Too Worried to Rest,' *The New York Times*, August 12, 2012, p. BU1.

75. *The Economist,* Editorial, January 30, 1999, pp. 17–18.

76. The numbers of day traders "swelled to more than 100,000 in the late 1990s." Ianthe Jeanne Dugan, 'For Day Traders, German Index Is Overnight Sensation,' *Wall Street Journal,* October 19, 2004, p. A1.

77. At the height of the Internet boom in 1999, there were estimated to be 40,000 online share-trading accounts in the UK. This figure was expected to "grow to 700,000 within four years," according to Fletcher Research. 'Day Trading: Gambling on the Edge,' *The Independent,* July 31, 1999, p. 21.

78. *The Independent,* July 31, 1999, op. cit.

79. In a legislative reaction to the presence of growing numbers of day traders, "new Federal rules in 2001 required that people trading stocks more than four times a week keep $25,000 in their accounts at all times." *Wall Street Journal,* October 19, 2004, op. cit.

80. 'A Premature Eulogy for Public Companies?' *Knowledge@Wharton*, October 10, 2012, http://knowledge.wharton.upenn.edu/article.cfm?articleid=3089

81. 'A Premature Eulogy for Public Companies?' *Knowledge@Wharton*, October 10, 2012, http://knowledge.wharton.upenn.edu/article.cfm?articleid=3089

82. Michael Powell & Danny Hakim, 'The Lonely Redemption of a Wall Street Critic,' *The New York Times*, September 16, 2012, p. 27.

83. Jeff Sommer, 'A Mutual Fund Master, Too Worried to Rest,' *The New York Times*, August 12, 2012, p. BU1.

84. 'Wait a second,' *The Economist,* Editorial, August 11, 2012, p. 10.

85. Candace Browning, 'Companies should drop quarterly earnings guidance,' *Financial Times*, March 20, 2006, p. 13.

86. John Kay, 'Cutting costs so often leads to cutting corners,' *Financial Times*, June 23, 2010, p. 9.

87. *Business Ethics,* Spring 2004, pp. 4–5, op. cit.

88. This tax has its roots in the Tobin Tax that was first proposed by the Nobel Laureate economist James Tobin in 1972. For more information, see: 'Is It Time for a Trading Tax?' *Knowledge@Wharton*, October 26, 2011, http://knowledge.wharton.upenn.edu/article.cfm?articleid=2864 and '11 euro states back financial transaction tax,' *The Daily Yomiuri*, October 11, 2012, p. 6.

89. Alfred D. Chandler, *The Visible Hand: The Managerial Revolution in American Business*, Harvard University Press, 1977, p. 10.

90. See: Issues: Executive Compensation in Chapter 6.

91. For alternative ideas on how to incentivize longer term perspectives among shareholders, see: Julia Werdigier, 'A Call for Corporations to Focus on the Long Term,' *The New York Times*, May 15, 2012, p. B9, and Richard Lambert, 'Sir Ralph's lessons on how to end short-term capitalism,' *Financial Times*, May 23, 2011, p. 11.

92. John Kay, 'Beauty in markets is best judged by the beholder,' *Financial Times*, June 10, 2009, p. 9.

93. John Maynard Keynes, *The General Theory of Employment, Interest and Money*, Harcourt Brace and Co., 1936, p. 156.

94. Roberto C. Goizueta, 'You are tomorrow's leaders,' Remarks at Emory University's Business School graduation ceremony, May 13, 1996, http://www.goizueta.emory.edu/aboutgoizueta/quotes/calling_full.html

95. Richard Milne, 'The jovial locust killer,' *Financial Times*, November 1/November 2, 2008, p. 7.

96. 'Shooting the Messenger: Quarterly Earnings and Short-term Pressure to Perform,' *Knowledge@Wharton*, July 21, 2010, http://knowledge.wharton.upenn.edu/article.cfm?articleid=2550

97. Sumantra Ghoshal, 'Bad Management Theories Are Destroying Good Management Practices,' *Academy of Management Learning & Education*, Vol. 4, No. 1, March, 2005, pp. 79–80.

98. For examples, see: Andrew Hill, 'Real value looks past quarterly reporting,' *Financial Times*, April 19, 2011, p. 10; Michael Skapinker, 'Banks will be judged by actions not words,' *Financial Times*, October 5, 2010, p. 13; and Andrew Ross Sorkin, 'Do Stockholders Really Know Best?' *The New York Times*, November 17, 2009, p. B1.

Chapter 3

CSR: WHOSE RESPONSIBILITY?

Whose responsibility is CSR? The term *corporate social responsibility* suggests that such behavior is the responsibility of corporations. But, where does the motivation for socially responsible behavior come from?

Should corporations act responsibly because they are convinced of the moral argument for doing so (irrespective of the financial implications of their actions) or should they act responsibly because it is in their self-interest? What is the point of a firm acting socially responsible if its key stakeholders do not care sufficiently to pay the price premium that is often associated with such actions? As the Malden Mills example in Chapter 1 indicates, the best intentions do not help a firm's stakeholders if the firm is bankrupt. The economic argument for CSR assumes that firms act most effectively when they are incentivized to do so. It assumes that for-profit firms are conservative—that they are more responsive to external stimuli and are less willing to initiate change proactively when there is little evidence that their actions will be rewarded in the marketplace. Importantly, it assumes that CSR maximizes both economic and social value when the firm's goals and society's expectations are aligned.

Chapters 1 and 2 present compelling strategic reasons for firms to integrate a CSR perspective throughout operations. Nevertheless, unprincipled behavior, even outright disregard for CSR, does not always have a direct and immediate impact. Sometimes stakeholders are willing to overlook socially *irresponsible* behavior because other issues are more pressing. A firm with unacceptable employment practices that are despised by employees, for example, may not reap the negative consequences of its actions if the jobs are vital to the well-being of the local community and there are no good alternatives. Should firms interpret the lack of push back against their actions as an invitation to uphold the status quo without consideration for the broader societal concerns about their operations?

A more difficult question arises when a CSR perspective fails to align the firm's interests with those of its stakeholders or the greater public good—i.e., when stakeholder interests conflict. What happens when stakeholders demand non-socially responsible behavior? What happens, for example, if consumers want to purchase a product that is not only bad for them (e.g., tobacco, alcohol, or fast-food), but is also bad for society (e.g., has greater health or resource implications)? What happens when consumers' primary concern is the lowest price, to the exclusion of all other concerns, such as the conditions in the factories where the product is made? If firms can be successful without implementing a CSR perspective, does this mean that CSR does not matter; or, at least, does not matter all of the time? And, what does this say in terms of whose responsibility it is to introduce CSR throughout the business community?

The focus of much of the CSR debate has been to urge firms to act proactively out of a social or moral duty. The label *CSR* itself talks about the *social responsibility* of corporations, without understanding that, often, there are no meaningful consequences for firms that do not act *responsibly* and that, in contrast, they are often rewarded economically for *not* pursuing CSR.[1] Unless their business suffers as a result of their actions, should firms be expected to change?

Discussion around the issue of CSR almost exclusively focuses on the responsibilities of business, while ignoring the responsibilities of stakeholders (consumers, in particular) to demand socially responsible action from firms. Anecdotal evidence suggests, for example, that consumers want the highest quality products at the lowest possible prices. If those products happen to coincide with an ethical message, then that is great, but consumers (on the whole) are willing to plead ignorance if it means getting their sneakers for $10 less:

> In the United Kingdom, ethical consumerism data show that although most consumers are concerned about environmental or social issues, with 83 percent of consumers *intending* to act ethically on a regular basis, only 18 percent of people act ethically occasionally, while fewer than 5 percent of consumers show consistent ethical and green purchasing behaviors.[2]

If, on the other hand, consumers began demanding specific minimum standards from firms and took their custom elsewhere if the firms failed to comply, those firms would be forced to change their practices and change them quickly. In the absence of such active consumerism, how can we expect businesses to introduce

CSR when doing so means they have to try and interpret what consumers say they want—opinions that often contradict the criteria those same consumers use to make their purchase decisions?

Just because stakeholders do not react immediately, however, does not mean that CSR is unimportant or is something that can be ignored for too long. Chapters 1 and 2 demonstrate that a firm's self-interest lies in meeting the needs of its broad range of stakeholders, not only its customers. Socially irresponsible behavior without immediate market consequences does not mean that the behavior is, or should be, condoned (or, that there will not be other, non-market consequences to their actions). Equally, business practices that are profitable today may not necessarily be profitable tomorrow. Short term success simply means that other issues take precedence . . . for now. As circumstances or societal expectations evolve, the lack of CSR may alter the firm's prospects. A vivid example comes from the recent Financial Crisis:

The Financial Crisis

In pursuit of process fees, brokers sold adjustable mortgages to those who could not afford them. These loans were then packaged and sold onto investors (in pursuit of annual bonuses), who didn't understand them or appreciate the associated risks. Given the AAA rating these securities were assigned by the credit-rating agencies (in pursuit of corporate fees), the mortgages continued to be sold to a growing percentage of the population. With insufficient oversight by regulators, these socially irresponsible actions were repeated for years. When housing prices declined and mortgage defaults soared, however, the lack of social responsibility by brokers, bankers, credit-rating agencies, and Wall Street resulted in dire consequences and bankruptcies for many firms that did not practice CSR.

The title of this chapter, "CSR: Whose Responsibility?" therefore reflects an important debate within the CSR community—Can firms safely ignore calls for reform as long as they are profitable? By definition, do profitable operations indicate that a firm is adding sufficient value (perceived or real) for key stakeholder groups, even if those needs have broader, negative consequences? What is the role of stakeholders in prompting firms to change and what is the role of firms to initiate change proactively? This chapter is designed to address these questions within the larger framework of strategic CSR. A central question is: Whose responsibility is it to bring about socially responsible behavior among firms? We examine why stakeholders may not always care about CSR or, even when they do care, why they may not demonstrate that concern with action. We propose that not only does CSR matter in its own right, but that the failure to be perceived as socially responsible by stakeholders will, if not now, at some point carry rational and economic repercussions for any firm—as the recent Financial Crisis revealed.

CSR: A CORPORATE RESPONSIBILITY?

The focus of much of the CSR debate (and captured by the term 'corporate social *responsibility*') is the assumption that firms have a responsibility to pursue goals other than profit maximization. This chapter explores this assumption in more detail. In particular, we propose the idea that the CSR community expects too much of firms; that firms *react* to change better than they *initiate* change and that, if society decides it wants greater social responsibility from firms, then perhaps it is a firm's stakeholders (and their consumers, in particular) that have an equal, if not greater, responsibility to demand this behavior. More importantly, stakeholders need to demonstrate that they will support such behavior. Firms that provide services that are not demanded by consumers will quickly go out of business. With CSR, as with many aspects of business, it does not pay firms to be too far ahead of the curve. If consumers, for example, demonstrate that they are willing to pay a price premium for CSR behavior (rather than reporting in surveys that they think firms should be more responsible, but basing their purchase decisions mainly on price), firms will quickly adapt. If consumers are not willing to pay this premium, however, is it in society's best interests for firms to bear the burden of producing such products?

Milton Friedman vs. Charles Handy

Two important articles on CSR frame this debate about the responsibility that a firm has to be socially responsible. The first article was published in *The New York Times Magazine* in 1970 by the Nobel Prize winning economist, Milton Friedman—'The Social Responsibility of Business is to Increase its Profits.'[3] In the article, Friedman argues that profit, as a result of the actions of the firm, is an end in itself. He believes strongly that a firm need not have any additional justification for existing and that, in fact, social value is maximized when a firm focuses solely on pursuing its self-interest in attempting to maximize profit:

> I share Adam Smith's skepticism about the benefits that can be expected from "those who affected to trade for the public good." . . . in a free society, . . . "there is one and only one social responsibility of business—to use its resources and engage in activities designed to increase its profits."[4]

The second article is a 2002 *Harvard Business Review* article by the influential British management author and commentator, Charles Handy.[5] In contrast to Friedman, Handy presents a much broader view of the role of business in society. For Handy, it is not sufficient to justify a firm's profits as an end in itself. For Handy, a business has to have a motivation other than merely making a profit in order to justify its existence—profit is merely a means to achieve a larger end. A firm should not remain in existence just because it is profitable, but because it is meeting a need that society *as a whole* values:

> It is salutary to ask about any organization, "If it did not exist, would we invent it? Only if it could do something better or more useful than anyone else" would have to be the answer, and profit would be the means to that larger end.[6]

On the surface, the positions taken by Friedman and Handy appear to be irreconcilable. Indeed, Friedman seems to go out of his way to antagonize CSR advocates by arguing that socially responsible behavior is a waste of the firm's resources, which legally belong to the firm's owners, its shareholders, and not the firm's executives:

> That is why, in my book *Capitalism and Freedom*, I have called [social responsibility] a "fundamentally subversive doctrine" in a free society.[7]

But, on closer analysis, how different are the arguments, really? Incorporating a strategic CSR perspective narrows the gap between these two commentators considerably. As outlined in Chapter 2, there are four components of strategic CSR: First, that firms incorporate a CSR perspective within their strategic planning process; second, that any actions they take are directly related to core operations; third, that they incorporate a stakeholder perspective; and, fourth, that they shift from a short term perspective to managing the firm's resources and relations with key stakeholders over the medium to long term. Consider again the following two questions:

- Does it make sense for a large financial firm to donate money to a group researching the effects of climate change because the CEO believes this is an important issue?
- Does it make sense for an oil firm to donate money to the same group because it perceives climate change as a threat to its business model and wants to mitigate that threat by investigating possible alternatives?

The action, a large for-profit firm donating money to a non-profit group, is the same. The difference is the relevance of the non-profit's activities to the firm's core operations. Most level-headed CSR advocates would consider the first a waste of money (incorporating Friedman's argument that the actions represent an inefficient allocation of resources in an area in which the firm has no expertise), while the second is a strategic recognition by the firm that it needs to address issues that are important to key stakeholder groups in the firm's operating environment. Taking the positions of Friedman and Handy in their entirety, a more insightful interpretation of their arguments is that, to the extent that it is in a firm's interests to meet the needs of its key stakeholders, strategy should incorporate all four levels of Carroll's CSR pyramid.[8] From Handy's perspective, this point is easy to argue, but Friedman also recognizes this. He qualifies his statement that a manager's primary responsibility is to the owners of the enterprise, who seek "to make as much money as possible," by noting that this pursuit must be tempered "while conforming to the basic rules of the society, *both those embodied in law and those embodied in ethical custom.*" In addition, a firm's actions are acceptable, only as long as it "engages in open and free competition *without deception or fraud*"[9] [emphasis added]. It is worth quoting Archie Carroll at length addressing this same issue in his foundational 1991 *Business Horizons* article:

> Economist Milton Friedman . . . has argued that social matters are not the concern of business people and that these problems should be resolved by the unfettered workings of the free market system. Friedman's argument loses some of its punch, however, when you consider his assertion in its totality. . . . Most people focus on the first part of Friedman's quote but not the second part. It seems clear from this statement that profits, conformity to the law, and ethical custom embrace three components of the CSR pyramid—economic, legal, and ethical. That only leaves the philanthropic component for Friedman to reject. Although it may be appropriate for an economist to take this view, one would not encounter many business executives today who exclude philanthropic programs from their firms' range of activities.[10]

CSR: A STAKEHOLDER RESPONSIBILITY?

The title of this chapter, 'CSR: Whose Responsibility?' raises the issue of whether stakeholders care about CSR. In particular, do stakeholders have an obligation to help ensure the business community adopts a CSR perspective? Should investors, regulators, and other stakeholders, for example, demand greater care in the issuing of loans from the finance industry? Should consumers demand higher wages for employees in the retail industry? Should firms expect overseas contractors to sign Codes of Conduct to ensure more responsible behavior throughout the supply chain? The point is to examine whether stakeholders have an obligation to help design the society in which they want to live and work. If society decides that financial bubbles and crises should be avoided, then it is fair to acknowledge they have a role in realizing this outcome. Similarly, if society decides that it does not want all of its jobs outsourced to low-cost environments, then it needs to pay the higher prices that will result from keeping those jobs at home. The responsibility is not solely with one group or another, but it is important to acknowledge that "we live in the house we all build."[11]

CSR Newsletters: Earthshare

Consider a full-page advert that appeared in *The New York Times* for the environmental activist group Earthshare.org (http://www.earthshare.org/). The ad can be viewed at: http://www.earthshare.org/psa/earthshare_printpsa_2008.pdf:

> Every decision we make has consequences. We choose what we put into our lakes and rivers. We choose what we release into the air we breathe. We choose what we put into our bodies, and where we let our children run and play. We choose the world we live in, so make the right choices. Learn what you can do to care for our water, our air, our land and yourself at earthshare.org.

What is attractive about the ad is the emphasis it places on individual responsibility, rather than merely haranguing firms for polluting too much. The headline of the ad (including capital letters and bold) captures the tone exactly: WE **LIVE** IN THE HOUSE WE ALL **BUILD**.

This emphasis is often absent from the CSR debate. Firms act much more quickly in response to key stakeholder demands (consumers, in particular) than they do when expected to initiate action that has no demonstrated support in the marketplace. In other words, if consumers stop buying a certain product because they disapprove of the way it was produced or some other action by the firm that produced it, that firm will quickly adapt or fail. In other words, stakeholders are as responsible for the corporations that survive and thrive in our society as the organizations themselves. It is not a perfect solution for the problems in our capitalist system, and firms are not absolved of all responsibility (and those firms that are able to differentiate themselves in relation to CSR will be more successful in the long term); it is just that more would be achieved that much faster in terms of CSR advocacy if an equal emphasis was placed on *stakeholder responsibility* (e.g., consumer education) as on *corporate responsibility*.

This idea is expressed in the concept of corporate *stakeholder* responsibility. If we are going to advocate for a *corporate* social responsibility (the responsibility on firms to act in accordance with stakeholder needs) and, in particular, if we are going to build the business case for CSR, we also need to advocate for a corporate *stakeholder* responsibility (the equal, if not more important, responsibility on a firm's stakeholders to hold that firm to account). Both sides of the responsibility coin are essential to the extent that, without one, we are unlikely to see enough of the other.[12]

> ### Corporate *Stakeholder* Responsibility[13]
>
> A responsibility among a firm's stakeholders to hold the firm accountable for its actions.

Consistently, for-profit firms have demonstrated that they are very good at reacting to market forces and economic incentives, and that they are *not* very good at predicting consumer trends or shifting markets in ways that counter demonstrated demand.

An alternative focus of the efforts of the CSR community, therefore, would be to shift the focus from firms to their stakeholders. In Chapter 1, we defined CSR as "a view of the corporation and its role in society that assumes a responsibility among businesses to pursue goals in addition to profit maximization and a responsibility among a firm's stakeholders to hold the organization accountable for its actions." In other words, there is a responsibility on stakeholders to hold firms to account that is *equal* to the responsibility on firms to act in a socially responsible manner. This more balanced approach is essential for generating meaningful change. Until stakeholders begin holding firms to account (i.e., governments start regulating effectively, suppliers start choosing business partners that treat them fairly, consumers start discriminating among firms based on their ability to maximize social value, etc.), firms are unlikely to be sufficiently motivated to generate a comprehensive shift to a sustainable economic model. The primary purpose of a business is to make a profit. As such, a business's risk tolerance for actions that undermine that purpose is limited. If, however, stakeholders are willing to translate their values, needs, and concerns into action that punishes those organizations that fail to meet those criteria and rewards those that exceed expectations, then CSR becomes a strategic necessity. Given such incentives, for-profit firms have demonstrated time and again that they are capable of rapidly changing the way they operate.

CSR Newsletters: Steve Jobs

In the aftermath of Steve Jobs' death, we were reminded of his 2005 commencement address to the graduating class at Stanford.[14] The speech is good (not great), but is remarkable for his views on death, which are summarized in a *Wall Street Journal* article:

> Jobs reflected at length on the undesirability of death from the individual point of view, and the usefulness of it from nature's point of view. He offered no comfort. . . . Jobs made it clear that he did not welcome death, but also that life could be more interesting knowing that death would be coming.[15]

In short, Jobs made the argument that the best way to ensure you live life to the full is to appreciate that your time is short and should not be wasted. As Jobs said to Stanford's 2005 graduating class, death is "life's change agent; it clears out the old to make way for the new." The comments reminded me of Joseph Schumpeter's work on creative destruction—we benefit when the weakest firms are replaced by new, innovative firms. In a similar way, Jobs was arguing that it is new life that innovates more readily than those who are older and, perhaps, more set in their ways. Jobs makes no mention of the value of wisdom and experience over youth and energy, but his point was clear and powerful, not least because he was willing to articulate it.

These ideas are directly relevant to the CSR debate. Death is clearly a personal event and matters to each of us individually and to those who are closest to us. Unless you are someone like Steve Jobs, however, your death is unlikely to matter more broadly. The predominant view of death from a personal perspective reflects the emphasis we place on the individual at the expense of the societal—a shift that occurred around the middle of the twentieth century. Today, we care more about ourselves and less about society, more about our rights and less about our responsibilities, more about our wellbeing and less about the impact the pursuit of that wellbeing may have on others. It is not clear we are individually better off as a result of this shift, but society suffers and ideas, such as CSR, face greater resistance.

Firms are good at making a profit. It is up to a firm's stakeholders to define the parameters of which actions are profitable and which are not. It would help companies considerably, therefore, if stakeholders were: caring, proactive, and transparent.

Caring Stakeholders

In order for CSR to be a stakeholder responsibility, stakeholders need to care sufficiently to warrant corporate action. The argument in favor of CSR presupposes that there are benefits for a company being perceived as a net contributor to the society in which it is based. At the very least, there should be economic disadvantages for firms that act contrary to the expectations of key stakeholders. Managers already understand the benefits of being perceived as an important and positive influence within a local community, as suggested by existing advertising campaign strategies and levels of corporate philanthropy. The extent to which that perceived image differs from societal expectations represents the potential for either an economic or social deficit, as depicted in Figure 3.1. These deficits suggest misalignment between the expectations of the firm's stakeholders (both internal and external) and what the firm delivers.

A firm that is successfully implementing a *strategic CSR* perspective (represented by the 45° line in Figure 3.1) is able to align the *economic value* its internal

Figure 3.1   The Strategic CSR Window of Opportunity

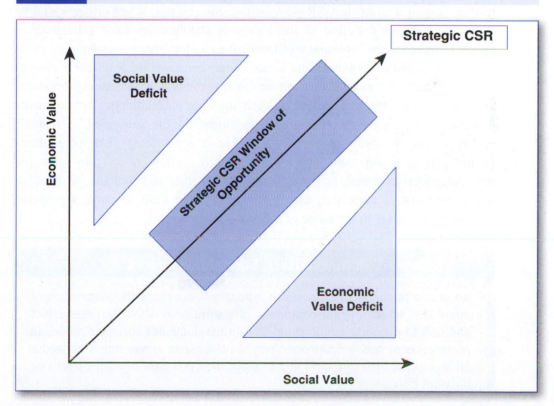

stakeholders seek with the broader *social value* that is sought by its various external stakeholders. Typically, the economic value sought is growing profits, which benefit organizational stakeholders such as shareholders and employees. To be considered legitimate over the medium to long term, however, the firm's pursuit of economic value should also provide social value to the firm's external stakeholders, such as the local community in the form of preserving local jobs or producing products that are safe to consume. The range of firm behavior that generates both economic and social value in sufficient quantities is termed the *Strategic CSR Window of Opportunity*.

This model is important because it emphasizes the need for balance. An unchecked, unbridled pursuit of economic value, without regard to the social consequences (e.g., such as a manufacturing process that generates excessive pollution), creates a deficit for the society in which the firm operates. Likewise, a firm that pursues social value too aggressively (e.g., Malden Mills in Chapter 1) may diminish its ability to generate economic value—causing a deficit in the form of slowed economic activity and lower returns to the owners. While actions that focus solely on profit maximization (economic) or philanthropic activity unrelated to the firm's core operations (social) add value, they do so in ways that fail to support a strategic CSR perspective. Simply put, when either social or economic value is deficient to some degree, stakeholders have a basis upon which to question the legitimacy of the firm as a member of society.

The alignment of economic and social value represents the implementation of a strategic approach to CSR throughout the organization. Restated, organizations must act in ways that are valued by their multiple stakeholders—not just their owners, employees, or any other single constituent. For the *Strategic CSR Window of Opportunity* to apply in practice, however, it is important that stakeholders evaluate firm actions and act to correct any deficit when they perceive one. Anecdotal evidence, however, questions whether stakeholders, in general, and consumers, in particular, care sufficiently about CSR to make significant short-term sacrifices in the name of a larger social cause:[16]

CSR Newsletters: Ethical Consumers

An article from *Ethical Corporation Magazine*[17] questions the assumption of many CSR advocates that consumers care sufficiently about business ethics and CSR to sustain a fundamental shift in the dominant economic model. In essence, consumers will say one thing in response to survey questions about ethics or CSR, then turn around and make their purchase decisions based on different principles:

For most people to choose an "ethical" product over a regular product, that product must not cost any more than an ordinary one, it must come from a reputed brand, require no special effort to buy or use, and it must be at least as good as its alternative.

In spite of a rise in availability of ethical products and producers willing to sell them, "[for] the majority of consumers, cheap products of decent quality remain the popular choice." If this is true, then "what incentives do businesses have in maintaining responsible or ethical standards?" While the article addresses the issue of reputation risk for firms, it also argues that the threat of regulation represents the strongest incentive for firms to reform ahead of consumer demands that they do so. Because consumers are unlikely to voluntarily sacrifice their current standard of living for a future, uncertain benefit (the article argues), governments will eventually be forced to act on their behalf:

... because the future will have to be one in which governments and regulators will have to take a much tougher line on the way externalities are priced by business.

The rational argument for CSR (Chapter 1) is not the most forceful (or uplifting) argument for sustainable change, but it might be the best one that we have!

Although many people say they want responsible companies, there is a limit to how much society and stakeholders are willing to impose their views. Consider consumers as one stakeholder group, for example. Although it appears that the numbers of socially concerned are growing (the Co-operative Bank's annual Ethical Consumerism Report estimates that, in the UK, "despite the economic downturn, sales of ethical goods and services have remained resilient, going up almost 9% last year from £43bn to £46.8," compared to 1999 "when annual ethical sales were just £13.5bn"),[18] a large component of consumer-driven economic pressure still demands that companies compete in terms of price or other, more traditional, characteristics, such as quality. As the *Financial Times* notes in commenting about the Ethical Consumerism Report, in spite of the increase since 1999, ethical spending in the UK still represents only "9 percent of the British public's spending, up from 3 per cent in 1999."[19]

To what extent, therefore, are investors, suppliers, and other stakeholders willing to sacrifice some short-term value in the name of longer-term sustainable value?[20] Are employees, creditors, regulators, and other key stakeholders always willing to exert influence when they enjoy some degree of leverage? Thomas Friedman of *The New York Times* captures this argument in a column about citizens demanding change from politicians, although the point holds if you substitute *corporations* for *leaders* and *consumers* for *citizens*:

> So what do we do? The standard answer is that we need better leaders. The real answer is that we need better citizens.[21]

Globalization provides powerful tools that stakeholders can use to represent their best interests, but only if they are willing to take advantage of the opportunity and demand change.

Proactive Stakeholders

Stakeholders encourage strategic CSR behavior when they represent rational or economic motives for the firm. Although this advocacy often comes from customers, investors, or other external activists, internal advocates (including founders, leaders, and employees) can also push a CSR agenda. Proponents of an economic argument for CSR believe that the most efficient means of maximizing profits is to ensure that companies meet the expectations of the widest possible range of these stakeholders. Though firms have motives to respond to stakeholder concerns, however, stakeholders also carry a responsibility to educate themselves about a firm's activities and respond appropriately.

Do stakeholders care *enough* to push their own agenda and be the fuel that drives corporations to become increasingly responsive in the 21st century? The revolution in communications technology, which fueled the growth of the Internet and global media industry, has presented stakeholders with the opportunity to mobilize and convey their collective message. They now have previously unimaginable abilities to monitor corporate operations and quickly disseminate any actions or information they feel do not represent their best interests. In this manner, the communications revolution has been a great leveler of corporate power.

As Figure 3.2 illustrates, globalization has facilitated a great expansion in corporate influence. Today, global companies span national boundaries, outsourcing large elements of operations off-shore, incorporating supply chain efficiencies, cutting costs, and growing their brands into cultural icons that span the globe: Think of Coke, Nike, or McDonald's, as examples, all of which regularly feature in surveys of the world's most important brands.[22] As a result, global corporations today are massive entities that wield significant power and influence:

> In the first half of [2011] alone, [Exxon Mobil's] profits were $21.3 billion. When the chief executive Lee Raymond stepped down a few years ago, his

Figure 3.2 The Two Phases of Globalization

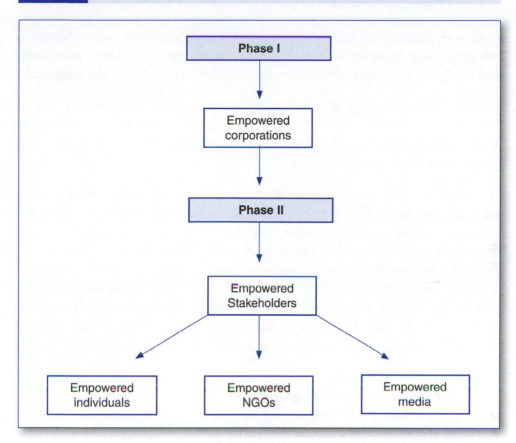

retirement package was worth $398 million. If revenue were counted as gross domestic product, the corporation would rank among the top 30 countries.[23]

Phase two of globalization, however, has been marked by countervailing pressures from stakeholders with access to increased sources of information and to increased means of acting on that information. Thomas Friedman, with greater historical perspective, refers to this as the:

. . . era of "Globalization 3.0," following Globalization 1.0, which ran from 1492 until 1800 and was driven by countries' sheer brawn, and Globalization 2.0, in which the key agent of change, the dynamic force of driving global integration, was multinational companies' driven to look abroad for markets and labor.... That epoch ended around 2000, replaced by one in which individuals are the main agents doing the globalizing, pushed by . . . "software [and a] global fiber-optic network that has made us all next-door neighbors."[24]

As a collective and armed with these tools of communication and mobilization, consumers have the power to shape the society they say they want. This is particularly true for a group of consumers that are as large as those that shop at Walmart every week:

> Does [Walmart's operating practices] matter? Only if consumers say it does, . . . Wal-Mart listens to "voters." If shoppers say they won't buy [a product] until Wal-Mart insists on higher standards from suppliers, then Wal-Mart will meet those demands.[25]

Many CSR advocates have relied on the moral argument for their cause, which boils down to the notion that businesses *should* act in a socially responsible manner because it is the *right* thing to do; however, values, such as judgments of right and wrong, are subjective, and can be subordinated within organizations to profit, sales, or other bottom-line considerations. Companies may wish or intend to act in a socially responsible manner for a variety of reasons, but they are more likely to commit consistently and wholeheartedly to CSR business practices if they are convinced of the rational or economic benefits of doing so. The evidence suggests that the dangers of not doing so for large corporations are growing exponentially:

> Multinationals are . . . more likely to suffer brand disasters that clobber their reputations, revenues, and valuations, as companies from BP to Nike to News Corp. can all attest. One study found that the five-year risk of such a disaster for companies owning the most prestigious global brands has risen in the past two decades from 20 percent to 82 percent.[26]

Stakeholder concerns become more evident and measurable for firms when key groups are willing to support their words with actions and communicate that intent clearly to firms.

Transparent Stakeholders

To the extent that they indicate which issues are on the minds of stakeholders, opinion surveys can serve as a useful tool. The message polls send, however, may not always be clear. The *Gallup* "Annual Honesty and Ethics poll," which rates "the honesty and ethics of workers in 21 different professions," for example, reveals that the public's perception of business executives is not very high. Figure 3.3 indicates that a review of the results from 1992 to 2010 shows the percentage of the U.S. public surveyed who rated business executives' ethics as "high" or "very high" never rises above 25% and is trending downwards.[27]

| Figure 3.3 | The Honesty and Ethics of Business Executives (1992–2010) |

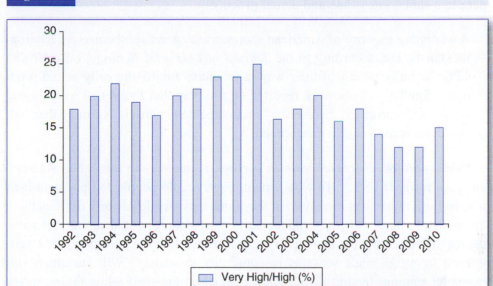

Source: USA Today (USAToday/GallupPoll,http://www.usatoday.com/news/polls/tables/live/2006-12-11-ethics .htm) and *Gallup* (Jeffrey M. Jones, "Lobbyists Debut at Bottom of Honesty and Ethics List," *Gallup*, December 10, 2007, http://www.gallup.com/poll/103123/Lobbyists-Debut-Bottom-Honesty-Ethics-List.aspx; Lydia Saad, "Nurses Shine, Bankers Slump in Ethics Ratings," *Gallup*, November 24, 2008, http://www.gallup.com/ poll/112264/Nurses-Shine-While-Bankers-Slump-Ethics-Ratings.aspx) Web sites.

The implicit accusation is that the current performance of executives is unacceptable. While people say they disapprove of unethical behavior, however, there appears to be a disconnect between perception and practice. A survey of MBA students by Donald McCabe, a professor at Rutgers University, for example, shows that "56 percent of MBA students admitted to cheating and, according to McCabe, they were doing it to 'get ahead.'"[28] This figure is little changed from a 2002 survey of 1,100 undergraduate students on 27 university campuses in the United States by the nonprofit organization Enactus[29] that identified a similar discrepancy between ideals and application:

> Some 59% [of college students polled] admit cheating on a test (66% of men, 54% of women). And only 19% say they would report a classmate who cheated (23% of men, but 15% of women).[30]

The pessimistic (or realistic, depending on your perspective) view of human nature held by Dov Charney, America Apparel's CEO, is that "to get what you want, you must appeal to people's self-interest, not to their mercy." Charney's approach to business, at least in relation to the teenage market segment to which American Apparel appeals, lies in understanding this gap between people's stated intentions and actual practice:

> A whopping majority of American shoppers may consider themselves environmentalists, but, according to the *Journal of Industrial Ecology*, only 10% to 12% "actually go out of their way to purchase environmentally sound products." Similarly, *Brandweek* reported on a survey that found that even among consumers who called themselves "environmentally conscious," more than half could not name a single green brand.[31]

Public opinion, expressed through surveys, is one way to measure a society's attitudes towards CSR.[32] To what extent, however, do people tell pollsters their true feelings rather than merely what they think they should say or what they think the pollster wants to hear? Undoubtedly, most people would agree that some degree of responsibility among firms is a desirable trait; however, does self-interest outweigh one's sense of responsibility to society? Will customers, for example, continue buying the cheapest product on the shelf while failing to ask the necessary questions to determine whether a company is socially responsible? Will other stakeholders question whether pronouncements of social responsibility are merely superficial public relations attempts to raise the company's profile? An indicator of hope for a future in which CSR becomes a more prominent part of business is the degree to which individual and corporate responsibility is an integral component of the education of future corporate leaders: To what extent are ethics and CSR classes entering the business school curriculum?

The *Beyond Grey Pinstripes* biennial survey by the Aspen Institute[33] is designed to measure progress in this area: "Our mission is to spotlight innovative full-time MBA programs that are integrating issues of social and environmental stewardship into curricula and research." The organization's 2011/2012 report, which assesses schools in four areas: relevant coursework, student exposure, business impact, and faculty research, reported that 'The percentage of schools surveyed that require students to take a course dedicated to business and society issues has increased dramatically over time: 34% in 2001; 45% in 2003; 54% in 2005; 63% in 2007; 69% in 2009; 79% in 2011."[34]

Net Impact[35] is another example of progress. The organization, originally founded as Students for Responsible Business in 1993, boasts a growing membership of "MBAs, graduate students, and professionals" who constitute:

> . . . a community of more than 30,000 changemakers who are using our jobs to tackle the world's toughest problems. We put our business skills to work for good throughout every sector, showing the world that it's possible to make a *net impact* that benefits not just the bottom line, but people and planet too.

An important factor fueling the rise in business and society courses at universities (captured in the Aspen Institute's MBA rankings) and the growth in activist organizations (such as Net Impact) is PRME—the United Nations six Principles of Responsible Management Education, which have now been adopted by almost 500 business schools and approved by all major education associations worldwide.[36] By committing to the principles, schools agree that:

> As institutions of higher education involved in the development of current and future managers we declare our willingness to progress in the implementation, within our institution, of the following Principles, starting with those that are more relevant to our capacities and mission. We will report on progress to all our stakeholders and exchange effective practices related to these principles with other academic institutions.[37]

The PRME Six Principles[38]

Principle 1: **Purpose:** We will develop the capabilities of students to be future generators of sustainable value for business and society at large and to work for an inclusive and sustainable global economy.

Principle 2: **Values:** We will incorporate into our academic activities and curricula the values of global social responsibility as portrayed in international initiatives such as the United Nations Global Compact.

Principle 3: **Method:** We will create educational frameworks, materials, processes and environments that enable effective learning experiences for responsible leadership.

Principle 4: **Research:** We will engage in conceptual and empirical research that advances our understanding about the role, dynamics, and impact of corporations in the creation of sustainable social, environmental and economic value.

Principle 5: **Partnership:** We will interact with managers of business corporations to extend our knowledge of their challenges in meeting social and environmental responsibilities and to explore jointly effective approaches to meeting these challenges.

Principle 6: **Dialogue:** We will facilitate and support dialog and debate among educators, students, business, government, consumers, media, civil society organisations and other interested groups and stakeholders on critical issues related to global social responsibility and sustainability.

A growing awareness and acceptance of CSR and related ethical issues is a necessary component of meaningful change. The extent to which future business leaders are aware of the importance of CSR will increase the likelihood of its acceptance in a corporate setting. More important from a corporate perspective, however, is the extent to which a growing awareness of CSR affects the business bottom line. If the market rewards CSR-sensitive companies and CSR-insensitive companies are punished, that will provide the greatest incentives for leaders to integrate CSR policies into their strategic perspective and day-to-day operations.

In the next section of this chapter, an extended case study examines the perspectives of multiple stakeholders and how they influence Walmart's approach to CSR. Besides being the largest for-profit organization in the world, Walmart embodies the full range of domestic and international CSR concerns as it engages with stakeholders and expands globally. As such, this extended example illustrates the interconnections among corporate actions and consequences, from the perspective of customers, communities, shareholders, and other stakeholders, and demonstrates that CSR-related actions can release a cascade of effects that are tempered by economic, cultural, and other realities. The intent is not to praise or condemn, merely to highlight the breadth and depth of CSR, as seen from the perspective of this important firm.

THE WALMART PARADOX

A firm that captures wholeheartedly the debate over whether responsibility for CSR lies with the organization or its stakeholders (or both) is Walmart—the world's largest company and a test case for CSR:

Walmart

Some facts about the world's largest private-sector firm:

- Each week, Walmart serves more than 200 million customers.
- 90% of all Americans live within 15 miles of a Walmart.
- In 2011, Walmart registered $419 billion in sales.... If Walmart were a country, it would be the 25th largest economy in the world.
- If Walmart's more than 900 million square feet of retail space were spread out over one place it would take up roughly 34 miles — about 1.5 times the size of Manhattan.
- China's exports to Walmart accounted for 11% of the growth of the total U.S. trade deficit with China between 2001 and 2006.

- In 2010, CEO Michael Duke's annual salary of $35 million earned him more in an hour than his employees earned in an entire year working for $8.75/hour.
- In 2000, Walmart was sued 4,851 times — about once every 2 hours.[39]

As these facts indicate, Walmart is an extremely successful and influential company. As such, it is clear that Walmart delivers a great deal of value to the tens of millions of customers that shop at its stores every week:

A poll in Vanity Fair . . . asked readers which institution best symbolized America: 48 per cent chose Walmart. The rest of the vote was split among Google, Microsoft, the National Football League and Goldman Sachs.[40]

Walmart's track record, however, also reveals that other stakeholders are not as happy with the firm. A brief survey of news headlines indicates the negative feelings the company can generate and the concerns some groups have about its long-term influence:

Is Wal-Mart Too Powerful?[41]

The Wal-Martization of America[42]

Is Wal-Mart Good for America?[43]

At the foundation of Walmart's success is its business strategy of minimizing costs, which relies on many policies and decisions that affect stakeholders in different ways, but the effect is often perceived to be negative. Suppliers of Walmart, for example, complain that their margins are continually squeezed by the firm's unrelenting focus on cost reduction. Regulators complain that the state has to subsidize the low wages and benefits the firm pays its employees (even while they welcome the jobs the company provides). And, the steady flow of litigation against the firm attests to other stakeholders (from female employees to local communities in which Walmart has announced a new store) who object to some aspect of Walmart's business.[44]

These competing views of the firm, positive and negative, frame the Walmart Paradox. They explain why, whenever Walmart enters a new market, some greet it as a liberating force, while others see it as a conquering imperialist?

Wal-Mart Invades, and Mexico Gladly Surrenders.[45]

Walmart Invades India – Who's Next?[46]

The paradox that surrounds Walmart and the controversy generated by its success suggest why the company is a case-study in so many different business disciplines. Overall, does the company provide a net positive or net negative impact on the societies in which it operates? As one writer observed, "Wal-Mart might well be both America's most admired and most hated company."[47] And, this controversy has followed it around the world as it continues to expand at an ever increasing rate (as indicated by Figure 3.4). Today, Walmart uses global expansion as a source of growth that it can no longer generate in the saturated U.S. market ("Ninety-six percent of Americans live within 20 miles of a Walmart")[48] and now "operates more than 10,300 stores in 27 countries around the world."[49]

As a result of all this controversy, the argument *against* CSR offers up Walmart as its main case in point. Does the fact that consumers continue to shop at the store (on average, almost 30 million customers pass through Walmart's doors every day)[50] critically undermine the argument in favor of CSR? If the criticisms against the firm are true, while sales continue to grow, does this suggest that the majority of Walmart's stakeholders do not care sufficiently about CSR? Would Walmart be as successful, today, if they cared more? Would it be more successful?

Figure 3.4　Walmart Overseas (2010)

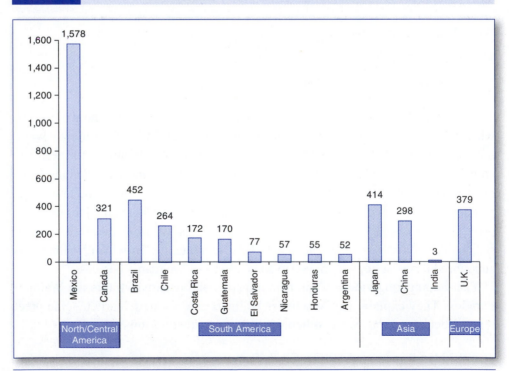

Source: Mariko Sanchanta, 'Wal-Mart Bargain Shops For Japanese Stores to Buy,' *The Wall Street Journal*, November 15, 2010, pB1.

IS WALMART GOOD FOR SOCIETY?

Is it healthy for an economy to have companies with the size and power of Walmart? Proponents of the pro-Walmart case credit the company with directly saving U.S. consumers billions of dollars because of the downward pressure it exerts on its own prices, and the price reductions it forces on competitors, on an annual basis:[51]

> The giant retailer is at least partly responsible for the low rate of U.S. inflation, and a McKinsey & Co. study concluded that about 12% of the economy's productivity gains in the second half of the 1990s could be traced to Wal-Mart alone.[52]

Walmart gives consumers what they indicate (with their shopping practices) they want—reasonable quality at low prices. Yet the methods by which Walmart achieves these cost savings and low prices are also having a lasting impact, often negative, in the eyes of other stakeholders. The Walmart paradox is magnified when the long-term impact of the company's policies are extrapolated. We suspect that the same people who complain about the number of U.S. jobs that are exported overseas, particularly manufacturing jobs, also form a significant percentage of Walmart consumers, to whom the company's low prices are so attractive:

> "Wal-Mart is a double-edged sword, and both edges are quite sharp," Bernstein of the Economic Policy Institute said. "On the price side, consumers wouldn't flood Wal-Mart if there wasn't something there they liked, the low prices. On the other hand, by sticking solidly to the low-wage path, they create tons of low-quality jobs that dampen wage and income growth, not just for those who work in Wal-Mart but for surrounding communities as well."[53]

The potential dangers for Walmart are many. What if consumers begin to worry about the impact the company is having on the economy and society more than they welcome the lower prices the company brings? Communities that worry about a megastore's impact on rural downtowns have already restricted Walmart's growth.[54] Will employees continue to apply for positions at Walmart if better paid alternatives exist? As the company continues to expand, will the government begin to fear the monopolistic characteristics of such a huge market influence? Suppliers are stakeholders who both relish Walmart's market scale and scope, yet fear their pricing pressures. How will these various stakeholder reactions affect Walmart's business strategy over the longer term? What is the outlook for the company from a CSR perspective?

Is Walmart Good for Society? Yes!

☺ Reasonable quality and low prices for consumers (lower inflation).
☺ Good jobs in economically deprived regions.
☺ Wide range of products.
☺ Redefinition of supply chain management (SCM) through technological efficiencies.
☺ Increased productivity.

Is Walmart Good for Society? No!

☹ Loss of domestic jobs to overseas suppliers.
☹ Strong opposition against collective representation of workforce.
☹ Relatively low employee wages and benefits.
☹ Competitors (and sometimes suppliers) go out of business, reducing competition and, ultimately, consumer choice.
☹ Litigation against the company brought by many stakeholder groups.

We elaborate on the salient characteristics of Walmart's operations and consider the impact of the firm's business decisions on its various stakeholders from five different perspectives: prices, suppliers, jobs, competitors, and quality and variety.

Prices

Walmart has grown to such an influential point that it now dominates any industry it enters by driving down prices and imposing punishing margins on its competitors. Walmart arrives at its low prices primarily by revolutionizing the management of supply chains and inventory within the retail industry. Now, thanks to Walmart's innovations, many firms are better able to manage the flow of goods and materials that form an interconnected chain from providers (such as subcontractors and suppliers), through the firm, to the customer. The company uses information technology to track products—from the supplier to the warehouse to the shelf to the cash register—and ensure, as soon as they are sold, that replacements are back on the shelf waiting for the next customer.

With this greater refinement in managing the flow of goods from suppliers around the world, it has become easier for firms like Walmart to seek the lowest-cost suppliers, wherever they operate. This practice pushes costs lower, even though it can cause disastrous results for domestic suppliers, including bankruptcy. The company's renowned satellite network ("the largest private satellite communication system in the U.S."),[55] together with its commitment to integrate radio frequency identification (RFID) technology throughout distribution and inventory systems, continues to push the technological boundaries of supply chain management.[56] Walmart's innovations create savings across the board, and it passes these savings on to customers in the form of lower prices. And, Walmart's impact is always industry-wide. One example of its revolutionary influence is the banking industry where, for a number of years, Walmart has been trying to expand its role as a financial institution, especially to the underserved or "unbanked" sections of society:

> The Federal Deposit Insurance Corporation estimates that 60 million Americans, most of them low-income, are underserved by local community banks and wind up using usurious check cashers, payday lenders and pawnbrokers for financial services.[57]

Understandably, the mainstream banks are petrified at the thought of Walmart's margin-lowering competition and have lobbied intensively to make sure the firm is prevented from fully entering the market:

> Four years ago, Wal-Mart abandoned its plans to obtain a long-sought federal bank charter amid opposition from the banking industry and lawmakers. . . . Ever since, Wal-Mart has been quietly building up à la carte financial services, becoming a force among the unbanked and "unhappily banked" as one Wal-Mart executive put it.[58]

This relentless driving down of costs above all else is good in the short term for consumers. In the long term, however, competition and quality can be diminished, as all elements of the production process become potential cost savings that need to be made to compete, from research and development (R & D) to the components used to make the product.

Suppliers

A tactic that Walmart uses to cut costs throughout operations is to place specific demands on its suppliers. It achieves this advantage by virtue of its size and importance in the economies in which it operates:

> Wal-Mart wields its power for just one purpose: to bring the lowest possible prices to its customers. At Wal-Mart, that goal is never reached. The retailer has a clear policy for suppliers: On basic products that don't change, the price Wal-Mart will pay, and will charge shoppers, must drop year after year.[59]

Walmart's size increases its importance for any of its 61,000 U.S. suppliers[60] that are 'lucky' enough to have the company as a client, and the company's growing influence among certain brands is astounding. In 2008, for example, 28% of Dial's total sales were made from Walmart stores.[61] Similar figures are true for Del Monte, Clorox, and Revlon, among others. This growing dependence, however, can be a double-edged sword for stakeholders who find themselves out of favor for whatever reason. From the point of view of suppliers (and also governments, see below), over-dependence on one company can cause societal harm or supplier collapse. In particular, such influence presents Walmart with disproportionate negotiating power:

> Wal-Mart is legendary for forcing its suppliers to redesign everything from their packaging to their computer systems. It is also legendary for quite straight-forwardly telling them what it will pay for their goods.[62]

Walmart is able to dictate the cost at which goods are supplied and enforces its demands by sourcing elsewhere, leaving the supplier unable to fill the gap left behind.

Jobs

Often in rural areas, Walmart is the only large employer in town, which gives the company additional clout:

> Wal-Mart's reputation for bringing a wide variety of goods to small towns and rural communities gives the company leverage over town councils and planning boards, which are often asked to grant zoning concessions or relax environmental standards. And, Wal-Mart's frequent position as the only big employer in town allows it leeway to hire workers at low wages.[63]

Walmart, however, vehemently denies that it creates only low paying jobs.[64] There is evidence that Walmart pays higher than average wages for its industry and also that "[Walmart's] average hourly wages exceed state minimums, sometimes by a considerable amount."[65] In addition, Walmart is known for promoting from within and the firm emphasizes the high percentage of senior managers who have risen through the ranks. What is not in doubt is the overwhelming number of people who apply for a job at Walmart when one is offered. If Walmart is as unattractive an employment option as it is reported to be, it would not continue to attract so much interest from job-seekers—when the firm opened a store in Chicago, for example, "25,000 people applied for 325 jobs."[66] Such numbers are not uncommon:

> If Wal-Mart were as greedy as its detractors say, it would never have attracted 8,000 job applicants for 525 places at a new store in Glendale, Ariz., or 3,000 applicants for 300 jobs in outlying Los Angeles.[67]

Nevertheless, alleged poor employment policies may well indicate some of the CSR-related dangers facing the company. When employees do have a choice, they may start choosing not to work for Walmart. A reputation as a poor employer leads to low morale, which reduces productivity, and causes higher turnover rates, which raise costs and disrupt service as new employees retrain. The operating practices that create such a reputation do not make good business sense in the long term as, in any given year, Walmart estimates that "about 44%" of its employees will leave[68] and half of all full-time employees leave within a year of joining the firm.[69] This means the firm has to hire hundreds of thousands new employees to replace them. And, where an employer's bad practices become inherent to the way the company conducts business, the fallout can have even more expensive repercussions:

> Questions over whether the retailer's relentless drive to cut costs is causing it to stray too close to the boundary of legality. . . . Many powerful businesses eventually run into issues that threaten to hold back their progress. . . . Could labor issues become the kind of thorn in the side for Wal-Mart that antitrust probes became for Microsoft?[70]

In December, 2008, for example, Walmart agreed to pay "at least $352 million, and possibly far more" to settle allegations that the firm forced employees to work unpaid overtime. The decision to settle, which was reported to have been prompted by the change in CEO from Lee Scott to Michael T. Duke, was described by lawyers "as the largest settlement ever for violations of wage-and-hour laws."[71]

Competitors

Another area of criticism that has been leveled against Walmart is in terms of the intense pressure its competitors face once a Walmart comes to town. The devastating impact the presence of a Walmart Supercenter is likely to have on existing local businesses is often cited in protests opposing the opening of a new store. While a new Walmart undoubtedly causes some small firms to go out of business, this has to be weighed against the jobs that become available at the new store, which offer better potential for advancement and a stable career. There is also evidence to suggest that the net jobs total following the opening of a Walmart store is positive. While some businesses close, they create space for other businesses to open:

> Creative destruction occurs when the introduction of a new idea or product results in the obsolescence of other products. New inventions, for instance, often result in the business failures of products supplanted by now-outdated technologies. This is unfortunate for the old businesses, but it benefits consumers and it frees money and resources that can then give rise to new businesses and further advancements.[72]

It is also worth keeping in mind that Walmart is only successful because consumers choose to shop there and choose not to shop at smaller vendors:

> . . . critics are wrong when they say that Wal-Mart puts little people out of business. We (consumers) put little people out of business. . . . We vote with our wallets, and we're the ones who choose Wal-Mart over local stores.[73]

Nevertheless, the lasting impression is of a huge multi-national putting small, independent stores out of business. Such stereotypes present ample ammunition to disgruntled stakeholders who seek to oppose a new Walmart when it comes to town.

Quality and Variety

Finally, an important component of Walmart's pricing strategy that enables it to lower prices is its policy of stocking the most profitable top tier products in an industry—the top 10% of best-selling toys from the biggest brands, for example. Walmart can afford to market these best sellers at lower margins (or even as loss-leaders) because of the volume and extra business they generate for the store. The concern for product quality and variety in the long term, however, is related to future research and development (R&D). By cherry-picking today's most profitable products and selling them at low margins, Walmart is taking away the profits that other industry-focused companies use to fund current and future R&D.

Without these profits, specialist producers are unable to finance the innovation that drives product development, creates choice, and produces the best-sellers of the next generation. As such, in buying at Walmart today at slightly lower prices, consumers may be ensuring future quality and variety will be diminished. If so, Walmart is also hurting its own future business strategy by narrowing the number of best-seller products it is able to market at low margins over time? The firm was accused of causing great dislocation within the toy industry during the 2003 holiday season, for example, leading to the bankruptcies of both F.A.O. Schwarz and KB Toys and reducing the margins of all the other major industry retailers, in particular Toys R Us:

> The toy war is merely the most recent manifestation of what is known as the Wal-Mart effect. To the company's critics, Wal-Mart points the way to a grim Darwinian world of bankrupt competitors, low wages, meager health benefits, jobs lost to imports, and devastated downtowns and rural areas across America.[74]

While quality and variety may suffer in the long run, however, there is also evidence to suggest that Walmart's short-term competitive influence on firms that survive benefits consumers. Although "competition from Walmart has been linked to bankruptcies of at least 25 supermarket chains," for example, it is also true that "local supermarkets reduce stockouts by an average of 10% and boost product variety after a Walmart supercenter opens nearby."[75]

WALMART IS NO. 1 . . . TODAY

In 2002, Walmart became the number one firm on the Fortune 500[76] and has remained as either number one or number two ever since.[77] In 2003 and 2004, Walmart also was named Fortune's *Most Admired Company in America*[78] and has routinely placed in the Top 50 firms on that list ever since.[79] It is the largest for-profit organization in the world and, as the discussion above indicates, in spite of its ongoing success, continues to generate both passion and loathing.

None of the issues discussed so far, however, solves the paradox that Walmart's promise to produce low prices and "Save money. Live better." appeals to the very workers who cannot afford to pay more. Many of these workers have had their wages driven down and their job security threatened because of Walmart's pursuit of ever lower costs, whether they work for the company itself, a supplier, a competitor, or another company in the affected labor pool.

A CSR perspective argues that Walmart's business model will only remain viable as long as the firm's attractions offset the consequences of its actions. Ultimately, a strategy of low prices that alienates stakeholders (even while satisfying customers) will erode the innovation, choice, and societal support necessary to operate. For a number of years from the 1990s into the 2000s, coalitions of unions, environmentalists, community organizations, state lawmakers, and academics planned coordinated attacks on Walmart to force it to change its policies and practices,[80] leading to the restriction of the firm's actions in some communities and industries.

CSR is an argument about business today in conjunction with an ability to understand what business will be about tomorrow. Today, Walmart is No. 1. But, in order to sustain its dominant market position, stakeholder theory argues that a CSR perspective should be integrated into the firm's strategic planning processes and throughout day-to-day operations. Absent this perspective, the firm is endangering its societal legitimacy, particularly among the key constituents (such as employees and local community zoning boards) that are crucial to its growth mandate. There is mounting evidence that Walmart understands this and has moved to change its perception among specific stakeholder groups.

WALMART AND SUSTAINABILITY

A key focus of Chapter 3 is what we refer to as 'The Walmart question.' If CSR is central to a firm's competitiveness in a global business environment, how is it that a firm like Walmart can apparently ignore calls for greater social responsibility from key stakeholders? The answer is that, perhaps it cannot. This is increasingly evident because Walmart's position regarding CSR has evolved drastically in the last decade, a position it was forced into taking because the "'constant barrage of negatives' in the US over everything from Wal-Mart's low wage business model to alleged discrimination against women [threatened] the company's ability to grow":[81]

> Walmart adopted sustainability as a corporate strategy in 2005. It was struggling mightily at the time. Bad headlines stalked the chain, as its history of mistreating workers and suppliers finally caught up with it. One analysis found that as many as 8 percent of Walmart's customers had stopped shopping at its stores. Grassroots groups were blocking or delaying one-third of its development projects. Stockholders were growing nervous. Between 2000 and 2005, Walmart's share price fell 20 percent.[82]

Today, however, particularly in relation to environmental and sustainability issues, Walmart is now considered by many to be a market leader.[83] The firm now works with the Environmental Defense Fund,[84] partners with Seventh Generation, Inc.,[85] and has even employed Adam Werbach, past president of the Sierra Club, as a consultant on environmental issues:

> I wholeheartedly believe in what Wal-Mart's doing. . . . Our goal . . . is to have Wall Street look at Walmart's green performance, and say, "Wow, do more of that."[86]

An early indication of the firm's dramatic change in policy and practice occurred when Walmart announced a $35 million campaign in partnership with the National Fish and Wildlife Foundation "to offset the amount of land [Walmart] develops to use for its stores and other facilities" over the next 10 years by purchasing 138,000 acres "of land in sensitive habitats" for conservation.[87] But, the real shift came in a speech given by then CEO, Lee Scott (*Wal-Mart: Twenty First Century Leadership*)[88] shortly after the devastation of Hurricane Katrina in and around New Orleans in the U.S. in August, 2005. In the immediate aftermath of the storm, Walmart was the first source of relief for residents. The firm had the distribution infrastructure to re-stock its stores with those supplies that were in demand with an efficiency that the federal and state governments were unable to match.[89] The experience was reported to have been a personal revelation for

Scott.[90] This sense of "a key personal moment"[91] was conveyed in the speech he subsequently delivered approximately two months later in October, 2005.[92]

In retrospect, this speech by Scott appears designed to achieve two goals. First, it served to reinforce Walmart's key core competence—identifying inefficiencies in the value chain and eliminating them to minimize costs. In this sense, this speech and Walmart's focus on sustainability, reinforces their existing business model. Second, however, the speech was also intended to re-position Walmart in the eyes of its various external stakeholders:

> To better understand our critics and Wal-Mart's impact on the world and society, [our top executives] spent a year meeting with and listening to customers, Associates, citizen groups, government leaders, non-profits and non-government organizations, and other individuals. . . . most of our vocal critics do not want us to stop doing business, but they feel business needs to change, not just our company, but all companies.[93]

In particular, Scott used the speech to commit Walmart to an overarching framework of three environmental goals:

Walmart's Environmental Goals[94]

1. To be supplied 100 percent by renewable energy.
2. To create zero waste.
3. To sell products that sustain our resources and environment.

As an initial step toward reaching these goals, Scott announced a number of specific quantifiable policy targets, such as "reducing greenhouse gases at our existing [stores] . . . by 20 percent over the next 7 years," "increasing our fleet efficiency by 25 percent in the next 3 years," "reducing our solid waste from U.S. [stores] by 25 percent in the next 3 years," and "working with suppliers to create less packaging overall, increase product packaging recycling and increase use of post-consumer material." Taken together, these commitments constitute a comprehensive sustainability policy about which Walmart appears to be both serious and sincere:

> [Hurricane] Katrina asked this critical question, and I want to ask it of you: What would it take for Wal-Mart to be that company, at our best, all the time?

What if we used our size and resources to make this country and this earth an even better place for all of us: customers, Associates, our children, and generations unborn?[95]

In essence, Walmart's consumers make short term purchase decisions based on price, with less emphasis placed on the longer term, broader societal consequences of those decisions. Implementing a stakeholder perspective reveals to Walmart that there are a broader set of stakeholders that they must pay attention to if it wants to remain viable over the long term. It is insufficient merely to be profitable in the short term. Importantly, however, as Walmart exposes itself to different ideas, it is discovering that responding to its stakeholders' demands need not diminish the firm's business model and may even enhance it. The turnaround has been dramatic:

> . . . after years of running afoul of the United States government on labor and environmental issues, Wal-Mart now aspires to be *like* the government, bursting through political logjams and offering big-picture solutions to intractable problems.[96]

An indication of Walmart's willingness to engage in a new start with its stakeholders was the introduction of a new logo and slogan in July, 2008:

CSR Newsletters: Save Money, Live Better

An article from *Businessweek*[97] dissects the meaning and consequences of Walmart's new logo:

> Something's up at Wal-Mart. Visitors to walmart.com will notice that the logo consumers have become accustomed to over the past 17 years is gone. . . . In its place: a new logo made up of rounded, lowercase characters. The hyphen has disappeared. And in place of the star is a symbol that resembles a sunburst or flower.

The article argues that the logo is an attempt by Walmart's to capitalize on its increasing reputation for progressive action in relation to environmental sustainability. The introduction of the new logo (changing from "Everyday low prices" to "Save money. Live better.") "coincides with CEO H. Lee Scott's goal of transforming Wal-Mart . . . into a more environmentally friendly corporation." The article also suggests, however, that the design will fall short of its intentions:

[Marty Neumeier, president of Neutron, a branding firm in San Francisco] adds that the image lacks the distinctive power of the most successful logos, such as Target's (TGT) bull's eye, . . . [Walmart's new logo] 'is designed so simply that there's no ownership to it,' . . . it could be used by almost any corporation.

One area where Walmart has the potential to deliver massive social value is in terms of stakeholder education. In order to care about CSR, first and foremost, stakeholders have to be aware of the issues, but also their ability to do something about them. Simply because of the scale and scope of Walmart's operations—not only the number of consumers it interacts with every week, but also the tens of thousands of suppliers that make the products sold in its stores—Walmart merely has to dip its toes in the water for it to make an immediate, meaningful impact:

[Mike Duke, Wal-Mart's CEO since February, 2009] has gone on record saying that "Wal-Mart and our supplier partners must operate in a more socially and environmentally responsible way wherever we do business . . . we at Wal-Mart are also committed to being a leader on sustainability." Using its vast size to influence entire supply chains to its advantage—the very practice that skeptics criticize as "bullying"—Wal-Mart is now leveraging this muscle to shift markets toward greener practices.[98]

A good example of Walmart's reach and influence is the firm's commitment to greatly reduce the waste packaging that is processed through its stores. The policy change reinforces the firm's environmental goals and had an immediate effect:

Our packaging team, for example, worked with our packaging supplier to reduce excessive packaging on some of our private-label Kid Connection toy products. By making the packaging just a little bit smaller on one private brand of toys, we will use 497 fewer containers and generate freight savings of more than $2.4 million per year. Additionally, we'll save more than 38-hundred trees and more than a thousand barrels of oil. Again, think about this with Wal-Mart's scale in mind: this represents ONE relatively simple package change on ONE private toy brand.[99]

Importantly, however, it also had dramatic ramifications for all the firms with whom Walmart does business:

[Walmart's] decision in 2006 to stock only double concentrate liquid laundry detergent led to the entire US detergent industry shifting to smaller, lighter bottlers by the start of [2008], saving millions of dollars in fuel costs.[100]

Literally, Walmart has the ability to change the world.[101] For 2007, for example, the firm announced a goal to sell 100 million compact fluorescent lightbulbs (CFL)—a doubling of the market for CFLs over the previous year's sales "to make clear how seriously Wal-Mart takes its new positioning as an environmental activist."[102] In typical fashion, Walmart reached its goal three months ahead of schedule;[103] in total, managing to sell:

137 million bulbs in 2007. . . . As of June 2009, Walmart and Sam's Club in the U.S. have sold more than 260 million CFLs. We estimate during the life of these CFL bulbs, our customers will save more than 7 billion dollars on their electric bills.[104]

And, Walmart's ambition is growing. In July, 2009, for example, Walmart's CEO announced a commitment:

. . . to create a global, industry-wide sustainable product index. The ambitious plan . . . aims to establish a sustainability rating system for each item on Wal-Mart's shelves. This will help shoppers understand the social and environmental impact of products. It should also drive innovation among suppliers.[105]

It is worth restating the enormity of the task Walmart has set itself: "to track the life cycle of every product it sells, measuring it on water use, greenhouse-gas emissions, and fair labor practices."[106] The complexity of the goal is astounding. Given Walmart's size and influence, however, it demands to be taken seriously. The subsequent "Sustainability Index"[107] has evolved into a consortium of firms, activists, and governmental agencies that "has attracted everyone from Monsanto to Disney, Seventh Generation to the EPA":[108]

The Sustainability Consortium drives scientific research and the development of standards and IT tools, through a collaborative process, to enhance the ability to understand and address the environmental, social, and economic implications of products.[109]

So, is Walmart promoting sustainability this aggressively because of a belief in the ethical, moral, rational, or economic arguments for CSR? In our assessment, Walmart would be wise if it is acting for all four reasons. The firm appears to realize that, even if specific stakeholders do not care or think about CSR in the short term, there are *ethical* and *moral* arguments for acting that win it support with other important groups. In addition, there are very *rational* arguments for pursuing a course of action that limits potential future constraints on the firm's business interests. Finally, Walmart also undoubtedly recognizes that implementing a CSR perspective assists the firm in its overall *economic* goal of providing goods to consumers as efficiently as possible—that waste is an inefficiency that drives up the cost of business. One of the benefits Walmart hopes to accrue from its work with the Sustainability Index, for example, is to better understand the processes by which the products it sells are made and distributed so it can extend its efficiencies (and cut costs) throughout the supply chain. To this end, in 2010 Walmart committed to "cut some 20 million metric tons of greenhouse gas emissions from its supply chain by the end of 2015 – the equivalent of removing more than 3.8 million cars from the road for a year."[110] In short, it is the combination of the ethical, moral, rational, and economic arguments for CSR that has resulted in Walmart's current sustainability vision:[111]

> [In October, 2008] Scott told analysts that Wal-Mart had shifted its position in the political spectrum so that it was able to "no longer be the whipping post for what is happening out there, but to take a leadership role."[112]

There is strong evidence that Walmart is genuine in its commitment to sustainability. There is also evidence, however, that the firm's performance is still being met with skepticism by some stakeholders. Due to the firm's narrow focus on sustainability (where it can cut costs) and a reluctance to adopt a broader CSR perspective (which sometimes involves higher costs), the overall firm's performance in relation to CSR remains open to challenge.

WALMART AND GREENWASH

Today, Walmart claims to be expanding its CSR policies beyond sustainability to encompass a "Global Responsibility."[113] There are suggestions, however, that the firm's progress, although significant, is not going as smoothly as initially thought. Three issues, in particular, suggest that, while Walmart has made some progress in areas in which it sees a cost-savings benefit to acting, there are other aspects of operations that have not changed and continue to act as a threat to the firm.

First, even though the massive class-action employment discrimination lawsuit against Walmart[114] was thrown out by the U.S. Supreme Court in 2011 (and was officially a 'victory' for the firm), the case was decided on a technical point of law (what constitutes a "class action"), rather than any vindication of Walmart's conduct.[115] The fact that this case has dragged on for over a decade and in spite of Walmart's half-hearted attempts to introduce "women-friendly plans" in the aftermath of the decision,[116] the company remains open to ongoing claims of sex discrimination by individual plaintiffs and sustains the image of a workplace that is not equally welcoming to all employees.

Second, the 'bribery in Mexico' scandal that was unearthed in 2012 in an in-depth report by *The New York Times*,[117] is damaging for Walmart because it details a pattern of behavior of corruption and suppression of information (which the firm was legally obligated to report to the U.S. federal government) that continued for a number of years, from 2005 to 2011:[118]

> Walmart's Mexican arm, Walmex, stands accused of greasing local officials' palms over several years to speed the granting of permits to open new stores. Managers at group headquarters in Bentonville, Arkansas, were apparently informed about the payments . . . in 2005. They launched a probe, but wound it down without disciplining anyone. They did not disclose any of this to the authorities until [December, 2011].[119]

The scandal is also revealing due to the importance of Mexico to Walmart's worldwide operations—"Today, one in five Wal-Mart stores is in Mexico, . . . where Wal-Mart now employs 209,000 people, making it the country's largest private employer."[120] The result of the bribery probe? In addition to legal challenges from pension funds[121] and protests at its 2012 annual meeting for endangering shareholder value,[122] Walmart faced stock market sanctions that wiped almost 5% off its market capitalization when "Jittery investors cut $10 billion from the value of [Walmart's] shares"[123] in the week following *The New York Times* article. And, in its 2013 fiscal year, "Walmart took a $157 million charge" against its internal investigation into the scandal.[124]

Third, and perhaps most damaging, as Walmart continues to implement its sustainability programs and proclaims its progress,[125] accusations of greenwash continue against the firm.[126]

Walmart's Sustainability "by the Numbers"[127]	
210	minimum number of new stores Walmart plans to open in the U.S. in 2012.
1.5 million	approximate metric tons of CO_2 saved each year by energy-efficiency improvements Walmart has made to U.S. stores built before 2006.
3.5-3.9 million	approximate metric tons of CO_2 emitted each year by Walmart stores built in the U.S. since 2006.
300	approximate number of years it would take for Walmart to reach 100 percent renewable energy at its current pace.

Partly this criticism arises due to Walmart's size and reach ("[Walmart's rural stores] contributed heavily to the more than 40 per cent increase in the amount of vehicle miles American households travel for shopping purposes since 1990"),[128] partly due to the firm's employment policies ("Wal-Mart Lowers Benefits for Employee Health Care"),[129] and partly due to the firm's continued success ("If Walmart continues to add stores at its current growth rate, its new stores alone will use significantly more energy than any of its energy-saving measures will save").[130] It is also clear, however, that the change in CEOs from Lee Scott to Mike Duke in 2009 may also have had ramifications for Walmart's CSR performance. As Jeffrey Hollender, co-founder and prior CEO of Seventh Generation, Inc. puts it:

Michael Duke became CEO in February 2009, replacing Scott. Duke joined Walmart in 1995. I believe that, from the day Duke started, the initiatives that Lee Scott championed, but never saw come to fruition, stalled and then slowly unraveled.[131]

More important than any specific incident, however, is what the collective pattern of behavior says about Walmart's business model and approach to CSR. It is true that Walmart attracts a lot of attention purely because it is so large and influential. It is also clear that the shift in company policy towards sustainability, in reaction to the sustained criticism the firm had been receiving, is remarkable. It is not clear, however, that Walmart's current business model is sustainable. Walmart still relies entirely on growth through expansion—high volume consumption in a disposal-oriented society. As it grows, although its commitment to sustainability ensures it consumes fewer resources than it otherwise would have done, Walmart's environmental footprint continues to expand and its CSR profile continues to draw criticism.

SO, WHOSE RESPONSIBILITY IS CSR?

The central question of this chapter is: Who is responsible for CSR? In order to answer this question, it is essential to understand stakeholder attitudes to CSR and to what extent these attitudes determine company action. Do firms have a responsibility to use their market position to educate stakeholders about CSR and create a point of competitive differentiation? Or, do stakeholders have a responsibility to educate themselves and demand change from firms in order to shape the society in which they wish to live? These are not easy questions, but they are central to the CSR debate. The extended Walmart case conveys the complexity of these issues. Walmart is an essential part of the global economy, today. Whether you love the store or refuse to shop there, understanding what Walmart does and why it does it (particularly in relation to CSR) is an important component of understanding the role of CSR in business today.

As such, the case study provides insight into Walmart's (sometimes fraught) relations with its stakeholders, particularly its customers and the communities in which it operates. What should have been apparent is that different stakeholders have different perspectives and that these different perspectives often lead to conflict. In other examples, corporate actions may be seen as less ambiguous with more direct consequences—think of Bhopal, India, where a Union Carbide plant accident killed thousands,[132] Enron's self-destruction due to the lack of social responsibility among its leaders that resulted in lost jobs and shareholder value (as well as criminal indictments), or the recent Financial Crisis that was fueled by irresponsible selling of subprime mortgages to people with little chance of repaying the loans, resulting in record foreclosures and evictions.

In these examples, among many others presented in this book, a lack of basic (let alone *strategic*) CSR led to universal condemnation, along with significant legal and market penalties. In most cases, however, the consequences to firm actions are more ambiguous. In general, firms that ignore societal tradeoffs face limits, as suggested by the "iron law of social responsibility" (Chapter 1). The stakeholder backlash to a firm's indifference to CSR, however, is not necessarily felt immediately—the tobacco and fast-food industries stand as prime examples (*The CSR Threshold*, Chapter 5). Nevertheless, a company that fails to reflect the evolving interests of its stakeholders is ultimately putting its reputation, its brand, and its future operations at risk.

The analysis presented in this chapter indicates that Walmart appreciates this sentiment more today than previously. Due to Walmart's selective approach to CSR, however, the firm remains a paradox that is central to the issues raised in this book. Walmart has made great strides in the last decade, but the firm retains a relatively narrow CSR perspective. Walmart focuses its efforts almost exclusively on environmental sustainability as a means of doing what it does best—reducing costs and passing those savings on to customers in the form of lower prices. As Walmart's senior vice president of sustainability stated "If this was not financially viable, a company such as ours would not be doing it."[133]

As we have discussed elsewhere, however, financial viability is not the most important question. The timeframe over which a return is expected is more pertinent. Strategic CSR will deliver financial benefits to the firm and enable it to retain its societal license to operate. But, not all those benefits will be short-term. Because of its continued selectivity in relation to the larger issues of social responsibility, therefore, Walmart will remain subject to stakeholder scrutiny and criticism. There is little evidence to suggest, for example, that Walmart would choose the socially responsible option in any situation where that decision would lead to a short-term increase in costs or where the financial savings were not apparent prior to the initial investment.

Central to the argument presented in this book is the idea that, when short-term perspectives allow economic necessity to take precedence over social concerns, the consequences will eventually catch up with the perpetrators. But, as the examples of the tobacco and fast-food companies illustrate, it is fair to say that firms in certain industries can delay the CSR day of reckoning for a significant period of time. This is because the threshold of concern varies for each stakeholder and within each industry. Stakeholders' CSR concerns depend on a unique mix of individual priorities and available options, both of which change over time. They also reflect the interwoven battle among conflicting constituent interests. In the short run, even a flagrant disregard for CSR may be ignored by some, or even all, stakeholders. On the other hand, reaction may be swift and unequivocal. Mostly, however, reactions will be mixed. Eventually, it is clear that firms suffer the consequences of stakeholder disillusionment for a perceived lack of commitment to CSR. Walmart has had its requests for zoning variations denied because its operations were deemed contrary to community interest, for example. Growing unionization efforts within the company's stores in the United States, Canada, and most dramatically in China,[134] seem at least partially attributable to revolt against its human resource policies. It will be interesting, for example, to see how Walmart responds to the challenges posed by the internal activism of employees that is driving the OUR Walmart campaign (http://forrespect.org/).[135]

So, finally, whose responsibility is CSR? Though a decisive answer must be hedged by the tradeoffs between stakeholder groups—as when company profits compete with paying a living wage to foreign factory workers—and differences between industries and cultures, it is apparent that firms need to work proactively and not merely react to what their stakeholders are telling them today. Stakeholder and broader societal concerns are fluid. What is *acceptable* today can become *unacceptable* very quickly. To some extents, therefore, while firms need to understand their stakeholders' needs today and meet those needs, they should also seek to exceed those needs in relation to CSR by anticipating how those needs will evolve tomorrow.

A broader consideration of the question 'CSR: Whose Responsibility?' therefore, leads to the conclusion that firms are best served by implementing a stakeholder perspective that seeks to meet the expectations of stakeholders, today and tomorrow. Certainly, the benefits to Walmart of their sustainability efforts so far indicate the value of fully-committing to a CSR perspective. As the employee charged with working with Walmart at the Environment Defense Fund put it "It is getting harder and harder to hate Walmart."[136] Many of Walmart's other stakeholders agree:

> By 2010, the number of Americans reporting an unfavorable view of Walmart had fallen by nearly half, from a peak of 38 percent in 2005, to 20 percent.[137]

What this relationship also reveals, however, is that a firm's stakeholders have a great deal of influence in shaping firm actions. As such, stakeholders have an incentive to use that influence to help shape the society in which they want to live. Just like we get the politicians we vote for, we get the businesses we buy from. Stakeholders (and customers, in particular) need to use their influence and purchasing power to reward the corporate behavior they support and withdraw support from companies that do not behave *responsibly*. If we do not demand change, we should not be surprised if firms do not deliver that change. Firms are incentivized to generate profits, so it is up to a firm's stakeholders to ensure that the best way to achieve those profits is to act in a manner that is socially responsible.

An holistic view of the organization and its interests (only possible with a stakeholder perspective combined with the goal of medium- to long-term viability), therefore, dictates that CSR should be central to a firm's strategic planning and implemented throughout operations. A commonsense view of stakeholder interests, however, suggests an equal investment in deciding what behavior is *responsible* and seeking to encourage more of that behavior by ensuring it is rewarded. In other words, there is a synergistic relationship between a firm and its range of stakeholders, which is reflected in terms of CSR by a joint responsibility to maximize favorable outcomes. Whether those outcomes are tangible or intangible, economic or social, responsibility is shared. CSR is not only a *corporate* responsibility; it is also a *stakeholder* responsibility.

NEXT STEPS

Of course, the answer to the questions raised by Walmart cannot be resolved definitively at this point. Much will depend on the decisions made by the company's 30 million daily customers. Nevertheless, it does seem that CSR concerns raised by Walmart's previous actions are altering the way the firm perceives its relations with its various stakeholders. As such, this case also provides insight into how firms integrate CSR into their strategic planning process and throughout operations. Next, Chapters 4 and 5 investigate these issues in greater detail. Chapter 4 puts CSR into strategic perspective and expands on the growing importance of CSR and its impact on corporate strategy. Finally, Chapter 5 will conclude Part I with a discussion of the issues that influence the implementation of CSR by firms.

QUESTIONS FOR DISCUSSION AND REVIEW

1. Who is *responsible* for CSR—firms or their stakeholders? Why?

2. List three points in favor of both Friedman's and Handy's view of the firm and its responsibilities? Which position to you agree with? Why?

3. Would you report a classmate you suspected of cheating at school? Why or why not?

4. If you were a member of Walmart's top management team, what arguments would you make to a community group that is trying to stop the building of a Walmart Supercenter in their community? If you were the leader of the community group resisting Walmart's expansion into your community, what arguments would you make to oppose the store?

5. Walmart argues that it provides valuable jobs to small communities and should be allowed to grow. Critics argue that these jobs are often low paying, with few benefits. What is your position? Is a low paying job better than no job at all?

6. Would you ever consider boycotting a certain brand or store because of the parent company's actions or stance on a particular issue? Illustrate with an example.

7. Compare Walmart's new and old logos:

| Old logo | New logo |

Which do you prefer? What is your impression of Walmart's new logo and slogan?[138] Do you get the sense that Walmart is genuine in its commitment to sustainability issues, or is it just an example of corporate *greenwash*?

STUDENT STUDY SITE

Visit the Student Study Site at **www.sagepub.com/chandler3e** for additional learning tools.

NOTES AND REFERENCES

1. Recently, Pepsi discovered that there are significant market penalties to being 'too responsible' for its customer base: "It's been a rough few years for PepsiCo. Indra Nooyi, chairman and chief executive officer, has diligently tried to transform the company from a purveyor of sugar-laden bubbly beverages and salty snacks, into one that has healthier and more wholesome offerings. But performance has – pardon the pun – fizzled. Shares of PepsiCo have barely budged during her six-year tenure, while the stock price of rival Coca-Cola has nearly doubled in that time." Quoted in: 'Pop Quiz: Can Indra Nooyi Revive PepsiCo?' *Knowledge@ Wharton*, March 28, 2012, http://knowledge.wharton.upenn.edu/article.cfm?articleid=2966

2. Deborah Doane, 'The Myth of CSR: The problem with assuming that companies can do well while also doing good is that markets don't really work that way,' *Stanford Social Innovation Review*, Fall, 2005, p. 26.

3. Milton Friedman, 'The Social Responsibility of Business is to Increase its Profits,' *The New York Times Magazine*, September 13, 1970, http://www.colorado.edu/studentgroups/libertarians/issues/friedman-soc-resp-business.html

4. Milton Friedman, 'The Social Responsibility of Business is to Increase its Profits,' *The New York Times Magazine*, September 13, 1970, http://www.colorado.edu/studentgroups/libertarians/issues/friedman-soc-resp-business.html

5. Charles Handy, 'What's a Business For?' *Harvard Business Review*, December, 2002, pp. 49-55.

6. Charles Handy, 'What's a Business For?' *Harvard Business Review*, December, 2002, p. 52.

7. Milton Friedman, 'The Social Responsibility of Business is to Increase its Profits,' *The New York Times Magazine*, September 13, 1970, http://www.colorado.edu/studentgroups/libertarians/issues/friedman-soc-resp-business.html

8. See Figure 1.1, Chapter 1 and Archie B. Carroll, 'The Pyramid of Corporate Social Responsibility: Toward the Moral Management of Organizational Stakeholders,' *Business Horizons,* July–August, 1991.

9. Milton Friedman, 'The Social Responsibility of Business is to Increase its Profits,' *The New York Times Magazine*, September 13, 1970, http://www.colorado.edu/studentgroups/libertarians/issues/friedman-soc-resp-business.html

10. Archie B. Carroll, 'The Pyramid of Corporate Social Responsibility: Toward the Moral Management of Organizational Stakeholders,' *Business Horizons,* July–August, 1991, p. 43.

11. Earthshare, Summer, 2008, http://www.earthshare.org/psa/earthshare_print-psa_2008.pdf

12. The concept of corporate stakeholder responsibility presented here is different from the idea of 'Company Stakeholder Responsibility' advocated by Ed Freeman and colleagues, which is more similar to our concept of *strategic* CSR. See: R. Edward Freeman, S. Ramakrishna Velamuri & Brian Moriarty, 'Company Stakeholder Responsibility: A New Approach to CSR,' *Business Roundtable Institute for Corporate Ethics*, 2006, http://consciouscapitalism.org/library/pdf/resources_company.pdf

13. For a more detailed discussion of these ideas, see: Duane Windsor, 'Stakeholder Responsibilities: Lessons for Managers,' *Journal of Corporate Citizenship*, April 2002, pp. 19-35; Mike Barnett, 'Business & Society Version 3.0: Attending to What Stakeholders Attend to,' *Network for Business Sustainability*, February 21, 2012, http://nbs.net/business-society-version-3-0-attending-to-what-stakeholders-attend-to/; and David Chandler, 'Why Aren't We Stressing Stakeholder Responsibility?' *HBR Blog Network*, April 29, 2010, http://blogs.hbr.org/what-business-owes-the-world/2010/04/why-arent-we-stressing-stakeho.html

14. Steve Jobs' 2005 Stanford Commencement Address, http://www.youtube.com/watch?v=UF8uR6Z6KLc

15. Holman W. Jenkins, Jr., 'And One Last Thing . . . ,' *The Wall Street Journal*, October 8-9, 2011, p. A15.

16. For an argument that humans are innately focused on the short term, see: Peter Wilby, 'Humanity must recognize our entire way of life is chronically short termist,' *The Guardian*, June 1, 2007, p. 33.

17. Chandran Nair, 'Ethical consumers – Cop-out at the checkout,' *Ethical Corporation*, September 8, 2008, http://www.ethicalcorp.com/content.asp?ContentID=6074

18. 'The Co-Operative Bank's Ethical Consumerism Report 2011,' *Ethical Consumer Research Association*, 2011, p. 1. All the annual reports, since 2000 are archived at: http://www.goodwithmoney.co.uk/ethicalconsumerismreport

19. Andrew Bounds, 'Ethical goods prove popular despite downturn,' *Financial Times*, December 14, 2011, http://www.ft.com/cms/s/0/759e0b12-2666-11e1-85fb-00144feabdc0.html#axzz294AdrICS

20. We define *value* in its broadest sense to encapsulate both economic and social contributions to the common good. This encapsulates the idea that financial profit already incorporates much of the value to society added by the pursuit of profit (at a minimum, jobs, taxes, a product consumers value, but much more subtle and far-reaching value-added as well). It is inaccurate to say that firms that pursue profit do

not also add social value. *Economic value* and *social value* are closer to being synonymous than being mutually exclusive. However, defining value more broadly also recognizes that there are large numbers of externalities currently excluded from the market pricing mechanism that affect total value-added and are better encapsulated within the term *social value*.

21. Thomas L. Friedman, 'Advice From Grandma,' *The New York Times*, November 22, 2009, p. WK10.

22. 'Best Global Brands 2012,' *Interbrand*, http://www.interbrand.com/en/best-global-brands/2012/Best-Global-Brands-2012.aspx

23. Adam Hochschild, 'Well-Oiled Machine,' *The New York Times Book Review*, June 10, 2012, p. 20.

24. Warren Bass, 'A Brave New World in 9/11 Aftermath,' *Miami Herald,* April 10, 2005, p. 7M. Review of 'The World is Flat: A Brief History of the Twenty-First Century,' by Thomas L. Friedman, Farrar Straus Giroux, 2005.

25. Kathleen Parker, 'Attention, Wal-Mart shoppers: You have a say,' *Orlando Sentinel* (re-printed in the *Austin American Statesman*), January 30, 2006, p. A9.

26. Moisés Naim, 'Corporate Power is Decaying. Get Used to It,' *Bloomberg Businessweek*, February 21, 2013, http://www.businessweek.com/articles/2013-02-21/corporate-power-is-decaying-dot-get-used-to-it

27. Jeffrey M. Jones, 'Nurses Top Honesty and Ethics List for 11th Year,' *Gallup*, December 3, 2010, http://www.gallup.com/poll/145043/nurses-top-honesty-ethics-list-11-year.aspx; raw data at: http://www.gallup.com/poll/File/145031/Honesty_Ethics_Dec_3_2010.pdf

28. Archie Carroll, 'Survey says not many think highly of executives' ethics,' *Athens Banner-Herald*, January 7, 2007, http://www.onlineathens.com/stories/010707/business_20070107012.shtml

29. Enactus: "The world's best-known and most successful program helping university students to create community empowerment projects," http://enactus.org/

30. 'You Mean Cheating Is Wrong?' *BusinessWeek,* December 9, 2002, p. 8.

31. Rob Walker, 'Sex vs. Ethics,' *Fast Company Magazine*, Issue 124, April**,** 2008, pp. 54–56.

32. For an analysis of the awareness and importance of CSR to the public and other corporate stakeholders, see Jenny Dawkins & Stewart Lewis, 'CSR in Stakeholder Expectations: And Their Implication for Company Strategy,' *Journal of Business Ethics,* May 2003, Vol. 44, pp. 185–193: "Over ten years of research at MORI has shown the increasing prominence of corporate responsibility for a wide range of stakeholders, from consumers and employees to legislators and investors. . . . Traditionally, the factors that mattered most to consumers when forming an opinion of a company were product quality, value for money and financial performance. Now, across a worldwide sample of the public, the most commonly mentioned factors relate to corporate responsibility (e.g., treatment of employees, community involvement, ethical and environmental issues)."

33. http://www.beyondgreypinstripes.org/

34. 'Beyond Grey Pinstripes 2011-2012: Preparing MBAs for Social and Environmental Stewardship,' *The Aspen Institute Centre for Business Education*, 2012, http://www.beyondgreypinstripes.org/reports/BGP%202011-2012%20Global%20Report-small.pdf

35. http://netimpact.org/

36. See also: 50+20, Management Education for the World, http://50plus20.org/

37. http://www.unprme.org/the-6-principles/index.php

38. http://www.unprme.org/the-6-principles/index.php

39. Facts quoted from: Dina Spector & Ujala Sehgal, '16 Facts About Walmart That Will Blow Your Mind,' *BusinessInsider.com*, November 14, 2011, http://www.businessinsider.com/walmart-facts-earnings-2011-11

40. Christopher Caldwell, 'Listen to the Walmart moms,' *Financial Times*, July 10/11, 2010, p. 7.

41. *BusinessWeek,* October 6, 2003, op. cit., pp. 100–110.

42. Editorial, 'The Wal-Martization of America,' *The New York Times,* November 15, 2003, p. A12.

43. Steve Lohr, 'Is Wal-Mart Good for America?' *The New York Times,* December 7, 2003, Section 4, p. 1.

44. For example, see: Miguel Bustillo & Ann Zimmerman, 'In Cities That Battle Wal-Mart, Target Gets a Welcome,' *The Wall Street Journal*, October 15, 2010, p. B1.

45. Anthony Bianco & Wendy Zellner, 'Is Wal-Mart Too Powerful?' *BusinessWeek,* October 6, 2003, pp. 100–110.

46 Phil Butler, 'Walmart Invades India – Who's Next?' *profy*, February 20, 2007, http://profy.com/2007/02/20/walmart-invades/

47. *BusinessWeek,* October 6, 2003, op. cit., pp. 100–110.

48. Farhad Manjoo, 'Dot Convert,' *Fast Company Magazine*, December 2012/January 2013, p. 131.

49. 'Walmart Locations and Data,' October, 2012, http://news.walmart.com/walmart-facts

50. "Each week, Walmart serves more than 200 million customers at more than 9,600 retail outlets in 28 countries." See: Dina Spector & Ujala Sehgal, '16 Facts About Walmart That Will Blow Your Mind,' *BusinessInsider.com*, November 14, 2011, http://www.businessinsider.com/walmart-facts-earnings-2011-11

51. *BusinessWeek,* October 6, 2003, op. cit., pp. 100–110.

52. Charles Fishman, 'The Wal-Mart You Don't Know,' *Fast Company Magazine*, November 15, 2008, http://www.fastcompany.com/magazine/77/walmart.html

53. Constance L. Hays, 'When Wages Are Low, Discounters Have Pull,' *The New York Times,* December 23, 2003, pp. C1 & C4.

54. For example, see, John M. Broder, 'Stymied by Politicians, Wal-Mart Turns to Voters,' *The New York Times,* April 5, 2004, p. A12; Steven Malanga, 'The War on Wal-Mart,' *The Wall Street Journal,* April 7, 2004, p. A18; Ann Zimmerman, 'Wal-Mart Loses Supercenter Vote,' *The Wall Street Journal,* April 8, 2004, p. B7; and, providing some degree of balance in the coverage, George F. Will, 'Waging War on Wal-Mart,' *Newsweek,* July 5, 2004, p. 64.

55. 'Wal-Mart: Timeline of world's largest retailer,' CBC News, June 30, 2005, http://www.cbc.ca/news/background/walmart/

56. Matthew Malone, 'Did Wal-Mart love RFID to death?' *smartplanet*, February 14, 2012, http://www.smartplanet.com/blog/pure-genius/did-wal-mart-love-rfid-to-death/7459

57. 'Halls of Finance Fear Wal-Mart,' *The New York Times*, June 24, 2010, p. B2.

58. Andrew Martin & Stephanie Clifford, 'As People Shun High Street Bank Fees, Wal-Mart Unexpectedly Gains,' *The New York Times*, November 8, 2011, p. A1.

59. Charles Fishman, 'The Wal-Mart You Don't Know,' *Fast Company Magazine*, November 15, 2008, http://www.fastcompany.com/magazine/77/walmart.html

60. 'Wal-Mart's Merchandise Reflects Our "Store of the Community" Philosophy,' Merchandising Fact Sheet, September, 2009, http://walmartstores.com/FactsNews/FactSheets/

61. Charles Fishman, 'The Wal-Mart You Don't Know,' *Fast Company Magazine*, November 15, 2008, http://www.fastcompany.com/magazine/77/walmart.html

62. Charles Fishman, 'The Wal-Mart You Don't Know,' *Fast Company Magazine*, November 15, 2008, http://www.fastcompany.com/magazine/77/walmart.html

63. Sharon Zukin, 'We Are Where We Shop,' *The New York Times,* November 28, 2003, p. A31.

64. Wal-Mart reports "our average, full-time hourly wage for Walmart stores is $11.24 and is even higher in urban areas. The average full-time hourly wage is $11.66 in Atlanta, $12.55 in Boston, $11.61 in Chicago, $11.25 in Dallas, $11.43 in San Francisco and $11.50 in New York City." In 'Corporate Facts: Walmart By the Numbers,' Corporate Fact Sheet, September, 2009, http://walmartstores.com/FactsNews/FactSheets/

65. Miguel Bustillo & Ann Zimmerman, 'In Cities That Battle Wal-Mart, Target Gets a Welcome,' *The Wall Street Journal*, October 15, 2010, p. B1.

66. 'Sustainability Progress to Date 2007-2008,' http://walmartstores.com/sites/sustainabilityreport/2007/communityJobs.html

67. Steven Greenhouse, 'Can't Wal-Mart, A Retail Behemoth, Pay More?' *The New York Times,* May 4, 2005, http://wakeupwalmart.com/news/20050504-nyt.html

68. *BusinessWeek,* October 6, 2003, op. cit., pp. 100–110.

69. 'The New Age of Walmart,' *CNBC*, September 23, 2009.

70. 'Labor Issues a Thorn at Wal-Mart,' *Financial Times,* in *Miami Herald,* November 22, 2003, p. 2C.

71. Steven Greenhouse & Stephanie Rosenbloom, 'Wal-Mart to Settle Suits Over Pay for $352 million,' *The New York Times*, December 24, 2008, p. B1.

72. Andrea M. Dean & Russell S. Sobel, 'Has Wal-Mart Buried Mom and Pop?' *Regulation*, Spring, 2008, p. 40, http://www.cato.org/pubs/regulation/regv31n1/v31n1-1.pdf

73. Kathleen Parker, 'Attention, Wal-Mart shoppers: You have a say,' *Orlando Sentinel* (re-printed in the *Austin American Statesman*), January 30, 2006, p. A9.

74. *New York Times,* December 7, 2003, op. cit., Section 4, p. 1.

75. 'When Walmart Arrives, Other Supermarkets Shape Up,' *Harvard Business Review: The Daily Stat,* November 14, 2012, http://web.hbr.org/email/archive/dailystat.php?date=111412

76. The Fortune 500 is ranked according to the revenues of the firm.

77. In 2006, Exxon was named No.1; Walmart returned to the top spot in 2007 and 2008. Exxon and Walmart have shared the top two spots, occasionally changing places, ever since.

78. Corporate Fact Sheet—'Corporate Facts: Walmart By the Numbers,' September, 2009, http://walmartstores.com/FactsNews/FactSheets/

79. http://money.cnn.com/magazines/fortune/most-admired/

80. Steven Greenhouse, 'Opponents of Wal-Mart to Coordinate Efforts,' *New York Times,* April 13, 2005, p. 16.

81. Jonathan Birchall, 'Duke faces test of his political aptitude,' *Financial Times,* November 22/23, 2008, p. 9.

82. Stacy Mitchell, 'Walmart's greenwash: Why the retail giant is still unsustainable,' *grist,* November 7, 2011, http://grist.org/series/2011-11-07-walmart-greenwash-retail-giant-still-unsustainable/

83. For example, 'Erica L. Plambeck & Lyn Denend, 'The greening of Wal-Mart,' Stanford Social Innovation Review, Spring, 2008, pp. 53-59; 'Wal-Mart Celebrates Thanksgiving by Sourcing Local Food, Supporting Hunger-Relief, and Buying Wind Power,' *CSRWire,* November 26, 2008, http://www.csrwire.com/press/press_release/15548; and Danielle Sacks, 'Working with the Enemy,' *Fast Company Magazine*, Issue 118, September 2007, http://www.fastcompany.com/magazine/118/working-with-the-enemy.html

84. Stephanie Clifford, 'Unexpected Ally Helps Wal-Mart Cut Waste,' *The New York Times*, April 14, 2012, p. B1.

85. Ellen Byron, 'Adversary's Clean Start With Wal-Mart,' *The Wall Street Journal*, July 26, 2010, p. B9.

86. Danielle Sacks, 'Working with the Enemy,' *Fast Company Magazine*, September, 2007, p. 77.

87. Ryan Chittum, 'Wal-Mart to Give $35 Million for Wildlife Areas,' *Wall Street Journal,* April 13, 2005, p. B4; and Stephanie Strom, 'Wal-Mart Donates $35 Million for Conservation and Will Be Partner With Wildlife Group,' *New York Times,* April 13, 2005, p. A16.

88. Lee Scott, 'Wal-Mart: Twenty First Century Leadership,' October 24, 2005, http://walmartwatch.com/img/documents/21st_Century_Leadership.pdf

89 Editorial, 'Private FEMA: In Katrina's Wake, Wal-Mart and Home Depot Came to the Rescue,' *The Wall Street Journal*, September 10, 2005, http://www.opinionjournal.com/editorial/feature.html?id=110007238; Michael Barbaro & Justin Gillis, 'Wal-Mart at Forefront of Hurricane Relief,' *The Washington Post*, September 6, 2005, p. D1.

90. 'Message from Lee Scott,' http://walmartfacts.com/reports/2006/sustainability/companyMessage.html

91. Lisa Roner, 'Wal-Mart – An environmental epiphany?' December 7, 2005, http:// www.climatechangecorp.com/content.asp?ContentID=4009

92. For more background on the origination of Walmart's commitment to sustainability, see: Daniel Diermeier, 'The case study: A disaster can improve reputation,' *Financial Times*, March 24, 2011, p. 12.

93. Lee Scott, 'Wal-Mart: Twenty First Century Leadership,' October 24, 2005, http:// walmartwatch.com/img/documents/21st_Century_Leadership.pdf

94. Lee Scott, 'Wal-Mart: Twenty First Century Leadership,' October 24, 2005, http:// walmartwatch.com/img/documents/21st_Century_Leadership.pdf

95. Lee Scott, 'Wal-Mart: Twenty First Century Leadership,' October 24, 2005, http:// walmartwatch.com/img/documents/21st_Century_Leadership.pdf

96. Michael Barbaro, 'Wal-Mart: The New Washington,' *The New York Times*, February 3, 2008, http://www.nytimes.com/2008/02/03/weekinreview/03barb.html

97. Reena Jana, 'Wal-Mart Gets a Facelift,' *BusinessWeek*, July 3, 2008, http://news letters.businessweek.com/c.asp?713736&c55a2ee820194f0f&14

98. 'Wal-Mart Celebrates Thanksgiving by Sourcing Local Food, Supporting Hunger-Relief, and Buying Wind Power,' *CSRWire*, November 26, 2008, http://www.csrwire .com/press/press_release/15548

99. Lee Scott, 'Wal-Mart: Twenty First Century Leadership,' October 24, 2005, http:// walmartwatch.com/img/documents/21st_Century_Leadership.pdf

100. Jonathan Birchall, 'Big Box looks to small packages,' *Financial Times*, November 4, 2008, p. 16.

101. See: Orville Schell, 'How Walmart Is Changing China,' *The Atlantic*, December, 2011, http://www.theatlantic.com/magazine/archive/2011/12/how-walmart-is-changing-china/308709/

102. Charles Fishman, 'How Many Lightbulbs Does it Take to Change the World? One. And You're Looking At It,' *Fast Company Magazine*, September, 2006, http://www .fastcompany.com/magazine/108/open_lightbulbs.html

103. 'Wal-Mart Reaches 100-Million CFL Goal Three Months Early,' *Sustainable Life Media*, October 3, 2007, http://www.sustainablelifemedia.com/content/story/ strategy/10032007

104. Compact Fluorescent Light Bulbs Fact Sheet, 'Saving Money and Energy with CFLs,' Fact Sheets, August 29, 2009, http://walmartstores.com/FactsNews/FactSheets/

105. Rajesh Chhabara, 'Wal-Mart – Thinking outside the big box,' *Ethical Corporation*, September 7, 2009, http://www.ethicalcorp.com/content.asp?ContentID=6583

106. 'No. 9: Walmart,' *FastCompany Magazine*, March 2010, p. 66.

107. See: http://corporate.walmart.com/global-responsibility/environment-sustainability/ sustainability-index and The Sustainability Consortium, http://www.sustainability consortium.org/

108. Kate Rockwood, 'Will Walmart's 'Sustainability Index' Actually Work?' *FastCompany Magazine*, February 1, 2010, http://www.fastcompany.com/1518194/ will-walmarts-sustainability-index-actually-work

109. The Sustainability Consortium, http://www.sustainabilityconsortium.org/what-we-do/

110. Stephanie Rosenbloom, 'Wal-Mart Plans to Make Its Supply Chain Greener,' *The New York Times*, February 26, 2010, p. B3.

111. For more detail on Walmart's sustainability program, see: Lyn Denend & Erica Plambeck, 'Walmart's Sustainability Strategy (B): 2010 Update,' *Stanford Graduate School of Business*, Case: OIT-71B, October 15, 2010.

112. Jonathan Birchall, 'Duke faces test of his political aptitude,' *Financial Times*, November 22/23, 2008, p. 9.

113. http://corporate.walmart.com/global-responsibility/

114. This lawsuit was allowed to proceed as a class-action suit in June 2004. This decision, involving a lawsuit initially filed by six former employees who felt they were not treated equally to male employees, presents "the world's largest retailer with the prospect of fighting a lengthy legal battle or potentially paying a multibillion-dollar settlement. . . . [involving] as many as 1.6 million current and former female U.S. employees." (Ann Zimmerman, 'Judge Certifies Wal-Mart Suit as Class Action,' *Wall Street Journal,* June 23, 2004, pp. A1 & A6). See the website (http://www.walmartclass.com/) for information about this and other discrimination lawsuits against Walmart.

115. Adam Liptak, 'Supreme Court Tightens Rules in Class Actions,' *The New York Times*, June 21, 2011, p. A1.

116. Stephanie Clifford & Stephanie Strom, 'Wal-Mart to Announce Women-Friendly Plans,' *The New York Times*, September 14, 2011, p. B3.

117. See: David Barstow, 'Vast Mexico Bribery Case Hushed Up by Wal-Mart After Top-Level Struggle,' *The New York Times*, April 22, 2012, p. A1 and David Barstow & Alejandra Xanic von Bertrab, 'The Bribery Aisle: How Wal-Mart Used Payoffs To Get Its Way in Mexico,' *The New York Times*, December 18, 2012, p. A1.

118. Even when Walmart reported it had begun an internal investigation about the possible bribery allegations to The Justice Department, *The New York Times* claimed in its initial story that the firm did so only because it learned of the newspaper's investigations.

119. David Barstow, 'Vast Mexico Bribery Case Hushed Up by Wal-Mart After Top-Level Struggle,' *The New York Times*, April 22, 2012, p. A12.

120. David Barstow, 'Vast Mexico Bribery Case Hushed Up by Wal-Mart After Top-Level Struggle,' *The New York Times*, April 22, 2012, p. A12.

121. Stephanie Clifford, 'Pension Plan Sues Wal-Mart Official Over Failures,' *The New York Times*, May 4, 2012, p. B1.

122. Gretchen Morgenson, 'New York Pension Funds To Challenge Wal-Mart,' *The New York Times*, May 1, 2012, p. B1.

123. 'Walmart's Mexican morass,' *The Economist*, April 28, 2012, p. 71.

124. Ben DiPietro, 'Wal-Mart Records $157 Million Charge for Mexican Bribery Probe,' *The Wall Street Journal*, February 21, 2013, http://blogs.wsj.com/corruption-currents/2013/02/21/wal-mart-records-157-million-charge-for-mexican-bribery-probe/

125. 'Top 10 ways Walmart made a difference in 2011,' *2012 Global Responsibility Report*, http://www.walmartstores.com/sites/responsibility-report/2012/top10.aspx

126. See: Pratap Chatterjee, 'Greenwashing Walmart,' *CorpWatch Blog*, April 18, 2012, http://www.corpwatch.org/article.php?id=15707 and Stacy Mitchell, 'Walmart's greenwash: Why the retail giant is still unsustainable,' *grist*, November 7, 2011, http://grist.org/series/2011-11-07-walmart-greenwash-retail-giant-still-unsustainable/

127. Facts quoted from: Stacy Mitchell, 'Walmart's Greenwash,' *Institute for Local Self-Reliance*, March, 2012, p. 4.

128. Michael Skapinker, 'Virtue's reward?' *Financial Times*, April 28, 2008, p. 8.

129. Steven Greenhouse & Reed Abelson, 'Wal-Mart Cuts Some Health Care Benefits,' *The New York Times*, October 21, 2011, p. B1.

130. Michael Skapinker, 'Virtue's reward?' *Financial Times*, April 28, 2008, p. 8.

131. Jeffrey Hollender, 'Walmart's Sustainability Efforts Stall Under New Leadership' *TriplePundit*, March 28, 2012, http://www.triplepundit.com/2012/03/walmarts-sustainability-efforts-stall-new-leadership/

132. Mallen Baker, 'Bhopal: 25 years later the echoes are still loud,' *Ethical Corporation*, August 20, 2009, http://www.ethicalcorp.com/content.asp?ContentID=6562

133. Sindya N. Bhanoo, 'Those Earth-Friendly Products? Turns Out They're Profit-Friendly as Well,' *The New York Times*, June 12, 2010, p. B3.

134. 'Wal-Mart approves unions in China,' *BBC News*, November 24, 2004, http://news.bbc.co.uk/2/hi/business/4037423.stm; Harold Meyerson, 'Wal-Mart Loves Unions (in China),' *The Washington Post*, December 1, 2004, http://www.washingtonpost.com/wp-dyn/articles/A23725-2004Nov30.html

135. See: Ira Boudway, 'Walmart vs. Walmart,' *Bloomberg Businessweek*, December 17-23, 2012, pp. 54-59.

136. Corby Kummer, 'The Great Grocery Smackdown,' *The Atlantic*, March, 2010, http://www.theatlantic.com/magazine/archive/2010/03/the-great-grocery-smackdown/307904/. See also: Stephanie Clifford, 'Unexpected Ally Helps Wal-Mart Cut Waste,' *The New York Times*, April 14, 2012, p. B1.

137. Stacy Mitchell, 'Walmart's greenwash: Why the retail giant is still unsustainable,' *grist*, November 7, 2011, http://grist.org/series/2011-11-07-walmart-greenwash-retail-giant-still-unsustainable/

138. 'Walmart U.S. Refreshes Stores' Logo,' June 30, 2008, http://walmartstores.com/FactsNews/NewsRoom/8411.aspx

Chapter 4

CSR AS A STRATEGIC FILTER

There are three kinds of organizations: nonprofit, governmental, and for-profit. Each exists to meet different needs in society. Those needs may be altruistic, such as feeding the poor, in the case of a nonprofit; they may be civic, such as providing for the safety and security of the public, in the case of government agencies; or they may be primarily economic, such as organizing resources in ways that yield a surplus for the owners, called profit. In a free society, all organizations exist to meet societal needs in some form, or they eventually go away. Restated, no publicly traded company, government, or nonprofit initially sets out to do harm. Yet, as demonstrated in the first three chapters of *Strategic CSR*, harm is certainly one possible outcome from day-to-day actions. In the case of for-profit firms, these often unintended consequences spring not from the organization's goals themselves, but from the methods or strategies deployed to pursue these goals. As a result, it is important to understand the strategic context of CSR.

In fulfilling their mission and vision, organizations face constraints on their methods and results. The economics of survival, for example, requires each entity to produce the *results* that generate the sources of income they require to operate—donations for nonprofits, taxes for governments, or profits for firms. At the same time, these results must be attained by *methods* that are acceptable to the larger society. Leaders of all organizations constantly grapple with the trade-offs between methods and results. When these issues involve for-profits, CSR helps firms balance the methods they use and the results they seek. It does this by ensuring that profit-seeking businesses plan and operate from the perspective of multiple stakeholders.

The problem that decision makers face is straightforward: Which stakeholders and what issues *matter* under the broad heading of corporate social responsibility as it pertains to our organization? The simple answer depends on the for-profit's strategy. And, because these strategies vary widely, the right mix will differ from firm-to-firm and industry-to industry. It will also evolve over time as firms adapt both their strategy and execution to increasingly turbulent operational environments. As a result, the exact issues that any firm is likely to face at any given time are impossible to predict. What is constant and can be applied by any firm in any situation, however, is that a strategic lens offers the best viewpoint through which to study CSR.

CSR + A STRATEGIC LENS

Effective strategy results in providing businesses with a source of sustainable, competitive advantage. For any competitive advantage to be sustainable, however, the tactics used to implement a firm's strategy must be acceptable to the societies in which they are deployed. If they are not, social, legal, and other forces may conspire against the firm, as when legal and regulatory sanctions are levied against a manufacturer for polluting the air and water.

Both CSR and strategy are concerned primarily with the firm's relationship to the context in which it operates. Whereas *strategy* addresses how the firm competes in the marketplace (its operational context), *CSR* considers the firm's impact on relevant stakeholders (its societal context). *Strategic CSR* represents the intersection of the two. Thus, in order to implement a strategic CSR perspective throughout operations, it is essential that executives understand the interdependent relationships among a firm, its strategy, and its stakeholders that define the firm's environment and constrain its capacity to act.

As illustrated in Figure 4.1, a firm's vision, mission, strategy, and tactics are limited by three kinds of constraints—resource constraints, internal policy constraints, and environmental constraints.[1] First, a significant limitation on the firm's ability to act is its access to resources and capabilities—the human, social, and financial capital that determine what the firm is able to do. A second constraint is the firm's internal policies that shape the culture of the organization by requiring and forbidding specific actions. These policies, however, are internally enforced and can be changed relatively easily by management (a flexibility that is indicated in Figure 4.1 by the dashed line). Finally, an organization's environmental constraints are generated by a complex interaction of sociocultural, legal, and stakeholder factors, together with the influence of markets and technology. These forces further limit the firm's freedom to act by shaping the context in which the firm implements tactics to pursue its strategic goals that, in turn, enable it to perform its mission and strive toward its vision. Compounding the complexity of integrating CSR into the vision-mission-strategy-tactics linkages, therefore, is the ever-changing expectations of society.

| Figure 4.1 | Strategic Constraints and The CSR Filter |

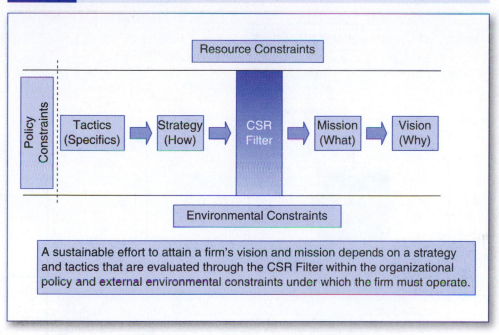

A sustainable effort to attain a firm's vision and mission depends on a strategy and tactics that are evaluated through the CSR Filter within the organizational policy and external environmental constraints under which the firm must operate.

As a result of this complexity, a sole focus on the linkage among vision, mission, strategy, and tactics is insufficient to achieve the firm's goals. Not only is such a narrow focus insufficient, however, it also represents potential danger. Tactical and strategic actions necessary to achieve the mission (and, thus, the vision) must be evaluated by first passing through a *CSR Filter*. The CSR Filter assesses management's planned actions by considering the impact of day-to-day tactical decisions and longer term strategies on the organization's constituents. A tactical or strategic decision that runs counter to stakeholder interests can undermine the firm's sustainable competitive advantage. At the extreme, such violations may even force the firm into bankruptcy—as happened to Malden Mills and Enron, albeit for very different reasons.

THE CSR FILTER

Strategy formulation links the firm's strengths with opportunities in its environment. The strategic decision making process faces limitations, however, which are presented in Figure 4.2.

First, a feasible strategy is limited by the firm's vision and mission, which are determined by the leadership. A plane manufacturer, such as Boeing or Airbus, is

Figure 4.2 Firm Strategy and The CSR Filter

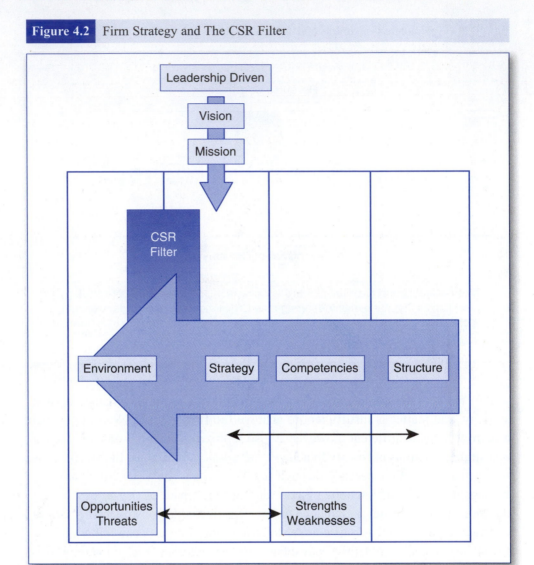

unlikely to make cars and trucks because these activities do not achieve its vision and mission, which is to make jet-powered, commercial planes. Second, the strategy is further limited by a firm's structure and competencies—organizational characteristics and competitive actions that aid the firm and set it apart from competitors. Boeing and Airbus, for example, which undoubtedly could make cars and trucks if they wanted, lack other resources, such as the network of dealerships necessary to sell cars and trucks nationwide. Third, whatever strategy the firm develops, it is enhanced by the CSR Filter, which identifies the range of strategies that is preferred by constituents. Above all, Boeing and Airbus must make planes in ways that do not harm their key stakeholders—their communities, employees, flyers, and other groups. In other words, before a competency-based strategy can be deployed, it must be developed within constraints and evaluated through a CSR Filter to assess its impact on those groups that are essential for the strategy to be a success.

There is an iterative relationship between the resulting strategy and organizational design. While strategy shapes design, it is also true that the firm's structure, roles, and reporting relationships should be configured to facilitate strategy. The *correct* organizational structure is a design that best supports effective execution of the strategy. For many firms, that means a departmental hierarchy organized around business units. In terms of implementing a CSR perspective throughout strategy and operations, therefore, the structure presents an additional opportunity to instill decisions made at the top (with a CSR Filter) throughout the organization.

The connection between a firm's internal strengths and its external opportunities is driven by the strategic axiom that success depends on a position of competing from strengths. For the strategist to connect strengths with opportunities in a globalizing business environment requires an intimate understanding of both internal and external factors. In order to remain competitive, therefore, it is essential for firms to employ a CSR Filter in formulating and implementing their strategies. Figure 4.2 demonstrates how the CSR Filter fits as an integral component of the strategy decision making process. In order to better understand the role of the CSR Filter in a firm's success, however, it is important to investigate the complex interplay among a firm's structure, competencies, and strategy in relation to the CSR Filter and operating environment.

Structure

The structure (the organizational design) exists to support the strategy of the firm. What architects say of a building, organization designers say of the firm's structure—form follows function. Thus, the *right* structure is the one that best supports the strategy. Because the optimal design is firm-specific, however, structure varies from industry-to-industry, as well as from company-to-company within an industry. When low cost strategies are pursued, for example, expertise is often concentrated into a *functional* organization design in which site location, store construction oversight, information systems, warehousing, distribution, store operations, and other similar activities are grouped together by their common functions into specialized departments. This functional grouping seeks to enhance specific areas of expertise and is scalable as the firm grows. The result is called a functional organization design.

In the case of Walmart, different parts of the company might pursue different structural designs. Support activities like accounting or finance, for example, may be grouped by function at corporate headquarters. At the same time, because Walmart is spread across many geographical areas, the store management oversight and distribution systems may be organized along geographical lines, such as a northeastern warehouse division or overseas store operations. At Nike, CSR is such an important function that it is built into the firm's structure in the form of a separate Corporate Responsibility department, headed by a vice president.[2]

Competencies

To facilitate an understanding of the firm's ability to build a sustainable competitive advantage, a clear distinction among *capabilities, competencies, core resources,* and *core competencies* is required:

Capabilities, Competencies, Core Resources, and Core Competencies

- **Capabilities** are actions that a firm can do, such as pay its bills, in ways that add value to the production process.
- **Competencies** are actions a firm can do very well.
- **Core resources** are the assets of the firm that are unique and difficult to replicate.
- **Core competencies** are the processes of the firm that it not only does very well, but is so superior at performing that it is difficult (or at least time consuming) for other firms to match its performance in this area.

It is the combination of a firm's core competencies (a valuable *process*, such as an efficient logistics operation) together with its core resources (a valuable *asset*, such as its people, capital, or technology) that form the foundation for a firm's long-term, sustainable competitive advantage. The source of Southwest's long-running success in the passenger airline industry, when most other airlines were losing significant amounts of money, for example, is the combination of its organizational culture (a core resource) together with its ability to operate its planes on a significantly more cost-effective basis, due to innovations such as its rapid turnaround time (a core competency). Similarly, consider how Walmart is able to manage the flow of goods from suppliers, through its stores, and on to its customers, often referred to as *supply chain management*.

Walmart's Supply Chain Management

Walmart has a *capability* of hiring employees; it has a *competency* to locate stores where they will be successful; it has a *core resource* of its logistics system, including the world's largest private satellite network; and it has a *core competency* of maintaining and distributing its inventory throughout the supply chain. In fact, Walmart is so very good at managing its supply chain that it minimizes both the amount of inventory it carries and the number of times items are out-of-stock in its stores. Other firms have the capability to maintain their inventory; some even have a competency at doing that, but none of Walmart's competitors are able to match its combination of core resources and core competencies that align in the firm's masterful supply chain management.

Strategy

Walmart's *vision* is to offer the best customer value in retailing, which gives rise to a *mission* of delivering groceries and other consumer products efficiently. That vision and mission are attained by a *strategy* of passing on cost savings to customers by continually seeking to roll back the firm's "everyday low prices." In turn, that strategy is built upon *core resources* and *core competencies,* which are the competitive weapons with which Walmart competes. Ultimately, how Walmart folds its resources and competencies into a strategy that it deploys vis-à-vis stakeholders determines the extent to which those stakeholders view Walmart as a valued partner and a socially responsible company.

Certainly, a firm like Walmart must advertise and do hundreds, even thousands of other activities. But its competitive advantage comes from its network of store locations, backed by an unmatched ability to manage and deliver its inventory in optimal ways. Towards this end, the firm's resources and competencies interact, reinforcing each other over time as experience enables the firm to refine its day-to-day operations. Without its exceptionally efficient and effective supply chain management, Walmart would not be a low-cost provider of groceries and other goods. But with these resources and competencies supporting its strategy, it creates a *virtuous cycle* in which the firm's lower prices attract more customers. More customers, in turn, mean greater volumes, which lead to increased economies of scale in operations and greater power in demanding price reductions from its suppliers. The result is even lower costs that allow Walmart to reduce prices further, which, in turn, continues the virtuous cycle by attracting still more customers. The increased economies of scale in distribution and purchasing perpetuate the cycle of still lower costs. Like all firms, therefore, Walmart's business level strategy rests upon the combination of core resources and competencies in ways that support its mission and vision.

A Firm's Business Level Strategy[3]

Business strategy: The strategy of a specific business unit within a firm that enables it to differentiate its products from the products of other firms on the basis of price or other factors (such as superior technology).[4]

Walmart employs a *low-cost* business strategy in order to compete. Mercedes-Benz, on the other hand, does not seek to produce the lowest-priced cars. Instead, it competes based on a *differentiation* business strategy. By making its products superior along the lines of safety, prestige, and durability, Mercedes-Benz (and other luxury goods producers) can charge a premium for the differentiation (real or perceived) that consumers receive. Apple is another firm that seeks to differentiate its products on the basis of some factor other than price—product design and technological innovation. For The Body Shop, their point of differentiation is not product quality so much as the social agenda and campaigns that the firm pursues. Consumers of The Body Shop's products gain value from this social agenda and by associating themselves with values to which they aspire, in addition to the functional value they gain from the firm's products (personal cosmetics and toiletries).

McDonald's, in contrast, strives for a focused strategy that embraces both low cost and product differentiation. Relatively low costs result from its high volume and standardization, leading to economies of scale; however, McDonald's also differentiates the product it offers by providing convenient service, putting it in the fast-food segment of the restaurant industry.

Firms that are able to establish a point of differentiation can then build a brand. Brands are valuable because they instill customer loyalty and enable the firm to charge an additional premium for their product and further increase potential profits. Whether that point of distinction is fashion, lifestyle, design, technical quality, product functionality, or social responsibility, a business level strategy of differentiation can be valuable for a firm. Companies that differentiate their products on the basis of low cost, however, may perceive CSR-related efforts as adding costs and, therefore, be less proactive regarding CSR.

Whether businesses compete on cost, differentiation, or a focused strategy that embraces either cost or differentiation (or both), strategy strives to add customer-focused value as a means of gaining a sustainable competitive advantage.

CSR Filter

Competencies molded into a strategy and supported by an efficient structure are necessary minimum conditions for success—but, increasingly, more is required. It is vital that firms also consider the stakeholder implications of their strategy and operations. The *CSR Filter* is a conceptual screen through which strategic and tactical decisions are evaluated for their impact on the firm's various stakeholders. Here, the intent is to take a viable strategy and make it *optimal* for the environment in which the strategy must be executed—even clever strategies can fail if they are perceived to be socially *irresponsible*. The CSR Filter therefore injects additional considerations into the decision mix, providing market opportunities and avoiding potential threats by encapsulating an understanding of the needs and concerns of the firm's major stakeholder groups. Together, these stakeholders form the larger context in which the firm operates and seeks to implement its tactics, strategy, mission, and vision.

The CSR Filter: Nike

Nike is a well-managed firm with an extremely valuable brand. Nike exploits its brand value to great effect in selling its lines of shoes, apparel, and other products. Each of its product lines, however, faces strong, high-quality competition from companies such as Adidas, Puma, and New Balance. If Nike's strategy of off-shore contract production leads to employer abuse in its factories (perceived or actual), consumers may shift their buying preferences to the firm's competitors. Even if Nike does not own or manage its overseas contract factories, negative publicity—such as a video clip or unfavorable report from an NGO highlighting human rights abuses—represents danger to Nike's otherwise effective business strategy of product differentiation.

Thus, Nike's offshore sourcing strategy must be constantly scrutinized through a CSR Filter. What is essential is to retain sight of what is core to the brand. Although manufacturing is a peripheral function for Nike, its brand value lies in the lifestyles it appeals to among the people who consume its products. As such, newspaper reports about sweatshop conditions in its overseas suppliers undermine the aspirational values Nike's consumers relate to and, as such, represent a direct threat to the firm. Nike's strategy before the mid-1990s was constructed without a CSR Filter. The firm has corrected that oversight and now employs a CSR Filter at the core of its strategic planning process.

Part II of this book identifies some of the many issues embedded in the CSR Filter. Beyond this, Part II also provides company-specific case-studies that outline the practical impact of these considerations, as well as online resources for further exploration. Together, these issues and cases provide insight into the dynamic operating environment that firms face today and that is driven by changing societal expectations. It is this dynamism that underscores the growing importance of CSR for firms and, therefore, represents a significant influence on company strategy. Although not all firms are able to create a business model that is as valuable as those of Walmart and Nike; ultimately, all successful strategies rest on a firm's ability to construct a sustainable competitive advantage within its operating environment.

Environment

Customers, competitors, economics, technology, government, sociocultural factors, and other forces all drive changes in the firm's operating environment. Often, these changes are gradual and imperceptible to all but the keenest observers. But, over time, their cumulative and interactive effects redefine the competitive environment and determine what organizational strategies and actions are deemed to be socially acceptable.

When the competitive environment demands a change in strategy, the existing resources and competencies of the firm may no longer be sufficient. If Walmart is seen as exploiting its low-paid workers, for example, the accompanying negative publicity may eventually harm its image. This can cause customers to shop elsewhere or cause communities to deny Walmart's applications for zoning variances needed to build or remodel stores. Evolving societal expectations require constant innovation of the firm's core resources and competencies, in areas such as public relations, advertising, and human resource management.

When environmental changes like these or others occur, leaders face a *make-or-buy* decision. Should the needed competencies be developed internally (*make*) or acquired from others outside the firm (*buy*)? Historically, many large businesses like Walmart have had the resources to develop the needed competencies internally through hiring and training. Today, the external environment is changing so rapidly that firms often buy the needed skills from others because the speed of execution is critical. If the decision makers decide to buy the necessary resources or competencies, leaders then face a second decision—whether to bring the needed skills within the organizational structure or to outsource them via contractual relationships with suppliers. When the activity is seen as a core resource or competency (e.g., managing inventory at Walmart or product design at firms like Apple[5] or Nike[6]), most companies capture that activity within the structure of the firm to strengthen this vital component of their strategic advantage.

If the activity is seen as peripheral, such as manufacturing sneakers or calculating and printing payroll checks, the firm will often outsource it for convenience or efficiency (even though, as the Nike example above indicates, this decision can also carry danger to the brand).

Either way, a business's structure and strategy must adapt in the face of a dynamic environment that is driven by constantly-evolving societal expectations. As Professor Archie Carroll observed,[7] this evolution of what is socially expected of organizations typically migrates from discretionary to ethical to mandatory (legal and economic).

Equal Pay

Over time, actions that were previously considered discretionary or ethical can be codified as laws or government rulings and, finally, as economic components of operations—in other words, minimum standards to which a firm needs to adhere in order to remain competitive. Many firms in the United States, for example, once blatantly paid women less than men for the same work. In spite of whatever justifications were applied, this behavior was within the discretionary decision-making authority of businesses.

Gradually, however, such discrimination came to be seen as unfair, even unethical. Then, in 1963, the federal government enacted the Equal Pay Act, which outlawed discrimination in pay based solely on an employee's gender. This legislation immediately served to limit this once discretionary area of management decision making. Today, diversity in the workplace is viewed as an economic imperative that enables firms to respond effectively to their consumers' needs.

Once society determines that a particular form of behavior has become unacceptable, the perceived abuse can lead to a legally-mandated correction, such as the Equal Pay Act. Consequently, the range of socially acceptable employment policies used to facilitate competitive strategies has changed greatly in the last half century as societies evolve.[8] Similar changes can be identified with regard to environmental pollution, product safety standards, financial record keeping, and scores of other previously discretionary behaviors. Once discretionary issues evolve into legal constraints, meeting societal expectations becomes an absolute requirement that is enforced by criminal or civil sanctions.

More difficult to identify are issues not yet subject to legal mandates, but which may still affect the firm. If leaders exercise discretionary authority to attain economic ends, but the actions are perceived to be socially irresponsible (even though they are legally permissible), the consequences may damage the firm. Such damage becomes evident in terms of lower sales, diminished employee recruitment and retention, evaporating financial support from investors and markets, and a host of other important relationships. What should a company do?

Strategic CSR bridges both the firm's economic and societal contributions. Ultimately, stakeholders have the right (even the responsibility) and the power to determine what is *acceptable* corporate behavior. Although, it is also true that societies benefit greatly from the innovation that businesses create in pursuit of profits. Nevertheless, in today's global environment, businesses are expected to pursue their strategies in ways that, at a minimum, do not harm others and, increasingly, are expected to address and solve social problems.[9] What makes this calculation so difficult for all organizations is that, as societies become more affluent and interconnected, the definition of *social harm* changes constantly.

As such, in terms of CSR, we argue that very little is discretionary any more. Past perspectives that viewed firms narrowly as profit engines have been altered beyond recognition both by globalization and growing social affluence. Highly interconnected societies have more knowledge and more choice, while wealthier societies have the resources to demand more *responsible* behavior from their firms. Developed economies around the world, for example, uniformly demand that car producers make safer and less polluting cars because they understand the implications of unsafe and polluting cars and can afford to pay for technological innovation.

In today's globalizing world, we believe that *shareholder* value can be maximized over the long term only if the firm addresses the needs of its primary *stakeholder* groups. Satisfying stakeholders is most efficiently achieved by adopting a CSR perspective as part of strategic planning and implementing that strategy throughout the day-to-day operations of the firm.

THE FIVE DRIVING FORCES OF CSR

As outlined in Chapter 1, there are five environmental forces that are driving CSR to the forefront of corporate strategic thinking: growing affluence, ecological sustainability, globalization, communications technologies, and brands. Any one of these drivers might be ignored by managers not convinced of the strategic benefits to the firm of CSR. Collectively, however, they are reshaping the business environment by empowering stakeholder groups. And, because each of these trends interacts with the others, the reinforcing effects mean that the environmental context will not only change, but will do so at an increasingly rapid rate—often in ways not foreseen by today's best strategists. Though each is discussed separately, their interactive effects heighten the importance of the CSR Filter for corporate strategy.

Affluence

CSR issues tend to gain a foothold in societies that are more affluent—societies where people have jobs, savings, and security and can afford the luxury of choosing between, for example, low-cost cars that pollute and high-cost hybrids that do not. As public opinion evolves and government regulation races to catch up, actions previously thought of as discretionary often become legal obligations.

Externalities

The Oxford English Dictionary defines an *externality* as:

> A side-effect or consequence (of an industrial or commercial activity) which affects other parties without this being reflected in the cost of the goods or services involved; a social cost or benefit.[10]

In the past, manufacturers have often been able to externalize some of their production costs to the larger society by polluting the environment. When the majority of people are desperately focused on the need for jobs to feed their families, pollution seems of limited concern. When most members of a society are desperately seeking food, shelter, and other necessities of life, CSR seems a luxury of little relevance.[11] As societies become increasingly affluent, however, the collective understanding of social issues, like pollution, grows; as does the ability of society to afford effective solutions.

It would be shortsighted, however, to assume that CSR is only applicable where there is affluence. Serious transgressions are always resisted by local stakeholders. As such, protests against international petroleum companies occur when operating standards are construed as harmful to the immediate community. In Nigeria, for example, residents in the Niger Delta continue to attack oil workers and sabotage equipment because the Nigerian government is not distributing the oil wealth, while pollution and deforestation continue. Though Shell and other companies comply with Nigerian law, they are being attacked (both at home and in Nigeria) by those who believe the company is doing harm.

Such protests demonstrate that, increasingly, stakeholders living in affluent societies are willing to hold multinational corporations to domestic standards in relation to their overseas activities in developing countries. As a result of such domestic pressure, for example, Nike requires its subcontractors in developing nations to provide wages and working conditions above the local norms.[12] Even so, activists continue to take Nike to task,[13] criticizing the pay and conditions of its subcontractors because local standards often are well below those that prevail in its home country, the United States. Other high-profile firms, such as Apple, have also become targets for campaigners. As such, although Apple has increased the level of CSR in its supply chain, the contrast with Nike's experience is still readily apparent:

CSR Newsletters: Apple

An article in *The Wall Street Journal*[14] comments on Apple's release recently of its annual audit of suppliers. The highlights:

- 62% weren't compliant with working-hours limits.
- 32% weren't compliant with hazardous-substance management practices.
- 35% failed to meet Apple's standards to prevent worker injuries.

It is not clear whether we should be shocked at the numbers or applaud Apple for its honesty. The initial impression, however, is one of greater scope and detail in the report:

The report is the most comprehensive on the subject in Apple's history, based on 229 audits of factories that do work for the company, the world's second-largest by market capitalization. While Apple has occasionally divulged selected suppliers, the new list covers those 156 companies that represent 97% of its materials, manufacturing and assembly spending.

Historically, Apple has not had a reputation for CSR that matches its reputation for product innovation. Perhaps this will be one area in which Apple's new CEO, Tim Cook, can improve on Steve Jobs' performance at the firm. On the other hand, however, maybe not. Transparency is one thing; performance is something else and this article[15] provides more evidence of Apple's tenuous relationship with CSR. In particular, *The New York Times'* investigation constitutes a detailed report on Apple's supply chain in China. The article is long, but one quote is particularly revealing: 'We're trying really hard to make things better,' said one former Apple executive. 'But most people would still be really disturbed if they saw where their iPhone comes from.'

Contrast this approach with the approach taken by Nike reported in an article that appeared in *Network for Business Sustainability*.[16]

In April 2005, Nike surprised the business community by suddenly releasing its global database of nearly 750 factories worldwide. No laws presently require a company to disclose the identity of its factories or suppliers within global supply chains. Yet, between the early 1990s and 2005, Nike went from denying responsibility for inhumane conditions in its factories to leading other companies in full disclosure — a strategic shift that illustrates how a firm can leverage increased transparency to mitigate risk and add value to the business.

Apple's response to *The New York Times'* investigation is posted online.[17] In addition, shortly following the report, Foxconn (Apple's main supplier in China) announced plans to significantly improve working conditions at its factories by increasing wages and reducing hours.[18] If it happens, this is important given that:

Foxconn, with 1.2 million Chinese employees, is one of China's largest employers. It assembles an estimated 40 percent of the smartphones, computers and other electronic gadgets sold around the world. Foxconn's decisions set standards other manufacturers must compete with.

The most important point made in the article, however, brought the focus back to where it ultimately resides—with the end consumers:

For that system to genuinely change, Foxconn, its competitors and their clients — which include Apple, Hewlett-Packard, Dell and the world's other large electronics firms — must convince consumers in America and elsewhere that improving factories to benefit workers is worth the higher prices of goods.

Developed country living standards are rapidly diffusing throughout the world. As more and more people clamor to enter the middle class (estimated to increase by "two or three billion people" over the next 40 years,[19] driven primarily by economic advances in China and India),[20] ever-rising societal expectations are accompanying their rising living standards. And, these rapidly developing economies understand that they cannot afford to progress along the same path as the one followed by the developed economies. This applies in terms of damage to the environment, but also in terms of restricting their own economic growth:

. . . the course of industrialization taken by Europe, America and other rich countries will not work for the rest of the world. Their route was "grow first, clean up later." . . . The idea that environmental concerns are mainly for the rich is still powerful and persistent. . . . But the costs of waiting for a clean-up are rising, under-mining the argument that poor countries cannot afford to go green. The Chinese Academy of Social Sciences reckons the total annual damage to China's economy from environmental degradation is the equivalent of 9% of GDP. The World Bank says bad sanitation and water pollution cost India 6% of national income.[21]

The obvious conclusion is that competitive strategies must consider the ever-shifting pattern of societal expectations that become emboldened by the greater choices affluence affords societies. What is clear is that, as the pace of progress gets ever-quicker, this task becomes more and more difficult:

After agriculture was invented 11,000 years ago, it took 4,000 years for it to supplant hunting and gathering as mankind's main source of food, 5,000 for cities to emerge, 6,000 for writing to develop and 7,000 for the invention of mathematics. After harnesses were devised to hitch oxen to plows, it took 4,000 years to adapt harnesses to the long necks of horses. But 66 years after the Wright brothers flew a distance shorter than the wingspan of a Boeing 747, a man stood on the moon, and mankind marveled at the modern pace of change.[22]

Sustainability

The effects of growing affluence and the changes in societal expectations that accompany it are enhanced by a growing concern for the resource constraints we are placing on the planet.[23] These constraints range from access to fresh water, to energy provision, to affordable food, to supplies of the rare earths that are essential to produce cellphones, computers, and other vital products. These resources, and many others, are being placed under increasing strain due to a fixed supply (we have only one planet) and a rapidly growing demand. In the autumn of 2011, the world population passed 7 billion people, and shows no signs of letting up:

The first billion people accumulated over a leisurely interval, from the origins of humans hundreds of thousands of years ago to the early 1800s. Adding the second took another 120 or so years. Then, in the last 50 years, humanity more than doubled, surging from three billion in 1959 to four billion in 1974, five billion in 1987 and six billion in 1998. . . . The United Nations Population Division anticipates 8 billion people by 2025, 9 billion by 2043 and 10 billion by 2083. India will have more people than China shortly after 2020, and sub-Saharan Africa will have more people than India before 2040.[24]

The scale and pace of this population growth places an enormous strain on the world's resources, causing commentators like Paul Ehrlich to predict "a collapse of global civilization."[25] Part of the reason for this is that, not only is the world's population becoming larger, but it is also becoming more concentrated. According to the United Nations:

> [In 2008] mankind became, for the first time in its history, a predominantly urban species. . . . Having taken around 200,000 years to get to the halfway mark, demographers reckon that three-quarters of humanity could be city-dwelling by 2050.[26]

And, due to its rapid economic growth, "most of the world's population increase in the next 40 years will be in developing countries."[27] As such, the natural environment will continue to bear the brunt of this resource depletion. In particular, climate change is an issue that has gained a great deal of visibility in recent years due to two events. First, the Stern Report, which was published by the UK government in 2006,[28] focused attention on the financial and economic consequences of deferring action today and waiting to see how bad things get. Second, the movie documentary, *The Inconvenient Truth*, essentially a souped-up powerpoint presentation by former U.S. Vice-President, Al Gore, brought climate change to the attention of a global audience.[29] The movie was awarded the 2007 Nobel Peace Prize as well as, perhaps more importantly for its mass public exposure, an Oscar for Best Documentary Feature.[30]

CSR Newsletters: The Most Terrifying Video You'll Ever See

The video in the url below condenses the convoluted, passionate, and often partisan debate about climate change into a straight forward argument:

http://video.stumbleupon.com/#p=p6o08udcmw[31]

The goal of the presentation is to remove the conflict over the science behind climate change and global warming from the debate and instead, reduce the argument to one of risk management. In other words, whether you believe in the science or not, the dangers of not acting far outweigh any dangers associated with acting.

Unlike the video's title implies, it is probably not the "most terrifying video" you'll ever see, but the author makes his case very well and the most important point is to focus on "the columns" rather than "the rows" (you'll have to watch the video to find out why!).

Although experts disagree about the speed of climate change and the likely extent of corrective action we will need to take, what is not in doubt is that human economic activity is depleting the world's resources and causing dramatic changes to the mix of gasses in the earth's atmosphere—changes that could become irreversible in the near future.

What is also clear is that internalizing the nature of the problem and the extent of action necessary to effect meaningful change, has implications for our entire economic system:

CSR Newsletters: The Story of Stuff[32]

The video in this url is a 20 minute video that focuses on sustainability. It is more polemical than it is objective and scientific, but it is entertaining and educational, and it makes some very important points:

http://www.storyofstuff.org/movies-all/story-of-stuff/

The most effective way of achieving the over-arching goal of the video (how to make a linear system more sustainable) lies in maintaining a focus on strategic CSR in its broadest interpretation. It is only by focusing on the system as a whole that meaningful and lasting change can occur.

Because waste is inherent to GDP growth—our economic model prefers us to replace our cars every three years rather than ten and to buy disposable products rather than ones we can re-use—and because the supply of raw materials is finite, it is essential that we use resources more effectively in order for our economic system to become sustainable.[33] Some CSR advocates see this fault in our economic model and call for a *revolution*. *Strategic CSR*, on the other hand, seeks *evolution*—to reform the current system so that capitalism maximizes both economic and social progress by integrating a CSR perspective into firm strategy and throughout operations.

As a result of the growing realization of the ecological changes that are occurring, firms that are seen as indifferent to their environmental responsibilities are likely to be criticized and penalized by stakeholders. Companies as diverse as General Electric (*Ecoimagination* program),[34] Unilever (firm-wide sustainable living program),[35] and Toyota (Prius hybrid car)[36] increasingly recognize this threat and are responding by innovating to meet stakeholder needs.

Other firms are "going green through the back door"—innovating on sustainability issues to generate operational efficiencies, without necessarily promoting these changes to consumers.[37] As illustrated in Chapter 3, for example, Walmart has become a market leader in issues related to sustainability, but they do it primarily for supply chain efficiency, not increased market share.[38] In addition, firms like Levi's (Better Cotton Initiative),[39] Starbucks (C.A.F.E. Principles),[40] Nike (Materials Sustainability Index),[41] and Home Depot (Forest Stewardship Council-certified wood)[42] reinforce the strategic value of being out ahead of an evolving issue:

> "Our data shows that most customers will not pay extra for sustainable wood and, in some cases, they consider 'green' wood a negative. We believe that FSC wood is the best way to go for both quality and sustainability reasons. . . . We do believe in educating our customers and employees about sustainability, but at the same time the voice of the customer is always our top priority. Thus including FSC wood without charging a price premium is the right thing to do, and thankfully, due to our enormous volume and purchasing power, we can make this equation work business-wise," [said Ron Jarvis, senior VP of Environmental Innovation, The Home Depot.][43]

The UK is a significant driver of innovation on this issue with firms competing on metrics such as food miles,[44] carbon footprints,[45] and recycling programs.[46] Indeed, the supermarket Tesco claims that, since 2009, its UK stores have sent zero waste to landfills:

> The United Kingdom's largest retailer says 100 percent of its waste from stores, offices and distribution centers across the country are now diverted from landfill – the result of aggressive recycling and treatment programs that include turning as much as 5,000 tonnes of old meat into heat and electricity each year.[47]

While there is much progress still to be made, where stakeholder awareness of environmental sustainability issues is high, progressive firms in this area can secure market share and competitive differentiation by being early innovators and adopters.

Globalization

Globalization is another force propelling the strategic value of CSR. Increasingly, corporations operate in a global business environment. They have prospered as a result:

Corporate Trends in a Globalized World[48]

In 1980, the world's largest 1,000 corporations:

- Generated revenues of $2.64 trillion ($6.99 trillion in 2010 dollars).
- Employed directly nearly 21 million employees.
- Had a total market capitalization of almost $900 billion (42.38 trillion in 2010 dollars)—equivalent to 33% of total world market capitalization.

In 2010, the world's largest 1,000 corporations:

- Generated revenues of $32 trillion.
- Employed directly 67 million employees.
- Had a total market capitalization of $28 trillion—equivalent to 49% of total world market capitalization.

And, multi-national firms will continue to prosper as the shift in global business moves away from the U.S. and becomes more evenly spread.[49] As the BRIC economies (Brazil, Russia, India, and China) continue to develop (making twice the contribution to global GDP growth of the G7 from 2011 to 2020)[50] and are joined by the CIVETS economies (Colombia, Indonesia, Vietnam, Egypt, Turkey, and South Africa), more and more consumers will join the global middle class and global firms will be best-placed to supply their consumer needs.[51]

The Internet, which drives this global environment, is a powerful enabling tool for communication and education, transportation, trade, and international capital flows. The Internet also, however, depersonalizes relations between individuals and reduces our sense of an immediate community. This, in turn, affects a business' sense of self-interest and can loosen the self-regulating incentive to maintain strong local ties. As Dr. Peter Whybrow[52] observes:

> Historically, . . . built-in social brakes reined in our acquisitive instincts. In the capitalist utopia envisioned by Adam Smith in the 18th century, self-interest was tempered by the competing demands of the marketplace and community. But with globalization, the idea of doing business with neighbors one must face the next day is a quaint memory, and all bets are off.[53]

In Adam Smith's[54] view of the eighteenth century world, all competition was local—the vast majority of products were produced and consumed within the same community. As a result, Smith reasoned, it would be in producers' self-interest to be honest because to do otherwise would threaten the reputations and goodwill on which ongoing trading within their community depends. As businesses grew in size, began selling to ever more distant markets, and dividing operations across geographic locations in order to minimize costs and maximize profits, Smith's fundamental assumption broke down. Firms were free to be bad employers in Vietnam or polluters in China because they sold their products in the United States or Europe and there was no way for Western consumers to know the conditions under which the products they were buying were produced. Disgruntled employees in Vietnam and local villagers in China were no threat to this business model, especially when even the worst jobs in the factories of multi-national firms were often the best jobs available and generating much-needed local economic progress. As globalization progresses, however, information is communicated more efficiently:

> . . . it took radio 38 years and television 13 years to reach audiences of 50 million people, while it took the Internet only four years, the iPod three years and Facebook two years to do the same.[55]

As a result, the world grows ever-smaller and societies are again approaching the conditions under which Smith first suggested self-interest will effectively regulate action. Once again, "all business is local,"[56] with the Internet allowing any individual with a cellphone to broadcast what they witness to anyone interested worldwide.

These ideas are expressed graphically in Figure 4.3 in terms of the three phases of stakeholder access to information—from industrialization, to international trade, to globalization. Adam Smith lived in a simpler time, when all information was local and kept firms honest. Due to the benefits of globalization, however, a similar access to information at a micro level is returning. As communication technology continues to innovate and power over its control is increasingly devolved to individuals, the ability of firms to manipulate stakeholder perceptions of their activities will decrease. As GE's vice-president of corporate communications reports:

> Every three seconds we see something posted online about GE – not all of it good – and so, if you're not out there engaging with people in discussion authentically, you're losing out.[57]

Globalization, therefore, transforms the CSR debate and magnifies its importance exponentially. A domestic context is not the only lens through which the issue of CSR should be viewed. Today, no multinational company can afford to ignore CSR. European consumers, for example, are just as likely to look to a company's operations in the United States, or elsewhere in the world, when judging to what extent a U.S. company's actions are acceptable and whether they are going

| Figure 4.3 | The Three Phases of Stakeholder Access to Information |

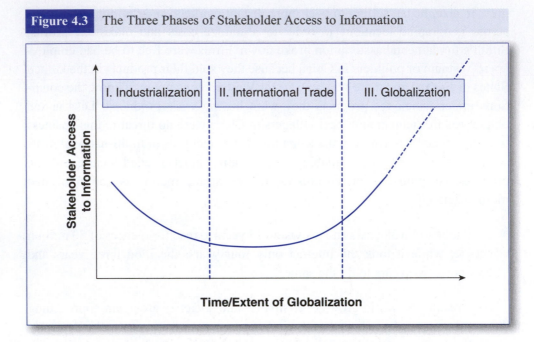

to buy the company's products. This is a lesson that the British bank, Barclays, learned when it continued to do business in Apartheid-plagued South Africa in the 1980s[58] and a lesson that the oil multi-national, Shell learned with its involvement with the Nigerian regime that executed Ken Saro-wiwa in the 1990s.[59] This trend will increase as global cultural differences lead to widely varying stakeholder expectations. Actions that may be acceptable, even required in one culture may be prohibited in another.

Discrimination

Discrimination based on gender is generally prohibited in developed societies, albeit with varying degrees of enforcement; however, in some cultures, like Saudi Arabia, women are segregated from male workers and encounter gender-based limitations on the type of work available to them.[60] A firm operating in Europe and Saudi Arabia may well be considered socially irresponsible and culturally insensitive if it applies the same HR policies across all operating locations. Yet, if women are treated differently in Saudi Arabia, criticisms may arise in Europe or elsewhere. The Swedish furniture giant IKEA learned this lesson in 2012 when it airbrushed women out of photos from the Saudi version of its catalog out of respect for local cultural sensitivities. The differences emerged after a reporter:

> ...compared the Swedish and Saudi versions of the catalogue and showed that women had been airbrushed out of otherwise identical pictures showcasing the company's products.[61]

> Ignoring inconsistencies in company practices can place multinational firms in very awkward positions. On the one hand, they must adapt their strategies to local expectations; but, on the other hand, strategies based on varying standards can leave the firm open to negative publicity, lawsuits, or other harmful outcomes at home.

CSR is more relevant today than ever before because of globalization. In terms of the relationship between corporations and their various stakeholders, this process of globalization appears to be progressing through two phases, as suggested by Figure 3.2 in Chapter 3.

Phase I of globalization greatly empowered corporations, enabling them to expand operations on a worldwide basis, shift manufacturing offshore, reform supply chain management, and develop powerful global brands. Merger and acquisition activities blossomed (because it was a quick way for companies to grow) and, as they grew, their power increased significantly. As globalization transcends national boundaries, the power of global firms expands further. Companies today are free to incorporate offshore to avoid paying higher tax rates in their home country. They are also increasingly able to move their manufacturing operations or production processes to lower-cost environments, often in countries with less rigorous labor and environmental regulations. In addition, corporations benefit from establishing global brands because of greater sales and worldwide customer loyalty. The brand's value proposition may entice consumers with price, reliable quality, status, or other features not available from competitors. Even regulating authorities may fear losing jobs, tax revenues, or public support by fighting back against a corporate power. Imagine, for example, if the European Union banned Microsoft products because of unfair or monopolistic operating practices.[62] Microsoft's leverage over both consumers and regulating authorities may be too strong for such an outcome to be politically or economically feasible.

Globalization, however, creates countervailing forces that are capable of curtailing corporations' expanding power (as depicted in Phase II of Figure 3.2 in Chapter 3).

Corporations are losing control over the flow of information that empowers NGOs and consumer activists to communicate and mobilize. A growing list of examples suggests that companies are no longer able to dictate the quality and quantity of information about their company and how that information affects the social debate. Nike,[63] GAP,[64] Coca-Cola,[65] and Google[66] are just a few examples of companies that have been damaged at some point by global information flows. Companies may be well advised to try to anticipate stakeholder needs and begin promoting operations from a CSR perspective, rather than fight against the free flow of information:

> Thanks to instant communications, whistle-blowers and inquisitive media, citizens and communities routinely put firms under the microscope. And the Internet is a central focus and organizing force for all these activities. . . . Transparency is on the rise, not just for legal or purely ethical reasons but increasingly because it makes economic sense. Firms that exhibit openness and candor have discovered that they can better compete and profit.[67]

This self-feeding cycle of globalization, triggering reactions that are met with reformulated strategies and CSR policies, may well be leading to a "tipping point"[68]—the point of critical mass after which an idea or social trend spreads wildly (like an epidemic) and becomes generally accepted and widely implemented. CSR may well have reached its tipping point largely due to globalization and will increasingly become a mainstay of strategic thinking for businesses, especially global corporations:

> . . . in a world where our demand for Chinese-made sneakers produces pollution that melts South America's glaciers, in a world where Greek tax-evasion can weaken the euro, threaten the stability of Spanish banks and tank the Dow, our values and ethical systems eventually have to be harmonized as much as our markets. To put it differently, as it becomes harder to shield yourself from the other guy's irresponsibility, both he and you had better become more responsible.[69]

Media

As presented in Figure 3.2 (Chapter 3), phase II of globalization suggests a shift in the balance of power concerning control over the flow of information back toward stakeholders in general and three important constituent groups in particular. First, the Internet has greatly empowered individuals because of the access it provides to greater amounts of information, particularly when an issue achieves a critical mass in the media. In every minute we spend online, it is estimated that we generate "100,555,555 emails; 72 hours of YouTube video; 138,889 tweets; 34,722 App Store downloads; 53,819 new Tumblr posts; [and] every two minutes, we snap as many photos as the whole of humanity took during the 1800s."[70] Second, globalization has increased the influence of NGOs and other activist groups because they, too, are benefiting from easily accessible and affordable communications technologies. These tools empower NGOs by enabling them to inform, attract, and mobilize geographically dispersed individuals and consumer segments, which helps to ensure that socially nefarious corporate activities achieve visibility worldwide. And third, new tools of communication and the demand for instantaneous information have enhanced the power of media conglomerates. Media companies have responded by increasing both their size and scope of operations. The combination of empowering the three stakeholder groups ensures that corporations today are unable to hide behind the fig leaves of superficial PR campaigns:

> We are approaching a theoretical state of absolute informational transparency. . . . As individuals steadily lose degrees of privacy, so, too, do corporations and states. . . . It is becoming unprecedentedly difficult for anyone, anyone at all, to keep a secret. In the age of the leak and the blog, of evidence extraction and link discovery, truths will either out or be outed. This is something I would bring to the attention of every diplomat, politician and corporate leader: the future, eventually, will find you out. . . . In the end, you will be seen to have done that which you did.[71]

The Internet is the means by which information is flowing ever more freely. And, as indicated in Figure 4.4, there is lots of it, with total Internet traffic rising 32,000,000% from 2000 to 2006:[72]

> Even if you still have to think twice about the meaning of "giga" and "tera" in computer-speak, you'd better get ready for "peta, "exa" and "zetta." These binary prefixes, which denote 1m, 1 billion and 1 trillion gigabytes respectively, will be used more and more often: the amount of digital data is exploding, with a staggering 1.8 zettabytes in 2011, up from 1.2 zettabytes in the previous year.[73]

It is increasingly apparent that two trends will dominate this future Internet growth: First, people will access the Internet via mobile devices (primarily cellphones and tablet computers); and second, they will share information via social media sites (such as Facebook and Twitter).

Mobile Devices: Cellphones and other mobile devices are now ubiquitous in almost any country that you visit in the world. In the U.S., only about 12% of all adults do not own a cellphone,[74] while the sales of tablets (the iPad in particular) have exceeded expectations. And, the rest of the world is catching up: "Ten years

Figure 4.4   The Flood of Global Digital Data

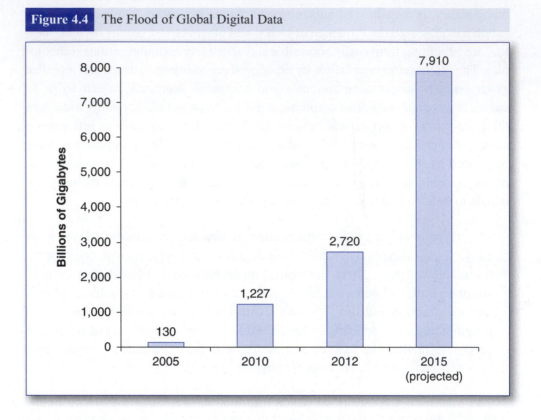

ago China had more mobile phones than America, [in 2011] it manufactured more and registered more patents, and in 2014 its retailers will sell more."[75] As a result, China Mobile is now the biggest mobile communications service company by sales.[76] Developing countries, in particular, will access the Internet via wireless technology (cellphones, text messaging, blogs, and social media sites),[77] rather than via the desktop computers and land telephone lines that were the foundation of the Internet in the developed economies.[78] For example, "Only 4% of households in Africa have Internet access, but more than 50% have cell phones":[79]

> In some African markets you can buy a daily dose of internet on a mobile phone for about the cost of a banana (i.e., less than ten American cents). This burgeoning connectivity is making Africa faster, cleverer and more transparent in almost everything that it does.[80]

To put the evolution of this technology more starkly so as not to underestimate the influence it will have on shaping future social interactions, according to a United Nations report:

India has more mobile phones than toilets. India's mobile subscribers totalled 563.73 million at the last count, enough to serve nearly half of the country's 1.2 billion population. But just 366 million people – around a third of the population – had access to proper sanitation in 2008.[81]

Social Media: As people access the Internet via their mobile devices, they are using social media to exchange information. Social media is perhaps more accurately described as "social technologies," of which there are two types—websites that "allow people to broadcast their ideas" (e.g., Twitter and its Chinese equivalent, Sina Weibo) and websites that allow people to "form connections" (e.g., Facebook and its corporate equivalent, LinkedIn):[82]

According to comScore, Twitter was the 28th most visited website in the U.S. with 38.2 million unique visitors in August. Among all U.S. websites, Facebook was No. 4 in traffic with 152.4 million unique users in August. Business-focused social site LinkedIn is ranked 26th with 40.9 million unique visitors.[83]

The amount of data being distributed via social media is staggering, with Facebook registering over 1 billion active users in 2012, while the number of tweets sent each day now exceeds 500m.[84] It is the interaction of these two media (cellphones and social media), however, where the potential for revolution is most apparent. The new kind of activism this technology is stimulating among consumers, activists, and NGOs, combined with the insatiable demand of global media conglomerates, is increasingly extending CSR concerns and awareness. And globalization continues to enhance the power of the Internet. Whether it is using Facebook and Twitter to overturn decades of totalitarian oppression in the Middle East or simply using GPS technology to play Pac-Man in the streets of New York ("Pac-Manhattan"),[85] the power of technology to mobilize strangers and unite them under a common agenda is growing daily:

Tick off the protests that characterized 2011, and you'll find that every one of them featured cell-phones, tweets, texts, Facebook, and YouTube. The immediacy and accuracy of information ramped up the speed of these activities and the intensity of the results. It you doubt that, here's this week's essay question: Comment on how the U.S. civil rights movement might have developed if the marchers in Alabama had used today's communications systems—and on how Libya might have turned out if the revolutionaries were stuck with 1955's technologies.[86]

The CNN Test

Simply put, "The Internet makes it possible to organize a global community around a certain issue in a split second."[87] A few giant media companies control large percentages of the information we receive across a wide range of media and their influence extends far beyond the watching public:

> The CNN test has been a criterion that causes CSR sensitive decision makers to ask, "How will this be viewed by watchers of CNN when broadcast around the world?" Even U.S. military commanders used this test to select bombing targets during the second Iraq war in 2003. This test shows the influence of the media in shaping government policy as well as public opinion today and why the CNN test is part of the CSR Filter for some organizations.

The result, as suggested by Figure 4.5, is an ever widening, free flow of information in a globalizing world that portends danger for entrenched interests everywhere. With "two billion people" already online and e-commerce sales at "$8 trillion a year,"[88] it is clear that the Internet has changed the way businesses operate. Reports of firms scrambling to form a 'social media policy,' together with multiple incidents of complaining customers and misfired tweets abound.[89] Harnessing this power and directing it at a corporate target has the potential to inflict significant damage to any firm's product, brand, or reputation. And it is becoming clear how these campaigns might evolve. Initiatives such as SeeClickFix (http://seeclickfix.com/) connects "iCitizens" with their local elected representatives to fix neighborhood problems,[90] while PolitiFact.org's (http://www.politifact.com/) Truth-O-Meter rates claims by politicians "on a six-level scale ranging from 'true' to 'pants on fire,'"[91] and Copwatch (http://www.copwatch.org/) monitors police activity and posts videos online to guard against abusive behavior.[92] It does not stretch the imagination too far to see how Copwatch easily becomes *Corpwatch*, using the same technology and community motivation to build campaigns against specific firms. The danger no longer lies in insufficient information, but being able to detect "whispers of useful information in a howling hurricane of noise."[93]

The relationship between stakeholders and the growing pool of information and communication is iterative (see Figure 4.5). As stakeholders gain access to larger amounts of information and communicate this information among each other, so they build support for particular issues and disseminate that information to other stakeholders.[94] This trend is already becoming apparent with the rapid growth in user-generated-content websites such as YouTube and Flickr. It is taking a step further with websites that allow users to rate and review the products and services

Figure 4.5 The Free Flow of Information in a Globalizing World

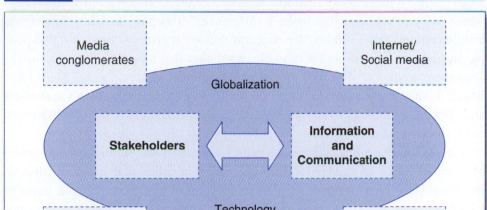

firms provide. Blogs that are dedicated to specific firms and their products, such as those targeting Apple (e.g., The Apple Blog, http://gigaom.com/apple/ or Apple Insider, http://appleinsider.com/) and Starbucks (e.g., Starbucks Gossip, http://star bucksgossip.com/) take this level of interaction between a firm and its stakeholders to another level—for good and for bad, depending on the firm and the extent to which it attempts to respond to the needs and demands of key stakeholder groups.

The result is that more and more consumers are researching firms and products online before making purchase decisions. Websites such as Good Guide (http://www.goodguide.com/), which "provides the world's largest and most reliable source of information on the health, environmental, and social impacts of consumer products," further utilize technology gains to aid their search.[95] Consumers are informed and they are willing to share their horror stories with millions of others.[96] Consequently, firms have an even more precarious hold on their reputations and need to be more responsive to stakeholders' concerns in order to protect them:

> Businesses spend millions to cultivate their reputations; now consumer evaluations can make or break them instantly. "The conventional wisdom is that a satisfied customer will tell one person and an unhappy person will tell 10," . . . That's now been upped by orders of magnitude.[97]

It is clear that the interaction of the Internet and social media is "shifting power from a few Goliaths to many Davids."[98] This technology offers stakeholders a means to hold firms to account, but only if they seek to do so. What is not clear is how fully stakeholders will take advantage of the information that is online. There are limits to virtual protest.[99] For example, while Change.org (http://www.change .org/) "is the web's leading platform for social change, empowering anyone, anywhere to start petitions that make a difference," it is hard to know how firms should respond to the stakeholder concerns that are registered there. If 5,000 people sign an online petition, for example, what does that mean? Will they refuse to shop there anymore? Will they protest at stores? And, if so, so what? For a large brand, 5,000 people widely diffused is a small percentage of the firm's customers and clicking a mouse is hardly an indication of personal conviction or willingness to sacrifice on behalf of a cause.

Success today assumes companies reflect accurately the values and aspirations of a broad range of stakeholder groups. For companies that promote lifestyle brands, such as Nike or Apple, this rule is even more significant. But, as noted in Chapter 2, just because a stakeholder feels affected by a firm's actions does not compel the firm to respond to those concerns. Corporations moving to take the initiative and meet the expectations of a broad range of stakeholders (while avoiding confrontation) need to put in place clear and open channels of communication that allow serious concerns to find their way through to the strategy and decision-making table.

A key component of this dialog can be partnering with NGOs (and other non-profits) to pursue projects of common concern. Both NGOs and consumers, with the help of the media, use the free flow of information to spread knowledge and build coalitions. These coalitions can occur spontaneously or as part of coordinated campaigns. One consistent feature, however, is their fluidity, encouraged by an ever-expanding technical capability, with groups bonding together for a particular issue then disbanding and joining other partners for a different issue. Besides avoiding conflict, developing a dialog with stakeholders offers potential benefit for firms. NGOs and nonprofits can help firms understand the rapidly evolving markets in which they operate, help them stay in touch with target consumers, and contribute in areas of product development.

In general, the firms most progressive in terms of CSR will be the ones that take external pressure for more responsible behavior, ethics, transparency, and social involvement and use it to re-vamp their strategic approach to business. Those firms best able to implement a strategic CSR perspective more genuinely throughout operations will be best placed to operate in a global business environment in which they no longer control the flow of information. In short, for companies to enjoy sustained success, CSR will increasingly form a central component of strategy and operations, particularly in relation to a firm's reputation and brand management.

Brands

Brands today are a focal point of corporate success and should be protected by integrating a strategic CSR perspective throughout the firm. Companies seek to establish strong brands because it increases their competitive advantage. In particular, we have identified three benefits of CSR to brands: Positive brand building, Brand insurance, and Crisis management.

Positive Brand Building: Anita Roddick, founder of The Body Shop, long championed the power of an influential global brand to enact meaningful social change. In doing so, she helped distinguish her business in the minds of consumers, gaining a strategic advantage. Whether you agree with the stance that The Body Shop adopts on a number of fair trade and other social issues,[100] many consumers are drawn to purchase the company's products because of the positions it takes. Its fair trade stance helps differentiate the firm's offerings and stands out in the minds of consumers. Similarly, Benetton has also set itself apart through advertising, using its voice to comment on the social issues that it thinks are relevant to its consumers.[101] Ben & Jerry's is another activist-alternative brand that pursues a similar strategy,[102] although its cult-like status has faded somewhat since being bought by Unilever in 2000.[103]

Brand Insurance:[104] Reflecting a socially responsible stance, George W. Merck, son of the pharmaceutical company's founder, announced, "Medicine is for the patients, not for the profits." This 'radical' corporate vision translates into an often cited example of the company donating the medicine Mectizan to combat the devastating disease, river blindness:[105]

> Twenty-two years ago, Merck started giving away a drug to treat river blindness, a devastating infectious disease endemic to certain countries in Africa and Latin America. The company has donated 2.5 billion tablets at a total cost of $3.75 billion over that time. Merck manages the program with the World Health Organization and other groups, and the effort is widely cited as a model of successful public-private partnerships. [In 2009], WHO announced for the first time that it sees evidence the disease will be eliminated in Africa with Merck's drug.[106]

It could be argued that Merck's actions bought a degree of insurance against attacks by social activists because of the company's up-front commitment to such a worthwhile, unselfish, and unprofitable cause. Perhaps this socially responsible viewpoint has enabled Merck to enjoy a relatively free run from the activist criticism visited on other pharmaceutical companies. The reputation it gained from this act has also been cited as a significant reason for the company's success in entering new markets, most notably Japan, where its socially responsible reputation preceded it. Yet even Merck's proactive CSR efforts may not save it from the economic and legal implications of Vioxx, a Merck product voluntarily withdrawn from the market in 2004 after a growing number of heart-related health problems among users.[107]

Crisis Management: Johnson & Johnson's transparent handling of the Tylenol crisis in 1982 is widely heralded as the model case in the area of crisis management.[108] J&J went beyond what had previously been expected of corporations in such situations, instigating a $100 million recall of 31 million bottles of the drug following a suspected poisoning incident. In acting the way it did, J&J saved the Tylenol brand, enabling it to remain a strong revenue earner for the company to this day:

> The cost [of the re-call] was a high one. In addition to the impact on the company's share price when the crisis first hit, the lost production and destroyed goods as a result of the recall were considerable. However, the company won praise for its quick and appropriate action. . . . Within five months of the disaster, the company had recovered 70% of its market share for the drug. The fact this went on to improve over time showed that the company had succeeded in preserving the long term value of the brand. . . . In fact, there is some evidence that [J&J] was rewarded by consumers who were so reassured by the steps taken that they switched from other painkillers to Tylenol.[109]

Brand value is critical to firms, whether on the local or global stage. Today, the value of the intangible brand may even exceed the value of the firm's tangible assets. The Coca-Cola brand, for example, is worth significantly more than half of the company's total market capitalization.[110] And, CSR is important to brands within a globalizing world because of the way brands are built: on perceptions, ideals, and concepts that usually appeal to aspirational values. CSR is a means of matching corporate operations with stakeholder values at a time when these values are constantly evolving. Given the large amount of time, money, and effort companies invest in creating brands, a good CSR policy has become a vital component of making it a success—an effective means of maximizing market appeal over the long term.

As such, it is essential that a firm is genuine in its marketing statements, particularly in terms of implementing CSR throughout operations, in order for the full benefits to be realized. For example, with a $200 million rebranding exercise, BP (the giant British Petroleum company) was able to reposition itself as the most environmentally and socially responsible of the integrated petroleum companies. The firm's progressive positions on climate change stood in stark contrast to ExxonMobil, which has faced NGO attacks, consumer boycotts, and activist-led litigation because of its decision to oppose the environmental movement.[111]

However, BP's disastrous environmental record in recent years (primarily involving the Deepwater Horizon Gulf oil spill in 2010, but also lethal accidents at key U.S. refineries in 2005, a serious spill in Alaska in 2006, and criticism about the extent of its investment in alternative energy sources),[112] has destroyed the firm's significant investment in building a positive brand image:

> These days, BP's stock trades about 25 percent below where it was before the disaster off the coast of Louisiana, about the same place it was a decade ago.[113]

Businesses today need to build a watertight brand with respect to all stakeholders. The attractiveness of a company—whether as an employer, producer, buyer, supplier, or investment—is directly linked to the strength of its brand. CSR affects all aspects of operations within a corporation because of the need to consider the needs of constituent groups. Each area builds on all the others to create a composite image of the firm and its brand in the eyes of its stakeholder groups, which has great market value.

THE MARKET FOR CSR

Central to the economic argument for CSR, therefore, is the notion that firms that best reflect the current needs of their stakeholders and anticipate how those needs will evolve over time will be more successful in the marketplace over the medium to long term.

CSR Price Premium

As demonstrated in Chapter 3, Walmart has found that adopting specific aspects of CSR (sustainability, in particular) need not undermine the firm's business model and can in fact enhance it. What Chapter 3 also demonstrates, however, is that Walmart is still taking the path of least resistance in the early stages of CSR implementation:

> "There is a substantial opportunity to make green pay," [Rand Waddoups, Wal-Mart's senior director of corporate strategy and sustainability] said. "We haven't even gotten to the low-hanging fruit yet. We are still picking up $1,000 bills off the floor."[114]

Walmart's business strategy relies on a core competence of minimizing costs and passing those savings on to customers. As such, there is little evidence to suggest that Walmart would choose the socially responsible option in any situation where that decision would lead to an increase in costs. This would threaten to undermine the laser-like focus on costs that Walmart executives have spent decades instilling in the firm's employees. What happens, therefore, when CSR increases costs and firms are forced to pass those costs increases on to their customers in the form of higher prices?

As indicated earlier in this chapter, firms that seek to differentiate their products on some feature other than low cost often charge a price premium for that product. Integrating a long-term stakeholder perspective throughout the firm can lead to an increase in costs and a reduction in short-term returns. What is also clear (as with most differentiated products), however, is that the market for these offerings is limited. A quick scan of public opinion polls and media articles about consumers' willingness to pay for ethical or environmental products reveals that, in the U.S., "35 percent said they are willing to pay extra for a green product, an increase from 27 percent in 2010 and 25 percent in 2009."[115]

Reports elsewhere, however, suggest such results are inflated. They also reveal an important shift in consumer opinion regarding expectations of businesses regarding CSR. A report in the UK, for example, notes that "only 22 percent of consumers around the world will pay more for 'eco-friendly' products even though 83 percent believe it is 'important for a company to have environmental programs.'"[116] Increasingly, consumers expect firms to be doing CSR, but they also expect not to have to pay extra for those activities. This new minimum requirement is reflected in a report in *Forbes Magazine* in the U.S.:

> Unfortunately, history has shown that the marketplace is not willing to pay extra [for sustainability products]. Consumers and the public instead expect sustainability as a baseline condition of business. They don't expect to pay for it. They are, however, more than willing to punish if it's not there.[117]

Firms should take two things away from this shift in market expectations regarding CSR. First, those firms that are genuine in their approach to CSR should ensure they understand the operational value that CSR offers. An important distinction, therefore, is between those firms that perceive CSR to be a cost and those that perceive it to be an opportunity.[118] Until firms understand that CSR is an opportunity with operational value above and beyond any potential short-term increase in sales, they have little chance of successfully implementing CSR throughout operations (Walmart understands this, although the firm's application of CSR is still too narrow). This reflects a broader stakeholder approach to CSR, rather than a narrow approach that focuses either on short-term shareholder value or consumer interests.

Second, it is clear that part of the reason for the skepticism among consumers regarding the value of CSR-related products is firms' prior marketing approach to their CSR activities. The combination of promises that were subsequently revealed to be misleading and the proliferation of CSR-related product labels, scales, and ratings designed to *educate* consumers about the socially responsible credentials of various firms and products (although more often confusing them) has left consumers skeptical when they are asked to pay the bill.

CSR Market Abuse

The market for CSR is complicated by the potential for abuse. Stakeholders, in general, and consumers, in particular, need to be vigilant. There is a gap between the information about a product that is known to the firm and the information that the consumer is willing and able to access about that product—in other words, "the information asymmetry between manufacturers and the buying public about the real social, health, and environmental impacts of consumer goods."[119] As the number of groups and individuals interested in CSR grows, so does the amount of information that is distributed by firms seeking to take advantage of consumer trends and sympathies. Some of this information will be accurate, while some will be misleading; some of the misleading information will be mistakenly so, while some will be deliberate. Either way, the proliferation of information is confusing for the firm's external stakeholders. In the face of such a barrage, most consumers disengage.[120] Whether deliberate or accidental, therefore, the effect is negative. As CSR becomes more profitable, the potential for *greenwash* increases:[121]

Greenwash[122]

Green-wash (green'wash', -wôsh') − verb: the act of misleading consumers regarding the environmental practices of a company or the environmental benefits of a product or service.[123]

Greenwash measures the extent to which firms are willing to jump on the CSR bandwagon and mislead consumers in the hope of financial gain. Research suggests that a significant percentage of CSR product marketing claims are false or misleading. In 2010, for example, the environmental marketing organization, Terrachoice, tested the veracity of the 12,061 environmental claims made on the labels of 5,296 consumer products:

More than 95% of consumer products claiming to be green were found to commit at least one of the "Sins of Greenwashing."[124]

The report identifies "seven sins"[125] that firms engage in when marketing the CSR components of their products. These sins include the Sin of the Hidden Trade-off, the Sin of No Proof, the Sin of Vagueness, the Sin of Irrelevance, the Sin of Lesser of Two Evils, the Sin of Fibbing, and Sin of Worshipping False Labels. Taken together, they indicate "both that the individual consumer has been misled and that the potential environmental benefit of his or her purchase has been squandered."[126] The accusation is that firms say the *correct* things, but do not necessarily alter the way they do business. As the report indicates, there are many examples to choose from and range from toilet paper,[127] to hybrid cars,[128] to the Olympics:[129]

> McDonald's may support sustainable fisheries, but its core business is still selling Big Macs. Big oil companies can talk all they want about reducing greenhouse emissions but they are still drilling for hydrocarbons.[130]

Moreover, as different groups push their own agendas and seek to have their CSR ranking, or their fair trade certification, or their environmental sustainability policy established as the standard, so CSR comes to mean different things to different people. While the market for CSR information and practices takes time to identify which ideas will emerge as the standard, the potential for confusion grows. Consumers, in particular, stand to be confused as different self-proclaimed experts bombard them with more information.

CSR Newsletters: Green Noise

An article in *The New York Times*[131] introduces the concept of "green noise":

> . . . static caused by urgent, sometimes vexing or even contradictory information [about the environment] played at too high a volume for too long.

> The idea of "green noise" adds value to the debate. While terms like "greenwashing" describe the conduct of firms, "green noise" presents a consumer perspective on the exponential growth in information on issues related to the environment and climate change that is often contradictory. The overall effect is to obfuscate, rather than clarify, whether deliberately or with good intentions:

> An environmentally conscientious consumer is left to wonder: are low-energy compact fluorescent bulbs better than standard incandescents, even if they contain traces of mercury? Which salad is more earth-friendly,

the one made with organic mixed greens trucked from thousands of miles away, or the one with lettuce raised on nearby industrial farms? Should they support nuclear power as a clean alternative to coal?

In outlining the concept of "green noise" the article also highlights the effect of this information overload on consumer behavior:

. . . consumers surveyed in 2007 were between 22 and 55 percent less likely to buy a wide range of green products than in 2006. The slipping economy had an effect, but message overload appeared to be a major factor as well.

There is an interesting relationship between the amount of information and effective decision making—the idea that more information is better, but too much leads to paralysis and, consequently, bad or non decisions. Information overload in relation to the environment or sustainability issues is likely to result in backlash from consumers.

To a certain extent, this confusion is unavoidable. Here, the CSR field is a victim of its own success. If CSR wasn't growing in popularity and acceptance, the issue of growing and contradictory information would neither exist nor matter. The goal, however, should be for a firm to have an honest and genuine conversation with its stakeholders about its CSR efforts—a conversation that Unilever is seeking through "five simple levers":

- Make it understood
- Make it easy
- Make it desirable
- Make it rewarding
- Make it a habit.[132]

The goal is to be not too far ahead of the market, and provide "solutions where you can take your customers with you. You can be one step ahead of them and take them with you. But if you're three steps ahead, you'll lose them."[133]

STRATEGIC CSR

The Strategic CSR Model, presented in Figure 4.6, visually summarizes the relationship between CSR and strategy. Corporate success assumes that *strategy*

Figure 4.6 The Strategic CSR Model

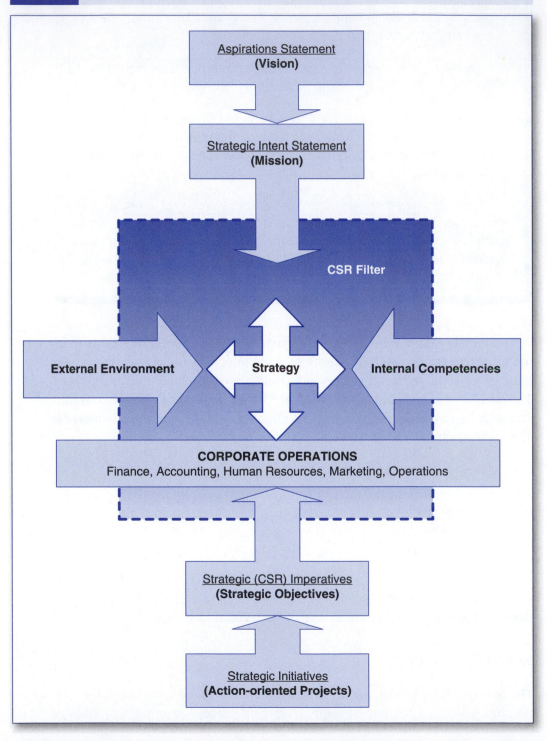

matches *internal competencies* with the *external environment* (stakeholder expectations), within the constraints of *mission* and *vision*. The implementation of strategy, however, rests upon *corporate operations* being successful. Finance, accounting, human resources, and other operational aspects must be executed effectively if the strategy is to be successful at matching competencies to market opportunities. To improve overall performance, therefore, leaders create *strategic objectives* that aim to strengthen these corporate operations. To ensure sufficient financial resources, for example, strategic objectives may be set for the accounting department to accelerate the collection of accounts receivables. Or, marketing might be tasked with the strategic objective of gaining five percent market share. These strategic objectives, however, must be viewed as strategic (must do) imperatives that enhance the firm's CSR goals; otherwise, the tactics and strategies may cause resistance among stakeholders. To achieve these strategic objectives that meet the firm's strategic imperatives, key players must undertake strategic initiatives in the form of *action-oriented projects*. The head of accounting, for example, might create a taskforce charged with a project that identifies and tracks clients who are slow to pay their bills. A similar action-oriented taskforce might also be created in marketing to evaluate the firm's advertising as a first-step to gaining market share. However these actor-oriented projects perform, they must do so by achieving strategic objectives in ways that are consistent with the firm's strategic CSR imperatives, otherwise larger threats to the firm's viability arise. As such, the firm's strategic perspective is surrounded by a *CSR Filter*.

As societies in general become more affluent, societal expectations evolve, and communication technologies become even more widespread, greater and greater demands for CSR will result—undoubtedly prompting more action-oriented projects intended to achieve strategic CSR imperatives. Certainly, ethical, moral and rational arguments exist for companies to act in a socially responsible manner; however, a strong economic incentive also exists to be perceived as a net contributor within a society. CSR, therefore, is a competitive differentiator that also acts as a form of brand insurance, in which the brand represents the perception of the company by each of its key stakeholder groups.[134] This economic argument surfaces daily in firms' advertising and public relations campaigns and is, perhaps, the strongest reason for the implementation of CSR to ensure the long-term viability of the organization. The sophisticated level to which the crisis management industry has evolved in advanced economies further demonstrates the value of reputation. In addition, increasingly, investors "are willing to give higher valuations to companies that are deemed good citizens. Put another way, investors give some companies with good track records the benefit of the doubt."[135]

Companies understand the value of being perceived as friendly neighbors and good corporate citizens. Until now, however, managers have largely confined this concern to public relations departments because they were able to control the information that shaped the public face of the corporation. Figure 3.2 (Chapter 3) and Figures 4.3 and 4.5 illustrate why this situation is changing as the momentum, in terms of information control, swings away from companies and toward their various constituent groups. As globalization progresses, the Internet and global media will further democratize and feed the exchange of information in all free societies. Thus, strategic CSR represents substantive actions, the results of which can flash around the world in an instant.

Firms need to reflect the concerns of society through genuine engagement. Ideally, progressive companies seek to stay ahead of these evolving values and are able to meet new stakeholder demands as they arise. Significantly, core constituent groups are increasingly acquiring the information necessary to see past superficial advertising campaigns, as well as the means to communicate their message and mobilize where necessary. The balance of power and influence is transferring from corporations to their stakeholders because of this shift in control of the flow of information. An effective and genuine CSR perspective, communicated broadly to stakeholders, allows firms to take advantage of these changes and maximize their economic performance in an increasingly globalizing world.

Central to the practical impact of CSR, therefore, is the ability to persuade business leaders that CSR offers strategic and, therefore, economic benefits. Firms can only maximize *shareholder* value in a globalizing world by utilizing strategies that address the needs of key *stakeholders*. CSR, driven by stakeholder theory, delivers these results. It is a means of allowing firms to analyze the total business environment and formulate appropriate organizational strategies. It can protect the firm and its assets, while also offering a point of competitive differentiation. When the business community perceives CSR as more of an opportunity than a threat,[136] CSR will receive greater attention from 21st century leaders.

NEXT STEPS

This chapter outlines in more detail the relationship between strategy and CSR. Constructing strategy using a CSR Filter offers firms the most effective means of navigating an increasingly complex, global business environment. In order for firms to receive the benefit of a CSR perspective, however, there also needs to be a focus on implementation. Without comprehensive and effective implementation, combined with support from the highest levels of the organization, the best laid plans will fall short of their potential. Chapter 5 offers guidance for firms on this issue. It provides insight in terms of the short-, medium-, and long-term aspects of implementation and concludes Part I of *Strategic CSR*.

QUESTIONS FOR DISCUSSION AND REVIEW

1. Why is it important to view CSR from a strategic context?

2. Why are large, multinational firms more likely to be concerned about CSR?

3. How do structure, competencies, strategy, and the external environment combine to create a successful organization?

4. Why are lifestyle brands more susceptible to CSR than companies that seek to differentiate their products with a business level strategy of low cost?

5. What advantages does a *CSR Filter* provide? If you were CEO of a firm, how would you go about applying a CSR Filter—what form might it take? Can you think of a company that is successfully utilizing a CSR Filter today?

6. What are the five environmental forces propelling greater interest in CSR? Explain using real-life examples to illustrate your points. Do you see emerging forces that may reshape CSR in the future?

7. Why does *greenwash* present a danger to CSR? Have a look at p. 10 of Terrachoice's 2010 report 'The Sins of Greenwashing.' Which of the seven sins do you think is the most important (http://sinsofgreenwashing.org/index35c6.pdf)? Think of a firm that is committing that sin—what is misleading about the firm's actions?

STUDENT STUDY SITE

Visit the Student Study Site at **www.sagepub.com/chandler3e** for additional learning tools.

NOTES AND REFERENCES

1. The flip side of each of these "constraints" are opportunities for the firm to build a sustainable competitive advantage.

2. http://nikeinc.com/pages/responsibility; http://www.nikeresponsibility.com/; Nike's Sustainable Business Report: http://www.nikeresponsibility.com/report/

3. Michael E. Porter, *Competitive Strategy*, The Free Press, 1980.

4. A firm's business level strategy stands in contrast to its corporate level strategy, which is the strategy of the firm as a whole. Strategy at this level involves decisions such as the businesses in which the firm will compete and whether or not to enter into partnerships with other firms via joint ventures, mergers, or acquisitions.

5. http://tofslie.com/work/apple_evolution.jpg

6. http://www.computerweekly.com/galleries/237328-4/The-Nike-Trash-Talk-Award-winning-product-design-of-2009.htm

7. Carroll, Archie B., 'A Three-Dimensional Conceptual Model of Corporate Performance,' *Academy of Management Review,* 1979, Vol. 4, No. 4, pp. 497–505.

8. Same sex partner employee benefits will likely be the next form of discrimination to be corrected by legal mandate. Many progressive firms today are proactively implementing such policies so as to avoid being forcefully sanctioned by litigation as the tide of social acceptability turns. See: Kathryn Kranhold, 'Groups for Gay Employees Are Gaining Traction,' *Wall Street Journal*, April 3, 2006, p. B3.

9. Michael E. Porter & Mark R. Kramer, 'Strategy & Society,' *Harvard Business Review*, December, 2006, pp. 78-92 and Michael E. Porter & Mark R. Kramer, 'Creating Shared Value,' *Harvard Business Review*, 89: 62-77, 2011.

10. OED website, January 2013, http://www.oed.com/view/Entry/66996?redirectedFrom=externality#eid

11. This phenomena was reflected in the recent Financial Crisis and Great Recession, when issues like climate change dropped down the list of economic and social priorities in developed economies, such as the U.S. and UK: "The proportion of adults reporting that they are willing to change their behaviour to limit climate change has fallen from 77% in 2006 to 72% in 2010 and 65% in 2011." In: 'Public attitudes to climate change and the impact of transport in 2011,' *Department of Transport*, January 26, 2012, p. 4. Full report is available at: http://assets.dft.gov.uk/statistics/releases/climate-change-and-impact-of-transport-2011/climate-change-2011-report.pdf

12. Aaron Bernstein, 'Nike's New Game Plan for Sweatshops,' *BusinessWeek*, September 20, 2004, http://www.businessweek.com/magazine/content/04_38/b3900011_mz001.htm

13. For an overview, see: 'Nike Campaign,' *Center for Communication & Civic Engagement*, http://depts.washington.edu/ccce/polcommcampaigns/Nike.htm. For a current example of an anti-Nike campaign, see: 'Sweatfree Communities,' *Global Exchange*, http://www.globalexchange.org/campaigns/sweatshops/nike/

14. Jessica E. Vascellaro & Owen Fletcher, 'Apple Navigates China Maze,' *The Wall Street Journal*, January 14-15, 2012, p. B1.

15. Charles Duhigg & David Barboza, 'In China, Human Costs Are Built Into an iPad,' *The New York Times*, January 26, 2012, p. A1, B10-B11.

16. Bushra Tobah, 'Just Do It: How Nike Turned Disclosure Into An Opportunity, *Network for Business Sustainability*, January 23, 2012, http://nbs.net/knowledge/just-do-it-how-nike-turned-disclosure-into-an-opportunity/

17. http://9to5mac.com/2012/01/26/tim-cook-responds-to-claims-of-factory-worker-mistreatment-we-care-about-every-worker-in-our-supply-chain/

18. http://www.nytimes.com/2012/02/20/technology/pressures-drive-change-at-chinas-electronics-giant-foxconn.html

19. 'Shoots, green and leaves,' *The Economist*, June 16, 2012, p. 68.

20. 'The emerging-world consumer is king,' *The Economist*, January 5, 2013, p. 53.

21. 'Shoots, green and leaves,' *The Economist*, June 16, 2012, p. 68.
22. George Will, 'The Fourth Great Awakening,' *The Bryan Times*, June 1, 2000, p. 4.
23. For more detailed discussion of issues related to the environment, see the 'Sustainability' Issue in Chapter 8.
24. Joel E. Cohen, '7 Billion,' *The New York Times*, October 24, 2011, p. A19.
25. Juliette Jowit, 'Paul Ehrlich: A Prophet of Global Population Doom who is Gloomier than Ever,' *The Guardian*, October 23, 2011, http://www.guardian.co.uk/environment/2011/oct/23/paul-ehrlich-global-collapse-warning
26. 'The joy of crowds,' *The Economist*, July 28, 2012, p. 73.
27. 'Shoots, green and leaves,' *The Economist*, June 16, 2012, p. 68.
28. http://www.sternreview.org.uk/ or http://www.occ.gov.uk/activities/stern.htm
29. http://www.climatecrisis.net/
30. Gore followed up the movie with a manifesto for 'sustainable capitalism' (Al Gore & David Blood, 'Toward Sustainable Capitalism,' *The Wall Street Journal*, June 24, 2010, p. A21) and continues to work and campaign for policy change in the field of sustainability (Carol D. Leonnig, 'In Al Gore's passion, two shades of green,' *The Washington Post* in *The Daily Yomiuri*, October 14, 2012, p. 6).
31. This video is also available at: http://www.youtube.com/watch?v=zORv8wwiadQ
32. For more videos on different aspects of our economic model from the same authors, see: http://www.storyofstuff.com/
33. See the following two articles for interesting discussions about the central role of continuous growth in our economic models: Andrew Marr, 'Charles: right or wrong about science?' *The Observer*, May 21, 2000, http://www.guardian.co.uk/theobserver/2000/may/21/focus.news and Steven Stoll, 'Fear of fallowing: *The specter of a no-growth world*,' *Harper's Magazine*, March, 2008, pp. 88-94.
34. http://ge.ecomagination.com/
35. http://www.unilever.com/sustainable-living/
36. http://www.toyota.com/prius-hybrid/
37. Jennifer Schwab, 'Slipping Green Through the Back Door,' *Sierra Club*, August 21, 2012, http://www.sierraclubgreenhome.com/uncategorized/slipping-sustainability-through-the-back-door/
38. Lee Scott, 'Wal-Mart: Twenty First Century Leadership,' October 24, 2005, http://walmartwatch.com/img/documents/21st_Century_Leadership.pdf
39. http://www.levistrauss.com/sustainability/product/cottonraw-materials
40. http://www.starbucks.com/responsibility/sourcing/coffee
41. http://www.nikeresponsibility.com/infographics/materials/index.html
42. http://www6.homedepot.com/ecooptions/stage/index.html
43. Jennifer Schwab, 'Slipping Green Through the Back Door,' *Sierra Club*, August 21, 2012, http://www.sierraclubgreenhome.com/uncategorized/slipping-sustainability-through-the-back-door/
44. Joanna Blythman, 'Food miles: The true cost of putting imported food on your plate,' *The Independent*, May 31, 2007, http://www.independent.co.uk/environment/green-living/food-miles-the-true-cost-of-putting-imported-food-on-your-plate-451139.html

45. http://www.walkerscarbonfootprint.co.uk/

46. See: http://www.recycle.co.uk/ or http://www.recycle-more.co.uk/

47. 'Tesco Gets Rid of Garbage: Zero Waste Goes to Landfill in UK,' *Reuters*, August 11, 2009, http://www.reuters.com/article/gwmBuildings/idUS302721664320090811

48. Adapted from Toby Webb, 'Global Drivers and Trends in Sustainable Business,' *The Smarter Business Blog*, September 24, 2012, http://tobywebb.blogspot.jp/2012/09/gobal-drivers-and-trends-in-sustainable.html

49. While, in 1999, 19 of the top 25 S&P 500 corporations in terms of market capitalization were U.S. firms, by 2009, this number had dropped to 14. Most notably, four corporations from China had entered the top 25 firms, as well as one firm from Brazil. See: 'New Sectors and Regions Dominate the World's Top 25 Companies,' *The Wall Street Journal*, December 20, 2009, p. R4.

50. 'How the BRICs were baked,' *The Economist*, December 10, 2011, p. 86.

51. South Africa is not the only African country with significant growth potential. Already, throughout the African continent, there are over 500 African companies with $100 million in annual revenues, while about 150 companies have $1 billion in annual revenues.

52. Peter Whybrow is the Director of the Semel Institute of Neuroscience and Human Behavior at the University of California at Los Angeles.

53. Summarized by Irene Lacher, 'In New Book, Professor Sees a "Mania" in U.S. for Possessions and Status,' *The New York Times,* March 12, 2005, p. A21.

54. For more information about Adam Smith, as well as examples of his work (in particular, *The Theory of Moral Sentiments*), see: http://www.adamsmith.org/adam-smith/

55. Alan Murray, 'The End of Management,' *The Wall Street Journal*, August 21-22, 2010, p. W3.

56. See the review of the book, 'All Business is Local' by John Quelch & Katherine Jocz, in 'Local heroes,' *The Economist*, January 14, 2012, p. 83.

57. 'Why Companies Need to be Prepared for Online Criticism,' *Ethical Corporation Magazine*, 2012, http://reports.ethicalcorp.com/reports/smcc/infographic.php

58. Margaret Ackrill & Leslie Hannah, *Barclays: The Business of Banking, 1690–1996*, Cambridge University Press, 2001.

59. 'Royal Dutch/Shell in Nigeria (A),' *Harvard Business School Press*, [9-399-126], August 10, 2006.

60. For information on the development of CSR in countries like Saudi Arabia, see: 'First study on corporate Saudi Arabia and CSR,' *CSRWire.com*, March 29, 2007, http://www.csrwire.com/press/press_release/15949

61. Ben Quinn, 'Ikea Apologises Over Removal of Women from Saudi Arabia Catalogue,' *The Guardian*, October 2, 2012, http://www.guardian.co.uk/world/2012/oct/02/ikea-apologises-removing-women-saudi-arabia-catalogue

62. 'Microsoft loses anti-trust appeal,' *BBC News*, September 17, 2007, http://news.bbc.co.uk/2/hi/business/6998272.stm

63. Debora L. Spar, 'Hitting the Wall: Nike and International Labor Practices,' *Harvard Business School Press*, [9-700-047], September 6, 2002.

64. 'GAP Hit by 'Sweatshop' Protests,' *BBC News*, November 21, 2002, http://news.bbc.co.uk/2/hi/business/2497957.stm

65. ''Killer Coke" or Innocent Abroad?' *BusinessWeek*, January 23, 2006, http://www.businessweek.com/magazine/content/06_04/b3968074.htm; Nandlal Master, Lok Samiti, & Amit Srivastava, India: Major Protest Demands Coca-Cola Shut Down Plant,' *GlobalResearch.ca*, April 8, 2008, http://www.globalresearch.ca/index.php?context=va&aid=8591

66. 'Google Censors Itself For China,' BBC News, January 25, 2006, http://news.bbc.co.uk/2/hi/technology/4645596.stm

67. Don Tapscott & David Ticoll, 'The Naked Corporation,' *The Wall Street Journal,* October 14, 2003, p. B2. Tapscott and Ticoll are coauthors of 'The Naked Corporation: How the Age of Transparency Will Revolutionize Business,' Free Press, 2003.

68. Malcolm Gladwell, 'The Tipping Point: How Little Things Can Make a Big Difference,' Little Brown, 2000, http://www.gladwell.com/. See also: Malcolm Gladwell, 'The Tipping Point,' *The New Yorker Magazine*, June 3, 1996, http://www.gladwell.com/pdf/tipping.pdf

69. Thomas L. Friedman, 'A Question from Lydia,' *The New York Times*, May 16, 2010, p. WK10.

70. Francesco Muzzi, 'The World's 50 Most Innovative Companies,' *Fast Company Magazine*, March 2013, p. 144.

71. William Gibson, 'The Road to Oceania,' *The New York Times,* June 25, 2003, p. A27.

72. Ben Schiller, 'The Environmental Impact Of Your Pointless Googling,' May 7, 2012, *Co.exist FastCompany Magazine*, http://www.fastcoexist.com/1679794/the-environmental-impact-of-your-pointless-googling

73. Ludwig Siegele, 'Welcome to the yotta world,' *The Economist: The World in 2012*, p. 124.

74. Anton Troianovski, 'Living Without a Cellphone,' *The Wall Street Journal*, September 28, 2012, p. B5.

75. Emma Duncan, 'Asia's catching up. Let's see if there's anything on the telly,' *The Times* in *The Daily Yomiuri*, January 8, 2012, p. 8.

76. 'SoftBank eyes ¥1tril. Spring deal,' *The Daily Yomiuri*, October 13, 2012, p. 1.

77. "Grameen Telecom (GTC) was established in 1995 as a not-for-profit company established by Dr. Muhammad Yunus for improving the standard of living and eradication of poverty from rural Bangladesh with the help of Grameen Bank," http://www.grameentelecom.net.bd/

78. In Africa, for example, "57% of tweets are sent from mobile phones." See: '#AfricaTweets,' *The Economist*, February 4, 2012, p. 52.

79. Bill Clinton, 'The Case for Optimism,' *Time Magazine*, October 1, 2012, http://www.time.com/time/magazine/article/0,9171,2125031,00.html

80. 'It's a hit,' *The Economist*, May 12, 2012, p. 57.

81. 'India has more mobile phones than toilets: UN report,' *The Daily Telegraph*, April 15, 2010, http://www.telegraph.co.uk/news/worldnews/asia/india/7593567/India-has-more-mobile-phones-than-toilets-UN-report.html

82. 'Schumpeter: Too much buzz,' *The Economist*, December 31, 2011, p. 50.

83. 'Can Twitter Monetize the Cultural Zeitgeist?' *Knowledge@Wharton*, October 2, 2012, http://knowledge.wharton.upenn.edu/arabic/article.cfm?articleid=2869

84. Ludwig Siegele, 'Welcome to the yotta world,' *The Economist: The World in 2012*, p. 124.

85. Warren St. John, 'Quick, After Him: Pac-Man Went Thataway,' *The New York Times,* May 9, 2004, Section 9, p. 1.

86. Rushworth M. Kidder, 'Protest 2011,' *Ethics Newsline*, December 12, 2011, http://www.globalethics.org/newsline/2011/12/12/protest-2011/

87. Michael Elliott, 'Embracing the Enemy Is Good Business,' *Time,* August 13, 2001, p. 29.

88. 'Schumpeter: Too much buzz,' *The Economist*, December 31, 2011, p. 50.

89. Elizabeth Holmes, 'Tweeting Without Fear,' *The Wall Street Journal*, December 9, 2011, p. B1.

90. Anya Kamenetz, 'iCitizen,' *FastCompany Magazine*, December 2010/January 2011, pp. 117–120 & 145.

91. 'Fun at the FactFest,' *The Economist*, November 26, 2011, p. 43.

92. 'Don't shoot,' *The Economist*, December 10, 2011, p. 34.

93. 'Schumpeter: Too much buzz,' *The Economist*, December 31, 2011, p. 50.

94. Yasmin Crowther, 'Swimming in social media's fast changing tide,' *Ethical Corporation Magazine*, August 22, 2012, http://www.ethicalcorp.com/communications-reporting/swimming-social-media%E2%80%99s-fast-changing-tide

95. 'Values for money,' *The Economist*, November 19, 2011, p. 66.

96. For examples of stakeholders creating websites to criticize the firms they particularly dislike, see: http://walmartsucksorg.blogspot.com/, http://ibmsucks.org/, or http://targetsucks.blogspot.com/

97. Anya Kamenetz, 'On the Internet, Everyone Knows You're a Dog,' *Fast Company Magazine*, December 2008/January 2009, pp. 53-55.

98. 'Schumpeter: Too much buzz,' *The Economist*, December 31, 2011, p. 50.

99. See: Toby Webb, 'Tablets and twitter will only take campaigners so far,' *Smarter Business Blog*, October 10, 2011, http://tobywebb.blogspot.jp/2011/10/tablets-and-twitter-will-only-take.html and Peter Knight, 'Letter from America: Is social media just old news rehashed?' *Ethical Corporation Magazine*, September 1, 2011, http://www.ethicalcorp.com/communications-reporting/letter-america-social-media-just-old-news-rehashed

100. 'Our Values & Campaigns,' http://www.thebodyshop.com/_en/_ww/values-campaigns/index.aspx

101. http://www.benettongroup.com/en/whatwesay/campaigns.htm

102. http://www.benjerry.com/activism/mission-statement/

103. James Austin & James Quinn, 'Ben & Jerry's: Preserving Mission and Brand within Unilever,' *Harvard Business School Press*, [9-306-037], January 18, 2007.

104. William B. Werther & David Chandler, 'Strategic Corporate Social Responsibility as Global Brand Insurance,' *Business Horizons*, Vol. 48, Issue 4, July 2005: 317–324.

105. http://www.merck.com/corporate-responsibility/access/access-developing-emerging/mectizan-donation-riverblindness/

106. Arlene Weintraub, 'Will Pfizer's Giveaway Drugs Polish Its Public Image?' *BusinessWeek*, August 3, 2009, p. 13.

107. http://www.merck.com/newsroom/vioxx/

108. Although J&J's response to the Tylenol crisis remains a best-practice model for crisis management, there is evidence to suggest that the firm has strayed from its core principles in recent years. See: 'Patients versus Profits at Johnson & Johnson: Has the Company Lost its Way?' *Knowledge@Wharton*, February 15, 2012, http://knowledge.wharton.upenn.edu/article.cfm?articleid=2943 and Alex Nussbaum, David Voreacos & Greg Farrell, 'Johnson & Johnson's Quality Catastrophe,' *Bloomberg Businessweek*, March 31, 2011, http://www.businessweek.com/magazine/content/11_15/b4223064555570.htm

109. Mallen Baker, 'Companies in Crisis: What to Do When It All Goes Wrong,' CSR Case Studies in Crisis Management: Johnson & Johnson, http://www.mallenbaker.net/csr/CSRfiles/crisis02.html

110. Coca-Cola's brand is consistently ranked number 1 in value in *BusinessWeek's* annual brand survey. In 2008, the brand was estimated to be worth $66.667 billion and was ranked number 1 for the eight straight year, http://images.businessweek.com/ss/08/09/0918_best_brands/2.htm; Burt Helm, 'Best Global Brands,' *BusinessWeek,* September 18, 2008, http://www.businessweek.com/magazine/content/08_39/b4101052097769 .htm

111. "A survey carried out by the UK's Royal Society found that in 2005 ExxonMobil distributed $2.9m to 39 groups that the society said "misrepresented the science of climate change by outright denial of the evidence."' In: David Adam, 'Exxon to Cut Funding to Climate Change Denial Groups,' *The Guardian*, May 28, 2008, http://www.guardian.co.uk/environment/2008/may/28/climatechange.fossilfuels

112. Mallen Baker, 'Companies in the News: BP,' October, 2007, http://www.mallenbaker.net/csr/CSRfiles/bp.html

113. Eduardo Porter, 'When Public Outperforms Private In Services,' *The New York Times*, January 16, 2013, p. B1.

114. Cathryn Creno, 'Wal-Mart's Sustainability Efforts Draw Praise,' *The Arizona Republic*, May 26, 2008, http://www.azcentral.com/business/articles/2008/05/26/20080526biz-greenretailers0526-ON.html

115. 'Harris Poll: Young Adults Willing to Pay Extra for Green Products,' *Green Retail Decisions*, May 31, 2012, http://www.greenretaildecisions.com/news/2012/05/31/harris-poll-young-adults-willing-to-pay-extra-for-green-products

116. 'Only 22 percent of consumers willing to pay more for green,' *The Independent*, September 2, 2011, http://www.independent.co.uk/environment/only-22-percent-of-consumers-willing-to-pay-more-for-green-2348201.html

117. Gregory Unruh, 'No, Consumers Will Not Pay More for Green,' *Forbes Magazine*, July 28, 2011, http://www.forbes.com/sites/csr/2011/07/28/no-consumers-will-not-pay-more-for-green/

118. David Grayson & Adrian Hodges, *Corporate Social Opportunity!*, Greenleaf Publications, 2004.

119. Karen K. Nathan, 'Behind the Label: The case for eco-disclosure,' *Barron's*, August 3, 2009, p. 32. Review of the book by Daniel Goleman, *Ecological Intelligence: How Knowing the Hidden Impacts of What We Buy Can Change Everything*, Broadway Business, 2009.

120. Alina Tugend, 'Too Many Choices: A Problem That Can Paralyze,' *The New York Times*, February 27, 2010, p. B5.

121. For ideas about the determinants of greenwashing, see: Magali A. Delmas & Vanessa Cuerel Burbano, 'The Drivers of Greenwashing,' *California Management Review*, Fall 2011, Vol. 54, No.1, pp. 64-87.

122. For another definition of *greenwashing* and related information, see: http://www.triplepundit.com/topic/greenwashing/

123. *Terrachoice*, http://sinsofgreenwashing.org/

124. http://sinsofgreenwashing.org/findings/greenwashing-report-2010/index.html

125. 'The Sins of Greenwashing,' *Terrachoice*, 2010, p. 10, http://sinsofgreenwashing.org/index35c6.pdf

126. Dan Mitchell, 'Being Skeptical of Green,' *The New York Times*, November 24, 2007, p. 5.

127. Sarah Nassauer, 'To Scream Green, Dyeing Paper a Light Brown,' *The Wall Street Journal*, January 25, 2012, p. D3.

128. Nick Bunkley, 'Payoff for Efficient Cars Takes Years,' *The New York Times*, April 5, 2012, p. B1.

129. Daniel Nelson, 'Greenwashing the Olympics,' *CorpWatch*, July 4, 2012, http://www.corpwatch.org/article.php?id=15748

130. Joe Nocera, 'The Paradoxes of Businesses as Do-Gooders,' *New York Times*, November 11, 2006, p. B1.

131. Alex William, 'That Buzz In Your Ear May Be Green Noise,' *The New York Times*, June 15, 2008, http://www.nytimes.com/2008/06/15/fashion/15green.html

132. Mallen Baker, 'Marketing and marketers: Use the dark arts for good,' *Ethical Corporation Magazine*, December 11, 2011, http://www.ethicalcorp.com/communications-reporting/marketing-and-marketers-use-dark-arts-good

133. Mallen Baker, 'For emerging trends in corporate social responsibility,' *Business Respect – CSR Dispatches*, No. 185, October 8, 2012, http://www.businessrespect.net/page.php?Story_ID=2747

134. William B. Werther & David Chandler, 'Strategic Corporate Social Responsibility as Global Brand Insurance,' *Business Horizons*, Vol. 48, Issue 4, July 2005: 317–324.

135. Paul J. Lim, 'Gauging That Other Company Asset: Its Reputation,' *The New York Times,* April 10, 2004, p. A18.

136. David Grayson & Adrian Hodges, *Corporate Social Opportunity!*, Greenleaf Publications, 2004.

Chapter 5

IMPLEMENTING CSR

The first four chapters of this book set out the case for CSR within the global economy, detailed the stakeholder model that is central to strategic CSR, addressed the issue of who has responsibility for CSR, and analyzed the importance of building a firm's strategy using a CSR Filter. This final chapter of Part I provides insights as to what a firm must do to integrate strategic CSR into its culture, strategy, and everyday operations. That is, *when* and *how* does a company become more socially responsible? When should a company begin to adopt CSR as a driver of its business, for example? Is there a standard point of organizational evolution at which this should occur, or does it differ from company-to-company and among industries? How should management construct CSR policies that can then trickle down throughout the firm? How will stakeholders distinguish between a genuine CSR strategy and a cynical attempt to create positive public relations or, worse, misleading *greenwash*?

We address the *when* by focusing on the *CSR Threshold*, a tipping point that triggers firms to move toward strategic CSR. Then, we turn to the *how* by outlining the design, timing, and implementation of strategic CSR, introducing the necessary corporate infrastructure and key policy ideas in the form of a comprehensive plan of action for a firm seeking to implement CSR throughout operations. Finally, we provide an outline of what the ideal result—a values-based business operating within a framework of *conscious capitalism*—might look like.

THE CSR THRESHOLD

The decision of *when* to implement a CSR policy is compounded by *why, where*, and *how* it should be implemented, not to mention *who* should oversee the process. The industry context complicates things further because of the varied stages of acceptance of CSR by different competitors. Another level of complexity, differences among countries and cultures, ensures different firms will approach CSR in vastly different ways. Although the value of CSR within specific industries and firms is becoming increasingly accepted, the point at which such a policy becomes ripe for implementation (or unavoidable to those unconvinced of the benefits) varies. Thus, *when* depends on many factors that include the CEO's attitude toward CSR, the firm's industry and actions of competitors, and the cultural environment in which the firm is operating.

Companies can pursue an effective CSR policy of either offense ("corporate social opportunity")[1] or defense (CSR as "brand insurance").[2] The innovative, proactive CEO who is convinced of the intrinsic value of CSR sees it as an opportunity to maximize core competencies and identify new competitive advantages. Examples abound: From Nike's FlyKnit Racer, an athletic shoe with an upper made from a single thread that reduces weight and waste,[3] to the wide range of products licensed under Bono's Product (RED) brand,[4] to Anheuser-Busch's efficient recycling policies,[5] firms seeking CSR can find lots of innovative ideas with which to work and plenty of profit-oriented reasons to put them into practice. Companies with a progressive and innovative mind-set see benefits that range from being an attractive employer (helping retention and recruitment), to greater acceptance among government agencies (such as needed zoning and tax relief), to better relations with social activists (such as Greenpeace). Timberland, for example, believes that its "Path of Service" program, which grants "full-time staff an annual benefit of (up to) 40 paid hours and part-time staff an annual benefit of (up to) 20 paid hours for community service,"[6] raises morale and increases retention, therefore lowering training costs while inducing new skills and stoking corporate pride.[7] In short, an effective CSR program improves a firm's relations with both its external and internal stakeholders.

In terms of defense, CSR still has value by avoiding criticism and other attacks on the firm or its products. In this instance, CSR is a rational choice that acts like a brand insurance policy, minimizing or offsetting stakeholder disillusionment in response to perceived lapses in CSR.[8] A good example of this approach is the USCAP (United States Climate Action Partnership, http://www.us-cap.org/), formed by a group of energy and manufacturing firms, which "supports the introduction of carbon limits and trading" as a means of mitigating federal legislation designed to control carbon emissions.[9]

Either approach (offense or defense) assumes an up-front investment in creating CSR policies; *when* to introduce CSR into the strategic process, however, depends on the driving force behind its implementation. For those managers convinced of CSR's strategic potential, there is no time like the present. Innovative ideas and policies that maximize market opportunities, minimize costs, and increase productivity can produce immediate benefits. For managers yet to be persuaded by the CSR argument, however, the temptation exists to delay as long as possible. Worse, cynical managers might see CSR as merely a public relations exercise or, worse still, postpone hard CSR choices by assuming they can avoid the expense altogether. Perhaps this is analogous to someone who imagines that, as long as they remain healthy, they will be able to avoid outlays for health insurance.

Nevertheless, a crisis point can arise. Once reached and stakeholder backlash becomes sufficient to warrant the introduction of a reactionary CSR policy, however, it may be too late. As mentioned in Chapter 3, Walmart announced in 2011 that it would create "new programs aimed at helping women-owned businesses and women workers."[10] Though commendable, this announcement was made within three months of the U.S. Supreme Court's decision on the decade-long class-action lawsuit filed against Walmart claiming sex discrimination employment policies. As such, the announcement, which amounted to commitments totaling only "a small percentage of Wal-Mart's overall budget," served primarily as a reminder of the alleged discrimination and not the good that such policies might do to support female business owners.[11]

Complicating matters further, this threshold of when to act ebbs and flows with public perception and media spin, which can change with the next news cycle. Even more confounding is the variability that exists among industries, cultures, and nations, as well as among companies within the same industry.

In summary, firms introduce CSR for different reasons. Implementing CSR proactively throughout the firm can generate multiple business advantages and may yield additional benefits associated with first-mover status. In addition, the genuine implementation of CSR, whether for offensive or defensive reasons, generates insurance-like benefits that render CSR lapses less damaging if committed due to factors outside the firm's control. Whatever the motivation, there is a *CSR Threshold* in every industry that acts as a point of no return. The sooner CSR is introduced, the less likely a firm is to cross this "tipping point,"[12] which varies for each company (depending on whether it is the market leader or a smaller player) and within each industry (some industries are more susceptible to stakeholder backlash than others). The variable nature of this threshold suggests why some companies perceive CSR to be of greater importance to their firm at different points in time. Still, why is it that different firms and industries have different CSR Thresholds? An important part of the answer lies in the company's business level strategy.

Variation Among Companies

Analyzing a company's business level strategy reveals how it distinguishes its products in the marketplace. Its value proposition is captured in its strategy and attracts stakeholder groups, particularly customers. In turn, the firm's strategy has a direct impact on the CSR Threshold for that company within its industry.

Figure 5.1 The Business Level CSR Threshold

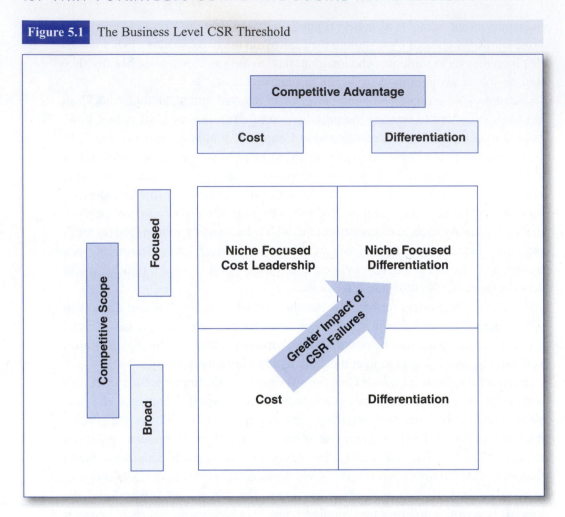

Consider these comparisons in light of Figure 5.1. Walmart's strategy probably raises its CSR Threshold; that is, the firm has more CSR leeway and can "get away with" more because its value proposition is based on a business level strategy of low cost. A Walmart shopper, for example, is unlikely to be surprised to discover that the company favors products manufactured overseas in low cost environments, rather than higher cost products made by U.S. employees. For a company like The Body Shop, however, which has built its reputation and customer base largely on the social justice issues it advocates (such as no animal testing and fair trade), the CSR Threshold at which customers, media, and society react may have a much lower tipping point. Thus, The Body Shop's stakeholders are more likely to have a lower threshold of tolerance for perceived CSR violations. Restated, a Body Shop customer would expect the company to live up to the values that attracted them to shop at the store in the first place, which translates into a lower

CSR Threshold for the firm. One CSR error by The Body Shop, for example, may well be equal, in terms of stakeholder perception, to multiple CSR oversights by Walmart.

As suggested by Figure 5.1, business level strategies can be divided into those that pursue low costs and those that pursue differentiation. The low cost approach suggests an ability to deliver products or services at a price below that of competitors. The products that Walmart sells, for example, are not fundamentally different from those of its competitors. Instead, the firm gains its competitive advantage from its "everyday low prices," which enable its customers to "Save money. Live better." Walmart is able to generate its low prices because of a laser-like focus on minimizing costs throughout the value chain. Differentiation strategies, in contrast, offer the customer something unique, such as a luxury car from Rolls Royce, for which there is an associated price premium.

These low-cost and differentiation strategies can be further categorized as either broad (targeting a large market segment, such as the automobile market) or narrowly focused (e.g., targeting only consumers seeking to purchase luxury cars). As a result, Walmart has a scope of business that can be labeled *broad,* while Rolls Royce's products are *focused*. Overall, therefore, Rolls Royce's business strategy offers a *differentiated* product, focused on the *niche* market of luxury cars, whereas Walmart's strategy pursues *cost leadership* (low costs) across a *broad* base of customers.[13] An alternative strategy is pursued by a firm like McDonald's, which seeks a focused strategy of low cost (cheap food) *and* differentiation (fast, convenient service).[14]

Whether a company pursues a cost- or differentiation-based strategy shapes the firm's CSR Threshold—the point at which CSR becomes a necessary component of strategic success. The most vulnerable strategy will be focused differentiation, particularly for those products dependent on lifestyle segmentation—products that are targeted at specific customers based on aspirational values. Nike, for example, makes a determined effort to associate its products (athletic apparel and shoes) with people who have a positive, outgoing, and physically active lifestyle. If, however, Nike is seen as socially irresponsible by its target customers, they are less likely to want to associate their identity with these products. Market segments, or niches, such as lifestyle brands, are especially valuable to a company because they often rest more heavily on subjective impressions tied up within shifting social trends, rather than objective price and quality comparisons. Such customers are often willing to pay a greater premium for the product. Yet, paradoxically, those able to pay this premium are precisely those with the widest range of alternatives, backed by the resources to make different choices. The subjective base on which lifestyle brand allegiance lies, therefore, also presents a danger to these firms. A CSR-related transgression that might inflict limited harm on a firm relying on a broad, cost-based strategy, could prove significantly damaging to one reliant on a strategy of focused differentiation. The petroleum industry, where consumers draw less distinction between similar gasoline from different companies, offers a good example. The nature of this industry allows ExxonMobil to adopt a lower CSR profile than Shell without penalty.[15] This implies a higher CSR Threshold for ExxonMobil because it has both lower visibility among environmentalists and it is difficult to differentiate its products (in terms of technical quality and performance) from those of Shell.

As different companies move across the chart in Figure 5.1 (in the direction of the shaded arrow) from cost- to differentiation-based strategies, the CSR Threshold that they face is likely to fall. That is, a business level strategy of differentiation is likely to make those firms more susceptible to stakeholder backlash. This increases the importance of an effective and well-implemented CSR policy within the firm. A similar tendency is visible when analyzing the industries within which these firms operate.

Variation Among Industries

Different industries also evoke different stakeholder emotions. Although there are likely to be differences within the apparel industry, for example, between a firm that sells unbranded clothing based on low costs (a higher threshold) and a firm using a focused differentiation strategy that offers a "lifestyle brand" (a lower threshold), the industry as a whole (with its reputation for sweatshop labor in developing countries) may have a lower threshold than industries where the connection between product, brand, and customer aspirations is weaker.

In the financial or banking industry (with its strategy of broad differentiation), for example, the CSR Threshold is relatively higher than for apparel. Here, it is generally harder for consumers to identify a victim or accurately quantify the degree of harm caused by any CSR violation. While firms benefit from striving to meet the needs and demands of their stakeholders, in general, and their customers, in particular, this relationship is more easily open to abuse for those firms that profit by selling products that their consumers do not fully understand. In the case of the financial and banking industries, "the logic of the industry rewards complexity."[16] And, even when they perceive a bank to be acting in a way they do not support, consumers are sometimes relatively powerlessness to act. When the First National Bank of Chicago decided to charge all customers $3 for every transaction they conducted that was not online, for example, there was significant stakeholder backlash. The result?

. . . the bank lost a percentage of its customers, but its profits went up by 28 percent. Why? There was indeed a big move to cheaper electronic transactions, and the customers they lost were generally the unprofitable ones they were only to happy to gift to their competitors. So what about the right of those customers to get a decent service? What about the social role that banking provides and their public duty?[17]

This perception is changing, however, due to the recent Financial Crisis, which resulted in generous government-backed bailout payments for financial firms. In spite of these publicly-financed payments, these firms retained excessive compensation levels for a sizeable proportion of employees. In spite of the traditionally lower threshold than for other industries, therefore, the Financial Crisis (and the public reaction to the financial industry's behavior throughout) suggests that this industry has moved significantly closer to its CSR Threshold.

The issues that determine the CSR Threshold for an industry are more complicated than those for individual companies, with specific industries being more vulnerable than others. Indeed, a number of industries have already passed through their CSR Threshold, causing companies that operate within those industries to take significant corrective action. One example is the fast-food industry and its relatively recent conversion to the benefits of health foods.[18] Another example, the tobacco industry, passed through its CSR Threshold long ago. To see Philip Morris on its website warning against the dangers of smoking, the health consequences of consuming their products, and recommending tips on how to give up smoking,[19] is to know that the industry has long since passed the point of no return in terms of its CSR Threshold.

Variation Among Cultures

CSR Thresholds driven by different cultural expectations further complicate firms' operating environment. Even among developed economies, there are stark differences. For example, it was legal action in the United States that determined the CSR Thresholds for the tobacco, fast-food, and asbestos industries. In Europe, instead of litigation-driven activism, NGO and nonprofit activism has largely driven the CSR agenda. Again, examples abound and include Greenpeace's campaigns against Shell's operations in Nigeria,[20] Friends of the Earth's campaigns against Monsanto and genetically modified foods,[21] and Oxfam's work (both with and against) Starbucks and its fair trade coffee program.[22]

In much of the developing world, however, the perception of CSR has traditionally revolved around issues of corporate philanthropy, an issue that consumes only a fraction of the CSR debate in developed economies.[23] This is changing, however, as the late C.K. Prahalad's work on the value of bottom-of-the-pyramid consumers[24] and Muhammad Yunus' work with Grameen Bank (for which he and the bank were jointly awarded the Nobel Prize for Peace in 2006) have transformed perceptions of developing economies among multi-national firms, as well as transformed perceptions of CSR within the developing economies.[25] In addition to CSR evolving in different ways in each area, it also developed at different speeds, with Europe adopting CSR before most other regions, followed by North America, and with developing countries adopting CSR later, although there has been a great deal of activity in recent years.

The 2011 *Newsweek* Green Rankings, which set out to evaluate "the key sustainability drivers for companies in each of these regions"[26] begins to demonstrate this phenomenon empirically: "Is the same value assigned to being 'green' in Europe, North America, and Asia-Pacific?" The article compares the performance of European, U.S., and Asian companies along the rankings' different metrics, with a clear pattern emerging:

> First and foremost is the issue of disclosure, where Europe takes the clear lead. Of the top 100 global disclosure scores featured in the 2011 Green Rankings, Europe accounts for 65% (though it only represents one-third of the companies ranked), compared to 19% for North America and 10% for Asia-Pacific. . . . European companies, most notably Northern European companies, have also taken the lead in environmental management, though the regional discrepancy is much narrower in this category.

Where the U.S. has taken the lead, in terms of "environmental impact," the report argues that the driver is the greater propensity to environmental crises, which likely prompt litigation, forcing U.S. firms to take more drastic action in response:

> 45 percent of the significant environmental controversy assessments assigned to the global 500 list implicated U.S. companies alone, which represent less than one-third of the global list. The silver lining there is that some of the most innovative environmental initiatives to date have been launched in reaction to controversies, paving the way for long-term strategic approaches to sustainability that would outlive tarnished reputations.

This difference in approach to environmental issues is most likely due to a matter of resource dependency. The U.S. is self-sufficient in natural resources in a way that Europe is not. Since the U.S. has more resources, it has less need to preserve them (from an economic, not environmental, perspective). Given the ingrained way of life that has not generally included resource preservation, the U.S. is finding it more difficult to adapt to the consolidating global view that resources are not unlimited and, therefore, need to be preserved.

Although these historical differences among cultures are real and have consequences for firms, globalization and the free flow of information help drive down CSR Thresholds across the board (reducing stakeholder tolerance and increasing the chance of backlash). As the news media and blogosphere continue to expose corporate CSR transgressions and people are better able to compare conditions across cultures, societal tolerance for irresponsible behavior is lowered.

This greater availability of information helps forge a more recognizable link between stakeholders and a specific company or product. Furthermore, as levels of affluence and living standards rise generally, and it becomes apparent that problems like climate change are transnational, the CSR Threshold is likely to become lower still as issues of societal necessity evolve into greater social choice and demands for change. Reporting on relative levels of corruption among countries, for example, highlights environments where CSR transgressions are more likely and suggests areas where even greater controls are needed. Transparency International's annual Corruption Perceptions Index,[27] which was first published in 1995 and "ranks countries and territories according to their perceived levels of public sector corruption,"[28] is the best guide to how different countries perform in terms of this issue:

> The 2011 Corruption Perceptions Index shows that public frustration is well founded. No region or country in the world is immune to the damages of corruption, the vast majority of the 183 countries and territories assessed score below five on a scale of 0 (highly corrupt) to 10 (very clean.) New Zealand, Denmark and Finland top the list, while North Korea and Somalia are at the bottom.[29]

The combination of globalization, rising living standards, and media applications of first-world standards to developing-world operations suggests that an effective CSR policy is increasingly necessary for all firms and will grow in importance as these trends continue into the future. The *CSR Threshold* model presented here argues that the different points at which CSR jumps onto the radar screens of leaders in different industries and cultures, and between different companies, varies based on a host of strategic and stakeholder factors. Best practice in response to the uncertainty suggests a proactive CSR policy that provides economic benefit to the firm, as well as a means of avoiding, or at least minimizing, negative publicity and societal backlash.

CSR: INTEGRAL TO THE FIRM

A research sample of 515 firms studied by Boston College's Center for Corporate Citizenship emphasizes the value of CSR to small, medium, and large corporations:

> Like financial controls and human resource management, corporate citizenship is integral to keeping a business healthy. Most accept the notion that businesses have responsibilities that go beyond the traditional making money, providing jobs, and paying taxes. Most respondents report that their commitment is rooted in tradition and values; eight of ten say corporate citizenship helps the bottom line; and more than half indicate it is important to their customers. The attitude about and commitment to corporate citizenship by small- and medium-sized business leaders are just as strong as they are in the largest corporations.[30]

The study also found that good corporate citizenship was driven by a variety of internal and external forces. Traditions and values, reputation or image, and business strategy were internal forces, with consumers forming the most significant external pressures and cited by more than 50% of the respondents. Lack of resources and a lack of executive commitment, however, were perceived to be the greatest barriers to good corporate citizenship. Encouragingly, only 9% of respondents reported seeing no benefit to the firm for good corporate citizenship.[31]

These findings are supported by anecdotal evidence from a variety of top firms. Companies such as Nike,[32] Starbucks,[33] Microsoft,[34] Timberland,[35] and others have grouped CSR related activities into CSR, Corporate Responsibility, Sustainability, or Ethics and Compliance departments. Those that are most successful are led by senior executives in the firm, such as Nike's Vice President, Sustainable Business and Innovation.[36] Though not all firms have interwoven CSR into their operations to this extent, these kinds of internal organizational structures are likely to be increasingly common as CSR grows in importance. In spite of progress by individual firms, however, there is still great room for improvement. *The Economist*, in a special report on CSR, notes that in spite of the increased profile of CSR in recent years, firms are still slow to grasp the full implications of what it means for day-to-day operations:

> Since there is so much CSR about, you might think that big companies would by now be getting rather good at it. A few are, but most are struggling.[37]

As we begin to understand more about how firms react to pressures for greater CSR, we understand more about their learning stages and how they translate that learning into action. Simon Zadek, the founder and CEO of AccountAbility,[38] has made an important contribution to this effort by identifying the five stages of learning that organizations go through "when it comes to developing a sense of corporate responsibility."[39]

The Five Stages of CSR Learning

1. Defensive (to deny responsibility)
2. Compliance (to do the minimum required)
3. Managerial (to begin integrating CSR into management practices)
4. Strategic (to embed CSR within the strategy planning process)
5. Civil (to promote CSR practices industry-wide).[40]

It is relatively easy to map this list onto the *CSR Threshold* model outlined above. While an industry or culture might be approaching its threshold (the point at which CSR becomes a strategic imperative), there is still likely to be variance among firms and the attitudes to CSR of individual executives. While some firms will long ago have recognized the benefits of a CSR perspective and be safely in the strategic or civil stages of learning, there will be others that lag behind in either the defensive or compliance stages. Assuming that a firm has decided to implement CSR, therefore, how does it actually go about becoming socially responsible?

IMPLEMENTATION: SHORT TO MEDIUM TERM

The urgency with which CSR policies are implemented depends on the perceived CSR Threshold and the priority the issue holds for the firm's leaders. The implementation process itself is about common sense policies that represent a means to integrate a stakeholder perspective throughout operations. The ultimate goal should be for CSR to form an integral component of the firm's culture, as reflected in day-to-day operations. The challenge is to move to a position at which all employees approach their work using a *CSR Filter* (see Figure 4.2). The following steps offer an overview of how any firm can further the integration of CSR into its operating practices and organizational culture over the short to medium term.

Executive Investment

For implementation to be successful, the CEO must actively sponsor CSR. Executive ownership of this issue is the foundation of an effective CSR policy and is central to ensuring that CSR is institutionalized as a core component of day-to-day operations. Ideally, the CEO will consider himself or herself the chief CSR officer.[41] At a minimum, the CEO must remain in touch with the company's CSR performance by receiving regular updates, while granting a clear line of access to the top for the CSR officer. This commitment from senior management is crucial for effective implementation. Executives must exhibit leadership to infuse a stakeholder perspective. Otherwise, any CSR policy or statement will quickly become a hollow gesture. A perfect example is Enron—a firm that went bankrupt because of fraudulent financial practices on a massive scale. Consider the firm's "award-winning" *Code of Ethics*:[42]

Look at this list of corporate values: Communication. Respect. Integrity. Excellence. They sound good don't they? Strong, concise, meaningful. Maybe they even resemble your own company's values, the ones you spent so much time writing, debating, and revising. If so, you should be nervous. These are the corporate values of Enron, as stated in the company's 2000 annual report. And as events have shown, they're not meaningful; they're meaningless.[43]

Ethics at Enron

As officers and employees of Enron Corp., its subsidiaries, and its affiliated companies . . . we are responsible for conducting the business affairs of the Company in accordance with all applicable laws and in a moral and honest manner.[44]

Enron stands on the foundation of its Vision and Values. Every employee is educated about the Company's Vision and Values and is expected to conduct business with other employees, partners, contractors, suppliers, vendors and customers keeping in mind respect, integrity, communication and excellence. Everything we do evolves from Enron's Vision and Values statements.[45]

Employees of Enron Corp., its subsidiaries, and its affiliated companies (collectively the "Company") are charged with conducting their business affairs in accordance with the highest ethical standards. An employee shall not conduct himself or herself in a manner that directly or indirectly would be detrimental to the best interests of the Company or in a manner that would bring to the employee financial gain separately derived as a direct consequence of his or her employment with the Company. Moral as well as legal obligations will be fulfilled openly, promptly, and in a manner which will reflect pride on the Company's name.[46]

Language is important and its ability to shape behavior should not be underestimated. Clearly, however, a well-crafted position statement is not enough; neither is top-management's superficial support. Ostensibly, CSR and ethics at Enron had support: CEO Kenneth Lay signed-off on all the documents. The point is that not only must the move to inject a CSR perspective be supported by senior executives, but that commitment must be genuine and reinforced on a day-to-day basis to avoid accusations of "empty rhetoric."[47] In spite of its market leading position on CSR today, for example, early on, Nike was also reluctant to embrace CSR:

> Initially, the Nike response was a textbook example of how not to handle corporate social responsibility (CSR). In the 1997 documentary The Big One, Michael Moore raised the issue of underage workers with a clearly uncomfortable Phil Knight. "Tell it to the United Nations," was his response.[48]

Consider, however, that:

> A well-led organisation will always seek to create the optimal value in all its relationships. In a way, that is simply good leadership. The most impressive corporate leaders have always been those whose vision of a successful business stretches beyond the product and the profits to their positive impact on the world around them.[49]

CSR Newsletters: Walmart vs. Apple

An article in *The New York Times*[50] discusses Apple's supply chain difficulties and makes the argument that Tim Cook (Apple's current CEO) is more engaged on this issue than his predecessor:

> Mr. Cook's appearance at a facility where Apple devices are made was an illustration of how differently Apple's new chief relates to an issue that first surfaced under his predecessor, Steven P. Jobs. Since Mr. Cook became chief executive in August, shortly before the death of Mr. Jobs, Apple has taken a number of significant steps to address concerns about how Apple products are made.

The article evokes an emerging narrative in recent coverage of Walmart[51] that the firm is beginning to slide on its commitment to sustainability:

> In October 2005, Walmart announced plans to transform itself into one of the greenest corporations in the world. Then-CEO Lee Scott called sustainability "essential to our future success as a retailer." I visited with Lee Scott numerous times between 2005 and 2008 to discuss, evaluate and advise on Walmart's sustainability strategy. Several years after

(Continued)

(Continued)

Scott's departure as CEO, something has gone seriously wrong. . . . Michael Duke became CEO in February 2009, replacing Scott. Duke joined Walmart in 1995. I believe that, from the day Duke started, the initiatives that Lee Scott championed, but never saw come to fruition, stalled and then slowly unraveled.

The contrast between the two articles identifies the importance of the CEO in supporting a firm's commitment to CSR. In particular, the articles present a stark contrast between two firms that appear to be moving in opposite directions on CSR by demonstrating how a change from a disengaged CEO to an engaged CEO (i.e., the shift from Steve Jobs to Tim Cook at Apple) can alter a firm's CSR profile, while the reverse shift (i.e., the change from Lee Scott to Mike Duke at Walmart) can undermine a lot of good work.

Today, progressive CEOs, such as Paul Polman of Unilever, Howard Schultz of Starbucks, and Yvon Chouinard of Patagonia all understand that there is not only a legal imperative to be a "responsible corporate officer,"[52] but also an ethical, moral, rational, and economic motivation, too. Sustainable businesses are operated over long-term horizons and that, anything less will jeopardize operations:

It used to be said that the problem with business is that it only thinks two quarters ahead. That is no longer the case – companies are having to think decades ahead, to plan for resource scarcity and climate volatility and to lock in supply chain resilience.[53]

CSR Officer[54]

Top-management support must translate into tangible action. As *The Economist* notes, "It has become almost obligatory for executives to claim that CSR is 'connected to the core' of corporate strategy, or that is has become 'part of the DNA.'"[55] To be effective, however, CSR needs both visibility and sponsorship within the organization. Backing by the CEO equals sponsorship, and the creation of a *CSR Officer*[56] position, staffed by an executive with a direct reporting relationship to the CEO and/or board of directors, creates visibility. Influencing the organizational culture toward greater CSR requires time and effort. Given other demands, CEOs are forced to delegate their efforts to a CSR officer. This CSR executive needs to formulate the direction that the company will pursue in terms of CSR. Thus, the champion must have access to the highest levels of decision making to ensure a CSR perspective is part of the strategic direction of the company. Starbucks[57] and Nike[58] provide good examples of this approach:

> [Since the position was established in 1998, Nike's vice president for Sustainable Business and Innovation has] overall responsibility for managing Nike's global corporate responsibility function, including labor compliance, global community affairs, stakeholder engagement and corporate responsibility strategic planning and business integration. She will report to Nike's Brand President.[59]

The CSR officer defines, implements, and audits the firm's CSR policies across functional boundaries. This includes assisting with legal and regulatory compliance, as well as compliance with discretionary certifications, such as the ISO (International Organization for Standardization) standards, which include ISO 9000 standards for quality management and ISO 14000 standards for environmental management,[60] as well as ISO 26000 guidelines for social responsibility.[61] It will undoubtedly also include responding to the numerous requests firms receive to complete surveys tied to "the proliferation of non-financial performance metrics,"[62] such as CSR and sustainability rankings.[63] As activist organizations increasingly hold firms accountable for their operations, "managers at major U.S. employers receive literally thousands of pages of surveys each year on their social, environmental, governance, and ethics policies."[64]

Perhaps the most famous of these is *Fortune Magazine's* Most Admired Firm rankings,[65] although many others, such as the *CRO Magazine's* 100 Best Corporate Citizens,[66] the Global Reporting Initiative,[67] and indexes produced by social responsibility research firms such as KLD Research & Analytics[68] are also becoming established within the CSR field. The rankings constitute signals to external constituents about the work that the firm is doing in relation to CSR. Although the surveys are no doubt tedious and time-consuming, "all seeking information tailored to the needs of their specific ratings framework,"[69] performing well in these rankings may well be of strategic advantage to the firm.

Implementing CSR Throughout the Value Chain

In broad terms, the implementation of strategic CSR by a firm can be divided into three focal areas:

Supply chain: Pre-firm production, such as raw materials extraction, supplier manufacturing, and outsourcing.

(Continued)

(Continued)

Operations: Within-firm production, including all aspects of the internal value chain, such as transportation, logistics, and design.

Consumption: Post-firm production, such as consumption and post-consumption recycling.

In addition, a CSR officer should innovate—such as the introduction of a Stakeholder Relations Department in place of the existing Investor Relations Department or create a CSR sub-committee of the Board on which both the CEO and President sit—to ensure the organizational design reinforces the firm's CSR commitments. Most importantly, however, the position must focus on contributing to strategy formulation. The most effective way to do this is to appoint the CSR officer to a key operations committee. For example, at Nike, the VP for Sustainable Business and Innovation works with buying departments to ensure products are high quality and on-time (traditional operations metrics), but also produced in line with the firm's CSR criteria.[70] Operations is where the CSR officer can hope to make the most progress in terms of fully integrating CSR throughout all aspects of the business.

All these policies need a firm-wide perspective to ensure effective implementation and dissemination of benefits and goals. Ideally, the CSR officer must create awareness with a blend of rewards, as well as penalties for employees who act in contrary ways. Thus, the CSR position is all encompassing. In particular, the CSR officer should be part risk manager, part ethics officer, part compliance and crisis manager, part brand builder and insurer, and part beacon bearer.[71] Additionally, the CSR officer will need to develop contingency plans for unexpected CSR crises. Ideally, the long term goal for all departments is to grow a CSR perspective:

> . . . ultimately, whilst we are professionalizing corporate social responsibility, adding new impenetrable jargon and making it a place fit for experts, we are missing the real deal. This is not a specialist part of business per se, it is business as usual.[72]

In the short term, however, this effort must begin with a focal point in the form of a corporate officer whose contribution to the strategic decision-making process starts from a CSR perspective. Over time, CSR will become more integrated throughout the organization, and there is evidence to suggest that immediate managers are as important as senior executives in reinforcing CSR norms and practices throughout the organization.[73] But, initially at least, focused leadership, supported by the CEO, senior executives, and the Board, are all vital to strengthening the CSR perspective within the organizational culture.

CSR Vision

Equally important for the firm's CSR direction is a position statement. Cadbury's CSR vision statement, for example, is displayed prominently on its website and in its CSR reports:

> Cadbury Schweppes is committed to growing responsibly. We believe responsible business comes from listening and learning, and having in place a clear CSR vision and strategy. It also comes from having the processes and systems to follow through and an embedded commitment to living our values.[74]

All stakeholders (internal and external) need to understand the firm's CSR position and how that stance affects them. The value of a statement outlining the vision and mission for the organization is part of this awareness process, as detailed in Chapter 2. Ideally, CSR or sustainability will feature prominently in the firm's overall mission and vision statements, although this is still rare. Toyota, however, is a welcome exception:

> Vision: Toyota aims to achieve long-term, stable growth in harmony with the environment, the global economy, the local communities it serves, and its stakeholders.[75]

The same benefits of an effective vision statement also apply to specific aspects of a firm's policies. At a minimum, therefore, the firm should have a CSR vision statement:

The CSR Vision Statement

The development of an effective CSR position statement:

- *Engages* the organization's key stakeholders to determine their perspectives
- *Helps* map out a conflict resolution process that seeks mutually beneficial solutions
- *Involves* the CEO's necessary endorsement and active support
- *Reinforces* the importance of CSR through rewards and sanctions
- *Provides* policies on how CSR is to be implemented on a day-to-day basis

Performance Metrics

Collectively, top-management support, the creation of a senior executive CSR position, and the elaboration of the firm's CSR vision in a position statement address a critical element in implementing CSR— awareness. Although the intent of CSR may be noble, however, people tend to focus on "what is inspected not expected."

Economic Incentives

During the 18th century, when the British government was still shipping its criminals to Australia, sea captains were paid based on the number of people they carried on their ships. What the government found, however, was that many inmates were dying during the journey—up to one-third in some instances. Neither sending a Doctor onboard for the journey, nor raising the captains' pay increased the number of passengers who survived the trip. It wasn't until the government began paying captains based on the number of people who arrived in Australia (rather than the number of people who left the UK), that behavior changed and the survival rate greatly increased—to as high as 99%.[76]

Many CSR violations arise from decision makers at different levels of the organization who were sincerely trying to make good decisions, but had not been given the tools or incentives to make the *most appropriate* decision. Faced with a choice between a minor violation of company rules about pollution, for example, or meeting a key performance deadline, a decision maker at any level of the firm might make a tradeoff that results in a CSR backlash. Why? Because, in most firms, rewards (pay, promotions, and bonuses) are based on short-term economic performance, not CSR compliance. A 2008 survey of the organizational members of the Ethics & Compliance Officers Association, for example, reveals that, while 54.3% of firms included some ethics and compliance benchmarks as part of CEO performance evaluation and 58.2% did so for Managers, only 14.0% of firms did the same for Board Directors.[77] If an incentive is tied to meeting a goal and CSR is neither measured nor rewarded, reasonable people inside the firm may conclude that CSR is of secondary importance.

Nike's Subcontractors

Today, Third World subcontractors to Nike must comply with company employment standards that dictate pay, rest breaks, and other terms and working conditions. These standards are enforced by inspections. Those subcontractors who perpetuate sweatshop conditions contrary to Nike's requirements risk losing their production contracts, even if these firms are in full compliance with local human resource laws and practices.

For a long time, however, Nike's production demands contradicted the employment conditions outlined in its code of conduct for suppliers. It is ineffective to stipulate specific low cost and high production targets, if, at the same time, a firm is asking its suppliers to restrict employee overtime and pay living wages. Given such a choice, many suppliers will chose to meet Nike's production demands in order to keep their contracts with the firm. Often, this choice was made at the expense of working conditions in their factories.

Once Nike realized the counter-productive effects of this contradiction, however, the firm worked to ensure its incentive scheme for subcontractors more accurately reflected and supported its corporate responsibility goals.[78]

Rewards and measures serve a fundamental role in shaping organizational culture. The creation of CSR rewards and measures (particularly if those who apply the CSR standards are the same people who develop them), therefore, increases overall awareness and reinforces CSR as an integral part of the firm's strategy. These measures become part of the basis for auditing the firm's CSR performance.

Integrated Reporting

A genuine organization-wide CSR audit, with published results, integrated with the firm's financial documents, furthers awareness among both internal and external stakeholders about the central importance of the firm's CSR activities. Environmental audits, for example, are now widely conducted and documented in annual reports, because stakeholders began demanding greater accountability for the environmental consequences of businesses' actions. This is a legal requirement where climate change constitutes a material business risk for the firms.[79] Ideally, this integration should be extended to all non-financial measures and supported by regular firm-wide risk assessments, as is increasingly happening in both the UK and the U.S.:

Currently, 81 per cent of FTSE 100 companies [the largest 100 firms in the UK based on market capitalization] are producing stand-alone reports on corporate responsibility, sustainability, environment or similar.[80]

52 percent of Fortune 100 Companies included statements of CSR in their 2010 annual reports and 10-K.[81]

Evidence suggests this trend is growing worldwide. An "analysis of 3,400 companies across 34 countries and 15 industry sectors concluded that nearly every Global Fortune 250 (G250) company now reports its CR activity,"[82] as presented in Figure 5.2.

In general, poor countries often put economic needs ahead of non-financial controls. That is, poorer countries are more likely to permit firms to externalize environmental, safety, or other costs onto society—a tradeoff made to gain or retain jobs. The poorer a country, the more desperate it is likely to be for jobs and the more willing it may be to allow firms to avoid externalities such as pollution cleanup or worker safety. As societies develop and stakeholder choices increase, however, the willingness to accommodate undesirable behavior decreases. Although many firms recognize the importance of being held publicly accountable for the consequences of operations, this realization does not always permeate the countless tactical decisions made by employees every day. The result can be CSR transgressions—the avoidable *Exxon Valdez* accident in 1989 provides a well-known example, as individual and corporate poor judgment resulted in a shipwreck and massive oil spill in Alaska's pristine waters.[83]

Figure 5.2   CSR Reports by Firms (2008–2011)

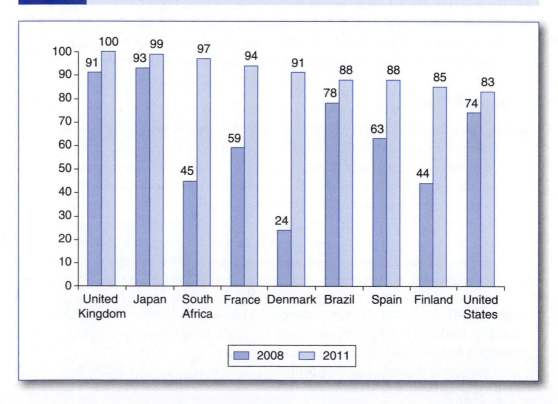

Figure 5.3 A Broader Perspective: The Triple Bottom Line

Figure 5.3 suggests the entirety of the CSR reporting process. A firm that wants to be transparent and accountable to all stakeholders should expand the scope of its annual report to incorporate the "triple bottom line,"[84] which measures a company's financial, environmental, and social performance. More and more firms are establishing this integrated reporting process. Since 1999 in the Netherlands and 2002 in France, for example, an evaluation of environmental and social risks, as related to operations, is legally mandated as part of a firm's financial reports.[85] Such reports serve two purposes: they provide measures to *internal* constituents, providing benchmarks to encourage further efficiency improvements; they also serve as a basis for communication with *external* constituents, providing feedback on prior commitments and statements on future intentions.

A good example of a company leading the way in CSR auditing and reports is Shell, which was prompted to reanalyze its business practices in 1995 following two separate NGO-orchestrated campaigns. The first campaign attacked the company's decision to sink the *Brent Spar* oil platform in the ocean; while the second campaign attacked the firm's failure to prevent the execution by the Nigerian government of an environmental activist, Ken Saro-Wiwa, who had been campaigning against Shell's operations in Nigeria. The stakeholder backlash over these two issues threatened Shell's underlying business model.[86] Following the intense international criticism Shell received for its reactions to these two high-profile events, "The company decided it needed to become a better global citizen."[87] One component of the drive to change the organizational culture and increase awareness of CSR was the *Shell Report:*

> The report has become famous for disclosing Shell's successes and failures in human rights and environmentalism, including oil spills and community protests, as well as the profits and losses of its multibillion-dollar business. . . . "I don't know any [other] oil company that produces anything as comprehensive and candid about its global social responsibility programs as the Shell Report," said Frank Vogl, co-founder of Transparency International. ". . . there is a tremendous level of sincerity behind what [the company] is trying to do."[88]

Other progressive companies are initiating product life-cycle assessments, using recent innovations to measure the carbon footprint (the total amount of carbon emitted during the life-cycle of a product, from production to consumption) for each of their products. Examples include Walkers in the UK[89] and Pepsi in the U.S.[90] The advantages for these firms are clear—in addition to understanding their value chain more completely and highlighting potential CSR transgressions before they read about them in the media, such analyses also identify waste, which carries the potential for cost savings. Such tools, "helped companies discover that vendors consume as much as 80% of the energy, water, and other resources used by a supply chain, and that they must be a priority in the drive to create sustainable operations."[91]

A final step, which is essential for validity, is to have an audit conducted, or at least verified, by an independent third party in the same way that an independent auditor verifies a company's financial reports.[92] Some form of objective verification lends credence to the information included. The sooner industry standards can be agreed upon and applied, the more meaningful CSR audits and reports will become. As one research study of NGOs concluded:

> Of the 56 NGOs surveyed . . . 79 percent find CSR reports "very" or "fairly' useful, but only 44 percent consider the reports "believable." . . . According to the survey, companies can gain credibility for their reports by disclosing poor sustainability performance, or significant challenges, or noncompliance with social or environmental laws or regulations. Other factors that boost confidence in CSR reporting include comprehensive performance metrics, third-party certification, and standardization of reporting.[93]

Organizations such as the International Integrated Reporting Committee (IIRC),[94] Ceres,[95] and the Global Reporting Initiative (GRI) are leading the effort to establish global standards for CSR and integrated reporting. With many examples of unsatisfactory reports,[96] however, agreed standards are still a long way from being realized:

> We currently have financial reporting. Well established. Clear audience. Clear set of rules. For what it captures (an incomplete picture) it captures well. And we have CSR/Sustainability reporting. Newly arrived and evolving. Multiple audiences. Vaguely expressed and debatable rules. It captures something important, but not yet well enough.[97]

Producing a CSR report is one thing; ensuring it is accurate, that it enables external observers to understand the extent of a firm's CSR activities,[98] and that firm performance is comparable across organizations,[99] represents another level of transparency altogether.

Ethics Code and Training

One way to encourage the desired CSR behavior throughout the firm is to record expectations and the boundaries of acceptable behavior in an Ethics Code and reinforce those rules and norms via regular ethics training. Both establishing the rules and then reinforcing them via training are essential to establishing a consistent culture throughout the organization:

> In 1995, [the Institute of Business ethics] estimated that six out of ten larger companies had codes of ethics (or similar). In 2010, the number is closer to 80% of the FTSE 100. . . . However, in this survey . . . only six out of ten UK companies provide training in business ethics for all their staff.[100]

Similar to a vision or mission statement for the firm, both the Ethics Code and ethics training program must by genuine and substantive in order to be meaningful. As the Enron example demonstrated, it is easy to say one thing (the *right* thing), yet do something different:

> By adopting its own code, a company can clarify for all parties, internal and external, the standards that govern its conduct and can thereby convey its commitment to responsible practice wherever it operates.[101]

In addition to an Ethics Code for their own operations, firms are also increasingly being held to account for the actions of their partners throughout the value chain. The business operations of suppliers, in particular, are a potential risk to a firm, especially when key elements of the production process are outsourced to low cost business environments. As discussed previously, Nike experienced first-hand the potential danger this presents to the brand when it ignored unacceptable working conditions in its own supply chain.[102] Other firms have also had to respond to accusations (fairly or unfairly) that they are insufficiently aware of the conditions under which their products are being made:

CSR Newsletters: Gap's Supply Chain

An article in *The New York Times*[103] reports on Gap's response to a piece of investigative journalism in October by the UK newspaper *The Observer* that uncovered evidence of under-age children making Gap clothes. The story is interesting on two levels. First, the speed and extent of Gap's response, which appears to be genuine:

> Gap said it would refine its procedures to ensure that items made in textile workshops in India were not being produced by children. It also announced a grant of $200,000 to improve working conditions. . . . the children who were found to be embroidering decorations on blouses for toddlers for Gap would be paid until they were of working age and then offered employment.

Second, the extent to which Gap could (or should) have been expected to avoid this problem. It appears that Gap's vendor had sub-contracted the embroidery work to a rural community center that had, in turn, sub-contracted the work to a smaller workshop in Delhi:

> While auditing in factories is relatively straightforward, checking conditions in the informal workshops where hand embroidery is done is harder because large contracts are often divided up among dozens of small workshops.

It is one thing for a firm to be held responsible for the business practices of an immediate supplier. It seems to be another thing altogether to expect Gap to know about a sub-contractor (a rural community center) that had again contracted out this order to a Delhi factory—three steps removed from the initial order by Gap. The extent to which a firm is responsible for the actions of its suppliers throughout its supply chain (as well as how that responsibility should be enforced) is an issue on which a consensus within the CSR community is yet to arise.

Firms rectify this lack of involvement in their supply chain by asking suppliers (and, where appropriate, distributors) to sign Codes of Conduct that adhere closely to the firm's ethics rules and norms as detailed in their internal Ethics Codes. While this is widely practiced by firms today, however, what is unclear is the extent of a firm's responsibility throughout its supply chain. Should firms be responsible for absolutely everything that occurs in their supplier firms, irrespective of how far removed that action is from any employee of the focal firm? Should Gap, for example, be held responsible for the actions of the sub-contractor of the sub-contractor of the firm's main sub-contractor in India (even though the number of these sub-sub-sub-contractors is in the tens of thousands)? What about the factories that process the cotton that is used by Gap's suppliers? What about the farmers who grow the cotton and the numerous hands through which the cotton passes before it even reaches a factory that sub-contracts to Gap?

This is an evolving area of debate within the CSR community, but is essential for the integrity of the supply chain. While it is generally agreed that a firm should be responsible for its immediate suppliers, it is less clear how far responsibility extends beyond this initial link. At present, the profile of the brand seems to be the best predictor of media exposure in the event of a supply chain *issue*, rather than the nature of the reported offense (see the *CSR Threshold*).

Ethics Helpline

A key component of the continuous internal reinforcement necessary for a CSR policy to remain effective is an anonymous feedback, complaint, or whistle-blowing procedure. This process should be available either internally or via a third party. This requirement in the U.S. was a key component of the Sarbanes-Oxley (SOX) Act of 2002.[104] In relation to business ethics, a notable component of the legislation compelled firms to establish a confidential reporting procedure (e.g., a toll-free telephone number or e-mail 'helpline') for employees to report ethical transgressions within the organization.[105] As a result, a number of independent companies have emerged offering to provide this service (often online) to firms wishing to contract it out:

> Shareholder.com[106] is typical of online services. Employees of a company that hires Shareholder.com can file their complaints with the . . . firm. The complaints then are forwarded electronically to the appropriate people back at the company—but only after all identifying information is stripped away.[107]

An independent third party performing this job guarantees the protection of employees' identities, which prevents retaliation from within the organization. This infrastructure encourages the reporting of any breeches of policy that can affect the company's stated CSR position. An ideal helpline also encourages positive feedback in the form of ideas from employees, who are often best placed to evaluate the organization's CSR policies in action.

Organizational Design

In order for all these CSR elements to coalesce into an effective CSR policy that represents stakeholder interests within the strategic decision-making process of the firm, a designed CSR framework is essential. The CSR effort must have visibility. Ideally, the day-to-day operationalization of CSR demands the direct involvement of top management, together with board commitment and oversight. Evidence among firms of the growing importance of CSR will be found when the Board of Directors puts CSR on the same level as other key corporate governance issues, such as the integrity of the firm's financial information. Further, the access of the CSR officer to the CEO, with a direct reporting relationship to the Board, suggests further operational support for CSR. In well-run, ethical, and socially responsible firms, tangible visibility for CSR within the organizational structure demonstrates the firm's genuine commitment in ways that mere memos, posters, hollow speeches, or press releases fail to do.

The danger is, of course, that while many firms will lag in terms of instituting the necessary structural support for CSR, others will establish structural positions, but then fail to provide the CSR Officer with the substantive support necessary to do their job. The Ethics and Compliance Officers Association, for example, estimates that 60% of Fortune 500 firms have adopted the Ethics and Compliance Officer (ECO) position (while 90% are estimated to have a Compliance Officer managing a firm-wide compliance program).[108] Anecdotal evidence has surfaced in the media, however, that many of these positions are considered to be "trendy" and serve mainly as "window dressing,"[109] and that, as a result, "many ECOs are set up for failure due to deficient resources, inadequate preparation, or insufficient authority."[110]

IMPLEMENTATION: MEDIUM TO LONG TERM

Beyond minimum start-up conditions for CSR, the firm must also seek to institutionalize and externalize the substance of its CSR policies. Over the medium to long term, the organization should communicate its perspective, while seeking feedback from stakeholder groups to both inform and involve them.

Stakeholder Involvement

All large, publicly held corporations have well-developed investor relations departments. They have become the norm because of the primacy shareholders have typically enjoyed as a company's main stakeholder, particularly in English-speaking economies. As a company's share price has become the key indicator of corporate and management success, keeping investors happy has become central to a CEO's ability to retain his or her job.

As part of moving CSR to the center of a company's strategic outlook, this two-way avenue of communication should be expanded to include a firm's broader set of stakeholders. One approach would be to change the focus of the investor relations department to become the *Stakeholder Relations Department*. Though the scope and skills of these two departments will vary, the expansion of the investor relations department would be a far more substantive move than merely changing the title on the door. The goal should be to develop relationships with all stakeholder interests, including employees, governments, the communities in which the firm operates, and the NGOs that seek to reform the firm's practices:[111]

> NGOs—nongovernmental organizations—have won significant influence over global companies. . . . [It is] a trend that—mostly quietly and behind the scenes—is defining our age. From companies like the coffee shop giant Starbucks (attacked for the treatment of workers on plantations and the price it pays for coffee), to Big Oil (a perennial target for environmentalists), to tuna canners (think dolphins), companies are increasingly changing their business practices when pressured by activists.[112]

As Paul Tebo, DuPont's corporate vice president for safety, health, and environment and "an advocate for social responsibility," more succinctly put it: "The closer [Dupont] can align with social values . . . the faster we will grow."[113]

Manage the Message

Strategic CSR that is genuine and substantive needs to be communicated to the firm's stakeholders. As such, a firm's PR department is an important medium through which the firm can communicate its CSR progress.[114] But, firms need to be careful as this is a sensitive area. Excessive self-promotion soon comes to be interpreted as a cynical effort of going through the CSR motions only to receive the public relations benefits and raises the specter of *greenwash*. Avoiding the impression of spin is crucial; however, it is also essential to let stakeholders know that the company values their input and interests. More importantly, firms do not want their identity defined by others via the media. The aim, therefore, is to meet stakeholder expectations by matching promises with reality. In particular, firms need to develop a strategy to deal with the rising importance of social media, which increasingly will be an important means by which stakeholders experience and evaluate the firm (see Chapter 4). As one of "The 36 Rules of Social Media," *FastCompany Magazine* reminds firms that "Your fans own your brand":[115]

> Social network websites account for over 22% of all time spent on the internet. . . . in this new age of social media and transparency, information on a brand's actions travel fast and brand managers must work harder to ensure consistency of the brand's values along their supply chain.[116]

Examples of companies that have failed to take the lead in determining their public perception are many. It is important that firms get it right. Often the perception of a company in the public mind, once created, is difficult to shift. For example, in spite of the company's recent progressive CSR work, Nike's initial failure to anticipate the reaction by its stakeholders to manufacturing offshore in low-cost environments and the failure to work closely with NGOs in this area has tagged it with an image that still prevails in many eyes. Go to Nike's corporate website[117] today, however, and it soon becomes apparent that the company has redefined the way it conducts its operations in relation to CSR and presents its corporate message to the outside world. Due to its early transgressions, however, Nike continually finds itself having to play catch-up, with some stakeholders refusing to grant the company any concessions at all.

Corporate Governance[118]

Corporate governance matters and is central to a firm's activities. It is the primary interface between the firm and its shareholders. The Board of Directors advises the CEO on strategy and the overall direction of the firm; the Board also acts in an oversight function, ensuring the owners' interests are protected. In terms of overall management of the firm "there is a premium associated with good governance."[119]

Transparency and *accountability* have become the watchwords of effective corporate governance, which has also become a vital aspect of effective CSR. Increased legal requirements reinforce this change in sentiment for all but the most narrow-sighted of corporate boards; however, equally important is the ability to move ahead of today's legal requirements and anticipate the legal expectations of tomorrow. Shareholder activism is increasing and is driving reform in this area of corporate law. Ensuring a company's policies and procedures are transparent, that its managers are accountable to external stakeholders, and that the process by which the policies are created and board members appointed is democratic, are all crucial to ensuring the traditional conflict between principal and agent is minimized.

Corporate governance will increasingly become the target of reforms prompted by insufficient attention to CSR. Following the financial and ethical scandals early in this century of Enron and others, Sarbanes-Oxley became law in 2002. In short, it places increased reporting requirements on firms, for which firms need to maintain additional records and issue additional reports. And, while it was only a few irresponsible firms that caused the scandals, the law was applied to all publicly-traded companies. More recently, the Financial Crisis revealed new scandals that resulted in the near total collapse of the world financial system. The result was the Dodd-Frank Act of 2010—increased scrutiny of corporate finance and investments, and more attention on the crucial oversight function of Boards of Directors.

These two waves of scandals in the first decade of the new century would have been less likely or less severe if CSR had been more widely practiced and Boards had more effectively integrated CSR into their operations. As such, these waves illustrate the *Iron Law of Social Responsibility* with the result of greater constraints on how corporations are governed. In future, the most effective Boards will form a CSR sub-committee on which both the CEO and President sit, introduce ethics and compliance benchmarks as part of Director (and senior executive) performance evaluation, and institute a direct reporting line from the CSR Officer to remain in touch with areas of risk throughout the firm. Such structural reforms go a long way to ensuring the organizational design reinforces the firm's CSR commitments, minimizes risk, and maximizes performance over the medium to long term.

Activism and Advocacy

Activism is an important way for a firm to establish a corporate identity that attracts stakeholders and fulfills the firm's mission and vision. Both The Body Shop and Ben & Jerry's, however, found that activism alone is insufficient to remain viable in the long run. In both cases, the founders were forced to cede operational control to professional managers as their firms grew in complexity. Activism of any sort, particularly CSR-related efforts, must support an economically viable business strategy. CSR-focused organizations benefit few if they are stuck in bankruptcy court. Economic viability and operating within society's legal parameters are minimum conditions for business survival. Activism does not preserve an operation if basic economical, legal, or other business fundamentals are missing.

That said, a sincere CSR focus throughout the firm helps further its viability over the long term by solidifying relationships with various stakeholders. Also, activism need not be confrontational, but advocating certain positions can help consolidate support for the firm. Engagement with other firms in the same industry in forming industry associations, for example, can help raise standards, while also protecting against potential threats:

> Consider the rumor that Adidas, Nike, Puma and other firms recently targeted by Greenpeace want to collaborate to create an industry-wide solution to toxic supply chain pollution. This might happen via an entity such as the Sustainable Apparel Coalition or another, similar mechanism. . . . It's an issue where the firms can't really compete, and where collaboration can deliver a solution to the perennial free-rider problem of a big player staying out of it. Greenpeace will be there to make sure they join in.[120]

Other examples include the Roundtable on Sustainable Palm Oil (RSPO) or the Fair Labor Association.[121] Corporate advocacy like this matters because, in cases like the Gap, Nike, and other 'lifestyle brands,' clear positions can help align the firm's actions with the values of customers who care. It may also serve as a potential defense, especially in more ambiguous circumstances, such as Gap's problems with the sub-sub-contractors of its primary sub-contractors in India (above). Beyond customer relations, corporate advocacy can win the support of other stakeholders—from employees, local communities, and government agencies. Such messages, however, must be consistent with the firm's mission and vision and extend from the boardroom and senior executives, via CSR professionals, throughout the organizational culture.

An overview of the different components of the implementation of CSR throughout an organization is presented in Figure 5.4.[122] Together, these different steps and policies represent a comprehensive plan of action for a firm seeking to implement a CSR perspective.

IMPLEMENTATION: EMBEDDING CSR

The primary CSR responsibility of the CEO is to support actively the integration of CSR into the organizational culture through the activities of the CSR Officer. The CSR Officer's role is to ensure congruity among the firm's CSR goals and its actions. In addition, other stakeholders can be expected to hold the firm accountable to the standards it has set for itself. Emboldened by technology, the free flow of information, and growing expectations for CSR, stakeholders will become increasingly assertive in ensuring their best interests are represented. And stakeholder activism may be the final piece of the CSR jigsaw puzzle that pushes CEOs and Boards past the CSR Threshold, ushering in a greater commitment to CSR. The real question is: Will that commitment by firms be proactive or reactive?

Figure 5.4 A Firm's CSR Plan of Implementation

Time Frame	Action	Summary
Short- to Medium Term	Executive Investment	The CEO must establish the necessary components of an effective CSR policy and ensure that CSR is institutionalized within the firm as a core component of day-to-day operating practice.
	CSR Officer	CSR needs both visibility and sponsorship within the organization. Backing by the CEO equals sponsorship, while the creation of a CSR officer position staffed by a company executive (and with a direct reporting relationship to the board of directors) creates visibility.
	CSR Vision	A CSR vision statement allows stakeholders (internal and external) to understand the firm's CSR position and how that stance affects them.
	Performance Metrics	The creation of rewards and measures that align the firm's production and corporate responsibility goals, increases awareness of CSR and its profile within the firm.
	Integrated Reporting	A genuine firm-wide audit, with published results, integrated with the firm's financial statements furthers awareness among internal and external stakeholders about the firm's CSR activities.
	Ethics Code and Training	One way to encourage CSR throughout the firm and its supply chain is to record expectations and the boundaries of acceptable behavior in an Ethics Code and ethics training for all employees, and a Code of Conduct for suppliers.
	Ethics Helpline	A key component of the continuous internal reinforcement necessary for a CSR policy to remain effective is an anonymous whistle-blowing procedure that is available to all stakeholders.
	Organizational Design	In order for all these CSR elements to coalesce into an effective CSR policy, tangible support for CSR within the organizational structure demonstrates the firm's genuine commitment.
Medium- to Long Term	Stakeholder Involvement	As part of moving CSR to the center of a company's strategic outlook, a two-way avenue of communication should be opened with the firm's broader set of stakeholders.
	Manage the Message	Strategic CSR that is genuine and substantive needs to be communicated to all stakeholders. Essential today is for a firm to establish an effective social media strategy.
	Corporate Governance	*Transparency* and *accountability* are essential for effective corporate governance, but need a committed Board of Directors with structural reforms that reinforce CSR throughout the firm.
	Activism and Advocacy	While no substitute for business fundamentals, corporate activism and advocacy helps define the firm's identity by solidifying relationships with its various stakeholders.

Strategic Planning

Though CSR involves the firm's overall direction and day-to-day activities, its implementation begins with the annual strategic planning process. This process identifies targeted goals, strategies to attain those goals, and an allocation of financial, human, and other resources in pursuit of those goals. Typically, long-range planning and goal setting begin early in the calendar (or fiscal) year of the firm. *Long range,* however, has vastly different meanings from one industry to another. For electricity utilities, for example, the planning horizon might stretch 10, 15, or more years into the future (given the complexity of estimating future electricity demand, designing, permitting, and building a base-load power plant, and connecting long distribution lines from facilities to users, with often contentious regulatory and hearing requirements coupled with a not-in-my-backyard mentality). In a consumer products firm, however, the long term might be measured in months, from idea to product introduction and obsolescence. A firm like Zara, the Spanish clothes retailer, for example, has constructed a value chain that allows it to move from design to production to display "in as little as two weeks."[123] The firm's production cycle is significantly faster than the industry average of several "months to bring new merchandise to market"[124] and has introduced the new term, "Fast Fashion."[125]

Nevertheless, the goal of long-range planning is to agree on the future objectives the firm will seek. In turn, business goals (growth rates, market share, and the like) must be translated into realizable objectives for each business unit and within these units for operating and support groups—from production to finance to human resource departments. Broad, overarching goals form the basis for specific strategies. A firm's CSR profile can play an important role in this respect. Though a CSR profile might not lead to immediate financial gains, it may be indispensable to hiring hard-to-find employees with unique skills. In fact, the ability to hire and retain key players may be necessary for survival (especially as the huge Baby Boomer generation retires and is replaced in the workplace by the Millennials or Generation Y), further justifying the allocation of time and resources toward socially responsible goals.

Long-term goals and their strategies for attainment must then be translated into more specific, short-term objectives. Ideally, short-term objectives are SMART, that is, Specific, Measurable, Attainable, Relevant, and Time-bound. Then, the resources necessary to implement these objectives are allocated. The unifying approach to resource allocation is the budget process. Usually done near the end of the fiscal or calendar year, the budget allocates resources (and, through salaries and capital budgets, people and investments) for the upcoming year.

Because this approach traditionally focuses on business investments selected on some objective basis (such as the payback period or return on investment), hard-to-measure objectives such as social responsibility may fail to register. And, because most firms seek multiple objectives, the relative importance of goals must be weighed by a correspondingly appropriate allocation of resources and rewards. CSR can fall through the cracks without an appropriate mandate from senior management or the board of directors and a dedicated CSR Officer.

The ease with which CSR can be overlooked in this planning process only serves to further emphasize the importance of adopting a methodical approach to ensuring uniform implementation throughout the firm. The integration of CSR within the strategic decision-making process and organizational culture along the lines outlined in this chapter goes a long way to ensuring CSR achieves the position of prominence that is increasingly necessary in today's global business environment.

Firm Action

At the firm level, CSR plans are meaningless unless they are translated into action. Press releases to the media, speeches to employees or trade groups, or assertions of CSR in annual reports are not the end goal. Necessary as these activities may be to raise awareness about CSR within the firm and the firm's broader stakeholder environment, CSR must be operationally integrated into day-to-day activities. For CSR to become integrated in this way requires a CSR Filter to be applied to the vision, mission, strategy, and tactics of the firm (see Figure 4.1). Granted, in a capitalist system, for-profit firms face an absolute economic imperative. Businesses do not exist merely to be nice to constituents; they exist to meet needs in society and this value is demonstrated via the profits generated by the firm. Increasingly, however, these societal needs include expectations beyond profit maximization. Ultimately, the viability of the firm— its ability to grow, increase shareholder wealth, and meet the needs of customers and other stakeholders—presupposes both an external and internal environment that is conducive to success.

With the primacy of economics, however, other components of the firm's activities can easily be relegated to a distant concern. The result may be a hostile environment that impairs the firm's performance, even its long-term viability. A CSR perspective, integrated throughout the organization, offers an alternative business approach, one that is more likely to provide the long-term stability companies require. In order to achieve this, however, executive support, a dedicated CSR Officer (at least until CSR is fully integrated into the organizational culture), a well-defined CSR position statement, CSR-focused performance metrics, an integrated report to relevant stakeholders, an ethics code and training for employees and suppliers, an ethics helpline available to internal and external stakeholders, and a structure that institutionalizes these elements are merely a beginning. Ideally, stakeholder involvement will include all affected groups to as great a degree as possible. Inclusion is more than just an attempt to co-opt relevant constituents. Whether internal or external, inclusion means giving stakeholders a voice and requires leaders that are both receptive and proactive to stakeholder concerns. Admittedly, the message must be managed, if for no other reason than to assure the firm's efforts are communicated and recognized. How else can stakeholders react and become involved in the process? With transparency and corporate advocacy added to the mix, a firm has the basic ingredients for the successful integration of a CSR perspective throughout operations.

The ultimate test, however, is the firm's actions. And for those actions to rise above mere "window dressing,"[126] CSR must form part of the firm's larger strategic plan. Here, concern must focus not only on the results, but also on the methods used. This focus must also be recalibrated to accommodate, as much as possible, the differing perspectives of the relevant stakeholders that the firm touches. Initially, both short- and long-term objectives are translated into action through the planning process. Then, plans are converted into budgets, which directly allocate financial and other resources. The way these actions are received by those most affected by them indicates the success of the process by which the socially responsible firm matches plans and intentions to actions and results.

CONSCIOUS CAPITALISM

The outcome of these plans, actions, and (hopefully) results, when extrapolated across a wide range of firms, is the *evolution*[127] of the dominant economic model. Rather than a narrow focus on short-term shareholder wealth, firms will exist to serve the needs and concerns of stakeholders, broadly defined, over the medium to long term. The result is a combination of the *Most Ethical Companies*[128] and the *Most Inspiring Companies*[129]—it is conscious capitalism:

Conscious Capitalism

"[An] emerging form of capitalism that holds the potential for enhancing corporate performance while simultaneously advancing the quality of life for billions of people."[130] Synonymous with *strategic* CSR, it is based on four principles that encourage the development of values-based businesses: Higher purpose, Stakeholder interdependence, Conscious leadership, and Conscious culture.

John Mackey, founder and co-CEO of Whole Foods Market, is the leading business proponent of conscious capitalism.[131] In his view,[132] there are four main principles that define conscious capitalism: Higher Purpose ("Why does the business exist?"), Stakeholder Interdependence ("the six major stakeholders are interdependent and the business is managed . . . to optimize value creation for all of them"), Conscious Leadership ("the quality and commitment of the leadership at all levels of the organization"), and Conscious Culture ("This naturally evolves from the enterprise's commitments to higher purpose, stakeholder interdependence, and conscious leadership").[133] As such, we see Mackey's conscious capitalism as synonymous with *strategic* CSR.[134] As Mackey reaffirms, "While there is nothing wrong with making money, indeed it is absolutely necessary for the enterprise to flourish; it is not by itself a very inspiring purpose for the enterprise."[135] Mackey is clear, however, in his belief that:

> Conscious capitalism is not primarily about virtue or "doing good." . . . Ordinary business exchanges are inherently virtuous. Business creates value for all of its major stakeholders that are exchanging with it and these acts of value creation are "good." . . . Many businesses do feel a sense of "social responsibility" and provide donations and support for the not-for-profit sector, and while such philanthropy is certainly commendable it is not the essence of "business virtue." Instead, I believe the argument can be successfully made that ordinary business exchanges aggregated collectively are the greatest creator of value in the entire world and that this value creation is the source of "business virtue."[136]

The goal is to build firms that are ethical and responsible, firms that are profitable because they inspire the stakeholders with whom they interact:

> ". . . . consumers are not only feeling inspired by certain businesses, but are acting inspired by spending more with these companies while evangelizing to others about their inspiring experience," says Terry Barber, chief inspiration officer for Performance Inspired. "We now see there is a validated set of drivers to inspiration and when these drivers are activated, it elevates employee engagement that shows up in the customer experience."[137]

Strategic CSR argues that success in today's globalized business environment is correlated highly with ethical, responsible, and inspiring behavior. Firms that respond to stakeholder needs and concerns in ways that win them over, and continue to win them over in an ongoing, virtuous cycle of positive exchange, will be the firms that define the twenty-first century. An important component of a conscious capitalist system, therefore, is businesses that reflect the system's core principles—in other words, values-based businesses.

Values-based Business

A values-based business is founded on the idea of CSR as an "opportunity,"[138] rather than a *responsibility* or *cost*. A genuine implementation of strategic CSR throughout operations lays the groundwork for the construction of such businesses. Values-based businesses stand for something positive, something that both defines and unites the organization. Following the steps outlined in this chapter, therefore, is an important means for firms to achieve this goal.

Values-based Business

A for-profit firm that is founded on a vision and mission based on social values and the other four principles that define conscious capitalism: Higher purpose, Stakeholder interdependence, Conscious leadership, and Conscious culture.

Values are important because they are shared beliefs that "drive an organization's culture and priorities and provide a framework in which decisions are made."[139] They therefore form the backbone of the firm. They are core to what the firm does and how it plans for the future. Based on principles similar to conscious capitalism, a values-based business assumes that profit alone is an insufficient driver of a successful company and motivator of people. In other words, a firm that merely layers CSR and ethics metrics as a component of performance evaluation on top of 'business as normal,' is focusing superficially on extrinsic, rather than intrinsic, motivation:

> The problem in my view is that such systems are actually counter-productive. They reinforce the view that payment is the only incentive scheme that matters and, therefore, if something is not financially rewarded it should not be done. This is a long way from the power of a genuinely values-led business. A genuine culture of values is based on a community of people that understand what is expected of them, what is seen to be right behaviour, and the responsibility they have to each other. As soon as you put money onto that, you remove the essence of what makes these values – and turn it simply into a group of individuals being personally rewarded to take actions that mimic those taken by those united by common values.[140]

As Peter Drucker noted, "profit for a company is like oxygen for a person. If you don't have enough of it, you're out of the game. But if you think your life is about breathing, you're really missing something." Throughout history, human beings have continually sought a deeper meaning to life that financial success alone cannot provide.[141] Values-based businesses speak to these needs. As John Mackey and Raj Sisodia write in their 2013 book, *Conscious Capitalism*:

> With few exceptions . . . entrepreneurs who start successful businesses don't do so to maximize profits. Of course they want to make money, but that is not what drives most of them. They are inspired to do something that they believe needs doing. The heroic story of free-enterprise capitalism is one of entrepreneurs using their dreams and passion as fuel to create extraordinary value for customers, team members, suppliers, society, and investors.[142]

Corporate Value Statements
Zappos' Core Values:[143]

As we grow as a company, it has become more and more important to explicitly define the core values from which we develop our culture, our brand, and our business strategies. These are the ten core values that we live by:

1. Deliver WOW Through Service
2. Embrace and Drive Change
3. Create Fun and A Little Weirdness
4. Be Adventurous, Creative, and Open-Minded
5. Pursue Growth and Learning
6. Build Open and Honest Relationships With Communication
7. Build a Positive Team and Family Spirit
8. Do More With Less
9. Be Passionate and Determined
10. Be Humble

Other examples of corporate values statements:[144]

- IBM: Dedication to every client's success; Innovation that matters, for our company and the world; Trust and personal responsibility in all relationships
- Timberland: Humanity. Humility. Integrity. Excellence.

(Continued)

(Continued)

- Omron: Challenge ourselves to always do better, Innovation driven by social needs, Respect for humanity
- Monster: One Monster, indivisible; Before us, the customer; Do the right thing; Innovate relentlessly; Excellence, served daily; Do well by doing good
- Novo Nordisk: Accountable, Ambitious, Responsible, Engaged with Stakeholders, Open and Honest, Ready for Change

These ideas of businesses founded around values have precedent within capitalism. Adam Smith in the *Theory of Moral Sentiments*,[145] for example, "gave an account of morality resting on empathy and conscience" and, in the process, addressed the great challenge of "how to order a society in which competition and ethical sensibility are combined."[146] Increasingly, firms are adopting these aims and using them to reform the way they conduct business:

> As Walmart grew into the world's largest retailer, its staff were subjected to a long list of dos and don'ts covering every aspect of their work. Now the firm has decided that its rules-based culture is too inflexible to cope with the challenges of globalisation and technological change, and is trying to instill a 'values-based' culture, in which employees can be trusted to do the right thing because they know what the firm stands for.[147]

Unfortunately, such organizations are rare. A survey conducted by the Boston Research Group aimed at learning more about the governance and leadership cultures inside firms, found that "Only 3% fell into the category of 'self-governance,' in which everyone is guided by a 'set of core principles and values that inspire everyone to align around a company's mission.'"[148]

CSR Newsletters: Adam Smith

An article in the *Financial Times*[149] by Jeffrey Sachs critiques Adam Smith's concept of the *invisible hand* ("self-interest, operating through markets, leads to the common good"). While the invisible hand works in principle, Sachs argues, in terms of maximizing social welfare because "the paradox of self-interest breaks down when stretched too far." In particular, Sachs identifies four ways in which "self-interest promotes competition, the division of labor, and innovation, but fails to support the common good":

First, self-interest fails when market competition breaks down. Second, self-interest can easily turn into socially unacceptable inequality. Third, self-interest leaves future generations at the mercy of today's generation. Fourth, self-interest leaves our fragile mental apparatus, evolved for the African savannah, at the mercy of Madison Avenue. Today there is evidence of both hopelessly addictive consumerism and brain numbing cultural forces.

Sachs concludes that, "For these reasons, successful capitalism has never rested on a moral base of self-interest, but rather on the practice of self-interest embedded within a larger set of values."

There is a lot going here. First, it is not clear that Sachs' "four ways" are really four ways, but more likely two ways. The second seems to be an outcome of the first, and the third is not specific to capitalism—however we decide to organize things in this life, future generations will bear the consequences of those decisions. The conclusion Sachs draws from the "flaws" he identifies in Adam Smith's model, however, is very important—the idea that capitalism can only "succeed" when embedded in a larger value system. In other words, some form of individual restraint is crucial. In many societies, that value system is provided by religion. Without that or any other form of civilizing restraint, capitalism can degenerate into raw selfishness and deceit.

Rectifying this paucity of values-based firms is central to reinvigorating public support for capitalism, which has suffered in recent years as a result of CSR transgressions that have caused widespread economic harm. Addressing the question of "Why capitalism has an image problem," Charles Murray argues that we need "to return to the vocabulary of virtue when we talk about capitalism" and, in particular, understand the responsibilities that accompany success:

Personal integrity, a sense of seemliness and concern for those who depend on us are "values" that are no better or worse than other values. . . . If it is necessary to remind the middle class and working class that the rich are not their enemies, it is equally necessary to remind the most successful among us that their obligations are not to be measured in terms of their tax bills. Their principled stewardship can nurture and restore our heritage of liberty. Their indifference to that heritage can destroy it.[150]

Joseph Nye of Harvard University addresses something similar when he talks about the CEO as the "tri-sector athlete"—a leader who is "good at private sector, public sector, social sector."[151] Such leaders are able to motivate the firm's stake-holders in terms that appeal across traditional dividing lines and draw on the multiple resources these stakeholders bring in order to collectively achieve the firm's goals. As such, the firm's employees are a core component of a values-based business. Firms such as, Southwest Airlines[152] and Johnson & Johnson[153] understand this. They place valuing their employees, both intrinsically and extrinsically, at the heart of what the firm does and stands for, believing that satisfied employees are the core to a successful business. As John Mackey puts it, "Happy team members results in happy customers, which results in happy investors."[154]

Figure 5.5 presents the strategic decision making model for a values-based business. While the core strategy process remains the same (tactics that inform the strategy, which serves to achieve the mission and vision), the firm's strategy is necessarily passed through the CSR Filter to ensure stakeholder concerns are placed front and center of the decision making process. Surrounding this core is a set of guiding values that frame the organizational culture, structure its priorities, and provide employees with a framework that they can use in day-to-day operations. It is the decisions that are made by employees every day that, over time, reinforce the guiding values and re-define the firm—what it stands for, what actions it takes, and, ultimately, whether it fails or survives and prospers.[155]

| Figure 5.5 | Conscious Capitalism |

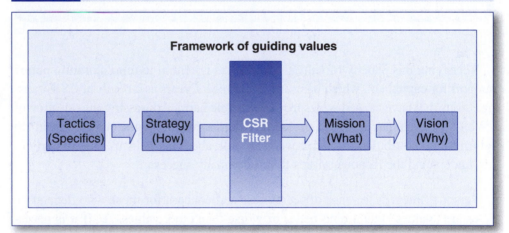

CSR Newsletters: Chick-fil-A

The problem with a values-based approach to CSR becomes apparent when a firm proudly announces its support for values with which you disagree. An article in *The Economist*[156] presents a good example of this and, in the process, summarizes an important critique of the CSR movement:

Conservatives sceptical of the corporate social responsibility (CSR) movement have often charged that CSR is a stalking horse for liberal causes that have failed to get traction through ordinary political channels. This charge finds some support, I think, in the fact that few in the media seem to see Chick-fil-A's Christian-influenced culture and business practices as an example of CSR, though obviously it is. Doesn't the demand that corporations act responsibly in the interests of society, in ways other than profit-seeking, directly imply that corporate leaders who find same-sex marriage socially irresponsible should do something or other to discourage it?

If we encourage a firm pledging to move to zero-waste manufacturing plants because the executives are concerned about climate change, then we must also allow a firm acting to prevent the widespread acceptance of same-sex marriage. Both are issues with passionate advocates who believe the realization of their position will benefit society:

> CSR, when married to norms of ethical consumption, will inevitably incite bouts of culture-war strife. CSR with honest moral content... is a recipe for the politicisation of production and sales.

In *Strategic CSR*, we focus on constructing an economic argument for CSR, with a particular focus on operational relevance (applicable to the zero waste example above; less obvious in terms of same-sex marriage). But, even there, the idea that a firm should seek to meet the needs and demands of its key stakeholder groups allows for the advocacy of beliefs that are important to those stakeholders (whatever the nature of those beliefs). Assuming that the action being advocated is not illegal, individual values differ and, as long as there are sufficient numbers of people willing to demonstrate support for a particular position, then a firm can make an economic argument for advocating on behalf of that position:

> People can run their businesses according to whatever principles they prefer. It's just stupid business for owners and managers who want to sell their firm's goods and services to people who don't happen to share their morals or politics, especially in cultures in which consumers are increasingly expected to vote with their wallets.

In other words, the only danger for Chick-fil-A is if they are on the wrong side of an issue that is moving strongly against them. Given the number of people who showed up at the firm's restaurants to support the firm's position, however, it is not clear this is the case:

(Continued)

(Continued)

Matters of moral truth aside, what's the difference between buying a little social justice with your coffee and buying a little Christian traditionalism with your chicken?

Unless we are willing to allow firms equally to support all issues that are important to key stakeholder groups, we are being hypocritical. Chick-fil-A's position is consistent with prior positions the firm has adopted and is important to many of the firm's customers.

As Bill Clinton wrote in an article on optimism in *Time Magazine*:

The truth is, the future has never had a big enough constituency—those fighting for present gain almost always win out. But we are now called upon to try to create a whole different mind-set. We are in a pitched battle between the present array of resources and attitudes and the future struggling to be born.[157] We need to build a better future. Strategic CSR will ensure that for-profit businesses, the engines of economic wealth and social progress, are at the vanguard of that movement.

NEXT STEPS

The varied stakeholder issues that define the scope of CSR are the focus of Part II of *Strategic CSR*. Taking advantage of the Internet, which is reshaping the role of CSR within the competitive business landscape, topical issues are identified and discussed. Throughout, relevant websites provide both the specifics and implications of these issues, as well as forming launch pads for deeper individual research and investigation.

QUESTIONS FOR DISCUSSION AND REVIEW

1. What is meant by the phrase "CSR as brand insurance?" Can you think of a firm that has benefited from CSR in this way?

2. Why do some firms, industries, and cultures have different "CSR Thresholds" than others? Illustrate your answer with examples for all three categories.

3. What role do stakeholders play in establishing the level of the CSR Threshold for a particular firm or within a particular industry? Think of an example firm and/or industry; what event do you think would push that firm or industry over its CSR Threshold?

4. Why is top-management support for CSR so critical? Can CSR be delegated? If so, why and to whom?

5. List four of the eight components of a firm's plan of action necessary to implement CSR over the short to medium term. What examples from business can you think of where firms have performed these actions successfully?

6. How does a firm avoid the perception that its CSR report is *greenwash*? Does it matter whether the reasons behind an action are genuine or cynical if the outcome is the same?

7. In your view, what does a values-based business look like? Think of an example from what you have seen or read in the news; what do you think would be different about working for a firm like that?

STUDENT STUDY SITE

Visit the Student Study Site at **www.sagepub.com/chandler3e** for additional learning tools.

NOTES AND REFERENCES

1. David Grayson & Adrian Hodges, *Corporate Social Opportunity! Seven Steps to Make Corporate Social Responsibility Work for Your Business*, Greenleaf Publications, 2004.
2. William B. Werther & David Chandler, 'Strategic Corporate Social Responsibility as Global Brand Insurance,' *Business Horizons*, Vol. 48, Issue 4, July 2005: 317-324.
3. http://www.nike.com/us/en_us/c/running/nike-flyknit
4. Alan Beattie, 'Spend, spend, spend. Save, save, save,' *Financial Times*, January 27, 2007, p. 18 and Marc Gunther, 'Better (Red) Than Dead,' *CSRWire*, August 5, 2008, http://greenbiz.com/blog/2008/08/03/better-red-dead
5. Anheuser-Busch claims that "we recycle 99 percent of the solid waste generated in the brewing and packaging process, including beechwood chips, aluminum, glass, brewers' grain, scrap metal, cardboard and many other items." http://anheuser-busch.com/index.php/our-responsibility/environment-our-earth-our-natural-resources/reduce-reuse-and-recycle/
6. http://responsibility.timberland.com/service/living-our-values/
7. For more details on this program, see 'Employee Relations' Issue in Chapter 6.
8. William Werther & David Chandler, 'Strategic Corporate Social Responsibility as Global Brand Insurance,' *Business Horizons,* Vol. 48, No. 4, 2005. pp. 317–324.
9. Jonathan Birchall, 'Business fights for tougher rules on emissions,' *Financial Times*, November 20, 2008, p. 4.

10. Stephanie Clifford & Stephanie Strom, 'Wal-Mart to Announce Women-Friendly Plans,' *The New York Times*, September 14, 2011, p. B3.

11. Stephanie Clifford & Stephanie Strom, 'Wal-Mart to Announce Women-Friendly Plans,' *The New York Times*, September 14, 2011, p. B3.

12. Malcolm Gladwell, *The Tipping Point: How Little Things Can Make a Big Difference*, Back Bay Books, 2002.

13. Although there are disagreements as to which categorization best fits different business models, what all these firms have in common is that their strategies seek to provide their customers with superior value.

14. In drawing these distinctions among firms, it is important to stress that the distinction between low cost and differentiation, and between broad and narrow, refers to a firm's *business level* strategies. As such, it is possible for a firm to have different strategies across its different business units. Apple's range of computers, for example, (for which the firm willingly exchanges high margins for continued low market share), targets a narrow segment of the total computer market, while its iPhones and iPads have a broader scope.

15. In July, 2008, ExxonMobil announced the largest ever quarterly profit for a publicly traded U.S. company: "The company's income for the second quarter rose 14 percent, to $11.68 billion, compared to the same period a year ago. That beat the previous record of $11.66 billion set by Exxon in the last three months of 2007. Exxon's profits were nearly $90,000 a minute over the quarter, . . . (The company calculates that it pays $274,000 a minute in taxes and spends $884,000 a minute to run the business.)" Clifford Krauss, 'Exxon's Second-Quarter Earnings Set a Record,' *The New York Times*, August 1, 2008, http://www.nytimes.com/2008/08/01/business/01oil.html

16. Mallen Baker, 'Financial services: Will banks ever treat customers fairly?' *Ethical Corporation*, April 1, 2008, http://www.ethicalcorp.com/content.asp?ContentID=5807

17. Mallen Baker, 'Financial services: Will banks ever treat customers fairly?' *Ethical Corporation*, April 1, 2008, http://www.ethicalcorp.com/content.asp?ContentID=5807

18. Richard Gibson, 'McDonald's Seeks Ways to Pitch Healthy Living,' *The Wall Street Journal,* May 27, 2004, p. D7.

19. http://www.philipmorrisusa.com/en/cms/Products/Cigarettes/Health_Issues/default.aspx

20. http://archive.greenpeace.org/comms/brent/brent.html and http://archive.greenpeace.org/comms/ken/

21. 'Who Benefits from GM Crops? AN Analysis of the Global Performance of GM Crops (1996-2006),' Friends of the Earth, January, 2007, http://www.foei.org/en/publications/pdfs/gmcrops2007execsummary.pdf; 'Monsanto Moves to Force-Feed Europe Genetically Engineered Corn,' Friends of the Earth, January 10, 2006, http://www.organicconsumers.org/ge/europecorn011106.cfm

22. Lisa Roner, 'Starbucks and Oxfam Team Up on Ethiopian Development Programme,' *Ethical Corporation Magazine,* October 18, 2004, http://www.ethicalcorp.com/content.asp?ContentID=2961 and Alison Maitland, 'Starbucks Tastes Oxfam's Brew,' *Financial Times* (U.S. Edition), October 14, 2004, p. 9.

23. See: Andrew Wilson, 'CSR in Emerging Economies: Lessons from the Davos Philanthropic Roundtable,' January 31, 2008, http://www.eef.org.ua/en/231.htm and 'First study on corporate Saudi Arabia and CSR,' *CSRWire.com*, March 29, 2007, http://www.csrwire.com/press/press_release/15949

24. C.K. Prahalad, 'The Fortune at the Bottom of the Pyramid: Eradicating Poverty Through Profits,' *Wharton School Publishing*, 2006; C.K. Prahalad & Allen Hammond, 'Serving the World's Poor, Profitably,' *Harvard Business Review,* September 2002, Vol. 80, No. 9, pp. 48–58.

25. Also see: Michael Hopkins, *Corporate Social Responsibility and International Development: Is Business the Solution?* Earthscan, 2007.

26. http://www.thedailybeast.com/newsweek/features/green-rankings/2011/international.html

27. http://www.transparency.org/research/cpi/overview

28. http://cpi.transparency.org/cpi2011/results/

29. http://cpi.transparency.org/cpi2011/results/

30. 'The 2005 State of Corporate Citizenship,' Center for Corporate Citizenship at Boston College, May 2005, http://www.bcccc.net/index.cfm?fuseaction=Page .viewPage&pageId=694&node%20ID%20=1&parentID=473

31. Ibid.

32. http://www.nikeresponsibility.com/

33. http://www.starbucks.com/aboutus/csr.asp

34. http://www.microsoft.com/about/corporatecitizenship/

35. http://www.timberland.com/corp/index.jsp?page=csr_civic_engagement

36. http://nikeinc.com/pages/executives

37. 'Just good business: A special report on corporate social responsibility,' *The Economist*, January 19, 2008, p. 4.

38. http://www.accountability21.net/

39. Simon Zadek, 'The Path to Corporate Responsibility,' *Harvard Business Review*, December, 2004, pp. 125-132.

40. Simon Zadek, 'The Path to Corporate Responsibility,' *Harvard Business Review*, December, 2004, pp. 125-132.

41. The Ethics and Compliance Officer Association in the United States (http://www .theecoa.org/) believes the CEO acronym should also stand for "chief ethics officer."

42. For example, "In 2000, Enron received six environmental awards. It had progressive policies on climate change, human rights, and anti-corruption" (David Gebler, 'Culture of Compliance,' *CRO Magazine*, http://www.thecro.com/node/68).

43. Patrick M. Lencioni, 'Make Your Values Mean Something,' *Harvard Business Review,* Vol. 80, No. 7, July 2002, pp. 113–117.

44. Memorandum from Kenneth Lay to All Employees, Subject: Code of Ethics, July 1, 2000.

45. Enron Corp's "Code of Ethics," p. 5.

46. Ibid, p. 12.

47. John Kay, 'Weasel words have the teeth to kill great ventures,' *Financial Times*, January 14, 2009, p. 9.

48. Derrick Daye & Brad VanAuken, 'Social Responsibility: The Nike Story,' July 25, 2008, http://www.brandingstrategyinsider.com/2008/07/social-responsi.html

49. A quote from Mark Goyder, 'Redefining CSR: From the Rhetoric of Accountability to the Reality of Earning Trust,' in Mallen Baker, '"Redefining CSR" report by Tomorrow's Company,' *Ethical Corporation Magazine*, August 1, 2003, http://www.ethicalcorp.com/content.asp?ContentID=900. The full report by Goyder can be accessed at: http://www.tomorrowscompany.com/uploads/Redef_CSRintro.pdf

50. Nick Wingfield, 'Fixing Apple's Supply Lines,' *The New York Times*, April 2, 2012, p. B1.

51. e.g., http://www.triplepundit.com/2012/03/walmarts-sustainability-efforts-stall-new-leadership/

52. See: 'Responsible Corporate Officer Doctrine: Executives Who Allow Misdeeds Face Career-Ending Consequences,' *JDSupra*, August 3, 2012, http://www.jdsupra.com/legalnews/responsible-corporate-officer-doctrine-00350/

53. Brendan May, 'Government: If only the political species faced extinction,' *Ethical Corporation Magazine*, January 31, 2012, http://www.ethicalcorp.com/governance-regulation/government-if-only-political-species-faced-extinction

54. The title of this position will vary considerably across firms and including Corporate Responsibility Officers, Sustainability Officers, and Ethics and Compliance Officers. The important point is that a position is created and that it has the substantive support of the CEO.

55. Daniel Franklin, 'The year of unsustainability,' The World in 2009, *The Economist*, November 19, 2008, p. 20.

56. This position, or its equivalent, has many titles—from Chief Sustainability Officer, to Chief Ethics & Compliance Officer, even to Chief Customer Officer ('The magic of good service,' *The Economist*, September 22, 2012, p. 78).

57. 'What Does It Mean to Be VP of CSR? A Conversation with Sandra Taylor of Starbucks,' *Business Ethics Magazine,* Summer 2004, p. 4.

58. Lisa Roner, 'Ethics Cited in Choice of New Nike Chief Executive,' *Ethical Corporation Magazine,* November 24, 2004, http://www.ethicalcorp.com/content.asp?ContentID=3248

59. 'Nike Names New VP of Corporate Responsibility,' Nike Press Release, October 20, 2004, http://www.csrwire.com/News/3154.html

60. http://www.iso.org/iso/management_standards.htm

61. http://www.iso.org/sr

62. Aaron Chatterji & David Levine, 'Breaking Down the Wall of Codes: Evaluating Non-financial Performance Measurement,' *California Management Review*, Vol. 48, Issue 2, 2006, p. 35.

63. Charles J. Fombrun, 'List of Lists: A Compilation of International Corporate Reputation Ratings,' *Corporate Reputation Review*, Vol.10, Issue 2, 2007, pp. 144-153.

64. Aaron Chatterji & David Levine, 'Breaking Down the Wall of Codes: Evaluating Non-financial Performance Measurement,' *California Management Review*, Vol. 48, Issue 2, 2006, p. 29.

65. http://money.cnn.com/magazines/fortune/mostadmired/2008/index.html

66. http://www.thecro.com/node/615

67. http://www.globalreporting.org/

68. http://www.kld.com/

69. Allen White, 'New rigorous ratings tool help investors and companies,' *Ethical Corporation Magazine*, August 10, 2012, http://www.ethicalcorp.com/business-strategy/new-rigorous-ratings-tools-help-investors-and-companies

70. Toby Webb, 'Podcast: Hannah Jones, VP sustainable business and innovation at Nike, on targets, performance, outlook and ambition,' *Ethical Corporation Magazine*, September 27, 2011, http://www.ethicalcorp.com/supply-chains/podcasts/hannah-jones-vp-sustainable-business-and-innovation-nike-targets-performance-

71. Here, it is important for the CSR Officer to balance the role of CSR Crusader (passionate believer) with the important role of a CSR Diplomat (grounded in economic and business realities) so as to win supporters within the firm. See: Aman Singh, 'Changing Business from the Inside Out: How to Pursue a Career in CSR and Sustainability,' *CSRWire*, August 16, 2012, http://www.csrwire.com/blog/posts/503-changing-business-from-the-inside-out-how-to-pursue-a-career-in-csr-and-sustainability

72. Mallen Baker, 'Corporate social responsibility: When the competent become the enemy of the good,' *Ethical Corporation*, February 25, 2008, http://www.ethicalcorp.com/content.asp?ContentID=5735

73. 'For Employee Buy-In, Supervisors Trump the CEO,' *Network for Business Sustainability*, March 3, 2013, http://nbs.net/knowledge/for-employee-buy-in-supervisors-trump-the-ceo/

74. Cadbury Schweppes CSR Report 2006, http://csr2006.cadburyschweppes.com/csrvision/csrvision.html

75. Toby Webb, 'Vision and mission: A barrier to sustainability strategy,' *Smarter Business Blog*, September 10, 2012, http://tobywebb.blogspot.jp/2012/09/vision-and-mission-barrier-to.html

76. David Kestenbaum, 'Pop Quiz: How Do You Stop Sea Captains From Killing Their Passengers?' NPR Radio, September 10, 2010, http://www.npr.org/blogs/money/2010/09/09/129757852/pop-quiz-how-do-you-stop-sea-captains-from-killing-their-passengers

77. David Chandler, *Organizations and Ethics: Antecedents and Consequences of the Adoption and Implementation of the Ethics and Compliance Officer Position*, Unpublished Dissertation, The University of Texas at Austin, Austin, TX, 2011.

78. See: Simon Zadek, 'The Path to Corporate Responsibility,' *Harvard Business Review*, December, 2004, pp. 125-132, for a detailed discussion of how Nike aligned its incentive scheme for sub-contractors with its corporate responsibility goals.

79. Mark Cohen, 'SEC Recognizes Climate Change as Material Business Risk,' *Resources for the Future*, February 5, 2010, http://common-resources.org/2010/sec-recognizes-climate-change-as-material-business-risk/

80. Rikki Stancich, 'Recession Ethics: CSR in a Downturn – Recession-proof Ethics Can Weather the Storm,' *Ethical Corporation Magazine*, March 5, 2008, http://www.ethicalcorp.com/content.asp?ContentID=5751

81. Aman Singh Das, '7 Conflicting Trends: Fortune 100 Annual Reports & CSR,' *Vault blogs*, July 18, 2011, http://blogs.vault.com/blog/in-good-company-vaults-csr-blog/7-conflicting-trends-fortune-100-annual-reports-csr/

82. 'UK ranks top in biggest global CR reporting survey ever published,' *Green Business News*, November 7, 2011, http://www.greenwisebusiness.co.uk/news/uk-ranks-top-in-biggest-global-cr-reporting-survey-ever-published-2770.aspx

83. The National Oceanic and Atmospheric Administration's Web site provides details of the *Exxon Valdez* oil spill at http://response.restoration.noaa.gov/spotlight/spotlight.html and images from the event at http://response.restoration.noaa.gov/photos/exxon/exxon.html. Another authoritative website is administered by the Exxon Valdez Oil Spill Trustee Council at http://www.evostc.state.ak.us/

84. The phrase *triple bottom line* was first introduced in 1994 by John Elkington of SustainAbility (http://www.sustainability.com/) "to describe social, environmental, and financial accounting." The term was used in conjunction with the launch of SustainAbility's "first survey benchmarking non-financial reporting." William Baue, 'Sustainability Reporting Improves, but Falls Short on Linking to Financial Performance,' *Social Funds*, November 5, 2004, http://www.socialfunds.com/news/article.cgi/article1565.html

85. Deborah Doane, 'Mandated Risk Reporting Begins in UK,' *Business Ethics Magazine,* Spring 2005, p. 13.

86. Elizabeth Becker, 'At Shell, Grades for Citizenship,' *New York Times,* November 30, 2003, Section 3, p. 2.

87. Ibid.

88. Ibid.

89. http://www.walkerscarbonfootprint.co.uk/

90. See: Andrew Martin, 'How Green is My Orange?' *New York Times*, January 21, 2009, http://www.nytimes.com/2009/01/22/business/22pepsi.html

91. Ram Nidumolu, C.K. Prahalad, and M.R. Rangaswami, 'Why Sustainability is Now the Key Driver of Innovation,' *Harvard Business Review*, September, 2009, p. 59.

92. Verité (http://www.verite.org/) is a good example of a firm that provides this verification service: "At Verité, we are committed to ensuring that people worldwide work under safe, fair and legal conditions. In over 60 countries around the world we provide governments, corporations, investors, factories, NGOs and workers with information on global working conditions and innovative programs to improve them."

93. William Baue, 'Survey Says: NGOs Believe Corporate Social Responsibility Reports That Reveal Faults,' *Social Funds,* November 14, 2003, http://www.socialfunds.com/news/article.cgi/1268.html

94. Mallen Baker, 'The truth and illusion of integrated reporting,' *Ethical Corporation Magazine*, October 3, 2011, http://www.mallenbaker.net/csr/page.php?Story_ID=2698

95. For example, see: Eric Marx, 'Ceres – Serious about reporting,' *Ethical Corporation*, June 12, 2009, http://www.ethicalcorp.com/content.asp?ContentID=6499

96. See: Toby Webb, 'Stakeholder engagement: Learning to listen,' *Smarter Business Blog*, November 5, 2011, http://tobywebb.blogspot.jp/2011/11/stakeholder-engagement-learning-to.html

97. Mallen Baker, 'Integrated reporting—The gulf between theory and practice,' *Ethical Corporation Magazine*, October 25, 2010, http://www.mallenbaker.net/csr/page.php?Story_ID=2637

98. Mark Goyder, 'Redefining CSR: From the Rhetoric of Accountability to the Reality of Earning Trust,' *Tomorrow's Company*, 2003, http://www.tomorrowscompany.com/uploads/Redef_CSRintro.pdf; Mallen Baker, '"Redefining CSR" report by Tomorrow's Company,' *Ethical Corporation Magazine*, August 1, 2003, http://www.ethicalcorp.com/content.asp?ContentID=900

99. Jon Entine, 'Reporting contradictions,' *Ethical Corporation*, June 7, 2009, http://www.ethicalcorp.com/content.asp?ContentID=6492

100. Simon Webley, 'Are corporate ethics programmes really 'alive'?' *Ethical Corporation Magazine*, June 28, 2011, http://www.ethicalcorp.com/governance-regulation/are-corporate-ethics-programmes-really-%E2%80%98alive%E2%80%99

101. Lynn Paine, Rohit Deshpandé, Joshua D. Margolis, and Kim Eric Bettcher, ''Up to Code: Does Your Company's Conduct Meet World-Class Standards?' *Harvard Business Review*, December, 2005, p. 123.

102. Debora L. Spar, 'Hitting the Wall: Nike and International Labor Practices,' *Harvard Business School Press*, [9-700-047], September 6, 2002.

103. Amelia Gentleman, 'Gap Vows To Combat Child Labor At Suppliers,' *The New York Times*, November 16, 2007, p. 6.

104. Also in 2002, both the NYSE and NASDAQ altered their listing requirements, compelling firms listed on the exchange to adopt and disclose both corporate governance guidelines and a code of business conduct and ethics for all employees, following SEC approval of standards for such reports.

105. Section 301.4b (2002: 776), http://www.404.gov/about/laws/soa2002.pdf

106. http://www.shareholder.com/. Another company providing a similar service is EthicsPoint Inc. (http://www.ethicspoint.com/), where "about 78% of the complaints channeled through [the company] had arrived via the Web," Phyllis Plitch, 'Making It Easier to Complain,' in the supplement, 'Corporate Governance: The Journal Report,' *The Wall Street Journal,* June 21, 2004, p. R6.

107. Ibid.

108. Personal correspondence with authors, December 2012.

109. Hannah Clark, 'Chief Ethics Officers: Who Needs Them?' *Forbes Magazine*, October 23, 2006, http://www.forbes.com/2006/10/23/leadership-ethics-hp-lead-govern-cx_hc_1023ethics.html

110. 'Leading Corporate Integrity: Defining the Role of the Chief Ethics & Compliance Officer (CECO),' *Ethics Resource Center*, 2007, http://www.ethics.org/resource/ceco

111. For examples of NGO campaigns and relations with firms, see: Toby Webb, 'Campaign groups will need to evolve their approach,' *Smarter Business Blog*, June 11, 2012, http://tobywebb.blogspot.jp/2012/06/campaign-groups-will-need-to-evolve.html

112. Michael Elliott, 'Embracing the Enemy Is Good Business,' *Time*, August 13, 2001, p. 29.

113. Marc Gunther, 'Tree Huggers, Soy Lovers, and Profits,' *Fortune*, June 23, 2003, pp. 98–104.

114. For a useful list of Dos and Don'ts in relation to "green marketing," see: 'How to look good green,' *Ethical Corp*, January 21, 2009, http://www.ethicalcorp.com/content.asp?ContentID=6298

115. Anjali Mullany, 'What Your Social Media Consultant Should Tell You,' *FastCompany Magazine*, September 2012, p. 73.

116. Paloma Lopez, 'Marketing: New sustainable skills for leading marketers,' *Ethical Corporation Magazine*, July 29, 2011, http://www.ethicalcorp.com/supply-chains/marketing-new-sustainable-skills-leading-marketers

117. http://nikeinc.com/

118. See the 'Corporate Governance' Issue in Chapter 6.

119. Paul J. Lim, 'Gauging That Other Company Asset: Its Reputation,' *New York Times*, April 10, 2004, p. A18.

120. Toby Webb, 'Big business collaboration around sustainability: Now it's getting interesting,' *Smarter Business Blog*, August 23, 2011, http://tobywebb.blogspot.jp/2011/08/big-business-collaboration-around.html

121. See: http://www.rspo.org/ and http://www.fairlabor.org/

122. For additional ideas regarding a comprehensive plan of implementation, it might also be helpful to read: Susan Graff, 'Six Steps to Sustainability,' *CRO Magazine*, June, 2007, http://www.thecro.com/node/520

123. Kerry Capell, 'Zara's Fast Track to Fashion,' *BusinessWeek*, June, 2008, http://images.businessweek.com/ss/06/08/zara/index_01.htm

124. Kerry Capell, 'Zara's Fast Track to Fashion,' *BusinessWeek*, June, 2008, http://images.businessweek.com/ss/06/08/zara/index_01.htm

125. Andrew McAfee, Anders Sjoman, & Vincent Dessain, 'Zara: IT for Fast Fashion,' *Harvard Business School Press*, [9-604-081], September 6, 2007; Store Wars: Fast Fashion, *BBC News*, June 9, 2004, http://news.bbc.co.uk/2/hi/business/3086669.stm

126. Hannah Clark, 'Chief Ethics Officers: Who Needs Them?' *Forbes Magazine*, October 23, 2006, http://www.forbes.com/2006/10/23/leadership-ethics-hp-lead-govern-cx_hc_1023ethics.html

127. An important note of concern relates to the issue of unintended consequences, which is one of the most important issues for the CSR community to face. When we try to subvert centuries of economic development, attempting to substitute social or altruistic motivation for economic incentives, we should tread carefully. That is why in *Strategic CSR*, we favor evolutionary, rather than revolutionary reform. It happens again and again—whether it is government subsidies or tax breaks for a particular kind of alternative energy, or a new technical innovation that interacts with some other factor (or is applied inappropriately) to generate some unexpected outcome. In

short, there is much that we do not understand about the social and economic forces that drive human behavior, and the relationship between these forces and societal-level outcomes. By definition, we can only base future projections on past experience and are constrained when we do so. When we propose solutions, we envisage the benefits and fail (or are unable) to fully understand all the risks. That does not mean that we should not try to implement change, but it does imply we should be humble in attempts to temper these highly-evolved forces.

128. Jacquelyn Smith, 'The World's Most Ethical Companies,' *Forbes Magazine*, March 15, 2012, http://www.forbes.com/sites/jacquelynsmith/2012/03/15/the-worlds-most-ethical-companies/

129. Jacquelyn Smith, 'America's 25 Most Inspiring Companies,' *Forbes Magazine*, September 25, 2012, http://www.forbes.com/sites/jacquelynsmith/2012/09/25/americas-25-most-inspiring-companies/

130. http://www.consciouscapitalism.org/

131. See: John Mackey & Raj Sisodia, *Conscious Capitalism: Liberating the Heroic Spirit of Business*, Harvard Business Review Press, 2013.

132. There are other perspectives; for example: James O'Toole & David Vogel, 'Two and a Half Cheers for Conscious Capitalism,' *California Management Review*, Vol. 53, No. 3, Spring 2011, pp. 60-82.

133. John Mackey, 'What Conscious Capitalism Really Is,' *California Management Review*, Vol. 53, No. 3, Spring 2011, pp. 83-85.

134. On the Conscious Capitalism Institute's website, the "Stakeholder Interdependence" principle is labeled "Stakeholder Orientation" (http://consciouscapitalism.org/learnmore/), bringing the concept even closer to the vision of strategic CSR that we present in this book.

135. John Mackey, 'What Conscious Capitalism Really Is,' *California Management Review*, Vol. 53, No. 3, Spring 2011, p. 83.

136. John Mackey, 'What Conscious Capitalism Really Is,' *California Management Review*, Vol. 53, No. 3, Spring 2011, pp. 85-86.

137. Jacquelyn Smith, 'America's 25 Most Inspiring Companies,' *Forbes Magazine*, September 25, 2012, http://www.forbes.com/sites/jacquelynsmith/2012/09/25/americas-25-most-inspiring-companies/

138. David Grayson & Adrian Hodges, *Corporate Social Opportunity!*, Greenleaf Publications, 2004.

139. Toby Webb, The case for re-evaluating values,' *Smarter Business Blog*, March 5, 2012, http://tobywebb.blogspot.jp/2012/03/case-for-re-evaluating-values.html

140. Mallen Baker, 'Paying the market rate for morality?' September 18, 2012, in *Business Respect – CSR Dispatches*, No. 185, October 8, 2012, http://www.mallenbaker.net/csr/post.php?id=451

141. Michael Skapinker, 'Why do business titans need to 'give back'?' *Financial Times*, November 30, 2010, p. 13.

142. Alan Murray, 'Chicken Soup For a Davos Soul,' *The Wall Street Journal*, January 17, 2013, p. A15.

143. See: http://about.zappos.com/our-unique-culture/zappos-core-values

144. Sylvia Kinnicutt, 'Corporate values statements – An integral part of corporate citizenship?' *Boston College Center for Corporate Citizenship*, January 5, 2010, http://blogs.bcccc.net/2010/01/corporate-values-statements-%E2%80%93-an-integral-part-of-corporate-citizenship/

145. Adam Smith published *The Wealth of Nations* in 1776, but it is his book, *The Theory of Moral Sentiments* (first published in 1759), that leads many observers to describe Smith as a moral philosopher, rather than an economist. For example, see: James R. Otteson, 'Adam Smith: Moral Philosopher,' The Freeman Ideas on Liberty, Vol. 50, Issue 11, November, 2000, http://www.thefreemanonline.org/features/adam-smith-moral-philosopher/

146. David Willetts, 'The invisible hand that binds us all,' *Financial Times*, April 25, 2011, p. 8.

147. 'The view from the top, and bottom,' *The Economist*, September 24, 2011, p. 76.

148. 'The view from the top, and bottom,' *The Economist*, September 24, 2011, p. 76.

149. Jeffrey Sachs, 'Self-interest, without morals, leads to capitalism's self-destruction,' *Financial Times*, January 18, 2012, http://theoligarch.com/capitalism_justice.htm

150. Charles Murray, 'Why capitalism has an image problem,' *The Wall Street Journal*, July 28-29, 2012, p. C1.

151. Quoting Dominic Barton, CEO of McKinsey & Co. in: Stefan Stern, 'A strategy for staying sacred,' *Financial Times*, August 16, 2010, p. 10.

152. See: Herb Kelleher, 'The business of business is people,' http://www.youtube.com/watch?v=oxTFA1kh1m8

153. http://www.jnj.com/connect/about-jnj/jnj-credo/

154. 'Mackey Speaks On The Business of Conscious Capitalism,' McCombs School of Business, March 28, 2011, http://www.today.mccombs.utexas.edu/2011/03/mackey-speaks-on-the-business-of-conscious-capitalism

155. This framework, within the overriding concept of *strategic* CSR, mirrors Mark Scwartz's Three Component VBA (Values, Balance, Accountability) Model, where Value = net social benefit; Balance = the inclusion of interests, values, and standards; and Accountability = transparency to all stakeholders. Thus, "Value + Balance + Accountability = Proper Role of Business in Society." See: Mark S. Scwartz, *Corporate Social Responsibility: An Ethical Approach*, Broadview Press, 2011, as reviewed by William C. Frederick, 'A Conceptual Toolkit for All Seasons,' October, 2012, http://williamcfrederick.com/articles%20archive/SwartzReview.pdf

156. 'Feathers flying,' *The Economist*, August 7, 2012, http://www.economist.com/blogs/democracyinamerica/2012/08/conscientious-consumption-and-culture-war

157. Bill Clinton, 'The Case for Optimism,' *Time Magazine*, October 1, 2012, http://www.time.com/time/magazine/article/0,9171,2125031,00.html

PART II

CSR: ISSUES AND CASE-STUDIES

Part II reveals the unique nature of *Strategic Corporate Social Responsibility*. Chapters 6, 7, and 8 explore the breadth and depth of corporate social responsibility (CSR) through 21 issues and case-studies, each of which serves as a practical introduction to a broader component of the CSR universe. Collectively, these issues and case-studies form a basis for discussion and debate that is enriched by online resources for further investigation.

The case-studies in Part II represent issues that range from corporate governance and NGOs to diversity and bribery; from sustainability and fair trade to microfinance and religion. They are a selection of some of the many issues that firms need to anticipate and react to every day. As such, they illustrate the direct impact of CSR on corporate behavior and strategic planning—decisions and actions that are made in a complex, ever-evolving economic and social operating environment. In other words, these issues can benefit or detract from the bottom line depending on a firm's approach. They shape stakeholder relationships with the firm via perceptions of the corporate brand, product, or behavior. For firms, the cumulative effect of these issues directly influences their chances of survival and, as such, they cannot be avoided by any organization that aims to be successful over the medium to long term.

To grasp the spectrum of CSR issues that affect corporate behavior, consider Figure II.1. We use this model to classify broadly the 21 issues of Part II into the three stakeholder groups that were initially presented in Chapter 2: Chapter 6 contains issues and case-studies primarily involving organizational stakeholders; Chapter 7, economic stakeholders; and, Chapter 8, societal stakeholders. First, stakeholders exist within the organization. Examples of organizational stakeholders include shareholders, employees, and managers. Taken together, these internal stakeholders constitute the organization as a whole and, therefore, should be its

Figure II.1   A Stakeholder Model

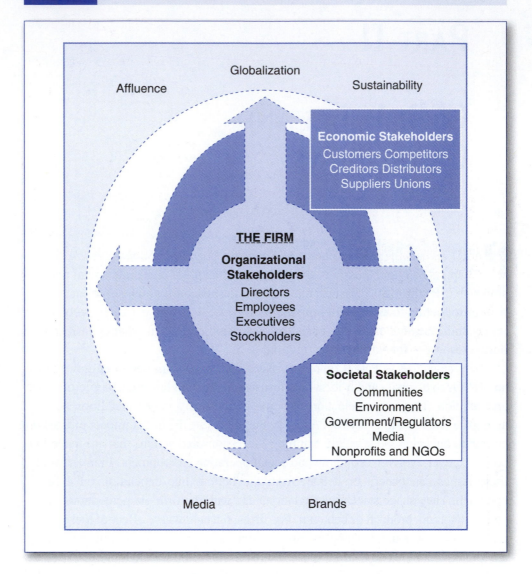

primary concern. In this chapter, the business functions and practices that affect organizational stakeholders are presented from a CSR perspective.

Second are economic stakeholders, examples of which include consumers, creditors, and competitors. The interactions that these stakeholders have with the firm are driven primarily by economic concerns. As such, these stakeholders fulfill an important role as the interface between the organization and its larger social environment. Not only do the issues in this section affect the financial/economic aspects of the organization, they create bonds of accountability between the firm and its operating context.

Third are those stakeholders that constitute the broader business and social environment in which the firm operates. Examples of societal stakeholders include government agencies and regulators, communities, and the natural environment. These societal stakeholders are essential for the organization in terms of providing the legitimacy necessary for it to survive over the medium to long term. Without the general consensus that it is *valued* by its broader society, no organization can expect to survive indefinitely.

Finally, the five driving forces of CSR (affluence, sustainability, globalization, media, and brands) frame this bull's-eye model of concentric circles. A central argument of *Strategic CSR* is that the emergence of these forces in recent years has changed the rules of the game for corporations—they have lead directly to a shift in control over the free flow of information from firms to their stakeholders (see Chapter 4). As such, these forces provide the overall context within which CSR and stakeholder theory have become essential components of the strategic and operating business environment for corporations today.

PART II STRUCTURE

Each issue in the three chapters of Part II is divided into seven sections:

- **CSR Connection:** A brief summary of the issue and its relevance to the broader CSR debate. This overview also includes an indication of the primary stakeholder groups driving each issue.
- **Issue:** A detailed discussion that identifies the central points and recent developments that make it a current topic of CSR interest.
- **Case-study:** An illustration of the issue via a real-life context and corporate action or reaction.
- **CEO Perspective:** A comment on each issue from a current or former chief executive.
- **Online Resources:** Links to the websites of organizations and other information sources that relate directly to the issue and case-study.
- **Pro/Con Debate:** A central component of the issue or case-study presented as a contentious statement for classroom debate.
- **Questions for Discussion and Review:** Five questions that provide guidance for further investigation and a starting point for in-depth discussion.

As demonstrated in Part I of *Strategic Corporate Social Responsibility*, CSR is a multi-faceted, dynamic subject. As such, the seven *Issues* for each of the three stakeholder groups presented in Part II (21 in total) are designed as introductions to a variety of CSR-related topics and are not intended to be comprehensive analyses of the subjects covered, many of which are complex. Similarly, each supporting *Case-study* is intended to be illustrative and does not cover every aspect of each issue within each demarcation. With this in mind, the *CEO Perspective* and *Online Resources* are provided as additional stimuli to support the *Pro/Con Debate* and the *Questions for Discussion and Review*, which can lead to whatever depth of discovery is relevant and appropriate. Within this framework, therefore, each issue is designed as a stand-alone topic of study, but is also part of the larger subject of CSR that is summarized in the *CSR Connection*.

The issues selected for inclusion in Part II illustrate CSR's practical and wide-reaching effects. As topical as today's newspaper headlines, they form the basis for active discussion and further inquiry using the resources provided. Many of the issues are broad, stretching across organizational, economic, and societal boundaries. As such, our goal here is to classify each issue in terms of its primary impact. Separately, these issues and case-studies are key elements of the contemporary CSR debate. Together, they represent the depth, breadth, and importance of CSR for firms today.

Chapter 6

ORGANIZATIONAL ISSUES AND CASE-STUDIES

CORPORATE GOVERNANCE

CSR Connection:	This issue reflects the central importance of boards of directors in ensuring organizational transparency, strategic oversight of the CEO, and the representation of shareholder interests.
Stakeholders:	Shareholders, Directors, Executives.

Issue

The duties of a board of directors are twofold:

Strategic advice: First, the board exists to provide the CEO and executive team with assistance in shaping the firm's strategy. Thus, a board filled with experienced officers from a variety of different firms and industries provides the firm's executives with a variety of knowledge on which to draw.

Oversight: Second, the board exists to represent shareholder interests. In this function, directors pursue the best interests of the firm's owners by monitoring the actions and performance of the CEO and executive team. The theory is that, to the extent that the interests of the shareholders and executives are aligned, the business will be managed in a way that best serves the shareholders. Given that shareholders are unable or unwilling to manage the firm on a day-to-day basis, the board's goal is to ensure the capital they have invested in the firm is well-managed on their behalf.

While it is difficult to evaluate the extent to which a board's strategic advice is sought and adhered to by the executive team (and even harder to know whether it altered fundamentally the fortunes of the firm), it is easier to know when a board has failed in its oversight role. The result of such a failure is often a transgression of some kind (often due to executive hubris or recklessness) that receives widespread media attention.

Scrutiny of the performance (and independence) of corporate boards has increased as a result of the corporate scandals in the early years of the 21st century. Scandals at Enron (2001), WorldCom (2002), Tyco (2002), HealthSouth (2003) and others, showed the damage that can occur when a weak board fails in its duty of oversight. These scandals raised the profile of corporate governance as an essential tool to limit executive excess. As a result of the public outcry at the corrupt practices brought to light by these corporate scandals, the U.S. legislature stepped in to regulate further the area of corporate governance. One result was the Sarbanes-Oxley (SOX) Act of 2002, a key provision of which is greater responsibilities for executive officers, holding them personally accountable for the actions of the organization:

> Under new federal sentencing guidelines after the Sarbanes-Oxley Act, corporate crooks can get life in prison if crimes involve some combination of the following: over 250 victims, a loss of at least $400 million, involvement of a public company, or threat to a financial institution's solvency.[1]

As such, the Act requires audit committee members "to be entirely composed of outside directors and chief executives to certify personally that a company's financial reports accurately reflect its financial condition."[2] Even for lesser transgressions, such as knowingly filing a false certification, in theory the director "can be fined $5 million or sent to prison for 20 years."[3] In spite of the good intentions embedded within the SOX legislation, however, it was unable to prevent the failure of Lehman Brothers in 2008 and what turned out to be the worst financial crisis since the Great Depression:

> Most major financial institutions in 2008 were more than compliant with SOX. Indeed, at the banks that collapsed, 80% of board members were independent, as were all members of their audit, compensation, and nominating committees. All the firms had evaluated their internal controls yearly, and the 2007 reports from their external auditors showed no material weaknesses in those controls. But that didn't stop the failures.[4]

Compounding the ineffectiveness of SOX to generate more effective governance, in the aftermath of the Financial Crisis, many of the strong provisions contained within the legislation have remained "largely unused":

After the financial crisis, [SOX's] certification rules seemed like a strong weapon against executives suspected of misleading investors. But prosecutors haven't brought any criminal cases for false certification related to the crisis. Regulators have brought only a handful of crisis-related civil allegations in that area.[5]

Many of the problems with poor governance come down to the structural characteristics of particular boards and the commitments and capabilities of individual directors:

Boards are often too large to operate effectively as decision-making groups. Members frequently lack sufficient expertise in the relevant industry. And most important, few members devote the time needed to fully understand the complexities of the company's global operations.[6]

And, where there is a failure of good governance, it is not clear that the directors responsible suffer significant consequences. In addition to not being imprisoned or fined when the firms they are responsible for collapse, it is also likely that the individuals involved will quite quickly get jobs on other boards. Analyses of the directors of firms like Enron, Bear Stearns, and Lehman Brothers, for example, indicate that almost all found other jobs (as directors on other financial firms or in academia) within a few years of the collapse of their old firms:

In part this reflects the old boy network of Wall Street, which keeps people in the same positions because of friendships. . . . The trend also underscores the decline in the importance of reputation on Wall Street—even since the time of Enron. Prior bad conduct simply is often not viewed as a problem.[7]

None of this bodes well for the future of corporate governance. This is important because, given the separation between ownership and control of the firm as a central tenet of capitalism, good corporate governance is essential to executive effectiveness and a firm's ongoing viability. Rather than being a theoretical ideal to which lip service is paid but not acted on, the ability of the board to hold a firm's executive team to account for the firm's actions is now recognized as a a key investment criterion in terms of evaluating corporations and establishing confidence. Publications such as *Businessweek's* ranking of the best and worst boards reflect this change in attitude toward the issue of corporate governance in the United States.

Principles of Good Governance[8]

Businessweek ranks corporate boards according to four principles of good governance:

Independence: The number of directors who were previously company executives or have existing business relationships with the company (e.g., consulting contracts).

Stock ownership: The amount of stock each member of the board owns in the company, therefore aligning personal interests directly with shareholder interests. *Businessweek* has stipulated an ideal minimum of $150,000 per director (excluding stock options).

Director quality: Directors should have experience in the same industry of the company's core business, as well as management experience of a similar-sized organization. "Fully employed directors should sit on no more than four boards, retirees no more than seven. Each director should attend at least 75% of all meetings."[9]

Board activism: Boards should meet regularly, should also meet without management present, and should show restraint in areas such as executive compensation.

The consequences for firms with good or bad boards can be significant as "the stocks of companies with the best boards [in *Businessweek's* study] outperformed those with the worst by 2 to 1. [In addition, during economic recessions] the Best Boards companies retained much more of their value, returning 51.7%, vs. -12.9% for the Worst Boards companies."[10]

The combination of the raised importance of corporate governance, together with the inconsistent performance of boards this century, has led to persistent calls for reform that reflect the importance of the board's oversight function. In the U.S., for example, there are growing calls for "a new culture of governance" that gives greater priority to hiring professional[11] instead of celebrity[12] directors. In the UK, The Financial Services Authority in the UK has been critical of the failure of boards to help avert the collapses of Northern Rock and the Royal Bank of Scotland during the recent Financial Crisis, "demanding change 'where the caliber/expertise/skills of non-executive directors [is] not good enough.'"[13]

Debates about the relative value of the different corporate governance rules and structures in the U.S. and the U.K. continue.[14] These differences between the two systems become apparent in relation to the separate roles of the CEO and the chair of the board.

Case Study: Split Chair/CEO

One of the most controversial determinants of the operational effectiveness of a corporate board is the issue of leadership: Should the jobs of CEO and chair of the board be legally separated? Traditionally in the United States, power is concentrated in one person who both chairs the board and is the top employee of the company, the CEO. In Canada, Britain, and continental Europe, however, the separation of these two jobs is standard practice. For corporate governance to be effective within an organization, the performance of the board of directors is crucial. And for this performance to be effective, the board's independence from management is important. Many in the United States are now arguing that the board cannot effectively monitor the CEO in terms of day-to-day operations if that same person is also the chair of the board:

> Andrew S. Grove, who is chairman of Intel Corp., while Craig R. Barrett is its CEO, made the point . . . this way: "The separation of the two jobs goes to the heart of the conception of a corporation. . . . If [the CEO is] an employee, he needs a boss, and that boss is the board. The chairman runs the board. How can the CEO be his own boss?" In a recent survey of board members from 500 large U.S. companies, McKinsey & Co. found similar views. Nearly 70% of respondents said a CEO should not run the board.[15]

The oversight role played by the board is growing in importance as investors (who rely on boards to protect their investments) are required to monitor and evaluate multinational organizations that produce increasingly complex financial statements. The position of chair of the board, as chief representative of investors, therefore, is also growing in importance. Add in the different skills required by both positions and the difficulty in having one person in both roles becomes more apparent. As a result, before 2003 in the U.S., "the share of companies separating the two jobs was rising about 2% annually. [And, in 2003], the share of companies whose CEOs didn't also hold the chairman's reins increased to 25% of the S&P 500 from 21% in 2002."[16] By 2011, however, in the S&P 500 "210 [42%] now split the two roles":

> There is, to be fair, an ongoing debate over whether there is any tangible evidence that having a separate chairman improves a company's performance. Yet it is mostly bosses who argue that it does not, while shareholders generally think it does.[17]

As shareholders become aware of the conflict of interest inherent in one person holding both positions, the backlash against companies that ignore calls for reform is increasing. Within the pharmaceutical industry, for example, shareholder resolutions tabled in 2005 garnered support for dividing the two roles and appointing an independent director chair of the board at Wyeth (39%); Eli Lilly & Co. (25%); Abbott Laboratories (17%); Merck & Co. (46.5%); and Pfizer Inc. (42.1%).[18] At Disney's 2004 annual general meeting, 43% of shareholders voted in favor of a no-confidence motion against then CEO, Michael Eisner. In response, the board removed him as chairman of the company (allowing him to retain his position as CEO) and appointed the respected politician, George Mitchell, in his place. In hindsight, this sea-change at Disney was credited as "a turning point for the movement for better corporate governance."[19]

In spite of the growing support for the idea of splitting the CEO and chair positions (and even for the CEO position to be shared by two people),[20] many corporations in the United States maintain unified responsibilities. As the quote above indicates, in 2011 the majority of firms in the S&P 500 still retained a combined CEO and Chair position. CEOs who covet both positions emphasize the efficiency value in doing so—one person can make decisions more quickly and decisively than two. Critics, on the other hand, note the power and ego-driven reasons for combining the CEO and Chair positions, while also pointing to research that suggests better decisions are made by diverse groups, even if the process is slower due to the checks and balances inherent with multiple sources of authority. Of particular concern to activists are firms with strong, dominant personalities at the top, such as the boards of "Viacom, CBS and Discovery Communications. . . . Coca-Cola and Nike," as well as Rupert Murdoch at News Corporation, which is "one of ten firms in the S&P 500 that particularly worry [corporate governance experts] GMI."[21] At News Corp's 2012 annual general meeting, "around two-thirds of independent votes cast were in favor of appointing an independent chair (stripping Mr. Murdoch of the role)."[22]

Although the ideal for corporate governance activists is an *independent* Chair (i.e., divided roles), one compromise that has grown in popularity as a result of the Sarbanes-Oxley (SOX) legislation is the appointment of a *lead* director of the board. This position is given to one of the board's independent directors (i.e., a director who is not an executive of the firm), who is expected to chair the board whenever there is a conflict of interest that requires the CEO to excuse him/herself from the conversation. It satisfies governance reformers because, in theory, it provides greater oversight of the CEO on sensitive issues such as compensation, while CEOs favor this compromise because it allows them to retain both the CEO and chair titles:

> The number of lead directors at S&P 500 companies rose to 247 in 2011, from 165 in 2006, ... Over the same period, the number of presiding directors [a position with narrower responsibilities] fell to 209 from 298.[23]

Similarly, the number of independent Chair positions is also rising:

> Under pressure from activist investors, more companies than ever are splitting the roles of chief executive and chairman. [In 2011] More than 20% of the companies in the S&P 500 Index [105 out of 500] have appointed an independent outsider as their chairman, up from 12% in 2007.[24]

As indicated in Figure 6.1, however, there are other ways that a U.S. firm can divide the CEO/Chair position that are more progressive than a lead director position (where the roles remain combined), but less satisfactory to governance activists than a fully independent Chair.

UK firms, however, have much less flexibility, with almost all firms adopting a divided role, with a CEO and "a chairman who is usually both part-time and

Figure 6.1 CEO/Chair Responsibilities Among S&P 500 Firms (2005–2010)

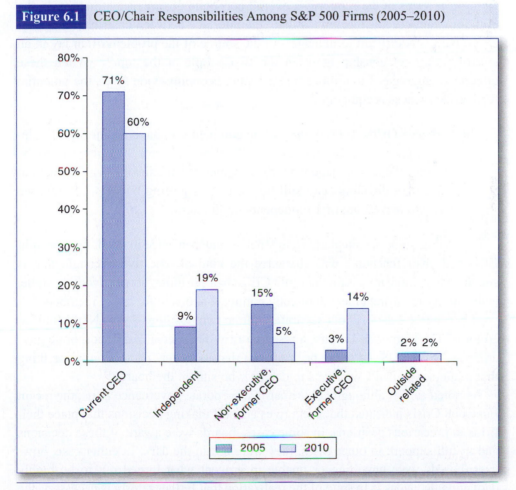

Source: Geoffrey Owen, 'A very British split at the top,' *Financial Times*, March 15, 2011, p. 10.

'independent' – that is, not someone who worked for the company before the appointment or had commercial links with it."[25] The change came about after a series of scandals at UK firms:

> In the early 1990s, Adrian Cadbury, the former chairman of Cadbury Schweppes, led a committee[26] that proposed reforms to improve governance and reassure the investor community after a series of high-profile scandals among British companies. One of the recommendations called for independent outside chairmen. Within a decade, most U.K. companies had adopted the recommendation due to pressure from regulators and investors.[27]

It is important to remember, however, that *independence* from the organization does not automatically mean *effectiveness*, either in terms of a board at a particular firm, or in terms of the economy's overall corporate governance structure. In the UK, for example, it is recognized that "the interface between chairman and chief executive . . . is difficult to manage. . . . the source of the problem often lay in an unsatisfactory relationship between the two people at the top."[28] When these effects are aggregated to a more fundamental, economy-wide level, the potential for ineffectiveness is compounded:

> The Sarbanes-Oxley Act requires public companies to have a majority of independent directors. . . . But the SEC still allows director nominations to be closely controlled by management. So as James McRitchie of Corp.Gov.net put it, independent directors "can still be the CEO's golfing buddies." Enron, we might recall, had 12 out of 14 independent directors.[29]

Given this, some are skeptical as to whether independence in itself, or even split CEO and chair functions, will guarantee the kind of objective oversight that is sought. Much more important than split CEO/chair positions, some advocates argue, is the ability for shareholders to directly nominate and vote for board members:[30]

"I don't give a damn about separation of the two positions," says Neil Minnow, editor of The Corporate Library, a research firm that specializes in corporate governance. "In the US, its never been proven that its better. There's only one thing that matters, and that's who gets to decide who sits on the board."[31]

As noted earlier, although not primarily a corporate governance issue, the recent Financial Crisis indicated that executives are still making decisions that place their firms in precarious positions. In some cases, boards were aware of these decisions and in full support; in other cases, they were left in the dark. In either case, however, boards were unwilling or unable to prevent what turned out to be highly damaging decisions.[32] In spite of the realization that further reform is necessary, the concern is that the desire to enact meaningful reform will fade as the attention of regulators, investors, and the public to these issues ebbs and flows in cycles.

Nevertheless, some look to recent developments as a sign of positive change. One of the fallouts from the Financial Crisis, for example, was strong public reaction to specific practices (such as high executive compensation) in the firms that received government financial assistance. Similar pressures resulted in Goldman Sachs reversing its publicly-stated position and appointing "an independent 'lead' director."[33] And, in the case of Bank of America, one consequence of this stakeholder reaction resulted in Ken Lewis, the firm's CEO, being forced out of his job as chair of the board:

The vote . . . was a stunning rebuke of Mr. Lewis' authority at the bank. . . . But it was also seen as a watershed moment for the US corporate governance movement, a sign that the European-style separation of the chairman and chief executive positions was gaining traction in North America.[34]

CEO Perspective

James Wolfensohn (World Bank)

Corporate governance is not designed just to avoid the next financial disaster. Effective corporate governance is also good for business. Academic studies have consistently shown that companies with independent boards of directors produce greater returns on shareholder equity, achieve higher profit margins and return more capital to their investors than competitors without independent boards. The shareholders of Enron learned the hard way that weak corporate governance can facilitate an environment in which fraud and mismanagement can occur. James Wolfensohn concluded when he was president of the World Bank that 'the governance of companies is more important for world economic growth than the government of countries.' Simply put, well-governed companies deliver better results.[35]

Online Resources

- CorpGov.net, http://www.corpgov.net/ and http://www.corpgov.net/links/links.html
- Dodd-Frank Corporate Governance Issues, http://www.sec.gov/spotlight/dodd-frank/corporategovernance.shtml
- Global Corporate Governance Forum (OECD & World Bank), http://www.gcgf.org/

- GMI Ratings, http://www3.gmiratings.com/
- International Corporate Governance Network, http://www.icgn.org/
- OECD Corporate Governance, http://www.oecd.org/corporate/
- PIRC (Pensions & Investment Research Consultants Ltd.), http://www.pirc.co.uk/
- PricewaterhouseCoopers, http://www.pwc.com/us/en/sarbanes-oxley/index.jhtml
- Public Company Accounting Oversight Board, http://www.pcaobus.org/
- Sarbanes-Oxley, http://www.sarbanes-oxley.com/
- The Corporate Library, http://www.thecorporatelibrary.com/
- United Nations Global Compact, Corporate Governance, http://www.unglobalcompact.org/docs/issues_doc/Corporate_Governance/Corporate_Governance_IFC_UNGC.pdf
- U.S. Securities and Exchange Commission, http://www.sec.gov/spotlight/sarbanes-oxley.htm

Pro/Con Debate

> **Pro/Con Debate:** The roles of CEO and chair of the board should not be divided among two people, but should be combined in one position.

Questions for Discussion and Review

1. What is the job of a corporation's board of directors? Whose interests *should* they serve? Whose interests *do* they serve? Which of their two main responsibilities do you think is the most important? Why?

2. Many CEOs complain that the result of recent legislation has been to complicate further the auditing process. Do you think that this is an area of law that can be left to market forces or do you think that, if corporations cannot regulate their own behavior, then it is the duty of government to step into the void?

3. Look at the four principles of good governance used by *Businessweek* to rank "The Best & Worst Boards." Which of these principles do you think is the most important? Why?

4. Are *independent* board members truly independent? What would you do to ensure the greater independence of board members?

5. What is your opinion of the causes of the recent Financial Crisis? What was the role of corporate governance and boards of directors?

CORPORATE RIGHTS

CSR Connection:	This issue analyses the entity that is the focus of this book—the corporation. In contrast to the corporation's responsibilities, what rights does it have as a legal person?
Stakeholders:	Corporation, Executives.

Issue

The corporation is the focus of much of the critical attention of CSR advocates. It is the organization blamed for many of the ills created by globalization and free trade. The attention reflects the high profile of the corporation in modern society:

> One hundred and fifty years ago, the corporation was a relatively insignificant entity. Today, it is a vivid, dramatic and pervasive presence in all our lives. Like the Church, the Monarchy and the Communist Party in other times and places, the corporation is today's dominant institution. But history humbles dominant institutions. All have been crushed, belittled or absorbed into some new order. The corporation is unlikely to be the first to defy history.[36]

In contrast to this picture of current dominance, but impending doom, *Fortune* magazine heralds the corporation as one of "the most significant innovations of the past 50 years":

> Without [corporations] and their proven ability to marshal and allocate resources, organize and harness the ingenuity of people, respond to commercial and social environments, and meet the ever more elaborate challenge of producing and distributing goods and providing services on a global scale, we would have far less innovation—and less wealth.[37]

This perspective is shared by Micklethwait and Wooldridge in their book, *The Company: A Short History of a Revolutionary Idea*:

> Hegel predicted that the basic unit of modern society would be the state, Marx that it would be the commune, Lenin and Hitler that it would be the political party. Before that, a succession of saints and sages claimed the same for the parish church, the feudal manor, and the monarchy. . . . they have all been proved wrong. The most important organization in the world is the company: the basis of the prosperity of the West and the best hope for the future of the rest of the world. Indeed, for most of us, the company's only real rival for our time and energy is the one that is taken for granted—the family.[38]

When we discuss a corporation's societal responsibilities, therefore, it is important to remember that, merely by existing—by providing a return on investment to shareholders, by providing jobs for employees and suppliers, by providing value to customers, and by paying taxes to government—the corporation is benefiting society. If you add to that mix the constant product innovation necessary to maintain sales and profits (in general, only products that are in demand are purchased), then the corporation, as a concept, can be considered an extremely positive and productive component of a healthy society. As Todd Stitzer, past CEO of Cadbury Schweppes, proclaimed:

> Remember Adam Smith's invisible hand? It is one of the most repeated phrases in the business world. But business has allowed society to forget a very simple fact: the hand that connects markets and balances supply and demand is ours. We are the people who put food on plates, books on shelves, music in people's ears and information online. We are the distributors and we are the creators of wealth.[39]

The corporation, however, can also do harm to the societies in which it operates. Doing all of the above does not ensure an organization's long-term viability and does not replace the need for an effective CSR policy implemented throughout the organization. Our discussion of Walmart in Chapter 3, for example, demonstrates that a company that is successful and producing products in demand can still be accused of behavior that is harmful to society as a whole. As a result, the positive aspects of Walmart's operations[40] are often lost among the negative publicity the company receives.[41]

Given all of this, to what extent is the corporation a positive factor in the CSR debate? To what extent is business essential to achieve the social agenda sought by CSR advocates? And, how can a corporation's contribution to the wider good be measured and evaluated?

CSR Newsletters: Legal Rights

An article in *The New York Times*[42] by Joel Bakan contrasts the progress of two relatively recently established, legally-protected entities—corporations and children. First, children, which emerged as a protected class towards the end of the nineteenth century:

> By the early 20th century, the "century of the child," as a prescient book published in 1909 called it, was in full throttle. Most modern states embraced the general idea that government had a duty to protect the health, education and welfare of children.

Second, corporations, which gained their status as a "legal—albeit artificial—person" in the twentieth century:

> Lawyers, policy makers and business lobbied successfully for various rights and entitlements traditionally connected, legally, with personhood.

Bakan, who co-authored the book and documentary, *The Corporation* (http://www.thecorporation.com/), argues that the interests of these two protected classes (children and corporations) are inherently in conflict:

> Century-of-the-child reformers sought to resolve conflicts in favor of children. But over the last 30 years there has been a dramatic reversal: corporate interests now prevail. Deregulation, privatization, weak enforcement of existing regulations and legal and political resistance to new regulations have eroded our ability, as a society, to protect children.

In particular, he identifies childhood obesity, electronic media, childhood medication, and toxic chemicals exposure as areas where corporate behavior is fundamentally controlling and damaging child development. He concludes that "our current failure to provide stronger protection of children in the face of corporate-caused harm reveals a sickness in our societal soul."

In addressing the *value* of the corporation to society, we are inherently determining what position it deserves in the social strata. Given that the ability to incorporate is a privilege bestowed by society, what rights should accompany the legal status of *corporation*? If we are going to argue that a corporation has *responsibilities* that we would like it to fulfill, we also need to grant *rights* that protect its ability to exist and do what is it designed to do—make money.

Case Study: Citizens United

A *corporation* is a fictitious legal person that is endowed with many of the functions of a human being. It can possess property, it can incur debts, it can sue and be sued, and it can be criminally prosecuted, fined, and, in theory, dissolved by the federal government. Under U.S. law, the Supreme Court has extended portions of the Bill of Rights to corporations, even while it has been less stringent in imposing many of the responsibilities of citizenship. The basis of these rights rests in the concept of *corporate personhood*. As Mitt Romney said during the 2012 Presidential campaign, "Corporations are people, my friend."[43]

> America's legal system has been forced to grapple with the meaning of corporate personhood more thoroughly than other countries' courts have done, because the constitution is so specific about the rights it bestows on people.[44]

This interpretation of the status of corporations in society is something that has evolved over time. It has changed so much that the politicians that were involved in the very earliest incarnations of the corporate form would be hard-pushed to recognize its modern equivalent. Originally, corporations faced a great deal of opposition from those (including Adam Smith) who perceived them as a dangerous invention, as indicated in comments by Sir Edward Coke, a jurist in the seventeenth century ("[Companies] cannot commit treason, nor be outlawed or excommunicated, for they have no souls")[45] and similar sentiments expressed by Lord Chancellor Edward Thurlow, a century later ("Corporations have neither bodies to be punished, nor souls to be condemned, they therefore do as they like").[46]

The idea of corporate personhood originated in a U.S. Supreme Court case, *Trustees of Dartmouth College v. Woodward* (17 U.S. 518, 1819). The case centered on a dispute between the college and the New Hampshire legislature's attempts to force it to become a public institution. In deciding in favor of the organization, the Court drew an important distinction between public and private charters and, in the process, reinforced the rights of the private organization to remain private (and, by definition, outside of the control of the state):

> In a ruling about the status of Dartmouth College in 1819, the Supreme Court found that corporations of all sorts possessed private rights, so states could not rewrite their charters capriciously.[47]

In keeping with this precedent, the Court continued to understand corporations as legal individuals. As such, over time, they began to increase the rights bestowed upon those individuals in line with constitutionally-protected individual rights:

> While corporations had been afforded limited rights, such as property ownership or contract-making, since the Renaissance, the idea that an inanimate entity was eligible for rights of personhood sprang from the 1886 case of *Santa Clara County v. Southern Pacific Railroad*. The corporation in this case was able to wield the newly minted 14th Amendment to argue that it, as a corporation, was entitled to the same tax benefits as individuals.[48]

This case, *Santa Clara County v. Southern Pacific Railroad* (118, U.S. 394, 1886), is often cited as the cornerstone of modern corporate rights in the U.S. It dealt with the issue of the taxation of railroad properties. Southern Pacific Railroad had refused to pay these California taxes because the rules under which they were levied were more stringent than the rules for personal taxation. Rather than the Court specifically deciding that corporations were individuals, however, the issue was taken as a starting point for the Justices' decision. In other words, this position was stated, rather than decided, which leaves its status as legal precedent somewhat precarious. This ambiguity is the source for much of the contentious debate around the legal rights of corporations today. Nevertheless, once the decision was published, corporations saw a chance to take advantage and they moved quickly:

> . . . . although the [14th Amendment to the Constitution] had been added to protect the rights of African Americans after the Civil War, only 19 individuals invoked it for protection between 1890 and 1910. Businesses, on the other hand, claimed 14th Amendment protection 288 times during that period.[49]

The concept of corporate personhood was extended more recently as a result of a 1976 Supreme Court case, *Buckley v. Valeo* (424, U.S. 1, 1976) where one of the most contentious corporate rights, freedom of speech, was strengthened.[50] In this case, the Court ruled explicitly that political donations were free speech and, as such, were constitutionally-protected behavior. This applied whether the donations were made by individuals or by organizations. And, it is this decision that lay the foundation for the controversial *Citizens United v. Federal Election Commission* (558 U.S. 310, 2010) decision, which was decided in 2010.

CSR Newsletters: Citizens United

An editorial in *The New York Times*[51] discusses "the rights of corporations" in relation to a case the U.S. Supreme Court was hearing at the time that, ultimately, was decided as *Citizens United v. Federal Election Commission* (558 U.S. 310, 2010):

> .... the court is considering what should be a fairly narrow campaign finance case, involving whether Citizens United, a nonprofit corporation, had the right to air a slashing movie about Hillary Rodham Clinton during the Democratic primary season.

Instead of deciding the case in terms of this narrow point of law, however, the Court decided to expand its consideration to include broader implications under the legal doctrine of "corporate personhood":

> The courts have long treated corporations as persons in limited ways for some legal purposes. They may own property and have limited rights to free speech. They can sue and be sued. They have the right to enter into contracts and advertise their products. But corporations cannot and should not be allowed to vote, run for office or bear arms. Since 1907, Congress has banned them from contributing to federal political campaigns—a ban the Supreme Court has repeatedly upheld.

It is clear that *The New York Times* does not think the Court's current view of corporate rights should be expanded (for an alternative perspective on the same case, see an op-ed article in *The Wall Street Journal*).[52] *The New York Times* also thinks a narrow interpretation of a corporation's rights represents a purer reflection of the original intent of the Constitution:

> John Marshall, the nation's greatest chief justice, saw a corporation as "an artificial being, invisible, intangible," he wrote in 1819. "Being the mere creature of law, it possesses only those properties which the charter of its creation confers upon it, either expressly, or as incidental to its very existence."

In particular, there are strong arguments to be made that corporations are not the same as individuals in their ability to amass resources that can then be used to distort the political debate. As such, the editorial argues that, in areas of political speech in particular, the Court should be wary of expanding corporations' Constitutional rights to allow these kinds of polemical statements to be made.

Citizens United was important because it dealt with the free speech rights of corporations. Like most rulings, however, there is the theory (which may be defendable) and the reality (which may be subject to abuse). This decision emphasizes this distinction by allowing corporations greater freedom to finance political ads/campaigns. As *The New York Times* editorial team put it:

> With a single, disastrous 5-to-4 ruling, the Supreme Court has thrust politics back to the robber-baron era of the 19th century. Congress must act immediately to limit the damage of this radical decision, which strikes at the heart of democracy.[53]

The core of the issue centers on whether corporations enjoy the same first amendment rights to free speech protection as individuals. Although the majority in the Supreme Court decision used well-established legal precedent to claim that they do, it is harder to understand why the decision to treat corporations as individuals was made in the first place:

> The founders of this nation warned about the dangers of corporate influence. The Constitution they wrote mentions many things and assigns them rights and protections—the people, militias, the press, religions. But it does not mention corporations.[54]

Criticism of the decision characterized the Supreme Court's decision to accept the case and use "a narrower, technical question" in order to elevate it "to a forum for striking down the entire ban on corporate spending" as "shameless judicial overreaching." In short:

> The majority is deeply wrong on the law. . . . It was a fundamental misreading of the Constitution to say that these artificial legal constructs have the same right to spend money on politics as ordinary Americans have to speak out in support of a candidate.[55]

The consequences of the decision are projected to alter the face of political campaigns, increasing the amount of money in politics, with direct consequences for the number of attack ads and favoring those candidates that support corporations. As such:

> The real solution lies in getting the court's ruling overturned. The four dissenters made an eloquent case for why the decision was wrong on the law and dangerous. With one more vote, they could rescue democracy.[56]

There is also a calmer perspective on what corporations can and cannot do in relation to political ad spending as a result of the Citizens United decision (and it is worth noting that the decision applies to all organizations, not only for-profit firms). This perspective argues that the consequences of the Court's decision will not be as momentous as some fear:[57]

> As the court noted, 26 states and the District of Columbia already permit independent corporate and union campaign spending. There have been no stampedes in those states' elections. Having a constitutional right is not the same as requiring one to exercise it, and there are many reasons businesses and unions may not spend much more on politics than they already do.[58]

More interesting and relevant to this discussion, however, is the Court's evolving position on which rights should be ascribed to corporations, in general. Even though the range of rights has been steadily increasing over time, progress is neither linear nor necessarily logical.

CSR Newsletters: Corporate Personhood

Constitutional law is interesting because of the immense impact the Supreme Court has on day-to-day life in the U.S. Clearly, appointing a Supreme Court Justice is one of the most important decisions a U.S. President makes because the effects last well beyond his/her time in office and affect society so broadly. While the Supreme Court is a highly influential and important branch of government, however, it does not mean it is efficient or, at times, even logical. However much it likes to ignore the reality, it is as political an institution (subject to the same biases, emotions, and inertial forces) as the other branches of the U.S. government. Of particular note are the inconsistencies of the judicial logic used to rationalize particular decisions and, presumably, win majority support among the Justices in different cases under different clauses of the constitution.

These thoughts were prompted by an article in *The New York Times*,[59] which reports on a 2011 Supreme Court decision in a case that focused on corporations' right to privacy in which the Court "ruled unanimously that corporations have no personal privacy rights for purposes of the Freedom of Information Act." While the intricacies of the arguments are fascinating, it is not clear why the same arguments were not used to deny corporations the right to free speech in the controversial Citizens United decision that removed limits on firms' donations to political campaigns.

The Citizens United decision is damaging because, although consistent with the legal definition of a corporation as an individual, it undermines the sanctity of the political process (and, for the same reason, other organizations, such as trade unions, should also be banned from making donations). If the Court is going to decide that a firm has the right to free speech, however, surely it must also decide that firms also have other rights that we attribute to individuals, such as the right to privacy. Instead, we get a convoluted semantic argument by Chief Justice Roberts (who wrote the majority opinion). Roberts' opinion, which "relied as much on dictionaries, grammar and usage as it did on legal analysis," debated the meaning of the word "personal" as a noun versus an adjective to justify a decision that appears to be inconsistent with recent precedent:

> "Adjectives typically reflect the meaning of corresponding nouns," he wrote, "but not always." He gave examples. "The noun *crab* refers variously to a crustacean and a type of apple, while the related adjective *crabbed* can refer to handwriting that is *difficult to read*," he wrote, quoting a dictionary. "*Corny*,' he went on, 'has little to do with *corn*."

A central component of the argument presented in this book is the recognition that corporations exist because their products are in demand and that, in general, it is in society's best interests to encourage healthy and wealthy corporations because they bring many benefits. An equally important component of our argument, however, is that, while demand for a product might be sufficient for short-term gain, it is insufficient for survival over the medium to long term. On top of a healthy foundation of an efficient organization and a profitable product, therefore, is the construction of an integrated, effective CSR policy that seeks to maximize stakeholder benefit over the medium to long term.

We, as a society, benefit if we are progressing. Corporations help us progress and generate much of the wealth on which we measure that progress. As such, for-profit firms are society's most important organizational form and therefore are central to future development. CSR helps corporations understand the dynamic environment in which they operate and chart a more sustainable path forward. In other words, CSR helps corporations maximize their potential and benefit the widest number of constituent groups. The concept of corporate personhood was developed with this goal in mind and, as such, is essential for the fluid operation of a market economy (firms need to be able to enter into contracts, to be able to sue and be sued, etc.):

> A development of the doctrine [of corporate personality] asserted that since companies could be liable for their debts, the individuals who ran the company were not. These institutional innovations made large scale economic organization possible.[60]

As such, the development of corporate personhood was an essential comple-ment to the concept of limited liability. Together, it can be argued that these inno-vations laid the foundation for the explosion in growth and prosperity among developed economies:

Until the mid-19th century companies (as opposed to partnerships) were regu-lated by corporate charters which laid down tight rules about what they could do. But reformers used the idea that companies, like people, should be captains of their own souls, to free them from these restrictions. The result of this lib-eration was an explosion of energy: Western companies turbocharged the indus-trial revolution and laid the foundations for mass prosperity.[61]

As a result, similar legal innovations have taken place in Europe and other developed economies, as well as in the U.S.:

[In Europe], corporations have been encouraged to assert the human rights conferred on individuals by the European Convention. Recent legislation in Britain created the new crime of corporate manslaughter. . . . [The larger issue] is that corporate personality is a reality, not just a legal construct. When people talk about the distinctive personality of Procter & Gamble or John Lewis we know immediately what is meant.[62]

In spite of this, however, the Supreme Court's inconsistent logic is in danger of getting itself in a mess. It is difficult for the Justices to continue to extend certain individual rights to corporations (like free speech), but not others (like privacy), unless it has a clear rationale for why it is drawing the distinction. At present, this rationale has not been made clear, but could be along the lines of only those rights that are essential "for the efficient functioning of business."[63] Already, the Court is perceived to be biased in favor of the business community:

During 1994-2005, some 56% of the cases supported by the [U.S. Chamber of Commerce] and considered by the court succeeded; the success rate during 2006-10 was 68%. In 2009-10 the side supported by the chamber won in 13 of 16 cases, five of those by the slimmest of majorities (5-4). . . . the Supreme Court ruled in a pro-business fashion in 29% of cases under Chief Justice Earl Warren (who served from 1953 to 1969). Under Warren Burger (1969-86) the figure was 47%. Between 1986 and 2005, under Chief Justice Rehnquist, it was 51%. Under Chief Justice Roberts it has risen to 61%.[64]

The danger for corporations is that, if the logic of personhood is extrapolated to its natural conclusion, then the rights that are granted should be accompanied with "onerous responsibilities."[65] Already many in the business community would point out that government regulation of business today is much higher than it has been historically.[66] In the absence of matching obligations, however, people will continue to question the privileges afforded to corporations. The inconsistency in the Court's decisions aggravates perceptions of bias and divides activists on where the boundary between corporate rights and societal responsibilities should lie. Many activist organizations, such as Move to Amend (https://movetoamend.org/) and Reclaim Democracy (http://reclaimdemocracy.org/), campaign in the U.S. for a constitutional amendment to redress the imbalance they see the Supreme Court as creating:

> We, the People of the United States of America, reject the U.S. Supreme Court's *Citizens United* ruling, and move to amend our Constitution to firmly establish that money is not speech, and that human beings, not corporations, are persons entitled to constitutional rights.[67]

Some among the Justices might well agree. In his dissent to Citizens United, for example, Justice John Paul Stevens argued that "because companies are without feelings, consciences or desires, they shouldn't benefit from laws that protect ordinary citizens."[68]

John Marshall (Chief Justice, U.S. Supreme Court, 1801–1835)

A corporation is an artificial being, invisible, intangible, and existing only in contemplation of law. Being the mere creature of law, it possesses only those properties which the charter of its creation confers upon it, either expressly or as incidental to its very existence. These are such as are supposed best calculated to effect the object for which it was created. Among the most important are immortality, and, if the expression may be allowed, individuality; properties by which a perpetual succession of many persons are considered as the same, and may act as a single individual. They enable a corporation to manage its own affairs and to hold property without the perplexing intricacies, the hazardous and endless necessity of perpetual conveyances for the purpose of transmitting it from hand to hand. It is chiefly for the purpose of clothing bodies of men, in succession, with these qualities and capacities that corporations were invented and are in use.[69]

Online Resources

- Adbusters, https://www.adbusters.org/
- Bakan, Joel, *The Corporation: The Pathological Pursuit of Profit and Power,* Free Press, 2004, http://www.thecorporation.com/
- Citizen Works, http://www.citizenworks.org/
- Corporation 20/20, http://www.corporation2020.org/
- GoodCorporation, http://www.goodcorporation.com/
- Move to Amend, https://movetoamend.org/
- Reclaim Democracy, http://reclaimdemocracy.org/corporate-personhood/
- The Center for Corporate Citizenship at Boston College, http://www.bcccc.net/
- *The Corporation,* http://www.thecorporation.com/
- Tomorrow's Company, http://www.tomorrowscompany.com/

Pro/Con Debate

> **Pro/Con Debate:** The corporation, as a legal person, should be extended the same individual rights as all other citizens.

Questions for Discussion and Review

1. Make a list of the rights of a corporation and a separate list of the responsibilities. Which is longer? Why do you think this is?

2. Can you imagine a world without corporations? What would we lose? What would we gain?

3. Go to the website for the movie documentary, *The Corporation* (http://www.thecorporation.com/). Have a look at the trailer posted on the site.[70] Is this kind of commentary helpful to those promoting CSR? Do you agree with the message it is conveying? Why, or why not?

4. What is your opinion of Citizens United? Was it the correct decision by the Court? Do you think the U.S. Constitution should be amended to read that "money is not speech, and that human beings, not corporations, are persons entitled to constitutional rights"?[71]

5. Have a look at Adbusters' "Corporate Logo Flag" as depicted on the Reclaim Democracy website (http://reclaimdemocracy.org/corporate-logo-flag-us-flag/).[72] What does this image represent to you? Is it a fair representation of reality or a distorted one?

EMPLOYEES

CSR Connection:	This issue investigates the benefit a firm receives when it meets the needs of one of its key stakeholders, its employees. A diverse organizational culture maximizes employee welfare, while also maximizing productivity and decision quality for the firm.
Stakeholders:	Employees.

Issue

Employees are an important stakeholder of the firm. To the extent that the organization fosters a feeling of commitment and loyalty within its workforce, the firm benefits. Employees are proud to work for organizations with an ethical reputation,[73] a sense that carries over into the quality of work that is produced:

> Evidence from the *Sunday Times'* "100 best companies to work for" list shows that the share prices of the quoted companies on the list outperform the FTSE All Share Index by between 10% and 15%, a result that is seen in every country that produces a list.[74]

This conclusion is reaffirmed by Gallup, which has been polling employees to determine their degree of engagement with their work and organization for many years:

> It is likely that organizations with engaged employees experience positive business performance, while workplaces with not engaged or actively disengaged employees are more likely to experience lower productivity.[75]

The Benefits of Motivated Employees

There are many causal-related benefits for companies that ensure their employees remain happy and healthy at work:

- Employee retention reduces costs associated with turnover—advertising, training, as well as lost productivity as the staff gain experience in their new positions:

(Continued)

(Continued)

Workers are six times more likely to stay in their jobs when they believe their company acts with integrity, according to Walker Information, a research company that measures employee satisfaction and loyalty at the workplace. But when workers mistrust their bosses' decisions and feel ashamed of their firm's behavior, four out of five workers feel trapped at work and say they are likely to leave their jobs soon.[76]

- Increased employee safety leads to reduced amounts of lost time and productivity due to injuries. Intel's approach to this issue makes both moral and business sense:

At Intel (No. 3), based in Santa Clara, Calif., good citizenship . . . includes careful attention to employee safety—so much that CEO Craig Barrett insists he be sent an e-mail report within 24 hours any time one of his firm's 80,000 employees loses a single day of work to injury. . . . In 2000, Intel's worldwide injury rate was just .27 injuries per 100 employees, compared to an industry average of 6.7.[77]

- Happy employees are productive and creative employees:

[At 3M, employees engage] in all sorts of frivolous activities, such as playing pinball and wandering about the campus. These workers are actually pushed to take regular breaks, as time away from a problem can help spark a moment of insight. . . . But this is just one reason for 3M's creative output. . . . The company also encourages its employees to take risks, not only by spending masses on research (nearly 8% of gross revenue), but also by expecting workers to spend around 15% of their time pursuing speculative ideas. Most of these efforts will fail, but some, such as masking tape, an early 3M concept, will generate real profit for the company. The reason why this approach works—and why it has been imitated by other crafty companies such as Google—is because many breakthroughs come when people venture beyond their area of expertise.[78]

The opposite effect, of course, occurs when employees are disenchanted and demotivated. To the extent that a firm treats its employees as a cost, something to be managed and minimized wherever possible (as encouraged by modern accounting convention), employees are likely to feel the organization deserves neither their loyalty nor 100 percent of their effort. To the extent that employees are valued by management and identified as the key to customer satisfaction (and, therefore, to increasing shareholder value), however, employees are likely to be more engaged, productive, and loyal. Unfortunately, it appears that modern corporations are better at engendering the first reaction among their employees than the second one:

> According to a 2011 Careerbuilder.com report, 76% of full-time workers, while not actively looking for a new job, would leave their current workplace if the right opportunity came along. Other studies show that each year, the average company loses anywhere from 20% to 50% of its employee base.[79]

And, this is not a pattern that can be attributed solely to economic hardship and the Financial Crisis. The danger is that corporations are undervaluing one of their key resources—the employees who enact their strategy and interact with customers on a day-to-day basis. Senior executives like to think of themselves as central to the firm's success, but the best strategy in the world is useless unless the firm has engaged employees who use their creativity and imagination to implement the strategy and conduct operations. A Gallup poll, first introduced in 2000 and designed to measure such engagement is not promising:

> The poll divided workers into three parts: "engaged" employees are those who are "emotionally attached to their workplaces and motivated to be productive." "Not engaged" employees are those who are "emotionally detached and unlikely to be self-motivated," while "actively disengaged" employees are those who "view their workplaces negatively and are liable to spread that negativity to others." In 2000, the poll indicated that 26% of employees were engaged, 56% not engaged and 18% were actively disengaged. In 2008, those figures came in at 29%, 51% and 20%; in 2010, at 28%, 53% and 19%; and in 2011, 29%, 52% and 19%.[80]

When companies ask for a 'bottom-line' benefit for implementing a comprehensive CSR perspective, employees are one of the most rewarding places to look. Creating a positive and inviting culture for employees takes some innovation, but best-practice models exist, and the return on the investment is tenfold. One example that is particularly effective in bolstering employee morale is an employee volunteer program:

> Today, more corporations are turning to hands-on volunteer projects to get their people motivated and working as a team. In many cases, participants say such activities help them forge bonds that remain even after they return to the office.[81]

In terms of employee loyalty and retention, employee volunteer programs revitalize employees. Such programs expose employees to a new environment away from their everyday position, allowing them to feel pride in their company and its standing within the community while also leading to the development of new skill sets.

Employee Volunteer Programs

Increasingly, firms are recognizing the benefits of employee volunteer programs and are prepared to dedicate increasing amounts of resources to ensure their success:

- **Accenture** – Loans employees to non-profits at discount rates.
- **Cisco Systems** – Places employees with education-related organizations for a year, at full salary.
- **Bain & Co.** – Supports employees who volunteer with local organizations, and pays for their time on full-time consulting projects.
- **Pfizer** – Pairs employees with health-related organizations to help with research and training.
- **Wells Fargo** – Pays employees to work with a school for as many as four months.[82]

In addition, AstraZeneca, HSBC, and KPMG all have dedicated employee volunteer programs in partnership with the UK's Volunteer Service Overseas (VSO) organization,[83] while IBM's Service Corps "sends young executives to help developing countries."[84] And, in response to the growing popularity of volunteer programs in the UK,[85] the British government (Home Office) designated 2005 as the Year of the Volunteer.[86] The bottom-line returns for firms from such programs are dramatic:

> Gallup estimates that actively disengaged employees cost more than $300 billion in lost productivity. Disengaged employees can hurt morale and erode the organization's bottom line. In contrast, engaged employees are more profitable, more customer-focused and easier to retain.[87]

One of the most celebrated employee volunteer programs is run by Timberland,[88] which reports the program's results along with the quarterly financial reports it releases in its annual *Corporate Social Responsibility Performance* reports.[89] The company's CEO, Jeffrey Swartz, inspired the volunteer program, which was launched in 1992.[90] Swartz saw the power the company possessed to evoke social change and also had the foresight to see the potential benefits this activism would bring. He also saw Timberland's employees as central to that success. The firm's *Path of Service*[91] volunteer program was the result:

> The program gives all Timberland employees 40 hours of paid leave each year for community service during the workweek. Service sabbaticals, which provide up to six months of paid time leave for employees to serve in capacity building roles in social justice organizations is the latest evolution of the Path of Service program.[92]

In response to a survey conducted by Timberland to learn more about the reception of the plan among employees, "79 percent of employees agree with the statement: 'Timberland's commitment to community is genuine and not a public relations vehicle.'" In addition, the survey "reveals that 89 percent of employees say community service is valuable to them, while 50 percent report that Timberland's volunteer programs influenced their decision to work for the company."[93] In general, research indicates that volunteerism at the workplace is a key driver for positive worker attitudes. One study finds that individuals who participate in employer-sponsored community activities are 30 percent more likely to want to continue working for that company and to help make it a success:[94]

> Accenture's program quickly became a draw for some employees. Hundreds applied, and those accepted now must wait weeks or months for an assignment. The program makes Accenture "more attractive as an employer," says Jill Smart, senior managing director of human resources.[95]

And, for Accenture, its program is not even one that will cost it any money. The firm is essentially running a social enterprise start-up that is designed to "break even financially":

> The company contributes, the employees contribute (via a cut in pay when they are doing it) and the client will pay a fee – although it is a fraction of the market cost.[96]

In return, Accenture benefits from greater employee loyalty, additional employee training, and improved relations with its community stakeholders.

Case Study: John Lewis Partnership

In addition to structuring an organizational culture that motivates employees, it is vital for firms to protect worker rights by embedding them within the organization's DNA. Doing so convinces employees they are truly valued and central to the firm's success.

Employee representation in the workforce has long been a cornerstone of a developed economy. Since the industrial revolution, in sectors as diverse as manufacturing, law enforcement, trucking, and education, labor unions have been the main source of protection for employee rights and interests. In the U.S., private sector employees gained the right to collective bargaining in 1935 with the passage of the National Labor Relationship (Wagner) Act.[97] This led to a rapid growth in union membership, to the point where, in the early 1940s, "one in five American workers belonged to a union. Some 10 years later, organized labor was at the peak of its power."[98] Since this time, labor union membership in the U.S. has been in steady decline:

> The Bureau of Labor Statistics said the total number of union members fell by 400,000 [in 2012], to 14.3 million, even though the nation's overall employment rose by 2.4 million. The percentage of workers in unions fell to 11.3 percent, down from 11.8 percent in 2011, . . . its lowest level since 1916, when it was 11.2 percent.[99]

Within this bigger picture, however, union membership is a tale of two contrasting sectors—private and public. As the economy in the U.S. has shifted from heavy industry and manufacturing to services, "union membership has fallen from 24% of private-sector workers in 1973 to a mere 7% in 2011." In contrast in the public sector, "union membership has risen from 23% in 1973 to 37% in 2011."[100] Private sector employees' rights and status in the organizational hierarchy have suffered in line with this decline in union membership:

> Today, fewer than one in 14 private sector workers belongs to a union, half the portion of 15 years ago. Where unions matter most—fighting for workers' share of the spoils of economic growth—they lost the battle long ago. Despite soaring worker productivity, the typical American worker takes home today only 2 percent more than a quarter of a century ago, after adjusting for inflation.[101]

William Greider argues in his book, *The Soul of Capitalism,* that this imbalance will not be corrected simply by reviving the union movement. Instead, a more fundamental change in organizational structure is required to remove the injustice and inequality that capitalism can generate. In other words, positively motivated employees are central to the goal of altering "the basic operating values of American capitalism so that the priorities of society [over the narrow financial priorities of stockholders] become dominant":

> Most Americans, in current life, go to work daily and submit to what is essentially a master-servant relationship inherited from feudalism. . . . The solution is for workers to own their work. The forms for doing so—employee-owned

firms, partnerships, cooperatives and other hybrids—are alive and growing. To be effective, they must incorporate not only employee ownership but collaborative decision making as well.[102]

An effective employee share-ownership scheme ensures that the workers', managers', and owners' interests are more closely aligned and that employees are likely to feel more committed to generating positive outcomes for the company as a whole. In spite of the criticism leveled at stock options—and their debatable impact on performance for top management—when awarded only to an elite few,[103] companies that distribute ownership throughout the organization see notable improvements in job motivation and satisfaction:

> Evidence suggests that smart use of options and other compensation do boost performance. Companies that spread ownership throughout a large portion of their workforce, through any form—options, Employee Stock Ownership Plans, or other means—deliver total shareholder returns that are two percentage points higher than at similar companies. . . . Better stock performance isn't the only benefit. Companies with significant employee ownership do better on a wide range of performance metrics, including productivity, profit margins, and return on equity, according to the studies.[104]

There are a number of arguments in favor and against employee-owned firms. A particularly well-known example in the UK is John Lewis, a department store that was founded in the early 1900s, but became employee-owned after the founder's death in 1928:[105]

> Its ownership structure dates back to 1929, when John Spedan Lewis, son of the founder, set up a profit-sharing scheme that became the John Lewis Partnership; a second settlement, made in 1950, transferred all his remaining shares into the partnership. John Lewis now has more than [81,000] employees, who are known as partners, and the success of the company is widely attributed to their loyalty and commitment.[106]

Employee-ownership is presented as an alternative form of for-profit organization that re-prioritizes the goals of the firm and generates much more of a social enterprise. Ownership can come in many forms, such as "cooperatives, employee-owned firms, social enterprises, and community land trusts," with proponents arguing that these alternatives are a fundamental reform of capitalism ("a permanent shift in the underlying architecture of economic power"). Equally importantly, they are scalable to a level where meaningful change could be introduced:

Consider, for example, the John Lewis Partnership (JLP) in England. It's the largest department store chain in the country, with 35 department stores and 272 Waitrose grocery stores. Revenues of this company are more than $11.5 billion. If placed into the Fortune 500 list of the largest U.S. corporations, JLP would settle in around 212—a little higher than Starbucks. It's 100 percent owned by its employees.[107]

In other words, employees feel invested *in* the company because they *are* the company. The firm's constitution, for example, states that "the purpose of the group is to ensure 'the happiness of all its members, through their worthwhile and satisfying employment in a successful business'":[108]

The John Lewis Partnership is built around the value of fairness. The founder, John Spedan Lewis . . . believed that traditional ownership was unfair because dividends paid to shareholders for doing nothing were obscene when workers barely earned subsistence wages. . . . If the ultimate perquisite of being an owner is the right to pocket some of the profit left after the bills are paid, then these employees are genuine owners. Each year, after the firm sets aside a portion of profits for reinvestment in the business, the remainder—generally between 40 and 60 percent of profit—is distributed to employees. . . . Here we begin to see what is revolutionary about the John Lewis Partnership. Employees in this firm are not a countervailing power. They're not legally outside the firm, negotiating with it. They are the firm.[109]

The result is a firm that feels different, yet performs as well, if not better, than its competitors:

The mood in [John Lewis'] stores is markedly different from any other company. The staff are more attentive and professional. They own the place and it shows. . . . John Lewis was recently named Britain's favourite retailer for the third year in succession . . . It's Christmas sales outstripped those of its rivals and Waitrose, its food arm, was the fastest-growing retailer.[110]

In spite of the many apparent advantages of this organizational structure, its long history ("Staff share-ownership schemes emerged in America in the 1920s"), and its favored status as "a more caring, cuddly capitalism," it has not been widely adopted beyond a few firms. This is strange, given that there are clear economic and competitive advantages to employee ownership:

Employee-owned companies are more productive and hardier in a recession, . . . [At John Lewis] Staff turnover is low; the shop beat many competitors on

Christmas sales. Firms with similar structures concur: Arup, an engineering outfit, attributes its business range and 'family feel' to being owned by its 10,000 employees.[111]

In spite of higher productivity and a more dispersed ownership, however, there are barriers to widespread application, including evidence that suggests employee-owned firms are no more socially responsible than firms with other ownership structures:

It does not prevent bad decisions: having a quarter of shares in employees' hands did not save Lehman Brothers from bankruptcy.[112]

Perhaps more importantly, minority employee ownership poses real risks to employees. While their job security is often higher, financially, their heavy investments in their own firm can easily leave them exposed to shifts in the firm's share price:

It is rash to put a worker's livelihood, savings and pension in one basket case; many employees lost everything when Enron, an energy-trading company, collapsed in 2001.

Ultimately, the disadvantages of employee ownership on an organization-wide level may outweigh the individual advantages that accompany increased involvement and commitment:

Companies that are wholly-owned by their staff may face barriers to growth. Many firms need a flexible capital base to expand—one reason the partnership model in banking declined. Employee mobility promotes innovation. At base, it is unrealistic to expect many bastions of capitalism to turn their shares over to their workforce.[113]

Similar ownership forms have been explored in other countries, such as the U.S.,[114] and employee protection has long been an important part of the economies of countries such as Germany and Japan. The hybrid forms of employee ownership that are most prominent in these countries, however, still face limitations in comparison for full employee-ownership:[115]

In the US, many companies have Employee Share Ownership Plans (ESOPs) and in a few cases the ESOP controls a majority of the shares, but these arrangements are rarely linked to joint decision-making. . . . In Germany, co-determination gives extensive consultation rights to employees through works councils and supervisory board membership, but does not usually involve employee shareholdings.[116]

In these systems, there remains the potential for a conflict of interests between employee interests and shareholder interests because ownership is not invested fully in the employees. Nevertheless, these hybrid models are still effective in flattening the organization's hierarchy and reducing inequality among employees. As owners' and workers' interests become better aligned, productivity generally increases, "as long as it is linked to a coherent package of work practices that reduce the level of supervision and give greater responsibility to employees."[117] This idea of reduced supervision—the elimination of layers of management—is beginning to take hold in a number of innovative firms and generating interesting consequences.

CSR Newsletters: Employees

An article in *The Wall Street Journal*[118] profiles an innovative approach to allocating annual performance bonuses among employees:

> Coffee & Power, a San Francisco odd-jobs start-up, granted each of its 15 full- and part-time employees 1,200 stock options this past January, to distribute among co-workers in whatever way they chose. A worker can plunk all his options onto one colleague or split them among the group, so individual bonuses are tied to how co-workers perceive each other's work.

Personnel decisions taken within companies (e.g., decisions to hire, fire, reward, and promote employees) are extremely subjective. We all are motivated by non-rational biases, prejudices, and incomplete information. What this idea is doing is substituting individual self-interest for the non-meritocratic decisions of managers and executives. Of course, such 'investment' decisions by employees will also be guided by the same biases and prejudices, but by democratizing or 'crowdsourcing' the process (by extending it to all employees), the opportunities for abuse are diminished. The program's rules reinforce this ethos:

> Workers cannot reward themselves, nor can they give options to company founders, who already have sizable shares. (The money or shares allocated to employees each quarter varies depending on company performance.) Employees only know what bonuses they receive, but don't learn who allocated what. The company makes public a distribution curve of all the bonus grants, with no names attached, so workers can see what the highest and lowest bonuses were.... The biggest surprise: the third-largest allocation went to the ninth-highest-paid person in the firm, a remote developer who handles small tasks and spends a lot of time helping others.

It is an interesting thought-experiment to see what applications this concept might have in other areas of the firm.

This idea of a flatter organization, with fewer bosses to closely control the workforce, has been explored at length by Gary Hamel in an article in the *Harvard Business Review*.[119] In spite of the value of managers, Hamel argues, the downside of what Alfred D. Chandler Jr. called the visible hand,[120] "is that the visible hand is inefficient and often ham-fisted." In response, Hamel promotes a vision of the organization where:

- No one has a boss.
- Employees negotiate responsibilities with their peers.
- Everyone can spend the company's money.
- Each individual is responsible for acquiring the tools need to do his or her work.
- There are no titles and no promotions.
- Compensations decisions are peer-based.[121]

It is these characteristics that define Morning Star Company, the world's largest tomato processor and the best-practice model of an organizational structure that Hamel sees elsewhere (in firms like W. L. Gore and Zappos),[122] but argues should be much more widely adopted. One example is the tech company, Valve Corp., a videogame maker in Washington state. Like many tech firms, Valve has a lot of perks for its employees, "One thing it doesn't have: bosses."[123] Reportedly, in the absence of hierarchical oversight, employees are motivated by the innovative structure, which seems to generate a culture that veers from anarchy to Communism:

At Valve, there are no promotions, only new projects. To help decide pay, employees rank their peers—but not themselves—voting on who they think creates the most value. . . . Firings, while relatively rare, work the same way: teams decide together if someone isn't working out. As for projects, someone typically emerges as the de facto manager, says Greg Coomer, a 16-year veteran of Valve who works on product design. When no one takes the lead, he adds, it's usually a sign that the project isn't worth doing.

Proponents argue that the "boss-less" approach can also be applied to larger, more traditional organizational structures, such as at GE, which "has run some aviation-manufacturing facilities with no foremen or shop-floor bosses" for a number of years.[124] W.L. Gore, however, provides perhaps the best example of how this approach can be implemented in practice:

Since it was founded in 1958, W.L. Gore has operated under what it calls a "lattice" management structure, which relies on teams in place of bosses and traditional chains of command. . . . Gore's 10,000 employees, who work mainly in engineering and manufacturing, take on leadership roles based on their ability to "gain the respect of peers and to attract followers," says Ms. Kelly, the CEO. Those who choose not to take the lead also are valued, she adds, noting that the company prides itself on staff "followership."[125]

CSR Newsletters: W.L. Gore

An article in the *Financial Times*[126] reports on an innovative management structure at W.L. Gore, the successful maker of Gore-Tex, where "You would think it is a pretty tight ship. But no. 'It's a very chaotic environment,' declares Terri Kelly, the company's chief executive officer." The founders of the 50-year old firm created a structure that minimizes layers of hierarchy:

> The corporate hierarchy at Gore, such as it is, is almost completely flat. No one gets to tell anybody else what to do. Decisions are reached by agreement, not diktat.

The result is a convoluted and sometimes unwieldy decision-making process. The firm's executives believe, however, that what they sacrifice in terms of speed, they make up for in terms of broad buy-in to decisions that are made. As Gore's CEO explains, "you have to sell your ideas, even if you're the CEO. You have to explain the rationale behind your decision and do a lot of internal selling." According to the article, the result is an environment that is more meritocratic, with only those ideas that enjoy broad support progressing:

> In Gary Hamel's book, *The Future of Management*, he quotes a Gore associate, Rich Buckingham, who sums up the company's approach. "We vote with our feet. If you call a meeting, and people show up, you're a leader."

CEO Perspective

Herb Kelleher (Southwest Airlines)

If the employees come first, then they're happy. . . . A motivated employee treats the customer well. The customer is happy so they keep coming back, which pleases the shareholders. It's not one of the enduring green mysteries of all time, it is just the way it works.

The core of our success. That's the most difficult thing for a competitor to imitate. They can buy all the physical things. The things you can't buy are dedication, devotion, loyalty—the feeling that you are participating in a crusade.[127]

Online Resources

- Accenture, Voluntary Service Overseas, http://www.accenture.com/us-en/company/citizenship/Pages/voluntary-services-overseas.aspx
- Employee-owned Companies, http://www.nceo.org/articles/employee-ownership-100
- Fair Labor Association, http://www.fairlabor.org/
- *Fast Company Magazine*, Employee Volunteer Programs, http://www.fastcompany.com/tag/employee-volunteer-programs
- John Lewis Partnership, http://www.johnlewispartnership.co.uk/about.html
- IBM Volunteer Program, http://www.ibm.com/ibm/responsibility/initiatives/volunteers.shtml
- Morning Star Company, http://morningstarco.com/index.cgi
- Salesforce.com, http://www.salesforce.com/foundation
- SERVEnet, http://www.servenet.org/
- The National Center for Employee Ownership, http://www.esop.org/
- Timberland's Path of Service, http://responsibility.timberland.com/service/
- Volunteer Service Overseas (VSO), http://www.vso.org.uk/
- W.L. Gore & Associates, http://www.gore.com/en_xx/aboutus/index.html
- Work Foundation, http://www.theworkfoundation.com/

Pro/Con Debate

> **Pro/Con Debate:** Employee-ownership is the best way to minimize inequality and increase morale among a firm's employees.

Questions for Discussion and Review

1. What are some of the benefits to companies from increased employee morale and loyalty? Do you agree that these benefits are likely to come from a volunteer program?

2. How can companies encourage employees to participate in volunteer programs and avoid the suspicion that "by volunteering, they are potentially derailing their chances for a promotion because of the time they'll spend out of the office"?[128]

3. Go to Timberland's main website (http://www.timberland.com/) and also the company's responsibility website (http://responsibility.timberland.com/).

Do you get the sense that Timberland is genuine in its commitment to CSR? Does that create a good impression of the company or not make much difference in your perception of it?

4. What is your impression of the John Lewis Partnership? Is it a good firm? Is it a successful firm? Are those two things (good and successful) the same? Would you like to work there? Why?

5. Do we have a *right* to a job, or is it a *privilege* that has to be earned?

EXECUTIVE PAY

CSR Connection:	This issue reflects the importance of the conflict between a company's *principals* (shareholders) and *agents* (managers) to understanding the stakeholder approach to CSR.
Stakeholders:	Executives, CEOs, Directors, Shareholders.

Issue

Principal/agent theory describes the inherent tension that exists between the owners of an organization (collectively, the *principals*, which include the shareholders and their representatives, the board of directors) and the managers (the *agents*), whom the owners appoint to operate the business on their behalf and protect their investment.

The conflict of interest that arises between these two groups is a problem that has plagued limited liability joint stock companies ever since they were established in the Companies Act of 1862.[129] The concept of *limited liability*, contained within the legislation, allowed people to invest in companies, but *limit* their *liability* to the amount of that investment, thus avoiding any additional responsibility for the firm's debts. We take this for granted today, but, at the time, it was revolutionary and provoked considerable resistance. Commentators, such as Adam Smith, saw limited liability as a subsidy from the state that gave corporations an advantage over other, purer, business forms.[130] One outcome of this innovation was that limited liability corporations encouraged the emergence of a class of investors who had the money to support various ventures, but did not have the time or expertise to become involved in day-to-day management. What emerged in their place was a class of professional managers who managed the investors' money on their behalf. Almost immediately, however, the issue arose of how best to ensure the managers were managing the investors' money with the investors' best interests in mind—how best to protect "shareholder value":[131]

> [Adam] Smith, in his 1776 classic, *The Wealth of Nations*, said he was troubled by the fact that corporations' owners, their shareholders, did not run their own businesses but delegated that task to professional managers. The latter could not be trusted to apply the same "anxious vigilance" to manage "other people's money" as they would their own, he wrote, and "negligence and profusion therefore must prevail, more or less, in the management of such a company."[132]

One of the safeguards put in place to guard against this eventuality and guarantee good governance was the appointment of a board of representatives with the power to oversee managers' actions, as well as provide advice where possible (the board of directors). Over time, however, relations between the principals' representatives (the board) and their agents (managers) shifted from one that was paternal to one that became fraternal. As a result, lines of interest became blurred—particularly in cases where the CEO was also the Chair of the board and where directors served at the CEO's pleasure. Compounding this tension between executives and directors was the gradual shift in corporate outlook as a firm's share price became the pre-eminent determinant of executive performance. As the influence of investors increased, executives altered their outlook from managing the firm's relationships with its many stakeholder groups over the medium to long term, to focusing on its relationships with shareholders and short term measures of success (for example, emphasizing quarterly earnings reports in order to bolster a company's share price):

> Before the 1980s one tenet of corporate governance was that company management served several constituencies: shareholders, yes, but also employees, customers, and perhaps others too. . . . But the shareholder-value crowd insisted that the only clientele that mattered was stockholders. If they were rewarded, then all other players would reap benefits as a byproduct of an even higher stock price. This mantra of shareholder value, however, could be taken to an extreme and perverted . . . [becoming] a handy all-purpose justification for mass firings, shoddy products, and the dumping of chemicals into rivers.[133]

Ultimately, in its modern reincarnation, this conflict between principal and agent corrupted the original goals of corporate governance. As executive oversight weakened, so CEO power and influence increased. Eventually, unchecked power resulted in hubristic excess and the corporate scandals that peppered the business world around the turn of this century:

> The Enron scandal—and those at WorldCom, Tyco, Adelphia and others— exposed a glaring flaw in the oversight of America's top executives. . . . In the textbooks, capitalism works because corporate managers are kept in check by shareholders, who operate through directors they elect. The truth, however, is that many American directors are handpicked and handsomely compensated by the very executives they oversee.[134]

Even with the legislative reforms that followed these scandals (primarily Sarbanes-Oxley in 2002), governance did not improve and produced yet another crisis of confidence:

> When the world's largest financial institutions had to be rescued from insolvency in 2008 by massive injections of governmental assistance, many blamed corporate boards for a lack of oversight. This was a problem we had supposedly solved nearly a decade ago, when blatant failures of corporate governance (remember Enron?) prompted Congress to pass the Sarbanes-Oxley Act. The new rules had seemed promising. The majority of a board's directors had to be independent, which would, in theory, better protect shareholders. Senior executives were required to conduct annual assessments of their internal controls for review by external auditors, whose work would be further reviewed by a quasi-governmental oversight board. The recent financial meltdown, however, has made it clear that the new rules were insufficient.[135]

The central question of this Issue, therefore, remains the same as it was for Adam Smith: What is the best way to align the interests of the owners of the organization (the principals) with those of the agents entrusted to operate the organization on the owners' behalf? In the 1990s, stock options became the new Holy Grail—by awarding executives options, the theory held that they would have a direct interest in the performance of the company. If the company performed well, stock prices would rise and the executives would benefit personally; however, this theory was quickly shown to be flawed as some executives saw the short-term stock price as their most important focus (maximizing personal benefit), rather than the long term health of the firm.

Case Study: Stock Options

A key component of the principal/agent conflict is the contentious issue of executive compensation. A significant assumption inherent in the granting of stock options is that executives' are best incentivized by paying them as much as possible. The reasoning goes that both shareholders and executives seek to maximize personal financial gain—shareholders via a higher share price and executives via higher levels of compensation. If executives can be paid in a way that meets their needs, while also meeting the needs of shareholders, then the two sets of interests will be aligned. One solution that became popular in the early- to mid-1990s was stock options. The result of this shift in executive compensation was an explosion in the amounts of money paid to CEOs, which has continued to today. A list of the top CEO compensation packages in the first decade of the twenty-first century is presented in Figure 6.2.

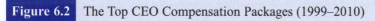

Figure 6.2 The Top CEO Compensation Packages (1999–2010)

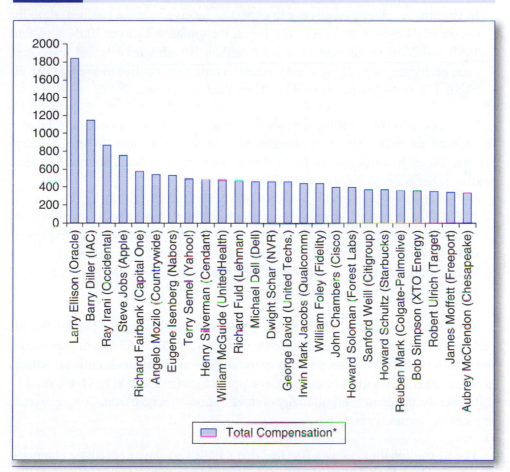

* Includes salary, bonus, restricted stock options, and other compensation (US$mn).

Source: 'The Decade's 25 Top Earners,' *The Wall Street Journal*, July 27, 2010, p. A16.

A detailed analysis of compensation among the top 200 highest-paid CEOs in 2011 reveals that, in spite of the recession and Financial Crisis, "rewards at the top are still rich – and getting richer." In particular, "Median pay of the nation's 200 top-paid CEOs was $14.5 million [in 2011]."[136] In short, CEO compensation continues to grow exponentially and these numbers only include the CEOs of publicly-traded companies, "it does not capture the many billions that have been earned by top hedge fund managers and private-equity dealmakers in recent years."[137] In addition, these expanding compensation packages are not limited to for-profit firms, with the highest-earning nonprofit CEOs[138] and university presidents[139] routinely receiving compensation packages in excess of $1 million.

Although the pay disparity between executives and employees is greatest in the U.S., this phenomenon is common throughout developed economies:

> In Britain, . . . chief executives can expect to receive average compensation in excess of £4.5m ($6.9m) [in 2012]. Pay at the top grew by over 300% between 1998 and 2010. At the same time, the median British worker's real wage has been pretty stagnant. These trends mean the ratio of executive to average pay at FTSE 100 firms jumped from 47 to 120 times in 12 years.[140]

More specifically, what the data show is that, in addition to becoming larger, the nature of executive compensation has shifted over time. While initially focused on cash compensation (either salary or bonuses), firms are increasingly finding other ways to reward their CEOs:

> A $90,000 area rug, a pair of guest chairs that cost almost as much, a $35,000 commode and a $1,400 trash can—these are just a few of the expenses from a remodeling of John Thain's office when he took over as Merrill Lynch's chief executive officer . . . . The total bill came to an astonishing $1.2 million— about the price of five average single-family homes.[141]

This trend is reflected in Figure 6.3, which presents the average breakdown of the different components of CEO compensation in 2011. CEO compensation today is less and less about pay and more and more about stock options, which now make-up 21.8% of CEO compensation packages (in addition to 41.4% stock).

Ironically, this growth in popularity of stock options emerged from Congressional attempts to limit executive pay:

> The $1 million limitation on [the tax] deductibility of senior executive compensation, which became law in 1993, resulted in many companies *increasing* CEO salaries to $1 million.[142]

Figure 6.3	Components of CEO Compensation (2011)

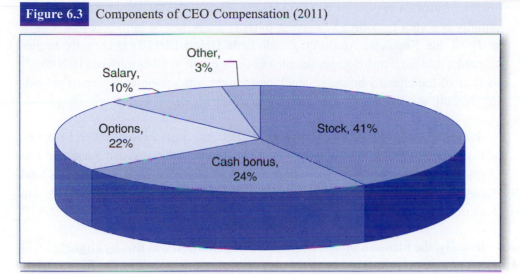

Source: 'The Decade's 25 Top Earners,' *The Wall Street Journal*, July 27, 2010, p. A16.

Rather than a ceiling for pay, as Congress had intended, however, the $1 million became the floor and de facto standard by which a CEO was judged. The differentiator then became the amount of the executive's compensation that was tied to *performance*. And stock options, which grant employees the right to purchase company stock at a fixed price at a future point in time, became the method of choice. Firms could afford to pay CEOs ever-increasing amounts of this form of *performance-related pay* because they had a minimal impact on a firm's accounts:

> In recent years, especially during the halcyon days of the technology boom, stock options were handed out liberally with no direct impact on companies' bottom lines, because most of these options, which critics contend impose a real economic cost on companies, weren't booked as expenses. They simply were referenced in footnotes in annual reports.[143]

Attempts to expense stock options following the ethics scandals of the turn of the century (forcing companies to attribute a value to the options and treat that value as an expense that counts against earnings) met with resistance by business. Small technology firms, in particular, argued that they need options to attract talent—they are generally younger organizations and less likely to have the established cash flows necessary to pay higher salaries or other traditional forms of compensation. In addition, there are a number of technical difficulties with expensing stock options. Principally, these involve what value to assign to them, as it is unknown when and at what price and future date they will be vested. This uncertainty often results in CEOs receiving very different amounts of pay than initially reported by a firm.[144] Having initially attempted to introduce this reform in 1991, the Financial Accounting Standards Board (FASB) eventually implemented a rule for firms to expense stock options given to all employees in 2005.[145] In spite of the change, however, stock options remain a popular means of providing executives with high levels of compensation:

> Some 34% of bosses exercised them in 2010, up from 23% in 2009. Frits van Paasschen of Starwood Hotels and Resorts Worldwide cashed in a bundle he was given when the firm's shares were in a ditch in February 2009, pushing his total pay up from $2.9m in 2009 to $17.4m in 2010. He was granted roughly 1m shares at an exercise price of $11.39. By the end of 2010 they were worth $60.[146]

Initially, the idea behind options-based compensation was that by aligning CEO and top management interests more closely with the interests of the firm's shareholders (via the firm's share price), management would be incentivized to maximize company performance. This, in turn, would lead to maximum sustainable growth for the company and share price over time. In practice, however, some CEOs focused on raising the company's share price in the short term, sometimes irrespective of the legality or honesty of their actions or the long-term impact on the firm's interests:

> These huge [compensation packages] bolster a system in which executives have incentives to manage the numbers for short-term gain and personal payout . . . . Exorbitant compensation feeds the worst instincts and egos of powerful CEOs, fueled by their desire to win at all costs and resulting, too often, in the cutting of ethical corners.[147]

This desire to maximize personal gain without regard for the firm's well-being was also apparent in the 2006 stock options backdating scandal, where firms agreed to executives' demands to backdate their stock options to the point when the share price was at its lowest:

> A key purpose of stock options is to give recipients an incentive to improve their employer's performance, including its stock price. No stock gain, no profit on the options. Backdating them so they carry a lower price would run counter to this goal by giving the recipient a paper gain right from the start.[148]

Ultimately, governance experts remain unconvinced that stock options effectively align the interests of the firm's owners and its managers:

A stock price is simply the consensus of investor expectations about the future performance of the company, and linking compensation to it is an incentive for executives to focus more on raising investor expectations than improving actual performance. While we might imagine that real performance drives expectations of future performance, the link is exceedingly tenuous.[149]

As a result of these different distortions of the main purpose behind stock options, their value essentially fell out of correlation with company performance.

Executive Compensation and Firm Performance

Compensation researcher Equilar studied 450 companies in the Standard & Poor's 500 and found something curious: The worst-performing companies in 2002 were those that gave their chief executives the biggest option grants in 2001. The median grant for those CEOs was $9.4 million. Median shareholder return the next year: -50%. CEOs with the best performances received much smaller grants—the median size was $3.7 million—and delivered returns of 17%.[150]

In the past decade, companies that granted 90% of all options to CEOs and a few top managers performed worse than those that distributed options more evenly and fairly among employees. There is no justification for increasing the compensation of CEOs from 40 times that of the average employee in the 1960s to nearly 600 times today.[151]

Consider: If you had invested $10,000 in the stock market (as represented by the Standard & Poor's average of 500 stocks), you would have more than doubled your money over 10 years, accumulating $22,170 by the end of 2002, despite the bear market. . . . But if you were investing in the companies with the highest-paid executives over the same period of time, the value of your investment would have fallen 71 percent to $2,899.[152]

How a company approaches the issue of stock options as a component of executive compensation, therefore, is an important indicator of that company's approach to transparency, corporate governance, and reporting financial statements and company information.[153] In short, it speaks to the firm's approach to communicating with its stakeholders. Many of the scandals that have plagued corporate America resulted from a lack of these characteristics. Many of the problems revolved around violating the spirit, if not the letter (although that happened too), of the law and deceiving investors for personal, self-motivated corporate gain:

> Pay isn't just about recruitment and retention. It's also a form of communication about a company's culture and values, which can impact a company's relation-ship with its employees, its brand reputation, and ultimately its share value.[154]

The recent Financial Crisis further highlighted the large compensation packages paid to the CEOs and senior executives of large firms and the failure of stock options to resolve the principal/agent conflict. As such, the mood shifted against stock options as the preferred performance-related component of executive pay. Too many executives, from the severance package "worth roughly $210 million" of Robert Nardelli, who resigned as CEO of Home Depot in January 2007,[155] to the 59.42% shareholder defeat of Shell's 2009 executive pay plan,[156] to the "outrageous" bonuses of $165 million (later revised up to $218 million)[157] paid to the financial services group at the insurance giant AIG during the height of the Financial Crisis,[158] the public perception was that executives were being paid for failure:[159]

> . . . a major reason for public outrage, the outlandish $165 million in bonuses that were paid to a few hundred executives at AIG—in a division of the com-pany that lost $100 billion! That's the teetering industrial giant into which taxpayers have poured about $170 billion in aid with another $30 billion to come. One can only wonder whether they would have received bigger bonuses if they lost $200 billion.[160]

In spite of these compensation packages, many commentators argue that "American chief executives are not overpaid"[161] and that "CEOs deserve their pay."[162] Part of the reason for this is the idea that CEOs are losing power and influ-ence within the corporate hierarchy—less likely to be appointed jointly as Chair of the board, for example.[163] One way in which this trend is expressed is in terms of CEO tenure, which, due to increased pressures for immediate performance returns (partly caused by excessive compensation), is decreasing:

> Corporate chiefs may earn much more than before, but tenure at the top has become more precarious. In 1992 a U.S. Fortune 500 CEO had a 36 percent chance of retaining his job for the next five years; in 1998 that chance was down to 25 percent. . . . the tenure of the average American CEO has declined from close to 10 years in the 1990s to about five and a half years. . . . In 2011 alone, CEOs at 14.4 percent of the world's 2,500 biggest listed companies left their jobs.[164]

Moving forward, the goal for those seeking reform of executive compensation should be to refocus incentives on the long-term health of the company and ensure these incentives are diffused throughout the organization. Although there are reported benefits to the practice, a number of companies have stopped giving out earnings estimates to investors as one way of reducing pressure on the short-term share price:[165]

Critics worry that a lack of guidance could lead to more earnings surprises, greater stock volatility, or even less vigorous oversight of management. In fact, it's a great leap forward. Successful strategies are not executed in three-month time slots. By refusing to play the quarterly guessing game, companies reduce the focus on short-term performance. That lessens incentives for accounting shenanigans aimed only at juicing the numbers.[166]

Today, reformers are pushing for executive compensation packages with policies and practices that, as always, seek to close the gap between the interests of agents and those of the firm's principals. As Shell's CEO admitted in 2009 as he called for reform of executive compensation in response to the "shareholder revolt" against his controversial pay increase:

You have to realize: if I had been paid 50 per cent more, I would not have done it better. If I had been paid 50 per cent less, then I would not have done it worse.[167]

Executive Compensation Reforms

Possible reforms include, but should not be limited to:

- Full and clear disclosure to stakeholders of executive compensation packages.[168]
- Binding shareholder votes on compensation packages—so-called "say-on-pay" votes introduced in the U.S. as a result of Dodd-Frank (2010). Remuneration Reports have been required for listed firms in the UK since 2002 and non-binding votes have been compulsory since 2006; these will be binding from 2013.[169] As a result, the average CEO in the UK "earns a little more than half what his or her U.S. counterpart makes."[170] In the U.S., say-on-pay votes are slowly gaining traction: "In 2012, a majority of shareholders voted against

(Continued)

(Continued)

executive pay packages at 2.2% of the companies that held . . . votes. That's up from 1.3% in 2011, the first full year such votes were held."[171]

- A salary cap for cash compensation similar to the "internal pay equity provision" of Dodd-Frank (2010).[172] Whole Foods, for example, has a cap of "19 times the average pay [in the firm]," which it considers sufficient "to make the compensation to our executives more competitive in the marketplace."[173]

- Packages that include a range of incentives designed to encourage short-, medium-, and long-term performance, with performance measured in operational excellence (e.g., revenues, market share, customer service, etc.), rather than share price, "executive compensation should be tied more closely to corporate debt [e.g., deferred compensation, defined-benefit pensions, or company bonds] . . . these types of incentives protect bond-holders' interests and the value of the firm, particularly when a company's solvency is in question."[174]

- Tie CSR and sustainability metrics to senior executive pay. Good examples of firms that have embraced this include Puma,[175] and Akzo Nobel and Marriott.[176] In general, however, firms have been reluctant to do this to date: "Among Europe's 300 largest companies, the percentage is under a third (28%). [And, those that have], have done so in a way that could be best described as 'opaque.'"[177]

- Capping of potential payouts of total compensation (including performance-related components) to limit excessive risk-taking. Along these lines, the EU intends to introduce a cap on executives' bonuses that cannot exceed the value of base pay, along with binding shareholder say-on-pay votes.[178]

- Empower compensation committees with the ability to revise packages according to new circumstances as they arise.

- Encourage long term executive ownership with restricted stock (versus options with short-term vesting periods), which helps better "align bosses' interests with shareholders.'[179]

- Introduce clawback[180] policies that allow a percentage of compensation to be recovered in the event that a firm is forced to restate earnings at a future date: "Nearly three-fourths of Fortune 100 companies had such rules in place in 2009, up from 18% in 2006."[181]

- Institute voting rules that allow for directors to be replaced directly by shareholders, particularly those that sit on the compensation committee of the board.[182]

There is hope that a more effective form of executive compensation is emerging from all the damage done since 2000—first, with Enron and related corporate scandals and, more recently, with the Financial Crisis and popular disillusionment with the finance industry:[183]

> According to Equilar Inc., . . . roughly 70% of total compensation for S&P 500 CEOs [is] in the form of long-term incentives, typically earned over three years or more and predominantly tied to shareholder return.[184]

For this to be true, however, will require more vigilant boards of directors to resist the temptation to chase celebrity CEOs and continue to award them excessive compensation packages. In reality, for all the new rules that are put in place following every crisis, there is little sense that anything is changing:

> The fact that executive compensation increased more than 12 percent in the first year after say-on-pay was introduced doesn't give much comfort.[185]

This phenomenon of ever-rising CEO compensation is based largely on an argument that firms have to pay the 'going rate' in order to secure the *best* leaders. Similarly, firms have to keep raising the pay of their current CEO if they are to stop that person from jumping ship to another firm with a higher pay check. There is new research from the University of Delaware, however, to suggest that this argument is false—that external hires are much less effective CEOs than internal hires, even though internal hires are paid less.[186] In other words, being a successful CEO in a particular industry requires skills that are not easily transferable:

> There is no conclusive empirical evidence that outside succession leads to more favorable corporate performance, or even that good performance at one company can accurately predict success at another. . . . In short, executive skills cannot pass the most basic test of generality: transferability.[187]

CEO Perspective

Peter Drucker

"Real leaders, Drucker observed, are leaders of teams showing respect for people and their work. Nothing destroys that as efficiently as excessive CEO compensation. He maintained that the appropriate pay range was 20 to 25 times what the rank and file earned – it's now in the hundreds. That level of

(Continued)

(Continued)

inequality foments disillusionment among mid-level managers, as he said in a 2004 Fortune interview, and corrodes mutual trust between the enterprise and society. Excessive compensation, he wrote in 1974, is designed to create status rather than income. 'It can only lead to political measures that, while doing no one any good, can seriously harm society, economy, and the manager as well.' And when a financial benefit accrues to managers who lay people off, he stated in 1996, 'there is no excuse for it. No justification. This is morally and socially unforgivable, and we will pay a heavy price for it."[188]

Online Resources

- AFLCIO, Executive PayWatch http://www.aflcio.org/Corporate-Watch/CEO-Pay-and-the-99
- Center On Executive Compensation, http://www.execcomp.org/
- Citizen Works—Expense Stock Options, http://www.citizenworks.org/corp/options/options-main.php
- Financial Accounting Standards Board, http://www.fasb.org/
- How do stock options work? http://money.howstuffworks.com/personal-finance/financial-planning/stock-options.htm
- International Accounting Standards Board, http://www.iasb.org/
- myStockOptions.com, http://www.mystockoptions.com/
- Securities and Exchange Commission, Executive Compensation, http://www.sec.gov/answers/execomp.htm
- Securities and Exchange Commission, Say-on-Pay, http://www.sec.gov/news/press/2011/2011-25.htm

Pro/Con Debate

Pro/Con Debate: Stock options are an effective way of solving the principal/agent problem.

Questions for Discussion and Review

1. What is your opinion about the current level of executive compensation? Do you agree with the statement: "Pay peanuts, get monkeys. Pay obscenely huge amounts, get obscenely greedy monkeys"?[189] Are executives

being paid the "market rate" or is some factor distorting the market for top executives?

2. What is the issue at the core of the principal/agent conflict? Are stock options a good form of employee or manager compensation? Do they begin to heal the inherent conflict that exists between principals and agents?

3. In 2011, Tim Cook, CEO of Apple, earned a total compensation of $378 million. In other words, that is $1 million a day, "roughly $42,000 an hour. Or $700 a minute. Or $12 a second." "Is any C.E.O. worth $1 million a day?"[190] Is it OK to pay a CEO any amount, as long as the net benefit the CEO brings to the organization exceeds her/his compensation?

4. Some companies award stock options to all employees. Starbucks is a good example of the loyal employees and good press coverage such a policy can generate. Have a look at this Starbucks video explaining how the company's *Bean Stock* program works (http://vimeo.com/36572039). Would such a policy encourage you to join one company over another, or is salary level still the most important determining factor in deciding between compensation packages?

5. Look at the list of possible *Executive Compensation Reforms* above. Which of these ideas do you think is most likely to alter behavior and better align the interests of both principals and agents? Why?

INVESTOR ACTIVISM

CSR Connection:	This issue reflects the rise in investor activism in recent years. It is a growing, if controversial, area within CSR, to which firms will face increasing pressure to respond. To what extent are investors willing to discriminate among companies and sacrifice short-term returns in order to pursue socially responsible investing strategies?
Stakeholders:	Shareholders, Investors.

Issue

There are two types of *investor activists*:

- Institutional investors—professional investors who manage large blocks of a firm's shares, such as hedge, pension, or mutual funds and who are driven largely by concerns of maximizing shareholder price. A good example of an institutional investor is Carl Icahn, whose battles with the management of firms such as General Motors, Time Warner, or, more recently, Netflix make front page news.[191]

- NGOs, other socially concerned groups, and individual investors—social activists who usually hold smaller blocks of a firm's shares, but who attempt to influence firm action on specific issues that reflect the social values that are important to them and their members. Some good examples of such groups include TIAA-CREF (http://www.tiaa-cref.org/) the teachers' and college professors' pension fund, the Interfaith Center on Corporate Responsibility (http://www.iccr.org/), but can also include groups such as Investors Against Genocide (http://www.investorsagainstgenocide.org/).[192]

While, from a CSR perspective, the second group has traditionally been the more relevant group of activist investors, as risk management becomes a more mainstream area of concern for firms and socially responsible mutual funds grow in importance (in terms of dollar amounts), the distinction between these two groups has blurred. On specific issues in relation to specific firms, both groups can easily find themselves seeking the same change in firm behavior. As a result, it is interesting to investigate instances where these two groups see overlapping interests. It is not clear, for example, whether demands for greater transparency and accountability from these groups (on issues such as corporate governance, executive pay, and green house gas emissions) lead necessarily to changes in corporate behavior. In addition, what opportunities exist for individual investors who seek to make investments that are consistent with their values? What is clear, however, is that both groups are becoming more vocal in their public criticism of executives and the decisions they take on behalf of their firms,[193] and new legislation is giving them the powers to take action:

In the US, the financial regulation bill . . . gives the Securities and Exchange Commission the authority to grant shareholders proxy access to nominate directors and provides investors with a non-binding vote on executive pay and golden parachutes. In the UK, the new Stewardship Code sets out the responsibilities for investors to increase their engagement with management and boards.[194]

This increased activity is apparent from the volume and subject of shareholder resolutions that are tabled at firms' annual general meetings (AGMs) and voted on by both institutional investors and social activists:

During the 2012 proxy voting season, investors successfully used shareholder resolutions to spur action on corporate sustainability challenges such as climate change, hydraulic fracturing and supply chain and water availability risks.

Of the nearly 110 resolutions tracked by Ceres in 2012, 44 proposals resulted in U.S. companies making commitments to tackle environmental and social risks in their operations and supply chains.[195]

This voting pattern signals a rise in the number of resolutions being filed that has been occurring for a number of years; in particular, since the corporate scandals around the turn of the century. It is prevalent across a broad range of issues and is becoming harder and harder for firms to dismiss:

> . . . investor support for environmental and social resolutions had been growing steadily over the past decade, from an average of 9 percent in 2001 to 18 percent in 2010. [In 2011] 82 resolutions were supported by votes of 20 per cent or more. '[Companies] cannot ignore it if a quarter or a third of their shareholders are asking for something.'[196]

As this engagement continues to gather strength ("The number of shareholder proposals . . . grew by 3 percent [in 2012] to 595"),[197] it signals what the *Financial Times* refers to as "the trend towards investor activism amid a crisis of confidence in corporate America." That crisis in confidence is driven by many factors, not least of which is a concern to protect investments, but it also appears to be more than purely financial return. Investors today "are no longer content merely to make money, but want to ensure they are doing so responsibly."[198] Similarly, *The New York Times*, refers to this trend as the "changing face of shareholder activism":

> While proxy season has long been the domain of labor unions and activist investors with large personalities and forceful demands, increasingly it is mutual funds and other more tempered institutional shareholders who are criticizing lavish pay packages and questioning corporate governance. Emboldened by new regulations—and angered by laggard stock performance and recent scandals—this new crop of activists is voting down company policies and backing proposals to reform corporate boards.[199]

The SEC stipulates a threshold of only 3 percent of shareholder votes for a proposition to be deemed to have sufficient support for it to be resubmitted for a vote the following year. This threshold rises to 6 percent for the proposal to be carried over for a second year, and 10 percent for a third year.[200] The reason this threshold is low is due to the dispersed nature of shares (with any one shareholder unlikely to hold a significant stake in the enterprise) and the reluctance of institutional investors which hold more than 50% of all listed corporate stock in the United States (about 60% in the largest 1,000 corporations)[201] to vote for dramatic change:

> In most cases, an investor with 3% ownership in a company would be one of the top shareholders and thus even single digit votes may gain considerable attention from a company. Social proposal votes more than 10% are difficult to ignore and often result in some action by the company to address the shareholders area of concern. Votes that receive 20-30% or more have garnered strong support from mainstream institutional investors and send a clear cut signal to management. Only the least responsive of companies is willing to ignore one out of every three or four of its shareholders.[202]

As a result of the concentration of shares controlled by institutional investors, it is the votes of these shareholders that constitute the largest blocs of votes cast at AGMs. They are highly influential and traditionally tend to vote with the company's management. This is changing, however, as individual shareholders become increasingly strident in expressing their opposition to failed executive performance, while institutional investors are taking more of an interest in protecting their holdings. Alternative shareholder resolutions that seek directly to challenge board recommendations, as well as votes of 20 percent and up in support of these resolutions, are becoming increasingly common. As pressure continues on institutional investors to ensure corporate governance minimizes risk and reflects societal values, the number of votes approaching and exceeding the 50 percent barrier will increase:

> [In 2012] About 27% of Barclays's shareholders voted "no" in [shareholder votes on executive pay plans]. Credit Suisse shareholders delivered a similar rebuke, with nearly one-third voting against the Swiss bank's compensation plans. . . . [These votes] came less than two weeks after a majority of Citigroup Inc. shareholders [55%] voted against the pay of top executives including CEO Vikram Pandit, whose pay jumped to $14.9 million last year from $1 in prior years.[203]

One example of shareholder pressure resulting in policy change occurred when Dell announced the launch of a recycling campaign ("Asset Recovery" program) to help customers dispose of their computers. Correct dismantling ensures the toxic chemicals they contain do not end up in landfill waste sites. Dell announced plans to charge customers $49 per computer for this service. The company was pressured into this move by a proxy-session campaign to improve recycling efforts by all the major computer manufactures instigated by the Calvert Group and the As You Sow Foundation:

Dell, which has been blasted for not taking a lead role in keeping toxic-laden PCs from ending up in landfills, will set specific recycling targets, disclose its progress to the public, and make sure its recycled goods are handled properly. Dell also pledged to study how to use its direct distribution model to lower the cost of recycling tech waste.[204]

In general, however, a firm is not bound by the result of a shareholder vote, even if the total is a majority of votes cast. Legislation in place in the UK since 2002, for example, requires companies to produce a remuneration report every year, which then must be voted on at the AGM. This produces a great deal more information for shareholders and investors on issues surrounding various elements of a corporation's remuneration package for its senior executives, such as contract terms, take-over clauses, and pension arrangements, as well as *golden parachute* clauses that are inserted into CEO contracts and result in large payments in the event that the company is taken over. Such information has previously been very difficult for interested parties to discover; however, "while voting on it is mandatory, the company is not obliged to make any changes even if the report is rejected, and no heads will roll."[205] The reason for these nonbinding votes (which apply to all shareholder votes, not only those related to compensation) is the prevalence of *plurality voting*:

Under majority voting rules, directors typically need an affirmative vote of more than 50% of the shares voted at a company's annual meeting. Under plurality rules, all of the top vote getters are elected, no matter how few "for" votes they get, so long as there are no alternative nominees with a more favorable tally.[206]

And, the reasons there are almost always no alternative nominees is that current rules make it very difficult for a slate of candidates not endorsed by the firm's executive team to stand. Without competing candidates, *shareholder democracy* becomes an empty term:

Until recently, those elections were Stalinesque: Only one slate of candidates was on the ballot, and while shareholder could without their support, withheld votes didn't count. As long as one shareholder supported each director, those directors prevailed.[207]

In effect, the results were rigged heavily in favor of the status quo before the election even occurred, being criticized by some as "more predictable than that of the North Korean politburo":[208]

Until recently, the votes of small investors—the ones who didn't just throw their ballots in the trash—were largely meaningless. . . . Say you withhold a vote for a candidate running uncontested. It doesn't matter, since directors can win without a majority. And if you chose not to vote? Your broker is allowed to cast your ballot without your permission, and brokers typically vote in line with management.[209]

As a result, almost invariably, management's slate of directors is elected.[210] In one year's worth of director elections, for example the "Institutional Shareholder Services, a proxy advisory firm, says only 14 out of 14,000 board candidates were rejected by a majority of votes cast in elections."[211] These wasted votes did not go unnoticed and calls for reform in the U.S. have existed for many years. Finally convinced that fundamental shareholder powers were not a threat but assist in corporate oversight and governance, the Securities and Exchange Commission instigated a review of *proxy access* soon after the scandals that occurred in the early years of this century. The goal was to enhance the ability of shareholders to nominate alternative candidates in competitive elections for directors. In 2010, the SEC announced the results from its review:

> In a decision years in the making, the SEC voted 3-2 in favor of the "proxy access" rule, which requires companies to include the names of all board nominees, even those not backed by the company, directly on the standard corporate ballots distributed before shareholder annual meetings. To win the right to nominate, an investor or group of investors must own at least 3% of a company's stock and have held the shares for a minimum of three years.[212]

CSR Newsletters: Greed

A blog posting by Mallen Baker[213] cuts through much of the comment over recent shareholder votes rejecting executive pay packages suffered by many firms. In 2012, companies from Aviva to Barclays to Citigroup all had strong protest votes registered against executive compensation packages as a result of increased requirements on firms to put senior employee compensation to a vote at the firm's annual general meeting:

> It's an interesting point to note, that suddenly shareholders have become lauded as this group that has the power to stick it to the greedy bad bosses.

Baker, however, recognizes that, rather than a long-awaited exercise in shareholder democracy, this is a case of one highly-criticized group holding another highly-criticized group to account. Or, as Baker puts it:

> For [shareholders], the point is more one of disappointment that they are not earning similarly high returns through the value of the shares that they own. If they were, they would smile warmly on inflated executive bonuses because they had been 'earned.'

Baker reminds us not to kid ourselves that shareholders are acting on behalf of the wider, social interest:

> This is not a benign force for good. It is the demand of shareholders for "above average" returns that drove many of the financial institutions to bring in high-risk high-return policies in the first place, which led to the financial crisis. Now they complain that the bosses at Aviva have "destroyed shareholder value."

As such, rather than a liberation, Baker pierces the rhetoric behind these new "say-on-pay" requirements:[214]

> We may think they are now meting out the justice we have been so long denied by giving certain individuals a huge roasting. Actually, they are standing up for their right to demand financial performance that is unreasonable in the face of the current state of the marketplace. The fact that some of those individuals may deserve their roasting (others were just in the wrong place at the wrong time) shouldn't get in the way of the fact that the process is simply keeping us on the path that caused the problems in the first place.

In general, it is true that "Companies cannot be properly accountable to their shareholders unless the latter can express their opinion in proportion to the capital they have at risk."[215] Nevertheless, the burst of shareholder democracy sparked by the SEC decision, ultimately, did not even last a year, with a Federal Appeals court throwing out the rule after the U.S. Chamber of Commerce and the Business Roundtable sued to repeal it:[216]

> [In overturning the rule, the] court issued a harsh rebuke to the SEC, saying it didn't adequately analyze the costs to U.S. companies of fighting in contested board elections. It also said the agency failed to back up its claim the rule would improve shareholder value and board performance. The decision doesn't block the SEC from starting over and issuing a new rule, but legal experts said it sets a high bar for a revamped rule to give shareholders the right to nominate directors.[217]

Many firms, however, are beginning to see that listening and talking with concerned stakeholders offers the path of least resistance regarding sensitive issues and may even help them interact with their multiple stakeholder groups:

In recent years, more companies have adopted a "majority rules" requirement, meaning a single vote can no longer elect the entire board, even if all other votes are withheld. . . . And starting [in 2010], brokers can no longer vote shares held in their customers' accounts without permission. On top of that, more voter resources are beginning to sprout on the Web that aim to educate smaller investors, demystify the issues on the ballot and make voting easier.[218]

In addition, firms are increasingly consulting with shareholders ahead of votes, surveying their opinion to gauge what package structure would be most acceptable. In its 2009 proxy, for example, Amgen "directed shareholders to a 10-question online survey [about the firm's compensation plan]. Queries include whether the plan is based on performance and whether the performance goals are understandable."[219] Also in 2009, Prudential Financial "created a link on its Web site so investors could comment on its compensation plan."[220] Extending this trend further, companies like Herman Miller are beginning to hold AGMs online only in order to involve a greater percentage of shareholders in the process, as well as save money:

Those with annual "e-meetings" included Warner Music Group Corp., Applied Minerals Inc. and Nutrisystem Inc. . . . During the meetings, investors—who log into a website through a 12-digit control number linked to their brokerage accounts—vote and pose questions electronically.[221]

Hewlett-Packard is being particularly progressive, essentially replicating the SEC rule requirement for shareholder rights to nominate alternative director candidates:

The Palo Alto, Calif., technology giant will give its stockholders the chance to approve so-called proxy access through a bylaw vote at its 2013 annual meeting. If the measure passes, investors who own at least 3% of H-P shares for at least three years would be allowed to nominate up to 20% of the company's directors, the company said. The vote would be binding, meaning H-P would be bound by the results.[222]

Or, at least, the news is a qualified good "as only four H-P shareholders own [the required 3% of shares in] the technology company, according to filings."[223]

Gradually, however, shareholder representation is increasing and firms are becoming more responsive to the demands of one of their most important stakeholders. One way in which investors can hold management to account is by investing in tailored funds that reflect the interests they value. In terms of CSR, socially responsible investment (SRI) funds seek to achieve this. The rise of *impact investing* has also generated a great deal of interest and innovation, such as the rise of social impact bonds.

Case Study: Social Impact Bonds

To what extent are investors limiting their investments to companies deemed to be operating in an ethical and socially responsible manner? Such investments are often referred to as impact investing and one example of this is socially responsible investment (SRI) funds:

> An investment is considered socially responsible because of the nature of the business the company conducts. Common themes for socially responsible investments include avoiding investment in companies that produce or sell addictive substances (like alcohol, gambling and tobacco) and seeking out companies engaged in environmental sustainability and alternative energy/clean technology efforts. Socially responsible investments can be made in individual companies or through a 'socially conscious mutual fund or exchange-traded fund (ETF).[224]

Socially responsible investing is not a new idea, but it is becoming increasingly common as societal pressures on firms for more socially responsible behavior grow and investors attempt to apply these same values to their financial portfolio:

> The mutual-fund industry began offering products based on this idea in the 1970s, and Morningstar Inc. recently identified 199 mutual funds and 23 exchange-traded funds as socially responsible. Among the industries these funds typically shun are those connected to tobacco, alcohol, pollution, weapons and authoritarian regimes.[225]

An important debate that speaks to the potential for SRI funds to influence firm behavior is the question of whether SRI funds are any more or less successful than regular investment funds. If true, this would suggest a connection between socially responsible behavior and superior firm performance. Critics claim SRI funds are ineffective and that ethical or virtuous stocks do not outperform either regular mutual funds or so-called *sin* stocks. Those who support SRI funds, however, counter with numbers that support their case:

> . . . nearly two-thirds of 160 socially responsible mutual funds offered by member companies of the Social Investment Forum outperformed their benchmark indexes and beat the Standard & Poor's 500-stock index in 2009 by significant margins.[226]

Although still a relatively small fraction of total investments, the assets invested in SRI funds are growing rapidly in terms of number, size, and influence, as are mutual funds claiming to be socially or environmentally responsible. In 2007, for example, "more than $2.7trillion—about 11% of all assets under professional management—were in some kind of socially responsible investment."[227] Over the next three years, however, "social investing enjoyed a growth rate of more than 13-perecent."[228] As a result:

> Nearly one out of every eight dollars under professional management in the United States today—12.2% of the $25.2 trillion in total assets under management tracked by Thomson Reuters Nelson—is involved in sustainable and responsible investing. . . . 250 socially screened mutual fund products in the US, with assets of $316.1 billion. By contrast, there were just 55 SRI funds in 1995 with $12 billion in assets.[229]

Strong SRI growth is also evident in the UK, where "funds invested with a socially responsible focus have grown from £1bn to £746bn ($1,260bn, €897bn) in 12 years."[230] And, more broadly, SRI is increasing in Europe as well:

> Total sales for the SRI sector for December, 2008, were €999.4m ($1.3 bn) to take its overall value to €35.4bn. Significantly, total SRI fund sales came out at 10% of the total European equity fund sales figure of just over €10bn in December, which suggests SRI fund sales are holding up well and increasing in comparison to their mainstream peers during the current economic market crisis.[231]

One of the underlying drivers of this growth is the professionalization of the SRI industry, which is reflected in its commitment to a market return on investment:

> Public pension plan managers . . . now "go out of their way to make clear that they are no longer willing to sacrifice returns for social considerations." . . . A requirement that an investment yield a "market rate of return" is a feature of nearly every definition of social investing, the report said.[232]

CSR Newsletters: SRI Funds

An article in the *Financial Times*[233] discusses the pros and cons of SRI—socially responsible investing. The general point is that, while SRI might not always outperform the market, and rarely changes the world, it is often able to mirror the market. This means that:

> It looks possible to screen out morally-questionable investments and still match the market. . . . So it need not hurt your wallet.

What is most interesting is the use of "social screens" by funds that rule out investments in certain "types" of firms, such as tobacco firms, or arms manufacturers, etc. When such categories of firms are automatically excluded, however, it invariably hurts the performance of these investment funds:

The Domini 400 social index, maintained the Boston index group KLD, is the clearest expression of this philosophy. It applies social screens, but tries to match the S&P 500 after making its exclusions. Since early 2005, when tobacco began to rebound, it has underperformed the S&P significantly, but for several years earlier this decade the two indices tracked each other closely.

While different products have different social benefits and consequences, some of which we should aim to avoid, it is unhelpful to use such a blunt instrument to brand a firm either totally good or bad in terms of CSR. Almost all firms that remain profitable are providing some degree of social benefit. Tobacco firms, for example, employ people, pay taxes, and support the local economy, above and beyond whatever harm their product does.

It is OK for someone trying to evaluate a firm's overall "CSR score" to add up the pros and the cons and declare that the cons outweigh the pros, but it is less rational to not even consider the pros by declaring a firm's product the be-all-and-end-all of its contribution to society. If a more holistic approach is adopted, it is likely that there will be some tobacco firms that are more or less socially responsible than others, which is a degree of subtlety that the CSR evaluation debate is far away from at present.

As the discussion immediately above suggests, across the range of impact investing funds (from faith-based, to ethical, to SRI, to sustainability) there are two kinds of investment strategies—*exclusion funds*, which screen out certain firms based on specific criteria, and *best-in-class funds*, which aim to mirror the market by selecting the best performers in each industry. While exclusion funds will not invest in any firms from specific industries, best-in-class funds evaluates firms based on relative performance, rather than some absolute ideological basis.

The result is a wide-range of different investment opportunities, tailored to individual investors' goals and personal values and beliefs, such as "green bonds":

> . . . according to Climate Bonds Initiative (CBI), an NGO, between $10 billion and $30 billion of bonds related to renewable-energy projects have been issued. Bonds that are explicitly advertised as green, mostly issued by the World Bank and other multilateral lenders, are easier to count. Around $5 billion-worth have been issued; by one estimate, they could amount to $30 billion by 2015.[234]

The Swiss investment firm, Naissance Capital has established the Women's Leadership Fund, with the goal of "investing in companies with a high number of women in senior roles."

> The fund is an example of growing interest in gender diversity in companies and is based on several studies suggesting that businesses with a higher proportion of women in senior positions perform better. [235]

Another example of a growing area of investment vehicles focuses on religious index funds, such as the Stoxx Europe Christian Index, which was launched in the aftermath of the Financial Crisis and constructed to meet "demand by investors for so-called ethical stocks in the wake of the financial crisis."

> The Stoxx Europe Christian Index comprises 533 European companies that only derive revenues from sources approved "according to the values and principles of the Christian religion." BP, HSBC, Nestlé, Vodafone, Royal Dutch Shell and GlaxoSmithKline are among the companies in the index. Only groups that do not make money from pornography, weapons, tobacco, birth control and gambling are allowed to be listed.[236]

In reaction to the growth of SRI funds and the doubt that they make a difference, some analysts have begun a backlash against ethical or environmental funds. One demonstration of this is the development of *sin* funds (focusing on companies in the tobacco, alcohol, gambling, defense, and oil extraction industries) that aim to provide superior returns to investors:

> [USA Mutuals] new Vice Fund went on sale to the public in [2002], advertising itself as a "socially irresponsible fund" that will invest clients' assets in tobacco, gambling, liquor, in addition to defence. . . . According to the fund's prospectus, only tobacco stocks under-performed the Standard & Poor's 500 index over the last five years. The largest gainer was alcoholic-beverage stocks. They gained 62.57% over the five years, compared with an 11.8% gain for the S&P 500.[237]

Anecdotal evidence suggests that there is empirical justification for investing in sin stocks. This is partly because many of these industries are mature and do not have large costs associated with growth and R&D, but it is also because many of these products satisfy basic human needs and desires and, as such, will always be in demand:

Only three Standard & Poor's 500 stock index subindustries posted an increase in average price performance during the 11 market declines associated with recessions since World War II: Alcoholic Beverages, Household Products, and Tobacco. I guess that's the reason for the old Wall Street saying "When the going gets tough, the tough go eating, smoking and drinking."[238]

Tobacco stocks, in particular, have performed well since the Financial Crisis, paying high dividends to shareholders:

Over the past five years, Altria and Reynolds have beaten the broad market, once dividends are included, by 128% and 98%, respectively. Lorillard has edged the market by 124% since its spinoff from Loews Corp. in 2008. Their main attraction: an average dividend yield of 4.7%, which is more than three times the yield on 10-year, U.S. Treasury notes.[239]

As a result, the Vice Fund has grown into a serious attempt to rival the reach and impact of SRI funds. According to USA Mutuals, since its inception in 2002, the Vice Fund (VICEX) has outperformed the S&P 500 Index, returning 9.15% to the S&P 500 Index's 6.71%.[240] While there is much debate over the financial consequences to fund performance from excluding certain firms and industries as part of an investment strategy, more objective research suggests that, at the very least, while there may not be a significantly advantageous return from SRI funds, there is no disadvantage to investing in funds that employ a CSR Filter and that "in the long run, there's no statistical difference in performance between SRI and non-SRI funds."[241] Other commentators, however, argue that the level of return is not the issue. What is more misleading is the idea that investing in an SRI fund advances the CSR causes in which the investor believes:

. . . socially responsible investing oversimplifies the world, and in doing so distorts reality. It allows investors to believe that their money is only being invested in "good companies," and they take foolish comfort in that belief. Rare is the company, after all, that is either all good or all bad. To put it another way, socially responsible investing creates the illusion that the world is black and white, when its real color is gray.[242]

Overall, the question of how good measures of social responsibility SRI funds really are remains a valid critique of the SRI industry. As such, one innovation that has emerged in recent years is designed specifically to channel the consequences of impact investing[243] more directly towards social progress with quantifiable outcomes—Social Impact Bonds:

Social Impact Bonds (SIBs), also known as "Pay for Success Bonds," are essentially financial instruments in which investors can front working capital for nonprofits that deliver social programs – a way to connect the social sector with the capital markets. If the nonprofit meets predefined metrics, public-sector savings are realized and the government then pays investors back their principal plus a rate of return. However, if the savings are not realized, the investors get no repayment. In terms of investment risk, then, these vehicles are more like an equity investment than a typical bond purchase.[244]

In short, "private investors—typically foundations—pay the costs of a new program in its early years, and the government later repays the investors, often with a bonus, as long as the program meets its goals. If it fails, taxpayers pay nothing."[245] SIBs were first introduced in the UK and initially focused on reducing recidivism rates among prisoners, which are as high as 60% for short-term prisoners:[246]

In 2011, Peterborough Prison in the United Kingdom issued one of the first social impact bonds anywhere in the world. The bond raised 5 million pounds from 17 social investors to fund a pilot project with the objective of reducing re-offending rates of short-term prisoners. The relapse or re-conviction rates of prisoners released from Peterborough will be compared with the relapse rates of a control group of prisoners over six years. If Peterborough's re-conviction rates are at least 7.5% below the rates of the control group, investors receive an increasing return that is directly proportional to the difference in relapse rates between the two groups and is capped at 13% annually over an eight-year period.[247]

In addition to the UK where SIBs are gaining a great deal of interest,[248] these financial instruments are also growing in countries like Australia,[249] and also in the United States where, in 2011, "President Obama earmarked $100 million for various pilot programs involving SIBs in his 2012 budget proposal."[250]

In Massachusetts, work is under way to use SIBs to address recidivism rates among young people as well as the chronically homeless. And in New York City, Goldman Sachs is putting up $9.6 million for a SIB aimed at reducing recidivism rates among young inmates at Rikers Island prison.[251]

The Goldman Sachs project in New York, in co-ordination with Bloomberg Philanthropies, is the first SIB project to be implemented in the U.S.[252] Similar to the UK project, the focus is on prisoners, but the involvement of Goldman Sachs and the firm's statement that their investment "is not a charitable donation"[253] raises the stakes for SIBs:

> If recidivism rates drop by 10 percent, Goldman gets its money back. The bank could make up to $2.1 million if the rates fall further. (Bloomberg Philanthropies is guaranteeing $7.4 million of the loan, leading some to say the New York City deal is not a true test of the bonds' appeal to commercial investors.)[254]

The results of the project will be known in 2016, which raises some of the problems that critics have identified with SIBs. First, is the issue of identifying which programs are suited to this sort of financing, but, second, is the issue of how best to measure success. Many of the lead times on these sorts of projects are long (which will not fit some investors' timeframes for a meaningful return), but they also deal with intractable social problems that do not always lend themselves to easy measurement:

> In addition, SIBs bring with them higher costs – expenses that include paying a third party to evaluate results, for example – when compared to simply delivering the services directly.[255]

Nevertheless, this is an innovative time for impact investing as foundations, charities, NGOs, and governments are increasingly "taking [their] cues from Wall Street and Silicon Valley," adopting venture capital tactics to invest in projects and social enterprises that promise "both social and financial benefits."[256] Ultimately, this range of investment vehicles, such as SRI funds and, more recently, Social Impact Bonds, demonstrates the potential social value of the finance sector, which has been less evident in recent years:

> A small fraction of the ingenuity devoted to the construction of complex financial instruments that no one should want could advantageously be applied to the construction of less complex instruments that meet the needs of the Big Society.[257]

CEO Perspective

Jack Welch (GE)

Jack Welch, former CEO of GE, condemned firms' primary focus on shareholder value, even though he was closely associated with such a focus during his time at GE, in a series of articles: first, in the *Financial Times* and, second, in *BusinessWeek*. In the *Financial Times* article, Welch said that "On the face of it, shareholder value is the dumbest idea in the world.... Your main constituencies are your employees, your customers and your products."[258] In the *BusinessWeek* follow-up article, Welch confirmed that "I was asked what I thought of 'shareholder value as a strategy.' My response was that the question on its face was a dumb idea. Shareholder value is an outcome—not a strategy."[259]

Online Resources

- As You Sow, http://www.asyousow.org/
- Calvert Social Investment Fund, http://www.calvertgroup.com/sri.html
- Ceres, Investor Network on Climate Risk (shareholder resolutions), http://www.ceres.org/incr/engagement/corporate-dialogues/shareholder-resolutions
- Climate Bonds Initiative, http://climatebonds.net/
- Domini 400 Social Index, http://www.domini.com/
- Dow Jones Sustainability Indexes, http://www.sustainability-index.com/
- Ethical Investment Research Service, http://www.eiris.org/
- FTSE 4 Good, http://www.ftse4good.com/
- Hang Seng Corporate Sustainability Index, http://www.hsi.com.hk/HSI-Net/HSI-Net
- Interfaith Center on Corporate Responsibility, http://www.iccr.org/
- Investors Against Genocide, http://www.investorsagainstgenocide.org/
- New Alternatives Fund, http://www.newalternativesfund.com/
- Nonprofit Finance Fund, http://payforsuccess.org/
- Pax World Funds (http://www.paxworld.com/)
- ProxyDemocracy, http://proxydemocracy.org/
- Social Finance, http://www.socialfinance.org.uk/
- SocialFunds.com, http://www.socialfunds.com/

- The Forum for Sustainable and Responsible Investment, http://ussif.org/projects/advocacy/
- SRI World Group, http://www.sriworld.com/
- STOXX Europe Christian Index, http://www.stoxx.com/indices/index_information.html?symbol=SXCHP
- United Nations Principles for Responsible Investment, http://www.unpri.org/
- USAMutuals Vice Fund, http://www.usamutuals.com/vicefund/

Pro/Con Debate

> **Pro/Con Debate:** Social Impact Bonds are an effective means to solve social problems.

Questions for Discussion and Review

1. Do you own any shares of a company? If so, do you vote at the company's annual general meeting (either in person or by proxy)? Is it important for shareholders to be actively involved with the companies they own? Why, or why not?

2. What are your thoughts about increasing demands for firms to hold say-on-pay votes on executive compensation packages? Is it a good idea or unnecessary interference in the day-to-day management of the firm? Should the votes be binding?

3. When considering an investment in a mutual fund, would you consider the CSR profiles of the companies in which the fund invested? What about SRI funds? Why, or why not?

4. Would you think twice about investing in a *sin fund* if historical returns showed greater growth potential than SRI funds? What is the justification for your decision?

5. Choose any one of the social investment fund companies listed in the *Online Resources* subsection. What is your opinion of their home page and their stated mission and values? Are these funds a force for *good*, or are they merely lulling gullible investors into a false sense of security by allowing them to think they are investing with a conscience?

SOCIAL ENTREPRENEURSHIP

> **CSR Connection:** This issue covers those firms that overtly combine the profit motive with a social mission. It also highlights the difficulties that can arise when the founders of such firms retire or when ownership is transferred to a larger firm with competing priorities.
>
> **Stakeholders:** Owners, Founders, CEOs.

Issue

Social entrepreneurs fashion themselves as capitalists with a *heart*. They form organizations that are guided by considerations other than *profit*. They see their mission of solving a social problem as a point of differentiation in the market—something that consumers will support because they value the mission that the entrepreneur has outlined. Famous examples of firms with strong social missions include: Tom's of Maine (http://www.tomsofmaine.com/), "putting the good of community and planet first;" Nau (http://www.nau.com/), "a force for change;" Product (RED) (http://www.joinred.com/), "fighting for an AIDS free generation;" and Naked Juice (http://www.nakedjuice.com/), "dedicated to preserving our planet;" and many more.[260] Social entrepreneurs (like all entrepreneurs) see themselves as revolutionaries—challenging the status quo; only social entrepreneurs also see their success as a means for "taking on the world's social problems."[261] As Nau CEO, Chris Van Dyke, puts it:

> We're challenging the nature of capitalism. . . . We started with a clean whiteboard . . . [and] believed every single operational element in our business was an opportunity to turn traditional business notions inside out, integrating environmental, social, and economic factors. Nau represents a new form of activism: business activism.[262]

CSR Newsletters: Toms Shoes

An article in *The Wall Street Journal*[263] reviews the autobiography of Blake Mycoskie, the founder of Toms Shoes (http://www.toms.com/). Mycoskie's innovation with Toms is the promise to donate one free pair of shoes to needy children for every pair of Toms shoes purchased.[264] The autobiography is titled

Start Something That Matters and, among other things, is the story of Mycoskie's founding of Toms in 2006 in Argentina:

> While in Argentina he came across a shoe called the alpargata, a kind of espadrille, and thought it would sell well in the United States. On the same trip, he met an American woman who was running a shoe drive, to deliver shoes to poor Argentine children. Twang went his entrepreneurial synapses: "Why not create a for-profit business to help provide shoes for these children?"

The reviewer is skeptical of the *social entrepreneur* label Mycoskie uses throughout the book, which generates a useful insight:

> Though General Electric builds power plants and life-saving medical equipment and Exxon heats homes in winter and keeps the world moving with its fuel, they are decried as the villains of society, while the "social" entrepreneurs are venerated for giving us hemp shirts and organic greens.

While it is important to recognize the incontrovertible social value those for-profit firms have generated, Toms achievements are pretty impressive, too:

> [In 2010] the company reported that, with the help of charities and other groups, its giveaways had passed the million-pair mark.

The advantage of a business model such as Toms (which now also includes eye glasses: http://www.toms.com/eyewear/), however, is that value is more likely to be added without the damage that the products of a traditional for-profit firm such as Exxon can also cause. The reviewer, ultimately, is also persuaded:

> Having given away a million pairs of shoes—to children who, when barefoot, might be vulnerable to hookworm, tetanus and other soil-borne ailments—buys Mr. Mycoskie the credibility he needs. I finished the book not only wanting to buy a pair of Toms but also wanting to 'start something that matters' myself.

What is the important insight of the book that, ultimately, is worth building a business around?

People yearn to do meaningful work.

Social entrepreneurs, who claim to be the founders of "a whole new, distinct fourth sector" of organizations,[265] however, face two issues that remain unresolved within CSR. First, is there a market for compassion? Will consumers prefer a social product over its market equivalent in sufficient numbers to sustain the organization? In other words, will consumers pay a *CSR premium* for a product? And second, how can such organizations retain their social mission and operating practices when the founder leaves or ownership is transferred to a for-profit parent that might not pursue the same goals with the same set of priorities? Issues of relevance and legacy are central to the discussion about social entrepreneurs.

The first issue facing social entrepreneurs relates to the size of the market for CSR goods. While this is definitely growing, it is still not very big. In addition, while successful social entrepreneurs attract a lot of attention and there is a lot of activity in this area,[266] the overall influence of the group of social entrepreneurs, in terms of market share, is not very large. It is relatively easy to have high percentage growth if the base amount is small. This is not due to a lack of effort or vision, but more to do with our modern consumer society where, "although 85% of US consumers claim they buy green, fewer than 8% actually do. . . . [and] although eight in 10 vacation travellers consider themselves 'eco-conscious,' only one in 10 books travel based on green considerations."[267] The United Nations Environment Programme is even more pessimistic, reporting that "only four percent actually purchase ethically even though 40 percent say they will."[268] Identifying similar findings:

> A 2008 study funded by the UK Economic and Social Research Council found that 30% of consumers reported they were very concerned about environmental issues but they struggled to translate this into purchases. As a result, the market share for "ethical foods," one of the most visible segments of the green market, has yet to crack 5%.[269]

Reflecting the limited size of the market for CSR goods is the idea that consumers are not uniform in their goals or willingness to support a social cause with their purchase decisions and, in fact, can be broken down into several sub-groups. One study, conducted in the UK, divides the market into four different types of consumers:

> The first, about 8 per cent of the total, are committed cause-driven purchasers. A second group, accounting for 30-35 per cent, want to purchase ethically but are not really sure how and are looking to retailers to help them. The third group, also about 30-35 per cent, feel the same, but doubt that their individual purchases can make much difference. The fourth group, the remainder, are completely uninterested, often because they are too poor to think about much more than putting food on the table for their families.[270]

In short, eco- or ethical consumers remain a marginal component of the overall market. As David Vogel puts it in his book, *The Market for Virtue*:

> . . . . consumers will only buy a greener product [if] it doesn't cost more, comes from a brand they know and trust, can be purchased at stores where they already shop, doesn't require a significant change in habits to use, and has the same level of quality, performance, and endurance as the less-green alternative.[271]

As a result, "'ethical consumers,' . . . no matter where you look, are simply not revolutionizing markets and company product and service line-ups at any kind of scale."[272] Yet, it is *revolution* that social entrepreneurs advocate. Supporters of social entrepreneurship argue that it is the only way that certain intractable social problems can be addressed. They contend that social entrepreneurs fill the gap between problems that the market has avoided and philanthropy has been unable to solve, such as "ways of tackling disease, poverty and environmental damage."[273] As a result of their limited reach, however, critics remain unconvinced that social entrepreneurs are adding any more (or even the same amount of) social value than regular for-profit firms with traditional for-profit motivations:

> [B]usinesses that have wrapped themselves in a social cloak—such as Body Shop, the cosmetics retailer, or the growing number of organizations offering carbon offsets for air travelers—simply salve the consciences of customers who would do more for the environment by reducing their overall consumption.[274]

The second issue facing social entrepreneurs relates to the threat to the social mission following a decision to sell the firm or a founder's decision to retire—"the legacy problem":[275]

> Stewardship means a sense of responsibility for that which you own and handle every day. . . . With the separation of ownership from control in the listed company, stewardship does not disappear, but it does erode.[276]

In essence, many social entrepreneurs who build firms around social missions that enjoy consumer support are victims of their own success. Once those firms secure a sufficiently large slice of the market, they automatically become a potential acquisition for larger firms with capital to invest and very different priorities:

> Pret a Manger . . . agreed to sell a third of its business to McDonald's; Pepsi swallowed PJ Smoothies . . . ; Cadbury Schweppes bought Green & Black's organic chocolate . . . ; Go Organic and Ben & Jerry's are now owned by Unilever – and the list goes on.[277]

In spite of promises made at the time of acquisition, the acquired firm and its founders (who are often replaced by professional managers as part of the purchase) have very little leverage if the situation changes at some future point. Essentially, in agreeing to sell the firm, the social entrepreneur loses the power to control its character and the values by which it operates:

> Tensions are inevitable when big corporations acquire companies with a quirky image. Multinationals are sprawling concerns, accustomed to gobbling up $1bn-plus acquisitions from which they cut costs and reap synergies by plugging the new products into existing infrastructure. Cult brands, by contrast, are all about devoted customers and staff, esoteric ways of doing business.[278]

In order to avoid such tensions, Gary Erickson, CEO and founder of Clif's Bars, turned down a "generous buyout offer" for his firm:

> Erickson walked away from millions not because he had dreams of taking Clif public, or because he thought he could command a higher price. Rather, he decided that a corporate parent would ultimately destroy the company. . . . Unilever gobbled up the famously iconoclastic Ben & Jerry's. Coca-Cola owns juice purist Odwella. Dean Foods runs soy milk pioneer White Wave and dairy brand Horizon Organic. But [Clif founder Gary] Erickson aspires to be a market leader while remaining private and staying true to ideals of corporate social responsibility.[279]

A good example of some of the issues that can arise is Unilever's "$326 million hostile takeover" of Ben & Jerry's in 2000.[280] Although, today, the relationship between Ben & Jerry's and Unilever is reportedly good (as indicated by Ben & Jerry's b-corp certification in 2012), the transfer of ownership was highly contentious at the time and involved the estrangement of founder, Ben Cohen.[281] Other examples abound:

> Green & Black's . . . remains keenly aware that its chocolate is dwarfed by Kraft's $1bn-plus brands. That also makes it harder to incentivise management, and is one reason why the chocolate maker [in 2010] sought to disentangle itself through a management buy-out. . . . PepsiCo was forced to write off PJ Smoothies, the UK's number two smoothie maker at the time of the 2005 acquisition, a decision the US company delicately describes as "economic." But the drink maker was in essence the casualty of a switch in focus as PepsiCo concentrated on its own chilled drinks, Tropicana and Copella.[282]

The conflict emerges from the contrasting missions. Firms that place profit first and foremost are, in general, seeking to please a different set of stakeholders than those organizations that place their social mission as a higher priority than making money. It is not that these two goals cannot co-exist (the argument we present in this book presupposes that they can); it is rather that, given current management perspectives, the different orientations make conflict, at some point, more likely. To the extent that a firm is public, as well as for-profit, the points of potential conflict increase still further. As such, it is generally recognized that "that it is easier to have a company founded on values and integrity when it is privately owned than when it is listed." The reason for this is that "values are not something that you try to smuggle into the working culture of the company when the shareholders aren't looking."[283]

In spite of these stories and while recognizing the risks, others contend that the fears are overblown—that the firms that acquire these social businesses have an interest in protecting the brand value associated with their investment:

> Such is the emotion invested in small ethical brands. Body Shop, Ben & Jerry's, Green & Blacks—these are the darlings of corporate responsibility. One by one, bigger brands have swallowed them up. But each time, concerns over their future seem to have been exaggerated.[284]

Threats to the integrity of an organization's social mission, however, do not only come from an acquisition or founder retirement. Accusations of a *sell-out* also occur when an organization with a social mission lends its name and reputation to a for-profit firm for a marketing campaign. Pleasing grass-roots members, many of whom are die-hard believers in the organization's mission and less willing to compromise with organizations that they perceive to be *the enemy*, can be challenging at the best of times.

CSR Newsletters: The Sierra Club

An article in *Fast Company Magazine*[285] analyses the partnership between Clorox and the Sierra Club that places the Sierra Club's logo on all of the products in Clorox's line of cleaning products—Green Works. In exchange, the Sierra Club receives a percentage of the profits from sales. Although Clorox has benefited handsomely from "one of the most successful launches of a new cleaning brand in recent memory":

> .... within the Sierra Club, the reaction to the deal has been contentious, with emails flying back and forth and charges that [Sierra Club Executive Director] Pope's executive committee has sold out . . . the awkward pairing with Clorox underlines both the huge potential upside for major brands discovering green and the danger for nonprofit environmental groups plunging headlong into the for-profit world.

(Continued)

(Continued)

On the face of it, the Sierra Club seems to have the most at risk in forming this relationship with a firm whose core product many environmentalists believe to be fundamentally opposed to their concept of "sustainability." The article notes that Clorox had been working on sustainable ingredients "for nearly a decade." Even after improvements in cost and availability, however, the firm still faces a difficult challenge in persuading environmentalists that their products really can be green.

While difficult, however, the Sierra Club's attitude when approached by Clorox is the attitude that many NGOs need to have if they are truly invested in realizable change. While there will always be a role for antagonists and idealism is fine, reality inevitably means incremental progress. That is not to say, however, that the Sierra Club is handling everything as well as it should:

With no independent scientific assessment of Green Works products, and with an undisclosed amount of money changing hands, what does that Sierra Club seal on the back of the bottle really mean?

Ultimately, "For Clorox, it's nothing but upside. For the Sierra Club, it's risking—if not undermining—its most valuable asset: its independent reputation." This skeptical tone is continued in this second article:[286]

Transparency and accountability are double-edged. Embedded in an organisation's culture they can burnish credibility and encourage progressive innovation. But if the promise does not match the practice, the greenwashing backlash can cause considerable brand damage.

Case Study: The Body Shop

In addition to the two central issues facing social entrepreneurship outlined above, a third issue arises for those organizations with particularly zealous founders: To what extent can companies that claim to be ethically conscious and socially responsible live up to the high standards they claim or hold to others?

The Body Shop, with its high-profile founder, Anita Roddick, became a global retailing force on the back of its image as a progressive, conscience-driven, campaigning corporation:

Ms. Roddick, who founded the Body Shop from a single store in Brighton in 1976 and built a global brand by banging the drum for a more ethical approach to business, including using recycled packaging and natural ingredients not tested on animals. She has often railed against the mores of big corporations and what she sees as the frustrating demands of the beauty industry on women.[287]

Today, the firm continues to be successful, "employing about 10,000 people in some 2,500 stores in over 60 countries, and selling well over 1,200 different beauty products around the globe."[288] Many of its consumers are drawn to the company because of its activism as much as the quality and range of its products:

A growing number of companies such as the Body Shop, a global skin- and hair-care retailer, make corporate virtue part of their value proposition: Buy one of our products, the Body Shop tells its customers, and you improve the lives of women in developing countries, promote animal rights, protect the environment, and otherwise increase the supply of social responsibility.[289]

As the ever-provocative Roddick, who once described corporate executives as "robber barons,"[290] put it:

Today's CSR movement doesn't explain how to put its ideas into practice and ignores a truth that nobody wants to discuss: if it gets in the way of profit, businesses are not going to do anything about it. When we are measured by a financial bottom line that does include human rights, social justice and workers' justice, then something will change.[291]

One of the first issues the company focused on, and became famous for campaigning against, was the issue of using animals for the testing of human cosmetic products:

The use of animals to test cosmetics and toiletries products and ingredients continues around the world today. It is estimated that over 35,000 animals are used in cosmetics tests every year throughout the European Union alone. In some cases the tests can cause suffering and even death. The Body Shop believes cosmetics testing on animals is unethical, unnecessary and should be banned.[292]

Peta

Although not a company, PETA (http://www.peta.org/) is still an organization that should strive to remain transparent and accountable to as many of its stakeholders as possible. Any organization that fails to meet consistently the needs and goals of a significant proportion of its stakeholders is unlikely to remain viable over the long term:

(Continued)

(Continued)

People for the Ethical Treatment of Animals (PETA) is the largest animal rights organization in the world, with more than 3 million members and supporters. PETA focuses its attention on the four areas in which the largest numbers of animals suffer the most intensely for the longest periods of time: on factory farms, in the clothing trade, in laboratories, and in the entertainment industry.[293]

Not many people would argue with most of PETA's goals. Many, however, take issue with the extent to which the organization takes its point of view (elevating the rights of animals to a status that is equal, or sometimes above, those of humans) and also the methods by which it attempts to convey its message and achieve its goals (direct, often violent, action). Accusations have also been made that, while trying to improve its own public face, PETA finances other much more radical operations:

The FBI lists the group and its counterpart, the Animal Liberation Front [ALF], as domestic terrorists. The government has said the two groups are responsible for more than 600 cases of ecoterrorism around the country, such as spray-painting buildings, breaking windows, and burning fur farms.[294]

A significant section of The Body Shop's customers are loyal to the firm because of the ethical stand it adopts. There is evidence, however, to suggest that there may be a degree of public relations gloss, even greenwash, regarding some of the company's historical positions and not quite as much substance as many customers believe. As some commentators suggest, for example, "Is the Body Shop's social conscience just a sham?"[295] The Body Shop's official position on animal testing, for example, is outlined in its 2011 *Values Report*:[296]

Our Promise: We are as committed today to our Against Animal Testing policy as we ever were. And that's guaranteed. None of our suppliers' sources of ingredients that are used in our products have been tested or re-tested on animals for cosmetics purposes since 31st December 1990.

Although The Body Shop may not itself use ingredients that have been tested on animals, or even source from companies that have tested on animals, the firm clearly continues to benefit from the knowledge gained by others who have previously used animals to test the same ingredients and ensure they are safe for human use:

> During 1989, The Body Shop switched from "not tested on animals" to "against animal testing" labeling after a lawsuit by the German government. The lawsuit claimed that Body Shop labeling was misleading, since their products' ingredients may have been tested on animals.[297]

It is the knowledge gained from testing on animals that makes it such a vital component of the research process. In fact, as a cosmetics company, it would be irresponsible for The Body Shop to do anything other than use this knowledge. The firm could not make a new shampoo, for example, unless it was confident that the ingredients would not make people blind if it got into their eyes. As such, the company's claims of innocence with regard to animal testing are disingenuous at a minimum and probably misleading to a significant percentage of its customers:

> Although the Body Shop maintains that they are against animal testing, they do not always make clear that many of the ingredients in their products have been tested on animals by other companies, causing much pain and suffering to those animals.[298]

In addition, its claims relating to animal testing is only one of multiple issues that have been raised by various campaigning and interested parties:

> Beyond balance-sheet woes, the company that likes to insist it puts principles before profits has been buffeted for [years] by allegations, which Roddick angrily denies, that it has misled the public about everything from its stand against animal testing to the ingredients of elderflower eye gel.[299]

The wide-ranging criticisms of Roddick, who at the time claimed "The stories were all fabrications,"[300] continued after her decision to sell the Body Shop to L'Oreal in 2006 for £652 million (from which, she received a net £130 million)[301] and her death in 2007.[302] In fact, critics saw the sale as additional evidence to support their suspicions about Roddick and her motives:

> L'Oréal, which makes Maybelline mascara, Lancôme skin cream and Armani and Ralph Lauren fragrances, claims to have stopped testing finished products on animals since 1989, but activists argue that ingredients are still not monitored. Ruth Rosselson, at Ethical Consumer Magazine, said: "I for one will certainly not be shopping at Body Shop again. L'Oréal has yet to show its commitment to any ethical issues at all." Other animal protection groups called for a boycott.[303]

In relation to social entrepreneurship, the criticisms Roddick received through-out her groundbreaking career (and, to be clear, she was a successful woman who changed the debate about business in the UK) indicate the double-edged sword of a holier-than-thou approach to business:

> What is Roddick's real legacy? . . . She will be remembered as a one-of-a-kind innovator, but when the solemnity subsides and the history books are finally written, she is not likely to be remembered as the world's most socially responsible executive.[304]

CEO Perspective

Anita Roddick (The Body Shop)

Consumers have not been told effectively enough that they have huge power and that purchasing and shopping involve a moral choice.

All through history, there have always been movements where business was not just about the accumulation of proceeds but also for the public good.

I want to work for a company that contributes to and is part of the community. I want something not just to invest in. I want something to believe in.

If you think you're too small to have an impact, try going to bed with a mosquito.

I am still looking for the modern equivalent of those Quakers who ran successful businesses, made money because they offered honest products and treated their people decently . . . This business creed, sadly, seems long forgotten.

Online Resources

- *Animal People*: "Body Shop Animal Testing Policy Alleged 'a Sham,'" http://www.animalpeoplenews.org/94/8/body_shop.html
- AnitaRoddick.com, http://www.anitaroddick.com/
- Ashoka, 'What is a Social Entrepreneur?' http://www.ashoka.org/social_ entrepreneur
- McSpotlight, 'What's Wrong with the Body Shop?' (http://www.mcspotlight. org/beyond/companies/bodyshop.html) and a reply by The Body Shop to the accusations (http://www.mcspotlight.org/beyond/companies/bs_reply.html)
- PBS—What is Social Entrepreneurship? http://www.pbs.org/opb/thenew heroes/whatis/
- PETA—People for the Ethical Treatment of Animals, http://www.peta.org/

- Sage, 'The Body Shop,' http://knowledge.sagepub.com/view/greenbusiness/n13.xml
- Schwab Foundation for Social Entrepreneurship, http://www.schwabfound.org/
- The Body Shop, http://www.thebodyshop.com/
- The Humane Society of the United States, http://www.humanesociety.org/

Pro/Con Debate

> **Pro/Con Debate:**   All business people are social entrepreneurs.

Questions for Discussion and Review

1. What is your definition of a *social entrepreneur*? How is it different from a *regular* entrepreneur? Is this something that you see yourself becoming?

2. Is *social entrepreneurship* "the future of business" or a phenomenon that, ultimately, must give way to 'the supremacy of the profit motive'?

3. What are the two main issues with social entrepreneurship highlighted in this Issue? Which of these issues do you think is the most dangerous to the case for social entrepreneurship? Why?

4. Think of an example of a corporation that you feel has been hypocritical in terms of its ethical or CSR stance. What is your reaction to the company's actions? Would you consider boycotting the products of a company that you felt had acted in a socially irresponsible way? How about one you felt had acted in a hypocritical way?

5. Read the essay titled, "Body Shop Animal Testing Policy Alleged 'a Sham'" (http://www.animalpeoplenews.org/94/8/body_shop.html). Then compare it with the Body Shop's website dealing with the same issue (http://www.thebodyshop-usa.com/values/AgainstAnimalTesting.aspx). Which of the two accounts do you believe? Does The Body Shop's stance on this issue matter?

WAGES

> **CSR Connection:**   This issue reflects the importance of wages as a highly tangible component of a firm's relationship with one of its key organizational stakeholders, its employees.
>
> **Stakeholders:**   Employees.

Issue

One of the concerns expressed with capitalism is that, in spite of all its efficiencies in creating innovation and opportunity, "what it's not good at is distributing the fruits, because the logic in the boardroom . . . is always cut your labor costs to improve your quarterly [numbers] and your profit margins for shareholder value."[305] Employees, in particular, are sometimes treated as a means to an end, rather than being a valued partner in the process:

> Layoffs. Downsizing. Rightsizing. Job cuts. Separations. Terminations. Workforce reductions. Off-shoring. Outsourcing. Whatever the term, getting rid of employees can be a necessary and beneficial strategic move for companies to make.[306]

While firing employees may be necessary, however, it is only beneficial if it is done in a constructive, meaningful manner. Unfortunately, many companies rely on a straightforward forced ranking process (that lists employees from best to worst) and then firing a certain percentage at the bottom of the list. This process is easy and it is unproductive. It is implemented by firms that do not take the time to assess the value of individual employees more effectively and that do not care about the impact their policies have on the morale of those who remain who are left wondering, "Will I be next?":

> The method, sometimes called "rank and yank," was pioneered by Jack Welch when he ran General Electric Co. from 1981 to 2001. Today, an estimated 60% of Fortune 500 firms still use some form of the ranking, though they might use gentler-sounding names like "talent assessment system" or "performance procedure."[307]

By reducing labor costs (minimizing wage levels, outsourcing, and/or cutting positions), however, are companies also reducing the overall health of the communities within which they are based and hope to sell their products? In other words, by cutting costs in the short term, is a firm undermining the market on which it depends for its long-term survival?

> The same workers who've been let go are the same people who have consumed the goods and services . . . They are not just a factor in the means of production. They're not only the consumers, they're the shareholders. So when you [sack] them . . . you slowly lose the purchasing power to empty inventories and long-term savings in the form of institutional pension funds to invest in the stocks and bonds of these companies.[308]

The same argument, that sacked employees lead to consumers with less discretionary income, applies to the economy as a whole in terms of overall wage growth—it is difficult for the economy to be strong when unemployment is high and wage growth is low:

> From 1948 to 1973, the productivity of all nonfarm workers nearly doubled, as did average hourly compensation. But things changed dramatically starting in the late 1970s. Although productivity increased by 80.1 percent from 1973 to 2011, average wages rose only 4.2 percent and hourly compensation (wages plus benefits) rose only 10 percent over that time, according to government data analyzed by the Economic Policy Institute. At the same time, corporate profits were booming. In 2006, the year before the Great Recession began, corporate profits garnered the largest share of national income since 1942, while the share going to wages and salaries sank to the lowest level since 1929. . . . In Germany, still a manufacturing and export powerhouse, average hourly pay has risen five times faster since 1985 than in the United States.[309]

The effort to minimize the cost of production is a legitimate business strategy. But corporations must also come to terms with the fact that the employees whose wages they squeeze can also be the customers on whom they rely for sales.

Henry Ford[310]

Nearly a century ago, Henry Ford drew no distinction between his employees and his customers. Challenging the conventional wisdom that the best way to maximize profits was to tailor your product to the wealthiest segment of society, Ford decided to market his black Model T as the car for "America's Everyman":

> For Ford, mass production went hand in hand with mass consumption. His benchmark for worker compensation was whether his own workers could afford to buy the product they were making. He offered a $5-a-day minimum wage for *all* his workers (crashing through the race barriers of the day)—twice the prevailing automobile industry average.
>
> In doing so, Ford created a *virtuous circle.* Workers flocked to his factory to apply for positions. If they managed to secure one of Ford's coveted jobs, then in time they too would be able to afford one of his cars. The company flourished based on the twin pillars of a desirable product and a highly motivated employee base. "By the time production ceased for the Model T in 1927, more than 15 million cars had been sold—or half the world's output."

Firms need also to consider the reputation implications of cutting jobs, as well as the damage to morale of those remaining employees and what effects that has on future productivity. In March 2007, for example, Circuit City was roundly criticized for cutting 3,400 jobs (7% of the firm's workforce). The rationale behind the "wage management initiative" was that the fired employees were overpaid, so the firm immediately re-advertised their jobs at a lower wage:

> The company did not disclose specifics, but *The Baltimore Sun* reported that the laid-off workers, known as "associates," made 51 cents more per hour above what the company had set as market wages. . . . The company said, however, that the people who lost their jobs received severance packages and could reapply for their old jobs, at lower pay, but had to wait 10 weeks to do so.[311]

What was the result of Circuit City's "series of changes to improve financial performance largely by realigning [its] cost and expense structure"?[312] The firm filed for bankruptcy in October, 2008, and liquidated its remaining stores and inventory in January, 2009.[313]

An alternative corporate perspective argues that, in spite of accounting convention, employees should be treated as an *asset*, rather than a *cost*. In this view, employees, as with any asset, will grow and improve with investment. In other words, there is a strong business argument for ensuring that employees are respected as a core component of the firm's mission that can assist the organization achieve its goals, rather than a potential barrier that might prevent it from achieving those goals. An analysis of the relationship between the "dollars spent on employee skills" and firm performance supports the value of this approach—"firms that made large investments in employee development subsequently outperformed the stock market. Indeed, training and development expenditures per employee proved to be an important leading indicator of future stock prices."[314] This view of employees as an asset, rather than a cost, is supported by firms such as Costco, the warehouse membership-based retailer:

> "From day one, we've run the company with the philosophy that if we pay better than average, provide a salary people can live on, have a positive environment and good benefits, we'll be able to hire better people, they'll stay longer and be more efficient," says Richard Galanti, Costco's chief financial officer.[315]

There are a number of other firms that share Costco's willingness to invest in their employees, believing that the motivation and loyalty such policies generate outweigh the potential cost savings gained by lower wages. At Zappos, an online retailer of shoes and handbags, for example, customer service is the firm's number one priority. As such, the firm makes sure that its employees are highly motivated and share the firm's values:

> After a few weeks of intensive training, new call-center employees are offered [$2,000] on top of what they have already earned to that point if they want to quit. The theory . . . is that the people who take the money "obviously don't have the sense of commitment" Zappos requires from its employees. The company says about 10 percent of its trainees take the offer.[316]

Although there are many components to employee satisfaction, rate of pay is one of the most important and contentious. At Whole Foods Market, for example, there is a reason why the firm is consistently ranked as one of *Fortune Magazine's 100 Best Companies to Work For*:[317]

> It is an open, relatively non-hierarchical organization. The pay of every employee is known, and even senior executives receive no more than 19 times the average wage. New recruits are voted in through a process of peer appraisal after a four-week probationary period.[318]

At John Lewis, the pay differential is larger, but there is still a defined limit that prevents the disparity between senior executives and junior employees from growing too large:

> [The founder's son] Spedan Lewis ensured that all staff would benefit from an annual share of profits, and that pay would be regulated according to a ratio. The highest paid staff member cannot earn more than 75 times the average wage of the shop-floor salesperson.[319]

In the absence of a firm's progressive approach to wage levels, it is clear that the significant drop in trade union membership in recent years has contributed to workers' loss of bargaining power that might otherwise protect the wages they receive.[320] In the absence of any constraints, however, what is an acceptable wage rate to pay employees that balances the need to maintain efficient operations and also helps create a consumer base that supports sales? Different people and ideologies suggest different solutions:

- A minimum wage (determined by the government).
- An average wage for the job and industry (determined by the market).
- A living wage[321] (determined by nonprofits and NGOs).

An example of the discrepancies that these three different calculations can create is seen when the federal hourly minimum wage in the United States ($7.25 per hour)[322] is compared with the government's 2012 poverty threshold annual wages for a family of four of $23,050 ($11.08 per hour for a single earner working a 40 hour week, 52 weeks a year):[323]

The real value of the minimum wage peaked in 1968. Had it kept pace with rising living costs, the minimum wage would exceed $10.50 per hour today. Meanwhile, the U.S. economy has been reorganizing over the past 30 years away from middle-wage jobs in manufacturing and construction and toward low-paying jobs in the rapidly expanding service, retail and restaurant industries.[324]

According to the Living Wage Action Coalition, a living wage will necessarily vary according to the local cost of living: "A living wage in rural Louisiana is around $9.33, while in Washington, DC it is closer to $15 an hour."[325] This discrepancy partly accounts for why state minimum wages in the U.S. differ from the federal minimum and also vary among themselves. Washington state, for example, has a minimum wage of $9.19, Connecticut's minimum wage is $8.25, and Massachusetts' minimum wage is $8 per hour, while Wyoming has a minimum wage of only $5.15 per hour.[326] It is also surprising that only ten U.S. states tie increases to their minimum wages to the rate of inflation. A history of the changes in the federal minimum wage in the U.S., since its introduction at $0.25 via the Fair Labor Standards Act of 1938[327] to its current level of $7.25 (set in 2009), is presented in Figure 6.4.[328]

Figure 6.4   The Federal Hourly Minimum Wage in the U.S. (1938–2009)

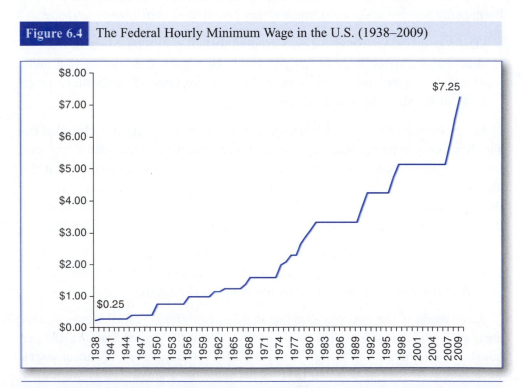

Source: 'Federal Minimum Wage Increase for 2007, 2008, & 2009,' *Labor Law Center*, July 24, 2009, http://www.laborlawcenter.com/t-federal-minimum-wage.aspx

In contrast to other countries, the federal minimum wage in the U.S. is low, both in terms of average wages within the U.S. and in comparison to national minimum wages elsewhere. The national minimum wage in the UK, for example, is £6.19 (approximately $9.33):[329]

America's minimum wage has long been low by international standards, equalling just 38% of the median wage in 2011, close to the lowest in the OECD. . . . The wage was last raised, to $7.25 per hour, in 2009. Since then its real value has slipped back to where it was in 1998. Twenty states now have minimum wages above the federal rate, compared to 15 in 2010, according to the Economic Policy Institute, a liberal research group.[330]

Case Study: McDonald's

McDonald's is a huge multinational company, whose brand is reportedly more recognized worldwide than the Christian cross.

McDonald's
Some facts about the world's largest fast-food firm: • McDonald's daily customer traffic (62 million people) is more than the population of Great Britain. • McDonald's sells more than 75 hamburgers every second. • Americans alone consume one billion pounds of beef at McDonald's in a year – five and a half million head of cattle. • McDonald's hires around 1 million workers in the US every year. • According to company estimates, one in every eight American workers has been employed by McDonald's. • McDonald's is the world's largest distributor of toys, with one included in 20% of all sales. • For the next three years, McDonald's is going to open one restaurant every day in China.[331]

At present, McDonald's has restaurants in 119 countries, with ongoing plans to expand that include opening 2,000 stores in China by the end of 2013.[332] Although there are regional variations in its menus (including vegetarian restaurants in India),[333] essentially, McDonald's has prospered by standardizing its product:

How many of us have wandered into a McDonald's overseas just to find a taste of home?[334]

The firm has also standardized its employment policies. As a result, whether accurate or not, and in spite of the company's passionate arguments to the contrary, McDonald's has become associated with low-wage, dead-end jobs. The company has become so associated with this type of employment that the Oxford English Dictionary has included the definition of a *McJob* since its 11th edition:

Mc.Job \m¶k-'jäb\ *n* (1986): a low-paying job that requires little skill and provides little opportunity for advancement.[335]

> ### CSR Newsletters: McJob
>
> Two articles from the *Financial Times* frame a valiant attempt by McDonald's in the UK to banish the term "McJob" from the dictionary:
>
> > . . . . a term the Oxford English Dictionary describes as "an unstimulating, low-paid job with few prospects, esp. one created by the expansion of the service sector."[336]
>
> McDonald's position, it turns out, deserves some sympathy because, in the UK at least, the firm has established a reputation as a good employer:
>
> > It has featured regularly in most of the main "good employer" league tables, and recently won Caterer and Hotelkeeper magazine's "Best place to work in hospitality" award. . . . Eighty per cent of McDonald's UK branch managers joined the company as hourly paid "crew members," as did half the company's executive team. Compared with some other companies in the service sector, McDonald's is serious about training and development. It is also more "female-friendly" than most: 40 per cent of managers and 25 per cent of the company's executives are women.[337]

Given McDonald's trials and errors in the past with efforts to change its public image,[338] the firm has begun to learn its lesson. Instead of continuing with its initial reaction to the McJob label by trying to refute and disown it, McDonald's now embraces the McJob (it is trademarked by the firm).[339] A McDonald's career, the firm argues, is "something to be proud of."[340] This is in spite of operating in the restaurant industry, which is dominated by high annual turnover ("over 100 percent")[341] and entry-level positions:

McDonald's is a dominant player in an industry that is among the lowest-paying in the U.S. The median wage for workers in food preparation and serving is $8.89 an hour—a little more than half the $15.95 median hourly wage for all occupations, according to the Bureau of Labor Statistics. The median annual wage in the sector is $20,800—less than half the median annual salary of $43,400 for all occupations.[342]

As McDonald's now argues, however, a starting position at one of its franchises can also be the beginning of a career as "More than half of McDonald's franchisees and 75 percent of restaurant managers started at entry-level jobs."[343] Of course, as indicated by a restaurant industry analyst, McDonald's is limited in its ability to improve conditions for its employees by the nature of the product that it produces:

> The thing that people forget is that if you want to spend $1 on food McDonald's can't have huge labor costs. . . . So part of the strategy of keeping food prices low is that labor costs have to be kept low, too.[344]

The relative purchasing power of a McDonald's wage is instructive. A study, conducted by *Asian Labor Update*,[345] aimed to compare the relative value of the wages paid to McDonald's employees[346] in various Asian countries. How long would each individual need to work to be able to buy a Big Mac sandwich at the McDonald's that employed him or her?

> Taking extreme examples, an Australian cleaner could buy three Big Macs after working for one hour, whereas a Pakistani cleaner would have to work for more than fourteen hours to buy the same burger.[347]

In Australia, where, at the time of the report, McDonald's staff worked for A$10.61 (US$5.60) per hour, it cost A$3.00 (US$1.58) to purchase a Big Mac. In Pakistan, however, where the company's staff worked for PR13 (US$0.22) per hour, a Big Mac cost PR185 (US$3.08). The difference between wage rates and the cost of a Big Mac produces the difference in purchase parity. The countries covered in the report included Australia, China, Hong Kong, India, Malaysia, New Zealand, Pakistan, Philippines, South Korea, Sri Lanka, and Thailand. Significant differences were identified. Wage rates ranged from a staff member who worked for IRs5.60 (US$0.11) per hour in India to the higher wages paid to McDonald's Australian employees: A$10.61 (US$5.60) per hour. In terms of the cost of burgers, Big Mac prices ranged from MR4.30 (US$1.13) in Malaysia, to NZ$3.95 (US$1.72) in New Zealand.

Rather than hourly wages, *The Economist* produces an annual Big Mac Index, which collates the price of a Big Mac across different countries and, it claims, "closely tracks the purchasing power parity rates calculated by more sophisticated methods."[348] The magazine has collected the data since 1986 and uses it to calculate the relative values of different currencies:

> A McDonald's Big Mac contains 29 grams of fat and a surprisingly large quantity of useful economic information. . . . In January [2012] a Swiss Big Mac cost $6.81, compared with $4.20 in America and just $2.44 in China, hinting at an overvalued franc relative to the dollar and an undervalued yuan. . . . Converting McWages into a common currency generates a surprisingly good picture of international differences in the cost of labour for simple, well-defined tasks. McWages are roughly comparable across the rich world, though rigid minimum-wage laws in western Europe make it a bit of an outlier. Among emerging economies, wages vary from 32% of the American level in Russia to about 6% in India, enormous gaps for functionally identical work.[349]

By dividing the local wage by the local price of a Big Mac, *The Economist* generates a measure of "Big Macs per hour (or BMPH)," which calculates the relative purchasing power of a single currency unit. By this measure in 2012, someone in Western Europe or Canada can buy 2.2 BMPH; in Russia, 1.2 BMPH; in Eastern Europe and South Africa, 0.8 BMPH; in China, 0.6 BMPH, and in Latin America and India, 0.4 BMPH:[350]

> Buy a Big Mac in Norway and it will set you back $7.20. Treat yourself to the very same culinary delight in China and your bank balance will be only $1.95 lighter. . . . The theory of purchasing power parity (PPP) suggests that if a Big Mac costs $4 in the US and £3 in the UK then, all things being equal, $4 should be of equivalent value to £3. By this token, the currencies of China, Malaysia, Thailand, Indonesia, Taiwan, Egypt and South Africa are all at least 30 per cent undervalued against the US dollar [in 2010].[351]

These differences reflect the different stages of economic development of the varied countries. In addition, the differences in purchase parity—how long each worker has to work to purchase a burger—reflect the different perceptions of a McDonald's meal within each country. In a developed country like Australia, McDonald's food is considered low-cost fast-food. In a developing country, like India, however, McDonald's is more exotic and, therefore, relatively more expensive. Nevertheless, the results are instructive in terms of the value of the same amount of work performed in different countries and cultures. This perspective also puts a new twist on Henry Ford's benchmark for worker compensation—whether his own workers could afford to buy the product they were making!

The issue of relative value is important in an age when Western consumers often judge a multinational corporation's operations overseas by domestic standards, rather than the local standards facing the company in that overseas country. The result is often difficult for the company that believes it faces a no-win situation. Nike, for example, has to manage a global network of over 700 independent supplier factories. To what degree is the company responsible for what happens within the operations of each of those independent organizations?

> The relationship is delicate. . . . NGOs have berated firms such as Nike for failing to ensure that workers are paid a "living wage." But that can be hard, even in America. . . . In developing countries, the dilemma may be even greater: "In Vietnam, [Nike's] workers are paid more than doctors. What's the social cost if a doctor leaves his practice and goes to work for [Nike]? That's starting to happen."[352]

Even within countries, the value of a particular job can change according to the relative context:

> Economic conditions matter. Job seekers might sneer at jobs at fast-food franchises in fast-growing Las Vegas, for example, where they can land lucrative positions as waiters in casinos. But they might covet them in a struggling textile town in the Carolinas.[353]

The combination of globalization, outsourcing, and the worldwide Financial Crisis is forcing changes in the labor market in developed economies. Low wage jobs that are transferable (such as manufacturing) are being outsourced,[354] replaced by machines,[355] or rendered obsolete,[356] while low wage jobs that are non-transferable (service jobs, such as gardening or waitressing) are stuck in a low-skill, low-wage cycle. In contrast, pay and conditions for skilled positions are rising—the result is growing income disparity and social stratification:

> The upper 1 percent of Americans are now taking in nearly a quarter of the nation's income every year. In terms of wealth rather than income, the top 1 percent control 40 percent. Their lot in life has improved considerably. Twenty-five years ago, the corresponding figures were 12 percent and 33 percent. . . . While the top 1 percent have seen their incomes rise 18 percent over the past decade, those in the middle have actually seen their incomes fall. For men with only high-school degrees, the decline has been precipitous— 12 percent in the last quarter-century alone. All the growth in recent decades— and more—has gone to those at the top.[357]

As such, another relative measure of wage levels for company employees, and an equally important indicator of the health of a firm, is the amount paid to corporate executives. What is an acceptable rate to pay top management? It seems that pay scales are relative and arbitrary:

Just how much do you have to pay a guy to run an outfit with 170,000 employees that's critical to our national defense? If he's the CEO of Boeing (which actually has 167,000 employees), the answer is $4 million plus lots of incentive compensation. If he's the Commandant of the U.S. Marine Corps (which actually has 174,000 employees), the answer is $169,860. Even Boeing's chief financial officer makes 10 times that much.[358]

Ironically, one study found that "chief executives of companies that had the largest layoffs and most underfunded pensions and that moved operations offshore to avoid U.S. taxes were rewarded with the biggest pay hikes."[359] As Peter Drucker wrote, somewhat hopefully, in a 1977 article criticizing "excessive" executive pay:

It is a business responsibility, but also a business self-interest, to develop a sensible executive compensation structure that portrays economic reality and asserts and codifies the achievement of U.S. business in this century: the steady narrowing of the income gap between the "boss man" and the "working man."[360]

The argument for a *fair* pay structure could be made on behalf of all of a firm's employees—as indicated by a *Wall Street Journal* headline:

Happy Workers Are the Best Workers.[361]

CEO Perspective

Henry Ford (Ford)

There is one rule for industrialists and that is: Make the best quality of goods possible at the lowest cost possible, paying the highest wages possible.

We try to pay a man what he is worth and we are not inclined to keep a man who is not worth more than the minimum wage.

Online Resources

- Asia Monitor Resource Center (AMRC), *Asian Labor Update*, http://www .amrc.org.hk/
- Create Jobs for USA, http://www.createjobsforusa.org/
- Fairness Initiative on Low-wage Work, http://www.lowwagework.org/
- Green America, http://www.coopamerica.org/programs/sweatshops/
- Labor Law Center, http://www.laborlawcenter.com/
- Living Wage Action Coalition, http://www.livingwageaction.org/
- Living Wage Calculator, http://livingwage.mit.edu/
- Low Pay Commission, http://www.lowpay.gov.uk/
- McDonald's Careers, http://www.mcdonalds.com/usa/work.html
- McSpotlight, 'What's Wrong with McDonald's?' http://www.mcspotlight .org/campaigns/translations/trans_uk.html
- National Labor Relations Board, https://www.nlrb.gov/
- The Foundation of Economic Trends, http://www.foet.org/
- U.S. Department of Labor, Bureau of Labor Statistics, http://www.bls.gov/
- U.S. Department of Labor, Wage and Hour Division, http://www.dol.gov/ esa/whd/flsa/
- United for a Fair Economy, http://www.faireconomy.org/

Pro/Con Debate

> **Pro/Con Debate:** Businesses have a responsibility to pay their employees a *living wage.*

QUESTIONS FOR DISCUSSION AND REVIEW

1. Is any job (at any wage) better than no job? Does your answer change if you apply the question to a worker in a developing, rather than developed country?

2. What is a fair wage? What does *fair* mean? What is the lowest hourly wage for which you would be willing to work? Think of some of the jobs you have done—would you have worked harder if your pay had been higher?

3. Is it a good idea for companies to apply a pay-scale ratio whereby the highest and lowest wage levels within an organization are kept within a certain ratio (such as in the Whole Foods Market example illustrated above)?

4. Where would you rather shop—Walmart/Sam's Club or Costco? If you answered 'Walmart' based on the price of its products, would you be willing to pay a higher price if you knew that the extra money would go directly to the firm's employees? If you answered 'Costco,' is it OK that the firm pays its employees above-market wages and passes those costs on to you, the customer, in terms of higher prices?

5. Respond to the following quote concerning Nike's relationship with its global network of over 700 independent supplier factories:

> The relationship is delicate. . . . NGOs have berated firms such as Nike for failing to ensure that workers are paid a 'living wage.' But that can be hard, even in America. . . . In developing countries, the dilemma may be even greater: "In Vietnam, [Nike's] workers are paid more than doctors. What's the social cost if a doctor leaves his practice and goes to work for [Nike]? That's starting to happen."[362]

STUDENT STUDY SITE

Visit the Student Study Site at **www.sagepub.com/chandler3e** for additional learning tools.

NOTES AND REFERENCES

1. 'Quick Takes,' *Business Ethics Magazine,* Summer 2003, p. 8.
2. Gary S. Becker, 'What the Scandals Reveal: A Strong Economy,' *BusinessWeek,* December 30, 2002, p. 30.
3. Michael Rapoport, 'Law's Big Weapon Sits Idle,' *The Wall Street Journal,* July 30, 2012, p. C3.
4. Robert C. Pozen, 'The Case for Professional Boards,' *Harvard Business Review*, December 2010, p. 52.
5. Michael Rapoport, 'Law's Big Weapon Sits Idle,' *The Wall Street Journal,* July 30, 2012, p. C3.
6. Robert C. Pozen, 'The Case for Professional Boards,' *Harvard Business Review*, December 2010, p. 52.
7. Steven M. Davidoff, 'On Boards, Little Cause for Anxiety,' *The New York Times*, August 3, 2011, p. B1. See also: Steven M. Davidoff, 'Despite Liability Worries, Serving at the Top Has Little Risk,' *The New York Times*, June 8, 2011, p. B5.
8. 'Principles of Good Governance,' *BusinessWeek,* October 7, 2002, http://www .businessweek.com/magazine/content/02_40/b3802005.htm
9. 'Principles of Good Governance,' *BusinessWeek,* October 7, 2002, http://www .businessweek.com/magazine/content/02_40/b3802005.htm

10. *BusinessWeek,* October 7, 2002, pp. 104–114, op. cit.

11. Robert C. Pozen, 'The Case for Professional Boards,' *Harvard Business Review*, December 2010, p. 58.

12. Steven M. Davidoff, 'Handicapping the Investment of IAC in Chelsea Clinton,' *The New York Times*, October 5, 2011, p. B6.

13. Kate Burgess, 'Criticism of board intensifies,' *Financial Times*, January 20, 2009, p. 21.

14. Tony Chapelle, 'Which set of company rules are OK? US-style of UK?' *Financial Times Special Report: Corporate Governance*, June 18, 2009, p. 1.

15. 'Don't Let the CEO Run the Board, Too,' *BusinessWeek*, November 11, 2002, p. 28.

16. Phyllis Plitch, 'Post of Lead Director Catches On, Letting CEOs Remain Chairmen,' *Wall Street Journal,* July 7, 2003, p. B2B.

17. 'Mickey Mouse Governance,' *The Economist,* October 15, 2011, p. 79.

18. Paul Davies, 'Drug Firms Urged to Split Top Jobs,' *Wall Street Journal,* April 22, 2005, p. C3.

19. 'Mickey Mouse Governance,' *The Economist,* October 15, 2011, p. 79.

20. John Gapper, 'Two chiefs can be wiser than one,' *Financial Times*, April 21, 2011, p. 11.

21. 'The doofus factor,' *The Economist*, September 17, 2011, p. 69.

22. 'Fazed and refused,' *The Economist*, October 20, 2012, p. 61.

23. Liz Rappaport, 'Lead Directors Gain Clout As Counterweight to CEO,' *The Wall Street Journal*, March 28, 2012, p. A6.

24. Joann S. Lublin, 'More CEOs Sharing Control at the Top,' *The Wall Street Journal,* June 7, 2012, p. B1.

25. Geoffrey Owen, 'A very British split at the top,' *Financial Times*, March 15, 2011, p. 10.

26. See: The Cadbury Committee, Judge Business School, University of Cambridge, http://www.jbs.cam.ac.uk/cadbury/report/committee.html

27. Nell Minow, 'Independent Chairmen Are Smart Investments,' *Bloomberg*, July 17, 2012, http://www.bloomberg.com/news/2012-07-17/independent-chairmen-are-smart-investments-nell-minow.html

28. Geoffrey Owen, 'A very British split at the top,' *Financial Times*, March 15, 2011, p. 10.

29. Marjorie Kelly, 'Eureka: An Opening for Economic Democracy,' *Business Ethics Magazine,* Summer 2003, p. 4.

30. For discussions of this issue, see: Floyd Norris, 'Greater Say on Boards Holds Risks,' *New York Times*, May 22, 2009, p. B1; 'A much needed shareholder victory,' *Financial Times Editorial*, May 22, 2009, p. 8; and 'Creating 'a Bigger Mess?' Battle Lines Are Drawn on the Proxy Access Rule,' *Knowledge@Wharton*, September 2, 2009, http://knowledge.wharton.upenn.edu/article.cfm?articleid=2331

31. Greg Farrell, 'Separation of functions still has a way to go,' *Financial Times Special Report: Corporate Governance*, June 18, 2009, p. 3.

32. Justin Baer, 'Executives face up to inevitable changes,' *Financial Times Special Report: Corporate Governance*, June 18, 2009, p. 1.

33. Liz Rappaport, 'Goldman Bows to Pressure on Board,' *The Wall Street Journal*, March 28, 2012, p. A6.

34. Greg Farrell, 'Separation of functions still has a way to go,' *Financial Times Special Report: Corporate Governance*, June 18, 2009, p. 3.

35. Frank Aquila, 'Corporate Governance: Don't Rush Reforms,' December 8, 2009, http://www.businessweek.com/investor/content/dec2009/pi2009128_869797.htm

36. 'The Corporation,' Movie-documentary, http://www.thecorporation.tv/about/. The documentary is summarized in the *Wall Street Journal* as "a documentary that functions as a 2½-hour provocation in the ongoing debate about corporate conduct and governance." 'The Corporation,' July 9, 2004, p. W2.

37. Brent Schlender, 'The New Soul of a Wealth Machine,' *Fortune,* April 5, 2004, pp. 102–110.

38. John Micklethwait & Adrian Wooldridge, 'The Company: A Short History of a Revolutionary Idea,' Modern Library, 2003, pp. xiv–xv.

39. Todd Stitzer, 'Business must loudly proclaim what it stands for,' *Financial Times*, June 1, 2006, p. 11.

40. "Wal-Mart, the most prodigious job creator in the history of the private sector in this galaxy, has almost as many employees (1.3 million) as the U.S. military has uniformed personnel. A McKinsey company study concluded that Wal-Mart accounted for 13 percent of the nation's productivity gains in the second half of the 1990s, which probably made Wal-Mart about as important as the Federal Reserve in holding down inflation. By lowering consumer prices, Wal-Mart costs about 50 retail jobs among competitors *for every 100 jobs Wal-Mart creates*. Wal-Mart and its effects save shoppers more than $200 billion a year, dwarfing such government programs as food stamps ($28.6 billion) and the earned-income tax credit ($34.6 billion)." In George F. Will, 'Democrats vs. Wal-Mart,' *The Washington Post,* September 14, 2006, p. A21.

41. For example, http://walmartwatch.com

42. Joel Bakan, 'The Kids Are Not All Right,' *The New York Times*, August 22, 2011, p. A19.

43. Philip Rucker, 'Mitt Romney says 'corporations are people' at Iowa State Fair,' *The Washington Post*, August 11, 2012, http://www.washingtonpost.com/politics/mitt-romney-says-corporations-are-people/2011/08/11/gIQABwZ38I_story.html

44. 'Peculiar people,' *The Economist*, March 26, 2011, p. 78.

45. Sir Edward Coke (1552-1634). Quoted in: John Micklethwait & Adrian Wooldridge, *The Company: A Short History of a Revolutionary Idea*, Modern Library, 2003, p. 33.

46. Lord Chancellor, Edward Thurlow (1731-1806). Quoted in: John Micklethwait & Adrian Wooldridge, *The Company: A Short History of a Revolutionary Idea*, Modern Library, 2003, p. 33.

47. John Micklethwait & Adrian Wooldridge, *The Company: A Short History of a Revolutionary Idea*, Modern Library, 2003, p. 45.

48. Martha C. White, 'Idea of company-as-person originated in late 19th century,' *The Washington Post*, January 31, 2010, http://www.washingtonpost.com/wp-dyn/content/article/2010/01/30/AR2010013000030.html

49. Martha C. White, 'Idea of company-as-person originated in late 19th century,' *The Washington Post*, January 31, 2010, http://www.washingtonpost.com/wp-dyn/content/article/2010/01/30/AR2010013000030.html

50. See also: *Cohen v. California* (403 U.S. 15, 1971).

51. 'The Rights of Corporations,' Editorial, *The New York Times*, 22 September 2009, p. 30.

52. Theodore B. Olsen, 'The Chance for a Free Speech Do-over,' *The Wall Street Journal*, September 7, 2009, http://online.wsj.com/article/SB100014240529702035 85004574393250083568972.html

53. 'The Court's Blow to Democracy,' Editorial, *The New York Times*, January 22, 2010, p30. For more background, see these related news articles that appeared in *The New York Times* on the same day as the announcement of the Court's decision: http://www.nytimes.com/2010/01/22/us/politics/22scotus.html and http://www.nytimes.com/2010/01/22/us/politics/22donate.html

54. 'The Court's Blow to Democracy,' Editorial, *The New York Times*, January 22, 2010, p. 30.

55. 'The Court's Blow to Democracy,' Editorial, *The New York Times*, January 22, 2010, p. 30.

56. 'The Court's Blow to Democracy,' Editorial, *The New York Times*, January 22, 2010, p. 30.

57. For more comment on the influence of Citizens United on campaign spending in the 2012 U.S. Presidential election, see: 'Money trouble,' *The Economist*, September 29, 2012, p. 35; Eric Lipton & Clifford Krauss, 'Fossil Fuel Ads Dominate TV In Campaign,' *The New York Times*, September 14, 2012, p. A1; and Eduardo Porter, 'Unleashing Corporate Contributions,' *The New York Times*, August 29, 2012, p. B1.

58. Jan Witold Baran, 'Stampede Toward Democracy,' Editorial, *The New York Times*, January 25, 2010, http://www.nytimes.com/2010/01/26/opinion/26baran.html

59. Adam Liptak, 'Justices' Ruling Is Wrapped in an English Lesson,' *The New York Times*, March 2, 2011, p. 15.

60. John Kay, 'Punish the directors and let the train driver go free,' *Financial Times*, May 18, 2011, p. 4.

61. 'Peculiar people,' *The Economist*, March 26, 2011, p. 78.

62. John Kay, 'Punish the directors and let the train driver go free,' *Financial Times*, May 18, 2011, p. 4.

63. 'Peculiar people,' *The Economist*, March 26, 2011, p. 78.

64. 'Corporations and the court,' *The Economist*, June 25, 2011, p. 75.

65. 'Peculiar people,' *The Economist*, March 26, 2011, p. 78.

66. 'Corporations and the court,' *The Economist*, June 25, 2011, p. 75.

67. https://movetoamend.org/

68. Martha C. White, 'Idea of company-as-person originated in late 19th century,' *The Washington Post*, January 31, 2010, http://www.washingtonpost.com/wp-dyn/content/article/2010/01/30/AR2010013000030.html

69. Chief Justice John Marshall, *Trustees of Dartmouth College v. Woodward* (17 U.S. 518, 1819).

70. http://www.thecorporation.com/index.cfm?page_id=46 also on YouTube: http://www.youtube.com/watch?v=xa3wyaEe9vE

71. https://movetoamend.org/

72. Also at: http://www.adbusters.org/cultureshop/corporateflag

73. *The Economist,* April 22, 2000, op. cit.

74. Newsdesk, 'The great company contribution,' *Ethical Corporation Magazine,* October 5, 2004, http://www.ethicalcorp.com/content.asp?ContentID=2884

75. Nikki Blacksmith & Jim Harter, 'Majority of American Workers Not Engaged in Their Jobs,' *Gallup Wellbeing*, October 28, 2011, http://www.gallup.com/poll/150383/Majority-American-Workers-Not-Engaged-Jobs.aspx

76. David Batstone, 'Saving the Corporate Soul—and (Who Knows?) Maybe Your Own,' Jossey-Bass, 2003, p. 3.

77. Peter Asmus, '100 Best Corporate Citizens of 2003,' *Business Ethics Magazine,* Spring 2003, pp. 6–10.

78. 'Throwing muses,' *The Economist*, March 17, 2012, p. 93.

79. 'Declining Employee Loyalty: A Casualty of the New Workplace,' *Knowledge@Wharton*, May 9, 2012, http://knowledge.wharton.upenn.edu/article.cfm?articleid=2995

80. 'Declining Employee Loyalty: A Casualty of the New Workplace,' *Knowledge@Wharton*, May 9, 2012, http://knowledge.wharton.upenn.edu/article.cfm?articleid=2995

81. Martha C. White, 'Doing Good on Company Time,' *New York Times*, May 8, 2007, p. C6.

82. Loretta Chao, 'Theory & Practice: Sabbaticals Can Offer Dividends for Employers,' *Wall Street Journal*, July 17, 2006, p. B5.

83. Rhymer Rigby, 'Time out to help less fortunate is its own reward,' *Financial Times*, July 21, 2009, p. 10.

84. John Bussey, 'Are Companies Responsible for Creating Jobs?' *The Wall Street Journal*, October 28, 2011, p. B1.

85. "[The UK's Home Office] estimates that the number of Britons engaged in 'active community participation' rose from 18.8 million to 20.3 million between 2001 and 2003." Simon Kuper, 'Office Angels,' *FT Weekend,* December 31, 2004 to January 2, 2005, p. W2.

86. http://www.yearofthevolunteer.org/

87. Bushra Tobah, 'Help Employees Help You: Five Research-based Ways to Boost Engagement,' *Network for Business Sustainability*, March 19, 2012, http://nbs.net/help-employees-help-you-five-research-based-ways-to-boost-engagement/

88. http://responsibility.timberland.com/service/

89. http://responsibility.timberland.com/reporting/report-archive/

90. For a detailed history of the origins of Timberland's volunteer program, see: Avery Yale Kamila, 'Timberland goes beyond philanthropy: Building value for community and brand with volunteers,' *Ethical Corporation*, February 13, 2004, http://www.ethicalcorp.com/content.asp?ContentID=1659

91. Note: Timberland was acquired by VF Corporation in 2011 and the Path of Service program celebrated its 20th anniversary in 2012 (http://responsibility.timberland.com/service/).

92. http://www.huffingtonpost.com/jeffrey-b-swartz

93. For a detailed history of the origins of Timberland's volunteer program, see: Avery Yale Kamila, 'Timberland goes beyond philanthropy: Building value for community and brand with volunteers,' *Ethical Corporation*, February 13, 2004, http://www.ethicalcorp.com/content.asp?ContentID=1659

94. Batstone, op. cit., p. 87.

95. Loretta Chao, 'Theory & Practice: Sabbaticals Can Offer Dividends for Employers,' *Wall Street Journal*, July 17, 2006, p. B5.

96. Rhymer Rigby, 'Time out to help less fortunate is its own reward,' *Financial Times*, July 21, 2009, p. 10.

97. Note: Public sector unions were excluded from this legislation. See: Paul Moreno, 'How Public Unions Became So Powerful,' *The Wall Street Journal*, September 12, 2012, pA15 and Maury Klein, '1st PAC used $600,000 to elect Roosevelt, boost Unions,' Bloomberg in *The Daily Yomiuri*, October 13, 2012, p. 15.

98. Eduardo Porter, 'Unions' Past May Hold Key To Their Future,' *The New York Times*, July 18, 2012, p. B1.

99. Steven Greenhouse, 'Share of the Work Force in a Union Falls to a 97-Year Low, 11.3%,' *The New York Times*, January 24, 2013, p. B1.

100. 'Poking Walmart, choking Twinkies,' *The Economist*, November 24, 2012, p. 74.

101. Eduardo Porter, 'Unions' Past May Hold Key To Their Future,' *The New York Times*, July 18, 2012, p. B8.

102. William Greider, 'Beyond Scarcity: A New Story of American Capitalism,' *Business Ethics Magazine*, Fall, 2003, pp. 9–11.

103. See: *Issues: Executive Pay* later in this chapter.

104. Nanette Byrnes et al., 'Beyond Options,' *BusinessWeek*, July 28, 2003, pp. 36–37.

105. For a complete history of the firm, see: http://www.johnlewispartnership.co.uk/about/our-founder.html

106. Geoffrey Owen, 'When the workers take over,' *Financial Times*, April 28, 2011, p. 10.

107. Marjorie Kelly, 'Can There Be 'Good' Corporations?' *Yes! Magazine*, April 16, 2012, http://www.yesmagazine.org/issues/9-strategies-to-end-corporate-rule/can-there-be-201cgood201d-corporations

108. Andrew Hill, 'A rather civil partnership,' *Financial Times*, January 20, 2012, http://www.ft.com/intl/cms/s/0/30ca497e-438a-11e1-9f28-00144feab49a.html

109. Marjorie Kelly, 'Can There Be 'Good' Corporations?' *Yes! Magazine*, April 16, 2012, http://www.yesmagazine.org/issues/9-strategies-to-end-corporate-rule/can-there-be-201cgood201d-corporations

110. Michael Skapinker, 'Staff ownership can save a company's soul,' *Financial Times*, February 9, 2010, p. 13.

111. 'The feeling is mutual,' *The Economist*, January 21, 2012, p. 62.

112. 'The feeling is mutual,' *The Economist*, January 21, 2012, p. 62.

113. 'The feeling is mutual,' *The Economist*, January 21, 2012, p. 62.

114. For a good example of a U.S., employee-owned firm, see CH2M Hill: http://www.ch2m.com/corporate/about_us/employee_ownership/default.asp

115. For detailed case-studies of the processes by which two firms (Tullis Russell, a papermaking firm in Fife, Scotland and Trace, a business software company in London) became employee-owned, see: Geoffrey Owen, 'When the workers take over,' *Financial Times*, April 28, 2011, p. 10 and Richard Tomkins, 'Sold to the lowest bidder,' *Financial Times: Life & Arts*, December 8/9, 2007, p. 1. For a comprehensive comparison of employee-owned organizations across different countries and cultures, see: Henry Hansmann, *The Ownership of Enterprise*, Harvard University Press, 2000.

116. Geoffrey Owen, 'When the workers take over,' *Financial Times*, April 28, 2011, p. 10.

117. Geoffrey Owen, 'When the workers take over,' *Financial Times*, April 28, 2011, p. 10.

118. Rachel Emma Silverman, 'My Colleague, My Paymaster,' *The Wall Street Journal*, April 4, 2012, p. B1.

119. See also: 'Going Boss-free: Utopia or 'Lord of the Flies'?' *Knowledge@Wharton*, August 1, 2012, http://knowledge.wharton.upenn.edu/article.cfm?articleid=3059

120. Alfred D. Chandler, Jr., *The Visible Hand: The Managerial Revolution in American Business*, Harvard University Press, 1977.

121. Gary Hamel, 'The Big Idea: First, Let's Fire All the Managers,' *Harvard Business Review*, December 2011, pp. 4–13.

122. For example, see this case-study about Zappos: Winter Nie & Beverley Lennox, 'Creating a distinct corporate culture: How to embed a sense of passion,' *Financial Times*, February 17, 2011, p. 10.

123. Rachel Emma Silverman, 'Who's the Boss? There Isn't One,' *The Wall Street Journal*, June 20, 2012, p. B1.

124. Rachel Emma Silverman, 'Who's the Boss? There Isn't One,' *The Wall Street Journal*, June 20, 2012, p. B1.

125. Rachel Emma Silverman, 'Who's the Boss? There Isn't One,' *The Wall Street Journal*, June 20, 2012, p. B1.

126. Peter Marsh & Stefan Stern, 'The chaos theory of leadership,' *Financial Times*, December 2, 2008, http://us.ft.com/ftgateway/superpage.ft?news_id=fto120120081556345506

127. http://www.logomaker.com/blog/2012/05/21/9-inspirational-quotes-on-business-by-herb-kelleher/
128. Pound & Moore, op. cit.
129. Micklethwait & Wooldridge, op. cit., pp. xvi & xviii.
130. Micklethwait & Wooldridge, op. cit.
131. The term "shareholder value" was introduced in a 1981 *Harvard Business Review* article by an accounting professor, Alfred Rappaport, who designed an index "to determine the value-creating prospects for alternative strategies at the business unit and corporate levels." In: Alfred Rappaport, 'Selecting strategies that create shareholder value,' *Harvard Business Review*, Vol. 59, Issue No. 3, 1981, pp. 139–149. Ironically, given the short-term focus of much of business today, Rappaport's goal was "to get corporate executives to pay less attention to accounting earnings and focus instead on economic earnings. . . . It was an argument for paying attention to what created value over time instead of stressing out about quarterly earnings." In: Justin Fox, 'Ignore Your Investors!' *Fortune Magazine*, June 8, 2009, p. 20.
132. Joel Bakan, *The Corporation: The Pathological Pursuit of Profit and Power*, Free Press, 2004, p. 37.
133. Andy Serwer, 'Wall Street Comes to Main Street,' *Fortune,* May 3, 2004, pp. 132–146.
134. Alan Murray, 'Political Capital: CEO Responsibility Might Be Right Cure for Corporate World,' *Wall Street Journal,* July 13, 2004, p. A4.
135. Robert C. Pozen, 'The Case for Professional Boards,' *Harvard Business Review*, December 2010, p. 52.
136. For a full breakdown of the compensation packages of all 200 CEOs in 2011, see: Nathaniel Popper, 'C.E.O. Pay, Rising Despite the Din,' *The New York Times*, June 17, 2012, p. BU1.
137. Nathaniel Popper, 'C.E.O. Pay, Rising Despite the Din,' *The New York Times*, June 17, 2012, p. BU9. "The top 25 hedge-fund managers regularly earn more as a group that all 500 S&P CEOs put together." In: 'Bargain bosses,' *The Economist*, September 8, 2012, p. 67.
138. Stephanie Strom, 'Nonprofit Salaries Under a Microscope,' *The New York Times*, July 27, 2010, p. A10.
139. Lauren Etter, 'More Get $1 Million to Lead Colleges,' *The Wall Street Journal*, November 15, 2010, p. A6.
140. 'Bosses under fire,' *The Economist*, January 14, 2012, p. 11.
141. Ray Fisman, 'In Defense Of the CEO,' *The Wall Street Journal*, January 12-13, 2013, p. C1.
142. Richard R. Floersch, 'The Right Way to Determine Executive Pay,' *Wall Street Journal*, March 5, 2009, p. A15.
143. Gene Colter, 'Stock Options Lose Appeal as an Option,' *Wall Street Journal*, October 12, 2004, p. C3.
144. 'Bargain bosses,' *The Economist*, September 8, 2012, p. 67.

145. 'How New Accounting Rules Are Changing the Way CEOs Get Paid,' *Knowledge@ Wharton*, May, 2006, http://knowledge.wharton.upenn.edu/index.cfm?fa=print Article&ID=1465

146. 'Pay up,' *The Economist*, June 18, 2011, p. 74.

147. Arthur Levitt Jr., 'Money, Money, Money,' *Wall Street Journal*, November 22, 2004, Op-ed page.

148. Charles Forelle & James Bandler, 'The Perfect Payday,' *Wall Street Journal*, March 18-19, 2006, p. A1.

149. Roger Martin, 'Reward real growth, not expectations,' *Financial Times*, August 3, 2010, p. 10.

150. Louis Lavelle, 'Wretched Excess: Mega Options, Mega Losses,' *BusinessWeek,* June 23, 2003, p. 14.

151. Editorial, 'What We Learned in 2002,' *BusinessWeek,* December 30, 2002, p. 170.

152. Kathy Kristof, 'Shareholders Should Look for Signs of Excessive Exec Pay,' *Miami Herald,* June 22, 2003, p. 6E.

153. For example, see: Kate Burgess & Richard Milne, 'Floored Boards,' *Financial Times*, June 2, 2009, p. 12 and Josh Martin, 'Committees strive to achieve the right mix,' *Financial Times Special Report: Corporate Governance*, June 18, 2009, p. 3.

154. Richard R. Floersch, 'The Right Way to Determine Executive Pay,' *Wall Street Journal*, March 5, 2009, p. A15.

155. 'Home Depot CEO Nardelli quits,' *Associated Press*, January 3, 2007, http://msnbc .msn.com/id/16451112/

156. Robin Pagnamenta & Helen Power, 'Shell's pay committee bears the brunt of growing investor anger,' *The Times*, May 20, 2009, p. 38.

157. 'AIG bonus payments $218 million,' *Reuters*, http://www.reuters.com/article/ newsOne/idUSTRE52K19L20090321

158. Alan Beattie, 'Summers' 'outrage' at AIG bonuses,' *Financial Times*, March 15, 2009, http://www.ft.com/cms/s/0/31bafc52-1192-11de-87b1-0000779fd2ac.html

159. Eric Dash, 'The Lucrative Fall From Grace,' *The New York Times*, September 30, 2011, p. B1.

160. Clarence Page, 'Is the honeymoon over?' *Chicago Tribune*, in the *Daily Yomiuri*, March 31, 2009, p. 17.

161. 'Bargain bosses,' *The Economist*, September 8, 2012, p. 67.

162. Robert B. Reich, 'CEOs Deserve Their Pay,' *The Wall Street Journal*, September 14, 2007, p. A13.

163. 'The wheel of fortune,' *The Economist*, May 26, 2012, p. 70.

164. Moisés Naim, 'Corporate Power is Decaying. Get Used to It,' *Bloomberg Businessweek*, February 21, 2013, http://www.businessweek.com/articles/2013-02-21/ corporate-power-is-decaying-dot-get-used-to-it

165. Baruch Lev, 'The Case for Guidance,' *The Wall Street Journal Report: Leadership in Corporate Finance*, February 27, 2012, p. R3.

166. Nanette Byrnes, 'Earnings Guidance: Silence Is Golden,' *BusinessWeek,* May 5, 2003, p. 87.

167. Carola Hoyos & Michael Steen, 'Outgoing Shell chief calls for executive pay reform,' *Financial Times*, June 9, 2009, p. 1.

168. Kara Scannell & Joann S. Lublin, 'SEC Asks Firms to Detail Top Executives' Pay,' *The Wall Street Journal*, August 1, 2007, p. B1.

169. Julia Werdigier, 'Shareholder Votes on Pay To Be Binding in Britain,' *The New York Times*, June 21, 2012, p. B4.

170. Joanna L. Ossinger, 'Poorer Relations: When it comes to CEO pay, why are the British so different?' *Wall Street Journal*, April 10, 2006, p. R6.

171. Vipal Monga, 'Boards Cozy Up to Investors,' *The Wall Street Journal*, January 8, 2013, p. B7.

172. Leslie Kwoh, 'Firms Resist New Pay-Equity Rules,' *The Wall Street Journal*, June 27, 2012, p. B8.

173. John McKay, CEO of Whole Foods, 'Final Word: "I no longer want to work for money," *Fast Company*, February, 2007, p. 112. See also: Alaina Love, 'Dousing the Passion for Greed,' *BusinessWeek*, October 23, 2009, http://www.businessweek.com/managing/content/oct2009/ca20091023_069551.htm

174. 'Why It Pays to Link Executive Compensation with Corporate Debt,' *Knowledge@ Wharton*, July 7, 2010, http://knowledge.wharton.upenn.edu/article.cfm?articleid=2533. See also: Alex Edmans, 'How to Fix Executive Compensation,' *The Wall Street Journal Report: Leadership in Corporate Finance*, February 27, 2012, p. R1. The EU has drafted plans to explore this option in the finance industry—see: Alex Barker & Patrick Jenkins, 'Bankers' bonuses should be paid in debt, Brussels review proposes,' *Financial Times*, October 2, 2012, p. 1.

175. James Wilson & Richard Milne, 'Puma gives the boot to cardboard shoeboxes,' *Financial Times*, April 14, 2010, p. 17.

176. Michael Skapinker, 'Replacing the 'dumbest idea in the world,' *Financial Times*, April 13, 2010, p. 13.

177. Oliver Balch, 'Executive Remuneration: Fat Cats vs. the Future,' *Ethical Corporation's Management Blog*, January 18, 2011, http://crmanagementblog.blogspot.com/2011/01/executive-remuneration-fat-cats-vs.html. See also: Richard Milne & Michael Steen, 'Executive bonuses tied to green targets,' *Financial Times*, February 24, 2010, p. 16.

178. John O'Donnell & Sinead Cruise, 'Europe moves towards Swiss-style executive pay curbs,' *The Globe and Mail*, March 6, 2013, http://www.theglobeandmail.com/report-on-business/international-business/european-business/europe-moves-toward-swiss-style-executive-pay-curbs/article9355210/

179. 'Pay up,' *The Economist*, June 18, 2011, p. 74.

180. In July, 2009, the Securities and Exchange Commission in the U.S. extended its use of the clawback law to include executives who had benefitted from fraud or misstated earnings in their firm, even if they were not personally involved: Joanna Chung, 'SEC toughens stance with first 'clawback' move,' *Financial Times*, July 29, 2009, p. 3.

181. Joann S. Lublin, 'Law Toughens 'Clawback' Rules for Improper Pay,' *The Wall Street Journal*, July 26, 2010, p. B6. Unfortunately, reports indicate that these

clawback clauses are rarely, if ever, used by firms (see: Gretchen Morgenson, 'Clawbacks Without Claws,' *The New York Times*, September 10, 2011, http://www.nytimes.com/2011/09/11/business/clawbacks-without-claws-in-a-sarbanes-oxley-tool.html

182. Carol Hymowitz, 'Sky-high Payouts to Top Executives Prove Hard to Curb,' *Wall Street Journal*, June 26, 2006, p. B1.

183. For an example of one CEO's compensation package that "wins praise from compensation critics," see: Joann S. Lublin, 'Valeant CEO's Pay Package Draws Praise as a Model,' *Wall Street Journal*, August 24, 2009, p. B4.

184. Richard R. Floersch, 'The Right Way to Determine Executive Pay,' *Wall Street Journal*, March 5, 2009, p. A15.

185. Steven M. Davidoff, 'Furor Over Executive Pay Is Not the Revolt It Appears to Be,' *The New York Times*, May 2, 2012, p. B5.

186. See: Maxwell Murphy, 'The Inside/Outside Pay Gap,' *The Wall Street Journal*, September 11, 2012, p. B6 and 'The trouble with superheroes,' *The Economist*, October 1, 2011, p. 74.

187. Charles M. Elson and Craig K. Ferrere quoted in: Gretchen Morgenson, 'Pamper 'Em or Lose 'Em? Not So Fast,' *The New York Times*, September 23, 2012, p. BU2.

188. Michael Hiltzik, 'Peter Drucker's revolutionary teachings decades old but still fresh,' *Los Angeles Times*, December 31, 2009, http://articles.latimes.com/2009/dec/31/business/la-fi-hiltzik31-2009dec31

189. Mallen Baker, 'Remuneration – Value society, Mr. President,' *Ethical Corporation,* March 11, 2009, http://www.ethicalcorp.com/content.asp?ContentID=6391

190. Natasha Singer, 'In Executive Pay, a Rich Game of Thrones,' *The New York Times*, April 7, 2012, http://www.nytimes.com/2012/04/08/business/in-chief-executives-pay-a-rich-game-of-thrones.html

191. See: Dawn C. Chmielewski, 'Carl Icahn calls Netflix's poison pill measures 'poor governance," *Los Angeles Times*, November 5, 2012, http://www.latimes.com/entertainment/envelope/cotown/la-et-ct-icahn-questions-netflix-poison-pill-20121105,0,925822.story and Gene G. Marcial, 'Carl Icahn's Cure for Corporate America,' *BusinessWeek*, November 18, 2005, http://www.businessweek.com/bwdaily/dnflash/nov2005/nf20051118_0496.htm

192. Bill Baue, 'Investing in … Genocide?' *CSRwire.com*, March 31, 2009, http://www.csrwire.com/News/14977.html

193. For example, see: Kate Burgess, 'Investors are taking a share in revolution,' *Financial Times*, May 6, 2009, p. 15.

194. Anthony Goodman, 'Investors should be careful what they wish for,' *Financial Times*, July 20, 2010, p. 10.

195. Brian Bowen, 'Shareholder Resolutions Spur U.S. Companies to Act on Sustainability During 2012 Proxy Season,' *Ceres*, July 10, 2012, http://www.ceres.org/press/press-releases/shareholder-resolutions-spur-u.s.-companies-to-act-on-sustainability-during-2012-proxy-season

196. Ed Crooks, 'Shareholders lead eco-crusade,' *Financial Times*, March 8, 2011, p. 15.

197. Ben Protess & Katherine Reynolds Lewis, 'Changing Face of Investor Activism,' *The New York Times,* June 8, 2012, p. B1.

198. Sheila McNulty, 'Shareholder Activists Hijack Exxon's AGM,' *Financial Times,* May 9, 2003, p. 17.

199. Ben Protess & Katherine Reynolds Lewis, 'Changing Face of Investor Activism,' *The New York Times,* June 8, 2012, p. B1.

200. Quoted by an officer from the Investor Responsibility Research Center on *The NewsHour With Jim Lehrer,* PBS, June 10, 2003.

201. http://corpgov.net/news/archives/archived996.html

202. 'Understanding Shareholder Votes,' *As You Sow*, November 2012, http://www.asyousow.org/csr/understandingvote.shtml

203. David Enrich, 'Barclays Shareholders Vent on Pay,' *The Wall Street Journal*, April 28-29, 2012, p. B2. See also: Julia Werdigier, 'Amid Shouts of Hecklers, Barclays' Board Apologizes to Shareholders,' *The New York Times*, April 28, 2012, p. B2.

204. Andrew Park, 'Dell Gets Greener,' *BusinessWeek,* May 5, 2003, p. 89.

205. *The Observer,* May 25, 2003, op. cit.

206. Maxwell Murphy, 'Snubbed By Holders, Directors Keep Posts,' *The Wall Street Journal*, June 12, 2012, p. B1.

207. Alan Murray, 'Pivotal Fight Looms for Shareholder Democracy,' *Wall Street Journal*, November 22, 2006, p. A2.

208. Jerri-Lynn Scofield, 'Shareholder Rights – Minority Rules' *Ethical Corporation Magazine*, November 1, 2010, http://www.ethicalcorp.com/stakeholder-engagement/analysis-shareholder-rights-minority-rules

209. Tara Siegel Bernard, 'Voting Your Shares May Start To Matter,' *The New York Times*, March 6, 2010, p. B1.

210. The proxy review by the SEC continues, but progress is being made. For one example concerning shareholders' ability to nominate directors, see: Deborah Brewster, 'Investors in boardroom victory,' *Financial Times*, May 21, 2009, p. 15 and Stephen Labaton, 'S.E.C. Proposes to Widen Investors' Say on Boards,' *New York Times*, May 21, 2009, p. B3.

211. Dennis K. Berman, 'Boardroom Defenestration,' *Wall Street Journal*, March 16, 2006, p. B1.

212. Jessica Holz & Dennis Berman, 'Investors Gain New Clout,' *The Wall Street Journal*, August 26, 2010, p. A1.

213. Mallen Baker, 'Greedy bosses get punished by ... um ... greedy shareholders,' May 7, 2012, http://www.mallenbaker.net/csr/post.php?id=438

214. See: 'SEC Adopts Rules for Say-on-Pay and Golden Parachute Compensation as Required Under Dodd-Frank Act,' January 25, 2011, http://www.sec.gov/news/press/2011/2011-25.htm

215. Peter Montagnon & Roderick Munsters, 'One share, one vote is the way to a fairer market,' *Financial Times*, August 14, 2006, p. 11.

216. One context in which the value of greater shareholder democracy can be questioned is during a hostile takeover of the firm. At these moments, it is not clear that shareholders are better placed than executives to determine the future of the organization. This phenomenon was demonstrated by Kraft's takeover of Cadbury's in the UK in 2010. While politicians and the majority of public opinion wanted the firm to remain British, the global set of institutional investors who owned the majority of the firm's shares determined their value was maximized by the sale of the firm. The fallout from the takeover led directly to legislative changes in UK corporate law to further constrain future hostile takeovers. See: Anousha Sakoui, 'The unappetizing consequences of a hostile acquisition,' *Financial Times*, May 24, 2011, p. 9 and Roger Carr, 'Cadbury: Hostile bids and takeovers,' University of Oxford, February 16, 2010, http://www.sbs.ox.ac.uk/newsandevents/news/Pages/RogerCarrCadbury.aspx

217. Jessica Holz, 'Court Deals Blow to SEC, Activists,' *The Wall Street Journal*, July 23, 2011, http://online.wsj.com/article/SB10001424053111903554904576461932431478332.html

218. Tara Siegel Bernard, 'Voting Your Shares May Start To Matter,' *The New York Times*, March 6, 2010, p. B1.

219. Phred Dvorak, 'Companies Seek Shareholder Input on Pay Practices,' *Wall Street Journal*, April 6, 2009, p. B4.

220. Phred Dvorak, 'Companies Seek Shareholder Input on Pay Practices,' *Wall Street Journal*, April 6, 2009, p. B4.

221. Joann S. Lublin, 'Online Annual Meetings Begin to Click,' *The Wall Street Journal*, November 14, 2011, p. B7.

222. Joann S. Lublin & Ben Worthen, 'H-P Activist Investors Make Proxy Progress,' *The Wall Street Journal*, February 6, 2012, http://online.wsj.com/article/SB1000142405297020466220457720174373422890.html

223. Joann S. Lublin & Ben Worthen, 'H-P Activist Investors Make Proxy Progress,' *The Wall Street Journal*, February 6, 2012, http://online.wsj.com/article/SB1000142405297020466220457720174373422890.html

224. Investopedia, November 2012, http://www.investopedia.com/terms/s/sri.asp#axzz2Bq0ujozQ

225. Chris Gay, 'Are Bank Stocks 'Responsible'?' *The Wall Street Journal,* February 6, 2012, p. R6.

226. David Bogoslaw, 'Social investing Gathers Momentum,' *BusinessWeek,* February 3, 2010, http://www.businessweek.com/investor/content/feb2010/pi2010023_247094.htm

227. John Tozzi, 'New Legal Protections for Social Entrepreneurs,' *Bloomberg BusinessWeek,* April 22, 2010, http://www.businessweek.com/investor/content/feb2010/pi2010023_247094.htm

228. 'Sustainable and Responsible Investing Facts,' *US SIF*, November 2012, http://ussif.org/resources/sriguide/srifacts.cfm

229. 'Sustainable and Responsible Investing Facts,' *US SIF*, November 2012, http://ussif.org/resources/sriguide/srifacts.cfm

230. Chip Feiss, 'Social enterprise – the fledgling fourth sector,' *Financial Times*, June 15, 2009, p. 11.

231. 'SRI fund sales hit 1 billion euro mark in December 2008,' *NaturalChoices.co.uk*, February 26, 2009, http://www.naturalchoices.co.uk/SRI-fund-sales-hit-1-billion-euro?id_mot=1

232. David Bogoslaw, 'Social investing Gathers Momentum,' *BusinessWeek,* February 3, 2010, http://www.businessweek.com/investor/content/feb2010/pi2010023_247094.htm

233. John Authers, 'There are clear arguments for a clear conscience,' *Financial Times*, July 28, 2007, p. 16.

234. 'A dull shade of green,' *The Economist,* October 29, 2012, p. 87.

235. Richard Milne, 'Fund to focus on role of women,' *Financial Times,* October 26, 2009, p. 17. See also: Julia Werdigier, 'Fund Plans to Invest in Companies With Women as Directors,' *The New York Times*, October 27, 2009, p. B7.

236. David Oakley, 'Vatican-backed index aims to meet demand for ethical stocks,' *Financial Times,* April 27, 2010, p. 13.

237. Jem Bendell, 'Have you seen my business case?' *Ethical Corporation,* November 2, 2002, http://www.ethicalcorp.com/content.asp?ContentID=264

238. Sam Stovall, 'Tobacco Stocks: A Classic Defensive Play,' *BusinessWeek,* January 29, 2008, http://www.businessweek.com/investor/content/jan2008/pi20080129_262388.htm

239. Spencer Jakab, 'How Much Is Left in This Pack of Smokes?' *The Wall Street Journal,* July 24, 2012, p. C1.

240. As of September 30, 2012, http://www.usamutuals.com/vicefund/docs/VICEXcomplete.pdf

241. Barbara Kiviat, 'Heart on One's Sleeve, Eye on Bottom Line,' *Miami Herald,* January 19, 2003, p. 3E.

242. Joe Nocera, 'Well-meaning But Misguided Stock Screens,' *New York Times*, April 7, 2007, p. B1.

243. For a more general discussion of the different components of *impact investing*, together with example projects, see: 'Happy returns,' *The Economist*, September 10, 2011, p. 84.

244. 'Social Finance's Tracy Palandjian on the Next Generation of Responsible Investing,' *Knowledge@Wharton*, March 14, 2012, http://knowledge.wharton.upenn.edu/article.cfm?articleid=2956

245. David Leonhardt, 'What Are Social-Impact Bonds?' *The New York Times*, February 8, 2011, http://economix.blogs.nytimes.com/2011/02/08/what-are-social-impact-bonds/

246. Caroline Preston, 'Getting Back More Than a Warm Feeling,' *The New York Times: Giving Special Section*, November 9, 2012, p. F1.

247. Investopedia, November 2012, http://www.investopedia.com/terms/s/social-impact-bond.asp

248. 'Commerce and conscience,' *The Economist*, February 23, 2013, p. 71.

249. See: 'Social Impact Bonds: Can This New Asset Class Create More Than a Win-Win?' *Knowledge@Wharton*, March 15, 2011, http://knowledge.asb.unsw.edu.au/article.cfm?articleid=1359

250. 'Social Finance's Tracy Palandjian on the Next Generation of Responsible Investing,' *Knowledge@Wharton*, March 14, 2012, http://knowledge.wharton.upenn.edu/article.cfm?articleid=2956

251. 'Social Impact Bonds: Can a Market Prescription Cure Social Ills?' *Knowledge@Wharton*, September 12, 2012, http://knowledge.wharton.upenn.edu/article.cfm?articleid=3078

252. David W. Chen, 'Goldman to Invest in City Prison Program, Reaping Profit if Recidivism Drops,' *The New York Times*, August 2, 2012, p. A14.

253. 'Being good pays,' *The Economist*, August 18, 2012, p. 28.

254. Caroline Preston, 'Getting Back More Than a Warm Feeling,' *The New York Times: Giving Special Section*, November 9, 2012, p. F1.

255. 'Social Impact Bonds: Can a Market Prescription Cure Social Ills?' *Knowledge@Wharton*, September 12, 2012, http://knowledge.wharton.upenn.edu/article.cfm?articleid=3078

256. Stephanie Strom, 'Philanthropists Take On Big Problems by Enlisting Capitalists,' *The New York Times*, December 12, 2012, p. F19.

257. John Kay, 'Time for the Big Society to get down to the nitty-gritty,' *Financial Times*, February 23, 2011, p. 9.

258. Francesco Guerrera, 'Welch condemns share price focus,' March 12, 2009, http://www.ft.com/cms/s/0/294ff1f2-0f27-11de-ba10-0000779fd2ac.html

259. 'Jack Welch Elaborates: Shareholder Value,' March 16, 2009, http://www.businessweek.com/bwdaily/dnflash/content/mar2009/db20090316_630496.htm

260. Stephanie Strom, 'Make Money, Save the World,' *New York Times*, May 6, 2007, p. BU1.

261. Steve Hamm, 'Capitalism with a Human Face,' *BusinessWeek*, December 8, 2008, p. 49.

262. Polly LaBarre, 'Leap of Faith,' *Fast Company Magazine*, June, 2007, p. 98.

263. Philip Delves Broughton, 'Doing Good By Shoeing Well,' *The Wall Street Journal*, September 9, 2011, p. A17.

264. See also: Christina Binkley, 'Charity Gives Shoe Brand Extra Shine,' *The Wall Street Journal*, April 1, 2010, http://online.wsj.com/article/SB10001424052702304252704575155903198032336.html

265. Chip Feiss, 'Social enterprise – the fledgling fourth sector,' *Financial Times*, June 15, 2009, p. 11.

266. "[UK] government estimates put the number of social enterprises in the UK at 55,000, with a turnover of £27 billion, contributing about £8 billion to the UK's gross domestic product and employing more than 500,000 people." In: Steve Coomber, 'New business is modeled on old-fashioned mutual interest,' *The Times*, July 24, 2007, p. 6.

267. Jon Entine, 'Eco marketing: What price green consumerism?' *Ethical Corporation Magazine*, September 1, 2011, http://www.ethicalcorp.com/environment/eco-marketing-what-price-green-consumerism

268. 'When do consumers say 'no' to green?' *Network for Business Sustainability*, June 24, 2011, http://nbs.net/knowledge/when-do-consumers-say-no-to-green/

269. Jon Entine, 'Eco marketing: What price green consumerism?' *Ethical Corporation Magazine*, September 1, 2011, http://www.ethicalcorp.com/environment/eco-marketing-what-price-green-consumerism

270. Michael Skapinker, 'There is a good trade in ethical retailing,' *Financial Times*, September 10, 2007, http://us.ft.com/ftgateway/superpage.ft?news_id=fto09102007 1414102552

271. David Vogel, *The Market for Virtue: The Potential and Limits of Corporate Social Responsibility*, Brookings Institution Press, 2005, p. 49.

272. Toby Webb, 'The Ethical Consumer at Scale Myth,' *Smarter Business blog*, January 30, 2012, http://tobywebb.blogspot.com/2012/01/ethical-consumer-at-scale-myth-why-do.html

273. Andrew Jack, 'Beyond charity? A new generation enters the business of doing good,' *Financial Times*, April 5, 2007, p. 11.

274. Andrew Jack, 'Beyond charity? A new generation enters the business of doing good,' *Financial Times*, April 5, 2007, p. 11.

275. Marjorie Kelly, 'Cover Story: The Legacy Problem,' *Business Ethics Magazine*, Summer, 2003, http://www.esopbuilders.com/articles/the-legacy-problem.pdf. For details of succession stories at four iconic firms (Disney, Walmart, Ford, and Microsoft), see: Joe Light & Scott Thurm, 'Disney, Walton, Ford, Gates: Tales of When Legends Leave,' *The Wall Street Journal*, August 26, 2011, p. B1.

276. Mark Goyder, 'Ownership and sustainability – Are listed companies more responsible?' *Ethical Corporation,* July 14, 2008, http://www.ethicalcorp.com/content.asp?ContentID=6004

277. 'Virgin, Ben & Jerry's, O2, BP, Starbucks to Discuss How They Brand Their Values,' *Ethical Corporation* Press Release, *CSRwire.com*, September 27, 2005, http://www.csrwire.com/press/press_release/22741

278. Louise Lucas, 'Preserve your unique flavor,' *Financial Times*, February 8, 2011, p. 12.

279. Melanie Warner, 'Solo Climb,' *Business 2.0*, December, 2004, p. 152.

280. Christopher Palmeri, 'From Ice Cream to Nuclear Freeze,' *BusinessWeek*, August 24, 2006, http://www.businessweek.com/investor/content/aug2006/pi20060824_523626.htm

281. Christopher Palmeri, 'From Ice Cream to Nuclear Freeze,' *BusinessWeek*, August 24, 2006, http://www.businessweek.com/investor/content/aug2006/pi20060824_523626.htm

282. Louise Lucas, 'Preserve your unique flavor,' *Financial Times*, February 8, 2011, p. 12.

283. Mallen Baker, 'CSR: Is it time to change the ownership of our best companies?' *mallenbaker.net*, January 12, 2010, http://www.mallenbaker.net/csr/page.php?Story_ID=2569

284. John Russell, 'Body Shop takeover – Ethical business as usual,' *Ethical Corporation Magazine,* March 11, 2007, http://www.ethicalcorp.com/content.asp?ContentID=4936

285. Anya Kamenetz, 'Cleaning Solution,' *Fast Company Magazine*, September, 2008, pp. 120-125, http://www.fastcompany.com/magazine/128/cleaning-solution.html

286. Jon Entine, 'Sell-out at the Sierra Club,' *Ethical Corporation Magazine*, September 1, 2008, http://www.ethicalcorp.com/content.asp?ContentID=6055

287. David Teather, 'Roddick nets £130m from Body Shop sale,' *The Guardian*, March 17, 2006, http://www.guardian.co.uk/business/2006/mar/18/highstreetretailers.retail

288. Sage, The Body Shop, http://knowledge.sagepub.com/view/greenbusiness/n13.xml

289. Roger Martin, 'The Virtue Matrix,' *Harvard Business Review*, March 2002, Vol. 80, No. 3, pp. 68–75.

290. Jon Entine, 'Queen of Green Roddick's 'unfair trade' started when she copied Body Shop's formula,' *The Mail on Sunday*, September 15, 2007, http://www.mailonsunday.co.uk/pages/live/femail/article.html?in_article_id=482012&in_page_id=1879

291. Tony Dawe, 'Business takes on board the need for social responsibility,' *The Times*, July 24, 2007, p. 3.

292. The Body Shop's Web site, http://www.thebodyshop.com/bodyshop/index.jsp, December, 2002.

293. PETA's website, http://www.peta.org/about/default.aspx, November 2012.

294. Emily Gersema, 'PETA Denies Accusation of Supporting Violence,' *Miami Herald,* February 16, 2003, p. 26A.

295. Saulo Petean, 'Broken Promises,' December, 1996, http://www.brazzil.com/p16dec96.htm

296. 'Animal Protection Principles,' *2011 Values Report*, http://www.thebodyshop-usa.com/values-campaigns/assets/aatprinciples.pdf

297. Aisha Ikramuddin, 'The Cosmetic Mask: Decoding Cruelty-Free,' June 30, 2007, http://healthychild.org/blog/comments/the_cosmetic_mask_decoding_cruelty_free

298. 'What's Wrong With The Body Shop?–A Criticism of "Green Consumerism,"' London Greenpeace, March, 1998, http://www.mcspotlight.org/beyond/companies/bodyshop.html

299. Charles Wallace, 'Can the Body Shop Shape Up?,' *Fortune,* April 1996, http://money.cnn.com/magazines/fortune/fortune_archive/1996/04/15/211474/index.htm

300. Jon Entine, 'Queen of Green Roddick's 'unfair trade' started when she copied Body Shop's formula,' *The Mail on Sunday*, September 15, 2007, http://www.mailonsunday.co.uk/pages/live/femail/article.html?in_article_id=482012&in_page_id=1879

301. David Teather, 'Roddick nets £130m from Body Shop sale,' *The Guardian*, March 17, 2006, http://www.guardian.co.uk/business/2006/mar/18/highstreetretailers.retail

302. For example, see: Rajeev Syal, 'Body Shop ethics under fire after Colombian peasant evictions,' *The Guardian*, September 12, 2009, http://www.guardian.co.uk/world/2009/sep/13/body-shop-colombia-evictions

303. David Teather, 'Roddick nets £130m from Body Shop sale,' *The Guardian*, March 17, 2006, http://www.guardian.co.uk/business/2006/mar/18/highstreet retailers.retail

304. Jon Entine, 'Queen of Green Roddick's 'unfair trade' started when she copied Body Shop's formula,' *The Mail on Sunday*, September 15, 2007, http://www.mailonsunday.co.uk/pages/live/femail/article.html?in_article_id=482012&in_page_id=1879

305. Interview of Jeremy Rifkin by David Batstone, 'The Future of Work,' first published in *Business 2.0 Magazine,* reprinted by Right Reality Inc., February 10, 2004, http://www.business2.com/b2/

306. 'Short-Circuited: Cutting Jobs as Corporate Strategy,' *Knowledge@Wharton*, April 4, 2007, http://knowledge.wharton.upenn.edu/article.cfm?articleid=1703

307. Leslie Kwoh, "Rank and Yank' Retains Vocal Fans,' *The Wall Street Journal*, January 31, 2012, p. B6.

308. Interview of Jeremy Rifkin by David Batstone, 'The Future of Work,' first published in *Business 2.0 Magazine,* reprinted by Right Reality Inc., February 10, 2004, http://www.jobpostings.net/articleDetail.cfm?id=286

309. Hedrick Smith, 'When Capitalists Cared,' *The New York Times*, September 2, 2012, http://www.nytimes.com/2012/09/03/opinion/henry-ford-when-capitalists-cared.html

310. Quoted from David Batstone & David Chandler, 'Ford's Success Formula Not Followed to a T,' *Atlanta Journal-Constitution,* December 17, 2004, http://www.sojo.net/index.cfm?action=sojomail.display&issue=041216. See also: Lee Iacocca, 'Henry Ford,' *Time 100,* http://www.time.com/time/time100/builder/profile/ford.html and 'In 1913, One Ad Changed the Face of America's Middle Class,' Ford ad in *Fortune,* February 9, 2004.

311. 'Short-Circuited: Cutting Jobs as Corporate Strategy,' *Knowledge@Wharton*, April 4, 2007, http://knowledge.wharton.upenn.edu/article.cfm?articleid=1703

312. 'Short-Circuited: Cutting Jobs as Corporate Strategy,' *Knowledge@Wharton*, April 4, 2007, http://knowledge.wharton.upenn.edu/article.cfm?articleid=1703

313. Parija B. Kavilanz, 'Circuit City to shut down,' *CNNMoney.com*, January 16, 2009, http://money.cnn.com/2009/01/16/news/companies/circuit_city/

314. Lauri Bassi & Daniel McMurrer, 'Are Employee Skills a Cost or an Asset,' *Business Ethics Magazine*, Fall 2004, p. 20.

315. Ann Zimmerman, 'Costco's Dilemma: Be Kind to Its Workers, or Wall Street?' *Wall Street Journal,* March 26, 2004, p. B1.

316. 'What's Online: Shoe Seller's Secret of Success,' *New York Times*, May 24, 2008, p. B5.

317. *Fortune Magazine*, http://money.cnn.com/magazines/fortune/bestcompanies/

318. Stefan Stern, 'Authoritarian boss belongs in the past,' *Financial Times*, September 13, 2007, p. 12.

319. Andrew Hill, 'A rather civil partnership,' *Financial Times*, January 20, 2012, http://www.ft.com/intl/cms/s/0/30ca497e-438a-11e1-9f28-00144feab49a.html

320. See also: Steven Greenhouse, 'Low-Wage Workers Are Often Cheated, Study Says,' *New York Times*, September 2, 2009, p. A11.

321. For more information about a "living wage," see: Rajesh Chhabara, 'Wages—Working for a living,' *Ethical Corporation*, June 30, 2009, http://www.ethicalcorp.com/content.asp?ContentID=6519

322. U.S. Department of Labor, September, 2009, http://www.dol.gov/dol/topic/wages/minimumwage.htm

323. U.S. Department of Health & Human Services, November, 2012, http://aspe.hhs.gov/poverty/12poverty.shtml

324. Mary Kay Henry & Christine L. Owens, 'Hardworking Americans should not be living in poverty,' *CNN*, July 25, 2012, http://www.cnn.com/2012/07/25/opinion/henry-owens-minimum-wage/index.html

325. 'What's a Living Wage?' *Living Wage Action Coalition*, November 2012, http://www.livingwageaction.org/resources_lw.htm

326. 'Minimum Wage Laws in the States,' *U.S. Department of Labor*, January 1, 2013, http://www.dol.gov/whd/minwage/america.htm. A table showing how states' minimum wages have evolved over time is at: http://www.dol.gov/whd/state/stateMinWageHis.htm

327. For this legislation's history, see: Jonathan Grossman, 'Fair Labor Standards Act of 1938: Maximum Struggle for a Minimum Wage,' *U.S. Department of Labor*, http://www.dol.gov/oasam/programs/history/flsa1938.htm

328. For additional data, see: Tara Kalwarski & David Foster, 'The Minimum Wage Rises—And is Outpacing Inflation,' *BusinessWeek*, August 3, 2009, p. 15.

329. November 2012, http://www.lowpay.gov.uk/

330. 'Trickle-up economics,' *The Economist*, February 16, 2013, p. 30.

331. Source: Gus Lubin & Mamta Badkar, '15 Facts About McDonald's That Will Blow Your Mind,' *BusinessInsider.com*, January 24, 2011, http://www.businessinsider.com/15-facts-about-mcdonalds-that-will-blow-your-mind-2011-1

332. Heidi Schuessler, 'McDonald's Around the World,' *msn.com*, http://local.msn.com/travel/slideshow.aspx?cp-documentid=252049980

333. Annie Gasparro & Julie Jargon, 'In India, McDonald's Plans Vegetarian Outlets,' *The Wall Street Journal*, September 5, 2012, p. B7.

334. Heidi Schuessler, 'McDonald's Around the World,' *msn.com*, http://local.msn.com/travel/slideshow.aspx?cp-documentid=252049980

335. This definition is from the Oxford English Dictionary. "[The] new entry for 'McJob' in the 11th edition of [Merriam-Webster's] collegiate dictionary, which . . . defines the term as a dead-end occupation." Quoted in, 'Review & Outlook: Thinking Outside the Bun,' *Wall Street Journal,* November 14, 2003, p. W15.

336. Stefan Stern & Jenny Wiggins, 'New definition would be just the job for McDonald's,' *Financial Times*, March 20, 2007, p. 1.

337. Stefan Stern, 'McJob: a fulfilling role with great prospects,' *Financial Times*, March 20, 2007, p. 10.

338. For a detailed discussion of the "McLibel case," which commentators have called "The most expensive and disastrous public relations exercise ever mounted by a multinational company," see: Judy Kuszewski, 'Reputation damage writ large,' *Ethical Corporation Magazine*, July 6, 2010, http://www.ethicalcorp.com/communications-reporting/mclibel-reputation-damage-writ-large

339. See: United States Patent and Trademark Office, http://tsdr.uspto.gov/#case Number=73480984

340. Full-page ad by McDonald's in *The New York Times*, September 18, 2012, p. A7.

341. John W. Schoen, 'McDonald's wants to redefine the McJob,' *msnbc.com*, August 4, 2011, http://www.msnbc.msn.com/id/42420858/

342. John W. Schoen, 'McDonald's wants to redefine the McJob,' *msnbc.com*, August 4, 2011, http://www.msnbc.msn.com/id/42420858/

343. John W. Schoen, 'McDonald's wants to redefine the McJob,' *msnbc.com*, August 4, 2011, http://www.msnbc.msn.com/id/42420858/

344. Quoted in: John W. Schoen, 'McDonald's wants to redefine the McJob,' *msnbc.com*, August 4, 2011, http://www.msnbc.msn.com/id/42420858/

345. 'How long McDonald's cleaners must work to buy a Big Mac,' *Asian Labour Update,* Issue No. 42, January–March, 2002, http://www.amrc.org.hk/alu_article/wages/how_long_mcdonalds_cleaners_must_work_to_buy_a_bigmac

346. Specifically, cleaners, or the nearest equivalent worker for which the necessary data was available.

347. *Asian Labour Update,* January–March, 2002, op. cit.

348. 'Fast food for thought,' *The Economist,* July 30, 2011, p. 12.

349. 'Burgernomics to go,' *The Economist,* June 9, 2012, p. 83.

350. 'Burgernomics to go,' *The Economist,* June 9, 2012, p. 83.

351. Steve Johnson, 'Big Mac index gives more than a taste of true worth,' *Financial Times: FTfm – Investing in forex,* October 4, 2010, p. 16.

352. 'Doing Well by Doing Good,' *The Economist,* April 22, 2000, http://www.economist.com/node/304119

353. 'Are Franchises Bad Employers? A Closer Look at Burger Flippers and Other Low-paid Jobs,' *Knowledge@Wharton*, September 5, 2007, http://knowledge.wharton.upenn.edu/article.cfm?articleid=1801

354. 'Should Manufacturing Jobs Be 'Re-shored' to the U.S.?' *Knowledge@Wharton*, September 26, 2012, http://knowledge.wharton.upenn.edu/article.cfm?articleid=3082

355. Steve Lohr, 'More Jobs Predicted for Machines, Not People,' *The New York Times*, October 24, 2011, p. B3.

356. 'The Obsolete Jobs Club,' *Bloomberg Businessweek*, February 6-12, 2012, pp. 22–23.

357. Joseph E. Stiglitz, 'Of the 1%, by the 1%, for the 1%,' *Vanity Fair*, May 2011, http://www.vanityfair.com/society/features/2011/05/top-one-percent-201105

358. Andrew Tobias, 'How Much Is Fair?' *Miami Herald,* Parade Magazine, March 2, 2003, p. 10.

359. Kathy Kristof, 'Study ties biggest CEO raises to largest layoffs,' *Miami Herald,* August 30, 2003, p. 1C.

360. Peter Drucker, 'An American Sage,' *Wall Street Journal*, November 14, 2005, p. A22.

361. Steven Kent, 'Happy Workers Are the Best Workers,' *Wall Street Journal*, September 6, 2005, p. A20.

362. 'Business Ethics: Doing Well by Doing Good,' *The Economist,* April 22, 2000, pp. 65–68.

Chapter 7

ECONOMIC ISSUES AND CASE-STUDIES

CORRUPTION

CSR Connection:	This issue, on both an individual and an organizational level, presents a significant challenge for multinational corporations.
Stakeholders:	Suppliers, Customers, Governments, Employees, Company.

Issue

The World Bank Institute estimates that bribes alone drain the equivalent of more than $1 trillion annually from the legitimate global economy of $30 trillion. That estimate does not include the embezzlement of public funds or the diversion of assets, which might double the total cost of corruption:[1]

> Corruption is a fact of life; [Transparency International] reports that, in their world poll, eight out of 10 people say political parties are corrupt, one out of four people report paying bribes in the past year to the police, and 50% of the people say their government's anticorruption measures are ineffective. Additionally, six out of 10 people say corruption has increased in the last three years. . . . Political parties, legislatures, and the police are seen as being corrupt or extremely corrupt, and now religious institutions have joined this unethical group.[2]

Both research and anecdotal evidence demonstrate that bribery is worldwide, with "no region or country . . . immune to the damages of corruption."[3] Reports also show that corruption is endemic at both the individual and organizational level.

Individual Corruption

Although corruption is endemic, degrees of corruption vary from region-to-region and from country-to-country. As such, individual expectations and attitudes towards corruption are also relative, with many citizens resigned to the levels of corruption they experience on a daily basis. A 2013 study into corruption throughout Latin America, for example, found that:

> . . . an average of about 20 percent of the region's people say they have been asked to pay a bribe by a policeman or another public official in the past year, compared with 5 percent in the United States and 3 percent in Canada. . . . in some Latin American countries like Haiti, Bolivia and Ecuador, the number of people who say they were asked to pay bribes [in 2012] surpasses 40 percent . . . according to the poll of 40,000 people in 26 countries.[4]

The extent to which corruption permeates a society constitutes a real economic burden for the members of that society, as well as for the companies that operate there. And, if anything, studies show that the problem is worsening in many countries, in spite of anticorruption campaigns by governments designed to change norms and perceptions. Prior studies in Mexico, for example, indicate that "the average Mexican household pays 7% of its annual income on bribes to get public services":[5]

> [In Mexico] corruption exists at all levels, from magnates to street vendors. It seems easier to get something done with a bribe than to fill out myriad forms and wait in lines to confront evasive civil servants. According to a recent study, companies shell out approximately 10 percent of their earnings to corrupt officials. In the last 30 years, the Mexican economy has lost more than $870 billion to corruption, crime and tax evasion.[6]

In India, where micro-level corruption is a particular problem,[7] a poll designed to identify Indians' experiences with bribery reported that "88% said it was impossible to register a property in India without paying bribes; 76% reported having to bribe an official to procure or renew a factory license; 52% paid a bribe to clear a customs check at an airport."[8]

To what extent do these local cultural and societal practices cause conflict when judged by the values of a different society? As globalization spreads and international business becomes more common, businesspeople travel more and come into contact with others from different countries and societies. In the process, they discover that what may be acceptable at home, may or may not be acceptable overseas (and vice-versa). These issues become important for large corporations that operate overseas subsidiaries whose employees can face the prospect of conforming to local expectations regarding *facilitation payments* in order to complete everyday tasks. In such circumstances, their ability and/or willingness to pay bribes will largely be determined by their company's internal compliance controls—to what extent bribes are expressly forbidden and effective controls and incentives are in place to discourage payments:

> Bribery involves two parties, not one. Lambasting officials in poor countries for their sticky fingers is usually easier (and less open to legal challenge) than investigating those who suborn them. . . . Based on questions to 3,000 businessmen, [Transparency International's Bribe Payers Index] ranks 28 countries (accounting for 80% of global trade and investment) by the perceived likelihood of their companies paying bribes. Russia and China scored worst by a hefty margin. Dutch and Swiss companies were seen as the cleanest, with Belgium, Germany and Japan close behind. Construction and industries involving government contracts, unsurprisingly, were the dirtiest.[9]

Ultimately, although bribery is an individual act, it is encouraged (or discouraged) based on a corporation's culture. Nevertheless, because an organization cannot go to jail, courts are increasingly holding individuals accountable for illegal actions taken on behalf of the firm.

Corporate Corruption

Historically, the United States has taken the lead in attempting to curtail the bribery of foreign government officials. This often left U.S. companies operating on an uneven playing field, too often forced to choose between bribing an official in contravention of U.S. law, or refusing to bribe and losing an overseas government contract. Simply put, until recently, it was illegal for U.S. corporations to bribe foreign officials, but companies from other countries were not held to the same legal standard. Some countries, "including France and Germany, even allowed companies to take tax deductions for bribes they paid."[10]

This is changing now as other governments and multinational organizations have begun acting to curb corruption through a number of international treaties and conventions. In 2002, the UK took up the issue of payments by major oil companies to foreign governments in conjunction with the rights to extract oil in those countries, partly in response to growing evidence of systemic corruption. The International Monetary Fund (IMF), for example, estimates that, "in Angola alone, \$1bn of oil revenue goes missing every year while three-quarters of the country's population lives in absolute poverty."[11] In addition in 2010, the UK passed the UK Bribery Act, which is widely recognized as an important step forward in the fight against corruption:

> Even countries best known as sources and recipients of corrupt payments are trying to meet international standards, at least on paper. Saudi Arabia has set up an anti-corruption agency. China, India and Indonesia have passed anti-bribery laws. So too has Russia.[12]

In spite of all this activity, however, meaningful progress (in terms of reduced incidences of bribery) is less easy to secure. For example, the UK initiative on transparency regarding payments within the oil industry (which is known as the Extractive Industries Transparency Initiative) was, on the surface, a success— "As many as three dozen countries, in Africa and elsewhere, agreed to publish details of payments from oil and mining companies. But the scheme was voluntary; the worst offenders either refused to join or dragged their feet."[13] And, in 2012, the OECD publicly rebuked countries such as France[14] and Australia[15] for not doing more to enforce those regulations that do exist. They are not alone:

> Transparency International complains that Germany, Japan and Saudi Arabia have not yet ratified a UN convention on bribery. 21 of the 38 states that signed the OECD anti-bribery convention, including Australia, Brazil, Canada, Mexico, South Africa and Turkey, show "little or no enforcement" of it. Attempts to get the G20 . . . to tighten rules on transparency and bribery have also bogged down.[16]

A failure by governments to act, while highlighting the difficulty in making real progress, also steers attention away from many of the smaller, private facilitators of corruption, such as the "banks that handle corrupt payments and lawyers who advise clients how to get around anti-bribery laws,"[17] who are equally instrumental in moving illegal payments around the globe.[18] Overall, this frustration with progress is best highlighted by Transparency International, whose Corruption Perceptions Index (first published in 1995) is credited with raising the profile of this issue as an international policy concern, and which continues to identify bribery and corruption as integral components of business around the world:

> Did you know that a global poll of business executives found two in five have been asked to pay a bribe when dealing with business institutions? Half of these

estimated that corruption raised project costs by at least 10 per cent. One in five of the executives claimed to have lost business because of bribes by a competitor. More than a third felt that corruption was getting worse. Moreover, politicians and officials in emerging economies are estimated to receive bribes of between $20bn and $40bn annually—equivalent to some 20-40 per cent of official aid.[19]

This is no less true than in the United States. While the Foreign Corrupt Practices Act (1977) has for many years been the gold standard for anticorruption legislation, the U.S. continues to score poorly on Transparency International's list of least corrupt nations, ranking only 19th out of 176 countries and territories in 2012.

Case Study: FCPA

To what extent are global corporations being held accountable in domestic courts for actions committed overseas?

Who a company chooses to do business with is not an ethical issue, right? Wrong.[20]

Over the past two decades more than 150 lawsuits have been brought against American and foreign corporations accused of violating international law . . . in more than 60 foreign countries.[21]

One of the key issues involved in this argument centers on "the extent to which the United States should compel the application of U.S. laws and regulatory standards to activities in other countries."[22] This issue is a growing phenomenon that is causing headaches for many corporations that are being accused of having applied different standards to their operations overseas, either directly or in conjunction with disreputable companies or governing regimes.

Prosecuting corruption committed by U.S. firms overseas based on domestic U.S. law represents an extension of this idea that U.S. firms should be held to the same expectations and legal standards wherever in the world they are operating. The Foreign Corrupt Practices Act (FCPA), passed in the U.S. in 1977, seeks to do this in relation to corruption. The legislation is designed to prevent bribes being paid by U.S. firms (including foreign firms registered in the U.S.) to foreign government officials in order to obtain or keep business. The FCPA emerged as part of the fallout from the Watergate scandal and Congressional investigations into the fall of the Nixon Presidency that uncovered slush funds that were being used by multinationals to secure overseas contracts:

Investigations by the Senate and the Watergate Special Prosecutor forced companies such as 3M, American Airlines and Goodyear Tire & Rubber to admit that they or their executives had made illegal contributions to the infamous Committee to Re-Elect the President. Subsequent inquiries into illegal payments of all kinds led to revelations that companies such as Lockheed, Northrop and Gulf Oil had engaged in widespread foreign bribery. Under pressure from the SEC, more than 150 publicly traded companies admitted that they had been involved in questionable overseas payments or outright bribes to obtain contracts from foreign governments. . . . Congress responded to the revelations by enacting the FCPA in late 1977. For the first time, bribery of foreign government officials was a criminal offense under U.S. law, with fines up to $1 million and prison sentences of up to five years.[23]

Initially, however, rather than act as a deterrent, the legislation merely pushed bribery underground, a move that was aided by the unwillingness of successive U.S. Administrations to ensure its adequate enforcement. This changed in 2005:

> . . . when former Federal Reserve Chairman Paul Volcker released the final results of the investigation he had been asked to conduct of the Oil-for-Food Program. Volcker's group found that more than half of the 4,500 companies participating in the program . . . had paid illegal surcharges and kickbacks to the government of Saddam Hussein. Among those companies were Siemens, DaimlerChrysler and the French bank BNP Paribas.[24]

Part of the confusion regarding the legislation in past years has related to what is and is not acceptable behavior. Firms complain that the wording of the legislation is so broad (Is paying for a client's dinner prohibited?) and insensitive to cultural differences (In many countries, token gift-giving is an essential part of the culture.) that it leaves the best-intentioned firms unable to know when they are breaking the law. As the SEC has stated:

> . . . bribing a government official to secure a huge government contract that would have otherwise gone elsewhere is one thing. Another is bribing a government official to make him do what he is supposed to do without a bribe. Another is bribing a chief of state to change the tax laws with regular political contributions entirely legal in that country.[25]

While so-called *facilitation payments*, have long been considered permissible under the FCPA,[26] more substantial bribes to win contracts have been considered clear transgressions. Where the line is drawn between facilitation payment and outright bribe, however, is not clear. In the past, there has also been less social stigma associated with bribe payments and, as a result, corporate bribery has continued unabated:

Whereas the bribery revelations of the 1970s elicited a public outcry, [more] recent cases have generated little comment. . . . Companies like Chevron pay their fine and go right on using their ad campaigns to present themselves as paragons of virtue.[27]

With the rise of international terrorism since the start of this century and a greater understanding of how global money flows finance such operations, however, today there is a much greater sensitivity to corruption by large corporations.

CSR Newsletters: Chiquita

Two articles from *CorpWatch* and *The Economist* about Chiquita Brands, the multi-national banana producer, provide pause for thought. The first article[28] reports that Chiquita will face charges in Federal Court in the U.S. regarding its role in making payments (opponents say "bribes," defenders say "payments to protect employees") to "right wing death squads" in Colombia:

> Cincinnati-based Chiquita has been growing bananas in Colombia since 1899. For over four decades these operations have been under attack . . . Court documents show that Chiquita executives paid off [two terrorist] groups. FARC was paid between $20,000 and $100,000 a month. Chiquita has also admitted to making over 100 payments totaling $1.7 million to the AUC . . . over seven years.

In contrast, the second article[29] bemoans the fact that, although Chiquita has recently made "huge efforts to promote social responsibility and sustainability" (e.g., partnering with the Rainforest Alliance), it has not received sufficient recognition for its efforts:

> Chiquita has signed and largely upheld a global agreement with local and international food unions. It has embraced sustainable farming techniques and allows products to be certified for environmental and other standards. Last year it promised to promote more women and to ensure there is no sexual harassment on the plantations it owns and buys from.

Chiquita's progress is particularly notable in contrast to the absence of similar efforts by its main competitors, Dole and Del Monte, neither of which have "been interested in following Chiquita in signing a global union agreement."

(Continued)

(Continued)

So, what are we to make of this? It is true, for example, that Chiquita volunteered the information about its activities in Colombia that were subsequently used against it in court (information the firm's prosecutors would not otherwise have been able to obtain). Chiquita's actions appear genuine, along with the claim that HQ was taken by surprise at what was going on in Colombia. It is also true that rumors suggest it was not the only firm engaging in bribery in the region, but it is the only firm that has voluntarily come forward. Should we punish firms for revealing flaws as part of their effort to become more socially responsible (thus, discouraging other firms from making similar commitments)? Or, should we be lenient on past corporate actions that flouted laws, regulations, and social norms?

Hmmmm.........., not easy. The conundrum is reminiscent of the challenge faced by the Truth and Reconciliation Commission that was set up in the aftermath of Apartheid in South Africa to encourage a full accounting of the crimes and atrocities that occurred during that period (http://www.justice.gov.za/trc/). While at times being very hard to swallow, such institutions can allow for the sort of progress and change that is essential for firms today. That does not make the process any easier to swallow, however.

Nevertheless, if we believe that social responsibility will be more effective when it is perceived by firms to be in their best interests, rather than bluntly mandated by government regulators, we will need to start swallowing and reward those firms that are willing to stick their necks out with our encouragement.

In recent years, the U.S. Justice Department has increased its efforts to prevent and punish corporate bribery by pursuing investigations against U.S. firms, as well as against foreign-based firms with a significant U.S. presence:

The crackdown under the Foreign Corrupt Practices Act . . . now extends across five continents and penetrates entire industries, including energy and medical devices.[30]

Similar to the political environment that gave rise to the FCPA in 1977, it is the increase in corporate scandals, starting with the Enron scandal around the turn of the century, that is prompting the government to act:

[The Enron scandal] led to tougher financial laws, like requiring top executives at publicly traded companies to certify that their firms' books were accurate, which in turn forced them to pay closer attention to payments made overseas. The 2010 Dodd-Frank law further heightened pressure by giving corporate whistle-blowers a financial incentive to report violations. . . . The department and the S.E.C. also began increasing fines by requiring companies to disgorge profits as a condition of settling cases without an indictment. That drove up fines to record levels, including $800 million paid by Siemens in 2008.[31]

While, from its passage in 1977 until around the turn of the century, there were only a few prosecutions under the FCPA every year ("The Department of Justice and the Securities & Exchange Commission together initiated, on average, three prosecutions per year"),[32] in contrast, "in recent years, [FCPA] enforcement has soared to 48 actions in 2010, from just two in 2004."[33] This dramatic shift is reinforced in Figure 7.1, which shows the companies involved in the top 10 largest settlements secured under the FCPA, all of which have occurred since 2008.

| Figure 7.1 | 10 Largest FCPA Settlements |

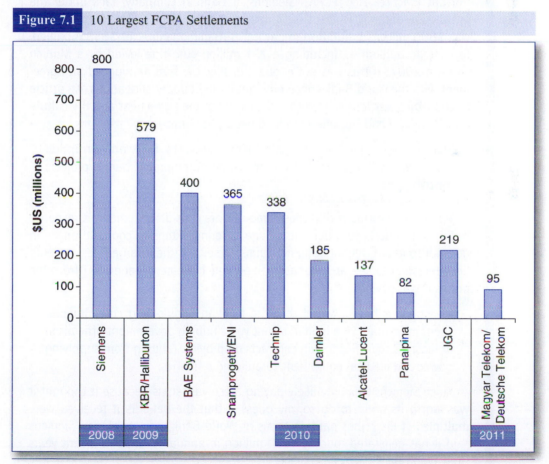

Source: Leslie Wayne, 'Foreign Firms Most Affected By a U.S. Law Barring Bribes,' *The New York Times*, September 4, 2012, p. B1 & B5.

As indicated by Figure 7.1, the financial and reputation costs of a serious transgression are significant, but they extend beyond the fine itself:

A spokesman at Siemens, which paid the largest foreign-bribery fine to date, said the cost of addressing its own corruption allegations was nearly as much as its total fine of 1.22 billion euros ($1.7 billion), including fines to the German government. . . . A Siemens spokesman said in an email that it's wise for a company "to have an adequate compliance system in place and a corporate culture that stands for clean business."[34]

CSR Newsletters: Siemens

In 2008, Siemens paid the largest penalty ever imposed under the Foreign Corrupt Practices Act (FCPA). Siemens, a German company, falls under the jurisdiction of the FCPA because it operates in the U.S. The fine Siemens paid was $800 million, in addition to paying "596 million euros, or $839.4 million, to German authorities, including a 201 million euro fine levied by a Munich court in 2007." If this was not enough, in July, the firm announced an agreement with the World Bank concerning additional bribery allegations. An article in *The Wall Street Journal*[35] details the extent of the agreement and the culture of bribery that had become ingrained within the firm:

Siemens AG . . . [agreed] to pay $100 million to help anticorruption efforts and to forgo bidding on any of the development bank's projects for two years.

What is interesting is that these amounts are considered lenient—a response to Siemen's efforts to rebuild its image, offering extensive cooperation in an attempt to resolve all outstanding claims. In spite of these large fines, it would be interesting to see an estimate of how much Siemens benefitted from the bribes it was paying:

Investigators have alleged that the German engineering conglomerate spent more than $1 billion in recent years bribing government officials in at least 10 countries to win contracts on projects ranging from supplying power and medical equipment to building refineries.

Since Siemens was only likely paying these vast sums because it thought it was worth its while to do so, my guess is that the benefits it received were multiples of the bribes paid. In terms of World Bank projects alone, "Siemens said it has generated roughly $160 million in annual revenue in recent years from World Bank-financed projects."

Perhaps crime does pay!?

In most cases, FCPA investigations result in a fine and a private settlement with the Department of Justice because it is deemed to be potentially ruinous for a firm to be indicted by the federal government.[36] In 2011, however, three employees from Lindsey Manufacturing Co. were convicted under the FCPA for paying bribes in Mexico. The surprising thing is that this is "the first time a company has been convicted at a U.S. trial in a foreign bribery case."[37]

As noted earlier, this increase in FCPA enforcement is in line with increased attempts by other countries and global institutions to institute anti-corruption measures. Among these efforts, the UK Bribery Act (enacted in 2010 and implemented in 2011) is the best example of a national government taking this issue seriously and attempting to go beyond the FCPA. As such, while the legislation is similar to the FCPA in some respects, in key areas, it goes further:

> The Bribery Act covers any company that conducts business in Britain, regardless of where the company is based. It goes beyond the FCPA by not just prohibiting illicit payments to foreign officials, but also bribes between private businessmen. It applies even if the individual who makes the payment doesn't realize the transaction was a bribe, legal experts say.[38]

The Bribery Act, which is described as "the FCPA on steroids," consolidates various UK rules and policies concerning bribery. It also extends the reach of government oversight and the possible punishments for transgressions by raising "the maximum penalty for bribery to 10 years in prison from seven, and sets no limits on fines."[39] The Act also bans "grease payments" ("small bribes common in some countries to get mail service, phone hook-ups or other services that otherwise would be delayed") that are permitted under the FCPA, as long as they are declared. Also different from the FCPA, the Act covers bribery both at home and abroad, and contains a "'compliance defence' that allows a company to avoid the harshest penalties if the wrongdoer is a junior employee and the firm otherwise has a strict anti-bribery policy" in place.[40]

In the U.S., in addition to the FCPA, the Dodd-Frank Act (2010) increases the pressure on firms by providing financial incentives for whistleblowers to report bribery,[41] collecting "334 reports in its first seven weeks."[42] Increasingly, it is essential that companies ensure they have effective compliance programs to ensure they are protected. Also, in the oil industry in particular, the SEC is improving the process started by the UK's Extractive Industries Transparency Initiative, requiring "The 1,100 resource companies listed on American stock exchanges, which make up half the global industry by value, . . . to publish all payments to foreign governments above $100,000."[43]

Most importantly, however, in 2012, the Department of Justice finally released detailed guidance on the FCPA, providing illustrations and much greater explanation in terms of defining what is legal and illegal under the law.[44] Although not providing "the firm policy pronouncements sought by the U.S. Chamber of Commerce and other critics of the law," the guidance represents "the most comprehensive effort to date by the [U.S. government] to dispel confusion surrounding their enforcement of the 1977 antibribery law."[45]

All the legislative activity and increased enforcement, in the U.S. and UK in particular, provides reason for hope.[46] As firms improve their compliance programs to avoid being caught by stricter government enforcement, so their exposure to corruption and bribery diminishes:

> [In 2012] companies reported they were affected by bribery and corruption over the last year, down from 19% in 2011. The decrease comported with the study's overall finding: A drop to 63% from 80% in the proportion of companies saying their exposure to fraud, in general, had increased in the last year.[47]

Nevertheless, it is still true that enforcement is inconsistent from year-to-year and also concentrated in only a few regions of the world. According to Transparency International:

> Of the top seven countries that actively enforce foreign bribery laws, all are located in the West. . . . The U.S. was by far the most active enforcer with 275 cases completed as of 2011, and 113 investigations underway. The rest of the top seven was rounded out (not in order) by: Germany, U.K., Italy, Switzerland, Norway and Denmark.[48]

Unfortunately, bribery remains a good investment for a company, generating "an average return of 10-11 times the value of the bung paid out to win a contract," which is why effective legislation and improved enforcement are crucial.[49] Bribery is not quite the oldest profession, but it appears to be just as persistent.

Transparency International

Looking at the Corruption Perceptions Index 2012, it's clear that corruption is a major threat facing humanity. Corruption destroys lives and communities, and undermines countries and institutions. It generates popular anger that threatens to further destabilise societies and exacerbate violent conflicts. The Corruption Perceptions Index scores countries on a scale from 0 (highly corrupt) to 100 (very clean). While no country has a perfect score, two-thirds of countries score below 50, indicating a serious corruption problem. Corruption translates into human suffering, with poor families being extorted for bribes to see doctors or to get access to clean drinking water. It leads to failure in the delivery of basic services like education or healthcare. It derails the building of essential infrastructure, as corrupt leaders skim funds. Corruption amounts to a dirty tax, and the poor and most vulnerable are its primary victims.[50]

Online Resources

- Business Anti-Corruption Portal, http://www.business-anti-corruption.com/
- Caux Round Table Anti-Corruption Measures, http://www.cauxroundtable .org/index.cfm?&menuid=92
- Combatting Corruption in the Private Sector (EU, 2003), http://eur-lex. europa.eu/LexUriServ/LexUriServ.do?uri=CELEX:32003F0568:EN:HTML
- Criminal Law Convention on Corruption (Council of Europe, 1999), http:// conventions.coe.int/Treaty/en/Treaties/Html/173.htm
- Dow Jones State of Anti-Corruption Compliance Survey, http://www.dow-jones.com/pressroom/smprs/djrcsurvey2012.html
- Extractive Industries Transparency Initiative, http://eiti.org/
- Foreign Corrupt Practices Act, 1977, http://www.justice.gov/criminal/fraud/fcpa/
- Inter-American Convention Against Corruption (Organization of American States, 1996), http://www.oas.org/juridico/english/treaties/b-58.html
- I Paid a Bribe, http://www.ipaidabribe.com/
- Organization for Economic Co-operation and Development (OECD), http:// www.oecd.org/corruption/
- The UK Bribery Act Guidance, http://www.justice.gov.uk/downloads/ legislation/bribery-act-2010-guidance.pdf
- The World Bank, http://www1.worldbank.org/publicsector/anticorrupt/
- Trace International, http://www.traceinternational.org/
- Transparency International, http://www.transparency.org/
- United Nations Convention Against Corruption (2004), http://www.unodc .org/documents/treaties/UNCAC/Publications/Convention/08-50026_E.pdf
- United Nations, Declaration against Corruption and Bribery in International Commercial Transactions (1996), http://www.un.org/documents/ga/res/51/ a51r191.htm

Pro/Con Debate

> **Pro/Con Debate:** Penalizing corruption places firms at a competitive disadvantage because firms from different countries are held to different standards.

Questions for Discussion and Review

1. How legitimate is it for companies to operate with different standards in different countries and cultures? Was it reasonable that, until 1999, German law not only permitted bribery overseas, but even made it a tax-deductible expense for corporations? Do you think the FCPA places an *unfair* burden on U.S. firms or the UK Bribery Act is similarly *unfair* for British firms?

2. *Corruption* means different things to different people. Some people argue that political campaign contributions are just another form of corruption. What is your reaction to this statement?

3. Why do you think corruption is more prevalent in some countries than others? What should a company do when operating in such an environment? Is it better to abide by local custom or try to impose standards and values from home?

4. Before reading this case, were you aware of the FCPA? Were you also aware that you can be held personally liable for illegal actions that you take on behalf of your company, even if you were just following orders? How have your views about bribery changed since reading the case?

5. If you were faced with the choice of paying a bribe to facilitate a routine transaction or missing a performance target at work, which would you choose? Why?

ETHICAL CONSUMPTION

> **CSR Connection:** This issue debates the extent to which customers are willing to base their purchase decisions on values, over the above concerns about price, and hold firms accountable when they transgress those values.
>
> **Stakeholders:** Customers, Suppliers, Company.

Issue

To what extent does a corporation's integration of a CSR perspective generate returns in terms of increased sales and brand loyalty? To a large extent, the value to a firm of ethical or socially responsible behavior depends on two things—first, customer *evaluations* of that behavior and, second, customer *responses* to that behavior, particularly if it causes an increase in the price of a product.

In terms of customer evaluations of firm behavior, a firm's brand has become the primary vehicle to communicate the organization's values, its goals, and how it intends to achieve them. Customers, in particular, draw inferences about firms based on their perceptions of brands—they expect brands to be responsive to their needs as well as reliable indicators of quality:

> Initially, product attributes were the source of reputations. Corporations like Coca-Cola and Gillette had reputations based strictly on what they made. In the mid-1990s, as competition intensified, . . . [brand management] became more customer-focused, and marketers used approaches that appealed to [customers'] emotions. . . . [Today], reputation is based on trust.[51]

Underpinning the brand loyalty that companies try to build, therefore, are stakeholder perceptions of the company and the products it produces. How a company is perceived by the societies within which it is based and operates goes a long way to determining whether that company is welcomed or rejected by that society—the loyalty of local consumers, the company's employees, suppliers, relationships with local interest groups, the relevant regulating authorities, and so on. While a positive evaluation represents a valued asset for the firm, a negative evaluation raises the risk of consumer boycotts, organized by activist NGOs. While customer evaluations play a large role in the success of a company, however, it is not clear to what extent CSR and ethics form a large component of customers' positive perceptions of brands.

Studies suggest that as consumers become more sophisticated, different approaches from companies are needed to maintain brand loyalty. Straightforward marketing and advertising is now no longer enough. As societies develop and become more affluent, CSR advocates believe that customers want to become responsible members of their communities and purchase products from companies that reflect their beliefs and values (what Yvon Chouinard of Patagonia calls "dollar democracy").[52] As such, the goal of an effective CSR policy is to ensure the company is both welcomed and successful. Increasingly, it is becoming impossible to separate the two.

CSR Newsletters: Ethical Brands

What is most interesting about two articles from the *Financial Times*[53] about ethical brands is the different kinds of firms that make up the Top 10 lists in the U.S. and the UK:

U.S.	UK
1. Coca-cola	1. Co-op (including Co-op Bank)
2. Kraft	2. The Body Shop
3. Procter & Gamble	3. Marks & Spencer
4 = Johnson & Johnson	4. Traidcraft
4 = Kellogg's	5 = Cafédirect
4 = Nike	5 = Ecover
4 = Sony	7 = Green & Black
8 = Ford	7 = Tesco
8 = Toyota	9. Oxfam
10 = Levis	10. Sainsbury's
10 = Starbucks	

While the U.S. Top 10 is made up exclusively of large, multi-national firms that have adopted CSR within existing everyday operations, the UK Top 10 includes a number of smaller, social activist organizations that were formed in order to achieve their social responsibility mission statement. Although the survey results in the articles make it clear that "ethical consumption" is on the rise, however, it is less clear on how firms should react:

> . . . . the first problem for businesses in assessing a shift in attitudes towards consumption is that the public is not sure what an ethical brand is. In food, the label can signify organic, locally grown or subject to fair trade agreements. In beauty, it can designate free from animal testing or produced from "natural" ingredients. Products that are fuel-efficient, recycled, produced in unionised conditions or not linked to the tobacco or arms industries are all marketed as ethical.

In addition, while people might say that they prefer "ethical brands," it is by no means clear that they will pay for that privilege because "what people say and what they do can be completely different." What is clear, however, is that inaction by firms is dangerous given the power to mobilize and act that currently lies with stakeholders:

> . . . . after independent consumer watchdogs, consumers were most likely to use the web to assess ethical brand claims. And the rise of internet commentary on brands might accelerate corporate willingness to stake out high profile ethical positions rather than allow bloggers to shape their reputations for them.

In terms of customer responses to firm behavior (a willingness to reward socially responsible behavior by favoring those firms that best meet societal expectations), we are constrained by our desire to consume and our fixation on price. In short, while there are any number of studies that suggest consumers are willing to buy green or CSR products, there are many others that suggest consumers are quite capable of saying one thing, while doing another.[54] Most individuals, when asked, want to think of themselves as ethical and also convince the person asking them that this is the case. When it comes time to purchase, however, we seem either to be unwilling or to lack the appropriate knowledge to put our ethical aspirations into practice. It seems that our best intentions are easily distracted and there is a limit for firms that rely too heavily on the market segment of ethical consumers:

> In the beginning, American Apparel put a "sweatshop free" label on its t-shirts. But sex turned out to be a better sell than good labor practices. Lessons in the limits of altruism.[55]

As such, in spite of the success of brands like Seventh Generation, "Green products of any brand account for less than 2 percent of the overall market."[56] In other words, the evidence suggests that ethical products remain a niche market:

> Everyone wants to buy "green" products, right? After all, we tell ourselves, we care about the environment and the resources left to future generations. However, research shows that while 40 percent of consumers say they are willing to buy 'green products,' only 4 percent actually do so when given the option.[57]

To a large extent, it is true that statistics follow lies and damned lies in degrees of deception. This is mostly because good empirical research is very difficult and time consuming. It is a lot easier to take shortcuts—particularly when the shortcuts generate the results that you were looking for in the first place:

> The Lifestyles of Health and Sustainability annual survey estimates that 13-19% of American adults are dedicated green buyers – a $290bn market. The US-based Cone Communications estimates that 70% of American consumers consider the environmental impact of their purchasing. The UK and Europe show similar numbers. According to marketing experts, however, these figures are wildly overstated, reflecting attitudes, not buying patterns.[58]

A stark indicator of the willingness for firms to engage in *greenwash* (either intentionally or unintentionally), together with the willingness of consumers to be deceived by these actions (either willingly or unwillingly), seems endless:

[In 2008], as green fever was peaking in Hollywood – green was declared the new black – Vanity Fair published its annual "Go Green" issue timed to Earth Day. Muckraked.com estimated that the issue, printed on non-recycled paper, used 2,247 tonnes of trees and produced 4,331,757 pounds of greenhouse gases, 13,413,922 gallons of wastewater and 1,744,060 pounds of solid waste. Vanity Fair scrapped the green theme issue in 2009.[59]

The idea that we can consume ourselves towards a *better* society provides false hope. Even with the best of intentions, the unintended consequences of our actions are either minimized or ignored altogether:

CSR Newsletters: The Jevons Paradox

An article in *The New York Times*[60] makes you want to throw your hands up in resignation. It focuses on the unforeseen consequences of energy efficiency, particularly in consumer products, such as appliances or cars. While the article does not dispute the more efficient use of energy by these products, it makes a compelling argument that the net energy consumption as a result of their use is often zero (i.e., unchanged) or even positive (i.e., an increase in overall energy use):

> The problem is known as the energy rebound effect. While there's no doubt that fuel-efficient cars burn less gasoline per mile, the lower cost at the pump tends to encourage extra driving. There's also an indirect rebound effect as drivers use the money they save on gasoline to buy other things that produce greenhouse emissions, like new electronic gadgets or vacation trips on fuel-burning planes.

There is a term for these unforeseen consequences – the Jevons Paradox. It was "named after a 19th-century British economist who observed that while the steam engine extracted energy more efficiently from coal, it also stimulated so much economic growth that coal consumption increased." A related term for this ability to convince ourselves that the best way to solve our excessive resource depletion of the Earth is to consume more things is 'The Prius Fallacy.'[61] By substituting one (possibly) greener product for another, we kill two birds with one stone—we satisfy both our psychological and material needs. What we fail to realize, however, is that even as we innovate, rather than reducing our environmental impact, the unintended consequence is often the opposite.

While generally dismissed by environmentalists today, there are important policy implications from this work:

> . . . . if your immediate goal is to reduce greenhouse emissions, then it seems risky to count on reaching it by improving energy efficiency. To economists worried about rebound effects, it makes more sense to look for new carbon-free sources of energy, or to impose a direct penalty for emissions, like a tax on energy generated from fossil fuels. Whereas people respond to more fuel-efficient cars by driving more and buying other products, they respond to a gasoline tax simply by driving less.

The issue of unintended consequences is one of the most important for the CSR community to face – particularly in relation to sustainability. It happens again and again; whether it is a government subsidy or tax break for a particular kind of alternative energy, or a new technological innovation that interacts with some other factor (or is applied inappropriately) to generate an unexpected result.

In short, good intentions that seek to subvert market forces and established market practices often result in net neutral or other counterproductive outcomes.

In order to alter this pattern of behavior, it is essential that we draw the connection between the price of a product and the social consequences of cost minimization and externalization by the firm. Then, it is essential that we act:

> Modern technologies allow us to shop in real time, often worldwide, for the lowest prices, highest quality, and best returns. . . . Yet, these great deals come at the expense of our jobs and wages, and widening inequality. . . . Great deals can also have devastating environmental consequences. . . . Other great deals offend common decency. We may get a low price or high return because a producer has cut costs by hiring children in South Asia or Africa who work 12 hours a day, seven days a week, or by subjecting people to death-defying working conditions. As workers or as citizens most of us would not intentionally choose these outcomes but we are responsible for them.[62]

Getting this issue right is huge for CSR, partly because our economic model is built around consumption and growth ("domestically-produced goods and services drives about 40% of economic activity"),[63] and partly because we consume so much. Just in terms of clothes, "Americans buy 20 billion garments a year, an average of 64 garments a person. When the Chinese are consuming at the same rate, that's more than 80 billion garments a year."[64] And, the corollary of buying more is that we also discard more:

> On average, each of us throws 54 pounds of clothes and shoes into the trash each year. That adds up to about 9 million tons of shoes, jackets and other wearables that are sent into the waste stream annually, according to the U.S. Environmental Protection Agency.[65]

As one fashion magazine editor puts it:

> The reality is: a T-shirt is a T-shirt is a T-shirt. . . . It costs the planet the same thing whether you have paid £200 for it or £1 for it. It does the same amount of damage. A T-shirt is equivalent to 700 gallons of water, gallons of chemical waste, so much human labor. But it used to be that we could do with three T-shirts a year. Now we need 30. Sometimes it's actually cheaper to throw away clothes than to wash them. That has got to be wrong.[66]

As a result, it is quantity, not quality or price, that determines the impact our shopping habits have on the planet.

> To eco-cynics green consumerism is the ultimate oxymoron. . . . The genuine solution, of course, is to buy less—by significantly reducing consumption of goods and resources.[67]

Rather than simply imploring consumers to consume less, a more realistic approach is to encourage incremental changes by both firm and customer. Companies should not be expected to move too far ahead of the market (to do so would be commercial suicide). But, enlightened companies should see the commercial value in differentiation that takes advantage of consumer values. After all, research indicates that, in spite of their shopping habits, the majority of consumers feel that companies have a responsibility to "address key social and environmental issues beyond their local communities."[68] This knowledge, however, should be placed in context:

1) Most consumers want to do the right thing. They want clean air and clean water, healthful food to eat, litter-free parks and beaches to play in, and energy to run their lives;

2) Whether it be keeping their bathtub clean, saving for retirement, driving the speed limit or eating healthfully, all consumers tend to overstate virtuous behavior to pollsters. . . . And;

3) just like for *all* products, most consumers will only pay a premium when products demonstrate genuine added value.[69]

Companies have a market incentive to structure operations in ways that take advantage of these tendencies. Customers are more likely to purchase ethically when they receive sufficient information with which to evaluate a firm or its products, when there is a moral alignment between their values and those of the firm or product goals, and when they perceive that they are receiving value that compensates for any price premium associated with the purchase.

CSR Newsletters: Moral Limits

In 2012, Michael Sandel of Harvard University published the book *What Money Can't Buy: The Moral Limits of Markets*. Sandel teaches a hugely popular course at Harvard titled 'Justice,' a semester-long series of classes that are available online (http://www.justiceharvard.org/). Over the summer, Sandel was interviewed on the PBS Newshour by its economics correspondent, Paul Solman.[70] The interview was good, as is the book, but one quote by Sandel stood out:

> Over the last three decades, we've actually drifted, without quite realizing it, from having a market economy to becoming a market society.

Sandel went on to explain what he meant by the distinction between a "market economy" and a "market society":

> A market economy is a tool, a valuable and effective tool, for organizing productive activity. But a market society is a place where almost everything is up for sale. It's a way of life where market values seep into almost every sphere of life, and sometimes crowd out or corrode important values, non-market values.

This insight resonated. Sandel gave multiple interviews to promote his book and, in all of them, he struggled to define the line of what is morally acceptable

(Continued)

(Continued)

and what is unacceptable. The approach of the interviewers always seemed to be: "Is this action OK?" "Well, what about this?" "And, what about this?" etc., etc. To his credit, Sandel stated that he is not trying to define the line of acceptability in determining morally appropriate behavior, but making the broader point that:

> ... the question that worries me is, when almost everything in our public life, not just access to the fast lane, is sold off to the highest bidder, something is lost. Money comes to matter more and more in our society. And against the background of rising inequality, that takes a toll on the commonality of our civic life. ... My concern is with the accumulated effect. Are we cheapening important social goods and civic goods that are worth caring about?

Ultimately, however, a weakness in Sandel's argument is that it is relative rather than absolute. He is not arguing from a point of principle (i.e., an action is absolutely right or wrong), more that too much of an action is harmful, but some of it is OK. Although expedient, this weakens the point he is making. Adopting this approach makes drawing the line between right and wrong, between acceptable and unacceptable behavior, extremely difficult to do (as demonstrated in the interviews he gave). Worse, it becomes a subjective exercise, which allows each of us to rationalize what we deem to be OK. Again, while it is easy to understand why he adopted this less stringent standard, the result is less helpful in the broader sense because behavior becomes determined by the individual, rather than some aggregated sense of what is socially most beneficial.

One other criticism relates directly to the book's title. It is not really the moral limits of *markets* that Sandel is concerned with, but the application of a dollar-value to goods and services that were previously valued in different ways. For example, in Chapter 1, Sandel focuses on how we can now increasingly pay to cut the queue (think paying extra to go through airport security faster, or ticket scalpers that re-sell highly sought after tickets above face value). Sandel critiques economists' justifications for such actions on the basis that it is not only *willingness* to pay that demonstrates demand for a product, but also *ability* to pay (poorer people are less able to do so than richer people). Sandel contests that queues are more democratic and, therefore, more morally justifiable.

What Sandel does not appreciate, however, is that queuing for something is also a market—a market valued in time, rather than money. While the poor student can argue that s/he cannot afford the *money* to buy tickets for a popular concert or sporting event, the wealthy CEO can argue with equal justification that s/he cannot afford the *time* to queue for the same ticket. Queuing or paying both serve the same function—to ration a scarce product using a scarce resource (for the student, money is scarce, but for the CEO, time is scarce). As such, it is not the moral limits of *markets* that Sandel should be targeting, but the moral limits of *money*. While both markets (money and time) have their moral limits, an increasing focus on one type of market over another (i.e., money over time) favors one group of society (the money rich) over another (the money poor), but Sandel's queues similarly favor a different group (the time rich over the time poor). The ultimate effect is demonstrated by Thomas Friedman who added his commentary on Sandel's book:

Throughout our society, we are losing the places and institutions that used to bring people together from different walks of life. Sandel calls this the 'sky-boxification of American life,' and it is troubling. Unless the rich and poor encounter one another in everyday life, it is hard to think of ourselves as engaged in a common project. At a time when to fix our society we need to do big, hard things together, the marketization of public life becomes one more thing pulling us apart.[71]

At present, our perception of the *value* of something in our society is determined largely by the monetary amount that is placed on that thing. Related to this discussion about the level of materialism in our society, therefore, is an appreciation that this was not always the case. Our understanding of the role of money as a valuation tool has shifted over time. Historically:

The notion of price was attached to the notion of value, which was kind of like a moral concept . . . The idea that there had to be some morality to how much things were worth in the marketplace drove the understanding of prices until the 17th century . . . That the price of that thing had to be the value of the labor that had gone into it . . . But [this perspective] totally forgot the idea that actually the price of something in a marketplace is a transaction. There is a buyer who values something and a seller who will be willing to make that transaction at that given price or not.[72]

Over time, our understanding has shifted from the idea of price as an assessment of "effort to produce" to price as an assessment of "willingness to pay." In other words, the focus of value has shifted in favor of the consumer—what the individual is willing to give up (the dollar value of a market transaction), instead of what should be charged for the product or service (some sense of absolute value that is determined by the resources used during the production process). As Sandel's book reminds us, however, the transition is not yet complete. One example is our valuation of things like blood:

> Other experiments show that paying people for doing something actually reduces their other motives for doing it—the most famous example being blood donation, which is often found to decline if payment is involved. It is hard for some economists to understand that human nature is more complex than their models. But most people like to feel they are giving of themselves and giving more than is expected.[73]

Another example is grass roots campaigns that are designed to support local, independent stores instead of nationwide chains. In towns such as Webster, Massachusetts, groups of residents use social media to band together as *cash mobs*—"A group of residents—local business supporters—show up at a predetermined small business at a certain date and time and spend money. How much money? Ten dollars is suggested."[74] The same principle has expanded to include *dish mobs* that target restaurants.[75] Similarly, some firms, such as Marks & Spencer in the UK, see the commercial potential of tapping into this underlying consumer goodwill. As one example of M&S's Plan A,[76] the firm has partnered with Oxfam to encourage UK consumers to recycle their old clothes:

> Anyone who heads down to an Oxfam store with a bag of unwanted clothes gets a £5 shopping voucher. The idea has been a roaring success with us, the consuming public. Oxfam has collected over seven million garments—that's an item from almost one in every eight UK residents.[77]

Ultimately, however, unless consumers are willing to translate opinions and preferences into concrete action in ways similar to the examples above, there is little to suggest the firms will do more than they are currently doing. Customers need to demonstrate to firms that there is market value in producing products that are priced according to their full social and environmental impact. The issues of blood diamonds and conflict minerals present an excellent example of products and raw materials on which customers should be demanding change.

Case Study: Conflict Minerals

"Little is known of Sierra Leone, and how it connects to the diamonds we own."

—Kanye West[78]

To what extent are consumers aware of the origin of the products they buy? To what extent are we aware that our purchase decisions at home have significant consequences for the livelihoods of individuals elsewhere? This is important because there is evidence to suggest that our demand for luxury products in the West (which are discretionary and could be sacrificed without a significant decline in living standards), for example, can result in death and poverty in developing countries:

[A report by Worldwatch Institute] cites diamonds, tropical woods and the mineral coltan, used in cellular phones and other electronic products, as examples. Worldwatch claims that wars fought over these valuable materials "have killed or displaced more than 20 million people and are raising at least $12 billion a year for rebels, warlords, repressive governments, and other predatory groups around the world."[79]

One example highlighted is the international trade in so-called conflict, or *blood*, diamonds, which the United Nations defines as "diamonds that originate from areas controlled by forces or factions opposed to legitimate and internationally recognized governments, and are used to fund military action in opposition to those governments, or in contravention of the decisions of the Security Council."[80] Definitive numbers indicating the extent of this problem throughout the diamond industry are difficult to calculate. While the diamond industry "estimates that conflict diamonds represent 4 per cent of the total trade in rough diamonds. Others put the figure closer to 14 per cent."[81] Where everyone agrees, however, is that this illegal trade in diamonds represents a significant problem both in moral and commercial terms:

Conflict diamonds . . . have funded brutal wars in Liberia, Sierra Leone, Angola, Democratic Republic of Congo and Côte d'Ivoire that have resulted in the death and displacement of millions of people. Diamonds have also been used by terrorist groups such as al-Qaeda to finance their activities and for money-laundering purposes.[82]

As awareness of this issue began to seep into the public consciousness (in particular, following the release of Kanye West's *Diamonds From Sierra Leone* in 2005 and the movie *Blood Diamond*, starring Leonardo DiCaprio, in 2006),[83] the negative publicity began to have an impact on industry-wide sales, which "dropped 15% to 20% in Europe" in a decade.[84] Combined with the threat of increased competition from synthetic diamonds, which have improved to the point where it is impossible for consumers to discern the difference, some companies within the industry decided to take a stand on this issue. The driver behind this was the recognition of the threat to the core business, combined with the belief that differentiation will lead to a sustainable competitive advantage:

> In the mid-1990s, when "conflict diamonds" first became an issue, 'we felt as an industry that we blew it, [Michael J. Kowalski, Chairman and CEO of Tiffany & Co.] said. "We should have seen it coming, we should have acted sooner" . . . [In 1999] Tiffany helped create a "chain of custody" for diamonds as well [as its gold and silver supply chains]. As a founding member of the World Diamond Council . . . Tiffany pledged to try and eliminate the trade of diamonds in underdeveloped countries where it contributes to conflicts and exploitation, particularly of children. . . . It really is about our social license to continue to do business.[85]

As both peer-group and public pressure continued to mount, diamond producing countries also began to see the threat posed by tainted diamonds and launched "an international certification system designed to stop 'blood diamonds' from reaching world markets."[86] This agreement became the Kimberley Process in 2000 and the Kimberley Process Certification Scheme (KPCS) in 2002 with the intention of tracking diamonds as they move along the supply chain, enabling every stone to be identified at any point. Enforcement of the voluntary KPCS began in January 2003, since when all imported diamonds handled by participating countries and companies have been required to be accompanied by "a certificate of origin and countries or traders that fail to comply will be barred from the international diamond trade."[87]

A key component of the momentum driving the establishment of the KPCS was the role of the United Nations General Assembly, which, in December 2000, "adopted, unanimously, a resolution on the role of diamonds in fuelling conflict, breaking the link between the illicit transaction of rough diamonds and armed conflict, as a contribution to prevention and settlement of conflicts (A/RES/55/56)."[88] As the process gathered international support, legislation was introduced in Washington to help prevent U.S. consumers, who "purchase 65 to 70 percent of the world's diamonds,"[89] getting caught up in this trade and also bring U.S. law into alignment with that of other countries that took a stance on this issue. The Clean Diamond Trade Act was signed into law by President George W. Bush on April 25, 2003, and commits U.S. companies to participate in the Kimberley Process:

> The [legislation] is meant to curb the trade in rough diamonds from mines controlled by antigovernment rebel groups in Sierra Leone, Angola and the Democratic Republic of Congo, who traded the stones for arms during civil conflicts that killed 3.7 million people. The smuggling of illegal diamonds also is said to be a source of funding for the al Qaeda terrorist network.[90]

In 2004, a further step was taken in trying to chart more accurately the movement of diamonds through the supply chain when the Jewelers of America, the national association of retail jewelers, launched "a new corporate responsibility initiative,"[91] including a "Supplier Code of Conduct"[92] and a "fair-trade" mark for diamonds. "The quality of diamonds has long been measured by the four Cs: carat, colour, clarity and cut. The new mark will indicate that a diamond has achieved the fifth C standard, that of cleanliness."[93] Progress continued, to the point where, on July 9, 2004:

> . . . the first case of successful industry self-regulation against trade in so-called "conflict diamonds" took place when Congo-Brazzaville was punished for failing to prove the source of its diamond exports. . . . by being expelled from the [Kimberley] Process (the first country ever to be thus censured). As a result, legal trade in its diamonds should cease. It is a test case for the industry.[94]

However, although initially promoted as a multi-national solution to the problem, since this early momentum in 2003 and 2004 the Kimberley Process has proven to be ineffective. With a voting procedure that requires unanimity and with members pursuing political agendas, the KPCS has become reluctant to punish even the most egregious transgressor countries.[95] As a result, in 2011, Global Witness abandoned the Kimberley Process, due to its "refusal to evolve and address the clear links between diamonds, violence and tyranny has rendered it increasingly outdated."[96] Global Witness was one of the primary campaigners against blood diamonds and was the first advocacy group to leave the KPCS, citing "egregious" violations of the spirit and letter of the KPCS framework:

> Global Witness had expressed concerns about how the Kimberley Process was operating for some time; it said the final straw was the decision last month to allow Zimbabwe to export diamonds from the Marange fields, where there

have been reports of widespread human rights abuses by government security forces.[97]

In spite of countries and companies willingly signing-up to the KPCS (today, "the KP has 54 participants, representing 80 countries . . . [that] account for approximately 99.8% of the global production of rough diamonds"),[98] the diamond industry remains tainted. Problems range throughout Africa, from Sierra Leone, to Zimbabwe, to the Democratic Republic of the Congo, and Angola, where funds from diamond sales help perpetuate "a conflict that has claimed as many as 5 million lives since 1996."[99] The main evidence that a largely unregulated market continues to flourish is the number of diamonds that are smuggled in order to hide their true origin and which "may account for 10% of the $12-billion-a-year diamond trade":[100]

> The Kimberley Process mission . . . has been so narrowly defined that the monitoring group has been unable to clean up the diamond business in any meaningful way. What's more, an institution that came into being to regulate the ultimate Darwinian industry has turned out to be just as morally compromised as the business it was supposed to purify, offering little more than what one critic calls a "feel-good PR exercise."[101]

It is not clear whether companies like DeBeers, which stated in its 2011 *Report to Society* its belief that "the ethical integrity of diamonds underpins their financial and emotional value,"[102] and Tiffany & Co., which celebrated its 175th Anniversary in 2012, are concerned. One reason for this may be that a lack of consumer support is thought to be one of the main reasons why the KPCS remained ineffective:

> Work is going on behind the scenes, but do the consumers actually care? "It is surprising that on the whole people are not interested in the provenance of diamonds," says Bob Gannicott, CEO of Aber Corporation. . . . As Global Witness says: "If consumers were more demanding and governments more committed, the Kimberley Process could work."[103]

In addition to diamonds, campaigners have targeted rubies and jade from Burma,[104] emeralds from Zambia,[105] and gold from many African nations.[106] All are precious stones that are being mined and processed in ways that support corruption and human rights abuses. In spite of these jewels having strong markets in developed countries (which ensures abuses continue), it is hard to capture consumers' attention because they are not high frequency purchases. In other words, while consumers as a whole buy a large number of diamonds every year, individually, most people do not buy diamonds very often. As such, in order to broaden the appeal of their message, campaigners have begun to focus on similar abuses in the extraction and processing of rare earths (the set of 17 chemical elements—the fifteen lanthanides plus scandium and yttrium) and other metals. These raw materials are essential components of everyday products, such as cellphones and other consumer electronics. As a result, more people buy them in larger quantities and more frequently (although they are not always aware of it) than they buy diamonds. Campaigners hope to gain wider publicity for the conditions under which these rare earths and metals are mined, therefore, because they are such essential components of modern society.

In 2010, the Dodd-Frank Wall Street Reform and Consumer Protection Act was passed in the United States. Although the law was designed as a legislative response to the Financial Crisis and focused on issues such as regulating the trading of complex financial derivatives, it also contained an important clause that related to conflict minerals. In particular, the clause required "issuers with conflict minerals that are necessary to the functionality or production of a product manufactured by such person to disclose annually whether any of those minerals originated in the Democratic Republic of the Congo or an adjoining country."[107] The rule was due to be implemented on January 1, 2013, with first reports due to the SEC by May 31, 2014.

In essence, the rule was designed to force firms to account for all aspects of their supply chain to identify which had products that contain conflict minerals (i.e., certain raw materials that were mined in the Congo or nearby countries). By requiring firms to report this information to the SEC, the regulatory agency was also beginning a process whereby consumers also become aware of the origins of key components in products that they purchase on a regular basis:

> Conflict minerals include coltan, cassiterite, gold and wolframite, and while you may not be familiar with some of these, they are widely used in electronics. Your cellphone may very well contain them.[108]

In response, many companies have criticized the legislation as being costly to implement and impossible to enforce. Even those firms that do not have these minerals in their products have to confirm that is the case. Multinational companies have complex supply chains that can involve tens of thousands of independent firms across their complete range of products (Kraft, for example, has reported that it has approximately 100,000 suppliers).[109] As a result, while the SEC estimates "the initial compliance cost to be $3 billion to $4 billion, with continuing costs of $207 million to $609 million a year," industry association estimates are higher, "pinning the cost at $8 billion to $16 billion."[110] Another concern related to the definition of a conflict mineral:

> The agency had to deal with how to treat recycled conflict minerals, what exactly it means for conflict minerals to be necessary for a product and how hard companies must work to review their supply chains, among other issues. All in a world where gold mined anywhere is hard to trace. As you might expect with a complex issue, a complex rule has resulted. The S.E.C.'s release explaining its conflict minerals rule is 356 pages long. Companies are going to have to spend millions just to understand the rules.[111]

All these costs are imposed on U.S. companies, while companies from other countries avoid them. Nevertheless, the legislation is an important step forward in creating ethical supply chains, while giving consumers (and investors, in particular)[112] the information they need to become ethical consumers.[113] Understanding the source of the products we buy every day and how our purchase decisions can have life and death consequences elsewhere in the world provides important insight into the global economy and the range of issues that fall within the CSR umbrella. Of course, political intrusions into economic decisions usually have their own unintended consequences as well and "the law's stiff requirements have led most U.S.-based companies to boycott Congolese minerals since April [2011], depriving thousands of Congolese of their livelihoods.[114]

CEO Perspective

Gareth Penny (De Beers)

The product we sell stands for the deepest of human emotions: love and commitment. So we have taken the view that we are enormously proud of what De Beers and its partners are doing today. We want people to know that with any diamond they buy, that product is not only deeply meaningful to them but, in terms of the contribution that it is making, to Africa. If we can tell our story across the world, it is positive for us, and the industry, and for Africa.[115]

Online Resources

- Adbusters, http://www.adbusters.org/
- ADiamondisForever.com, http://www.adiamondisforever.com/
- Cash Mobs, http://cash-mobs.com/

- De Beers Group, http://www.debeersgroup.com/
- Earthworks, http://www.earthworksaction.org/issues/detail/conflict_minerals
- Global Witness, http://www.globalwitness.org/conflict-diamonds
- Jewelers of America, http://www.jewelers.org/
- Kimberley Process, http://www.kimberleyprocess.com/
- No Dirty Gold, http://www.nodirtygold.org/
- Responsible Jewelry Council, http://www.responsiblejewellery.com/
- World Diamond Council, http://www.worlddiamondcouncil.com/
- Worldwatch Institute, http://www.worldwatch.org/

Pro/Con Debate

Pro/Con Debate: Firms have a duty to be transparent and educate consumers about the consequences of their purchase decisions, while consumers have a duty to apply their values and principles in making purchase decisions and not base the decision on price alone.

Questions for Discussion and Review

1. Are you an 'ethical consumer'? Why or why not?

2. Think of a company with a brand that you like and one with a brand that you dislike. What accounts for the difference between the two? Is CSR related at all?

3. Given the size of its operations, De Beers is the most important company in the diamond industry. What interest might it have in seeing the Kimberley Process either work or fail?

4. Diamonds are already very expensive. Would you be willing to pay more to ensure the integrity of the diamond you were buying? Why, or why not?

5. What is your reaction to the following quote?

   Ah, a diamond! Does that mean it must be love? Or that your suitor has paid a massively over-inflated price for a cheap and common stone, whose value is artificially manipulated by a single company founded by Britain's greatest colonialist, a stone whose profits have recently funded the bloodiest of violent conflicts in Africa, and whose entire modern tradition was invented by an expensive marketing campaign in the mid-20th century?[116]

ETHICAL SOURCING

> **CSR Connection:** This issue reflects the growing consumer support for companies that are perceived to have healthy supply chains. From a strategic perspective, fair trade allows firms to secure stable supplies of essential raw materials, while signaling a commitment to suppliers.
>
> **Stakeholders:** Suppliers, Consumers.

Issue

Although much of CSR enables firms to operate more efficiently and, therefore, reduce costs,[117] other aspects of CSR cost firms money, at least in the short term. To operate in a socially responsible manner means to do things the *right* way, which is not always the easiest or the cheapest way. As such, an important debate within the CSR movement is the extent to which consumers are willing to pay a price premium for CSR. While consumers often say they want to purchase from firms that are ethical and socially responsible,[118] to what extent do their purchase decisions support these statements?

Related to this question, to what extent do companies have an interest in operating an ethical supply chain? Is there any added value to purchasing products from suppliers at prices that are *fair* (therefore ensuring their suppliers' medium-term wellbeing), rather than at prices that are dictated by the market? What is the extent of the market in developed economies for products with ingredients that have been purchased in this way from developing economies? More specifically, what exactly is *fair* trade?[119]

> Fairtrade is about better prices, decent working conditions, local sustainability, and fair terms of trade for farmers and workers in the developing world. By requiring companies to pay sustainable prices (which must never fall lower than the market price), Fairtrade addresses the injustices of conventional trade, which traditionally discriminates against the poorest, weakest producers. It enables them to improve their position and have more control over their lives.[120]

The fair trade movement began "in the Netherlands in the late 1980s as a way to organize small farmers producing various commodities into cooperatives and to improve their incomes by pressuring buyers to pay guaranteed minimum prices."[121] Price guarantees help small farmers overcome unstable commodity prices, which affect a wide range of raw materials. One product that Western consumers use daily and is readily associated with the fair trade movement is coffee, which was the first consumer product to be certified using the *Fairtrade* label.[122] Although fair trade began with coffee, however, it rapidly expanded to include many different kinds of foods and, over time, retail sales have increased dramatically. Figure 7.2, for example, presents retail sales in the UK in £ million for a range of fair trade products, from 2001 to 2011:

Figure 7.2	Retail Sales of Fair Trade Products in the UK , 2001–2011

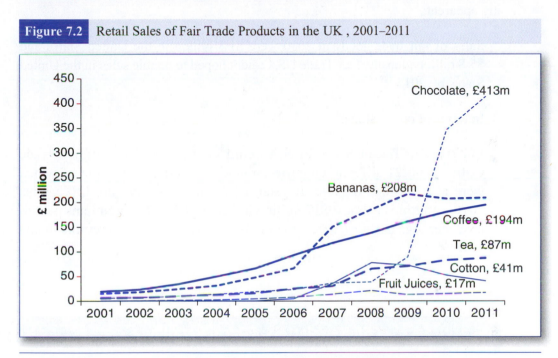

Source: The Fairtrade Foundation website, January 2013, http://www.fairtrade.org.uk/what_is_fairtrade/facts_and_figures.aspx

Although primarily intended to improve the living standards of workers in developing economies, an important additional goal of fair trade is to educate "developed-world consumers to gain a greater awareness of those on the far end of the supply chain."[123] And, it is clear that there is a percentage of the consumer market that is willing to pay "above market prices for commodities such as coffee, bananas and chocolate, if he knows that this premium will be spent on higher wages for those who did the planting, picking and packing."[124] Overall, for example, the UK market for fair trade certified products is growing rapidly, reaching a total of £1.3 billion in retail sales in 2011, up from only £50 million in 2001:[125]

The UK is one of the world's leading Fairtrade markets, with more products and more awareness of Fairtrade than anywhere else. Around 20% of roast and ground coffee, and 20% of bananas sold in the UK are now Fairtrade.[126]

Fair trade, therefore, is not just about coffee, but encompasses a growing range of consumer products, such as sugar, fruit, cotton, palm oil, and chocolate. The range of products available is largely determined by the willingness of the market to support them. In the UK, this currently translates to "more than 4,000 certified fair-trade products."[127] In the U.S., which operates under a competing fair trade certification scheme (Fair Trade USA),[128] similar growth patterns are also becoming apparent:

Sales of fair trade goods in 2010 were $1.3 billion in the United States and $5.8 billion globally. Fair Trade USA said it hoped to double sales in the United States by 2015.[129]

In terms of coffee alone:

In 2011, Fair Trade USA certified a record 138 million pounds of Fair Trade Coffee from 22 different countries around the world, 52 percent of which were also certified organic. In total, coffee imports were up 32% versus 2010, resulting in almost $17 million in Fair Trade coffee premiums paid to producer organizations, a new record for Fair Trade premium returns in one year.[130]

CSR Newsletters: Ethical Retailing

An article in the *Financial Times*[131] reviews the extent of the market for "ethical retailing." In spite of the common perception among executives that consumers do not make purchase decisions based on their best intentions, there is growing evidence to suggest that this is now changing, even though Fairtrade-certified products "are still equivalent to only 2.6 per cent of Tesco's revenues and 0.6 per cent of Wal-Mart's." In general, the UK's ethical retail market is relatively mature and research indicates that it can be divided into four separate categories:

The first, about 8 per cent of the total, are committed, cause-driven purchasers. A second group, accounting for 30-35 per cent, want to purchase ethically but are not really sure how . . . The third group, also about 30-35 per cent, feels the same, but doubt that their individual purchases can make much difference. The fourth group, the remainder, are completely uninterested.

> Although these data demonstrate progress, they also highlight the limitations of this market. These category numbers mean that the "completely uninterested" group is at least twice the size of the "committed, cause-driven consumers," possibly three times as big. At the end of the day, there is nowhere near a majority of consumers who are willing to place social responsibility concerns above more traditional considerations in arriving at their purchase decisions. The overwhelming sense, therefore, is that any gains made are still occurring at the periphery and are as much about relieving first-world consumer guilt than re-shaping the underlying business model to instill a permanent strategic CSR perspective. In other words, "by publicising their initiatives the supermarkets help consumers feel they have done the world a good deed." Along these lines, the final quote in the article is the most enlightening because it demonstrates the danger associated with this issue for firms:
>
> A smart retailer is half a step ahead of the consumer. Ten steps ahead and you're out of business.

In spite of the speed at which the market for fair trade goods has grown, it is important to remember that the overall market segment to which such goods appeal is limited, capturing only "0.01 per cent of worldwide food and beverage sales in 2009."[132] To what extent fair trade has mass market appeal, therefore, remains an open question. In general:

> Purchasing levels of green and ethically-produced goods are linked to levels of affluence. For the majority of consumers, price overrides ethical considerations as the key factor in their decision-making.[133]

Beyond a limited market, there are three main criticisms of fair trade. The first of these is that fair trade, as a pricing mechanism, represents a distortion of the market by encouraging over-production in areas that are not economically sustainable. This argument ignores the choice being exercised by the willing consumers to whom such products are being sold:

> Buying Fairtrade chocolate no more distorts the chocolate market than buying a Louis Vuitton handbag distorts the handbag market. In both cases buyers are sending signals: that they are prepared to spend more on a bag with a prestigious label, or on chocolate that provides cocoa growers with a better life.[134]

A related counterpoint against this criticism that fair trade encourages ineffi-ciency is that world market prices for many commodities are not set on an open and free market, with many Western producers benefiting from large government quotas and subsidies. In terms of cotton, for example:

Eleven million growers raise cotton today [in West Africa]. . . . those millions of black farmers are undercut by the 35,000-or-so mainly white farmers in the former slave states of Texas and the American south. Some $4bn dollars a year in federal government handouts encourages high-cost American farmers to dump subsidized cotton on the world market, depressing its price.[135]

As such, the ultimate argument advanced by economists against *fair* trade is, in fact, an argument in favor of *free* trade. Many supporters of fair trade would prefer to see free trade, which they believe would have a wider, quicker, and longer last-ing impact in favor of farmers worldwide than any artificial designation of what may or may not constitute *fair*:

Poor people are poor because they do not participate sufficiently in the world international trading system. They are not poor because they are unjustly treated when they do.[136]

Trade subsidies and quotas prevent farmers from the developing world from competing on a level playing field. As such, action to reduce these market ineffi-ciencies would have a much greater impact than any artificial fair trade market, which is dismissed as a phenomenon created to appease consumer consciences. As such, advocates of fair trade often use the words of Adam Smith to justify their arguments, noting that developed economies could do much more for farmers in developing countries by dropping all barriers to trade and extensive support pro-vided by governments to domestic producers:

What is prudence in the conduct of every family can scarce be folly in that of a great kingdom. If a foreign country can supply us with a commodity cheaper than we ourselves can make it, better buy it of them with some part of the produce of our own industry, employed in a way in which we have some advantage.[137]

The second criticism of fair trade is that, because it appeals to consumers' better instincts and makes "shoppers feel good about themselves and the food they are buying,"[138] it is open to abuse by firms that want to appear more socially responsible than they actually are.[139] These accusations are often made against supermarkets and other Western retailers, suggesting they use fair trade to gain additional revenue for themselves, while passing on only small amounts to the farmers who produced the raw materials. There is some validity to this argument, with studies indicating that "between 10 per cent and 25 per cent" of the price premium of an average fair trade product reaches the farmer who produced the raw product and certification standards vary and are often poorly enforced.[140] Similarly, other reports indicate that "probably only about 9 cents of the $3.10 cost of an average fairly traded 100g bar of chocolate goes to Africa or a poor country."[141] The counterpoint to this argument is stakeholder (particularly consumer) vigilance. Some progressive retailers "realize the danger to their brand of being perceived as Fairtrade profiteers"[142] and have pledged not to increase margins on fair trade products. With some justification, however, they also note that one cause of the higher prices of fair trade products is the initial costs involved in establishing a fair trade supply chain:

> The [Marks & Spencer] Fairtrade cotton T-shirt, for example, retails at £8, a pound more than a conventional equivalent. But a lot of the difference reflects limited availability of Fairtrade cotton and the cost of running small batches of cotton through the supply chain—problems that M&S expects to shrink as the volume of Fairtrade cotton buying increases.[143]

In order to counter this effect and negate the criticism that Western retailers are unduly profiting from Fairtrade products, there is growing support for the idea of *equitrade*, which offers a more equitable distribution of the economic benefits of ethical retailing:

> Whereas Fairtrade provides help to a relatively small (though growing) number of farmers, Equitrade tries to raise the quality of life for the majority of poor people by carrying out the processing operations, where most of the profits are made, in the poor countries themselves. Malagasy Foods, for example, has . . . started harvesting and processing chocolate in Madagascar. It thereby ensures that 40 per cent of its income stays in Madagascar, with an extra 11 per cent benefiting the country through tax.[144]

A similar example is Good African Coffee, which was the first African packaging and roasting factory to export coffee directly to the UK.[145] Both fair trade and equitrade have advantages and disadvantages:

> Fairtrade demonstrably helps the groups of people whom it targets, and works through cooperatives that guarantee environmental and social standards and that demand democratic decision-making over how the extra money earned is distributed. Equitrade stimulates the wider economy, but is less accountable and assumes that the manufacturer treats the cocoa bean growers or other farmers and suppliers fairly.[146]

Finally, the third criticism of fair trade is that, for consumers who want to support CSR companies and causes, and for whom issues such as "food miles"[147] are important, buying a local product is more ethical and sustainable than sourcing one from thousands of miles away. While there is some truth to this point, making the *best* choice becomes a matter of prioritization. Whether, for example, a consumer's support for local farmers in the West adds more or less social value than the same support for poor farmers in Africa is a personal judgment.

CSR Newsletters: Fair Trade

What is interesting about an article from *Ethical Corporation Magazine*[148] is not that the Fair Trade coffee company (AMT) lost its license to operate coffee kiosks at London railway stations to a competitor that doesn't stock any Fair Trade coffee. What is interesting is that the reason the firm lost relates back to a strategic decision not to pass on its higher supply chain costs to its customers, which has a direct impact on profits.

It is not clear whether this is due to a managerial misstep, or a lack of confidence that UK consumers are willing to pay the price premium associated with Fair trade coffee. Either way, it is not good news for AMT and potentially has implications for the fundamental CSR business model. For example, it is fine for AMT to say that "We can sleep at night knowing that the people picking our beans that go in our cups are being looked after – unlike the high street guys who are trying to take over the world," but the reality is that "The closures slashed a hefty £6 million off AMT's £15 million revenue in one fell swoop."

Firms that differentiate their products on some aspect other than price (i.e., quality, technology, design, etc.) charge a corresponding price premium because, in general, the products are more expensive to produce and the consumers who buy such products are less price sensitive than consumers who make their purchase decisions based primarily on price. The same laws of economics apply to firms that want to differentiate their products based primarily on socially responsibility, which often incurs a higher cost structure.

Due to the awareness surrounding the Fair Trade brand in the UK ("Four-fifths of UK consumers now recognise the Fairtrade brand, according to the Department for Environment, Food and Rural Affairs") and the likely small increase in price per cup involved, it seems fair to assume that UK consumers place a higher importance on CSR issues than most and would be willing to pay the difference. But, that will not help AMT if the firm goes out of business without testing to see whether or not this is true.

For an increasing number of firms, the positives of fair trade outweigh any real or perceived negatives. These firms increasingly see fair trade as more of a good business decision than an act of charity. Beyond improved consumer perceptions of the firm and its products, fair trade is a means by which firms can build long-term relationships with suppliers and guarantee a more stable supply of higher quality products that are essential to their business.

The UK company Cadbury is one such company. In 2009, in partnership with the Fairtrade Foundation, Cadbury made an important decision to supply all of the cocoa beans it uses to make chocolate from Fairtrade sources.[149] Another example is Hershey's, which in 2012 followed Cadbury's example and committed to source 100% certified cocoa by 2020, ensuring the crop is grown to "the highest internationally recognized standards for labor, environment and better farming practices."[150] The advantages of such moves extend not only to the specific company, but ripple out to other producers and consumers throughout the industry:

> Currently, certified cocoa accounts for less than 5 percent of the world's cocoa supply, according to Hershey. As the largest chocolate manufacturer in North America, Hershey says its 2020 purchasing commitment should significantly expand the global supply of certified cocoa, particularly from West Africa, which produces about 70 percent of the world's cocoa.[151]

Ultimately, firms like Cadbury and Hershey's have determined that their best interests lie in forming long-term relationships with suppliers who are incentivized to continue supplying a product that these firms rely on for a core part of their business. This is a message that continues to resonate as fair trade becomes an established way to source ethically and is increasingly demanded by consumers. Starbucks is another firm that believes in the market value of fair trade.

Case Study: Starbucks

As one of the top five coffee buyers in the world,[152] Starbucks' actions have significant influence over the industry as a whole, but have also been a source of negative publicity for the company in the past. Among other things, Starbucks has been accused of profiting at the expense of coffee growers, whose livelihoods rise and fall in line with the wildly fluctuating global market price for coffee, which can generate a situation where the market price of coffee falls below the cost of production.[153]

Coffee was not only the first consumer product to by widely available as a Fairtrade certified product; it is also one of the most popular. Today, fair trade coffee makes up "20 per cent of the UK retail sales of ground coffee"[154] and "70% of the [total] US fair trade market."[155] Due to high-profile NGO campaigns and firm responses, public awareness about fair trade issues is growing. In addition to the growing popularity of fair trade products in Europe, for example, according to Fair Trade USA, awareness about fair trade is also growing among U.S. consumers, albeit more slowly:

> While the [fair trade community], which was established in Europe over 50 years ago, has achieved 80% market awareness of Fair Trade products among consumers there, consumer awareness of Fair Trade stands at just 34% in the U.S.[156]

As a result of the combination of growing awareness of fair trade, in general, and the growing popularity of fair trade coffee, in particular, Starbucks has attracted a lot of attention from fair trade campaigners who began campaigning for change at Starbucks "in February 2000 when the activist NGO Global Exchange launched a protest at the company's annual meeting, demanding that Starbucks sell Fair Trade coffee."[157]

In response, Starbucks has been at the vanguard of developing the profile of fair trade products in the U.S. ever since.[158] Today, the company works closely with suppliers to help them convert to sustainable practices and offers long-term purchasing contracts as an incentive to do so. This approach helps Starbucks meet the needs of the fair trade industry, as well as increase the quality of the product it buys and then resells in its stores. In particular, in 2004, Starbucks launched the Coffee Agronomy Company.[159] It is based in Costa Rica and positioned as "the flagship vehicle for Starbucks' sustainable supply chain commitment." Soon after, the company launched its Coffee and Farmer Equity (CAFE) Practices guidelines, which "spell out Starbucks' expectations for its suppliers on economic, social and environmental issues."[160]

Starbucks' CAFÉ Practices[161]

When Starbucks implemented C.A.F.E. Practices, it had six objectives in mind:

1. Increase economic, social, and environmental sustainability in the specialty coffee industry, including conservation and biodiversity.

2. Encourage Starbucks suppliers to implement C.A.F.E. Practices through economic incentives and preferential buying status.

3. Purchase the majority of Starbucks coffee under C.A.F.E. Practices guidelines by 2007.

4. Negotiate mutually beneficial long-term contracts with suppliers to support Starbucks growth.

5. Build mutually beneficial and increasingly direct relationship with suppliers.

6. Promote transparency and economic fairness within the coffee supply chain.

Starbucks developed CAFE in conjunction with the environmental charity Conservation International.[162] The goal for suppliers in conforming to the guidelines is to be certified as a Starbucks' *preferred supplier*, which contains specific price guarantees by Starbucks over and above current market prices.[163] The internal logic behind Starbucks' action made it a clear operational and strategic decision:

> To support [its] high growth rate, it was clear that an integral part of the company's future success would come from meeting increased demand through a secure supply of high-quality coffee beans. Coffee beans constituted the bread and butter of Starbucks' business—the company had to ensure a sustainable supply of this key commodity.[164]

In the broader picture, the business case for fair trade throughout the coffee industry is convincing:

> Sure, by creating a healthier supply chain, [Starbucks] might end up helping some of [their] competitors. . . . But in the end, it helps the industry. And a healthier industry is better for us, better for the consumer, for the environment, for everyone.[165]

These results have been repeated elsewhere, particularly in Europe. In September 2004, for example, Marks & Spencer, the well-known UK retailer, announced it would source all of the coffee it serves in its coffee shops from fair trade sources. The decision doubled the amount of fair trade coffee on sale in UK coffee shops. In addition, McDonald's has been sourcing all its coffee served in the UK from fair trade and sustainable sources since 2007 and, elsewhere in Europe, Nestlé's Nespresso "premium coffee brand . . . has pledged to source 80% of its beans from farms meeting strict social and environmental standards by 2013."[166]

As a result of this rapid change in the global coffee industry, in recent years, Starbucks has faced the combination of a rapidly evolving competitive market and wildly fluctuating commodity prices.[167] Starbucks has always faced competition on *price* (people could always buy coffee cheaper elsewhere), but now the firm is also facing real competition on *quality* as fast-food U.S. firms such as McDonald's and Dunkin' Donuts seek to eat into Starbucks' core target market at home, as well as abroad.[168] In the U.S., for example, Dunkin Donuts has been serving fair trade only coffee in its stores since 2003 and McDonald's is also looking to expand the amount of fair trade coffee that it serves.[169]

This growing competition strikes at the heart of Starbucks' business model. Ultimately, what is Starbucks' product? Is it *quality coffee*; or the *coffee-house experience* that Howard Schultz (Starbucks' CEO) tried to bring back to the U.S. from a 1983 trip to Milan, Italy; or is it the location—a *third place* between home and work? When there is deterioration in the economy, can Starbucks justify the price premium it charges based on experience alone (if competitors are catching up in terms of quality, yet offering products at a cheaper price)? Either way, the company is increasingly being pushed to innovate and fair trade coffee is seen as an area where Starbucks can continue to push industry best practice:

> [In September, 2009] Starbucks stores in the UK and Ireland . . . began serving 100% Fairtrade Certified and Starbucks Shared Planet verified coffee in all of their espresso-based beverages. Every one of the two million visitors per week can walk away with a Fairtrade Certified Cappuccino, Latte or Mocha and help support small-scale farmers and their communities in developing countries around the world.[170]

Today, Starbucks' website tracks the firm's progress regarding its ethical sourcing practices and performance since 2000 when it began purchasing fair trade coffee:

> Since then we've paid over $16 million in Fairtrade premiums (on top of the purchase price of green coffee), which are used by producer organizations for social and economic investments at the community and organizational level. . . . Starbucks bought over 428 million pounds of coffee in fiscal 2011. Some 86% of that—367 million pounds worth—from C.A.F.E. Practices-approved suppliers. We paid an average price of $2.38 per pound for our premium green (unroasted) coffee in 2011—up from $1.56 per pound in 2010. . . . The reach of the program is vast, spanning 20 countries, affecting over 1 million workers each year and encouraging responsible practices on 102,000 hectares each year.[171]

In order to put those numbers in context, a useful point of reference is Green Mountain Coffee Roasters, which produces brands like Tully's Coffee and Newman's Own Organics. Green Mountain Coffee has long been recognized as one of the world's 100 Best Corporate Citizens[172] and, according to Fair Trade USA, is claimed as "the world's largest purchaser of Fair Trade Certified coffee."[173] In 2011, the company imported over 50.3 million pounds of raw coffee, 24 percent of its total.[174] In comparison, however:

> [Conservation International] and Starbucks have been working together for more than 14 years, developing and applying the comprehensive set of environmental, social and economic guidelines Starbucks uses to source ethical coffee. . . . In 2011 Starbucks bought 86 percent of its total coffee this way—367 million pounds worth. By 2015, all of Starbucks coffee will be third-party verified or certified, either through C.A.F.E. Practices, Fairtrade, or another externally audited system.[175]

Closely associating itself with fair trade coffee is a straightforward business decision for Starbucks. It enables the firm to deflect criticism, help win those customers who are willing to pay for the value-added by the fair trade certification label, and, most importantly, helps secure supplies of the high quality coffee beans that are central to the firm's business model. In short, fair trade is a point of differentiation for Starbucks that will help it expand further into those markets where it is not yet established. A good example is the Scandinavian countries, which are the largest per capita consumers of coffee in the world (at 26.7 pounds per person, for example, Finnish people consumer three times the amount of coffee that Americans consume, 9 pounds, and four times the average annual consumption per person in the UK, 6.7 pounds). Equally importantly, the "Nordic nations . . . tend to pride themselves on ethical business practices."[176]

CEO Perspective

Howard Schultz (Starbucks)

Companies should not have a singular view of profitability. . . . There needs to be a balance between commerce and social responsibility. . . . The companies that are authentic about it will wind up as the companies that make more money.[177]

Online Resources

- Commitment to Ethical Cocoa Sourcing, http://www.laborrights.org/stop-child-labor/cocoa-campaign/resources/861
- Common Code for the Coffee Community, http://www.sustainable-coffee.net/
- Conservation International, http://www.conservation.org/
- Ethical Trading Initiative (ETI), http://www.ethicaltrade.org/
- Fairtrade Foundation, http://www.fairtrade.org.uk/
- Fair Trade Labeling Organization (FLO), http://www.fairtrade.net/
- Fair Trade USA, http://www.fairtradeusa.org/
- International Cocoa Initiative, http://www.cocoainitiative.org/
- International Labor Rights Forum (ILRF), http://www.laborrights.org/
- National Coffee Association (NCA), http://www.ncausa.org/
- U.S. Fair Labor Association, http://www.fairlabor.org/

Pro/Con Debate

> **Pro/Con Debate:** *Equitrade* is preferable to fair trade; free trade is preferable to both.

Questions for Discussion and Review

1. Do you believe in *fair trade*? Why, or why not? What does *fair* mean?

2. Are you happy to pay a price premium for CSR products?

3. What do you think explains the fact that, in Europe, "the market for Fair Trade Certified products is three times larger in dollar sales than it is in the U.S."?[178]

4. Do you know what the Fairtrade symbol looks like? Can you name a Fairtrade product that you have bought recently? Why did you buy that product?

5. Did you know about Starbucks' involvement in this issue and the Fairtrade products the company sells? Does it make you more likely to shop there? Do you think this is something the company should publicize? Is there any downside to doing so?

FINANCIAL CRISIS

> **CSR Connection:** This issue views the global economic system through the eyes of the Financial Crisis. What challenges does the crisis present to the global economy and capitalist system? What is the role of CSR in the crisis? And, what changes should the CSR movement advocate in response?
>
> **Stakeholders:** Consumers, Creditors, Debtors, Investors, Company, Government.

Issue

"And I sincerely believe, with you, that banking establishments are more dangerous than standing armies; and that the principle of spending money to be paid by posterity, under the name of funding, is but swindling futurity on a large scale."

—Thomas Jefferson[179]

In many ways, the dramatic economic events that began towards the end of 2007,[180] which have widely been reported as, alternatively, "the most serious financial crisis since the Great Crash of 1929"[181] or the "Great Recession,"[182] brought into focus the comprehensive nature of CSR. From individual greed and the abdication of responsibility, to organizational fraud and the mismanagement of resources, to governmental failure to monitor and adequately regulate the financial system, the crisis emphasized the many interlocking factors that make CSR such a complex issue. At the same time, however, and with the benefit of hindsight, these events also demonstrated how straightforward CSR can be. At its simplest, CSR is not rocket science. It is often common sense combined with an enlightened approach to management and decision making. To look back at some of the decisions taken by key players that contributed to the economic crisis and try to rationalize why they were taken, however, represents an exercise in exasperation. As Thomas Friedman of *The New York Times* noted:

What do you call giving a worker who makes only $14,000 a year a nothing-down and nothing-to-pay-for-two-years mortgage to buy a $750,000 home, and then bundling that mortgage with 100 others into bonds—which Moody's or

Standard & Poors rate AAA—and then selling them to banks and pension funds the world over?[183]

Essentially, the crisis resulted from the cumulative effects of multiple bad decisions by many individuals who had lost their sense of perspective:[184]

. . . how so many people could be so stupid, incompetent and self-destructive all at once.[185]

. . . the scale of stupidity and greed at the big banks defies belief.[186]

. . . a near total breakdown of responsibility at every link in our financial chain, and now we either bail out the people who brought us here or risk a total systemic crash.[187]

. . . how could the people who sold these [products] have been so short-sightedly greedy? . . . how could the people who bought them have been so foolish?[188]

At various stages, key actors suspected the *system* was unsustainable, but had no self-interest in advocating for change. As Citibank's Chuck Prince said in 2007, shortly before his ouster as CEO later that year, "As long as the music is playing, you've got to get up and dance. We're still dancing."[189]

In general, the economic crisis was driven by three main factors: First, the housing market bubble, which was fueled by low interest rates and easy access to mortgages; second, the underpricing of risk, particularly by investors on Wall Street; and, third, the failure (or inability) of the regulatory infrastructure to police the increasingly liquid global financial market. As such, blame for the crisis can be shared widely—from the individuals that sold mortgages that had attractive commissions, but were unlikely to be re-paid, to the organizations that allowed these sales to continue because they were passing on the risk, to the regulators who failed to oversee the markets it was their responsibility to monitor, to the investors who developed complex securities and other financial instruments that they knew no one (not even themselves) fully understood, right down to the people who failed to question whether it was wise to apply for one hundred percent mortgages on hugely inflated home prices with little or nothing down, purely on the belief that house prices would continue to rise and that, anyway, they would be able to re-finance in a couple of years. All of these decisions were taken within an atmosphere of over-dependence on the *market* as the ultimate arbiter that relieved individual actors of the personal responsibility attached to many of their day-to-day decisions.

While the crisis was inherently an invention of the U.S. financial markets and regulators, however, for it to have the global reach that it did required the buy-in of the rest of the world. Everyone was happy to play along while the market was going up. The resulting backlash against the status quo following the crash, therefore, represents a challenge to the spread of globalization shaped largely by U.S. liberal capitalism (e.g., deregulation, free international money flows, self-correcting markets, and the efficient pursuit of profit in the form of shareholder returns):

> This suspicion of Anglo-Saxon economic liberalism cut across the usual political boundaries. Right wing industrialists disliked it, but so did left-wing labor unions. Chinese communists felt threatened, but so did Green Party activists in Germany. . . . The critique of U.S. liberalism . . . is shared by a diverse group that includes French President Nicolas Sarkozy, German Chancellor Angela Merkel, Chinese Prime Minister Wen Jibao and Russian President Dmitry Medvedev.[190]

What is not clear, is how effective or self-sustaining this critique will be and whether, in conjunction with any shift in economic ideology, there will be a corresponding shift in global political power. The dominant feature of the U.S. economic model prior to the crisis was an inherently unstable combination of excessively low savings and excessively high borrowing. This surplus of credit was being used to finance an unsustainable level of consumption—unsustainable because the U.S. was consistently spending more than it saved. That money had to come from somewhere and most of its came from China. As such, the only real, long-term solution to the crisis is a re-balancing of demand and supply within the global economy, which represents a shift in influence from the borrower to the lender:[191]

> [The crisis] is not only a crisis of capitalism or of a particular form of capitalism after all, it's one of U.S. economic and global power as well. . . . the fact that [the meeting to discuss a global response to the crisis] is one of the G-20 rather than the Group of Seven—and that its most important meetings are between Obama and Chinese President Hu Jintao—is a symbol of the decline of U.S. economic power exposed by the crisis.[192]

The sense is that the times have changed and U.S. capitalism, as the driving force behind globalization, will have to change with them:

> . . . even a newspaper as inherently pro-business as [*The Economist*] has to admit that there was something rotten in finance. The basic capitalist bargain, under which genuine risktakers are allowed to garner huge rewards, seems a poor one if taxpayers are landed with a huge bill for it.[193]

And change is what we need, and quickly. It is five years since Lehman Brothers filed for bankruptcy protection to signal the beginning of "the greatest threat to the international capitalist system since the Great Depression of the 1930s."[194] Lehman's bankruptcy is important because "it was the moment when everything changed."[195] It is worth remembering because "it was a signal that deep problems had enveloped our economy—problems that wouldn't be solved quickly or easily." CSR, ultimately, represents the solution to these problems:

> Prior to Lehman, it was easy to believe that housing prices could only go up and that we could always rely on debt to maintain our standard of living. We shrugged as manufacturing jobs disappeared . . . and good middle-class jobs became harder to find. We didn't talk much about income inequality. Nor did we care much that Wall Street had developed a mercenary trading culture, which had little to do with providing capital for companies, ostensibly its reason for being. Post-Lehman, economic reality set in.[196]

The debate that has emerged within the CSR community regarding the future shape of capitalism reflects this shift in the content and tone of discussions about the global economy. Bill Baue, contributing editor of *CSRwire.com*, for example, highlights the intersection of the economic and environmental crises:

> The economic meltdown of 2008 mirrors the simultaneous environmental meltdown fueled by the climate calamity – both share common roots, and many in the Corporate Social Responsibility (CSR) community believe they share a common salvation. At the most basic level, the global economy is melting down because the belief in perpetual growth, propped up by deregulation and outright fraud, has smacked up against the finite nature of reality. Likewise, our atmosphere is literally melting our ecosystems, primarily because of the growth curve of fossil fuel emissions and carbon concentrations. . . . The most likely savior scenario likewise entwines economy and environment: a "green" recovery promises to create good jobs and strong companies while transitioning to a low-carbon energy infrastructure powered by renewable resources such as wind and solar.[197]

A similar argument was presented to a much larger audience by Thomas Friedman in *The New York Times*:

> What if the crisis of 2008 represents something much more fundamental than a deep recession? What if it's telling us that the whole growth model we created over the last 50 years is simply unsustainable economically and ecologically

and that 2008 was when we hit the wall—when Mother Nature and the market both said: "No more."?[198]

In early 2009, articles with titles such as "Is Capitalism Working?"[199] "The End,"[200] and "The End of the Financial World As We Know It"[201] began to appear. This sense of seismic change was reinforced by a major series of articles in the *Financial Times* about the crisis and its consequences for the global economic order. The goal of the series, which was titled the "Future of Capitalism" and had contributions from the newspaper's top economic columnists as well as invited articles by experts such as Paul Kennedy, Nigel Lawson, and Amartya Sen, was to assess the consequences of the crisis, given that "Assumptions that prevailed since the 1980s embrace of the market now lie in shreds. The scope of government is again widening and the era of free-wheeling finance is over." Representative of the debate was this comment by Martin Wolf in the opening article in the series:

> It is impossible at such a turning point to know where we are going. . . . Yet the combination of a financial collapse with a huge recession, if not something worse, will surely change the world. The legitimacy of the market will weaken. The credibility of the US will be damaged. The authority of China will rise. Globalisation itself may founder. . . . The era of financial liberalization has ended. Yet, unlike the 1930s, no credible alternative to the market economy exists. . . . Where we end up, after this financial tornado, is for us to seek and determine.[202]

Combined with Bill Gates' call for "creative capitalism"[203] and Muhammad Yunus' book, "Creating a World Without Poverty,"[204] the sense is that we are at a point of "inflection"[205] in the economic history of our planet. While we might not notice measurable change immediately, the intellectual shift indicates that, whatever the shape globalization takes moving forward, it will be different than what it was prior to the crisis.[206]

CSR Newsletters: Moral Hazard

Two articles from the *Financial Times* touch indirectly on issues related to social responsibility within the global financial system. In particular, they focus on the decline in global stock markets and discuss possible causes of the recession that analysts were projecting at the time. In the first article,[207]

(Continued)

(Continued)

George Soros uses the presence of moral hazard to highlight the failure of a pure market ideology:

> [Market] Fundamentalists believe that markets tend towards equilibrium and the common interest is best served by allowing participants to pursue their self-interest. It is an obvious misconception, because it was the intervention of the authorities that prevented financial markets from breaking down, not the markets themselves.

The article accuses governments of creating a system that is unsustainable. In order to avoid the damage to the broader economy that would result from undermining the positions of global financial traders, Soros notes that governments and central banks have averted their eyes from the moral hazard that is an inherent part of the financial system:

> Every time the credit expansion ran into trouble the financial authorities intervened, injecting liquidity and finding other ways to stimulate the economy. That created a system of asymmetric incentives also known as moral hazard, which encouraged ever greater credit expansion.

The second article by Martin Wolf[208] paints an even more complicated interaction of causes that range from a "fundamentally defective financial system," "rational responses to incentives," "the short-sightedness of human beings," overly-loose US monetary policy, and "the massive flows of surplus capital" around the globe. The article also highlights the role of governments in sustaining a system that has become too important to fail, the knowledge of which advantages traders significantly. Unfortunately, he concludes that politicians, with all their human weaknesses (primarily the short term driver of self-preservation), are unlikely to change anything any time soon:

> Those who emphasise rationality can readily point to the incentives for the financial sector to take undue risk. This is the result of the interaction of "asymmetric information"—the fact that insiders know more than anybody else what is going on—with "moral hazard"—the perception that the government will rescue financial institutions if enough of them fall into difficulty at the same time. There is evident truth in both propositions: if, for example, the UK government feels obliged to rescue a modest-sized mortgage bank, such as Northern Rock, moral hazard is rife.

The resulting economic reality led initially to various forms of protest, most notably the Occupy Wall Street movement (http://occupywallst.org/), which initially started with a tweet by Adbusters (#occupywallstreet)[209] and took root in Zuccotti Park in Lower Manhattan, but soon spread worldwide. The failure of this movement to organize and sustain its momentum does not diminish the foundation on which it was founded. An important indicator of change, therefore, will be whether the intellectual driving force behind Occupy Wall Street that challenged the legitimacy of the *efficient market* can be corralled into a meaningful platform for reform.

Along these lines, the evolving thoughts of Alan Greenspan, Chair of the U.S. Federal Reserve from 1987 to 2006, on the policing role of market forces is instructive. In 1963, Greenspan wrote that it would be self-defeating (and, therefore, highly unlikely) for firms "to sell unsafe food and drugs, fraudulent securities, and shoddy buildings. It is in the self-interest of every businessman to have a reputation for honest dealings and a quality product." By 2008, in testimony to the U.S. Congress' House Committee on Oversight and Government Reform, however, Greenspan admitted the error in this line of thought:

> Those of us who have looked to the self-interest of lending institutions to protect shareholders' equity, myself included, are in a state of shocked disbelief.... This modern [free market] paradigm held sway for decades. The whole intellectual edifice, however, collapsed in the summer of last year.[210]

Greenspan's shift demonstrates the limits of the free market approach (the "efficient market hypothesis")[211] in the face of incentives that significantly distort the checks and balances that are theoretically in place. As the *Financial Times* summarized, "The intellectual impact of the crisis has already been colossal. The "Greenspanist" doctrine in monetary policy is in retreat. . . . Finance has already changed irrevocably."[212]

As such, the Financial Crisis focuses the debate back onto the personal ethics of decision makers and those organizations that foster leaders willing to make the best decisions in the long term interests of their organizations and their stakeholders. Together with the debate about what the crisis holds for the global political power balance and the form of capitalism that will drive globalization forward, the crisis also injects an element of cross-cultural understanding into an increasingly online and interconnected global business environment, where decisions taken by firms in one country have implications that can reverberate around the world. In the process, this crisis crystallizes a number of questions that highlight the importance of CSR: What does it mean for society when widespread business failure results in broad social and economic harm? How will this affect the environment in which we seek jobs and launch the firms of the future? How will societal expectations of these firms change (if at all) and how should the business community respond? And, what obligations do we have as individuals, organizations, governments, or societies to avert similar crises in the future?

Case Study: Countrywide

Countrywide is a good example of how bad things had become, in terms of corporate irresponsibility within the financial industry, prior to the downturn:

> More than any other lending institution, Countrywide has become synonymous with the excesses that led to the housing bubble.[213]

Countrywide,[214] founded in 1969 by Angelo Mozilo and David Loeb, was a mortgage lender that aggressively sought to expand its market share by "promoting homeownership for as many Americans as possible."[215] As the firm became more successful, however, particularly in the early 1990s, external pressures to maintain that success led to the search for growing numbers of customers and increasing amounts of money to loan them. Initially, the growth strategy continued and, by 2006, "Countrywide had 800 consumer branches, 54,000 employees and about $200 billion in assets."[216] But, as the pursuit of ever-greater growth became more difficult, the temptation to compromise Countrywide's loan qualification standards became too great. It proved to be a short step from granting mortgages to customers who met standard qualifications, to a more liberal interpretation of those standards, to the development of riskier financial products that would expand the potential pool of applicants:

> When the great refinancing wave of 2003 came to a close, [Countrywide] scrambled to maintain volume by offering riskier types of loans and encouraging Americans to pull the equity out of their house and spend the proceeds.[217]

At the height of the boom, the subprime mortgage industry in the U.S. had clearly lost all sense of proportion so that, "In Bakersfield, Calif., a Mexican strawberry picker with an income of $14,000 and no English was lent every penny he needed to buy a house for $720,000."[218] The result was higher default rates and, as a consequence, higher rates of home repossessions:

> Between 2005 and 2007, which was the peak of sub-prime lending, the top 25 subprime originators made almost $1,000bn in loans to more than 5m borrowers, many of whom have [since] had their homes repossessed.[219]

In Countrywide's case, the pursuit of profit without consideration for the societal implications led to a rapid growth in Alt A and subprime mortgages (mortgages given to under-qualified homeowners) that triggered the financial crisis. The blame should be spread far and wide ("Some commentators pointed to the SEC changing a rule in 2004 to expand the amount of debt that banks could carry. Others cited Congress's 1999 repeal of the Glass-Steagall Act, which threw open banks' doors to investment banking"),[220] but ultimately, it was the system that was at fault. Individual mortgage brokers were only responding to incentives that had been devised to encourage short-term revenue maximization, rather than a longer-term focus on the sustainable expansion of the housing market:

> Countrywide, determined to gain market share, kept making high-risk loans well into 2007 as the housing market began to crumble. . . . The managers also believed that their bonuses would rise indefinitely, or at least as long as the company continued to expand. . . . Greed and wishful thinking prevailed.[221]

Mallen Baker argues that, within the financial industry, the potential for this kind of abuse is higher than in other industries. While firms, in general, benefit from striving to meet the needs and demands of their customers, he suggests that this relationship is weaker for those firms that sell products that their consumers do not necessarily need and do not fully understand:

> If someone wants a tin of beans from a supermarket, they can immediately see whether that retailer has the product actually in stock, and they can pretty easily compare the price of that tin of beans with identical products being sold elsewhere. But, if you could fleece the customer and knowingly sell products that don't wholly meet their needs, but are immensely profitable, would you do it?[222]

Baker's accusation is that the underlying logic of the financial sector is confusion (of the consumer), combined with a fundamental legitimacy (people know, in principle, that it is important to save and invest money):

> Many banks in different countries will offer a basic deposit account to put your money into which is free if you stay in credit. They will also provide a number of outlets for you to withdraw cash for free as well. . . . Beyond that, the logic of the industry rewards complexity.[223]

The result of this short-term focus and rapid expansion of the mortgage market was a service that undermined trust and proved to be very costly for Countrywide.

While costly for this particular firm, however, it became disastrous when extrapolated to the level of the national and global economic system:

> It took Fannie [Mae] and Freddie [Mac] over three decades to acquire $2 trillion in mortgages and mortgage-backed securities. Together, they held $2.1 trillion in 2000. By 2005, the two [Government-sponsored Enterprises] GSEs held $4 trillion, up 92% in just five years. By 2008, they'd grown another 24%, to nearly $5 trillion. . . . [Critics estimate that] $1 trillion of this debt was subprime and "liar loans," almost all bought between 2005 and 2007.[224]

In terms of the U.S. housing market, large numbers of excessive mortgages loaned to people who were unable to repay the loans or keep up payments resulted in large numbers of foreclosures and repossessions. The recession that followed the bursting of the housing bubble exacerbated this problem. By early 2009, "1 million owners [had] lost homes since 2006 and 5.9 million more expected to do so over the next four years."[225] By 2011:

> The Standard & Poor's/Case-Shiller 20-city index of prices has fallen back to where it was in 2003. Housing prices in Phoenix are at 2000 levels, and Las Vegas is revisiting 1999. . . . With the homeownership rate possibly headed to its pre-bubble level of 64 percent from 69 percent at the peak, . . . the nation needs 1.6 million fewer homes than it now has. . . . Three of 10 homes . . . are now sold for a loss. American homeowners have equity (market value minus mortgage debt) equal to 38 percent of their homes' worth, down a third since 2005 and half what it was in 1950.[226]

While Countrywide became the face of the mortgage-fueled asset bubble in the U.S., therefore, it was by no means the only transgressor. In addition to the role played by Fannie Mae and Freddie Mac, who, in 2008, owned "almost half of all American mortgages,"[227] Washington Mutual faced similar accusations of improper lending practices, with equally devastating consequences:

> At WaMu, getting the job done meant lending money to nearly anyone who asked for it—the force behind the bank's meteoric rise and its precipitous collapse [in 2008] in the biggest bank failure in American history. On a financial landscape littered with wreckage, WaMu . . . stands out as a singularly brazen case of lax lending. By the first half of [2008], the value of its bad loans had reached $11.5 billion, nearly tripling from $4.2 billion a year earlier.[228]

A similar fate occurred at the mortgage lender Northern Rock, which became the face of the financial crisis in the UK. Northern Rock's collapse and eventual nationalization prompted the first run on a British bank since 1866. The mortgage lender was eventually nationalized in February 2008[229] with a large capital injection by the British government:

> [Northern Rock] had seen its debt to the government balloon to £29.6bn at the end of 2007 as it struggled to survive, while its savings deposits, decimated by the run on the bank by anxious customers, shrank by almost £14bn in six months to £10.5bn.[230]

The damage in the UK was not limited only to Northern Rock, however. Ultimately, the "losses that UK banks suffered in 2008-2009 wiped out roughly half of the economic value added – wages, salaries, and gross profits – that the banking sector generated between 2001 and 2007."[231] All of this occurred, in spite of warning signs by prominent, independent observers:

> As early as 1993, the Interfaith Center on Corporate Responsibility was filing shareholder resolutions raising red flags on predatory subprime lending.[232]

The industry, as a whole, experienced all the signs of a bubble, the aftermath of which generated dramatic headlines such as "Sex, Lies, and Mortgage Deals."[233] As a society, we should have picked this up earlier and acted to diffuse it. As such, the mortgage-fueled asset bubble and the corresponding financial crisis highlight the central role of CSR in today's global business environment. It is a lens through which excesses can be minimized, risk can be mitigated, and social value can be maximized. When organizations lack a CSR perspective they endanger themselves, but they can also cause great harm to society. Countrywide Financial and Merrill Lynch, for example, the biggest firms in their market space, have disappeared as independent entities due to the socially *irresponsible* manner in which they were run. A short-term profit maximization mindset, without socially-oriented guiding principles (i.e., without CSR), is a moral issue for individual employees and an issue of survival for the organization:

> The price was attractive. There was money to make on the deal. Was it responsible? Irrelevant. It was legal, and others were making money that way. And the consequences for the banking system if everybody did it? Not our problem. Now we are paying the price in trillions of dollars for that imprudent attitude. . . . Responsibility means awareness of the system consequences of our actions. It is not a luxury, it is the cornerstone of prudence.[234]

Unscrupulous individual decision making, combined with executives' abdication of their fiduciary responsibilities to protect the long-term interests of shareholders, add up to irresponsible levels of risk that, ultimately, threatened the existence of many firms:

> On June 25, 2008 California Attorney Jerry Brown Jr. sued Countrywide Financial, CEO Angelo Mozilo, and president David Sambol, for "engaging in deceptive advertising and unfair competition by pushing homeowners into mass-produced, risky loans for the sole purpose of reselling the mortgages on the secondary market." . . . [and devised specific schemes] to mislead and deceive borrowers into taking out risky, costly and complex subprime and adjustable rate mortgage (ARM) loans that were inappropriate for most homeowners.[235]

After increasing an amazing 25,000 percent from 1982 to August 2007, Countrywide's share price "plummeted more than 90 percent, to around $4, in February 2008. At the nudging of government officials, Bank of America bought the lender for $4 billion, or roughly $4.25 a share, in July 2008.[236] In order to purchase Countrywide, BofA received approval from the Federal Reserve's Board of Directors and, "on October 16, 2008, Countrywide announced it would delist its stock."[237] Why BofA purchased Countrywide is not clear. The acquisition, together with the firm's assumption of responsibility for Countrywide's bad debts, contributed towards a $1.79bn loss in the fourth quarter of 2008—the bank's first quarterly loss in 17 years,[238] as well as adding $20bn to the $25bn in bailout money the firm had already received from the U.S. government.[239] On April 27, 2009, Bank of America 'quietly retired' the Countrywide brand:

> BofA bought Countrywide in [2008] in a deal valued at $4.1bn after the biggest US mortgage lender ran aground on multi-billion-dollar losses. The bank is renaming Countrywide's operations as part of Bank of America Home Loans, ending four decades of a brand established by Angelo Mozilo, former chief executive.[240]

CSR Newsletters: Goldman Sachs

In a blog entry,[241] the comedian, Andrew Borowitz, presents a cutting commentary to the Occupy Wall Street protests. It is a mock "Letter to Investors," supposedly from Lloyd Blankfein, Goldman Sachs' CEO:

> Up until now, Goldman Sachs has been silent on the subject of the protest movement known as Occupy Wall Street. That does not mean,

however, that it has not been very much on our minds. As thousands have gathered in Lower Manhattan, passionately expressing their deep discontent with the status quo, we have taken note of these protests. And we have asked ourselves this question:

How can we make money off them?

The answer is the newly launched Goldman Sachs Global Rage Fund, whose investment objective is to monetize the Occupy Wall Street protests as they spread around the world. At Goldman, we recognize that the capitalist system as we know it is circling the drain – but there's plenty of money to be made on the way down.

The letter continues to provide details about the firm's proposed Global Rage Fund, which sounds like a good investment:

The Rage Fund will seek out opportunities to invest in products that are poised to benefit from the spreading protests, from police batons and barricades to stun guns and forehead bandages. Furthermore, as clashes between police and protesters turn ever more violent, we are making significant bets on companies that manufacture replacements for broken windows and overturned cars, as well as the raw materials necessary for the construction and incineration of effigies.

What is clever and telling about the spoof letter is that it is not hard to imagine someone at Goldman Sachs thinking something similar to these thoughts (and even perhaps writing them down). Most good comedy contains at least an element of truth!

In June, 2009, the Securities and Exchange Commission in the U.S. charged Mozilo and his top two executives with fraud, "alleging that they misled investors about the financial condition of the mortgage company in the months leading up to its sale to Bank of America":[242]

In October 2010, Mr. Mozilo agreed to pay $22.5 million to settle federal charges that he misled investors about Countrywide's risky loan portfolio. The settlement was the largest penalty levied by the Securities and Exchange Commission against a senior executive of a public company. As part of the deal,

Mr. Mozilo, who did not admit or deny wrongdoing, also agreed to forfeit $45 million in 'ill-gotten gains.'[243]

In terms of the firm's legacy for Bank of America, the acquisition continues to represent a drain on profits as the bank moves to wind down its involvement in the mortgage market.[244] In terms of various costs and fines related to Countrywide, Bank of America has paid $17.7 billion in losses in the bank's loan and insurance business, $22 billion in mortgage-security repurchases settlements, $8.4 billion in loan modification settlements, $600 million in pension fund settlements, $108 million in a settlement with the Federal Trade Commission, and $67.5 million in fraud-suit settlement involving Angelo Mozilo. And, "Bank of America still faces the prospect of billions of dollars in fines from U.S. and state regulators investigating foreclosure procedures. That mess could cost about $7.4 billion."[245] In short:

['Buying Countrywide] turned out to be the worst decision we ever made,' said one Bank of America director who voted for the Countrywide deal.[246]

CEO Perspective

Angelo Mozilo (Countrywide)

Countrywide was one of the greatest companies in the history of this country. . . . [I am] proud of what we accomplished. . . . [Countrywide's stock grew] 25,000 percent over 25 years – a much better performance than Warren Buffett at Berkshire Hathaway. This is documented.[247]

Online Resources

- Adbusters, https://www.adbusters.org/
- Countrywide Watch, Center for Responsible Lending, http://www.responsiblelending.org/mortgage-lending/research-analysis/unfair-and-unsafe.html
- Federal Reserve, Financial Crisis, http://www.federalreserve.gov/newsevents/lectures/about.htm
- Federal Reserve Bank of St. Louis, Financial Crisis Timeline, http://timeline.stlouisfed.org/

- International Monetary Fund—Financial Crisis, https://www.imf.org/external/np/exr/key/finstab.htm
- Mallen Baker's website, http://www.mallenbaker.net/csr/
- Martin Wolf's blog at the *Financial Times*, http://blogs.ft.com/economistsforum/
- Mortgage Bankers Association, http://www.mbaa.org/
- Occupy Wall Street, http://occupywallst.org/
- Summit on the Future of the Corporation, http://www.summit2020.org/
- World Bank—Financial Crisis, http://www.worldbank.org/financialcrisis/

Pro/Con Debate

> **Pro/Con Debate:** The Occupy Wall Street campaign was a success.

Questions for Discussion and Review

1. In your view, what were the main causes of the Financial Crisis?

2. Given your answer to question 1, what are the main solutions? What form of global economic system should we be striving to create?

3. What role does CSR play in the crisis—what were the CSR lapses that helped cause the crisis and how does CSR help us find a solution? View Bill Gates' speech at 2008 World Economic Forum at Davos at: http://www.youtube.com/watch?v=Ql-Mtlx31e8. What do you think?

4. What reforms would you recommend to a mortgage lender in terms of its employee incentives to ensure it avoids Countrywide's mistakes? In general, how do you motivate sales people who work on commission (as the majority of mortgage brokers did in the run-up to the Financial Crisis)? How can a company encourage them to sell products that are in their customers', rather than their own, interests?

5. How many credit cards do you carry? What loans have you taken out? Do you think that reform of the credit-fueled economic model in the U.S. is essential for a more equitable global economy? In general, to what extent is it *fair* to ask the U.S. to make any sacrifices in its standard of living for the benefit of the rest of the world?

MICROFINANCE

CSR Connection:	This issue reinforces the idea that finance and personal (micro) loans encourage entrepreneurship and other positive social outcomes. It also explores the limits of the microfinance business model.
Stakeholders:	Creditors, Debtors, Entrepreneurs, Governments.

Issue

One of the biggest barriers to development in any area of the world is access to finance. This barrier is even greater in developing economies and in poorer communities in the developed world. This lack of provision is a result of large financial institutions that ignore poorer economic regions and consumers at "the bottom of the pyramid"[248] who, traditionally, have not been thought of as a profitable target market. Why is this so? Are poorer people more of a credit risk? Does the bureaucracy involved in administering loans for smaller amounts offer lower and less attractive margins for the lenders? Is there a market for companies willing to loan in smaller amounts to more-difficult-to-reach, non-traditional customers and markets around the world?

One solution to the provision of finance in poorer economic regions is *microfinance*.[249] Microfinance is a broad term that encompasses the range of personal financial services (e.g., loans, accounts, insurance, and money transfers), but are provided on a smaller scale to meet the specific needs of poorer consumers. Micro-credit, or microloans, therefore, is a sub-component of microfinance, in which financial institutions provide small amounts of money, as a loan "without any collateral and often without any written contract,"[250] to finance specific entrepreneurial projects. In practice, however, *microfinance* has become the general term that is applied to those financial services provided to consumers who have traditionally been ignored by mainstream financial institutions.[251]

Case Study: Grameen Bank

Microfinance, which aims to serve the estimated 2.5 billion adults "lacking access to financial services,"[252] was "invented" in Bangladesh by the Bangladesh Rehabilitation Assistance Committee (BRAC). BRAC is "the largest NGO in the world by the number of employees and the number of people it has helped (three-quarters of all Bangladeshis have benefited in one way or another)."[253] An important part of the assistance the NGO provides is access to very small loans, which are then used to invest in entrepreneurial projects.

Although BRAC invented the concept of extending micro loans to the poorest people in society; today, the microfinance industry is synonymous with the name Muhammad Yunus and his Grameen Bank. It was Yunus who realized the potential mass application of microfinance. His vital contribution was to introduce effective accountability. Specifically, by targeting the loans to groups of women who knew each other (living in the same neighborhoods or villages) and holding weekly meetings to provide peer group support (and pressure) for those who were struggling to repay, Yunus generated very high loan repayment rates. The value of these high repayment rates (historically 97% and up) is that they allow him to lend money to people who have no collateral assets to guarantee a loan and, therefore, who cannot qualify for help from traditional financial organizations. With this business model, BRAC and Grameen have flourished ("Grameen has 8.4m borrowers and outstanding loans of over $1 billion; BRAC has 5m borrowers and loans of $725m"[254]), but it is Yunus who created a worldwide industry:

In the beginning, microfinance sought to alleviate poverty by giving out tiny loans to help people start small businesses. Popularized by Bangladeshi economist and Nobel Peace Prize laureate Muhammad Yunus and Grameen Bank, which he founded in 1983, the microfinance industry has since grown to hundreds of institutions serving more than 150 million borrowers worldwide.[255]

Grameen Bank by the Numbers[256]

Some statistics that reflect the growing reach and scale of microfinance, in general, and the success of Grameen Bank, in particular:

- More than 8 million customers.
- $10.3 billion lent since it began operations in 1976.
- Historical loan recovery rate of 97%.
- The bank "has doubled the number of its offices over the past 10 years to more than 2,900 and employees to some 23,000, including more than 13,000 loan officers, nearly all women."
- "The average loan balance per borrower is $123, with the cost per borrower over the years hovering between $8 and $13 annually."
- "As of 2009, Grameen had $1.5 billion of assets and a return on equity of 5.64%."

Today, Grameen has applied the same principles across numerous industries and has created a global empire:

Muhammad Yunus . . . founded Grameen Bank in 1983 to provide tiny loans to poor rural women. Grameen became a global model for microfinance. It also spawned 48 other firms in sectors that stretch from textiles to mobile phones. . . . the Grameen network [now] includes assets worth an estimated $1.6 billion.[257]

CSR Newsletters: Muhammad Yunus

An interview in *The New York Times*[258] with Muhammad Yunus provides interesting background information on how Grameen Bank's micro-credit system works, the impact it has had on the societies in which it operates, as well as Yunus' philosophy regarding the value of social entrepreneurship over charity and philanthropy:

Q. Can you talk a little about the relative merits of nonprofit microcredit versus it as a business model and whether that is more sustainable, perhaps?

A. First of all, I'm not in favor of nonprofit things. These are charities. I'm not involved in that. I don't particularly get excited about it. I'm talking about the business part of it where you do things so that you get your money back. . . . So one is a profit-maximizing business. The other is a social business. I'm on the social business side of it. If somebody wants to run it as a profit-maximizing business, welcome. This is competition. My mission is to get the person out of poverty rather than how much money I'm making out of it.

Microfinance is used to encourage entrepreneurial activity within poorer communities. Microloans (which can range from as little as $10, but are more normally defined as beginning at $50) have had a huge impact in many parts of the developing world. Ultimately, the aim is to "foster sustainable economic activity at the grassroots" in economic regions that otherwise have difficulty gaining access to adequate amounts of capital, such as Africa:

In Uganda . . . 245,000 families have borrowed from village banks run by international and local agencies. The money has been used to start everything from rabbit farms to grocery stores. Microlenders "are reaching more people than Uganda's entire commercial banking sector." . . . A bank started by FINCA [Foundation for International Community Assistance, which runs a global network of microcredit banks] . . . has 36,000 clients borrowing an average of $137—and boasts an 11% return on equity.[259]

In an attempt to raise the profile of microfinance and encourage greater provision of this service to the poorer regions of the world, the United Nations declared 2005 to be the International Year of Microcredit.[260] This recognition grew when the 2006 Nobel Peace Prize was awarded jointly to Grameen Bank and Yunus,[261] while annual awards such as the *Financial Times'* Sustainable Banking Awards highlight industry best practice. The main barrier to a more rapid expansion of microfinance, however, has historically been the high interest rates associated with such loans. These are caused by a lack of financers competing to make loans available to poorer clients and also by the high transaction costs associated with making many small loans. This is beginning to change, however, as the early success of microfinance, increased availability of efficient systems to manage the numerous loans, and relatively low risk associated with such high rates of repayment are beginning to generate greater interest from more mainstream financial institutions.[262]

Perhaps the most important driver of this growing interest from commercial operators is the industry's high loan repayment rates. Accion,[263] one of the leading nonprofits operating in the field of microfinance, for example, consistently achieves exceptionally high repayment rates on its micro-loans. Specifically, "Accion's network, operating in 23 countries, boasts a repayment rate of 97% on some $7.6 billion of loans to more than 4.7 million people."[264] In contrast, "U.S. credit card issuers typically charge off around 5% of outstanding balances."[265]

Accion in 2011[266]

- Active borrowers: 5.1 million.
- Active loan portfolio: $5.5 billion.
- Active savers: 2.1 million.
- Active savings deposits: $2.7 billion.

(Continued)

(Continued)

Accion (2001–2011)

- Total number of borrowers: 13.2 million.
- Total number of micro loans: 55.7 million.
- Total amount lent: $46 billion.
- Loan repayment rate (worldwide):   97 percent.

As a result of such high repayment rates, the opportunity to lend to a large and underserved percentage of the world's population represents an extremely viable business model. High rates of return rival those of commercial banks and range from "about 6% a year, with the best-performing funds returning three or four times that amount":[267]

> Studies conducted in India, Kenya and the Philippines found that the average annual return on investments by microbusinesses ranged from 117% to 847%, according to the United Nations.[268]

Traditionally, microfinance institutions have relied on aid and government lending to finance their activities. As such, the growing interests of more commercial banks is ironic, since it was their rejection of this market segment (i.e., very small loans to poorer borrowers) that led to the gap in provision that Yunus initially sought to fill.[269] In particular, funds for microfinance-backed projects are increasingly available via socially responsible investment funds,[270] venture capital,[271] and multinational banks:[272]

> Emerging markets bank Standard Charter, for example, in May [2008] had an outstanding microfinance portfolio of $180m. . . . In early October, New York-based Citigroup announced the opening of two micro-credit firms in China's Hubei province. . . . London headquarterd HSBC and Standard Chartered entered the Chinese microfinance sector last year.[273]

Multinational corporations that operate in consumer product markets also benefit indirectly from microfinance. By taking out small loans from microfinance institutions, local businesswomen form networks of intermediaries that sell products in hard-to-reach rural areas for firms such as Unilever and its Indian subsidiary, Hindustan Lever:

> Today, about 13,000 poor women [many of whom received start-up micro-loans] are selling Unilever's products in about 50,000 villages in India's 12 states and account for about 15% of the company's rural sales in those states. Overall, rural markets account for about 30% of Hindustan Lever's revenue.[274]

And, Yunus claims, it is microfinance's reliance on this *real* economy that insulated it from the Financial Crisis:

> The simple reason is because we are rooted to the real economy—we are not paper-based, paper-chasing banking. When we give a loan of $100, behind the $100 there are chickens, there are cows. It is not something imaginary.[275]

Increased innovation, aided especially by the spread of mobile phones, is allowing institutions to expand their potential customer base. Studies suggest that, in the near future, "mobile phone payment systems could be available to 15 per cent of the world's 3bn unbanked people."[276] In South Africa, for example, "Less than half of South Africans have bank accounts, but nine out of 10 own a mobile phone:"[277]

> Mobile technology has the potential to offer cheap no-frills banking, at low risk, because transactions are monitored in real-time, on widely-used, high-quality infrastructure.[278]

The potential for economic gain, tied to social progress, is great. As *The Economist* notes, "in a typical developing country, a rise of ten mobile phones per 100 people boosts GDP growth by 0.6 percentage points."[279] In spite of all this activity, however, there is evidence that demand for microfinance continues to outstrip available supply, which remains inconsistent from country-to-country. In 2009, according to the International Finance Corporation (part of the World Bank Group), the "penetration of microfinance in Brazil and Argentina is about 3 per cent. This means that for every 100 microenterprises that would be eligible for microfinance products, only three are currently being served. However, the rate in Paraguay, Chile and Peru is between 25 and 35 per cent. In Bolivia, . . . the IFC says penetration is more than 160 per cent."[280]

In response to this market opportunity, the danger is twofold: First, in the search for greater application, the purpose of microloans will be corrupted, with reports growing that "Microloans are most often used for something [other than entrepreneurial projects], such as financing the purchase of consumer durables or repaying debts to moneylenders."[281] And second, that as more and more for-profit institutions enter the market, they will distort the microfinance business model as they pursue economic returns over social value at ever-higher rates of interest:

> A credit crisis is brewing in "microfinance," the business of making the tiniest loans in the world. . . . "We fear a bubble, . . . Too much money is chasing too few good candidates." . . . In India, microloans outstanding grew 72% in the year ended March 31, 2008, totaling $1.24 billion, according to Sa-Dhan, an industry association in New Delhi.[282]

Ultimately, this quote proved prescient. Shortly afterwards, in 2010 and 2011, two incidents rocked the microfinance world—one in Bangladesh and one in India. The combination of the two events threw a shadow over the whole industry and threatened the gains Yunus had made in expanding access to finance for the poor. The first incident involved Yunus himself. Following an attempt to form a political party to promote reform within his native Bangladesh, Yunus experienced strong political backlash from entrenched powers who felt threatened by such a high-profile star in domestic politics. The Prime Minster, Ms. Sheikh Hasina, in particular, went out of her way to criticize the microfinance industry, in general, and Yunus, in particular:

> "Microlenders make the people of this country their guinea pig," she said. "They are sucking blood from the poor in the name of poverty alleviation."[283]

As a result of the political battle (which was stimulated by a dubious accusation of tax evasion against Yunus),[284] in April, 2011, Yunus was forced out of his position as head of Grameen Bank, officially for exceeding the legal retirement age for public employees. The court-ordered dismissal was accompanied with calls for reform of Grameen Bank's governance controls. A state-appointed committee, in particular, determined that Grameen had broken the law by expanding from a microfinance organization into "a business empire ranging from telecoms to solar lighting" and that Yunus was acting without effective oversight:

> The panel concluded that Grameen Bank's 12-member board of directors, of whom nine are elected representatives of the lender's impoverished women borrowers, was ill equipped to fulfill its oversight role, leaving the vast institution to run largely unchallenged by its charismatic founder.[285]

The second incident followed a controversial IPO by the Indian microfinance company, SKS Microfinance. Shortly prior to the August 2010 IPO, which raised a total of $358 million in capital and valued SKS at $1.5 billion, the firm's founder

(Vikram Akula) sold shares amounting to $13 million. The sudden display of wealth by Akula contrasted strongly with the poverty of most of the people who borrowed money from his firm and caused a backlash from Indian politicians who accused SKS and other microfinance organizations of "seeking 'hyper-profits' from the poor through over-lending and 'coercive' collection tactics."[286] As a result of the ensuing public debate about the expansion of for-profit firms into what had traditionally been a nonprofit space, collection rates plummeted across India and fundamental questions were raised that challenged whether microfinance was, in fact, beneficial for the poor. Firms were accused of pursuing rapid growth by lowering lending standards (in order to increase borrowers) and increasing interest rates (in order to raise profits), with the consequence that default rates and greater indebtedness also increased. As investigations were made, it became apparent that these concerns were not isolated:

> Already in the past two years, Morocco, Bosnia, Nicaragua, and Pakistan have all been hit by microloan repayment crises. The Consultative Group to Assist the Poor, a World Bank-linked group seeking to improve financial access for the disadvantaged, blames the upheavals on lending that devoted inadequate attention to borrowers' ability to repay.[287]

As SKS's share price dropped,[288] Akula was forced to resign from his post as Executive Chairman of SKS amid further calls for reforms of the microfinance industry and the firms that:

> . . . were earning record profits even as they charged poor women interest rates of 30 to 65 percent. There was also growing evidence that the micro-credit, even if it did give the poor a small boost, often did not lift them out of poverty. . . . And a sizable minority of borrowers appeared to have become overly indebted because of the ease with which they could borrow money from competing lenders.[289]

CSR Newsletters: Microfinance

An article in *The Wall Street Journal*[290] discusses some of the problems that have resulted from the recent explosion in growth of the microfinance industry. To some degree, microfinance is becoming a victim of its own success.

(Continued)

(Continued)

In general, the microfinance industry has been altered by the influx of for-profit firms that are attracted by a business model that relies on the high repayment rates that are typical within the sector. With profit as a stronger focus, however, these new microfinance lenders are increasing interest rates and introducing much more liberal criteria for extending credit. One consequence of this is the continued success of traditional moneylenders in India (who charge much higher interest rates), who are flourishing in spite of the success of microfinance. It turns out that the source of the high repayment rates for microfinance is also the source of the microlenders' ongoing success:

> Some microfinance borrowers say they need village moneylenders to help them pay their debts on time. . . . Peer pressure to pay back microfinance loans is intense, because microlenders almost always require borrowers to join small, tightknit groups. If one member defaults, none can get another loan. Microloans have a stellar repayment rate—close to 100%—and some analysts believe a hidden reason is the stopgap provided by moneylenders.

Borrowers are willing to put up with higher interest rates in order to get easier access to credit and avoid the social ramifications of failing to meet their microfinance commitments:

> . . . the moneylenders are virtually indistinguishable from the microlenders. They distribute knock-off versions of the microlenders' passbooks. Some use the same weekly repayment structure and door-to-door service as the microlenders do. The difference, however, is that the moneylenders give loans faster, without asking the women to form groups and serve as each other's guarantors, as microfinance lenders do in order to ensure a higher repayment rate. They also charge significantly more than the four microlenders serving the neighborhood.

In the aftermath of these two crises, debate in many countries (but primarily India and Bangladesh, which "together account for half of all borrowers")[291] focused on the operating practices of microfinance organizations. In particular, reforms were proposed to combat high default rates as a result of over-indebtedness (by stipulating maximum loan amounts), usury (by capping interest rates), and rapid industry growth (by drafting stricter regulations). From a CSR perspective, however, as the microfinance industry evolves, it provides a fascinating case-study of the limits of the profit motivation in areas which have traditionally not supported competitive markets. Public firms with large numbers of shareholders face pressures to grow. It is not profit, per se, that constrains the role of commercial firms in the microfinance industry, but the pressures to maintain year-on-year increases in profit that create bubbles and have particular limitations within social markets. Many decades ago, Muhammad Yunus had already thought through this problem and challenged the idea that for-profit firms could be effective guardians of the microfinance business model:

> Microfinance is mission-driven banking. When you float an IPO you are telling your investors there is a good opportunity to make money off poor people. The message is wrong, the direction is wrong. . . . Staunch believers of market forces keep saying competition will bring business to people who are now unreached. Over centuries, this has not happened. Competition never brought credit to the poor; it only took it to richer people. That is the route the IPO will take them.[292]

It will be interesting to see how the industry solves these tensions between the business (public and private), societal, and political forces in the coming years, especially as the stronger role for regulators that emerged from the turmoil is beginning to revive the industry.[293]

CEO Perspective

Muhammad Yunus (Grameen Bank)

When a destitute mother starts earning an income, her dreams of success invariably center around her children. A woman's second priority is the household. She wants to buy utensils, build a stronger roof, or find a bed for herself and her family. A man has an entirely different set of priorities. When a destitute father earns extra income, he focuses more attention on himself. Thus money entering a household through a woman brings more benefits to the family as a whole.[294]

Online Resources

- Association for Enterprise Opportunity, http://www.microenterpriseworks.org/
- Community Development Financial Institutions, http://www.cdfifund.gov/
- Community Investing Center, http://www.communityinvest.org/
- Community Reinvestment Act, http://www.ffiec.gov/cra/
- Consultative Group to Assist the Poor (CGAP), http://cgap.org/
- FINCA, http://www.villagebanking.org/
- Goldman Sachs, 10,000 Women, http://www.goldmansachs.com/10000women
- Grameen Foundation, http://www.grameenfoundation.org/
- Hand in Hand, http://www.hihseed.org/
- Microfinace Gateway, http://www.microfinancegateway.org/
- Microfinance Information eXchange, http://www.themix.org/
- Socialfunds.com, http://www.socialfunds.com/
- SKS Microfinance, http://www.sksindia.com/
- Women's World Banking Network, http://www.swwb.org/

Pro/Con Debate

Pro/Con Debate: Given the high loan repayment rates, commercial financial firms have a duty to enter the microfinance market.

Questions for Discussion and Review

1. Visit the Accion International website at http://www.accion.org/. What are your impressions and thoughts regarding the work this organization is doing?

2. Why do microfinance organizations have significantly higher repayment rates (97% and above) than for-profit banks in developed economies?

3. To what extent do you think there is a successful business model for microfinance in the developed economies (such as North America and Europe)?

4. What do you think of efforts by firms such as Goldman Sachs to become involved in the microfinance industry (e.g., http://www.goldmansachs.com/10000women)?

5. Given what you have read in the case, are you optimistic or pessimistic about the future of microfinance? Why is that so?

PROFIT

CSR Connection:	This issue forms an essential component of the CSR debate. The best of intentions aside, a bankrupt company does not benefit any of its stakeholders. Profits are essential to the survival of the firm and, as such, form a core component of the strategic CSR argument.
Stakeholders:	Customers, Company, Communities.

Issue

By definition, profit is what drives all *for-profit* organizations. The pursuit of profit underwrites market-based economies and forces companies constantly to innovate and progress by meeting society's developmental needs. Profit is also cited by business leaders as a reason for *not* being able to pursue CSR. In this perspective, CSR represents a short-term cost that the firm has a duty to minimize in order to be as profitable as possible and maximize returns to investors. The goal of *Strategic CSR* is to overcome this perceived divide between profit and CSR.

An argument for CSR as an essential component of firm strategy and operations, therefore, assumes that CSR and profit are not mutually exclusive goals. On the contrary, given today's globalized, online world, we argue that CSR is the most effective means to ensure long-term viability via the firm's social license to operate. As such, the merging of the pursuit of profit and integration of CSR within corporate strategy renders a *short*-term, profit-only approach increasingly untenable. Combined with the increasing pressure placed on companies today to perform consistently, over the *medium* to *longer* term, managers need to be as innovative and progressive as possible in implementing the firm's vision, mission, strategy, and tactics. Understanding the needs and concerns of customers is central to this task. The firms that are being most innovative in this respect cast a broader net in search of customers to serve:

> [For businesses] doing good does not necessarily rule out making a reasonable profit. You can . . . make money by serving the poor as well as the rich. . . . There is a huge neglected market in the billions of poor in the developing world. Companies like Unilever and Citicorp are beginning to adapt their technologies to enter this market. Unilever can now deliver ice cream in India for just two cents a portion because it has rethought the technology of refrigeration. Citicorp

can now provide financial services to people, also in India, who have only $25 to invest, again through rethinking technology. In both cases the companies make money, but the driving force is the need to serve neglected consumers. Profit often comes from progress.[295]

Is it OK for firms to profit from poverty? Where is the dividing line between a social mission and a valid market opportunity in an emerging market that also produces social progress? Is there any advantage in drawing such a distinction? Today, is it more helpful to think of all firms as having a social mission, but delivering varying degrees of added value?

CSR Newsletters: Intel

An article in *Fast Company Magazine*[296] contains a case study of Intel's effort to build its market presence in the developing world. Due to declining revenue in the U.S. and Europe, Intel has launched its World Ahead Program to explore market opportunities in the developing world. The scale of these potential markets underlies their importance to firms:

> Half of the global middle class lives in the developing world today. Within 25 years, that figure will be 90%, according to the World Bank's latest forecast. That will more than double, to 1 billion, the number of potential buyers for products that today are considered luxuries, including not only cars and refrigerators but also computers.

Equally interesting, however, is Intel's strategic approach to these markets—by defining its target markets a little more narrowly, the potential for success is increased:

> Intel is pursuing not the so-called bottom of the pyramid, or BOP—the billions of people who live on a few dollars a day or less—but the next billion, consumers who rank economically just below those it serves today.

This strategy differs from the BOP focus that drives much of the CSR debate on this issue. Intel seeks to deliver social value to those economies best able to afford its products over the short to medium term. As Intel's Chairman, Craig Barrett, bluntly notes, "We're not a charitable organization, . . . We're trying to foster the continued growth of our products."

It is estimated that "the richest 2 per cent of adults own more than 50 per cent of global assets, while the poorest half of the population holds only 1 per cent of wealth."[297] This means that 65% of the world's population, or 4 billion people, exist on less than $2,000 per year.[298] This section of the world forms Tier 4—the largest and bottom of the four-tier pyramid that comprises the world's population— the bottom of the pyramid (BOP). As such, these people represent a huge market segment that needs the help of the developed world, but also can pay their way in terms of buying essential and reasonably-priced products:

> Individually, the purchasing power of Tier 4 is limited. . . . But together it adds up to trillions. [Their] general wants and needs are familiar: securing better lives for their children, getting the best price for their labor, staying healthy, and having fun.[299]

Nevertheless, this "huge potential market,"[300] which the World Bank estimates to be worth "as much as $5 trillion" annually,[301] remains largely ignored by many companies.[302] What is required is an innovative approach by firms to deliver their products to places previously thought to be inaccessible, at prices previously thought to be unprofitable:

> But to be profitable, firms cannot simply edge down market, fine-tuning the products they already sell to rich customers. Instead, they must thoroughly re-engineer products to reflect the very different economics of BOP: small unit packages, low margin per unit, high volume. Big business needs to swap its usual incremental approach for an entrepreneurial mindset, because BOP markets need to be built not simply entered.[303]

A multinational that has done a lot of work in this area of "progressive profit" is Hewlett-Packard, which created e-Inclusion,[304] a business unit dedicated to creating market-based solutions to problems in developing economies using IT products:[305]

> When Hewlett-Packard launched its e-Inclusion division, which concentrates on rural markets, it established a branch of its famed HP Labs in India charged with developing products and services explicitly for this market . . . like speech interfaces for the Internet, solar applications, and cheap devices that can connect with the web. HP made e-Inclusion a business venture rather than a philanthropic one because it believes only systems that can sustain themselves economically can address the scale of the need—and in that scale is a business opportunity.[306]

For C. K. Prahalad ("perhaps the most visible proponent of the view that the globe's poor are a huge—and hugely untapped—market")[307] the business opportunity is clear.[308] It requires effort and commitment on the part of multinational corporations, but there are benefits in terms of top-line growth, reduced costs, and inspired innovation:

> If we stop thinking of the poor as victims or as a burden and start recognizing them as resilient and creative entrepreneurs and value-conscious consumers, a whole new world of opportunity will open up.[309]

CSR Newsletters: Cadbury's

An article in *The Wall Street Journal*[310] demonstrates how Cadbury's is expanding its presence in the confectionary market in India into the bottom of the pyramid:

> The candy maker's latest product for the low end of the Indian market is Cadbury Dairy Milk Shots. The pea-sized chocolate balls, which were introduced this year, are sold for just two rupees, or about four U.S. cents, for a packet of two, which weighs five grams—a fraction of an ounce. They have a sugar shell to protect them from the heat.

The potential for growth is significant:

> The British candy maker has been in India for more than 60 years and dominates the chocolate market. Still, it says, less than half of India's 1.1 billion people have ever tasted chocolate. Traditional milk-based sweets, or mithai, still dominate the industry here, where they are given and eaten at festivals.

> Although Prahalad's bottom-of-the-pyramid argument has been seized by CSR advocates as a potential hope for solving some of the developing world's social problems (and the article dutifully notes similar product targeting by firms such as Procter & Gamble and Unilever), given some of the more fundamental problems that face the poorer sections of India's society, it is hard to see how bringing chocolate to the masses constitutes social progress. The principle, however, is important—the greater the opportunity for the private sector to cater to the needs of consumers in developing economies, the greater the chance for the social progress that the private sector has instigated elsewhere.

It is important to note that Prahalad, who died in 2010, has his critics[311] who question the size of the market at the bottom of the pyramid, as well as the ability (and willingness) of multinational corporations to provide products that add significant social value:

> Much of the profitable business with lower-income markets involves products such as mobile phones, not the provision of basic nutrition, sanitation, education and shelter. . . . In addition, . . . claims about empowering people by providing means for them to consume cannot be taken at face value. The environmental impacts of changing consumption patterns also need to be looked at. . . . And we need to assess, if more foreign companies do come to serve lower income markets, might they not displace local companies and increase the resource drain from local economies?[312]

Nevertheless, it is also clear that Prahalad has had a significant influence on how firms perceive the developing world and that this has had a material impact (for better or worse) on the lives of people there.[313] Most importantly, Prahalad has helped envision a different perception of the developing world and how the developed world can and should interact with it:

> For decades, the main model of Third World aid has been the obvious: Give stuff to poor people—be it hydroelectric dams, surplus food or medical equipment. But Western countries have poured some $1.5 trillion into such efforts over the last 60 years, and more than 1 billion people worldwide still live on less than a dollar a day. . . . [Alternatively] If you design a useful product for a market rather than for charity's sake, the theory goes, the target population is more likely to actually want it and use it. If businesses can turn a profit making that product, it not only creates jobs but will keep getting made even if Western donors lose interest. And there should be colossal profits to be made: The world's poor don't have much money individually, but there are billions of them.[314]

Although all of the products being provided by multinational firms cannot be considered *essential*, there is increasing evidence that the work being done by for-profit firms, such as P&G (water),[315] Nestlé (food),[316] and Unilever (personal hygiene),[317] achieve socially beneficial outcomes (in particular in relation to public health), while also achieving for-profit goals.

Case Study: Unilever

This link between for-profit business and social progress is one that should not be in doubt. As John Mackey, CEO of Whole Foods Market notes:

In 1800, 85% of everyone alive lived on less than $1 per day (in 2000 dollars). Today only 17% do. If current long-term trend lines of economic growth continue, we will see abject poverty almost completely eradicated in the 21st century. Business is not a zero-sum game struggling over a fixed pie. Instead it grows and makes the total pie larger, creating value for all of its major stakeholders—customers, employees, suppliers, investors and communities.[318]

One of the reasons for this is that the products businesses produce enable people to pursue dreams and better their lives. A good example is mobile phones, which are becoming increasingly important in developing countries that do not have established infrastructure (such as fixed landlines) because they enable people to communicate and conduct business. Because these phones are so important, "people will skip a meal or choose to walk instead of paying for a bus fare so that they can keep their phone in credit."[319] For-profit firms produce products that fulfill peoples' aspirations, which is why economic development, rather than international aid, offers the best means for rapid social progress in the developing world.[320] And, thanks to Prahalad's work at the bottom-of-the-pyramid (BOP), multinational firms are beginning to realize the potential embedded within these non-traditional markets:

> Where do the world's poor live? The obvious answer: in poor countries. [Recent research, however, suggests] that the obvious answer is wrong. Four-fifths of those surviving on less than $2 a day . . . live in middle-income countries with a gross national income per head of between $1,000 and $12,500, not poor ones.[321]

This means that these people have disposable income; in other words, that they are consumers. As such, progressive firms have begun to explore how best to serve these markets:

> Hindustan Lever, the Indian consumer goods company 51% owned by Unilever, for example, knew that many Indians could not afford to buy a big bottle of shampoo. . . . So it created single-use packets (in three sizes, according to hair length) that go for a few cents—and now sells 4.5 billion of them a year.[322]

Unilever, in particular, has committed itself to implementing CSR as a core component of the firm's strategy and operations and has moved quickly to deliver its products to consumers in BOP markets. As part of this process, Unilever is increasingly exploring the tension between for-profit goals and non-profit priorities in the developing world:

In their work to promote handwashing, partners say Unilever tends to be in a hurry to get things done, while some donors and aid workers get entangled in their own red tape. . . . One of toughest challenges faced by Unilever's marketing experts has been to persuade partners that radio ads and roadshows need to be run at particular times of the year to be effective, and cannot always wait for consensus-building.[323]

Unilever's involvement in the campaign to increase hand washing in Uganda rests on the firm being able to get its branded soap (Lifebuoy) associated in the public's mind with hand washing. UNICEF's goal, however, is just to get people to wash their hands, but they benefit from the marketing and distribution expertise that accompanies private sector involvement. It is easy to see how the two organization's goals are compatible, while also introducing friction:

Donors would never pay for a branded campaign that told the suspicious residents of Muko to "wash your hands with Lifebuoy," Ms. Sidibe says, and some are not comfortable with a multinational brand on the same list as campaign supporters. "But they are realising it's the only way to keep us interested. It's important the brand gets recognised otherwise it's impossible to justify our involvement."[324]

CSR Newsletters: Unilever

In November 2010, Unilever launched its "sustainable living plan." As CEO, Paul Polman, announced at the launch, Unilever is an ambitious company that plans to grow:

> But growth at any cost is not viable. We want to be a sustainable business in every sense of the word. So we have developed a plan—the "Unilever Sustainable Living Plan"—that will enable billions of people to increase their quality of life—without increasing their environmental impact.

The plan was received well by the CSR community[325] due to specific targets that build on Unilever's prior CSR investments. In particular, the firm commits by 2020 to:

> Help more than 1 billion people improve their health and well-bring. Halve the environmental impact of our products. Source 100% of our agricultural raw materials sustainably.[326]

(Continued)

(Continued)

As an article in the *Financial Times* highlights,[327] Unilever sees this plan as integral to its business model and, as such, an important point of differentiation from its competitors:

> Unilever has a long history of doing well by doing good. William Lever, one of its founders, created Lifebuoy soap to encourage cleanliness and reduce infectious diseases in Victorian Britain. Today, in the developing world, 3.5m children under five die from diarrhea and respiratory infections. Teaching children to wash their hands is a way of reducing this toll. The company sees opportunities to save lives and sell soap.

What was striking about the announcement, however, was the framing of the document by Polman. Rather than focus on the cost savings to the firm in an attempt to justify the plan to investors, Polman instead issued a challenge:

> Unilever has been around for 100-plus years. We want to be around for several hundred more years. So if you buy into this long-term value-creation model, which is equitable, which is shared, which is sustainable, then come and invest with us. If you don't buy into this, I respect you as a human being, but don't put your money in our company.

Importantly, Polman stuck with this line, even in the face of a lukewarm reception by investors. In the period shortly after the announcement, "the Financial Times reported his company's shares were lagging behind both competitors' and the market." Rather than present any cause for concern, however, Polman responded by reinforcing his underlying message, while also stopping the issuing of earnings guidance to investors because "We certainly don't want to attract the investor base that wants higher and higher and quicker results against targets that we put out every 90 days." The decision to frame this announcement in an absolute moral argument, rather than a relative business argument, was refreshing, made all the more so by how unique it was:

> Ultimately, Unilever's pledge points to a new model of doing business: one in which economic growth is "decoupled" from negative social-economic costs. One company, however large, cannot shape the system. But it can signal the way.[328]

Part of the reason for Unilever's engagement is the potential to enter markets that remain relatively untouched by Western multinationals. An important incentive, therefore, is to move before the competition. P&G, for example, also sees the potential that these markets offer and is eagerly exploring how to build a business model to appeal to BOP consumers.[329] As part of its growth plan, P&G "is looking to tap roughly one billion additional consumers – most of them very poor women who live in developing countries."[330] What is clear for consumer products companies like Unilever and P&G, however, is that there are unique challenges in accessing these markets and adapting to new cultural and economic environments. These challenges range from product packaging (single portions, rather than family-size packets), to shop design and layout (smaller outlets), to different shopping habits (daily, rather than weekly trips):

> Reaching these customers isn't easy. In emerging markets, P&G estimates that 80% of people buy their wares from mom-and-pop stores no bigger than a closet. . . . Rather than stock up on full-size goods, which cost more per item, they buy small portions of soap, laundry detergent, and single diapers as they need them—even though the smaller sizes are usually sold at a premium. . . . P&G calls such locally owned bodegas, stalls and kiosks "high-frequency stores," because of the multiple times shoppers visit them during a single day or week.[331]

Improvements in logistics (distribution and supply chain management) are also essential in order to make inroads into BOP markets:

> Unilever has created a 45,000-strong army of female entrepreneurs who sell its products in 100,000 villages in 15 Indian states. Nespresso, a coffee pod-peddling arm of Nestlé, teaches its coffee suppliers to improve their yields. Procter & Gamble, a household goods firm, and Walmart, a retailer, use "sustainability scorecards" to encourage their suppliers to use less water, manage waste better and emit less greenhouse gases.[332]

These adaptations reflect an approach that demands businesses understand the markets they are attempting to enter. This requires them to listen, rather than instruct, and complement existing norms, rather than try and change them. BOP consumers have the same aspirations as consumers everywhere, but they have different expectations and needs that firms must respect if they are to be successful.[333] Getting all these different dimensions right has the added advantage of providing some insulation against the economic cycle in more developed economy markets:

Analysts have long argued that companies selling products and services to people earning less than $4 a day can outperform in tough times. This is because consumers still must buy food, soap, and other basic goods when the economy is bad, even as middle-class buyers cut back on discretionary items like fashion or gadgets.[334]

While these firms are pursuing goals associated with social development, however, it is also clear that it is the business model that is driving the expansion into emerging markets:

P&G expects developing markets to contribute 37% of its total revenues [in 2012], up from 34% in 2010 (and 23% in 2005). For Unilever, the share from developing markets is already up to 56% of sales, from 53% in 2010. . . . By 2020, Unilever expects developing markets to account for 70% of total sales.[335]

CEO Perspective

The Dalai Lama

When the Dalai Lama was asked about what surprises him most about humanity; he answered:

Man; because he sacrifices his health in order to make money; then he sacrifices his money to recuperate his health; and then he is so anxious about the future that he doesn't enjoy the present. As a result, he doesn't live in the present or the future; he lives as if he's never going to die, and then he dies having never really lived.

Online Resources

- Base of the Pyramid Protocol, http://bop-protocol.org/
- Executives Without Borders, http://www.executiveswithoutborders.org/
- Grassroots Business Fund, http://www.gbfund.org/
- HP Global Citizenship, http://www.hp.com/hpinfo/globalcitizenship/
- Inclusive Business, http://www.inclusivebusiness.org/
- Intel, World Ahead Program, http://www.intel.com/content/www/us/en/company-overview/world-ahead.html

- NextBillion.net—Development Through Enterprise, http://www.nextbillion .net/
- Unilever's Sustainable Living Plan, http://www.unilever.com/sustainable-living/
- World Resources Institute, http://www.wri.org/

Pro/Con Debate

> **Pro/Con Debate:** Firms operating at the bottom-of-the-pyramid are exploiting poor people by selling them consumer products that they do not need.

Questions for Discussion and Review

1. Is it OK for a for-profit company to profit from poverty?

2. Outline the opportunity that exists at the base of the pyramid. Can you think of a company and an existing product and how it can be modified to become profitable in the developing world?

3. Assuming a company found a profitable niche in serving the fourth tier (the four billion people at the bottom of the economic pyramid), how might such a breakthrough benefit the firm in selling to the developed world at the top of the economic pyramid?

4. Have a look at Unilever's Sustainable Living Plan (http://www.unilever .com/sustainable-living/). Before reading the case, were you aware of this initiative? Does it change your impression of Unilever at all? Is this plan CSR, or strategy, or both? Why?

5. What is your reaction to the following statement by Unilever's CEO, Paul Polman, at the launch of Unilever's Sustainable Living Plan?

   Unilever has been around for 100-plus years. We want to be around for several hundred more years. So if you buy into this long-term value-creation model, which is equitable, which is shared, which is sustainable, then come and invest with us. If you don't buy into this, I respect you as a human being, but don't put your money in our company.[336]

SUPPLY CHAIN

> **CSR Connection:** This issue highlights the complexities of CSR when dealing with conflicting values in different cultures. This is a particular problem for multinational corporations that source their products in many different countries, but need to try and satisfy all stakeholders.
>
> **Stakeholders:** Suppliers, Employees, Governments.

While the *Ethical Sourcing* issue earlier in this chapter presents the strategic advantages to the firm of an ethical supply chain, this *Supply Chain* issue covers the dangers to the firm of an unethical supply chain.

Issue

To what extent do business practices contribute to the community in which the organization is based and operating? Increasingly, firms are becoming more global, with markets in many different countries and cultures. One consequence is that companies are relocating operations offshore, which often means that jobs are lost at home and gained by the countries to which the companies relocate. Whether this represents an overall gain or loss for society in general, however, is not clear.

The upside of this aspect of globalization is that firms are able to locate operations in the region of the world that makes most business sense. These decisions can be justified in terms of distribution logistics (proximity to market) or simply in terms of efficiencies (lower costs and fewer regulations). This mix of determining factors can generate unusual situations where a Ford Mustang is assembled using parts largely manufactured outside of the U.S., while a Toyota Sienna is assembled in Indiana with 90% of its parts originating in the U.S. and Canada.[337] And, the longer a supply chain becomes, the more complex it becomes—to the point where "a shirt imported to the US from Hong Kong includes tasks of workers from as many as 10 countries":[338]

It is why Pascal Lamy, chief of the World Trade Organization, argues that terms like "made in America" or "made in China" are phasing out. The proper term, says Lamy, is "made in the world." More products are designed everywhere, made everywhere and sold everywhere.[339]

The complexity of today's global supply chains represents the daily operating reality for multinational firms in the twenty-first century:

> Wal-Mart counts about 60,000 suppliers. Tesco has some 6,000 in Britain alone. IBM's network is made up of 28,000 suppliers spread across 90 countries. Unilever has a solid claim to the biggest supply network, with 160,000 companies providing it with goods and services.[340]

The downside of this movement of operations affects the component of production that is often the least mobile—a firm's employees. As a result of growing blue-collar factory jobs in China and Southeast Asia to white-collar call-center and computer-programming jobs in India, many workers in developed economies are being forced to experience globalization up close and personal, to the extent that, "In the 10 years ending in 2009, [U.S.] factories shed workers so fast that they erased almost all the gains of the previous 70 years; roughly one out of every three manufacturing jobs — about 6 million in total — disappeared."[341]

> Corporations in the U.S. and Europe will move an additional 750,000 jobs in IT, finance, and other business services to India and other low-cost geographies by 2016, . . . [by which time], a total of 2.3 million jobs in finance, IT, procurement, and HR will have moved offshore. This represents about one third of all jobs in these areas.[342]

But, the downsides of outsourcing do not lie solely with domestic employees. Reports of horrendous working conditions and human rights abuses in overseas sweatshops appear regularly in the media.[343] And the worst cases of abuse overseas, where they occur, seem to fall disproportionately on those who are least able to defend themselves:

> The International Labour Organization (ILO) estimates that there are 122m economically active five to 14-year-olds in the Asia-Pacific region, with 44m of them in India, giving it the largest child workforce in the world.[344]

As such, while advocates of offshoring or outsourcing often point to the benefits the process brings to the workers in developing countries who now have jobs; ultimately, it is not clear whether these foreign employees benefit (from the jobs created)[345] or suffer (from the conditions in which they are forced to work),[346] or even whether better quality products and services are delivered at home.[347] Equally importantly, this massive shift in production logistics has occurred in a relatively short period of time. One indicator of this is that the U.S. now "makes 3% of the clothing its consumers purchase, down from about 50% in 1990."[348]

Though some of these jobs would have been lost anyway to automation as a result of technological progress, what effects have these rapid changes had on firms from a CSR perspective? To what extent does operating in a foreign environment, with different values and norms, render the corporation vulnerable to cultural conflict?[349] What role does outsourcing play for firms seeking to implement CSR throughout the supply chain? To what extent can an ethical supply chain, "from ethical purchasing through to proper disposal of the end product,"[350] be an asset for the firm and a force for positive societal change?[351]

The other side of this debate is whether an *unethical* supply chain is punished by a firm's stakeholders. What is the potential damage of a perceived abuse for the company in its home market, where observers and consumers judge the company by local values and expectations, rather than the standards of the foreign culture?[352] It is also worth asking: Are *sweatshops* necessarily bad? For example, people "in the West mostly despise sweatshops as exploiters of the poor, while the poor themselves tend to see sweatshops as opportunities."[353] The argument in favor of sweatshops, therefore, is that, in comparison to the alternatives facing many people living in developing economies, a factory job with a supplier for a Western multinational represents the opportunity for advancement:

> [Proponents of] labor standards in trade agreements mean well, for they intend to fight back at oppressive sweatshops abroad. But, while it shocks [Westerners] to hear it, the central challenge in the poorest countries is not that sweatshops exploit too many people, but that they don't exploit enough. Talk to those families [who live and scavenge in a garbage] dump, and a job in a sweatshop is a cherished dream, an escalator out of poverty, the kind of gauzy if probably unrealistic ambition that parents everywhere often have for their children.[354]

An important component of this argument, therefore, is the idea of cultural relativism—to what extent should actions in overseas countries be judged by the home country's moral, ethical, and religious standards, and to what extent should they be judged in terms of the historical and cultural context in which they occur? Western NGOs, in particular, are accused of actively campaigning against the opening of multi-national operations in developing countries based on Western notions of *acceptable* work conditions, but are not in a position to provide alternative sources of investment if the company is forced to withdraw:

> International NGOs in Guatemala train local leaders to "empower" minorities and indigenous groups and to denounce [extraction] mines as "neo-colonial" ventures. But the reality is that the very nature of the NGO saves it from having a real stake in the communities it affects through its activism. It can blow through town like a hurricane disrupting development and then be gone.[355]

CSR Newsletters: Supply Chain

An article in the *Financial Times*[356] addresses the issue of a firm's responsibility for its extended supply chain. It cites two examples in the UK (Primark and Tesco) where evidence suggests a systematic abuse of human (child laborers) and employment (low pay) rights in factories that supply both firms. The column then asks for advice from four different perspectives in response to the following questions:

> Is it ever possible for companies with suppliers in developing economies to guarantee that their goods have been produced in ethically acceptable conditions? And what kind of audit system could provide consumers with such a guarantee?

In relation to the first question, it was encouraging (in terms of its honesty) to see the position taken that consumers should not be surprised when they pay such relatively low prices for clothes and it then emerges that the clothes did not cost much to produce:

> Consumers massage their consciences, crying crocodile tears when an abused producer is found by an intrepid journalist, but show their true colours shopping for underwear.

In addressing the second question, the response was also refreshing (in terms of its perceptiveness), suggesting that (a) firms should not be surprised that suppliers in developing countries try and deceive auditors and (b) that they only have themselves to blame because, while firms might say that they want their suppliers to adhere to certain standards, they incentivize them to minimize costs. Until firms are serious about providing financial incentives for suppliers to adhere to their codes of conduct and punish transgressors, they are unlikely to see the kind of behavior they say they seek:

> That means engaging the supply chain in good corporate social responsibility practices rather than relying on spot checks. It means getting suppliers to recognise that adhering to sound employment practices is in their own interests and helping suppliers develop policies and practices that will make them a trusted supplier and build a long-term relationship.

(Continued)

(Continued)

The absence of a choice for many workers in the developing world is also a point well made:

Poor parents in India, Pakistan or Vietnam cannot choose between sending their children to a school or a factory. The real choice is between eating or going hungry.

While the column does not provide many specific answers, at least it is realistic in the situation facing firms, their suppliers, and employees throughout the supply chain.

In short, while there are multiple examples at the extremes, it is unclear whether these changes to the supply chains of global corporations represent an absolute *good* or *bad*, for either the firm or its employees. This is even less clear when there is no common point of reference:

When a corporation from an advanced economy does business in a developing country, it may . . . establish a level of corporate virtue consistent with the host country's civil foundation. Notoriously, Nike, by running its Southeast Asian athletic footwear plants and paying its workers in accordance with local customs and practices, opened itself to charges of operating sweatshops. In essence, it was accused of averaging down its level of corporate responsibility. Although the company protested that its conduct was virtuous by local standards, angry U.S. consumers made it clear that they expected Nike to conform to [the standards of] the U.S. civil foundation.[357]

The example of Nike is instructive because it demonstrates how far Western corporations have come in developing effective and ethical supply chains. Nike has long been plagued by allegations that it oversees sweatshop conditions in its factories abroad. The allegation was initially made against the company whether the factories are Nike owned and operated, or merely contractors producing shoes and clothing on behalf of the firm:

More than 90 percent of the Nike workers in Vietnam are girls or young women, aged 15 to 28. . . . A meal consisting of rice, a few mouthfuls of a vegetable and maybe some tofu costs the equivalent of 70 cents. Three similarly meager meals a day would cost $2.10. But the workers only make $1.60 a day.

And . . . they have other expenses. . . . To stretch the paycheck, something has to be sacrificed. Despite the persistent hunger, it's usually food.[358]

Today, in contrast, Nike is one of the most progressive global corporations in terms of its socially responsible supply chain. A significant reason for this, however, is the firm's past mistakes and attacks by NGOs that continue to this day.[359] Those attacks focus largely on the working conditions in Nike factories in South East Asia, which, as Phil Knight, Nike's Founder and CEO, admitted, "Produced considerable pain" for the firm in the late 1990s.[360] Although, initially, Nike was reluctant to reform,[361] today, the firm has become more proactive in arguing the positive impact of its operations and products worldwide. Nike has created a vice president for corporate responsibility and publishes CSR reports to institutionalize a commitment to CSR in its corporate structure and operations as well as help protect the company's brand against future CSR lapses. The on-going program of re-positioning its brand on issues of social responsibility appears to be paying-off for Nike as it once again dominates the U.S. running shoe market with 55% market share.[362] And, in many areas of CSR, the firm is now recognized as "a standard-setter for efforts to improve supply chain conditions and other companies have followed its lead on corporate responsibility."[363]

CSR Newsletters: Nike

It is characteristic of the media that good news takes a back seat to scandal, but an article from the *Associated Press*[364] is worth highlighting as an example of how far Nike has come regarding CSR. The article, buried deep in the sports pages of a local paper, reports Nike's voluntary disclosure of the mistreatment of workers at the factory of a Nike sub-contractor in Malaysia that included "squalid living conditions, garnished wages and withheld passports of foreign workers." Nike's response was impressive:

Nike said all workers are being transferred to Nike-inspected and approved housing . . . All workers will be reimbursed for any fees and going forward, the fees will be paid by the factory. All workers will have immediate access to their passports and any worker who wishes to return home will be provided return airfare.

Those executives that remain unconvinced of the value of CSR, however, are likely to remain skeptical as long as such proactive behavior remains unrecognized, while the slightest transgression is plastered all over the front pages.

This shift in approach to outsourcing is occurring at a time when there is an ongoing reassessment of the value of moving abroad everything that is not tied down. This is partly due to rising labor costs overseas, which "in China have recently been growing by around 20% a year,"[365] but also because executives are taking a broader perspective of this business decision. Firms are increasingly questioning the sense of short-term cost savings at the expense of exposing themselves to the danger of longer-term threats to reputation and other problems associated with logistics, customer service, and market flexibility:

> More and more U.S. businesses are realizing their decisions to move manufacturing jobs overseas wasn't all it was cracked up to be. . . . [As a result], 40 percent of manufacturing firms believe there is an increased effort to move manufacturing plants back to the U.S. from countries such as China and India. In addition, 38 percent of the companies researched indicated that their direct competitors have already brought manufacturing jobs back to the U.S. from overseas. . . . rising labor costs in emerging countries, high oil prices and increasing transportation costs and global risks, such as political instability, are the motivating factors in bringing manufacturing operations back home.[366]

In spite of this reassessment, however, it is also clear that *reshoring* will not solve all the employment issues caused by globalization ("if 10% of China's electronics production was moved to the U.S., China would lose 300,000 jobs. Yet, just 40,000 new jobs would be created in the U.S. Put another way, if all of China's manufacturing output was magically transported to the U.S. tomorrow, the U.S. unemployment rate would decline by only 2.75 percentage points after accounting for the effects of automation"),[367] even while it might help firms create more efficient and responsive supply chains.[368]

Case Study: Foxconn

Although some firms are reconsidering the value to their business of outsourcing; for others, outsourcing makes clear business sense. Apple is one of these companies. One reason for this is that, today, the best electronics in the world are made most efficiently in Asia. And, one company in particular does it bigger and better than anyone else:

> Foxconn (also known by its parent company's name, Hon Hai) is the world's largest contract manufacturer. . . . Across China, it employs 1.4m on 28 campuses. . . . In the past decade it has gone from being one of many invisible firms in the electronics supply chain to the world champion of flexible manufacturing. Barclays, a bank,

forecasts that the company's revenues will exceed NT$3.9 trillion ($134 billion) this year.[369]

Apple, along with many other major consumer electronics firms, is highly reliant on Foxconn. According to some reports, "about half of all consumer electronics sold in the world today are produced at [Foxconn's] mammoth factory campus in Shenzhen, China."[370] As such, the firm makes a large percentage of Apple's iPhones and iPads. While Foxconn is able to make those products well, however, they are also able to make them extremely efficiently:

Apple had redesigned the iPhone's screen at the last minute, forcing an assembly-line overhaul. New screens began arriving at the [Chinese] plant near midnight. A foreman immediately roused 8,000 workers inside the company's dormitories, according to the executive. Each employee was given a biscuit and a cup of tea, guided to a workstation and within half an hour started a 12-hour shift fitting glass screens into beveled frames. Within 96 hours, the plant was producing over 10,000 iPhones a day.[371]

In spite of the remarkable economic value Apple receives from outsourcing much of its production to firms such as Foxconn, like Nike before it, Apple has also received some negative press for its extended supply chain in Asia. In particular, as its biggest supplier, conditions at Foxconn's factories have drawn the greatest media attention[372] and have covered a range of issues related to employees striking,[373] rioting,[374] committing suicide,[375] being underage and underpaid,[376] and being poisoned.[377]

As a result of the press coverage and coinciding with the change in leadership from Steve Jobs to Tim Cook, Apple has moved to alter stakeholder perceptions of its commitment to an ethical supply chain by taking a number of steps to improve conditions at Foxconn's factories. First, Apple released a report that comprehensively assessed working conditions in firms "that represent 97% of its materials, manufacturing and procurement spending"—the most detailed report on its supply chain that Apple has released:

The report found 62% of suppliers violated Apple's working hours standards of 60 hours per week. . . . Apple also said it found 112 facilities that weren't properly storing, moving or handling hazardous chemicals. . . . Nearly a third of its suppliers didn't abide by Apple's standards on wages and benefits, the company said. The audits also found five facilities that employed underage workers.[378]

Second, Foxconn announced that it will improve working conditions for all employees at its factories—increasing wages, reducing overtime, and generally improving employees' working conditions.[379] Third, Apple announced a commitment to have all its supplier factories audited by the third party organization, the Fair Labor Association (FLA), along with a promise to stop working with those suppliers that "do not measure up to its labor and human rights standards."[380] Finally, following the FLA's audit, Apple and Foxconn agreed to implement the changes recommended—in particular in relation to pay and overtime. As Foxconn announced:

> "We will continue to support Apple's initiatives to ensure that its business partners are in compliance with all relevant China laws and regulations and the FLA's Workplace Code of Conduct." The recommendations included reducing work hours to a maximum of 40 hours a week and limiting overtime to a maximum of 36 hours a month—the legal maximum in China.[381]

A Sustainable Supply Chain – Mallen Baker[382]

Mallen Baker provides the outline of a broad framework of steps that firms can use to build a sustainable supply chain:

- Create a picture of what is out there...[identify] where the hidden issues lurk.
- Prioritise your engagement...start by identifying the areas of the biggest risk.
- Be clear about your own standards...what [are] the standards you would expect to enforce?
- Focus on ways to measure performance...What changed...? How do you know?
- And, as always, get top level buy-in...[senior management] have to get the strategic business case for prioritizing action in this area.

In spite of all the negative stories that have emerged in the Western press about Foxconn, its oppressive factory conditions, and its relationship with Apple, two points are worth keeping in mind. The first point concerns the effect these stories have had on public perceptions of Apple—arguably, "they have not impacted Apple's reputation one jot."[383] The second point is the position of Foxconn's employees, many of whom moved from the countryside in China to its big cities in pursuit of economic progress. In response to Foxconn's commitment to bring its overtime rules in line with Chinese laws, "allowing workers to work no more than nine hours of overtime a week" and improve health and safety conditions (which some fear will reduce margins and threaten jobs), employees are beginning to push back:

> Nets to catch would-be jumpers still sag ominously from Hon Hai Precision Industry Co.'s buildings. But two years after a spate of suicides at the Apple Inc. supplier's campus here, workers are more concerned about another measure designed to protect them: limits on overtime. . . . more than 15 workers on the Shenzhen campus said in interviews that they work more than the legal limit of nine overtime hours a week. A majority said they work 10 to 15 overtime hours and would prefer more, having left their distant homes to make money in this southern Chinese boomtown on the border of Hong Kong.[384]

Amid these conflicting incentives and pressures, Apple's commitment to its key supplier appears genuine. This is confirmed in subsequent press coverage of the progress being made at Foxconn's facilities[385] and is reinforced by Apple's public statements on its website:

> Apple is committed to the highest standards of social responsibility across our worldwide supply chain. We insist that all of our suppliers provide safe working conditions, treat workers with dignity and respect, and use environmentally responsible manufacturing processes. Our actions – from thorough site audits to industry-leading training programs – demonstrate this commitment.[386]

In acting to protect its reputation, Apple is merely the latest firm to learn from the trial and errors of earlier pioneers, such as Nike. For these firms, their reputations and the values around which their brands are built are core strategic assets. And, in some respects, the supply chain is more of a strategic issue for Apple, given that supplier contracts are usually longer in the consumer electronics industry than "the three-month terms common in the apparel business." This necessarily "gives Apple a much bigger stake in the long-term success of Foxconn as a supplier, and makes it less attractive to cut and run to a cheaper option."[387] As such, there is a clear strategic imperative for multinational firms today to respond to stakeholder concerns about the sustainability of their supply chains in ways that are transparent and acceptable in terms of standards applied by stakeholders, both at home and overseas:

> In April 2005, Nike surprised the business community by suddenly releasing its global database of nearly 750 factories worldwide. No laws presently require a company to disclose the identity of its factories or suppliers within global supply chains. Yet, between the early 1990s and 2005, Nike went from denying responsibility for inhumane conditions in its factories to leading other companies in full disclosure—a strategic shift that illustrates how a firm can leverage increased transparency to mitigate risk and add value to the business.[388]

In general, factory audits conducted by independent, third parties are increasingly being used by firms. In spite of the challenges ("At HP, for example, only seven of the 276 factories in its supply chain fully complied with its code of conduct at the last audit."),[389] audits are perceived as a solution whereby Western firms can continue to operate in low cost environments, local employees can continue to benefit from their presence, and NGOs can receive some assurance that the local employees are not being abused.[390] Best practice, pushed by firms such as Nike and GAP (and now Apple), dictates that firms should work with contractors to improve conditions when violations occur and, only in persistent cases, sever ties due to workplace violations.[391] Ultimately, for these firms that rely on effective supply chains, the potential risks far outweigh the short-term cost outlays:

> Some say Apple should copy an idea from Henry Ford [who] . . . paid his employees enough to afford a Model T. Will the workers who assemble iPads one day be able to own one? With wages soaring in China, that may not be a pipe dream. Given that wages account for only 2% of the retail price, bumping them up would hardly cripple Apple's margins. And removing the "sweatshop" stigma might help its global reputation.[392]

What is clear is that outsourcing is not going away, even as Apple investigates the possibility of bringing some production back to the U.S.[393] Establishing an efficient and effective supply chain is essential to firms seeking to reach markets worldwide. As their supply chains become longer, however, firms run into increasingly complex stakeholder conflicts. A CSR lens provides a means to navigate these complexities as firms seek to locate operations in the region that offers the best mix of location, employee skills, and lower costs. What is important from a CSR perspective is to ensure firms adhere to their legal and social obligations and that it is *best* practice, rather than *worst* practice, that is recognized and rewarded by stakeholders.

CEO Perspective

Tim Cook (Apple)

As a company and as individuals, we are defined by our values. Unfortunately some people are questioning Apple's values today, and I'd like to address this with you directly. We care about every worker in our worldwide supply chain. Any accident is deeply troubling, and any issue with working conditions is cause for concern. Any suggestion that we don't care is patently false and offensive to us. As you know better than anyone, accusations like these are contrary to our values. It's not who we are. . . . Every year we inspect more factories, raising the bar for our partners and going deeper into the supply chain. As we reported earlier this month, we've made a great deal of progress and improved conditions for hundreds of thousands of workers. We know of no one in our industry doing as much as we are, in as many places, touching as many people. . . . We will continue to dig deeper, and we will undoubtedly find more issues. What we will not do—and never have done—is stand still or turn a blind eye to problems in our supply chain. On this you have my word. You can follow our progress at apple.com/supplierresponsibility.[394]

Online Resources

- Apple Supplier Responsibility, http://www.apple.com/supplierresponsibility/
- China Labor Watch, http://www.chinalaborwatch.org/
- EICC Code of Conduct, http://www.eicc.info/eicc_code.shtml
- Electronic Industry Citizenship Coalition, http://www.eicc.info/
- Fair Labor Association, http://www.fairlabor.org/
- Foxconn CSR Report, http://www.foxconn.com/CSR_REPORT.html
- Institute for Supply Management, http://www.ism.ws/
- International Labor Organization, http://www.ilo.org/
- Labour Behind the Label, http://www.labourbehindthelabel.org/
- NikeWatch Campaign, http://www.oxfam.org.au/campaigns/labour-rights/nikewatch/
- Social Accountability International (SAI), http://www.sa-intl.org/
- Sweatshop Watch, http://www.change.org/sweatshop_watch
- Verité, http://www.verite.org/

Pro/Con Debate

> **Pro/Con Debate:** Working in a sweatshop is preferable to being unemployed in a country with no welfare safety net.

QUESTIONS FOR DISCUSSION AND REVIEW

1. Is a firm responsible for its supply chain? If so, how far down the supply chain does this responsibility extend—to immediate suppliers, the suppliers' suppliers, or beyond?

2. Should a firm's operations abroad be judged by the standards (legal, economic, cultural, and moral) of the country in which it is operating or by the standards of its home market?

3. Do you buy Apple products? If so, why? If not, why not? Why is Apple so successful?

4. Why does Apple continue to source its production from overseas firms such as Foxconn? What advantages does this generate for the firm? What are the disadvantages that result from the decision? Should Apple have been able to see these threats ahead of time and avoid them? Overall, do the benefits of Apple's decision outweigh the costs?

5. Is Apple a *good* company? Why or why not?

STUDENT STUDY SITE

Visit the Student Study Site at **www.sagepub.com/chandler3e** for additional learning tools.

NOTES AND REFERENCES

1. Bernadette Hearne, 'Analysis: The World Bank and Action on Corporate Corruption,' *Ethical Corporation,* May 20, 2004, http://www.ethicalcorp.com/content.asp?ContentID=2079

2. Theodore Gordon, 'An Ethics Report Card,' Ethics Newsline, October 15, 2012, http://www.globalethics.org/newsline/2012/10/15/ethics-report-card/

3. 'Corruption Perceptions Index 2011,' Transparency International, http://www.transparency.org/cpi2011/results

4. Andres Oppenheimer, 'Latin America's corruption starts at top,' *The Miami Herald,* February 9, 2013, http://www.miamiherald.com/2013/02/09/3224326/latin-americas-corruption-starts.html

5. David Luhnow & Jose De Cordoba, 'A Tale of Bribes and Romance Roils Mexican Politics,' *Wall Street Journal,* June 23, 2004, pp. A1 & A10.

6. Homero Aridjis, 'The Sun, the Moon and Walmart,' *The New York Times,* May 1, 2012, p. A21.

7. Mark Magnier, 'India leads the world in—shoplifting?' *Los Angeles Times* in *The Daily Yomiuri,* December 26, 2011, p. 10.

8. Paul M. Healy & Karthik Ramanna, 'When the Crowd Fights Corruption,' *Harvard Business Review,* January-February 2013, p. 125.

9. 'Supply side,' *The Economist,* November 5, 2011, p. 72.

10. Carol Matlack et al., 'Cracking Down on Corporate Bribery,' *BusinessWeek* online, December 6, 2004, http://www.businessweek.com/magazine/content/04_49/b3911066_mz054.htm?c=bwinsiderdec3&n=link11&t=email

11. Patrick Bartlett, 'EU Investigates Oil Giants,' BBC News, June 12, 2003, http://news.bbc.co.uk/1/hi/business/2984006.stm

12. 'Supply side,' *The Economist,* November 5, 2011, p. 72.

13. 'Show us the money,' *The Economist,* September 1, 2012, p. 14.

14. Samuel Rubenfield, 'OECD Rebukes France for Lack of Bribery Prosecutions,' *The Wall Street Journal,* October 23, 2012, http://blogs.wsj.com/corruption-currents/2012/10/23/oecd-rebukes-france-for-lack-of-bribery-prosecutions/

15. Samuel Rubenfield, 'OECD Slams Australia for Lack of Anti-Bribery Enforcement,' *The Wall Street Journal,* October 25, 2012, http://blogs.wsj.com/dealjournalaustralia/2012/10/26/oecd-slams-australia-for-lack-of-anti-bribery-enforcement/

16. 'Supply side,' *The Economist,* November 5, 2011, p. 72.

17. 'Supply side,' *The Economist,* November 5, 2011, p. 72.

18. In relation to this issue, in December 2012, the global bank HSBC agreed to pay $1.92 billion to the U.S. government as part of a settlement against allegations that the bank allowed its accounts to be used by criminals and terrorists to launder "hundreds of millions of dollars" over a number of years. See: Kevin McCoy, 'HSBC will pay $1.9 billion for money laundering,' *USA Today,* December 11, 2012, http://www.usatoday.com/story/money/business/2012/12/11/hsbc-laundering-probe/1760351/

19. Samuel Brittan, 'Worse evils exist than corruption,' *Financial Times*, September 18, 2009, p. 9.

20. *BizEthics Buzz,* December 2002. *BizEthics Buzz* is an online news report from *Business Ethics Magazine,* http://www.business-ethics.com/email_newsletter/sample.html

21. 'Law's long arm,' *The Economist*, October 6, 2012, p. 34.

22. George L. Priest, 'Supreme Wisdom,' *Wall Street Journal,* June 18, 2004, p. A10.

23. Philip Mattera, 'The New Business Watergate: Prosecution of International Corporate Bribery is on the Rise,' *CorpWatch blog*, December 18th, 2007, http://www.corpwatch.org/article.php?id=14859

24. Philip Mattera, 'The New Business Watergate: Prosecution of International Corporate Bribery is on the Rise,' *CorpWatch blog*, December 18th, 2007, http://www.corpwatch.org/article.php?id=14859

25. Paul Betts, 'Blame for corporate immorality goes beyond the board,' *Financial Times*, February 4, 2011, p. 14.

26. Although this is true under U.S. law, this is not the case in most countries: "Besides the U.S., only a handful of countries permit companies to make such payments, including South Korea, Canada and New Zealand." In: Dionne Searcey, 'Small-Scale Bribes Targeted by OECD,' *The Wall Street Journal*, December 10, 2009, p. A4.

27. Philip Mattera, 'The New Business Watergate: Prosecution of International Corporate Bribery is on the Rise,' *CorpWatch blog*, December 18th, 2007, http://www.corpwatch.org/article.php?id=14859

28. Pratap Chatterjee, 'Chiquita Banana To Face Colombia Torture Claim,' *CorpWatch blog*, March 30th, 2012, http://corpwatch.org/article.php?id=15697

29. 'Going Bananas,' *The Economist*, March 31, 2012, p. 74.

30. 'US Cracks Down On Corporate Bribes,' *The Wall Street Journal*, May 27, 2009, http://online.wsj.com/article/SB124329477230952689.html

31. Charlie Savage, 'Justice Dept. Issues Guidance on Overseas Bribes,' *The New York Times*, November 15, 2012, p. B10.

32. Alberto Gonzales, Richard Westling & William Athanas, 'Forecasting the Future of FCPA Enforcement,' *Corporate Counsel*, May 9, 2012, http://www.law.com/corporatecounsel/PubArticleCC.jsp?id=1202552821910&Forecasting_the_Future_of_FCPA_Enforcement&slreturn=20130004200529

33. Charlie Savage, 'Justice Dept. Issues Guidance on Overseas Bribes,' *The New York Times*, November 15, 2012, p. B10.

34. 'US Cracks Down On Corporate Bribes,' *The Wall Street Journal*, May 27, 2009, http://online.wsj.com/article/SB124329477230952689.html

35. Vanessa Fuhrmans, 'Siemens Settles With World Bank on Bribes,' *The Wall Street Journal*, July 3, 2009, p. B1.

36. See: 'The Business of Bribery,' *The Wall Street Journal*, October 2, 2012, p. B1.

37. Samuel Rubenfeld, 'Conviction in Foreign Bribery Case Is First in U.S. Trial,' *The Wall Street Journal*, May 11, 2011, p. B4.

38. Dionne Searcey, 'U.K. Law On Bribes Has Firms In a Sweat,' *The Wall Street Journal*, December 28, 2010, p. B1.

39. Dionne Searcey, 'U.K. Law On Bribes Has Firms In a Sweat,' *The Wall Street Journal*, December 28, 2010, p. B1.

40. 'A tale of two laws,' *The Economist*, September 17, 2011, p. 68.

41. Matthew Valencia, 'Year of the bounty hunter,' *The Economist: The World in 2012*, p. 147.

42. 'Too big not to fail,' *The Economist*, February 18, 2012, p. 22.

43. 'Show us the money,' *The Economist,* September 1, 2012, p. 14.

44. http://www.justice.gov/criminal/fraud/fcpa/guidance/

45. Joe Palazzolo, 'FCPA Guidance is Here!' *The Wall Street Journal*, November 14, 2012, http://blogs.wsj.com/law/2012/11/14/fcpa-guidance-is-here/

46. See: 'Squeezing the sleazy,' *The Economist*, December 15, 2012, p. 61.

47. C.M. Matthews, 'Companies Say Effects of Corruption Down, Survey Finds,' *The Wall Street Journal*, October 16, 2012, http://blogs.wsj.com/corruption-currents/2012/10/16/companies-say-effects-of-corruption-down-survey-finds/

48. C.M. Matthews, 'Foreign Bribery Enforcement Largely Limited to West,' *The Wall Street Journal*, September 6, 2012, http://blogs.wsj.com/corruption-currents/2012/09/06/foreign-bribery-enforcement-largely-limited-to-west/

49. 'You get who you pay for,' *The Economist*, June 2, 2012, p. 89.

50. 'Corruption Perceptions Index 2012,' Transparency International, http://cpi.transparency.org/cpi2012/results/

51. Barbara Kahn, quoted in: 'The Evolution of Reputation,' *BusinessMiami Magazine*, Spring 2010, p. 39.

52. Patt Morrison, 'Yvon Chouinard: Capitalist Cat,' *Los Angeles Times*, March 12, 2011, http://articles.latimes.com/2011/mar/12/opinion/la-oe-morrison-chouinard-031111

53. Carlos Grande, 'Ethical consumption makes mark on branding,' *Financial Times*, February 20, 2007, p24 and Carlos Grande, 'Businesses behaving badly, say – ETHICS,' *Financial Times*, February 20, 2007, p. 16.

54. See: T.M. Devinney, P. Auger & G.M. Eckhardt, *The Myth of the Ethical Consumer*, Cambridge University Press, 2010. Also, this effect is enhanced when action involves 'change' because humans instinctively value the status quo and fear the unknown: 'According to a study of referendums worldwide, voters almost always reject change: if the campaign starts with opinion evenly balanced, the status quo wins in 80 per cent of cases." Rachel Sylvester, 'Voters always know best, that's why it pays not to ask them,' *The Times* in *The Daily Yomiuri*, October 21, 2012, p. 8.

55. Rob Walker, 'Sex vs. Ethics,' *Fast Company Magazine*, Issue 124, April, 2008, pp. 54–56.

56. Stephanie Clifford & Andrew Martin, 'As Consumers Cut Spending, 'Green' Products Lose Allure,' *The New York Times Magazine*, April 22, 2011, p. B4.

57. Elayne Crain, 'Do Consumers Levy a 'Sustainability Penalty' on Certain Goods?' *McCombs Today*, Spring/Summer 2010, p. 5.

58. Jon Entine, 'Eco marketing: What price green consumerism?' *Ethical Corporation Magazine*, September 1, 2011, http://www.ethicalcorp.com/environment/eco-marketing-what-price-green-consumerism

59. Jon Entine, 'Eco marketing: What price green consumerism?' *Ethical Corporation Magazine*, September 1, 2011, http://www.ethicalcorp.com/environment/eco-marketing-what-price-green-consumerism

60. John Tierney, 'When Energy Efficiency Sullies the Environment,' *The New York Times*, March 8, 2011, p. D1.

61. See: http://strategiccsr-sage.blogspot.com/2012/09/strategic-csr-prius-fallacy.html

62. Robert Reich, 'We are all going to hell in a shopping basket,' *Financial Times*, January 16, 2012, http://www.ft.com/cms/s/0/2f0babbe-3e30-11e1-ac9b-00144feabdc0.html

63. Michael Mandel, 'Get It Straight: Consumer Spending is *not* 70% of GDP,' *Bloomberg Businessweek*, August 29, 2009, http://www.businessweek.com/the_thread/economicsunbound/archives/2009/08/get_it_straight.html

64. Suzy Hansen, 'How Zara Grew Into the World's Largest Fashion Retailer,' *The New York Times Magazine*, November 11, 2012, p. 35.

65. Susan Carpenter, 'Designers, brands take steps towards sustainable fashion,' *Los Angeles Times*, October 14, 2012, http://articles.latimes.com/2012/oct/14/image/la-ig-biodegradable-fashion-20121014

66. Masoud Golsorkhi, editor of Tank Magazine, quoted in: Suzy Hansen, 'How Zara Grew Into the World's Largest Fashion Retailer,' *The New York Times Magazine*, November 11, 2012, p. 35.

67. Jon Entine, 'Eco marketing: What price green consumerism?' *Ethical Corporation Magazine*, September 1, 2011, http://www.ethicalcorp.com/environment/eco-marketing-what-price-green-consumerism

68. Stuart Elliott, 'Glad Cuts the Hyperbole for Its New Green Trash Bag,' *The New York Times*, October 19, 2011, p. B6.

69. Jacqui Ottman, 'What Green Consumer Polls Should Really Be Asking,' May 4, 2012, http://www.greenmarketing.com/blog/comments/what-green-consumer-polls-should-really-be-asking/

70. Paul Solman, 'What Money Can't Buy and What it Shouldn't Buy,' June 11, 2012, http://www.pbs.org/newshour/bb/business/jan-june12/makingsense_06-11.html. The second part of the Solman interview can be seen at: http://www.pbs.org/newshour/businessdesk/2012/06/betting-on-death-creepy-or-not.html

71. Thomas Friedman, 'This Column is Not Sponsored by Anyone,' *The New York Times*, May 13, 2012, p. SR13.

72. Eduardo Porter – quoted in 'The price behind the choices we make,' *Marketplace. org,* January 10, 2011, http://www.marketplace.org/topics/business/big-book/price-behind-choices-we-make

73. Richard Layard, 'The case against performance-related pay,' *Financial Times,* April 18, 2011, p. 9.

74. Susan Shalhoub, 'Webster takes 'cash mob' concept to heart,' *telegram.com,* September 23, 2012, http://www.telegram.com/article/20120923/NEWS/109239916/0

75. Nick Leiber, ''Dish Mobs' Aim to Benefit Local Restaurants,' *Bloomberg Businessweek,* February 11, 2013, http://www.businessweek.com/articles/2013-02-11/dish-mobs-aim-to-benefit-local-restaurants

76. Marks & Spencer launched Plan A (http://plana.marksandspencer.com/) in 2007. The plan was named *Plan A* because there is no Plan B—i.e., no alternative to implementing a CSR perspective throughout all aspects of operations. Plan A consists of a 100 policy commitments spread over five commitment areas that the firm has pledged to achieve by 2012 and that promises to "change beyond recognition" the way M&S operates. In spite of an initial plan to spend £200 million on Plan A, by early 2009, M&S claimed that Plan A was "cost-neutral." For more detail about Marks & Spencer's Plan A and its value for the firm, see David E. Bell, Nitin Sanghavi, and Laura Winig, 'Marks and Spencer: Plan A, *Harvard Business School* [Case # 9-509-029], January 5, 2009.

77. Oliver Balch, 'The M&S Effect: Bin bags, business sense and Barry,' *Ethical Corporation's Management Blog*, May 13, 2011, http://crmanagementblog.blogspot.com/2011/05/m-effect-bin-bags-business-sense-and.html . See also: Mallen Baker, 'Will we shwop til we dwop at Marks and Spencer?' *mallenbaker.net*, May 2, 2012, http://www.mallenbaker.net/csr/post.php?id=437

78. Kanye West, 'Diamonds From Sierra Leone,' 2005.

79. 'News: Summary for December 2002,' *Ethical Corporation,* December 24, 2002, http://www.ethicalcorp.com/NewsTemplate.asp?IDNum=477

80. http://www.un.org/peace/africa/Diamond.html

81. Jonathan Clayton & Jan Raath, 'Mugabe's blood diamonds,' *The Times* in *The Daily Yomiuri,* June 6, 2010, p. 7.

82. Global Witness: Conflict Diamonds, January 2013, http://www.globalwitness.org/campaigns/diamonds/

83. Maria Doulton, 'A step in the right direction,' *Financial Times,* November 11, 2006, p. 13.

84. 'Diamonds to Get 'Ethical' Label,' *BBC News,* June 23, 2004, http://news.bbc.net.uk/1/low/business/3834677.stm

85. 'Tiffany & Co.: A Case Study in Diamonds and Social Responsibility,' *Knowledge @ Wharton,* November 2004, http://knowledge.wharton.upenn.edu/article/1074.cfm

86. *Ethical Corporation Magazine,* December 24, 2002, op. cit.

87. *Ethical Corporation Magazine,* December 24, 2002, op. cit.

88. http://www.un.org/peace/africa/Diamond.html

89. Tosin Sulaiman, 'Law Targets "Blood Diamonds,"' *Miami Herald,* May 8, 2003, p. 2A.

90. Tosin Sulaiman, 'Law Targets "Blood Diamonds,"' *Miami Herald,* May 8, 2003, p. 2A.

91. http://www.jewelers.org:8080/3.consumers/ethics/index.shtml

92. Lisa Roner, 'Jewelers of America Launch Corporate Responsibility Initiative,' *Ethical Corporation,* September 23, 2004, http://www.cthicalcorp.com/content.asp?ContentID=2820

93. Ethical Corporation Magazine, June 30, 2004, op. cit.

94. 'Special Report: The Diamond Cartel. The Cartel Isn't Forever,' *The Economist,* July 17, 2004, pp. 60–62.

95. For more on the failures of the KPCS, see: Mallen Baker, 'What can we learn from the dying throes of the Kimberley Process?' *mallenbaker.net,* October 25, 2011, http://www.mallenbaker.net/csr/page.php?Story_ID=2706 and Oliver Balch, 'Kimberley Process: Time to get tough,' *Ethical Corporation's Management Blog,* January 16, 2011, http://crmanagementblog.blogspot.com/2011/01/kimberly-process-time-to-get-tough.html

96. Global Witness: Conflict Diamonds, January 2013, http://www.globalwitness.org/campaigns/diamonds/

97. John Eligon, 'Advocacy Group Quits Coalition Fighting Sale of 'Blood Diamonds,"' *The New York Times,* December 6, 2011, p. A6.

98. Kimberley Process website, January 2013, http://www.kimberleyprocess.com/web/kimberley-process/kp-basics

99. Horacio Salinas, 'Bloody Shame,' *Fast Company Magazine,* December 2009/January 2010, p. 113.

100. Horacio Salinas, 'Bloody Shame,' *Fast Company Magazine,* December 2009/January 2010, p. 113.

101. Horacio Salinas, 'Bloody Shame,' *Fast Company Magazine,* December 2009/January 2010, p. 113.

102. 'Report to Society 2011,' *DeBeers Family of Companies,* 2011, p. 27.

103. Maria Doulton, 'A step in the right direction,' *Financial Times,* November 11, 2006, p. 13.

104. Raphael Minder, 'Burmese ruby ban likely to be undermined,' *Financial Times,* November 18, 2008, p. 6.

105. Claire Adler, 'Gemfields: Group leads charge for ethical emeralds,' *Financial Times Special Report: Watches & Jewelry,* June 12, 2010, p. 13.

106. See: No Dirty Gold Campaign, http://www.nodirtygold.org/

107. Securities and Exchange Commission, Conflict Minerals Final Rule, November 13, 2012, http://www.sec.gov/rules/final/2012/34-67716.pdf

108. Steven M. Davidoff, 'Humanitarian Effort in Congo Puts S.E.C. in Unintended Role,' *The Wall Street Journal,* August 28, 2012, http://dealbook.nytimes.com/2012/08/28/humanitarian-effort-in-congo-puts-wall-st-regulator-in-unintended-role/

109. Nick Elliott, 'Conflict Minerals Rules Could Reverberate Through Supply Chain,' *The Wall Street Journal,* September 14, 2012, http://blogs.wsj.com/corruption-currents/2012/09/14/conflict-minerals-rules-could-reverberate-through-supply-chain/

110. Steven M. Davidoff, 'Humanitarian Effort in Congo Puts S.E.C. in Unintended Role,' *The Wall Street Journal,* August 28, 2012, http://dealbook.nytimes.com/2012/08/28/humanitarian-effort-in-congo-puts-wall-st-regulator-in-unintended-role/

111. Steven M. Davidoff, 'Humanitarian Effort in Congo Puts S.E.C. in Unintended Role,' *The Wall Street Journal,* August 28, 2012, http://dealbook.nytimes.com/2012/08/28/humanitarian-effort-in-congo-puts-wall-st-regulator-in-unintended-role/

112. Oliver Balch, 'Conflict Minerals – Dodd-Frank Due Diligence,' *Ethical Corporation Magazine,* October 4, 2012, http://www.ethicalcorp.com/supply-chains/analysis-conflict-minerals-dodd-frank-due-diligence

113. Editorial, 'Conflict minerals,' *Financial Times,* August 27, 2010, p. 8.

114. Jason Stearns, 'Digging for the Truth About a Dirty Trade,' *The Wall Street Journal,* August 27-28, 2011, pC5. For additional insight into the unintended consequences of Dodd-Frank, see 'Digging for victory,' *The Economist,* September 24, 2011, p. 60 and David Aronson, 'How Congress Devastated Congo,' *The New York Times,* August 8, 2011, p. A17.

115. Gareth Penny was CEO of De Beers from 2006 to 2010. He is quoted here in: Vanessa O'Connell, 'De Beers Polishes Its Image,' *The Wall Street Journal,* July 7, 2008, p. B1.

116. Jonathan Clayton & Jan Raath, 'Mugabe's blood diamonds,' *The Times* in *The Daily Yomiuri,* June 6, 2010, p. 7.

117. The cost savings Walmart is able to secure by operating more sustainably that we discussed in Chapter 3 are a good example of this.

118. The 2009 *Conscious Consumer Report* from the branding consultancy BBMG, for example, notes that 67% of Americans agree that "even in tough economic times, it

is important to purchase products with social and environmental benefits," and also that 71% of consumers agree that they "avoid purchasing from companies whose practices they disagree with." Jack Loechner, 'Consumers Want Proof It's Green,' *Center for Media Research*, April 9, 2009, http://www.mediapost.com/publications/?fa=Articles.showArticle&art_aid=103504

119. For information about sustainable certification schemes that rival fair trade (e.g., Rainforest Alliance and Utz Certified), see: John Russell, 'Coffee sourcing: Nespresso points Nestlé towards sustainability,' *Ethical Corporation*, June 29, 2009, http://www.ethicalcorp.com/content.asp?ContentID=6518

120. The Fairtrade Foundation website, January 2013, http://www.fairtrade.org.uk/what_is_fairtrade/faqs.aspx

121. James E. Austin & Cate Reavis, 'Starbucks and Conservation International,' *Harvard Business School Case,* May 1, 2004, [9-303-055], p. 14.

122. Katy McLaughlin, 'Is Your Grocery List Politically Correct?' *Wall Street Journal*, February 17, 2004, pp. D1 & D2.

123. Andrew Stark, 'The Price of Moral Purity,' *The Wall Street Journal*, February 4, 2011, p. A13.

124. Andrew Stark, 'The Price of Moral Purity,' *The Wall Street Journal*, February 4, 2011, p. A13.

125. The Fairtrade Foundation website, January 2013, http://www.fairtrade.org.uk/what_is_fairtrade/facts_and_figures.aspx

126. The Fairtrade Foundation website, January 2013, http://www.fairtrade.org.uk/what_is_fairtrade/faqs.aspx

127. Deborah Ball, 'U.K. KitKats Shift to Fair Trade As Nestle Burnishes Reputation,' *The Wall Street Journal,* December 8, 2009, p. B6.

128. For a discussion of why there is a separate certification organization governing fair trade products in the U.S. and the tensions this causes between Fairtrade USA and Fairtrade International, see: Jon Entine, 'Ethical branding: Fairtrade laid bare,' *Ethical Corporation Magazine,* February 2, 2012, http://www.ethicalcorp.com/supply-chains/ethical-branding-fairtrade-laid-bare and also: William Neuman, 'A Question of Fairness,' *The New York Times,* November 24, 2011, p. B1.

129. William Neuman, 'A Question of Fairness,' *The New York Times,* November 24, 2011, p. B1.

130. Katie Barrow, 'Fair Trade USA's 2011 Almanac Shows Impressive Growth in Imports,' *LOHAS blog,* May 6, 2012, http://blog.lohas.com/blog/fair-trade-usa/fair-trade-usas-2011-almanac-shows-impressive-growth-in-imports

131. Michael Skapinker, 'There is a good trade in ethical retailing,' *Financial Times*, September 11, 2007, p. 15.

132. Michael Skapinker, 'No markets were hurt in making this coffee,' *Financial Times,* November 9, 2010, p. 11.

133. Quote from the 2005 *Green and Ethical Consumer* Report. In, Poulomi Mrinal Saha, 'Ethics Still Not Influencing UK Consumers,' *Ethical Corporation,* March 15, 2005, http://www.ethicalcorp.com/content.asp?ContentID=3557

134. Michael Skapinker, 'No markets were hurt in making this coffee,' *Financial Times*, November 9, 2010, p. 11.

135. Alan Beattie, 'Follow the thread,' *Financial Times*, July 22/23, 2006, p. WK1.

136. John Kay, 'Justice in Trade Is Not Simply a Moral Question,' *Financial Times* (U.S. edition), June 26, 2003, p. 13.

137. Adam Smith, quoted in 'Economic Focus: Too Many Countries?' *The Economist*, July 17, 2004, p. 75.

138. Katy McLaughlin, 'Is Your Grocery List Politically Correct?' *Wall Street Journal*, February 17, 2004, pp. D1 & D2.

139. Parminder Bahra, 'Tea workers still waiting to reap Fairtrade benefits,' *The Times*, January 2, 2009, http://www.timesonline.co.uk/tol/news/uk/article5429888.ece

140. Michael Skapinker, 'No markets were hurt in making this coffee,' *Financial Times*, November 9, 2010, p. 11.

141. John Vidal, 'New choc on the bloc,' *The Guardian*, June, 2005, http://www.guardian.co.uk/world/2005/jun/03/outlook.development

142. Alan Beattie, 'Follow the thread,' *Financial Times*, July 22/23, 2006, p. WK1.

143. Alan Beattie, 'Follow the thread,' *Financial Times*, July 22/23, 2006, p. WK1.

144. Peter Heslam, 'George and the Chocolate Factory,' *The London Institute for Contemporary Christianity*, September, 2005, http://www.licc.org.uk/engaging-with-culture/connecting-with-culture/business/george-and-the-chocolate-factory-203

145. http://www.goodafrican.com/. See also: Daniel Bergner, 'Can Coffee Kick-Start an Economy?' *The New York Times*, April 6, 2012, http://www.nytimes.com/2012/04/08/magazine/can-coffee-kick-start-an-economy.html

146. John Vidal, 'New choc on the bloc,' *The Guardian*, June, 2005, http://www.guardian.co.uk/world/2005/jun/03/outlook.development

147. James E. McWilliams, 'Food That Travels Well,' *New York Times*, August 6, 2007, http://www.nytimes.com/2007/08/06/opinion/06mcwilliams.html and Claudia H. Deutsch, 'For Suppliers, the Pressure Is On,' *New York Times*, Special Section: *Business of Green*, November 7, 2007, p. 1.

148. David Vetter, 'UK Fairtrade – Shunted into a siding,' *Ethical Corporation*, December 14, 2007, http://www.ethicalcorp.com/content.asp?ContentID=5583

149. 'Cadbury Dairy Milk commits to Going Fairtrade,' Cadbury Press Release, *CSRwire.com*, March 3, 2009, http://www.csrwire.com/News/14719.html. See also: Michael Skapinker, 'Fairtrade and a new ingredient for business,' *Financial Times*, March 10, 2009, p. 11.

150. 'Hershey to Source 100% Certified Cocoa by 2020,' *Environmental Leader*, October 8, 2012, http://www.environmentalleader.com/2012/10/08/hershey-to-source-100-certified-cocoa-by-2020/

151. 'Hershey to Source 100% Certified Cocoa by 2020,' *Environmental Leader*, October 8, 2012, http://www.environmentalleader.com/2012/10/08/hershey-to-source-100-certified-cocoa-by-2020/

152. "Starbucks Corporation was the world's largest specialty coffee retailer, with $6.4 billion in annual revenue for the fiscal year ended October 2, 2005. . . . By the end of 2005, Starbucks . . . boasted more than 10,000 stores—up from 676 a decade earlier—and roasted 2.3 percent of the world's coffee. Each day it opened an average of four stores and hired 200 employees." In 'Starbucks Corporate: Building a Sustainable Supply Chain,' *Stanford Graduate School of Business*, Case: GS-54, May, 2007, pp. 1–2.

153. Stanley Homes & Geri Smith, 'For Coffee Growers, Not Even a Whiff of Profits,' *BusinessWeek,* September 9, 2002, p. 110.

154. Michael Skapinker, 'No markets were hurt in making this coffee,' *Financial Times,* November 9, 2010, p. 11.

155. Jon Entine, 'Ethical branding: Fairtrade laid bare,' *Ethical Corporation Magazine,* February 2, 2012, http://www.ethicalcorp.com/supply-chains/ethical-branding-fair-trade-laid-bare

156. Andrew Downie, 'Fair Trade In Bloom,' *New York Times*, October 2, 2007, p. C5.

157. James E. Austin & Cate Reavis, 'Starbucks and Conservation International,' *Harvard Business School Case,* May 1, 2004, [9-303-055], p. 14.

158. Starbuck's policies regarding fair trade and ethical sourcing can be found at: http://www.starbucks.com/responsibility/sourcing/coffee

159. 'Starbucks Coffee Agronomy Company Opens in Costa Rica to Help Farmers Improve Their Coffee Quality,' *Starbucks Financial Release*, January 28, 2004, http://investor.starbucks.com/phoenix.zhtml?c=99518&p=irol-newsArticle&ID=489261

160. Oliver Balch, 'Peter Torrebiarte, Starbucks Coffee Agronomy Company,' *Ethical Corporation,* June 24, 2004, http://www.ethicalcorp.com/content.asp?ContentID=2263

161. 'Starbucks Corporate: Building a Sustainable Supply Chain,' *Stanford Graduate School of Business*, Case: GS-54, May, 2007, p. 4.

162. For more detailed information on Starbucks's C.A.F.E. Practices scorecard, see: http://www.scsglobalservices.com/files/CAFE_SCR_Genericv3.0_101812.pdf

163. Oliver Balch, 'Peter Torrebiarte, Starbucks Coffee Agronomy Company,' *Ethical Corporation,* June 24, 2004, http://www.ethicalcorp.com/content.asp?ContentID=2263

164. 'Starbucks Corporate: Building a Sustainable Supply Chain,' *Stanford Graduate School of Business*, Case: GS-54, May, 2007, p. 2.

165. Peter Torrebiarte, general manager of the Starbucks Coffee Agronomy Company, quoted in Oliver Balch, 'Peter Torrebiarte, Starbucks Coffee Agronomy Company,' *Ethical Corporation,* June 24, 2004, http://www.ethicalcorp.com/content.asp?ContentID=2263

166. John Russell, 'Coffee sourcing: Nespresso points Nestlé towards sustainability,' *Ethical Corporation*, June 29, 2009, http://www.ethicalcorp.com/content.asp?ContentID=6518

167. Javier Blas & Jenny Wiggins, 'Coffee and sugar prices stirred by shortages,' *Financial Times*, May 11, 2009, p. 13.

168. See: Brad Stone, 'The Empire of Excess,' *New York Times*, July 4, 2008, p. C1 and Jenny Wiggins, 'McDonald's lays the ground to mug Starbucks in Europe,' *Financial Times*, May 27, 2009, p. 13.

169. Andrew Downie, 'Fair Trade In Bloom,' *New York Times*, October 2, 2007, p. C1 and 'McDonald's to Sell Fair Trade Certified Coffee,' Oxfam America Press Release, *CSRwire.com*, October 27, 2005, http://www.csrwire.com/press/press_release/21423

170. 'Starbucks Serves up its First Fairtrade Lattes and Cappuccinos Across the UK and Ireland,' *Fairtrade Foundation*, September 2, 2009, http://www.fairtrade.org.uk/press_office/press_releases_and_statements/september_2009/starbucks_serves_up_its_first_fairtrade_lattes_and_cappuccinos.aspx

171. January 2013, http://www.starbucks.com/responsibility/sourcing/coffee

172. '100 Best Corporate Citizens 2007,' *The CRO Magazine*, http://www.thecro.com/?q=node/304. Note: Due to a change in methodology, 2007 was the last year that Green Mountain was eligible for inclusion in the rankings: '100 Best Corporate Citizens 2008,' *The CRO Magazine*, http://www.thecro.com/node/615

173. Andrew Adam Newman, 'This Wake-Up Cup is Fair-Trade Certified,' *The New York Times*, September 28, 2012, p. B3.

174. Andrew Adam Newman, 'This Wake-Up Cup is Fair-Trade Certified,' *The New York Times*, September 28, 2012, p. B3. See also: http://www.gmcr.com/csr/PromotingSustainableCoffee/Statement.aspx

175. 'Coffee and Farmer Equity (C.A.F.E.) Practices,' *Conservation International website*, January 2013, http://www.conservation.org/campaigns/starbucks/Pages/CAFE_Practices_Results.aspx

176. John D. Stoll, 'Starbucks Aims to Invade Nordic Region,' *The Wall Street Journal*, September 27, 2012, p. B8.

177. David A. Kaplan, 'Strong Coffee,' *Fortune Magazine*, December 12, 2011, p. 114.

178. Katy McLaughlin, 'Is Your Grocery List Politically Correct?' *Wall Street Journal*, February 17, 2004, pp. D1 & D2.

179. Thomas Jefferson, 'Letter to John Taylor, May 28, 1816, http://www.britannica.com/presidents/article-9116907

180. Some commentators have identified "June 12, 2007, when news broke that two Bear Stearns hedge funds speculating in mortgage-backed securities were melting down" as the starting point of the 2007-2009 economic crisis: Allan Sloan, 'Unhappy Anniversary,' *Fortune Magazine*, June 8, 2009, p. 14.

181. Lionel Barber, 'How gamblers broker the banks,' *Financial Times Special Report: The FT Year in Finance*, *Financial Times*, December 16, 2008, p. 1.

182. David Leonhardt, 'We're Spent,' *The New York Times*, July 17, 2011, p. SR1.

183. Thomas L. Friedman, 'The Great Unraveling,' *The New York Times*, December 17, 2008, p. A29.

184. See *Animal Spirits: How Human Psychology Drives the Economy, and Why It Matters for Global Capitalism* by George A. Akerlof & Robert J. Shiller (Princeton

University Press, 2009) for an excellent description of the varied motivations driving human behavior with respect to economic behavior and the financial markets.

185. David Brooks, 'An Economy Of Faith And Trust,' *The New York Times*, January 16, 2009, p. A27.

186. Luke Johnson, 'A tragedy for champions of free markets,' *Financial Times*, February 4, 2009, p. 10.

187. Thomas L. Friedman, 'All Fall Down,' *New York Times*, November 26, 2008, p. A31.

188. John Kay, 'What a carve up,' *Financial Times*, August ½, 2009, Life & Arts, p. 12.

189. Editorial, 'When the music stops,' The Guardian, November 6, 2007, http://www.guardian.co.uk/commentisfree/2007/nov/06/comment.business

190. David Ignatius, 'Obama's vision of new foundation should reassure summiteers,' *The Washington Post*, in *The Daily Yomiuri*, April 3, 2009, p. 17.

191. See Martin Wolf's excellent discussion of the causes and solutions of the economic crisis in the *Financial Times* at: http://blogs.ft.com/economistsforum/. A typical example: Martin Wolf, 'Choices made in 2009 will shape the globe's destiny,' *Financial Times*, January 7, 2009, p. 9.

192. Seumas Milne, 'Leaders still aren't facing up to scale of crisis,' *The Guardian*, in *The Daily Yomiuri*, April 3, 2009, p. 17.

193. 'Bashing the rich counterproductive,' *The Economist* (April 4-10 issue) in *The Daily Yomiuri*, April 5, 2009, p. 8.

194. Samuel Brittan, 'The key to Keynes,' *Financial Times*, August 22-23, 2009, Life and Arts, p. 13.

195. Joe Nocera, 'Two Days in September,' *The New York Times*, September 15, 2012, p. A23.

196. Joe Nocera, 'Two Days in September,' *The New York Times*, September 15, 2012, p. A23.

197. Bill Baue, 'Questions remain for CSR in 2009,' CSRwire.com, January 12, 2009, http://www.csrwire.com/press/press_release/22696

198. Thomas L. Friedman, 'The Inflection is Near?' *New York Times*, March 8, 2009, p. WK12.

199. 'A Question Revisited: Is Capitalism Working?' *Knowledge@Wharton*, March 4, 2009, http://knowledge.wharton.upenn.edu/article.cfm?articleid=2172

200. Michael Lewis, 'The End,' *Portfolio.com*, December, 2008, http://www.portfolio.com/news-markets/national-news/portfolio/2008/11/11/The-End-of-Wall-Streets-Boom

201. Michael Lewis & David Einhorn, 'The End of the Financial World As We Know It,' *New York Times*, January 4, 2009, p. WK9.

202. Martin Wolf, 'Seeds of its own destruction,' *Financial Times*, March 9, 2009, p. 7.

203. Bill Gates, 'Creative Capitalism: A Conversation with Bill Gates, Warren Buffett, and Other Economic Leaders,' Simon & Schuster, 2008. See also: Text of Gates' speech at 2008 World Economic Forum at Davos, http://www.microsoft.com/Presspass/exec/billg/speeches/2008/01-24WEFDavos.mspx

204. Muhammad Yunus, *Creating a World Without Poverty: Social Business and the Future of Capitalism*, Public Affairs, 2009. See also: Brad Buchholz, 'You may say he's a dreamer . . . ,' *Austin American-Statesman*, March 1, 2009, http://www.martinfrost.ws/htmlfiles/mar2009/yunus-maybe-dreamer.html

205. Thomas L. Friedman, 'The Inflection is Near?' *New York Times*, March 8, 2009, p. WK12.

206. Skeptics, on the other hand, advise caution and suggest that the talk of reform is premature: '"Capitalism with a conscience" promised on the sickbed may be quickly forgotten in recovery. Don't imagine the stake is through the neoliberal heart yet." Polly Toynbee, 'Brown should spend more to save young people,' *The Times*, in *The Daily Yomiuri*, April 6, 2009, p. 8.

207. George Soros, 'The worst market crisis in 60 years,' *Financial Times*, January 23, 2008, p. 9.

208. Martin Wolf, 'Why the financial turmoil is an elephant in a dark room,' *Financial Times*, January 23, 2008, p. 9.

209. William Yardley, 'The Branding of the Occupy Movement,' *The New York Times*, November 28, 2011, p. B1.

210. Donald Cohen, 'The Education of Alan Greenspan,' *The Huffington Post*, October 31, 2008, http://www.alternet.org/workplace/105414/the_education_of_alan_greenspan/

211. See: Justin Fox, *The Myth of the Rational Market*, Harper Business, 2009 and Richard Thaler, 'The price is not always right and markets can be wrong,' *Financial Times*, August 5, 2009, p. 7.

212. Editorial, 'A survival plan for capitalism,' *Financial Times*, March 9, 2009, p. 8.

213. Eric Lipton, 'Ex-lenders Profit from Home Loans Gone Bad,' *New York Times*, March 4, 2009, p. A1.

214. For more background information on the rise and fall of Countrywide, see: Gretchen Morgenson, 'How Countrywide Covered the Cracks,' *The New York Times*, October 17, 2010, p. BU1.

215. James R. Hagerty, 'Marketing Into a Meltdown,' *The Wall Street Journal*, January 7, 2009, p. A11.

216. Angelo Mozilo in deposition to a Congressional inquiry, September 2010. In: Ben Protess, 'From Ex-Chief, a Staunch Defense of Countrywide's Legacy,' *The New York Times*, February 18, 2011, p. B5.

217. James R. Hagerty, 'Marketing Into a Meltdown,' *The Wall Street Journal*, January 7, 2009, p. A11.

218. Quoting Michael Lewis, in Thomas L. Friedman, 'All Fall Down,' *New York Times*, November 26, 2008, p. A31.

219. Edward Luce, 'Subprime explosion: Who isn't guilty?' *Financial Times*, May 6, 2009, p. 3.

220. David Hechler, 'Risky Business,' *Corporate Counsel*, April 1, 2009, http://www.law.com/corporatecounsel/PubArticleCC.jsp?id=1202429141994

221. James R. Hagerty, 'Marketing Into a Meltdown,' *The Wall Street Journal*, January 7, 2009, p. A11.

222. Mallen Baker, 'Financial services: Will banks ever treat customers fairly?' *Ethical Corporation*, April 1, 2008, http://www.ethicalcorp.com/content.asp?ContentID=5807

223. Mallen Baker, 'Financial services: Will banks ever treat customers fairly?' *Ethical Corporation*, April 1, 2008, http://www.ethicalcorp.com/content.asp?ContentID=5807

224. Karl Rove, 'President Bush Tried to Rein in Fan and Fred,' *Wall Street Journal*, January 8, 2009, p. A13.

225. Brian Gow, 'Bank of America Works Out Countrywide Mortgages,' *BusinessWeek*, February 19, 2009, http://www.businessweek.com/magazine/content/09_09/b4121022492701.htm

226. 'The Housing Horror Show Is Worse Than You Think,' *Bloomberg Businessweek*, July 11-17, 2011, pp. 43-44.

227. Karl Rove, 'President Bush Tried to Rein in Fan and Fred,' *Wall Street Journal*, January 8, 2009, p. A13.

228. Petter S. Goodman & Gretchen Morgenson, 'Saying Yes to Anyone, WaMu Built Empire on Shaky Loans,' *New York Times*, December 28, 2008, p. A1.

229. 'Northern Rock to be nationalized,' *BBC News*, February 17, 2008, http://news.bbc.co.uk/1/hi/business/7249575.stm

230. Chris Tighe, 'Future looks brighter as the Rock begins to roll,' *Financial Times*, *Special Report: Doing Business in North-East England*, February 27, 2009, p. 2.

231. John Cassidy, 'Lessons from the collapse of Bear Stearns,' *Financial Times*, March 15, 2010, p. 11.

232. Bill Baue, 'CSRwire Reports Top Corporate Social Responsibility News of 2008,' *CSRwire.com*, January 12, 2009, http://www.csrwire.com/press/press_release/22696

233. Mara Der Hovanesian, 'Sex, Lies, and Mortgage Deals,' *BusinessWeek*, November 24, 2008, p. 71.

234. Mark Goyder, 'How we've poisoned the well of wealth,' *Financial Times*, February 15, 2009, http://www.ft.com/cms/s/da50a3ae-fa03-11dd-9daa-000077b07658.html

235. See: People v. Countrywide, Los Angeles Superior Court case number LC081846. Company Profile: Countrywide Financial (Subsidiary of Bank of America), *Crocodyl.org*, http://www.crocodyl.org/wiki/countrywide_financial_subsidiary_of_bank_of_america

236. Angelo Mozilo in deposition to a Congressional inquiry, September 2010. In: Ben Protess, 'From Ex-Chief, a Staunch Defense of Countrywide's Legacy,' *The New York Times*, February 18, 2011, p. B5.

237. Company Profile: Countrywide Financial (Subsidiary of Bank of America), *Crocodyl.org*, http://www.crocodyl.org/wiki/countrywide_financial_subsidiary_of_bank_of_america

238. Marketplace, *National Public Radio*, January 16, 2009.

239. William Cohen, 'The tattered strategy of the banker of the year,' *Financial Times*, January 20, 2009, p. 13.

240. Saskia Scholtes, 'BofA lays Countrywide brand to rest,' *Financial Times*, April 27, 2009, p. 17.

241. Andrew Borowitz, 'A letter from Goldman Sachs—Concerning Occupy Wall Street,' *The Borowitz Report*, October 17, 2011, http://www.borowitzreport.com/2011/10/17/a-letter-from-goldman-sachs/

242. Greg Farrell, 'Mortgage executives charged by SEC,' *Financial Times*, June 5, 2009, p. 1.

243. Angelo Mozilo in deposition to a Congressional inquiry, September 2010. In: Ben Protess, 'From Ex-Chief, a Staunch Defense of Countrywide's Legacy,' *The New York Times*, February 18, 2011, p. B5.

244. Jessica Silver-Greenberg & Peter Eavis, 'In Deal, Bib Bank Extends Retreat from Mortgages,' *The New York Times*, January 8, 2013, p. A1.

245. Dan Fitzpatrick, 'Banks Haunted by Houses,' *The Wall Street Journal*, June 30, 2011, p. C2.

246. Dan Fitzpatrick, 'Banks Haunted by Houses,' *The Wall Street Journal*, June 30, 2011, p. C2.

247. Angelo Mozilo in deposition to a Congressional inquiry, September 2010. In: Ben Protess, 'From Ex-Chief, a Staunch Defense of Countrywide's Legacy,' *The New York Times*, February 18, 2011, p. B5.

248. C.K. Prahalad & Allen Hammond, 'Serving the World's Poor, Profitably,' *Harvard Business Review,* September 2002, Vol. 80, No. 9, pp. 48–58.

249. A related term is *microfranchising*—"an economic development tool . . . [designed] to provide sound business opportunities and services to the poor by introducing scaled-down business concepts found in successful franchise organizations." See: 'What is MicroFranchising?' *Economic Self-Reliance Center, BYU*, http://marriott school.byu.edu/selfreliance/microfranchise/

250. Rajesh Chhabara, 'Microfinance – Banking on the poor,' *Ethical Corporation*, December 15, 2008, http://www.ethicalcorp.com/content.asp?ContentID=6263

251. It is important to highlight that microfinance services are needed not only in developing economies, but are also expanding in developed countries, such as the U.S. Sometimes labeled "community investing," microfinance began in the U.S. in the 1980s and is still expanding, with 362 microfinance institutions (MFIs) in 2011. As "nearly nine million U.S. households (or approximately 8% of all households) are unbanked, while another 21 million are 'underbanked,'" the need for greater access to capital and other financial tools (such as checking accounts and debit cards) is strong. MFIs such as Accion International (established in 1991, "the country's largest microlender with some 19,500 small business loans worth a total of more than $119 million as of January 2010") and Grameen America (2008) emerged to fill that need. Across the U.S. in 2008, "MFIs made some 9,100 loans with a total value of $100 million." See: 'American Offshoots: Will Microfinance Ever really Take Root in the U.S.?' *Knowledge@Wharton*, June 17, 2011, http://knowledge.wharton.upenn.edu/article.cfm?articleid=2797

252. The World Bank website, January 2013, http://web.worldbank.org/WBSITE/EXTERNAL/NEWS/0,,contentMDK:20433592~menuPK:34480~pagePK:6425704 3~piPK:437376~theSitePK:4607,00.html

253. 'The path through the fields,' *The Economist,* November 3, 2012, pp. 24-26.

254. 'The path through the fields,' *The Economist,* November 3, 2012, pp. 24-26.

255. 'Microfinance's Latest Challenge: Cutting Back on Over-indebtedness Among Its Poorest Clients,' *Knowledge@Wharton,* December 11, 2011, http://knowledge.wharton.upenn.edu/article.cfm?articleid=2895

256. 'The Ouster of Muhammad Yunus: Can Politics Destroy Grameen Bank?' *Knowledge@Wharton*, April 13, 2011, http://knowledge.wharton.upenn.edu/article.cfm?articleid=2753

257. 'Grabbing Grameen,' *The Economist,* January 28, 2012, p. 67.

258. Vikas Bajaj, 'Out to Maximize Social Gains, Not Profit,' *The New York Times,* December 9, 2006, p. A4.

259. Pete Engardio, 'A Way to Help Africa Help Itself,' *BusinessWeek,* July 21, 2003, p. 40.

260. http://www.yearofmicrocredit.org/

261. See a text and video of Yunus' acceptance Nobel Lecture at: http://nobelprize.org/nobel_prizes/peace/laureates/2006/yunus-lecture.html

262. Eric Bellman, 'Entrepreneur Gets Big Banks to Back Very Small Loans,' *Wall Street Journal*, May 15, 2006, p. A1.

263. http://www.accion.org/

264. http://www.fastcompany.com/social/2006/statements/accion.html

265. Eric Bellman, 'Entrepreneur Gets Big Banks to Back Very Small Loans,' *Wall Street Journal*, May 15, 2006, p. A1.

266. All data quoted from 'Accion 2011 Annual Report,' January 2013, http://www.annualreport.accion.org/

267. Rajesh Chhabara, 'Microfinance – Banking on the poor,' *Ethical Corporation*, December 15, 2008, http://www.ethicalcorp.com/content.asp?ContentID=6263

268. *Knowledge@Wharton,* April 20, 2005, op. cit.

269. Tim Harford, 'Conflicts of interest,' *Financial Times*, Life & Arts, December 6/7, 2008, pp. 1–2.

270. Rachel Emma Silverman, 'A New Way to Do Well by Doing Good,' *Wall Street Journal*, January 5, 2006, p. D1.

271. See Fergal Byrne, 'Matters of faith, hope & charity,' *Financial Times,* March 25/26, 2006, p. W3 and Catherine Holahan, 'Ebay: The Place for Microfinance,' *BusinessWeek*, October 24, 2007, http://www.businessweek.com/technology/content/oct2007/tc20071023_930086.htm

272. David Wighton, 'Citigroup plans to fund microfinance programme,' *Financial Times*, September 22, 2006, p. 18.

273. Rajesh Chhabara, 'Microfinance – Banking on the poor,' *Ethical Corporation*, December 15, 2008, http://www.ethicalcorp.com/content.asp?ContentID=6263

274. Cris Prystay, 'With Loans, Poor South Asian Women Turn Entrepreneurial,' *Wall Street Journal*, May 25, 2005, p. B1.

275. 'Sup-par but not subprime,' *The Economist*, March 31, 2009, p. 82.

276. Ross Tieman, 'Mobile phone operators revolutionise cash transfers,' *Financial Times*, June 3, 2008, p. 14.
277. Richard Lapper, 'A call to South Africa's masses,' *Financial Times*, January 7, 2009, p. 10.
278. Ross Tieman, 'Mobile phone operators revolutionise cash transfers,' *Financial Times*, June 3, 2008, p. 14.
279. 'Calling an end to poverty,' *The Economist*, July 9, 2005, p. 51.
280. Jonathan Wheatley, 'Small is beautiful for Latin America's pioneers,' *Financial Times*, February 27, 2009, p. 18.
281. William Easterly, 'Measuring How and Why Aid Works—Or Doesn't,' *The Wall Street Journal*, April 30-May 1, 2011, p. C5.
282. Ketaki Gokhale, 'A Global Surge in Tiny Loans Spurs Credit Bubble in a Slum,' *The Wall Street Journal*, August 13, 2009, p. A1.
283. Amy Kazmin, 'Cradle of microfinance rocked,' *Financial Times*, December 11/12, 2010, p. 4.
284. See, for example: Lydia Polgreen & Vikas Bajaj, 'Microcredit Pioneer Said to Be Forced Out of Bangladeshi Bank He Founded,' *The New York Times*, March 3, 2011, p. A9.
285. Amy Kazmin, 'Call to overhaul Grameen Bank,' *Financial Times*, April 27, 2011, p. 4.
286. Amy Kazmin, 'Small loan, big snag,' *Financial Times*, December 2, 2010, p. 11.
287. Amy Kazmin, 'Small loan, big snag,' *Financial Times*, December 2, 2010, p. 11.
288. Vikas Bajaj, 'Luster Dims For a Public Microleander,' *The New York Times*, May 11, 2011, p. B1.
289. Vikas Bajaj, 'Amid Scandal, Chairman of Troubled Lender to Quit,' *The New York Times*, November 24, 2011, p. B3.
290. Ketaki Gokhale, 'As Microfinance Grows in India, So Do Its Rivals,' *The Wall Street Journal*, December 16, 2009, p. 8.
291. Vikas Bajaj, '15 Years In, Microcredit Has Suffered a Black Eye,' *The New York Times*, January 6, 2011, p. B3.
292 'Capitalism vs. Altruism: SKS Rekindles the Microfinance Debate,' *Knowledge@Wharton*, October 7, 2010, http://knowledge.wharton.upenn.edu/india/article.cfm?articleid=4533
293 'Road to redemption,' *The Economist*, January 12, 2013, p. 65.
294. Muhammad Yunus, *Banker to the Poor: Micro-lending and the Battle Against World Poverty*, Perseus Books Group, re-produced by Accessible Publishing Systems PTY Ltd, 2010, p. 80.
295. Charles Handy, op. cit., p. 55.
296. David Foster, 'Intel's Amazon Ambitions,' *Fast Company* Magazine, February 2008, p. 86.
297. Chris Giles, 'Half the world's assets held by 2% of population,' *Financial Times*, December 6, 2006, p. 6.
298. C.K. Prahalad & Allen Hammond, 'Serving the World's Poor, Profitably,' *Harvard Business Review,* September 2002, Vol. 80, No. 9, pp. 48–58.

299. Cait Murphy, 'The Hunt for Globalization That Works,' *Fortune,* October 28, 2002, p. 164.

300. David Ignatius, 'World's poor represent huge potential market,' *Washington Post*, in *The Daily Yomiuri*, July 7, 2005, p. 11.

301. 'A market of 4 billion people,' *The Daily Yomiuri*, October 22, 2012, p. 5.

302. While the BOP market overseas is potentially lucrative for firms, there is also a sizeable market of poor people at home who can benefit from the skills in marketing, product design and packaging, and distribution that the firms develop overseas: "The same [BOP] logic is now being applied to the poorest Westerners (there are 46m Americans living in poverty and almost 50m still without health-care insurance)." In: 'Gold-hunting in a frugal age,' *The Economist*, December 15, 2012, p. 70. See also: 'The bottom of the pyramid,' *The Economist*, June 25, 2011, p. 80.

303. 'Face Value: Profits and Poverty,' *The Economist,* August 21, 2004, p. 54.

304. See: http://www.hp.com/e-inclusion/en/vision/mission. For HP's e-Inclusion announcement, see: http://www.hp.com/hpinfo/newsroom/press/2000/001012a.html. Note: "HP launched its e-inclusion initiative in 2000 and fulfilled its e-inclusion commitments in 2006, but we are still supporting many of the projects that evolved from this initiative" (http://h41111.www4.hp.com/globalcitizenship/uk/en/e-inclusion/project/index.html).

305. E-Inclusion "aims to deliver computer and Internet technology to the world's 4 billion poor people through sustainable microenterprises." *Fortune* writer David Kirkpatrick called e-Inclusion "the most visionary step I've ever seen a large tech company take." Marc Gunther, 'Can One Person Change A Major Corporation,' *Business Ethics Magazine,* Winter 2004, pp. 10-12.

306. Prahalad & Hammond, op. cit.

307. *Fortune,* October 28, 2002, op. cit.

308. C.K. Prahalad outlines his work and ideas in this area in a *Wall Street Journal* article: 'Aid is Not the Answer,' August 31, 2005, p. A8 and in his book: *The Fortune at the Bottom of the Pyramid: Eradicating Poverty Through Profits*, Wharton School Publishing, 2004.

309. C. K. Prahalad, quoted in 'Face Value: Profits and Poverty,' *The Economist,* August 21, 2004, p. 54.

310. Sonya Misquitta, 'Cadbury Redefines Cheap Luxury—Marketing to India's Poor, Candy Maker Sells Small Bites for Pennies,' *The Wall Street Journal*, June 8, 2009, p. B4.

311. See 'Will Corporations Really Help the World's Poor?' *Lifeworth* Press Release, *CSRwire.com*, January 31, 2005, http://www.csrwire.com/News/3483.html and Mallen Baker, 'Is there REALLY a fortune at the Bottom of the Pyramid,' *Ethical Corporation*, September 3, 2006, http://www.ethicalcorp.com/content.asp?ContentID=4458

312. '2004 Lifeworth Annual Review of Corporate Responsibility,' *Lifeworth*, 2005, p. 2.

313. 'Business Prophet,' *BusinessWeek Special Report*, January 23, 2006, http://www.businessweek.com/magazine/content/06_04/b3968089.htm

314. Vince Besier, 'Save the Poor. Sell them Stuff. Cheap!' *Miller-McCune*, May/June 2011, pp. 48–50.

315. Sarah Ellison & Eric Bellman, 'Clean Water, No Profit,' *Wall Street Journal*, February 23, 2005, p. B1 and Ellen Byron, 'P&G has big plans for the shelves of tiny stores in emerging nations,' *Wall Street Journal*, July 17, 2007, p. 16.

316. Jonathan Wheatley & Jenny Wiggins, 'Little by little Nestlé aims to woo Brazil's poor,' *Financial Times*, February 20, 2007, p. 6.

317. Barney Jopson, 'Unilever looks to clean up in Africa,' *Financial Times*, November 15, 2007, p. 18.

318. John Mackey, 'To Increase Jobs, Increase Economic Freedom,' *The Wall Street Journal*, November 16, 2011, p. A17.

319. 'Vital for the poor,' *The Economist*, November 10, 2012, p. 52.

320. Howard Sharman, 'Markets can work for development gain,' *Ethical Corporation Magazine*, May 25, 2012, http://www.ethicalcorp.com/stakeholder-engagement/view-middle-markets-can-work-development-gain

321. 'The geography of poverty,' *The Economist*, September 1, 2012, p. 74.

322. *Fortune,* October 28, 2002, op. cit.

323. Barney Jopson, 'Unilever looks to clean up in Africa,' *Financial Times*, November 15, 2007, p. 20.

324. Barney Jopson, 'Unilever looks to clean up in Africa,' *Financial Times*, November 15, 2007, p. 20.

325. See: Toby Webb, 'Unilever raises sustainability bar, but neglects the markets,' *The Smarter Business blog*, November 15, 2010, http://ethicalcorp.blogspot.com/2010/11/unilever-raises-sustainability-bar-but.html

326. Unilever provides regular updates on its performance in relation to these goals. See: 'Unilever reports on first year's progress against ground-breaking sustainable living plan targets,' *Unilever Press Release*, April 24, 2012, http://www.unilever.com/mediacentre/pressreleases/2012/unilever-reports-slp-progress.aspx

327. Michael Skapinker, 'Long-term corporate plans may be lost in translation,' *Financial Times*, November 23, 2010, p. 13.

328. Oliver Balch, 'Unilever: Sustainable living planned,' *Ethical Corporation Magazine*, December 3, 2010, http://www.ethicalcorp.com/communications-reporting/unilever-sustainable-living-planned

329. For example, see: Jennifer Reingold, 'Can P&G Make Money in Places Where People Earn $2 a Day?' *Fortune Magazine*, January 17, 2011, pp. 86-91.

330. Ellen Byron, 'Emerging Ambitions,' *The Wall Street Journal*, July 16, 2007, p. A1.

331. Ellen Byron, 'Emerging Ambitions,' *The Wall Street Journal*, July 16, 2007, p. A1.

332. 'Good business; nice beaches,' *The Economist*, May 19, 2012, p. 76.

333. See: Jennifer Reingold, 'Can P&G Make Money in Places Where People Earn $2 a Day?' *Fortune Magazine*, January 17, 2011, pp. 86-91; Erik Simanis, 'At the Base of the Pyramid,' *The Wall Street Journal*, October 26, 2009, p. R7; and V. Kasturi, Michael Chu & Djordjija Petkoski, 'The Globe: Segmenting the Base of the Pyramid,' *Harvard Business Review*, June 2011, http://hbr.org/2011/06/the-globe-segmenting-the-base-of-the-pyramid/

334. Eric Bellman, 'Multinationals Market to the Poor,' *The Wall Street Journal*, July 24, 2012, p. B8.

335. 'Fighting for the next billion shoppers,' *The Economist*, June 30, 2012, p. 65.

336. Michael Skapinker, 'Long-term corporate plans may be lost in translation,' *Financial Times*, November 23, 2010, p. 13.

337. Jathon Sapsford & Norihiko Shirouzu, 'Mom, Apple Pie and . . . Toyota?' *Wall Street Journal*, May 11, 2006, p. B1.

338. Glenn Hubbard, 'Offshoring can benefit workers of all skill levels,' *Financial Times*, September 28, 2006, p. 19.

339. Thomas L. Friedman, 'How Did the Robot End Up With My Job?' *The New York Times*, October 2, 2011, p. SR11.

340. Toby Webb, 'Supply Chain Stats,' *The Smarter Business blog*, October 1, 2012, http://tobywebb.blogspot.com/2012/10/supply-chain-stats.html

341. Thomas L. Friedman, 'Average is Over,' *The New York Times*, January 25, 2012, p. A25.

342. The Hackett Group, '750,000 Jobs Lost to Outsourcing by 2016,' *Product, Design & Development*, March 29, 2012, http://www.pddnet.com/news/2012/03/750000-jobs-lost-outsourcing-2016

343. For example, see: Declan Walsh, 'Anger Rolls Across Pakistani City in Aftermath of Factory Fire,' *The New York Times*, September 14, 2012, p. A6.

344. Jo Johnson, 'India extends prohibitions on employing children,' *Financial Times*, August 3, 2006, p. 4.

345. See: Andrea Tunarosa, 'What Do NGOs Have Against Poor Guatemalans?' *Wall Street Journal*, July 21, 2006, pA15 and Glenn Hubbard, 'Offshoring can benefit workers of all skill levels,' *Financial Times*, September 28, 2006, p. 19.

346. See: Sam Chambers, 'China's factories—Exploitation ain't what it used to be,' *Ethical Corporation*, August 30, 2006, http://www.ethicalcorp.com/content.asp?ContentID=4458; 'Secrets, Lies, and Sweatshops,' *BusinessWeek*, Cover Story, November 27, 2006, http://www.businessweek.com/magazine/content/06_48/b4011001.htm; and Richard McGregor, 'We must count the true cost of cheap China,' *Financial Times*, August 2, 2007, p. 7.

347. Tracey Taylor, 'A Label of Pride That Pays,' *New York Times*, April 23, 2009, p. B4.

348. Pia Catton, 'Beware False Thrift,' *The Wall Street Journal*, June 23-24, 2012, p. C10.

349. For an interesting example of firms being caught in the middle of a cultural clash, see the scandal that erupted in 2012 following IKEA's decision to delete photos of women from its catalogs in Saudi Arabia (Reuters, 'IKEA slammed for female-free Saudi catalog,' *The Daily Yomiuri*, October 4, 2012, p. 1)—a decision for which the firm apologized (Anna Molin, 'IKEA Regrets Cutting Women From Saudi Ad,' *The Wall Street Journal*, October 1, 2012, http://online.wsj.com/article/SB100008723963904445924045780302742003871360.html).

350. Dale Neef, 'Supply chain ethics: The devil is in the details,' *Ethical Corporation*, April 14, 2005, http://www.ethicalcorp.com/content.asp?ContentID=3629

351. For example, see: Kris Hudson & Wilawan Watcharasakwet, 'The New Wal-Mart Effect: Cleaner Thai Shrimp Farms,' *Wall Street Journal*, July 24, 2007, p. B1.

352. For example, see the controversy that surrounds the use of forced child labor in the harvesting of cotton: Toby Webb, 'Special Report Cotton: Corporate action on Uzbeki white gold,' *Ethical Corporation*, March 6, 2008, http://www.ethicalcorp.com/content.asp?ContentID=5760

353. Nicholas D. Kristof, 'In Praise of the Maligned Sweatshop,' *New York Times*, June 6, 2006, p. A21.

354. Nicholas D. Kristof, 'Where Sweatshops Are A Dream,' *New York Times*, January 15, 2009, p. A27.

355. Andrea Tunarosa, 'What Do NGOs Have Against Poor Guatemalans?' *Wall Street Journal*, July 21, 2006, p. A15.

356. 'Moral maze for retailers reliant on developing world suppliers,' *Financial Times*, July 2, 2008, p. 16.

357. Roger Martin, 'The Virtue Matrix,' *Harvard Business Review,* March 2002, Vol. 80, No. 3, pp. 68–75.

358. Bob Herbert, 'In America: Nike's Boot Camps,' *New York Times,* March 31, 1997, p. A15.

359. 'Sweatfree Communities,' http://www.globalexchange.org/campaigns/sweatshops/nike/; 'Don't Do It,' http://www.dontdoitarmy.com/

360. Debora L. Spar, 'Hitting the Wall: Nike and International Labor Practices,' *Harvard Business School Press*, [9-700-047], September 6, 2002, p. 11.

361. Derrick Daye & Brad VanAuken, 'Social Responsibility: The Nike Story,' July 25, 2008, http://www.brandingstrategyinsider.com/2008/07/social-responsi.html

362. Jane L. Levere, 'New Balance Celebrates Its Homemade Footprint,' *The New York Times*, April 5, 2012, p. B2.

363. Jonathan Birchall, 'Nike to strengthen efforts to combat worker abuse,' *Financial Times*, May 31 2007, p. 9.

364. Sarah Skidmore, 'Nike finds major violations at Malaysian factory,' *Associated Press*, August 1, 2008, http://www.newsvine.com/_news/2008/08/01/1713691-nike-finds-major-violations-at-malaysian-factory

365. 'The boomerang effect,' *The Economist Special Report: Manufacturing and Innovation*, April 21, 2012, p. 8.

366. Chad Brooks, 'What's Bringin US Jobs Back from Overseas?' *Yahoo! News*, October 2, 2012, http://news.yahoo.com/whats-bringing-us-jobs-back-overseas-154734351.html

367. 'Rethinking Re-shoring,' *Knowledge@Wharton*, January 21, 2013, http://knowledgetoday.wharton.upenn.edu/2013/01/rethinking-re-shoring/

368. Additional evidence to support this reshoring effect can be found in: 'Here, there and everywhere,' *The Economist Special Report: Outsourcing and Offshoring*, January 19, 2013.

369. 'When workers dream of a life beyond the factory gates,' *The Economist*, December 15, 2012, p. 63.

370. Charles Isherwood, 'Moral Issues Behind iPhone And Its Makers,' *The New York Times*, October 18, 2012, p. C1.

371. Charles Duhigg & Keith Bradsher, 'How the U.S. Lost Out on iPhone Work,' *The New York Times*, January 21, 2012, http://www.nytimes.com/2012/01/22/business/apple-america-and-a-squeezed-middle-class.html

372. Charles Duhigg & David Barboza, 'In China, the Human Costs That Are Built Into an iPad,' *The New York Times*, January 26, 2012, p. A1 and pp. B10-11.

373. Associated Press, 'Chinese iPhone workers strike at Foxconn plant,' *The Daily Yomiuri*, October 8, 2012, p. 5.

374. Paul Mozur, 'New Labor Attitudes Fed Into China Riot,' *The Wall Street Journal*, September 27, 2012, p. B1.

375. See: The Daily Show with Jon Stewart, http://www.thedailyshow.com/watch/mon-january-16-2012/fear-factory

376. David Barboza & Charles Duhigg, 'Apple Supplier Accused of Using Forced Student Labor,' *The Salt Lake Tribune*, September 11, 2012, http://www.sltrib.com/sltrib/money/54873765-79/foxconn-students-apple-labor.html.csp

377. David Barboza, 'Workers Poisoned at Chinese Factory Wait for Apple to Fulfill a Pledge,' *The New York Times*, February 23, 2011, p. B1.

378. Jessica E. Vascellaro & Owen Fletcher, 'Apple Navigates China Maze,' *The Wall Street Journal*, January 14-15, 2012, p. B1.

379. David Barboza & Charles Duhigg, 'Pressure, Chinese and Foreign, Drives Changes at Foxconn,' *The New York Times*, February 20, 2012, p. B1.

380. Charles Duhigg & Nick Wingfield, 'Apple, in Shift, Pushes an Audit of Sites in China,' *The New York Times*, February 14, 2012, p. B6.

381. Loretta Chao, James T. Areddy & Aries Poon, 'Apple Pact to Ripple Across China,' *The Wall Street* Journal, March 31-April 1, 2012, p. B3.

382. Mallen Baker, 'Making the sustainable supply chain puzzle simpler – five ways to start,' *mallenbaker.net*, November 14, 2011, http://www.mallenbaker.net/csr/page.php?Story_ID=2712

383. Mallen Baker, 'The tricky task of measuring a reputation,' *mallenbaker.net*, February 21, 2012, http://www.mallenbaker.net/csr/page.php?Story_ID=2723

384. Paul Mozur, 'Foxconn Workers: Keep Our Overtime,' *The Wall Street Journal*, December 18, 2012, p. B1.

385. Keith Bradsher & Charles Duhigg, 'Signs of Changes Taking Hold in Electronics Factories in China,' *The New York Times*, December 27, 2012, p. A1.

386. Supplier Responsibility at Apple, January 2013, http://www.apple.com/supplier responsibility/

387. Eduardo Porter, 'Dividends In Pressing Apple Over Labor,' *The New York Times*, March 7, 2012, p. B5.

388. 'Just Do It: How Nike Turned Disclosure Into An Opportunity,' *Network for Business Sustainability*, January 23, 2012, http://nbs.net/knowledge/just-do-it-how-nike-turned-disclosure-into-an-opportunity/

389. See also: 'When the job inspector calls,' *The Economist*, March 31, 2012, p. 73.

390. James Hyatt, 'China Checkup,' *CRO Magazine*, May, 2008, http://thecro.com/node/672

391. For example, see: Sean Ansett & Jeffrey Hantover, 'Bangladesh factory fires – The hidden dangers of subcontracting,' *Ethical Corporation Magazine*, February 5, 2013, http://www.ethicalcorp.com/supply-chains/bangladesh-factory-fires-%E2%80%93-hidden-dangers-subcontracting and Stephanie Kang, 'Nike Cuts Ties With Pakistani Firm,' *Wall Street Journal*, November 21, 2006, p. B5.

392. 'iPhones make Chinese eyes light up,' *The Economist*, July 28, 2012, p. 55.

393. 'The boomerang effect,' *The Economist Special Report: Manufacturing and Innovation*, April 21, 2012, p. 8 and Jessica E. Lessin & James R. Hagerty, 'Apple CEO Says Mac Production Coming to U.S.,' *The Wall Street Journal*, December 6, 2012, http://online.wsj.com/article/SB1000142412788732464010457816299244638 7774.html

394. Tim Cook, Internal e-mail to Apple employees, January 26, 2012, *CBS News*, January 27, 2012, http://www.cbsnews.com/8301-501465_162-57367367-501465/apple-cares-about-every-worker-in-its-supply-chain-says-tim-cook/

Chapter 8

Societal Issues and Case-studies

ACCOUNTABILITY

> **CSR Connection:** This issue tackles the problem of how to measure CSR. It emphasizes the importance of accountability and transparency in a firm's relations with its stakeholders, and explores the societal consequences of fully incorporating all externalities into (lifecycle) product pricing.
>
> **Stakeholders:** Society, Consumers, Investors, Company.

Issue

Do you think of CSR in terms of a dichotomy (i.e., a firm is either socially responsible or not)? Or, do you think of CSR in terms of a continuum (i.e., all firms are either more or less socially responsible, depending on a number of factors and the context in which they occur)? If it is the former, then CSR is relatively easy to measure and there are plenty of options out there that claim to measure the CSR profile of firms. If it is the latter, however, then CSR is very difficult even to conceptualize fully (with many dimensions), let alone measure accurately.

In general, dichotomous measures of CSR are unhelpful to those who advocate for greater CSR for two reasons: First, because they contain the biases of the measuring organization (e.g., excluding specific industries, such as tobacco or firearms); and, second, because CSR is more complicated than a simple *yes* or *no*. All firms contain *good* and *bad*; the value is in being able to capture accurately the *net effect*—On balance, is a firm better or worse than other firms? The difficulty lies in equating these effects across the spectrum of different firm activities. Is a *responsible* firm in the pharmaceuticals industry, for example, equivalent to a *responsible* firm in the airlines industry? It is impossible to answer this question meaningfully unless you use a standard evaluation system that captures all dimensions of actions across all firms and industries. As such, any attempt to use dichotomous ratings to measure a causal relationship between CSR and overall firm performance (the foundation of a business argument for CSR) is unlikely to generate reliable or valid results. It is essential for those who study CSR and seek to evaluate firms in this respect, therefore, to think of CSR as a continuum, rather than a dichotomy.

Once CSR is thought of in terms of a continuum, what is the best way to measure CSR? Is a tobacco firm that employs tens of thousands of people and pays significant taxes a *better* or *worse* firm (in terms of CSR performance) than a supermarket that sells food, but pays its employees low wages? Is a firearms manufacturer, whose products are used to defend national security, *better* or *worse* than a pharmaceutical firm that produces lifesaving drugs, but refuses to make them affordable in developing countries? In adding up the *good* and the *bad*, it is firms that have a *net positive value added* that are effectively incorporating social responsibility into everyday operations. Capturing all possible metrics in a way that is objective and permits comparability across firms and industries, however, is incredibly complex. As a result, 'How do we measure CSR?' is one of the most pressing and contentious areas of the CSR debate today. How can a company be held accountable for its CSR actions in a way that is objectively measurable, yet financially feasible? How can we develop an accurate and consistent measure of CSR that allows stakeholders to evaluate the social and environmental impact of different products and firms, and compare them to other products and firms (i.e., compare apples with oranges along common metrics)? And, if we can't measure CSR, how can we tell whether and when it matters? A *CSR report* by a firm provides some answers. A *CSR audit*, containing objective standards developed by an independent third party, provides additional information.

CSR reports are increasingly recognized as a critical tool for firms seeking to incorporate CSR into everyday operations and strategic outlook. They allow firms to set CSR goals (thus, helping establish expectations and minimum operating standards internally), measure progress in relation to those goals, and remain accountable to stakeholders by communicating both goals and progress transparently. Important advances in CSR reporting include: GAP's 2003 Social Responsibility report, which disclosed vendor violations of the firm's Code of Conduct; Nike's 2004 Corporate Responsibility report, which identified its complete list of worldwide supplier factories; Timberland's 2006 *Our Footprint* labeling scheme, which clearly listed the environmental and social impact of the production process for each of its products; Stoneyfield Farm's 2008 partnership with Climate Counts to measure carbon emissions; and Patagonia's 2009 *Footprint Chronicles*, which combines elements of all of the above.[1] As firms increasingly accept the idea of internal monitoring beyond financial metrics and engage with external audit and evaluation organizations, the field is beginning to converge on a universal standard:

> [The] Global Reporting Initiative (GRI) has become the default standard for sustainability reporting. Launched in 2002, the GRI is referenced by 95% of the DJSI Super Sector leaders, 78% of the FTSE4Good Global 100, and 70% of the Global 100 Most Sustainable Corporations.[2]

Multi-stakeholder CSR Reporting Frameworks

Over the last two decades, a variety of organizations have emerged to help promote more transparent relations among firms and their stakeholders via CSR reports and audits:

AccountAbility (http://www.accountability.org/), a British organization founded in 1995, has been at the forefront of the push to establish a credible objective means by which the CSR performance of companies can be evaluated. Its AA1000 series of principle-based standards are "the assurance standard of choice. [The 1000AS] is used by 26% of the Global 100 Most Sustainable Corporations and also 26% of the DJSI Super Sector Leaders."[3]

The *Carbon Disclosure Project* (https://www.cdproject.net/), founded in 2000, is a nonprofit organization with the primary mission of reducing greenhouse gases. To this end, it provides "global system for thousands of companies and cities to measure, disclose, manage and share environmental information."[4]

The *Ceres Principles* (http://www.ceres.org/about-us/our-history/ceres-principles) were created in 1989. The Principles is a ten-point code of environmental conduct that is to be "endorsed by companies as an environmental mission statement or ethic. Embedded in that code of conduct was the mandate to report periodically on environmental management structures and results.[5]

The *Fair Labor Association* (http://www.fairlabor.org/), founded in 1999, encourages multinational firms to allow their overseas factories to be audited by the FLA. Significantly, the FLA pushes to allow the final reports to be made public, something often resisted by corporations in the past. This occurred for the first time in June 2003.

(Continued)

(Continued)

Global Reporting Initiative (http://www.globalreporting.org/) is the leading light in the field. Founded in 1997, GRI works with the United Nations to realize its vision "that disclosure on economic, environmental, and social performance is as commonplace and comparable as financial reporting, and important to organizational success."[6]

GMI Ratings (http://www3.gmiratings.com/) formed in 2010, following the merger of The Corporate Library, GovernanceMetrics International, and Audit Integrity. Today, GMI Ratings claims to provide "the most extensive coverage of environmental, social, governance and accounting-related risks affecting the performance of public companies worldwide."[7]

The *Greenhouse Gas Protocol* (http://www.ghgprotocol.org/) was launched in 2001 out of a partnership between the World Resources Institute and the World Business Council for Sustainable Development. The Protocol claims to be "the most widely used international accounting tool for government and business leaders to understand, quantify, and manage greenhouse gas emissions."[8]

The *ILO Labour Standards* (http://www.ilo.org/global/standards/lang--en/index.htm) were introduced in 1919 with the goal of "promoting opportunities for women and men to obtain decent and productive work, in conditions of freedom, equity, security and dignity."[9] Today, they represent "a comprehensive system of instruments on work and social policy, backed by a supervisory system designed to address all sorts of problems in their application at the national level."[10]

International Integrated Reporting Committee (http://www.theiirc.org/) aims to "create a framework for integrated reporting that brings together financial, environmental, social and governance information in a consistent and comparable format."[11]

ISO 26000 (http://www.iso.org/iso/iso26000). Launched in 2010, the standard is intended to act as a guide for *appropriate* behavior and is not available as a certification process (unlike other ISO standards). The ISO 26000, however, is recognized as "the leading global multi-stakeholder forum for debate on what is meant by social responsibility and how it should be applied to organizations on a day-to-day basis."[12]

The *OECD Guidelines for Multinational Enterprises* (http://www.oecd.org/daf/internationalinvestment/guidelinesformultinationalenterprises/), were first adopted in 1976. They "provide voluntary principles and standards for responsible business conduct in areas such as employment and industrial relations, human rights, environment, information disclosure, combating bribery, consumer interests, science and technology, competition, and taxation."[13]

Social Accountability International (http://www.sa-intl.org/), founded in 1997, was one of the eight founding members of the auditing and accreditation alliance ISEAL (International Social and Environmental Accreditation and Labeling). ISEAL has an international focus and shows the willingness among accreditation organizations to move toward a set of internationally recognized standards. SA 8000, in particular, is "a global and verifiable standard designed to make workplaces more humane."[14]

The *United Nations Global Compact* (http://www.unglobalcompact.org/), launched in 2000, is a global initiative designed to encourage firms to align their policies with ten principles in areas such as human rights, anti-corruption, and the environment.[15] Since 2000, it has grown to "more than 10,000 participants, including over 7,000 businesses in 145 countries around the world."[16]

The *United Nations Guiding Principles on Business and Human Rights* (http://www.ohchr.org/Documents/Publications/GuidingPrinciplesBusiness HR_EN.pdf), also known as the Ruggie Principles, were endorsed by the UN Human Rights Council in 2011. The Guiding Principles "recommend how governments should provide greater clarity of expectations and consistency of rule for business in relation to human rights."[17]

The *Universal Declaration of Human Rights, UDHR* (http://www.un.org/en/ documents/udhr/index.shtml) was adopted by the UN General Assembly in 1948. The Declaration defines "the concept of human rights broadly, to include not only political rights but also social and economic rights. Universally accepted, the UDHR has formed the basis of many constitutions around the world. Moreover, the UDHR is cited in many corporate responsibility codes and principles."[18]

Verité (http://www.verite.org/), founded in 1995, is a major influence in the social auditing field as a nonprofit organization that works with firms, through factory inspections, to improve the working conditions throughout the supply chain.

Among the many different multi-stakeholder platforms and measurement tools (both at the macro, multi-institutional level and at the micro, individual brand level), GRI is pre-eminent:

Since its inception, the GRI has become a worldwide, multi-stakeholder network which includes representatives from business, civil society, labour, investors, accountants and others. Revisions to the framework take place through an exhaustive set of committees and subcommittees, [which, GRI claims, ensures] the credibility and trust needed to make a global framework successful.[19]

As CSR reporting moves from *"nice to have* to *can't avoid*,"[20] GRI is successful because it is indicator-based. As such, the GRI allows firms "to track their progress and to set objectives."[21] GRI has diffused to the point where "many countries now require them, either by law or as a condition of stock exchange listing."[22] And, while commentators have criticized earlier drafts of the GRI for being a box-ticking exercise that conveys much data but little meaning, the most recently issued consultation draft (G4) represents significant progress.[23]

When it is done effectively, transparency and honesty in all aspects of a firm's operations allow external observers to evaluate the organization, its managers, and policies. The reporting of a firm's activities in a misleading way, however, if discovered, can have a negative impact on the perception of that organization among external stakeholders. The different perceptions of BP and Exxon in the oil industry are instructive—while BP had spent a lot of money re-branding itself as "beyond petroleum," Exxon drew criticism from the CSR community due to its CEO's long-standing skepticism of climate change. Nevertheless, as we discovered with the 2010 Deepwater Horizon oil spill, performance outweighs branding in terms of environmental impact:

> Between 1997 and 1998 alone, . . . BP was responsible for 104 oil spills in the Arctic. And in 2008, BP received the largest fine in the history of the U.S. Chemical Safety and Hazard Investigation Board: $87 million for failing to correct safety hazards revealed in the 2005 Texas City explosion. As of June 2010, BP has had 760 such OSHA fines for "egregious, willful" safety violations. Meanwhile Exxon Mobil has had just one.[24]

Although CSR reporting has come a long way in recent years, therefore, it still suffers from the potential for *greenwashing* and the lack of authenticity that only an independent audit can provide. As such, it is important to recognize that, when we talk about a firm being *accountable* and CSR reporting as a means to that end, we are really talking about three separate steps, each of which need to be clear and transparent if the system as a whole is to be effective:

> First, standards—a set of requirements, usually taking a consensus-based approach. Second, certifications—providing assurance of conformity against this standard. And, third, the [consumer] labels themselves—on-pack marks that indicate conformance with the standard. This model came into being over 30 years ago, and . . . has changed very little in that time.[25]

As the field progresses and firms recognize the value of reporting or compliance as a source of legitimacy, the second step in that process, CSR auditing, is evolving rapidly. As a result, the field is moving beyond the foundation of the triple bottom line (which measures firm performance on various financial, environmental, and social metrics)[26] into the search for detailed, objective, and verifiable standards that allow stakeholders to compare different firms in different industries. In addition to presenting a more complete CSR perspective of a company's operations, establishing these standards represents an essential component for those seeking an holistic assessment of business risk:

> "We are not social activists; we're independent risk assessors," says George Dallas of S&P. The information in non-financial reports "contributes to building up a company's risk profile." And although it has still not been convincingly demonstrated that good environmental and social practices create value for shareholders, it is clear, says Mr. Dallas, that bad ones can destroy it.[27]

As the field develops, new tools are constantly being introduced to help observers evaluate different firms' operations from a CSR perspective. One way in which auditors can signal quality is via a recognized certification process, by which specific independent actors (such as the NGOs, Rainforest Alliance Network, Greenpeace, or the Forest Stewardship Council) audit and then certify that particular products are being produced and sourced in ways that meet established criteria. So, for example, McDonald's announced in 2013 that it would partner with the Marine Stewardship Council (MSC) "to show that the fish it serves is caught in an environmentally sustainable manner."[28] Along similar lines:

> Sainsbury's is the largest retailer of MSC certified fish in the UK and we offer twice as many MSC labelled products as our nearest competitor. All of the tuna in our sandwiches and sushi will be pole and line caught by the end of the year and we are the UK's largest retailer of RSPCA Freedom Food approved salmon.[29]

One of the most heralded developments in recent years was the negotiation of a voluntary standard for CSR by the International Organization for Standardization (ISO). The consultation phase for the Corporate Social Responsibility standard, ISO 26000, was initiated in 2005, with the standard launched worldwide in 2010.[30] The evolution of ISO 26000 represents both the political and practical challenges in attempting to measure CSR. Some commentators, for example, while supporting ISO 26000, caution against it being held up as the gold standard of CSR behavior. They argue that CSR is not like *quality* or *environmental performance*, which can be measured, but contains important qualitative components that are not easily quantified. This is the primary reason why ISO 26000 was developed as a *guide*, rather than as a *standard*:

> Fundamentally, CSR is about relationships. Stakeholders change their minds. They can punish you today for doing what they demanded yesterday. Building those relationships—and resolving the dilemmas that present themselves along the way is really more of an art than a science. It's not something that easily lends itself to a standards-based approach.[31]

Other commentators and some governments, however, are concerned that, what is guidance on the surface can quickly become a socially-accepted standard if widely adopted:

> ISO's brand recognition and credibility give it potential to make a positive contribution to social responsibility. ISO standards are voluntary, but they frequently become benchmarks for good practice among businesses. They are often referenced in supply chain requirements. And many are absorbed into national regulations and standards.[32]

As a result of this qualitative component of CSR, and notwithstanding the diffusion of GRI, progress towards a universally accepted CSR standard remains incremental at best. More than two years on from the launch of ISO 26000, for example, its value remains highly debated, with some dismissing the guide as a political process that produced a "limp noodle . . . [that consists of] little more than high-minded rhetoric":

> Let's be clear: the 26000 standard is nothing like the guidelines put forth by the ISO on other aspects of business. . . . ISO 26000 is both vague and highly political. Each section has a laundry list of daunting societal problems, mostly in developing countries, followed by a wish list of NGO-supported solutions, the bill for which would be picked up by developed countries. . . . The United States and India, which supported early drafts of ISO 26000, ultimately voted, along with three other countries, against the final version. Critics believe it contains problematic proclamations about contested notions of environmental impacts and employee and consumer rights, but no endorsement of shareholder rights.[33]

Critics complain that ISO 26000 is not nearly ambitious enough—that it is good as a basic outline or checklist and helps identify and define stakeholders, but is less effective in terms of how to implement the ideas. Importantly, there is little rigor and next to no enforcement. And, in the absence of a universal standard that can measure performance, CSR reports remain focused on processes, rather than focusing on outcomes. In general, CSR reports today:

> . . . [talk] about whether the company sets targets. [They talk] about whether the report follows the GRI guidelines. [They talk] about whether the report is assured by an independent third party. The only thing [they do not] talk about is how that company is actually performing on a social, environmental or economic scale. . . . By and large, CSR reports—whether GRI, independently assured, or printed on hemp with biodegradable ink, are not being accepted as providing useful evidence.[34]

CSR Newsletters: Puma

An article by Mallen Baker[35] highlights the futility of relying solely on quantitative metrics to capture a firm's CSR performance. The comment was initially prompted by a BBC News story,[36] which reported that Puma was "the world's first major corporation to publish details of the cost of its impact on the environment. . . . the combined cost of the carbon it emitted and water it used in 2010 was 94.4m euros ($134.3m; £82.8m)." Baker deconstructs this figure by questioning the assumptions that were necessary to generate a number that is supposed to represent the environmental damage done by Puma's operations:

> Let's suppose changes in average world temperature lead to the extinction of, let's say Blue Whales, and an obscure currently undiscovered insect in the Amazon. What valuation would we place on the Blue Whale, and how would we calculate it? On the potential economic value of products that might be extracted from it? On the basis of what someone would be prepared to pay for it's existence to be preserved? And what about the insect we never even heard of? Suppose it might hold the secret of a new pharmaceutical discovery? Or then again, it might not.

Baker's conclusion, however, is both instructive and presents an insightful comment on our willingness to trust numbers:

> So the figures are bogus. Unquantifiable. Why would the BBC cover such a story? Oh, yes, that's right. Because the figures have been produced by PwC amongst others. The magical power of auditors to give credibility to numbers.

(Continued)

(Continued)

In spite of the futility involved in this exercise to measure perfectly a firm's CSR profile, does that mean we have to throw our hands up in the air and surrender, returning to moral/ethical arguments designed to persuade executives to "do the right thing"? Baker's point that, as a society, we place great faith in the face-value of numbers (and are less likely to question the underlying methodology) provides the ammunition he needs to critique the figure Puma arrives at; it also, however, provides the logic for continuing the pursuit of effective metrics for measuring CSR activity.

To the extent that we can arrive at a standardized way of measuring what we agree should be measured, then we will be able to compare one firm's activity with another's. Whether those figures are 100 percent accurate is less important than whether any biases are applied equally to all firms. If they are, the measure represents a relative assessment of performance. Almost all measures involve subjective interpretations and assumptions, but have become accepted as objective statements of fact (albeit socially constructed). Placing a value on the extinction of the Blue Whale versus an unrealized pharmaceutical discovery will always involve some element of subjectivity (and, therefore, be open to contestation).

There is a great deal of value, however, in identifying a relative measure of which firms are better or worse performers. This speaks to continued investigation in this difficult area and the application of standardized measures across all firms. As Baker concludes, "the point is not the answer—it is that you haven't sufficiently well-defined the question."

The third step in the reporting process concerns the disclosure of goals and progress to external stakeholders (in particular, consumers). This usually involves a product label of some sort, ideally accompanied by the logo of a respected certifying auditor, which is either attached to the product or advertised at the point of sale. The goal is to convey some sense of the standards passed in order to earn the gold star, letter grade A, score of 5 (out of 5), or whatever method used by the producer to register quality in terms of CSR performance, such as Whole Foods' color-coded rating program to assess and support sustainable seafood products:

Similar to a stoplight, seafood is given a green, yellow or red rating. A green rating indicates the species is relatively abundant and is caught in environmentally friendly ways. Yellow means some concerns exist with the species' status or the methods by which it was caught. And a red rating means the species is suffering from overfishing, or the methods used to catch it harm other marine life or habitats. . . . Whole Foods also announced Monday that it will end sales of red-rated species by Earth Day 2013.[37]

As this example indicates, however, often these labels are instigated at the initiative of a particular company and may or may not conform with industry standards (even if such standards exist). As such, the main problem with these labels is not the absence of such measures, but the proliferation of efforts to measure CSR. In terms of *ecolabels* (labels designed to measure environmental impact), for example, there are currently estimated to be "400 and counting – and the move to mainstream for many (thus removing their value as a differentiator) is significantly reducing their value."[38] The problem comes, not from the good intentions of each organization, but from the varying methods they use to evaluate performance and the varying means they use to convey that information to consumers and other stakeholders. The result is confusion, rather than clarity. In North America alone, there are 88 such eco-labels.[39] As a result, the Federal Trade Commission has produced guidelines designed to increase the value of such certifications:

> The commission's revised "Green Guides" . . . warn marketers against using labels that make broad claims that cannot be substantiated, like "eco-friendly." Marketers must qualify their claims on the product packaging and limit them to a specific benefit, such as how much of the product is recycled. [40]

Of course, if all firms were socially responsible and worked to eradicate unsustainable or harmful practices from their supply chains, none of this would be necessary. One market-based approach to achieving this is to account for all costs in the pricing of products—lifecycle pricing.

Case Study: Lifecycle Pricing

As highlighted above, the value of being able to measure CSR is threefold for firms: it allows them to set goals; it allows them to measure progress; and it allows them to communicate that progress to their various stakeholders. A perfect example of the complexity of the measuring component and the benefits in terms of communication coincide in the work that is being done by Walmart (and other retailers, including "Gap, JC Penney, Levi Strauss, Nike, Marks and Spencer, Adidas, H&M," and many more)[41] to create a standardized *eco-label* for all products.[42] The goal is to have a label and unified evaluation metric that captures environmental impact ("from the greenhouse-gas emissions of an Xbox to the water used to produce your Sunday bacon")[43] on every one of the 100,000+ products in every Walmart Superstore (and, in theory, in every other store). The effort is monumental. As a result, it will change the game in terms of the extent to which firms are accountable for the products they produce:

> More than 200 clothing manufacturers and retailers have joined together to create an industry-wide sustainability rating, the Eco Index, which will assess the environmental impact of products along their entire life-cycle chain. . . . The Eco Index . . . provides three types of tools – guidelines, indicators and metrics . . . [that] enable any company to participate, whether seasoned in sustainability or not. Each tool assesses a product's impact within six life-cycle stages: materials; packaging; product manufacturing and assembly; transport and distribution; use and service; and end of life.[44]

The goal of the group (the Sustainable Apparel Coalition) is to connect the consumer with every stage of the production process ("giving them a much more detailed view into the supply of fabrics, zippers, dyes, threads, buttons and grommets that come together to form the clothing they buy, as well as what impact the creation of that clothing has on both people and the planet"),[45] while also giving companies what amounts to perfect knowledge of the supply chain:

> The coalition's tool is meant to be a database of scores assigned to all the players in the life cycle of a garment—cotton growers, synthetic fabric makers, dye suppliers, textile mill owners, as well as packagers, shippers, retailers and consumers—based on a variety of social and environmental measures like water and land use, energy efficiency, waste production, chemical use, greenhouse gases and labor practices.[46]

In order for this effort to be effective, however, the Eco Label project has to grapple with the idea of *lifecycle pricing*. What the group is doing is attempting to capture all of the impacts of the production process, at each step in the supply chain, and assign a quantitative value to that step. Although it is a lot more complicated than this (simply trying to avoid double-counting is, in itself, highly complex), in essence, they will add up the positive and negative values to arrive at a net impact score for each product. In short, the group is trying to measure externalities—costs that firms previously have often pushed onto others.

Externality

The Oxford English Dictionary defines an *externality* as:

> A side-effect or consequence (of an industrial or commercial activity) which affects other parties without this being reflected in the cost of the goods or services involved; a social cost or benefit.[47]

Lifecycle pricing, therefore, attempts to eradicate the idea of an externality—rather than being an effect that is not "reflected in the cost of the goods or services involved," the goal of lifecycle pricing is to incorporate (or internalize) all costs within the final price of the product. This is important because, "If prices reflected all the costs, including ecological costs spread across generations, the world would not face sustainability challenges; at least in theory."[48]

Figure 8.1 presents the six stages of the lifecycle framework: Extraction → Processing → Manufacture → Wholesale/Retail → Purchase/Consume → Dispose/Recycle. Between each stage there is transportation and storage, as well as inputs of energy, materials, and other resources that are used in the processing that occurs before and after the transition. Each stage also generates outputs, such as waste materials and other forms of pollution. The overall process should be valued in terms of the triple bottom line (financial, social, and environmental), as well as ethical considerations that are associated with decisions made throughout the system.

Lifecycle pricing supports the idea that we need to develop an economic model that is no longer founded on waste by accounting for total costs in pricing (i.e., similar to the idea of Pigovian taxes—"When an activity imposes costs on society, economists have long said that the activity should be taxed").[49] In other words, the price of a product should not only include the cost of production, but also include the costs associated with replenishing the raw materials used and disposing/recycling of the waste after consumption. Attempts to put a price on carbon reflect

Figure 8.1 The Product Lifecycle

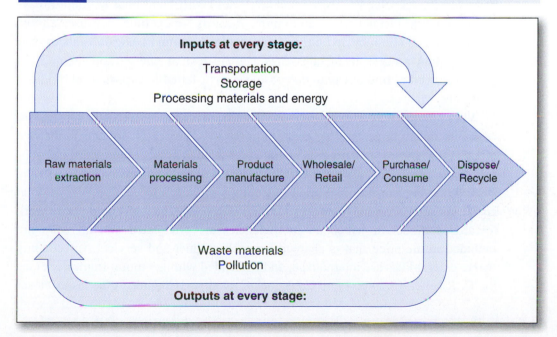

this process (either through a carbon tax or cap-and-trade program),[50] while firms' efforts to develop carbon footprints[51] provide a possible means of implementation.

There are a number of firms that are incorporating lifecycle pricing into their core business model. Nike is one good example, with its GreenXchange initiative,[52] "which open sources life cycle design methods."[53] But, perhaps the best example of a firm that has comprehensively attempted to integrate a lifecycle approach throughout operations is Interface carpets, whose inspirational founder and CEO, the late Ray Anderson, explained his journey in terms of the seven (+1) faces of *Mount Sustainability*: 1. Waste. 2. Emissions. 3. Energy. 4. Materials. 5. Transportation. 6. Culture. 7. Market. 8. Social equity.[54] In Anderson's vision, the peak of the mountain represents *sustainability*, which he defines as "take nothing, do no harm." The natural conclusion of such a *cradle-to-cradle*, closed-loop system throughout a firm's value chain is zero waste. Anderson expanded on his vision of the business logic of sustainability ("Project Zero," to be reached by 2020) at the TED conference in 2009.[55]

It is only by developing industry-wide standards within a lifecycle pricing model that we will move closer to understanding the holistic impact of our current economic system and business practices. What is not clear is the extent to which consumers want this information and will act on it. What is without doubt is that, as a society, we need to act, and act quickly. We have created an economic system based around convenience and waste—we spend money we do not have, on things we do not want, for purposes that are unimportant.[56] As a result, "the typical person discards 4.5 pounds of stuff per day, [only] 1.5 pounds of which are recycled."[57] Even recycling is an insufficient goal within a lifecycle framework. Instead, we need to move towards "upcycling" because "almost all products can be recycled only as low-grade reclaimed basic substances, and the recycling process itself consumes a great deal of energy and labor."[58] In short, we need to find a way to decrease our unsustainable exploitation of virgin resources.

What should be clear from the above discussion is that, as currently constituted, "markets fail to price the true costs of goods."[59] The reason for this is that the markets we have created are riddled with inefficiencies (what politicians call subsidies, tax breaks, loopholes, etc.). These inefficiencies introduce costs into the system that prevent the final price reflecting a product's true value (i.e., its total costs). As such, we need to reform our market system. The goal should be to work towards a model in which all inefficiencies are eradicated and all costs are included in the price that is charged for each product and service. An economy where externalities are internalized, and embedded within a moral framework (see the CSR Filter, Chapter 4 and Conscious Capitalism, Chapter 5) moves us closer to the economy Adam Smith envisioned and wrote about in his classic treatise *The Theory of Moral Sentiments*[60]—truly free markets filled with values-based businesses and vigilant stakeholders. Instead, we have a very different reality:

> Corporate welfare [by government] is the offer of special favors—cash grants, loans, guarantees, bailouts and special tax breaks—to specific industries or firms . . . . [estimated in the U.S. to be] $92 billion for fiscal 2006, which is more than the U.S. government spends on homeland security. That annual cost may have doubled to $200 billion in this new era of industry bailouts and subsidies. According to the House Budget Committee, the 2009 stimulus bill alone contained more than $80 billion in "clean energy" subsidies, and tens of billions more went for the auto bailout and cash for clunkers, as well as aid for the mortgage industry through programs to refinance or buy up toxic loans.[61]

If companies are forced to price finished products accurately, many of the cheap items in our disposable economy will become significantly more expensive and businesses will be incentivized to produce sustainable alternatives. The market remains the most effective means we know of allocating scarce and valuable resources in ways that maximize social outcomes. Rather than subsidizing specific industries, adequately pricing the *true* cost of a product allows for a less distorted competition of ideas in the marketplace that should also generate socially responsible outcomes.

People on both the left and the right tend to favor government intervention when it is in support of a cause in which they believe (e.g., subsidies for solar power on the left, tax breaks for oil firms on the right), but at least the left recognizes that it favors government intervention. Right-wing ideology, in contrast, preaches the free market, but then implements heavily subsidized intervention in contravention of that ideology. What the above quote about corporate welfare does not include, therefore, is the recognition that subsidies and quotas are only one component of the inefficient system of corporate subsidies we have created in the West:

> Economics 101 tells us that an industry imposing large costs on third parties should be required to "internalize" those costs. . . . [Extraction by] Fracking might still be worth doing given those costs. But no industry should be held harmless from its impacts on the environment and the nation's infrastructure. Yet what the industry and its defenders demand is, of course, precisely that it be let off the hook for the damage it causes. Why? Because we need that energy![62]

It is the combination of reduced government intervention (i.e., the removal of subsidies, quotas, tax breaks, etc.) *plus* the internalization of all externalities in pricing that allows a truly free market to emerge. One without the other is not free; at present, we have neither:

> So it's worth pointing out that special treatment for fracking makes a mockery of free-market principles. Pro-fracking politicians claim to be against subsidies, yet letting an industry impose costs without paying compensation is in effect a huge subsidy. They say they oppose having the government "pick winners," yet they demand special treatment for this industry precisely because they claim it will be a winner.[63]

In this light, a government tax on carbon is simply a means of accounting for the full environmental costs of oil/gas extraction, processing, and consumption. In other words, it is a means of creating the conditions for a *free* market. Once the level-playing field has been created (with more accurate prices for all forms of energy—traditional and alternative), then the market will determine which energy sources should drive our future economies. Ultimately:

> . . . markets are truly free only when everyone pays the full price for his or her actions. Anything else is socialism. . . . Our future will largely be determined by our ability to admit the need to end planetary socialism. That's the most fundamental of economics lessons and one any serious environmentalist ought to heed.[64]

CEO Perspective

Howard Schultz (Starbucks)

[In 2008, when Schultz returned to lead Starbucks] Our stock was in free fall. One day, I found myself on a phone call with one large institutional share-holder. He addressed the longstanding health coverage for our employees, which at the time cost $250 million. He said this would be the perfect time for Starbucks and me to cut health care. Many companies were doing this at the time, so I would be immune from any public outcry. I tried to describe to him that the essence of the brand is humanity, and our culture is steeped in two primary benefits that have defined who we are: comprehensive health-insurance coverage for our people and equity in the form of stock options, which we give to anyone who works more than 20 hours a week. I told him,

"This is a nonstarter at every level because you don't understand the essence of our company. After all these years, if you believe the financial crisis should change our principles and core purpose, perhaps you should sell your stock. I'm not building a stock. I'm trying to build a great, enduring company." We are a performance-driven organization, but we have to lead the company through the lens of humanity.[65]

Online Resources

- British Standard BS 8900, http://www.bsi-global.com/Shop/Publication-Detail/?pid=000000000030118956
- Center for Sustainable Innovation (CSI), http://www.sustainableinnovation.org/
- Cradle to Cradle Certification, http://www.c2ccertified.org/
- Ecolabel Index, http://www.ecolabelindex.com/
- EU Eco-Management and Audit Scheme, http://www.iema.net/ems/emas
- International Social and Environmental Accreditation and Labeling (ISEAL) Alliance, http://www.isealalliance.org/
- International Organization for Standardization (ISO), http://www.iso.org/ (ISO 14000, http://www.iso.org/iso/iso_14000_essentials and ISO 26000, http://www.iso.org/sr/)
- SustainAbility, http://www.sustainability.com/
- Sustainable Apparel Coalition, http://www.apparelcoalition.org/
- United Nations Millennium Goals, http://www.un.org/millenniumgoals/

Pro/Con Debate

Pro/Con Debate: In the absence of legislation, firms should incorporate all externalities/costs into the price of their products voluntarily.

Questions for Discussion and Review

1. Do you think of CSR in terms of a dichotomy or do you think of CSR in terms of a continuum? If it is the former, what advantages does this approach provide? If it is the latter, what implications does this have for those seeking to measure CSR?

2. Is a tobacco firm that employs tens of thousands of people and pays significant taxes a *better* or *worse* firm (in terms of CSR performance) than a supermarket that sells food, but pays its employees low wages?

3. Who benefits most from the publication of a CSR report—the firm or its stakeholders? What are the dangers of *greenwash*, where a firm inflates or misrepresents its CSR achievements in the hope of reputation benefits?

4. Why is it important that an audit of a company's operations be conducted by an independent organization? What benefits are there for a firm in working together with NGOs to conduct a social audit of operations? What are the dangers? Which approach would you use if a major client wanted you to demonstrate your CSR commitment?

5. Have a look at the following certification logos. Do you recognize any of them? Do you know what they measure? If you wanted to buy a product and one brand had one of these logos attached and another didn't, would it affect your purchase decision?

COMPLIANCE

CSR Connection:	This issue reflects an ongoing debate within CSR—The extent to which companies should be compelled, or encouraged to adhere voluntarily, to more socially responsible practices.
Stakeholders:	Government, Society, Company.

Issue

It is generally recognized that firms seek to pursue their best interests and that those interests are narrowly defined around profit maximization. What is debated, however, is the extent to which this focus on profit also maximizes the level of social value added by firms. And specifically, if the pursuit of profit does generate social value, how should that outcome be achieved? Should firms be free to pursue their self interest and let the market determine the nature of their actions (through interactions with consumers and competitors, for example) or should society impose specific actions on firms with the goal of achieving specific social outcomes (through government legislation and other forms of coercion)? In short, should CSR be voluntary or mandatory?

Those who support the *mandating* of specific actions argue that this is the only way to ensure firms will behave in a way that is socially acceptable. They believe that the only way to generate ideal outcomes is via coercion. In terms of encouragement, in the area of sustainability for example, they argue that "every example of major environmental progress—reducing acid rain, improving air quality, restoring the ozone layer—has been the result of national legislation or a global treaty;"[66] and, in terms of punishment, they argue that, for executives and other corporate employees, "Fines are meaningless. Only prison can change behavior."[67]

Unfortunately, the evidence in support of the business case for corporate social responsibility is weak. . . . [and, as such] corporations do not have sufficient incentive to devote the resources needed to ameliorate the problems corporate social responsibility is intended to address.[68]

Those who support the opposite position (*voluntary* action by firms), however, argue that additional regulation is a distraction and an added cost to business that generates less optimal social outcomes. In the U.S. healthcare industry, for example, they note that, due to excessive regulation, for every hour spent treating a patient, there is a corresponding increase in paperwork of at least the same amount of time. In 2013, "the number of federally mandated categories of illness and injury for which hospitals may claim reimbursement will rise from 18,000 to 140,000. There are nine codes relating to injuries caused by parrots, and three relating to burns from flaming water-skis."[69] As a result of such regulatory confusion and complexity, these people believe that it is only when an organization genuinely believes that CSR is in its best interests that it will commit sufficient resources to achieving that goal. Otherwise, firms will only find ways to avoid the rules ("Time and again, financial innovation finds a lucrative path around regulation"),[70] defeating the very purpose and effort invested in creating them. Working to encourage *voluntary* action on the part of companies, therefore, is the most effective way of producing genuine and meaningful change:

> Legislation is designed to enforce minimum standards. CSR is about best practice. . . . A government can no more legislate for best practice than it can repeal the laws of gravity.[71]

Voluntary vs. Mandatory

At one end of the spectrum is an argument in favor of legislation to control the worst excesses of firms:

> *Existing laws do not compel a high enough standard of social behavior. Companies will never do more than is required of them if the action is considered a cost to business. Therefore, new and stricter legislation is required to compel more responsible corporate behavior.*

At the other end of the spectrum is an argument in favor of encouraging voluntary action by providing incentives that demonstrates the value of compliance:

> *Companies should realize it is in their best interests to make sure the communities in which they do business accept them. It is those communities' expectations and shifting standards that will define what is and what is not acceptable behavior. Best practice cannot easily be defined or mandated. If CSR behavior is tied to success, then the profit motive will provide the ideal incentive for the necessary innovation.*

Needless to say, there are also several shades of gray between these two points of view at the extremes.

Compliance with stakeholder expectations goes to the heart of CSR because it largely dictates the degree to which a company is accepted by society. Those companies that add value will be welcomed and those that are perceived to be detracting from the general wellbeing will be criticized and even rejected. As such, there is a strong case for the strict regulation of a company's actions when they come into (potentially negative) contact with society. Left to its own devices and if it felt it could get away with it, for example, a firm transporting nuclear waste might be tempted to avoid undertaking all the costly precautions necessary to ensure a completely safe journey. As the discussion above suggests, however, there is an equally strong case to be made that a company has to be genuinely committed to implementing CSR in order for it to be effective and that no amount of regulation can dictate such commitment. Alan Greenspan, chairman of the Federal Reserve Board in the United States from 1987 to 2006, has long been an advocate of self-regulation, or voluntary compliance, within the finance industry:

> "It is in the self-interest of every businessman to have a reputation for honest dealings and a quality product," he wrote . . . in 1963. Regulation, he said, undermines this "superlatively moral system" by replacing competition for reputation with force. . . . [Greenspan] still admires the laissez-faire capitalism of the mid-19th century. At that time, competition, not regulation, kept financial markets honest. Banks, for example, issued their own currency whose value fluctuated with the issuer's reputation.[72]

Government regulatory interventions—such as producing a national currency and guaranteeing individual savings deposits—Greenspan argues, reduces "the incentive for bankers and businessmen to act prudently . . . [and makes] depositors less concerned about the reputation of the bank to which they entrusted their money."[73] Needless to say, the Financial Crisis has shaken Greenspan's unwavering faith in the self-correcting power of the market. Appearing before the House Committee on Oversight and Government Reform to give testimony on the crisis, Greenspan declared that "Those of us who have looked to the self-interest of lending institutions to protect shareholders' equity, myself included, are in a state of shocked disbelief."[74]

Many CSR advocates believe that voluntary change is central to a definition and clear understanding of CSR as "the voluntary integration of environmental and social considerations into core business operations over and above legal obligations, and is based on dialogue with stakeholders."[75] It is also true, however, that many companies would prefer to determine operational costs based on self-interest (i.e., as low as possible), rather than on what an objective evaluation indicates would be best for society in general, if money were no object. Hence the case for stricter legislation in specific areas acts as a safeguard for society's interests:

> Enron, for example, proudly presented its CSR credentials as a giant PR exercise while internally betraying them. Unless companies really own CSR it is only window-dressing, argue the voluntarists. . . . The best instrument is to show business that behaving well is good business, so that it adopts CSR willingly and internalizes it.[76]

As a general rule, people have argued for a place for regulation in areas of greatest interest to the largest number of people. In France, for example, "since 2002 all public companies have been required to report social and environmental information as part of the annual report."[77] As noted above, however, the trouble with excessive regulation is that it is very costly. The average cost to a public firm in the U.S. in order to comply with Sarbanes-Oxley legislation, for example, is estimated to be $2.3 million a year.[78] Where costs become too high, the advantages to firms of remaining public are reduced, and the dangers to society increase as firms shrink from the glare of public oversight. In 2012, for example:

> The number of public companies has fallen dramatically over the past decade— by 38% in America since 1997 and 48% in Britain. The number of initial public offerings (IPOs) in America has declined from an average of 311 a year in 1980–2000 to 99 a year in 2001–11. Small companies, those with annual sales of less than $50m before their IPOs—have been hardest hit. In 1980–2000 an average of 165 small companies undertook IPOs in America each year. In 2001–09 that number fell to 30. [79]

While too much regulation stifles entrepreneurship and encourages inefficiency, firms' best interests require an understanding that stakeholder definitions of acceptable behavior are dynamic. If firms ignore stakeholders' expectations, a potentially more damaging backlash of widespread, punitive regulation may stifle the business environment for all. Ironically, it is often those firms that have felt the brunt of the attention of CSR campaigners at some point in the past that are subsequently the most proactive regarding CSR. These companies understand more completely the self-interest in reacting positively to prior stakeholder backlash and instigating CSR protection to try and avoid similar problems in the future:

> Shell's experience with *Brent Spar* and in Nigeria convinced it to take relations with its stakeholders more seriously, becoming an exemplar of best practice in its environmental and social reporting.[80]

It is always difficult to tell, of course, whether these incidents prompt a company genuinely to reevaluate its operations and strategic perspective to incorporate the importance of CSR, or whether the company merely recognizes a need to *appear* concerned about issues that are potentially harmful. Shell's more recent CSR performance indicates this concern is valid. A 2009 study that looked at publicly available data in the oil industry to evaluate emissions reporting by six major oil companies on a scale of 1 (bad) to 5 (good) in terms of "the level of detail, frequency and coherency of emissions disclosures," for example, "scored Shell at

1.15 out of 5 on its carbon disclosures. That compares with 3.05 for BP, 2.76 for Exxon, 2.64 for Conoco-Phillips, 2.4 for Chevron and 2.03 for Total."[81] The debate between voluntary carrots and mandatory sticks as the most effective way to encourage CSR behavior continues. . . .

Case Study: Nudge

What is the most effective way to encourage recycling? Is it better to appeal to people's self-interest, arguing the importance of creating a sustainable economic model that minimizes the impact on the world's resources so that their children and their children's children can have a planet to inherit? Or, is it better to mandate specific actions that seek to alter behavior? Much of the argument presented in *Strategic CSR* is based on the assumption that it is only when firms become convinced of the self-interest inherent in socially responsible behavior that meaningful change will occur. In terms of individual consumer behavior in relation to recycling, however, there is evidence to suggest that mandated action is effective. There is also evidence to suggest that, if a shift in consumer behavior occurs, then firms will quickly adapt.

In the case of recycling by companies, some understand the value of voluntary action—that they can reduce costs and, therefore, increase efficiency, by recycling raw materials. As highlighted in Chapter 3, Walmart's work in this area is now considered best practice. This is partly to do with Walmart's size of operations, but it is also clear that the firm genuinely sees action on sustainability issues as a means of becoming more efficient and passing those lower costs on to customers as ever lower prices. Anheuser-Busch is another firm that has long been recognized as promoting recycling best practice. In 2003, the firm "recycled more than 97 per cent of the solid waste . . . —more than 5 billion pounds of material."[82] In 2005, it "decreased the amount of paperboard used to produce its packaging by almost 21 million pounds since 2002." In 2013, the firm recycles "99 percent of the solid waste generated in the brewing and packaging process, including beechwood chips, aluminum, glass, brewers' grain, scrap metal, cardboard and many other items."[83] In spite of this impressive level of operations, the overall recycling rate in the U.S., particularly in relation to plastics, is not encouraging, with only 1.44 of the 5.15 billion pounds of plastic bottles in the U.S. in 2009 recycled.[84] The amount of plastic produced every year that is used once and then disposed indicates the scale of the problem:

> It's estimated that half of the nearly 600 billion pounds of plastics produced each year go into single-use products. Some are indisputably valuable, like disposable syringes. . . . Yet many disposables, like the bags, drinking straws, packaging and lighters commonly found in beach clean-ups, are essentially prefab litter with a heavy environmental cost. [85]

As such, what action is being taken on sustainability-related issues in terms of individual consumers? Again, Walmart has made impressive inroads in encouraging a change in consumer behavior by prominently displaying products such as energy efficient light bulbs in its stores. Again, simply because of its size, the firm is able to reach a large percentage of the population:

> The company is changing a lot more than its trucks. For instance: Replacing incandescent bulbs in all the ceiling fans on display in the company's stores reaped savings of $7 million a year. Now Wal-Mart is using in-store displays to promote compact fluorescent bulbs to consumers, and has sold over 100 million of them - more than one per customer - saving enough energy to run a city the size of Philadelphia.[86]

Still, as noted above, overall recycling levels remain low. According to the Environmental Protection Agency in the U.S., for example, "While some 52% of paper, 36% of metals, and 22% of glass get recycled, only 7% of all plastics do."[87] An essential component of the recycling debate and the damaging environmental impact of consumerism, therefore, is the question of how best to reduce the use of plastic bags by individual consumers:

> After the plastic water bottle, you couldn't do much better than the plastic shopping bag as a symbol of American consumerism run amok. We go through 380 billion a year. An estimated 5.2% get recycled; in landfills, they could last 1,000 years. Bags are made from oil, and our bag habit costs us 1.6 billion gallons each year.[88]

CSR Newsletters: Paper or Plastic?

An article in *The Washington Post*[89] makes a depressing comparison between paper or plastic bags to see which imposes the greater environmental burden, in terms of production, consumption, and disposal, "The reality is that both paper and plastic bags gobble up natural resources and cause significant pollution." There are some surprising statistics, but the upshot of the paper vs. plastic debate is that neither is a good option:

> It takes more than four times as much energy to manufacture a paper bag as it does a plastic bag. The production of paper bags generates 70 percent more air and 50 times more water pollutants than production of plastic bags.

...it can cost $4,000 to process and recycle 1 ton of plastic bags. This can then be sold on the commodities market for about $32.

More often than not, bags collected for recycling never get recycled. A growing trend is to ship them to countries such as India and China, where they are cheaply incinerated under more lax environmental laws.

Paper is degradable, but it cannot completely break down in modern landfills because of the lack of water, light, oxygen and other necessary elements.

An editorial at *The Washington Post*[90] makes a similar point in response to a proposal to ban plastic shopping bags in Maryland:

The problem, opponents of the idea counter, is that paper bags are harmful, too: They cost more to make, they gobble up more resources to transport, and recycling them causes more pollution than recycling plastic. The argument for depriving Annapolis residents of their plastic bags is far from made.

It seems that in the contentious debate between paper and plastic, there is only one thing on which most people can agree:

Disposable shopping bags of any type are wasteful, and the best outcome would be for customers to reuse bags instead.

The extent of the problem is forcing some municipalities in the U.S., which have to clean-up the bags after they are (often) discarded, to take action.[91] In particular, state and local regulatory agencies in California,[92] Colorado,[93] Texas,[94] and Washington[95] states are all seeking to enact measures to reduce or eliminate the widespread consumption of plastic bags. While governments are increasingly taking action in this area, the success of such initiatives remain subject to the fluctuating price for recycled materials, which go down[96] as readily as they go up.[97] The corresponding wild fluctuations in the market price for specific recycled materials mean that it is sometimes cheaper for firms to dispose of them (to avoid storage costs) than sell them on the market.[98]

As such, the results of two interesting social experiments indicate that legislation mandating specific action carries the potential to produce much greater change in consumer behavior in a much shorter timeframe. First, IKEA introduced a policy of charging consumers for any bags they use and donating the money generated to a non-profit organization:

> The policy [in six months] cut bag consumption in the United States by more than 50%, far more than executives had expected. . . . In the United Kingdom, the policy . . . cut bag use by 95%.[99]

In a press release, IKEA announced the U.S. results on the first year anniversary of its plan to minimize the number of plastic bags used by its customers and, again, reported a marked change in consumer behavior. As a result, the firm decided to extend its policy and "IKEA will no longer offer plastic bags, and paper bags are not available in IKEA stores either."[100]

> With the introduction of its leadership "bag the plastic bag" program . . ., IKEA set a goal of reducing its US stores' plastic bag consumption by 50%; from 70 million to 35 million plastic bags in the first year. . . . Now it is one year since the program began and . . . more than 92% of their customers said no more plastic bags![101]

The second social experiment occurred in 2002 when the Irish government passed a tax on plastic bags, requiring that customers had to pay the equivalent of 33 cents for every bag they used. In a result very similar to the one experienced by IKEA, the tax had a dramatic and immediate impact on consumer behavior:

> Within weeks, plastic bag use dropped 94 percent. Within a year, nearly everyone had bought reusable cloth bags, keeping them in offices and in the backs of cars. Plastic bags were not outlawed, but carrying them became socially unacceptable—on a par with wearing a fur coat or not cleaning up after one's dog.[102]

The website http://reusablebags.com/ reports that "In January [2008] almost 42 billion plastic bags were used worldwide"[103]—that is in only one month! The IKEA and Ireland experiments show that dramatic change is possible, given the political will and the ability to approach problems innovatively. Other firms are seeking to build on IKEA's early success:

> Wal-Mart, long the target of environmentalists, is teaming with the [Environmental Defense Fund] in a so-called Global Plastic Shopping Bag Waste Reduction Program, which it says will reduce the number of shopping bags by 9 million by 2013.[104]

City governments from New York[105] to New Delhi[106] to Wales[107] also noted the rapid change in behavior and have announced similar schemes. Ireland is planning to build on the success of its scheme and extend similar taxes to influence other areas of consumer behavior, "proposing similar taxes on customers for A.T.M. receipts and chewing gum. . . . [In 2008], the government plans to ban conventional light bulbs, making only low-energy, long-life fluorescent bulbs available."[108] As a general rule, knee-jerk government intervention should be avoided, but the examples presented in this case indicate the potential for social policy to shift public behavior radically and quickly in a positive direction. What is also clear, however, is that mandated action has limits. That, while we will respond to coercion in certain circumstances, we are also not very good at following orders, even when they are in our best interests:

> Ever since Aristotle defined man as a rational animal, that has been seen as the very essence of our species. But the philosopher left a little room for interpretation. Did he mean man to be perennially rational, constantly raising himself above the beasts, or rather merely capable of such rationality, but infrequently demonstrating it? The latter is the more plausible.[109]

While proponents of mandatory regulation to encourage CSR have always focused on a mix of coercive incentives and strict punishments to achieve the goals they seek, the pathway towards encouraging voluntary behavior has been less clear. Recent thoughts in this area suggest a mix of economic and sociological tools. While financial incentives (economic) have always played a role, more recent behavioral research on suggests that peer group pressure (sociological) also plays an important part.

> "Economics is all about how people make choices; sociology is all about how they don't have any choices to make."
>
> —James Duesenberry[110]

As the quote above by James Duesenberry suggests, economists and sociologists have traditionally disagreed vehemently about the drivers of human behavior. The emergence of behavioral economics as a field of research offers a bridge between the two disciplines and, more importantly for *Strategic CSR*, offers a promising solution to the mandatory vs. voluntary debate:

> "Freakonomics" was the book that made the public believe the dismal science has something interesting to say about how people act in the real world. But "Nudge" was the one that got policy wonks excited.[111]

Nudge economics incorporates the biases and prejudices that inform our decisions into policies that encourage *optimal* social outcomes, while still retaining the *illusion* of choice:

Behavioural economists have found that all sorts of psychological or neuro-logical biases cause people to make choices that seem contrary to their best interests. The idea of nudging is based on research that shows it is possible to steer people towards better decisions by presenting choices in different ways.[112]

When deployed intelligently, the results of *nudges* ("simple, subtle cues that prompt people to make better decisions")[113] can be powerful:

In one trial, a letter sent to non-payers of vehicle taxes was changed to use plainer English, along the line of "pay your tax or lose your car." In some cases the letter was further personalised by including a photo of the car in question. The rewritten letter alone doubled the number of people paying the tax; the rewrite with the photo tripled it. . . . A study into the teaching of technical draw-ing in French schools found that if the subject was called "geometry" boys did better, but if it was called "drawing" girls did equally well or better. Teachers are now being trained to use the appropriate term.[114]

The key, therefore, lies in the choices offered and the ways in which they are presented. The crucial question should always be: What is the most effective way to produce the desired outcome? Take the healthcare issue of obesity, which has received a lot of attention in the U.S. and UK. Sometimes the best policy approach will be a consumption tax (e.g., "a per ounce tax on beverages with added sugar"),[115] sometimes it will be a ban on certain foods (such as excessive serving sizes[116] or trans-fat levels[117]), but sometimes it can be as simple as access and choice.

In order to understand how children (who tend to reject "heavy-handed nutri-tional policies" that restrict access to tasty burgers and fries) choose which foods for their school lunches, for example, researchers studied selection behavior in school cafeterias. What they found was that, simply by placing the less nutrition-ally beneficial foods in harder-to-reach places (e.g., placing fresh milk at the front of the counter and chocolate milk towards the back), they were able to alter dras-tically the selections the children made. Placing broccoli at the beginning of the food line, for example, "increased the amount students purchased by 10 percent to 15 percent," while encouraging the use of cafeteria trays resulted in higher vegeta-ble consumption ("students without trays eat 21 percent less salad but no less ice-cream").[118] The reverse psychology is employed by supermarkets that place chocolate and candy near the checkouts so that children will pester their parents to buy them at the point in time when they are most flustered (juggling their wal-let, while packing their bags) and, therefore, least likely to resist.[119]

The goal of behavioral explanations of human actions, therefore, is to explain them in terms of empirical examination rather than theoretical assumptions. There is now a great deal of research that highlights the value of behavioral economics for public policy because it demonstrates how human action can be shaped dramatically by applying the knowledge we have gained. In particular, it offers an effective way to achieve socially beneficial outcomes, while retaining the individual choice that is an essential component of an open society. This is what makes nudge economics such an important and fascinating CSR tool:

When you renew your driver's license, you have a chance to enroll in an organ donation program. In countries like Germany and the U.S., you have to check a box if you want to opt in. Roughly 14 percent of people do. But behavioral scientists have discovered that how you set the defaults is really important. So in other countries, like Poland or France, you have to check a box if you want to opt out. In these countries, more than 90 percent of people participate.[120]

And, nudge economics also has something to say about plastic bag use, showing not only the power of choice, but also the power of peer group pressure. In 2010, Washington DC imposed a five cent tax on disposable bags:

But more important than the extra cost was something more subtle: No one got bags automatically anymore. Instead, shoppers had to ask for them—right in front of their fellow customers. The result? Retail outlets that typically use 68 million disposable bags per quarter handed out 11 million bags in the first quarter of this year and fewer than 13 million bags in the second quarter, according to the district's Office of Tax and Revenue. That may help explain why volunteers for the city's annual Potomac River Watershed Cleanup day in mid-April pulled 66% fewer plastic bags from the Anacostia River than they did last year.[121]

CEO Perspective

Milton Friedman

If you put the federal government in charge of the Sahara desert, in five years there'd be a shortage of sand.[122]

Online Resources

- Bag It Movie, http://www.bagitmovie.com/
- Ban the Bag! http://www.banthebagspdx.com/
- EurActiv, http://www.euractiv.com/socialeurope/voluntary-vs-mandatory-remain-point-contention-csr/article-128568
- IIED—International Institute for Environment and Development, http://www.iied.org/
- ICIS.com, http://www.icis.com/Articles/2002/04/15/161455/csr-mandatory-or-voluntary-approach.html
- IKEA, the NEVER ENDING list, http://www.ikea.com/ms/en_US/about_ikea/our_responsibility/the_never_ending_list/index.html
- MyDD, http://www.mydd.com/story/2008/4/20/22529/4708
- Reuseit.com, http://reusablebags.com/
- Shell's *Brent Spar* Dossier, http://www-static.shell.com/content/dam/shell/static/gbr/downloads/e-and-p/brent-spar-dossier.pdf
- Shell Nigeria, http://www.shell.com.ng/
- Whole Foods Market, http://www.wholefoodsmarket.com/abetterbag/index.php

Pro/Con Debate

Pro/Con Debate: Plastic bags are less harmful to the environment than paper bags.

Questions for Discussion and Review

1. Which argument do you favor—persuading a company to incorporate a CSR perspective voluntarily or forcing them to change using legislation? Why? Which of these two approaches is ideal? Which is more realistic?

2. Google the terms *csr, mandatory, voluntary*. Have a brief look at some of the relevant documents this search produces. What is your sense of the argument that is playing out within the business world? Where would most firms like the balance to fall? Is that the same as the nonprofit organizations or NGOs that are also participating in the debate?

3. In 2003, the Norwegian government passed a law that was designed to force "listed companies to have women as 40 per cent of their directors."[123] At the

time "only 6 per cent of directors were female." The law came into effect in 2008 and, similar to the IKEA and Irish government social experiments outlined in the case, the results were dramatic: "[Today] the country now has the world's highest proportion of female board members. . . . 44 per cent of directors are women."[124] How well do you feel women are represented in executive and board positions in firms in your country? Do you think a similar law would improve things?

4. Have a look at this video, which shows Coca-Cola's "World's Largest Bottle-to-Bottle Recycling Plant" (http://www.youtube.com/watch?v=0f4Sl804HPM). What are your thoughts? Does it change your perception of the firm? Would you ever choose the drinks you buy because of action such as this?

5. Have a look at the UK newspaper *The Daily Mail's* "Banish the bags" campaign (http://www.dailymail.co.uk/news/article-519770). If you are not in the UK, can you imagine a similar campaign being waged by a newspaper in your country? If you are in the UK, did you know about the campaign? Was it a success? Why or why not?

CORPORATE RESPONSIBILITIES

CSR Connection:	This issue analyzes a company's *public purpose*—its responsibilities and obligations as determined by corporate law and founding corporate charters.
Stakeholders:	Society, Company, Executives, Directors.

Issue

What responsibilities and obligations do corporations have, as determined by their founding charters?

The corporation, as created by law, compels executives to prioritize the interests of their companies and shareholders above all others. The law forbids any other motivations for company actions, whether to assist workers, improve the environment, or help consumers save money. Corporate social responsibility is thus illegal—at least when it is genuine.[125]

This shareholder perspective became enshrined in U.S. popular perception after a Michigan Supreme Court case, *Dodge vs. Ford Motor Company*,[126] in which two brothers, John Francis Dodge and Horace Elgin Dodge (who, together, owned 10% of Ford's shares), sued Henry Ford because of his decision to distribute surplus profit to customers in the form of lower prices for his cars, rather than to shareholders in the form of a dividend. In deciding in the Dodge brothers' favor, the judge in the case:

> . . . reinstated the dividend and rebuked Ford—who had said in open court that "business is a service, not a bonanza" and that corporations should be run only "incidentally to make money"—for forgetting that "a business corporation is organized and carried on primarily for the profit of the stockholders"; it could not be run "for the merely incidental benefit of shareholders and for the primary purpose of benefiting others." *Dodge v. Ford* still stands for the legal principle that managers and directors have a legal duty to put shareholders' interests above all others and no legal authority to serve any other interests—what has come to be known as 'the best interests of the corporation' principle.[127]

This approach of shareholder supremacy and its legal foundations, however, is disputed. Rather than unambiguous corporate law, critics contend that this perspective has evolved over time in accordance with the values we choose to espouse as a society. As Lynn Stout explains in her analysis of corporate responsibilities as determined by legal precedent in the U.S., contrary to widespread perceptions and norms, there is no obligation on executives or directors to focus the firm's efforts primarily on maximizing shareholder value:

> . . . shareholder value ideology is just that—an ideology, not a legal requirement or a practical necessity of modern business life. United States corporate law does not, and never has, required directors of public corporations to maximize either share price or shareholder wealth. To the contrary, as long as boards do not use their power to enrich themselves, the law gives them a wide range of discretion to run public corporations with other goals in mind, including growing the firm, creating quality products, protecting employees, and serving the public interest.[128]

In particular, Stout argues that "we should stop teaching *Dodge v. Ford*" in our universities and business schools:

> In the past 30 years the Delaware courts have cited *Dodge v. Ford* as authority in only one unpublished case—and then not on the subject of corporate purpose [maximizing shareholder wealth], but on another legal question entirely.[129]

In spite of Stout's arguments, the myth of maximizing shareholder value is firmly entrenched in today's executive suite and boardroom. This position is very different from how corporations were initially envisaged, with *public purpose* as a founding requirement. Early corporate charters were granted by legislative bodies under strict rules—they were issued only for a limited period of time (the corporation would be wound-up after this period ended) and only to do a specific task that was sanctioned by public need (e.g., build a bridge over a river or construct a railroad):

> The early American states used chartered corporations, endowed with special monopoly rights, to build some of the vital infrastructure of the new country— universities (like America's oldest corporation, Harvard University, chartered in 1636), banks, churches, canals, municipalities, and roads. . . . In 1848, Pennsylvania's General Manufacturing Act set a twenty-year limit on manufacturing corporations. As late as 1903, almost half the states limited the duration of corporate charters to between twenty and fifty years. Throughout the nineteenth century, legislatures revoked charters when the corporation wasn't deemed to be fulfilling its responsibilities.[130]

In spite of these strict rules, the growth of corporations occurred rapidly around the turn of the nineteenth century:

> Whereas only 32 for-profit corporations had been chartered from the time of the first colonial settlement in 1607 through 1790, an astounding 287 were chartered from 1791 through 1800.[131]

Today, in contrast, politicians give corporate leaders significantly greater flexibility to meet shareholders' expectations. The legislation that removed the public purpose provision of a corporation's charter (or, its articles of incorporation) was designed to root out the corruption that had become inherent in the political power to award charters:

> The earliest, recognisably modern business corporation was the famous—or infamous—East India Company. Chartered on 31 December, 1600, its public purpose—"the advancement of trade"—was in fact nothing more glorious than the making of money for its proprietors.[132]

In working to treat "the corporation as simply another business form, available to all—just as a partnership or an unincorporated company" in the U.S. in the first half of the nineteenth century, Andrew Jackson deliberately eliminated "determinations of a 'public purpose' that warranted granting special privileges to a particular business organization. Theoretically, all corporations would receive the same privileges and immunities."[133] As such, while early corporations and business leaders would have accepted a social responsibility beyond profit maximization as an implicit contract with society in return for the right to operate, today's corporate executives understand incorporation as a right, rather than a responsibility. This reinforces the idea that the firm contributes to society simply by its continued existence, rather than the idea that the firm exists at the privilege of society, to which something is owed in return.[134] As suggested by Lynn Stout's work (discussed above), as well as empirical evidence that suggests courts do not necessarily favor shareholder interests over director actions,[135] however, this status quo is a social construction that has evolved over time. As such, it can be changed if, as a society, we decide it should be different. As Bill Clinton puts it:

> When I went to law school . . . in the 1970s, I was part virtually of the last generation of American law students and business students taught that corporations had a responsibility (because they had special privileges under the law, like limited liability) to their stakeholders (to their shareholders, their employees, their customers, and the communities of which they were a part). Then, starting in the late 1970s, that practice changed and all of a sudden the shareholders were way up here and all the stakeholders were down here. It had the ironic consequence of giving the most influence over corporate decisions to the stakeholders with the least concern about the long term profitability of the corporation and the greatest concern about the short term profitability. . . . We need to be competitive, . . . but we also need to try to create an ethic in America where the employees and the customers and the communities can [be represented] too and we need to make it easy for corporations to act that way again.[136]

To this end, the state government in Vermont is famous for creating the "Ben & Jerry's law" that was passed by the legislature in the run-up to Unilever's acquisition of the firm in 2000. The law allowed the Boards of Vermont firms to consider factors in addition to shareholder value when deciding whether to accept a takeover offer:

> . . . permitted a company's directors to reject a takeover bid if "they deem it to be not in the best interests of employees, suppliers, and the economy of the state." Thus, even when a company was offered a financial premium in a buyout situation, its directors where permitted to reject the offer based on the best interests of the State of Vermont.[137]

From a CSR perspective, what is the best approach to determine the responsibilities and obligations firms seek to fulfill? What prevents a firm from operating in the best interests of a broad array of stakeholders, rather than a narrow section of shareholders, who can only loosely be referred to as *owners*:

Owners carry responsibility. If I own a dog, and it bites a child, I am legally responsible. Shareholders provide capital to the business and acquire a right to a percentage of the profits of the business. They should get a fair return. But capital is not the only asset the business should value—it must protect its staff, its reputation and the continued favor of its customers.[138]

The firm has a responsibility to its shareholders, but they are only one of many stakeholders. Their interests are important, but there are many instances in which those interests are likely to be (or even *should* be) subservient to the interests of other important stakeholders:

> . . . people forgot (or never realized) that shareholders do not actually own the company; they own only its stock. This entitles them to get the residual assets of the company upon its breakup and to vote on resolutions at annual meetings and on the appointment of directors, but not to tell the firm what to do. A company is in law an independent person, and its directors have a fiduciary duty to the company as a whole—that is, to its workers and customers as well as its investors.[139]

What *should* a corporate charter look like and what is the most appropriate authority (federal vs. state government) to regulate this area of corporate law? What should the responsibilities of the firm be and what structure is best suited to achieve these outcomes?

Case Study: Benefit Corporations

Issues of corporate governance in the U.S. are currently regulated under state, rather than federal, law. Those who support this system argue that it encourages competition between states (to entice corporations to incorporate within their state) and, therefore, produces effective and efficient legislation. Critics of this system, however, rebut the benefits of interstate competition because the result is a race to the bottom as states bend over backwards to craft legislation that appeases corporations. States want firms to incorporate within their jurisdiction because of the lucrative fees and taxes they receive for each company that registers there, wherever the company is actually headquartered:

> Corporations don't have to incorporate where a firm is headquartered, or even where it employs the most people. Managers can go jurisdiction-shopping, looking for the most advantageous set of laws, since getting a corporate charter is easier than getting a driver's license.[140]

As a result, firms seeking to incorporate in the U.S. tend to choose Delaware. This is confirmed by the Delaware State government website, which claims that:

The State of Delaware is a leading domicile for U.S. and international corporations. More than 850,000 business entities have made Delaware their legal home. More than 50% of all publicly-traded companies in the United States including 63% of the Fortune 500 have chosen Delaware as their legal home.[141]

Delaware is perceived as having the *most advantageous* system of regulation for companies, which translates as having the least regulation. The state, whose 850,000 registered companies almost equals its population of approximately 900,000 people, also advertises additional benefits, such as "allowing even greater secrecy than offshore tax havens."[142] And it is easy to see why:

At a time when many states are being squeezed by a difficult economy, Delaware collected roughly $860 million in taxes and fees from its absent corporate residents in 2011. That money accounted for a quarter of the state's total budget.[143]

In terms of oversight, liability, responsibility, and regulation, Delaware is considered a friendly place to do business because the state has "long been reluctant to disturb the decisions of corporate boards."[144]

[Business] has been the business of Delaware since 1792, when the state established its Court of Chancery to handle business affairs. By the early 20th century, the state was writing friendly corporate and tax laws to lure companies from New York, New Jersey and elsewhere.[145]

As such, other states feel compelled to reproduce Delaware's lax environment, simply to keep companies currently headquartered there from moving to Delaware:

If another state wants to be more aggressive in fighting corporate crime or protecting shareholders, employees, or communities, it runs the risk that its companies will simply re-incorporate in Delaware. So most states end up mimicking Delaware law.[146]

One option to generate meaningful reform in the area of governing corporations would be for the federal government to take control of the process. The authority to do so is invested in the federal government under the Commerce Clause of the Constitution.[147] Doing so would allow either Congress or the Securities and

Exchange Commission (SEC) to raise the bar for all corporations without having to worry that companies would simply flee in protest to the state with the weakest rules.[148] A starting point for the federal government would be a law stating that corporations have to incorporate where they have the largest presence—i.e., where their true headquarters are, where they employ the most people, or where they have the greatest percentage of operations. This would make corporations more directly accountable for their actions to the community within which they actually operate. By introducing these changes, the government would also go a long way toward closing the loophole in the tax code that allows corporations to incorporate offshore (again, irrespective of where their headquarters are) to avoid paying the higher rates of corporation tax levied in the United States:

> Just £349 ($560) buys you a company in the Seychelles, with no local taxation, no public disclosure of directors or shareholders and no requirement to file accounts.[149]

And, it is not just small companies that try to avoid[150] government oversight and taxation through legal maneuvers:

> Starbucks, the Seattle-based international coffee chain, has been accused of tax avoidance in the UK. Between 1998 and 2011 the company has made £3 billion in sales but paid out just £8.6 million in taxes on its 735 stores in the country. In the last three years Starbucks did not pay a penny in taxes there.[151]

As a first step in this campaign toward federalization, various attempts have been made to introduce a *Code for Corporate Responsibility* at the state level, which would reform the law with regard to broadening directors' fiduciary duties. The potential impact of this simple, but far-reaching change to the law would be significant. The entire purpose of the corporation would necessarily shift and the new law would give stakeholders a tool by which to hold corporations accountable for their actions and policies. Forcing this multi-constituency approach would result in U.S. firms increasingly acting like European ones, as well as firms in Asian countries such as Japan, which tend to define their stakeholders more broadly and actively.

Groups in both Minnesota and California have begun to campaign for this change, with states such as Maine and Massachusetts also showing interest.[152] In 2004, legislation was introduced in California to put the new code into effect. Senate Majority Whip, Richard Alarcon's Good Corporate Citizen bill (SB 917) says that, while existing law "requires corporate directors to perform their duties in good faith and in a manner that is in the best interests of the corporation and its shareholders" and "provides for 'derivative lawsuits' by shareholders against corporate officers and directors for violations of these standards":

> This bill would provide that directors shall carry out these duties "in a manner that does not cause material damage to the environment, the public health and safety, the communities in which the corporation operates, the rights of the corporation's employees, and human rights."

In addition, in February 2009, Minnesota Senator John Marty and Representative Bill Hilty introduced a *Bill for Socially Responsible Corporations* into the Senate[153] and House,[154] respectively with the intention of creating "an alternative kind of corporation, the SR (socially responsible) corporation." The bill was re-introduced as the *Minnesota Responsible Business Corporation Act* in 2011.[155]

There are legitimate concerns regarding the implementation of these proposed laws. For example, "What happens if a company moves a plant to a more environmentally friendly facility, thereby helping the environment but harming the employees and community of the previous locality?"[156] What would be the consequences if investors sell their stock under these *anti-investor* policies in favor of firms in more *investor-friendly* countries? Also, what would be the proposed penalties for directors that fail the new test? Would they be individually liable for any damage or stakeholder complaint that ensued? Nevertheless, the idea that modern corporations should be compelled to register a *public purpose* that reflects a broader set of social responsibilities is receiving growing support.

A new "best interests of the corporation" principle?

A *BusinessWeek/*Harris Poll asked which of the following options was preferable:

Corporations should have only one purpose—to make the most profit for their shareholders—and pursuit of that goal will be best for America in the long run.

—or—

Corporations should have more than one purpose. They also owe something to their workers and the communities in which they operate, and they should sometimes sacrifice some profit for the sake of making things better for their workers and communities.

An overwhelming 95 percent of Americans chose the second proposition.... When 95 percent of the public supports a proposition, enacting that proposition into law should not be impossible.[157]

A new corporate structure (a new type of corporate charter) that is gaining in popularity is the Benefit Corporation (http://www.bcorporation.net/). Becoming a Benefit Corporation expands the fiduciary responsibilities of the firm's executives and directors by committing the organization to meet the needs of a broad range of stakeholders, beyond shareholders alone:

Benefit Corporations are a new class of corporation that 1) creates a material positive impact on society and the environment; 2) expands fiduciary duty to require consideration of non-financial interests when making decisions; and 3) reports on its overall social and environmental performance using recognized third party standards.[158]

CSR Newsletters: Patagonia

An article in *Environmental Leader*[159] reports Patagonia's decision to re-structure itself as a Benefit Corporation. It is the first company in California to do so:

> The legal status affords a company's directors legal cover to consider environmental and social benefits over financial returns.

California is one of twelve states (plus Washington D.C.) that have either passed or introduced legislation allowing B corporations (see: http://www .benefitcorp.net/state-by-state-legislative-status). In California, the law became effective on January 1, 2012. Once a law is passed in a state, then a firm can restructure itself as a Benefit Corporation. Whether in a state with such legislation, however, any company can apply for b-corp certification. This certification is awarded by B Lab (http://www.bcorporation.net/) to those firms that pass specific criteria related to the broader fiduciary responsibilities of a Benefit Corporation. In this case, B Lab is a nonprofit organization that acts "the same way TransFair certifies Fair Trade coffee or USGBC certifies LEED buildings."

Rather than an endpoint, therefore, becoming a Benefit Corporation (either the formal change of legal status or the certification) is the starting point of a process for firms that forces them to operate at higher standards of transparency and accountability. In order to enable this transformation, B Lab places specific reporting requirements on firms to ensure accurate information about operations is disseminated to stakeholders:

> Through a company's public B Impact Report, anyone can access performance data about the social and environmental practices that stand

(Continued)

(Continued)

behind their products. . . . As a result, individuals will have greater economic opportunity, society will move closer to achieving a positive environmental footprint, more people will be employed in great places to work, and we will have built stronger communities at home and across the world.

Although B Lab has only been established a few years, it has already made a substantial impact. As of early-2013, 693 firms have been certified as b-corps. These companies have combined revenues of over $4.2 billion and operate in 60 industries and 24 Countries:[160]

Companies include Seventh Generation, the maker of natural household and personal care products; Pura Vida, which sells organic, fair trade coffee; Etsy, the online market for handmade goods; and King Arthur Flour.[161]

The advantages of b-corp status are threefold: First, it protects against the possibility of lawsuits from shareholders seeking compensation for a perceived failure by the firm/executives/directors to maximize shareholder returns:

"Corporate law in the U.S. says your job is to maximize return for your shareholders," explains Jay Coen Gilbert, cofounder of B Lab, the nonprofit that created the B Corporation status. "So that's what you're legally bound to do. If you don't, you can get sued." Unless, that is, shareholders also have explicitly endorsed that larger purpose.[162]

Second, the b-corp structure embeds the values of a broader stakeholder perspective within the fabric of the company by instituting a structure that formalizes the mission in quantifiable goals. By adopting b-corp status, the firm is legally required to implement a stakeholder model:

Once a company is certified as a B Corporation, its board commits to considering environmental and social factors every time it makes a decision and has to hit specific social and environmental performance targets.[163]

Third, b-corp status protects the mission of a firm should the founder retire or the firm is sold to another firm. In such circumstances, protecting the original CSR mission becomes very difficult to guarantee. This problem surfaces whenever a social enterprise is taken over by a multi-national, such as when Green & Black's was sold to Cadbury (now Kraft) in 2005[164] and The Body Shop sold to L'Oreal in 2006:[165]

Mr. Chouinard argues that making a firm's social mission explicit in its legal structure makes it harder for a new boss or owner to abandon it.[166]

Proponents of reinstating some form of public purpose within a corporation's charter argue that it is when the business is being sold or broken up that a Benefit Corporation legal structure will make the most difference as directors will be able to consider a broad range of interests beyond shareholder value maximization (i.e., the best price). This asset would have been valuable for Ben & Jerry's (which announced its b-corp certification in 2012) during its sale to Unilever in 2000:

> Ben & Jerry's Homemade Inc. . . . sold to Unilever plc. in 2000, despite the objections of co-founder Ben Cohen and some directors. "There was a lot of pressure from the lawyers to sell," says Jeff Furman, a Ben & Jerry's director since the 1980s and its current chairman. If benefit corporations had existed back in 2000, the board probably wouldn't have agreed to the Unilever deal, Mr. Furman says.[167]

In the spirit of transparency, and as part of the certification process, Ben & Jerry's released its full B Impact Assessment in 2012:

> Highlights show that 45% of the cost of goods sold go toward investing in and supporting small scale suppliers through the Caring Dairy program; its lowest paid hourly worker receives 46% above the living wage, and between half and three quarters of staff took part in an organised community programme in the last year. Between 65%-80% of its staff are "satisfied" or "engaged" at work, and the highest paid individual earns between 16 and 20 times more than the lowest paid full time worker. . . . In terms of overall performance, Ben & Jerry's scored 93% of available points for its governance structure, 55% for environment and 45% for community.[168]

The growing number of firms willing to sign-up to become certified as Benefit Corporations reflects the interest in reforming the status quo and encouraging firms to become more socially responsible. B Lab's timeliness is reflected in the other legal alternatives for corporate structures that are emerging based around similar goals:

> California's B Corp legislation took effect alongside a new law creating the "flexible purpose company" (FlexC), which allows a firm to adopt a specific social or environmental goal, rather than the broader obligations of a B Corp. Another option in America is the low-profit limited-liability (LC3) company, which can raise money for socially beneficial purposes while making little or no profit. The idea of a legal framework for firms that put profits second is not confined to America. Britain, for example, has since 2005 allowed people to form "community interest companies." Similar laws are brewing in several European countries.[169]

The issue of the extent to which fiduciary responsibilities can include an expanded set of stakeholder considerations was considered comprehensively in the important *Freshfields Report* of 2005.[170] The report concluded that, while there appears to be relative flexibility across many jurisdictions for the inclusion of a broader set of stakeholder interests in management decisions, there is also considerable scope for legal challenges to those actions, particularly where they can be considered to have diminished firm profits. While establishing the firm as a Benefit Corporation would assuage such challenges to a degree, it is not clear where that leaves regular corporations that have received b-corp certification. As such, it will be interesting to see what happens when this new organizational structure and expanded fiduciary responsibilities are challenged in court. B Lab's goal is for this corporate structure to become a legitimate alternative to the current narrow focus on shareholder value. As corporate charters are reformed, so it is hoped that the changes will initiate widespread reform of the market economy:

> The key question to address is whether social entrepreneurs, B corporations and community interest companies can be managed in a way that enables them to reach scale. And how should they do so—is it best for each one to become big, or for small organisations to be replicated by the dozen?[171]

An equally important question, however, is: Do we need to invent new organizational forms, ones more effectively grounded in CSR principles, or can we fix the model that already has scale—our current corporate structure and small and medium-size businesses? Given the work of Lynn Stout (and others) discussed above, it is not clear that there is strong precedent within corporate law for shareholders to sue firms on the basis that their value has not been maximized. If true, the b-corp structure, while useful in focusing debate on the responsibilities of the firm and institutionalizing CSR principles throughout operations, is essentially redundant in a conceptual sense. Benefit Corporations promise to act in the interests of a broad range of stakeholders, but that is also a promise that regular firms can (and should) make within current legal and governance structures. In other words, it is not the organizational form that is preventing firms pledging to be more socially responsible, but the willingness of executives to make such commitments. The B-corp structure is a solution to a problem that may not exist.

That the b-corp structure is perceived to be an innovation indicates how far capitalism today has moved from the original public purpose of corporate charters. But, it does not necessarily follow that the underlying structure is in need of reform; more so that our current interpretation of those structures reflects our skewed priorities. As such, Benefit Corporations will only effect meaningful change if they are able to persuade CEOs and executives not already predisposed to CSR to change their organizational structure. Convincing firms like Patagonia and Ben & Jerry's (firms that are already examples of CSR best-practice) to become Benefit Corporations will not save the planet! We will know b-corps are here to stay when more intransigent firms decide there is value in altering their foundational charter documents.

CEO Perspective

Yvon Chouinard (Patagonia)

In 2012, Patagonia became the first company in California to become a Benefit Corporation:

'Patagonia is trying to build a company that could last 100 years,' said Patagonia founder Yvon Chouinard. 'Benefit corporation legislation creates the legal framework to enable mission-driven companies like Patagonia to stay mission-driven through succession, capital raises, and even changes in ownership, by institutionalizing the values, culture, processes, and high standards put in place by founding entrepreneurs.'[172]

Online Resources

- B-Lab, http://www.bcorporation.net/
- Benefit Corporation Information Center, http://benefitcorp.net/
- Citizens Works, Code for Corporate Responsibility, http://www.citizen-works.org/enron/corp_code-text.php
- Common Dreams NewsCenter, http://www.commondreams.org/
- Corporation 20/20, http://www.corporation2020.org/
- SOCENTLAW, http://socentlaw.com/
- Tomorrow's Company, http://www.tomorrowscompany.com/
- United Nations Environment Programme Finance Initiative (UNEP FI), http://www.unepfi.org/

Pro/Con Debate

Pro/Con Debate: Companies should incorporate in the location where they have their largest operational presence.

Questions for Discussion and Review

1. What is your opinion of the verdict delivered in *Dodge v. Ford Motor Company*? Was the judge correct to rule the way he did? If the case came before the court today, would the outcome be any different?

2. What are the arguments for having corporate governance issues regulated at the federal rather than state level? Do you support these arguments?

3. Develop an argument against the *Code for Corporate Responsibility*—is it persuasive?

4. Which of these two positions from the *BusinessWeek*/Harris Poll do you agree with: That "corporations should have only one purpose—to make the most profit for their shareholders" or that corporations should "have more than one purpose. They also owe something to their workers and the communities in which they operate, and they should sometimes sacrifice some profit for the sake of making things better for their workers and communities"? Why?

5. What are the advantages and disadvantages of a firm incorporating as a Benefit Corporation? If you were starting a firm, would you consider becoming a b-corp?

MEDIA

CSR Connection:	This issue analyzes the role of the media in an increasingly wired world that allows NGOs and nonprofit organizations to expose corporate actions they feel to be socially irresponsible. What is the role of the media in terms of CSR?[173] To what extent do the media have a responsibility to hold firms accountable for their actions?
Stakeholders:	Media/Journalists, NGOs.

Issue

The expansion of global media conglomerates and the spread of TV into every corner of the world are radically changing the way we consume news and information. In other words, the media "simply *is*—everywhere and all the time":[174]

Before the second world war, radio reached a mere 10% of the population, the print media no more than 20%. Now papers and TV both reach 90% of adults, and radio around 98%. The power of the media has effected a sea change in the development of public attitudes. As the raw material of politics, public opinion has become a mere reflection of the messages put out by the system, the producers of which insist unconvincingly that they follow what, in fact, they are creating . . . Without noticing it, we are abandoning representative democracy and marching towards opinion-led democracy.[175]

The Internet magnifies this trend, threatening traditional media (newspapers, in particular, but also TV)[176] and decreasing the time it takes for information to reach us:

We watch 60-second television commercials that have been sped up to fit into 30-second spots, even as we multitask our way through e-mails, text messages and tweets. . . . Changes that used to take generations . . . now unfurl in a span of years. Since 2000, we have experienced three economic bubbles (dot-com, real estate, and credit), three market crashes, a devastating terrorist attack, two wars and a global influenza pandemic.[177]

Life is lived today at a hectic pace. And, when a newsworthy event occurs, we know about it almost instantly. When a US Airways plane crash-landed in the Hudson River in New York on January 15, 2009, for example, a passenger on the ferry that went to the rescue of the plane's passengers took a photo of the plane with his cellphone (http://twitpic.com/135xa) and uploaded it instantly with the following message to Twitter, "There's a plane in the Hudson. I'm on the ferry going to pick up the people. Crazy."[178] This trend is important for news stations because the channel that breaks the story tends to hold the viewers. And for the media today, bad news is good news is entertainment:

This obsession with speed creates problems—we report rumors, with caveats, but mistakes are made . . . It's a complicated world. The media have a lot to say and not much time to say it. They also have to win audiences, so they sensationalize and simplify. Stalin said that every death is a tragedy; the death of a million, a mere statistic. That's how the media, albeit with different motives, work as well.[179]

Not only is news spreading more quickly, but how it is interpreted depends on the context. Activities around the world are viewed and judged by the standards where the news is absorbed, not where it occurred. When Al-Jazeera reports on

U.S. actions in the Middle East, for example, it does so for an Arab audience. In spite of President Obama giving his first interview with a foreign media outlet as president to Al-Jazeera's English channel,[180] the U.S. has little control over the way the country and its foreign policy is portrayed and interpreted in the streets and cafes of Baghdad or Lebanon. As an ad for Al Jazeera in *The New York Times* states:

> Bold and fearless journalism that doesn't shy away from the truth. We put the human being at the center of our news agenda and take you to the heart of the story. Exploring events that are often years, decades and even centuries in the making. Located at the center of the most complicated region in the world—get the real picture, every angle, every side. Al Jazeera.[181]

The speed at which news travels today and how it is ultimately interpreted should also be a point of both interest and concern for global corporations, who are already portrayed in a negative light in the media.[182] Firms can no longer trust they can control the flow of information (see Figure 4.5). No actions can be hidden and, if anything goes wrong, the whole world knows about it very quickly. When two employees from Domino's Pizza decided to film a prank video in the kitchen where they worked and upload it to YouTube, for example, the consequences were swift, both for the employees and for Domino's:[183]

> In a few days, thanks to the power of social media, [the two employees] ended up with felony charges, more than a million disgusted viewers, and a major company facing a public relations crisis. . . . By Wednesday afternoon, the video had been viewed more than a million times on YouTube. References to it were in five of the 12 results on the first page of Google search for "Dominos," and discussions about Domino's had spread throughout Twitter.[184]

Today, a firm needs to strive to maintain positive ties with a broad array of stakeholders, both internal and external. The internet and global media conglomerates make it relatively easy for individuals or NGOs to mobilize and spread their message to multiple audiences before firms even know a problem exists. The growth in importance of global brands, twinned with the rise of media conglomerates, leaves companies exposed to any consumer backlash against activities perceived to be unacceptable or running counter to the image a company's brand portrays.

Case Study: CNBC

> "Four hostile newspapers are more to be feared than 10,000 bayonets."
>
> —Napoleon Bonaparte[185]

The media is an essential part of the democratic society in which we live. Its role is to inform the public and hold those in power accountable to those they are supposed to serve. In an age of information overload and advertising revenue driven by viewer numbers, however, what information to present and how to present it is central to the integrity of the industry. The temptation to condense in order to capture people's attention soon leads to the need to entertain to keep them watching. Today, the news of the world is conveyed in 30-minute segments, squeezed between the weather, sports, and personal finance programs. *CNN Headline News,* without blushing, manages to fit the day's major news from around the world into a segment that used to be called "The Global Minute"! The news media often simplify the message and repeat news handed to them by PR departments. As Nick Davies writes in his book, *Flat Earth News*:

> In the end, the researchers found that only 12 percent of stories [in the five national UK newspapers—*The Times,* the *Guardian, The Independent,* the *Daily Telegraph,* and the *Daily Mail*] were based on material generated entirely by the papers' own reporters.[186]

The twenty-four-hour news cycle today is a CNN world of voyeurism and reality TV, where a firm's difficulties or ethical transgressions are everyone else's fascinating tidbits:

> Fear of embarrassment at the hands of NGOs and the media has given business ethics an even bigger push. Companies have learnt the hard way that they live in a CNN world, in which bad behavior in one country can be seized on by local campaigners and beamed on the evening television news to customers back home.[187]

CNN, launched in June 1980, came to prominence in the living rooms of the world and North America, in particular, during the first Gulf War. The station's willingness to push the envelope in what is expected of a 24 hour cable news channel's frontline reporters enabled them to carry on presenting after the competition had evacuated to safety:

> CNN had been a failing venture until the 1991 Gulf War, when it provided the only television coverage from inside Baghdad. That exclusive was possible only because every other network had pulled its correspondents to protect their lives. Tom Johnson, CNN's president at the time, wanted to do the same, but [Ted] Turner told him: "I will take on myself the responsibility for anybody who is killed. I'll take it off of you if it's on your conscience." No one was killed, but Mr. Turner's roll of the dice with other men's lives is no less jarring.[188]

The role CNN plays in conveying information to the public is now a legitimate consideration for the U.S. government when selecting military bombing targets during a war. This is particularly so when the targets are located in civilian or urban areas. As in all aspects of society today, rapidly developing technology allows more things to be done in a much shorter time frame. In a war, the information field commanders receive has multiplied exponentially, as has the speed in which they must decide what to do. When the wrong decision or a mistake is made, CNN is there to tell the world about it:

> When missiles do go awry, as happened when the United States accidentally struck the Chinese Embassy in Belgrade in May 1999 . . . there is alarm worldwide.[189]

The *CNN Test* is the assessment military commanders make when choosing potential targets for bombing during warfare today. This issue was the focus of a number of news items in the lead up to the second Iraq war (2003-2011):[190]

> Military commanders have long had legal advisers. But more than ever, attorneys are in the teams that choose the strategies, the targets and even the weapons to be used. . . . And legal issues aren't the only factors . . . Commanders must also worry about "the CNN test." Is the target worth all the loss of innocent life—and the inevitable outcry?[191]

Public opinion greatly influences a country's foreign policy (which, after all, is determined by politicians who need to be re-elected). And the media today plays a central role in shaping that public opinion. People react much more strongly to pictures that they see than to words that they read. With words, they have to use their own imagination, which requires effort; pictures are spoon-fed to the public via TV and, increasingly, the Internet. And, when the pictures are riveting, they're played over and over again until they become ingrained in the public conscience—known as the "CNN effect."[192] From Vietnam to the fall of the Berlin Wall, from the World Trade Center towers in New York to the Fukushima tsunami to the Arab Spring, TV footage personalizes the story, introduces emotions, and removes the larger context within which foreign policy decisions must be made. As such, the story that the news media convey is not always *complete* or *accurate*, but can be thought of more as *entertainment* that is "packaged for ease of dissemination and consumption."[193]

Nevertheless, CNN's successes have caused their competitors to respond in order to make their product more competitive. From BBC World to Al-Jazeera to Fox News,[194] cable news channels have re-shaped the way we watch TV and receive our knowledge about the world. It is perhaps not surprising, therefore, that, in the same way that the first Iraq war enabled CNN to establish itself in the ultra-competitive media market, the Financial Crisis enabled another cable network, CNBC, to find its identity:[195]

Partisanship aside, this is CNBC's equivalent of a war. Just as the first cable news channel, CNN, rose to prominence during the gulf war in 1991, and another one, the Fox News Channel, became a ratings leader in the period before the Iraq war in 2002 and 2003, CNBC is on a war footing. . . . the network's home audience started to surge in August 2007 as the upheaval began in the credit markets. They peaked in March 2008 when Bear Stearns was sold to JP Morgan Chase . . . After hitting a plateau that spring, the ratings soared [in fall 2008] when other investment banks collapsed, setting records for the network.[196]

The increased viewers the channel attracted in the aftermath of the Financial Crisis also helped its parent company, NBC, dominate the network news ratings in the U.S. at the time,[197] while securing "its fourth year of double-digit growth in operating profits"[198] in 2010. CNBC was successful because it was relevant—"It was news being made, all the time, in real time."[199] The role played by the station in reporting the crisis (both before and after it occurred), however, was not without its critics:

A showdown between a comedian who has become one of America's most challenging news commentators and a news commentator known for his comedic antics has shone the brightest spotlight on the media market's coverage since the financial crisis began.[200]

CSR Newsletters: CNBC

For those who missed Jon Stewart's lambasting of CNBC on *The Daily Show* in March 2009, his three part interview of Jim Cramer (host of Mad Money) is compelling TV:

http://www.thedailyshow.com/watch/thu-march-12-2009/jim-cramer-pt--1

As usual, Stewart employs comedy to great effect. In addition, however, he confronts Cramer with an honesty and directness that you rarely see on current affairs TV in the U.S. Stewart articulates succinctly the behavior of Wall Street that led directly to the Financial Crisis, but also skewers Cramer (and CNBC) for becoming part of the problem, rather than being the journalists they purport to be. As a result, the interview is both entertaining and uncomfortable to watch because Stewart so completely undermines what it is that must get Cramer out of bed every morning to do his show.

Stewart's analysis was all the more compelling because it challenged what it means to be a modern journalist in a democratic society. Beyond merely castigating CNBC (and, by implication, the business media as an industry) for failing to perform their role of oversight more effectively, Stewart accuses CNBC of complicity—knowing what was going on, but being overly concerned with their status as *insiders*, rather than maintaining their journalistic integrity. To what extent is journalism part of the establishment and to what extent do journalists have a civic responsibility to hold the great social institutions (e.g., politics and businesses) accountable for their actions? It is hard to do both:

> The problem here is not individuals but attitudes, including a media culture that causes some people, particularly in the entertainment-driven medium of television, to blur the line between entertainment, good journalism and sound analysis. . . . As long as everyone was making money, nobody wanted to hear the bad news.[201]

Jon Stewart advocates for impartiality and criticizes the partisan journalists who he believes fail to hold politicians to account:

> The problem with the media today is they are too wrapped up in the strategy of the Beltway. . . . They are worried about their connections within that world when what they need to be worrying about is their connection to us outside of that world. . . . We are the ones that they need to protect from this cynical game of right and left that is being perpetrated.[202]

As indicated by other commentators, the media, with all its flaws, is only capable of writing "a flawed first draft of history" as it unfolds.[203] It is debatable, however, whether creating an historical account is even given lip-service by today's media, which others have argued "doesn't exist to deliver programs to viewers; it exists solely to deliver audiences to advertisers."[204] This service is packaged in an increasingly partisan message that leaves channels like CNN, who at least claim to be objective, without a strong base of core viewers:

> Fox News assures conservative viewers that Democrats' gaffes [represent bad intentions], and Republicans' [represent a misunderstanding]. MSNBC, vice versa. CNN tries to be fair. Viewers hate that. Its ratings in America are sliding, while Fox and MSNBC are doing well.[205]

This shift towards partisan ideology and ratings maximization is precisely why the media continues to value attention-seeking anchors such as Jim Cramer, who demand the limelight with elaborate (and often misleading) bold pronouncements:

> There is only one Jim Cramer, host of CNBC's popular finance show Mad Money. His latest notable outburst came [in April, 2009]: "Right now, right here, on this show—I am announcing the depression [is] over!" He is going too far again.[206]

As the line between news and entertainment blurs, so the way that we understand world events and consume the news has also changed:

> Today's satirists are a substantial part of one of the great powers in free societies—the media—and, since the latter part of the 20th century, have substituted themselves for news. . . . In the US, programmes such as *The Daily Show with Jon Stewart* and *The Colbert Report* have displaced news and documentary as the main way in which young viewers learn about current events.[207]

This discussion does not diminish the concern firms should have about their loss of control over the free flow of information. If anything, it should heighten it because, today, the *truth* and *facts* are increasingly subjective points of disagreement that are spun to fit a specific agenda, rather than reflect reality. As we become increasingly interconnected and words and images are shared more freely, the ability to assert control is lost and it is not coming back. The Internet is anarchic at heart. As a result, firms need to do all they can to ensure relations with their myriad of stakeholders are as positive as possible, to ensure they do not become the next victim of this communication medium.

CEO Perspective

Rupert Murdoch (News Corporation)

The world is changing very fast. Big will not beat small anymore. It will be the fast beating the slow.[208]

Online Resources

- 10 × 10, http://tenbyten.org/10x10.html
- Accuracy in Media, http://www.aim.org/
- BBC World News, http://www.bbcworldnews.com/
- Business & Media Institute, http://www.businessandmedia.org/
- CNBC, http://www.cnbc.com/
- CNN, http://www.cnn.com/
- Independent Media Center, http://www.indymedia.org/
- Mad Money, http://www.cnbc.com/id/15838459
- mediachannel.org, http://www.mediachannel.org/
- Media CSR Forum, http://www.mediacsrforum.org/
- The Daily Show with Jon Stewart, http://www.thedailyshow.com/

Pro/Con Debate

> **Pro/Con Debate:**   The media today plays a valuable role holding the important institutions of our society (businesses, government, etc.) to account.

Questions for Discussion and Review

1. Do the media today *report* the news or *distort* the news? Do we watch *news* or *entertainment*? What do you think CNN's role, or the BBC's, should be? What about Al-Jazeera? Is news reporting today objective or is it necessarily culturally biased?

2. Should the armed services have to answer to CNN or any other news organization? Isn't that the responsibility of the civilian planners and politicians that shape the strategies that the armed services implement? Should the media's powers be restricted during wartime? Have embedded journalists helped the reporting of war or just upped the entertainment level closer to Hollywood special-effects levels?

3. What is the correct role of a media channel in a democratic society? Are they there to police society's institutions and hold them accountable based on their own biases and political agendas? Or, are they there to report the news objectively without taking sides? From what you know of CNBC, did they

perform well or badly in terms of reporting before, during, and after the Financial Crisis?

4. Watch the three parts of Jon Stewart's interview of Jim Cramer from CNBC's *Mad Money* (http://www.thedailyshow.com/watch/thu-march-12-2009/jim-cramer-pt--1). Do you think Stewart's questions are fair? What do you think about Cramer's answers? As a result of the interview, do you trust Cramer's stock advice more or less? Why?

5. What is your response to the following quote?

> In reality, news is entertainment. And, despite the public's acceptance of journalistic ideologies, most of the public watch or read news not to be informed or to learn the 'truth,' but precisely to be entertained.[209]

RELIGION

CSR Connection:	This issue places *religion* in a CSR context. To what extent is religion a unifying concept? How can firms incorporate religion into their operating and strategic outlook? What does it mean to be socially responsible with respect to religion?
Stakeholders:	Society, Customers, Employees.

Issue

What does it mean to be socially responsible with respect to *religion*? Beyond tolerance, how can firms respond to stakeholders' religious needs and interests without shifting the firm's position from issue-to-issue or seeming to favor one constituency over another? Where people disagree, how can firms respect that diversity to the advantage of all?

In the U.S., it is hard to collect definitive statistics about the nation's religious profile. Religion is a sensitive subject. Federal law, for example, prohibits the census from asking about someone's religious affiliation on anything other than a voluntary basis.[210] As such, what data there are tend to be self-reports, which are unreliable indicators of actual behavior.[211] There are interesting statistics available from other sources, however, with which a religious

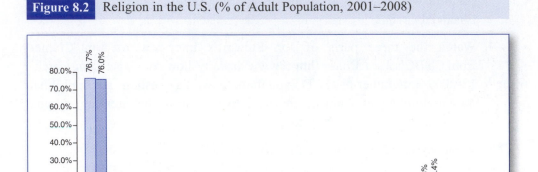

Figure 8.2   Religion in the U.S. (% of Adult Population, 2001–2008)

Source: 'The 2012 Statistical Abstract: Self-Described Religious Identification of Adult Population,' *United States Census Bureau*, January 2013, http://www.census.gov/compendia/statab/cats/population/religion.html

profile of the U.S. can be pieced together. The resulting picture indicates little change from 2001 to 2008.

The data presented in Figure 8.2 can be compared against numbers published by John Green from the University of Akron, who estimates that "White Evangelicals alone . . . make up 26% of the population. . . . When you add in Catholics, mainline Protestants, black Evangelicals, and other Christians, . . . nearly 80% of Americans are affiliated with a Christian church."[212] Some have interpreted these data as an indication that religion in the U.S., while still stronger than in most developed countries, is not as strong as it used to be. According to the most recent American Religious Identification Survey (ARIS):

> . . . the number of Americans who claim no religious affiliation has nearly doubled since 1990, rising from 8 to 15 percent. . . . the percentage of self-identified Christians has fallen 10 percentage points since 1990, from 86 to 76 percent. . . . A separate Pew Forum poll echoed the ARIS finding, reporting that the percentage of people who say they are unaffiliated with any particular faith has doubled in recent years, to 16 percent. . . . This is not to say that the Christian God is dead, but that he is less of a force in American politics and culture than at any other time in recent memory.[213]

It is also true, however, that in a country where "over one-third of Americans, more than 100m, can be considered evangelical," religion is deeply embedded in the social fabric:[214]

The number of Americans with faith in a spiritual being—nearly nine in 10—has not changed much over the past two decades, according to historical polling. . . . Eighty-five percent said religion is "very important" or "fairly important" in their own lives—a number that hasn't changed much since 1992.[215]

Of course, the degree of importance of religion in a country is more interesting as a relative measure. In the UK, the census includes questions about religious affiliation. As such, an accurate profile of the religious affiliation of the population is more readily available—it does not make easy reading for the Church of England:

Around 3% of English people attend an Anglican service at least once a month. Perhaps more significantly, according to the 2011 census, only 59% call themselves Christian, representing a drop of 13 points in a decade. By comparison, two in three young women, according to a poll by *More!* magazine, claim to have experimented with bondage or spanking. The concept of Christendom, a Christian realm that has endured since the time of Constantine the Great, is dying in Britain. In the most godless continent, it is one of the most secular countries.[216]

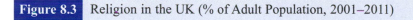

Figure 8.3 Religion in the UK (% of Adult Population, 2001–2011)

Source: '2011 Census,' *UK Government's National Statistics*, March 27, 2011, http://www.ons.gov.uk/ons/index .html

As the 2011 Census data in Figure 8.3 indicate, there are a significant number of people in the UK who identify themselves as having *no religion* (25.1%), which is a marked increase over the level in 2001 (15.1%). In the U.S., by comparison, the number of people claiming *no religion*, plus the very few willing to label themselves *atheists* of *agnostics*, does not exceed 15%. In a *Newsweek* poll in the U.S., for example, "Only 9 percent [of respondents] said they were neither religious nor spiritual."[217] This difference is reflected in everyday life, where religion plays a role in the U.S. to a degree that many British find difficult to relate:

A plaque at Chick-fil-A's headquarters in Atlanta says the company's mission is to "glorify God," which it does by serving chickenburgers and closing its 1,600 outlets on Sundays. The founder, Truett Cathy, once said that while "you don't have to be a Christian to work at Chick-fil-A . . . we ask you to base your business on Biblical principles because they work."[218]

Ironically, it is the U.S. (with a constitutionally-defined separation of Church and State) that is overtly religious, while the UK (where the head of State, the Queen, is also the head of the State Church of England) is more agnostic and atheist:

The latest British Social Attitudes Survey shows just 20% of the British public calling themselves members of the Church of England, down from 40% in 1983. Roman Catholicism (about one in ten of the population) is more stable. Half of the population say they have "no religion." More than half "never" attend a religious service. Non-Christian faiths are growing but small (6% of the population).[219]

In spite of this distinction, religion causes as many issues in the UK as the U.S.; the issues just tend to be of a different nature. In the U.S., for example, it is hard to imagine a candidate being elected President unless s/he is willing to state publicly (and often) his/her belief in God. After all, "over 40% of Americans say they would never vote for an atheist presidential candidate" and "several states still ban atheists from holding public office."[220] As a result, the top echelons of Constitutional institutions in the U.S. are dominated by piety, although the mix of religions can shift over time. During the Presidential election campaign in 2012, for example:

. . . not one person in a group of top political jobs—the presidential and vice-presidential nominees of both parties, the Supreme Court justices, the speaker of the House or the Senate majority leader—is a white Protestant. That group instead comprises nine Catholics (six justices, Mr. Ryan, Vice President Joseph R. Biden Jr. and Speaker John A. Boehner), three Jews (on the court), two

Mormons (Mitt Romney and Senator Harry Reid) and one African-American Protestant (President Obama).[221]

In the UK, in contrast, religion is detrimental to a successful political career. As Alistair Campbell, Tony Blair's press secretary, famously declared when the Prime Minister was asked a question about his Christianity, "We don't do religion!"

While in the U.S., the overly sensitive nature of the religious debate means that even a minor slight can have major ramifications, in the UK, it is the lack of sensitivity to issues surrounding religion that tend to be the problem. In 2006, for example, British Airways found itself in the media spotlight for suspending an employee for wearing "a small crucifix." In defense of its actions, and in the face of strong public criticism and accusations of "religious discrimination," BA parroted its "uniform policy," looking somewhat ridiculous in the process:

> BA says that, under its uniform policy, employees may wear jewelry—including religious symbols—but it must be concealed underneath the uniform. However, the airline says that items such as turbans, hijabs and bangles can be worn 'as it is not practical for staff to conceal them beneath their uniforms.'[222]

At around the same time, a government Minister drew attention to the secular nature of British society by criticizing a Muslim teacher who wore a veil during school lessons. The Minister, Jack Straw (then Leader of the House of Commons), suggested the veil helped create "parallel communities" within Britain[223] and that if he could choose, "he would prefer Muslim women not to wear veils which cover the face."[224]

Part of the explanation for the lack of religious sensitivity in the UK is the large (and growing) percentage of the population who do not believe in God. In 2009, for example, the Atheist Bus Campaign (http://www.atheistbus.org.uk/) launched a series of adverts on London's famous red buses to promote atheism in the country. Gaining the support of high-profile atheists, such as Richard Dawkins (famous for his book, *The God Delusion*),[225] the campaign was intended to present "a corrective"[226] to the overtly religious ads that had been displayed previously on the buses. The text of the ads read "There's probably no God. Now stop worrying and enjoy your life."[227] In contrast, in the U.S., where issues arise, it generally tends to be because of the overbearing influence of too much religion, rather than a lack of sensitivity to the issue. The political influence of the Christian Right, for example, is well-reported. What is less well known is the influence this same lobby has over corporate policy in the U.S.:

> Wal-Mart and Land's End have been forced to apologize for slighting Christmas. And the [American Family Association] has boasted that its complaints led to Ford yanking ads for Jaguar and Land Rover from gay publications.[228]

A similar fight over support for gay rights legislation in Washington state (protecting gays and lesbians against employment discrimination) saw Microsoft criticized by fundamentalist Christian groups. Microsoft eventually withdrew its support for the legislation under criticism from the gay and lesbian community.[229] The company later faced similar pressures over its support for legislation supporting employee benefits for same-sex partners.[230]

In the U.S., however, religion also has its lighter side, with commentators using humor to convey their message. The 'What Would Jesus Drive?' (WWJDrive) campaign (http://www.whatwouldjesusdrive.info/intro.php), for example, is organized and sponsored by the Evangelical Environmental Network (EEN), a biblically orthodox Christian environmental organization. The campaign seeks to reduce the numbers of SUVs, vans, and pickups on U.S. roads because of the environmental damage these vehicles cause. And, extending the transportation theme, the Atheist Bus Campaign reached the U.S. in 2010 in an attempt to influence Americans during the run-up to Christmas:

> In New York City, a large billboard promoting atheism at the entrance of the Lincoln Tunnel, which a local affiliate of American Atheists paid for, has generated controversy. (The message: "You know it's a myth. This season, celebrate reason!").[231]

In terms of stronger criticism, the controversial comedian Bill Maher, after drawing public ire by refusing to label the 9/11 terrorists *cowards*, decided to take on organized religion for an encore in a documentary titled *Religulous*. The film is effective because it:

> . . . takes savagely funny pot-shots at three of the major religions (Christianity, Judaism and Islam) and the apparently deluded 3.7 billion people who practice them. "We're looking at the zillions of religious people in the world," he says. "These are nice people who happen to need their myths to live by." We ask: "How does all this turn into suicide bombings, exorcisms and [molesting] children?"[232]

The strong distinction between the U.S. and Europe in terms of religion has deep historical roots that go back as far as records have been kept: "In 1584, census takers in Antwerp discovered that the city had a larger proportion of 'nones' than 21st-century America: a full third of residents claimed no religious affiliation."[233] Contrast that with the situation in the U.S. during colonial times:

> When conservative activists claim that America stands apart from godless Europe, they are not entirely wrong. The colonies were relatively unchurched,

but European visitors to the early republic marveled at Americans' fervent piety. Alexis de Tocqueville wrote in 1840 that the absence of an established state church nurtured a society in which 'Christian sects are infinitely diversified and perpetually modified; but Christianity itself is a fact so irresistibly established that no one undertakes either to attack or to defend it.'[234]

In the U.S., however, perhaps as a result of the growing criticism, there is some evidence that religion is weakening its hold on society since the most recent census data was released in 2008. Although it may simply be a realignment among those with *no religion*, Americans are increasingly willing to identify themselves as *atheists* "the past seven years have seen a fivefold increase in people who call themselves atheists, to 5% of the population, according to WIN-Gallup International, a network of pollsters. Meanwhile, the proportion of Americans who say they are religious has fallen from 73% in 2005 to 60% in 2011."[235] This is part of a worldwide trend as the number of people that publicly do not associate themselves with any organized religion is also rising:

> A global study of religious adherence released [in 2012] by the Pew Research Center found that about one of every six people worldwide has no religious affiliation. This makes the "unaffiliated," as the study calls them, the third-largest group worldwide, with 16 percent of the global population—about equal to Catholics.[236]

Irrespective of this trend, religion is an issue that firms find hard to ignore because it is important to so many of their stakeholders, both internal (employees) and external (society). In terms of the CSR debate, therefore, to what extent are religion and business compatible?

> Businesses should accept the diverse cultural traditions of their staff, provided they do not threaten their ability to succeed as businesses. Society should also accept that diversity, provided its expression does not threaten the core values of freedom, equality and the rule of law. . . . In the vast majority of cases [of conflict between a firm's pursuit of success and employee rights to religious expression], firms and employees should be able to find sensible compromises, without interference by government or the law.[237]

An appreciation of the world's religions helps firms implement tolerant and diverse policies that appeal to all stakeholders. As such, in addressing the question, "Is ethical capitalism possible?" Devin Stewart answers a resounding "yes":

Ethical principles that emphasize reciprocal rights and responsibilities have long characterized human societies. The Golden Rule is a feature of more than 100 world religious and cultural canons . . . . The ancient Egyptians and Greeks alike pointed to the moral worth of not doing to your neighbor "what you would take ill from him." The Golden Rule is found in both the Old and the New Testament, with the Great Commandment found in Levitivus: "Love thy neighbor as thyself." For Islam, the Golden Rule was offered in the last sermon of Muhammad: "Hurt no one so that no one may hurt you." Variations and extensions of the principle are also found in Buddhism, Hinduism, Taoism, and Jainism.[238]

Different groups recognize this common ground among all religions and seek to encourage it, rather than emphasize issues that demarcate religions. The Charter for Compassion is a good example of such an organization:

By recognizing that the Golden Rule is fundamental to all world religions, the Charter for Compassion can inspire people to think differentially about religion. The Charter is a collaborative project and everyone is encouraged to participate.[239]

In practice, religion has had a long association with business. A good example is the Quakers in the UK, who were "banned from careers in government, the church or law and with their pacifism barring a military career, they were forced into commerce":

Their high ethical standards meant they couldn't be involved with alcohol, gambling or making armaments. The grocery trade became a natural outlet for their energies. All the great English chocolate dynasties: Cadbury, Fry and Rowntree, were Quakers. Their belief in the brotherhood of man led to paternalistic employment practices. They built garden towns for their employees with creches, sporting facilities and healthcare. . . . they believed that cooperation and social provision were a necessary and natural adjunct to making money.[240]

In the U.S., "New England's Puritan settlers brought with them two ideas that have driven American society ever since: Calvinism and capitalism":

[Today] religious faith is on display in American business as perhaps never before, from Tyson Foods' "workplace chaplains [who] roam the corporate halls and processing floors" to the never-open-on-Sunday Chick-fil-A's policy of dedicating each new restaurant to God's glory. . . . "Corporations like Ford and Xerox sponsor spiritual retreats to spark creativity." Even companies with no overt religious or spiritual interests may be the site of spiritual expression, whether that means a Bible study in a conference room or a weekly meeting hosted by the Spiritual Unfoldment Society at the World Bank.[241]

Tom Chappell, the CEO of Tom's of Maine, presents a good example of how to incorporate religion into everyday working life.[242] In his case, the time he spent at Harvard Divinity School during a break from running his company provided him with:

> . . . "a worldview that I could use everywhere in life." More important, he says, he no longer felt he had to apologize for wanting to incorporate values more thoroughly into his business. After Harvard, he says, "I could argue quite confidently that a holistic view of what's good for society or nature was also good for consumers and shareholders."[243]

Books on Religion and Business

- Tom Chappell, *Managing Upside Down: The Seven Intentions of Values-centered Leadership*, William Morrow & Co., 1999.
- Douglas A. Hicks, *Religion and the Workplace: Pluralism, Spirituality, Leadership*, Cambridge University Press, 2003.
- Laura Nash and Scotty McLennan, *Church on Sunday, Work on Monday: The Challenge of Fusing Christian Values with Business Life*, Jossey-Bass, 2001.
- Ken Costa, *God at Work: Living Every Day with Purpose*, Continuum Books, 2007.
- Lake Lambert III, *Spirituality, Inc.*, New York University Press, 2010.

While there is certainly no conflict between capitalism and religion, in general, specific areas of business raise moral challenges for religious believers. Stefan Stern of the *Financial Times*, for example, argues that the finance industry is a particularly challenging forum in which to work, be successful, yet remain true to a strong moral and religious compass. He argues that this has been particularly so recently and sites a book by a vice-chairman of UBS bank, Ken Costa,[244] in support of his argument:

> During the last 30 years, being a Christian at work has, if anything, become more difficult. . . . Financial markets have become more volatile, decisions more complex and few choices are clear-cut. . . . The work place is the coal-face where faith is tested and sharpened by day-to-day encounters with ambiguities and stresses of modern commerce.[245]

As noted by The Right Reverend Justin Welby, Bishop of Durham at the time (and, since January 2013, the Archbishop of Canterbury), while chairing a government inquiry into "banking standards" in the UK, "Coming from a Christian point of view on human sinfulness and failure, the efficient market system doesn't work. . . . People don't make rational decisions in markets more than anywhere else."[246] Rather than evidence that these challenges make religion and finance incompatible, however, Costa finds plenty of support for his career choice in the Bible:

> He reminds us that in the Bible's parable of the talents (Luke 19: 11-27) it is the two servants who put the master's money to work who are rewarded, while the one who preserved the capital and took no risks is punished. And he quotes the great Methodist John Wesley, who told his followers: "Gain all you can, without hurting either yourself or your neighbor."[247]

More broadly, Dave Evans, co-founder of Electronic Arts, the videogame company, believes that "all of work—not just church work—is holy. . . . Work itself has value. It is a huge countercultural behavior to train yourself to value work for its own sake and to see it as a service to God."[248] But, it is in finance where different religions have strived most overtly to overcome any religious hurdles to participation and incorporate an industry-wide social responsibility.

Case Study: Islamic Finance

Evidence that the worlds of religion and finance are compatible (or, at least, that the market is capable of adapting to religious needs when there is sufficient potential profit at stake) can be seen in the rapid growth and acceptance of Sharia-compliant financial instruments.

CSR Newsletters: Corporate Personhood

An article in *The Wall Street Journal*[249] presents a new subset of the socially responsible investing (SRI) community—"religiously themed mutual funds":

> There are around 50 of these funds, with assets topping $17 billion, according to investment researcher Morningstar Inc., up from $500 million 10 years ago.

As usual with stories about SRI, the article follows its early enthusiasm with debate questioning the *wisdom* or *value* of such themed mutual funds. The story reflects, however, the seeming rising profile of religion within the CSR realm, which is reinforced by an article that appeared on the front page of the *Financial Times*[250] announcing the first leveraged buy-out in the West to be financed solely by bonds compliant with Sharia (Islamic) law:

> Now West LB, the German bank, has been appointed to arrange £225m of quasi-debt finance to back the LBO - but only that which accords with the Koran's opposition to interest and speculation.

In some ways, religion and capitalism are well-matched. This is particularly true in the United States, where capitalism is framed within a Judeo-Christian ethos and considered to be "a moral endeavor."[251] In addition, there is always the money:

> Religions rarely praise consumerism. But 2.2 billion Christians and 1.6 billion Muslims are a big market. Sales of books on the world's two biggest faiths are soaring, with interactive Korans and Bibles among the innovative products. [In 2011] sales of religious books in America grew by 8% in a declining industry.[252]

Religion and finance, however, have not always happily co-existed. Usury (the charging of excessive interest), which is the core issue that resulted in the emergence of *Sharia*-compliant financial instruments, has traditionally not been accepted by the major religions. The early Christian church, for example, banned the collection of interest on loans, on punishment of excommunication and condemnation to hell![253] The primary concern was that, by charging borrowers for borrowing money over a defined period, the lenders "were not trading in goods but in time, and this was God's":[254]

> Based on biblical passages—fallen man must live "by the sweat of his brow" (Genesis 3:19), Jesus' appeal to his followers to "lend, expecting nothing in return" (Luke 6:35)—medieval theologians considered the lending of money at interest to be sinful. Thomas Aquinas, based on Aristotle, considered usury—like sodomy—to be contrary to nature because "it is in accordance with nature that money should increase from natural goods and not from money itself."[255]

Dante's third rung of hell reserves a special distaste for the work of usurers:

The third ring—inside the first two—is a barren plain of sand ignited by flakes of fire that torment three separate groups of violent offenders against God: those who offend God directly (blasphemers: Inferno 14); those who violate nature, God's offspring (sodomites: Inferno 15-16); and those who harm industry and the economy, offspring of nature and therefore grandchild of God (usurers: Inferno 17). . . . Dante's emotional reactions to the shades in the seventh circle range from neutral observation of the murderers and compassion for a suicide to respect for several Florentine sodomites and revulsion at the sight and behavior of the lewd usurers.[256]

The corrupting influence, of course, is money (or, the pursuit of it). Money serves three essential purposes—it must be exchangeable, it must be stable (retaining value over time), and it must be a measure of worth. In different forms ("Tea, salt and cattle have all been used as money. In Britain's prisons, inmates currently favour shower-gel capsules or rosary beads"),[257] money has been used by human societies for millennia:

Electrum, an alloy of gold and silver, was used to make coins in Lydia (now western Turkey) in around 650BC. The first paper money circulated in China in around 1000AD. The Aztecs used cocoa beans as cash until the 12th century.[258]

As long as money has existed, in whatever form, there has been antipathy towards those who control access to it:

Hurling brickbats at bankers is a popular pastime. . . . Scorn for moneymen has a long pedigree. Jesus expelled the moneychangers from the Temple. Timothy tells us that "the love of money is the root of all evil." Muhammad banned usury. The Jews referred to interest as *neshek*—a bite. The Catholic church banned it in 1311. Dante consigned moneylenders to the seventh circle of hell—the one also populated by the inhabitants of Sodom and "other practisers of unnatural vice."[259]

The partner of *interest* is *credit*. Interest, today, is charged on loans that are made on the basis of credit, which is extended on the understanding that the borrower undertakes a future obligation to repay the loan. While Jesus might have appealed "to his followers to 'lend, expecting nothing in return' (Luke 6:35),"[260] however, financiers today are not so altruistic. In addition to their commitment to repay the debt, borrowers agree to pay a fee to the lender for the service that reflects the level of *risk* the lender is accepting in agreeing to loan the money to the borrower. This risk fluctuates based on variables such as the size of the loan, the likelihood of repayment, and competing demands for the funds. In addition, however, there is an unspoken element of mutual *trust*—I lend money to you because I trust that you will pay it back; I pay you with this banknote because you trust that the Treasury will honor it to the extent of its face value.

Financial Etymology

Company: The name *company* comes from a combination of the Latin words *cum* and *panis,* the literal translation of which originally meant "breaking bread together."[261]

Credit: "... the root of [the word] credit is *credo*, the Latin for 'I believe.'"[262]

Money: From the Latin moneta 'place for coining money, mint; coined money, money, coinage,' from Moneta, a title or surname of the Roman goddess Juno, in or near whose temple money was coined.[263]

Risk: "... derives from Tuscan *rischio*, the amount considered necessary to cover costs when lending money, i.e., a euphemism for interest.[264]

Without trust, our economic system breaks down, as the Financial Crisis demonstrated only too clearly. Today, the global economic system is underpinned by an interlocking financial system founded on credit. While trust underpins this model, however, it is also true that the profit incentive has distorted the relationship between lender and borrower. Some commentators have gone as far as to argue that it was "the legalization of usury" that was the cause of the Financial Crisis.[265] The root of the problem, according to this argument, is a 1978 U.S. Supreme Court case that prevented Minnesota from enforcing strict limits on the amount of interest charged on a credit card loan by an out-of-state bank.[266] In response to the case, other states quickly repealed similar laws in an attempt to prevent national banks from re-locating to other states, which led to the situation today where banks and credit card companies have an incentive to offer unlimited credit and charge high interest rates to customers who are unable to repay the loans plus interest:

[Following the U.S. Supreme Court's decision] No longer was a credit-worthy borrower the best customer. The bigger profits were made when credit card companies could charge 25 or 35 percent interest on an account that was only intermittently paid off. For payday lenders, interest rates could reach annual levels of 500 percent or higher, as long as the borrower was kept in a cycle of perpetual indebtedness.[267]

As Thomas Geoghegan,[268] an advocate for this position, argued in a television interview:

> You know, if you are Mr. Potter in *It's a Wonderful Life* and can only get six percent, seven percent on your loan, you want the loan to be repaid. Moral character is important. You want to scrutinize everybody very carefully. But if you're able to charge 30 percent or, in a payday lender case, 200 or 300 percent, you don't care so much if the loan—in fact, you actually want the loan not to be repaid. You want people to go into debt. You want to accumulate this interest.[269]

In contrast to modern-day Western finance, Islamic (or *Sharia*, literally, 'the way' and also known as *Shariah* or *Shari'a*)[270] law forbids the charging of interest (or *riba*). Money should only be used as a facilitator of business and the trade of goods; it cannot be used as a commodity to be traded or a tool for speculation. In other words, money should be used to create *things*, not just to create more *money* because "the Prophet Mohammed said debts must be repaid in the amount that was loaned. Money proffered must be backed by collateral, and if financial instruments are traded, they generally have to sell for face value, which deters banks from repackaging debt."[271] As a result, with a global population of 1.6 billion believers[272] and a total *halal* market reported to be worth $2.1 trillion,[273] there is a significant market of devout Muslim investors who have previously either compromised their principles and felt guilty about it, or who traditionally avoided modern finance because of its conflict with their beliefs. This has not only had personal limitations; some also believe it has affected the Muslim world as a whole:

> While ignored by many secular Muslims and the conventional banks that operate in most Muslim nations today, this ban [on usury] has long denied the benefits of modern banking to strict believers—contributing, some way, to the Muslim's world's relative decline after interest-based bonds and loans powered the West's industrial revolution.[274]

Now, many Muslims see Islamic finance as a way to compete and catch-up.[275] Banks enable this by developing financial products that, although based on alternatives to interest, aim to deliver similar investment returns. These alternatives "are technically based on profit-sharing, leasing or trading—all activities permissible in Islam because they involve entrepreneurial work rather than simply moneylending."[276] In order to determine whether a particular investment or financial product is *Sharia*-compliant, banks appoint boards of *Sharia* scholars (Muslim clerics) in order to advise in the development of such products and certify them as compliant when they are issued. The trouble is that many Islamic scholars are not trained in finance and those that are are in short supply and highly sort after:

> At present, devout Muslims will only buy such instruments if a recognized sharia scholar, such as a mullah, has issued a *fatwa* to approve it. . . . However, there are very few Islamic scholars who command enough religious respect to issue *fatwas*, understand the complexities of global structured financial products—and speak good enough English to read the necessary market documentation.[277]

Like all financial instruments, *Sharia*-compliant products run the spectrum from mortgages, to bonds (*sukuk*), to mutual funds and stocks, each with their own set of rules that enable them to remain compliant with Islamic law. A common method for devout Muslims to take out a *Sharia*-compliant mortgage, for example, is *ijara*. With *ijara*, instead of the bank lending the home buyer the money to buy the property and charging a fee (interest) until the loan is re-paid, a bank buys the property on behalf of the home buyer who then pays back the principal over time, while also paying a "lease payment" to use the property in the meantime.[278] Similarly, in order for Islamic bonds (*sukuk*)[279] to be *Sharia*-compliant, it is essential that they "don't pay interest, but instead give investors profits from an underlying business that backs a bond, to comply with a Koranic ban on interest payments."[280] Similarly, Muslim investors seeking to invest in stocks need to buy the stocks of firms (directly or indirectly through mutual funds) that are considered to be *Sharia*-compliant:

> To be sharia-compliant, companies can't run casinos or sell tobacco, alcohol, pork, or pornography, and debt can't exceed 30% of equity. Such rules leave more than half the companies in the Standard & Poor's 500-stock index—including Microsoft, Southwest Airlines, and Nike—in compliance.[281]

Even though the concept of Sharia-compliant funds was first developed in the 1960s,[282] in recent years, the size of the Islamic finance market has grown exponentially. In 2010 alone, "Islamic finance banking assets have risen by 8.9 per cent. . . . Since 2006, the industry has more than doubled in size"[283] and is now estimated to have "total assets of about $950bn."[284] As a result, the Islamic finance industry has moved into the mainstream, "Though Islamic banking still represents only 1 per cent of global banking assets, most observers expect this heady pace of growth to continue for many years."[285] One reason why growth projections are so strong is because "only a small percentage of Muslims, estimated at about 12 per cent of the 1.6bn globally, [currently] use Islamic finance."[286]

The rapid growth of the Islamic finance industry was initially fueled largely with money from the expanding oil countries of the Persian Gulf,[287] with Western banks (such as Citigroup, HSBC, and Deutsche Bank) only becoming interested once the potential became apparent and growing awareness prompted Muslim communities in the West to push for change. Among Muslim countries, however, even though the Dubai Islamic Bank was established in 1975, "the world's first Islamic bank,"[288] it is Malaysia that is credited as the leading source of expansion and product innovation.[289] In 1983, the Malaysian government passed an Islamic banking law and established Bank Islam, "which gave out the nation's first Islamic loans. . . . more than a decade before Saudi clerics followed suit."[290] In many ways:

> [Malaysia] is the world's most important Islamic-finance centre. Just over a fifth of the country's banking system, by assets, is *sharia*-compliant; the average for Muslim countries is more like 12%, and often a lot less. Malaysia dominates the global market for *sukuk*, or Islamic bonds. The country issued the world's first sovereign *sukuk* in 2002; in the first three quarters of 2012 it was responsible for almost three-quarters of total global issuance. Malaysia is also home to the Islamic Financial Services Board, an international standard-setting body. These are big achievements for a relatively small country of just 30m people, of whom only about 60% are Muslim. In neighbouring Indonesia, which is home to the largest Muslim population in the world, only about 4% of the financial sector is *sharia*-compliant.[291]

In the West, Britain has worked hard to market itself as a "global centre of Islamic finance,"[292] and is "the largest Islamic finance market in Europe, holding roughly US$19 billion in Islamic financial assets."[293] The UK, which has been completing Sharia-compliant transactions since the 1980s, "was the first European Union member to adapt its fiscal legislation to place conventional and Islamic finance on a level playing field," and opened "the first 100% Sharia-compliant retail bank in a non-Muslim country, . . . the Islamic Bank of Britain (IBB)."[294] The UK "is currently eighth among Islamic financial markets in the world,"[295] progress that has occurred in spite of international competition.[296] There have also been calls for a U.S. dollar denominated *Sharia*-compliant Treasury bond[297] as a way of healing rifts between Islamic communities and the West following the September 2001 terrorist attacks in the U.S.[298]

Along with a rapidly growing market for Islamic finance is a corresponding growth in organizations seeking to cater to an Islamic clientele. This growth extends from Citigroup (which "operates what is effectively the world's largest Islamic bank in terms of transactions. Some $6 billion of Citibank deals now have been structured and marketed in conformance with Islamic laws since starting out in 1996")[299] to the FTSE (which launched a series of Sharia-compliant indices[300] that are "designed to meet the requirements of Islamic investors globally")[301] to local "hometown" banks in Ann Arbor, Michigan, such as University Bank, and across the U.S.:

> University Bank's boomlet forms only part of a national trend. Institutions like Devon Bank in Chicago and Guidance Residential in Reston, Va., also offer mortgage alternatives. The Amana Funds, based in Bellingham, Wash., has several mutual funds operating on Islamic principles.[302]

Similarly, in response to the growing demand for *Sharia*-compliant financial products and a growth in firms willing to provide them, the demand for financiers who are trained in Islamic finance has also grown. Schools that offer MBA[303] and other Masters[304] degrees that comply with Islamic teachings have arisen to fulfill this need.

CSR Newsletters: MBAs and Islamic Finance

An article in the *Financial Times*[305] documents the growing interest in the business world surrounding the potential of Islamic finance and outlines the potential for an MBA incorporating training that revolves around *Sharia* law:

> The need for MBA graduates armed with a knowledge of Islamic norms has become increasingly pressing. Bankers working to put together deals involving Islamic finance point towards a fundamental skill gap in finding professionals who combine the knowledge of Islamic sharia (jurisprudence) principles with knowledge of the marketplace.

The article provides insight into the forces driving this interest (oil revenues and potential profit), while also accounting for those who think there is either insufficient interest or need at present. It also discusses how *Sharia* law forbids the use of interest-based financial transactions, but still allows investors to profit from specific kinds of investments:

> Islam seeks to promote the idea of partnership-type structures, where depositors provide money through a bank or other institution and bor-

(Continued)

(Continued)

rowers use that money for investment purposes. Profit or loss from the investment is supposed to be shared between the provider and the borrower, with the bank charging a fee for managing the transaction.

In other ways, investment vehicles based on *Sharia* principles (*sukuk*) sound similar to the SRI funds that have grown in popularity among western investors in recent years:

Other obvious prohibitions include investments in anything considered a vice under Islamic law, such as pork, investments in hotels where alcohol is served and outlets for gambling, as well as businesses involved with the trade of arms.

In 2009, Islamic finance was being heralded by advocates as offering a way forward for those wishing to re-model a global financial system founded on credit and the collection of interest.[306] Although Islamic banks, like the financial industry worldwide, have been negatively affected by the global recession, "No Islamic bank has failed during the [Financial] crisis."[307] Others, however, contend that the Islamic finance industry is really no different from Western finance and is merely subverting the rules in search of profit.[308] The argument continues that what Muslim clerics are doing by certifying products as Sharia-compliant is no different than steps taken throughout the ages to subvert the inherent tension between religion and capitalism:

In about 1220 a canonist named Hispanus proposed that, although usury was prohibited, a lender could charge a fee if his borrower was late in making repayment. The period between the date on which the borrower should have repaid and the date on which he did repay, Hispanus termed *interesse*, literally that which "in between is."[309]

The accusation is leveled that the Islamic finance industry is merely the latest evolution of financial products that are designed to conform to strict limitations on the surface, but, in fact, generate "window-dressing pseudo-Islamic financial instruments that [are] mathematically equivalent to conventional debt and mortgage contracts."[310]

The gestation of products within this very un-Islamic framework has resulted in the ultimate mutant, an Islamic personal loan at 7.9 per cent annual percent rate courtesy of the Islamic Bank of Britain. How different this is from the original vision of Muslim economists.[311]

CEO Perspective

Dan Cathy (Chick-fil-A)[312]

We don't claim to be a Christian business.... But as an organization we can operate on biblical principles. So that is what we claim to be.... [When asked if Chick-fil-A's success is attributed to biblical values, Cathy replied] I think they're inseparable. God wants to give us wisdom to make good decisions and choices.

[When questioned about Chick-fil-A's 'Closed on Sunday' policy, Cathy responded] It was not an issue in 1946 when we opened up our first restaurant. But as living standards changed and lifestyles changed, people came to be more active on Sundays.... We've had a track record that we were generating more business in six days than the other tenants were generating in seven [days].

We are very much supportive of the family – the biblical definition of the family unit. We are a family-owned business, a family-led business, and we are married to our first wives. ... our restaurants are typically led by families; some are single. We want to do anything we possibly can to strengthen families.

We intend to stay the course.... We know that it might not be popular with everyone, but thank the Lord, we live in a country where we can share our values and operate on biblical principles.[313]

Online Resources

- Accounting and Auditing Organization for Islamic Financial Institutions, http://www.aaoifi.com/
- American Atheists, http://atheists.org/
- American Family Association, http://www.afa.net/
- Association of Religious Data Archives, http://www.thearda.com/
- Bank Islam (Malaysia), http://www.bankislam.com.my/
- Charter for Compassion, http://charterforcompassion.com/
- European Islamic Investment Bank, http://www.eiib.co.uk/html/
- Evangelical Environmental Network, http://creationcare.org/
- Freedom From Religion Foundation, http://ffrf.org/
- FTSE Shariah Global Equity Index Series, http://www.ftse.com/Indices/FTSE_Shariah_Global_Equity_Index_Series/index.jsp
- INCEIF, The Global University in Islamic Finance, http://www.inceif.org/
- Interfaith Center on Corporate Responsibility, http://www.iccr.org/
- Islamic Bank of Britain, http://www.islamic-bank.com/

- Islamic Financial Services Board, http://www.ifsb.org/
- Jesus on Facebook, https://www.facebook.com/Jesus.page
- Jesus Daily on Facebook, https://www.facebook.com/JesusDaily
- National Religious Broadcasters, http://www.nrb.org/
- Pew Forum on Religion & Public Life, http://religions.pewforum.org/
- United Coalition of Reason, http://unitedcor.org/
- World Halal Forum, http://www.worldhalalforum.org/

Pro/Con Debate

> **Pro/Con Debate:** Religion is a private matter and does not belong in the workplace.

Questions for Discussion and Review

1. What role does religion play in your life? Do you feel the society in which you live is becoming more or less religious? Is this *good* or *bad*? Does it matter?

2. Have a look at photos of the Atheist Bus Campaign's adverts on London buses at: http://www.atheistbus.org.uk/bus-photos/. What is your reaction? Are they provocative or do you not understand what all the fuss is about?

3. Are you interested in a career in finance? Would you have any religious or moral concerns about working in the finance industry? Are there any jobs or industries that you would avoid based on your moral or religious values?

4. What is your reaction to the accusation that the Islamic finance industry is generating "interest-bearing loan[s] in all but name"? From what you have learned in the case, do you agree that Islamic financial products are *Sharia*-compliant, or are banks just finding ways to make people feel comfortable when investing their money with them?

5. Have a look at the website of the campaign "What Would Jesus Drive?" (http://www.whatwouldjesusdrive.info/intro.php). If he were alive today, what car would Jesus drive? Why?

SUSTAINABILITY

CSR Connection:	This issue rose to public prominence ahead of the broader issue of CSR. As such, environmental awareness, in the form of *sustainability*, remains a central component of the CSR debate.
Stakeholders:	Environment, NGOs, Governments, Consumers.

Issue

The issue of *environmental sustainability* raises a number of important questions that business and society are in the process of addressing: Do firms have a social responsibility to the environment? Beyond legal requirements, should firms internalize the environmental costs of operations (e.g., clean up the pollution their operations produce)? Should governments help with these costs? Should firms be allowed to deplete the earth's resources (i.e., remove more than they replenish) during production? Should firms support government-led efforts to place a minimum price (a tax) or a market price (a cap-and-trade scheme) on carbon? Should the price of a product, such as a car, contain the costs to the environment incurred during consumption? *Should* consumers be expected to pay a premium to ensure products are produced in a way that protects the environment? *Will* they pay this premium or continue to reward firms that find ways to avoid the full costs of production? In other words, What is *sustainability*?

CSR Newsletters: The Brundtland Report

This in-depth article in *Ethical Corporation Magazine*[314] chronicles the impact of the 1987 Brundtland Report, which was named after its main author, Gro Harlem Brundtland—Norwegian Prime Minister and chair of the UN's World Commission on Environment and Development. One of the key contributions of the report was to define the term "sustainable development" and identify the importance of sustainability for firms:

> "Sustainable development is development that meets the needs of the present without compromising the ability of future generations to meet their own needs," the report famously states in its oft-cited quote.

(Continued)

(Continued)

Beyond this, however, the report was also prescient in framing the importance of a business case for CSR-related practices. It formed an important step in the debate that has emerged around social responsibility and sustainability issues; and particularly regarding the role that society demands of for-profit organizations:

The Brundtland Report, which inspired the 1992 Earth Summit in Rio de Janeiro that resulted in the Climate Change Convention and in turn the Kyoto Protocol, acknowledged that many "of the development paths of the industrialized nations are clearly unsustainable." However, it held fast to its embrace of development toward industrialized nation living standards as part of the solution, not part of the problem. 'If large parts of countries of the global South are to avert economic, social, and environmental catastrophes, it is essential that global economic growth be revitalized,' the report stated.

The Brundtland Report popularized the term *sustainability*[315] and its definition has become the essential definition. While some people use the term interchangeably with broader issues related to CSR, however, the discussion about sustainability originated in response to resource utilization (in particular, the unsustainable rate of utilization). As such, today, most people understand *sustainability* to represent issues related to the natural environment:

Sustainability

Meeting the needs of the present without compromising the ability of future generations to meet their own needs.

One of the reasons this quote has become so widely accepted, however, is that it is extremely broad. This has the advantage of making it applicable to all organizations that are able to interpret it to suit their circumstances. Another interpretation of such versatility, however, is vagueness—because it can be context-specific, *sustainability* is also subject to varying levels of implementation. In practice, therefore, what does *sustainability* mean and, equally importantly, why should businesses care?

The myth is that financial issues are "hard" while social issues are "soft"— meaning: unimportant and irrelevant, because they don't impact investor money. . . . When society forces companies to internalize social costs, via legal or other penalties, social issues *become* financial issues—which is the way to get companies to sit up and take notice.[316]

Reports increasingly suggest that there is a growing financial risk for any corporation not conducting business in what is considered an appropriate manner by contemporary society:

> Munich Re, a large German insurance company, estimates that the effects of climate change could cost companies $300 billion annually by 2050 in weather damage, pollution, industrial and agricultural losses. . . . Companies may also face unexpected expenses resulting from future taxes, regulations, fines, and caps on products that produce greenhouse gases.[317]

While sustainability is therefore a means of managing risk, there are also many positive reasons for firms to act. As such, rather than wait for the government to impose restrictions on how they operate, many firms are voluntarily choosing to act now (with varying degrees of enthusiasm) in an attempt to access these benefits. In particular, carbon emissions and the market for carbon has become an area of increased firm activity.[318] Pepsi's decision, in association with the Carbon Trust,[319] to measure the carbon footprint through the lifecycle of one half gallon of its Tropicana orange juice is one example of many:

> PepsiCo finally came up with a number: the equivalent of 3.75 pounds of carbon dioxide are emitted to the atmosphere for each half-gallon carton of orange juice. . . . PepsiCo is among the first [in the U.S.] that will provide consumers with an absolute number for a product's carbon footprint, which many expect to be a trend.[320]

Figure 8.4 presents the details of Pepsi's attempt to measure the carbon footprint of its Tropicana Orange Juice. It is instructive that the majority of emissions occur during production (as opposed to distribution, packaging, and consumption). The value for firms in this respect, therefore, is in compiling a better understanding of their supply chain—identifying inefficiencies and communicating that information to stakeholders. These actions mirror earlier decisions by firms like Walkers and Cadbury in the UK,[321] which are demonstrating best practice in this area:

> The famous glass and a half of milk that goes into a Cadbury milk chocolate bar is responsible for 60% of the product's greenhouse gas emissions.[322]

In addition, many firms see economic opportunity in environmental awareness. In the U.S., for example, GE acted early to stake its claim to a significant share of

| Figure 8.4 | The Carbon Footprint of Tropicana Orange Juice |

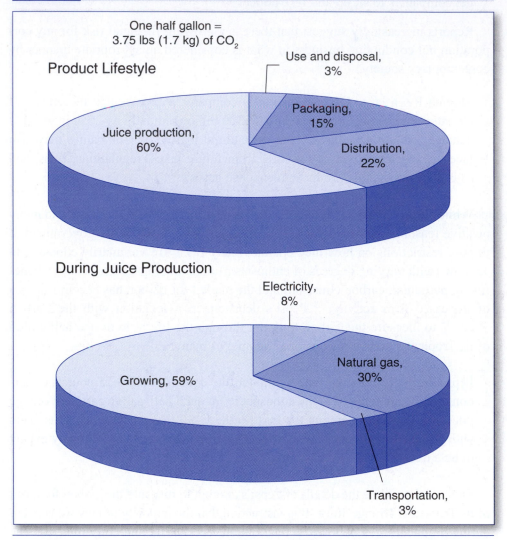

One half gallon =
3.75 lbs (1.7 kg) of CO_2

Product Lifestyle

Use and disposal, 3%

Packaging, 15%

Juice production, 60%

Distribution, 22%

During Juice Production

Electricity, 8%

Growing, 59%

Natural gas, 30%

Transportation, 3%

Source: Tropicana. Adapted from: Andrew Martin, 'How Green Is My Orange,' *The New York Times*, January 22, 2009, p. B1.

the sustainability market. GE, which appointed its first VP for corporate citizenship in 2002, launched its drive to capitalize on the shifting business context with its *Ecomagination* program in 2005:

"The world's changed," [GE CEO, Jeff] Immelt says. "Businesses today aren't admired. Size is not respected. There's a bigger gulf today between haves and have-nots than ever before. It's up to us to use our platform to be a good citizen. Because not only is it a nice thing to do, it's a business imperative."[323]

Other firms, such as Nike,[324] Dr. Hauschka,[325] and many others, have made sizeable bets that their future business model relies on *sustainability* becoming a necessary component of business in the twenty first century. As Walmart[326] has successfully demonstrated, an effective sustainability program *saves*, rather than *costs*, money[327] and, in the most progressive firms, is "a key component of long-term strategy."[328] General Motors has gone "landfill-free"[329] and Samsung has announced plans to invest $20 billion by 2020 because, "Just as electronics defined swathes of the 20th century, the company believes that green technology . . . will be central to the 21st."[330] According to the Carbon Disclosure Project, "More than two thirds of the top 500 companies in the world have now put climate change as a key focus in their strategy,"[331] while 53% of the S&P 500 and 57% of the Fortune 500 firms reported their sustainability performance in 2012.[332] In the case of Unilever, for example, the firm sees little distinction between a sustainability business model and economic success. As then CEO, Patrick Cescau stated:

> As environmental regulations grow tighter around the world, Unilever must invest in green technologies or its leadership in packaged foods, soaps, and other goods could be imperiled. "You can't ignore the impact your company has on the community and the environment," Cescau says. CEOs used to frame thoughts like these in the context of moral responsibility, he adds. But now, "it's all about growth and innovation. In the future, it will be the only way to do business."[333]

A 2009 article in *Harvard Business Review*, argued from an even stronger perspective that, for many firms, "sustainability is now the key driver of innovation":

> Executives behave as though they have to choose between the largely social benefits of developing sustainable products or processes and the financial costs of doing so. But that's simply not true. . . . sustainability is a mother lode of organizational and technological innovations that yield bottom-line and top-line returns. . . . smart companies now treat sustainability as innovation's new frontier.[334]

No firm demonstrates the progressive approach to transforming operations (or the financial benefits that can accrue as a result) as much as Interface carpets, the largest carpet-tile maker in the world. As the company's founder and CEO, the late Ray Anderson launched his attack on *Mount Sustainability* in the mid-1990s, measuring progress using Eco-Metrics[335] and developing innovations such as "plant-based carpeting."[336] The value for the firm of these innovations quickly became self-evident:

... by 2007 the company was, he reckoned, about halfway up 'Mount Sustainability.' Greenhouse-gas emissions by absolute tonnage were down 92% since 1995, water usage down 75%, and 74,000 tonnes of used carpet had been recovered from landfills. The $400m he was saving each year by making no scrap and no off-quality tiles more than paid for the R&D and the process changes. As much as 25% of the company's new material came from "post-consumer recycling." ... Most satisfying of all, sales had increased by two-thirds since his conversion, and profits had doubled.[337]

Ray Anderson was prompted to re-imagine Interface's day-to-day operations in response to the environmental harm that he realized is being done to the planet. After reading Paul Hawken's book, *The Ecology of Commerce*, Anderson understood the extent of the problem and, in particular, understood that business people like him would be judged by future generations as "thieves and plunderers of the planet"[338] unless something changed. In short, those economies that have developed the furthest, the fastest, have also been producing the most carbon emissions. And, given the unsustainable nature of our current business model, it is easy to appreciate how the individual decisions we take, every day (such as whether to turn on the air conditioning), aggregate to a planetary-wide problem: "America uses more electricity for cooling than Africa uses for everything."[339] Figure 8.5 presents the cumulative effect of these decisions in terms of different countries' carbon emissions from 1950-2007, while Figure 8.6 presents a comparison of total emissions per country in 1990 and 2007. It is clear that, while countries like the

| Figure 8.5 | Carbon Emissions by Country/Region (1950-2007) |

Source: Fiona Harvey & Sheila McNulty, 'Savings potential scales new heights,' *Financial Times*, August 21, 2009, p. 17.

Figure 8.6   Carbon Emissions by Country (bn. tons, 1990 & 2007)

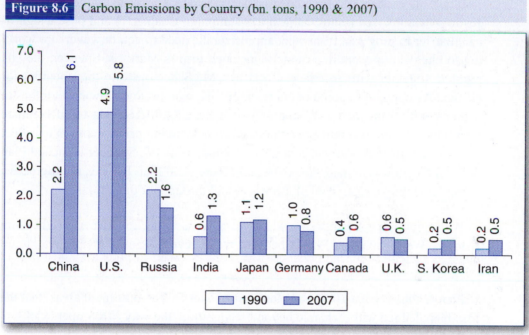

Source: 'Counting Carbon,' *The Wall Street Journal,* December 15, 2009, p. A10.

U.S. and Europe had previously been the primary culprits, they are increasingly being joined by countries such as China and India as access to 'luxuries' like air conditioning spreads.

The result is that, "the 13 warmest years for the entire planet have all occurred since 1998, according to data that stretches back to 1880"[340] and global temperatures in 2013 "are warmer than at any time in at least 4,000 years."[341] But the extent of the problem, in terms of unsustainable resource utilization, goes well beyond climate change to also include "ocean acidification; the thinning of the ozone layer; intervention in the nitrogen and phosphate cycles (crucial to plant growth); the conversion of wilderness to farms and cities; extinctions; the build up of chemical pollutants; and the level of particulate pollutants in the atmosphere."[342] As Thomas Friedman puts it, "The Earth is Full":

> . . . we are currently growing at a rate that is using up the Earth's resources far faster than they can be sustainably replenished, so we are eating into the future. Right now, global growth is using about 1.5 Earths. "Having only one planet makes this a rather significant problem," says [Paul] Gilding.[343]

Just because we can identify the problems, however, does not mean that change is easy, or even that we know what changes to make. Good intentions that seek to subvert market forces often lead to results that have net neutral or even negative results. This concept of unintended consequences is known to economists as the Jevon's Paradox (see Issues: Ethical Consumption, Chapter 7) and pose a significant barrier to progress. Firms that appreciate the need to act, however, are working to change our economic model. One such firm is Marks & Spencer, the UK retailer. Together with Interface, firms like M&S demonstrate the potential for change. As opposed to some retailers in the UK, who produce low cost clothes to compete with firms such as Walmart (Asda in the UK), M&S seeks to differentiate its products based on quality and charges a corresponding price premium to reflect the different market segment it targets. In 2007, Marks & Spencer launched Plan A.[344] The plan was named *Plan A* because there is no Plan B—i.e., no alternative to implementing a sustainable business model throughout operations:

> We're doing this because it's what you want us to do. It's also the right thing to do. We're calling it Plan A because we believe it's now the only way to do business.[345]

Plan A consists of a 100 point plan, spread over five commitment areas, that the firm has pledged will "'change beyond recognition' the way M&S operates:"

> Initiatives within the 100 point plan include transforming the 460-strong chain into a carbon neutral operation; banning group waste from landfill dumps; using unsold out-of-date food as a source of recyclable energy and making polyester clothing from recycled plastic bottles.[346]

In spite of an initial plan to spend £200 million over the five years of Plan A,[347] by the first half of 2009, M&S claimed that Plan A was "cost-neutral."[348] More importantly, based on progress during the first half of the plan's five years, three trends are apparent:

> Corporate responsibility guidance and the Plan A commitment have systematically embedded themselves into the company's management platform; clear package labels and effective outreach to third-party stakeholders are changing consumer behavior; and steady progress is being made towards fulfilling Plan A's five commitment areas of carbon emissions, waste, sustainable sourcing, ethical trading, and healthy lifestyles.[349]

In 2012, on the fifth anniversary of the 2007 launch, M&S announced that Plan A continues to demonstrate "its centrality to M&S's long-term corporate and commercial future. Already 138 commitments have been achieved, with a further 30 on course. Of all M&S products, 31% adhere to a Plan A commitment and a total of £185m in net benefits has been delivered."[350] As a result, "Plan A is still widely acknowledged as the most ambitious public sustainability declaration to come from a supermarket retailer."[351] The benefit to M&S, however, is evident not only in terms of reputation, but also in terms of added value:

- Energy efficiency savings: **£22m per year**
- Zero waste to landfill: **£6.3m** in 2011/2012
- Packaging reductions: **£16.3m** in 2011/2012
- Transport fuel efficiency: **£2.1m** in 2011/12
- Printing cost reductions: **£550,000** in 2011/12[352]

A central goal of *Strategic CSR* is to restore faith in the corporation. For all its faults, the corporation is uniquely placed to achieve many of the goals CSR advocates support. While the government and nonprofits also fill valuable social roles, it is the corporation that has the ability to allocate valuable and scarce resources in ways that encourage innovation and maximize social value. Those corporations that embrace CSR at all levels of operations, seeking to engage stakeholders to meet their needs and expectation, will be much better placed to survive and thrive over the medium to long term. In terms of sustainable resource utilization, in the absence of dramatic political action on a global basis, for-profit companies are, quite simply, our only hope:

> Ready or not, we are moving to a world of scarce resources, in which companies will increasingly need to consider their total return not just on assets and equity but on resources. They will have to monitor how much water, soil, and other natural resources they consume, as well as the payback they get from them. Companies that fail to calculate this equation will find themselves at the mercy of price increases and volatility, regulation, and social pressures, while those that master it will enjoy competitive advantage and gain market share.[353]

If for-profit firms do not reform our current economic model, and quickly, we will face a change in the planet's climate patterns that may well be irreversible. In that instance, we would rather not find out whether the worst predictions by scientists are likely to come true:

> Global warming isn't a prediction. It is happening. . . . If [we continue to exploit all known oil reserves], it will be game over for the climate. . . . concentrations of carbon dioxide in the atmosphere eventually would reach levels higher than in the Pliocene era, more than 2.5 million years ago, when sea level was at least 50 feet higher than it is now. That level of heat-trapping gases

would assure that the disintegration of the ice sheets would accelerate out of control. Sea levels would rise and destroy coastal cities. Global temperatures would become intolerable. Twenty to 50 percent of the planet's species would be driven to extinction. Civilization would be at risk.[354]

In other words, in spite of what M&S says, there is a Plan B; it is just not in anyone's interests to have firms pursue it.

Case Study: e-Waste

Waste is a central component of the economic model that drives the global economy. For the majority of for-profit firms, the more you buy of their product, the better they perform and the faster the economy grows. In other words, if you buy a product, the quicker you throw it away and buy another one, the better for all concerned. A huge assumption of this economic model, however, is that the world's resources are infinite. As a result, when a company extracts a raw material and converts it into something that consumers want to buy, the consumer pays only for the cost the firm incurred during the extraction and conversion. For the most part, there is no charge associated with the replenishment of the resource (for example, the cost of re-planting trees cut down to make paper), or the environmental costs incurred during consumption (for example, the CO_2 emitted when driving a car). Such costs are termed *externalities*—costs incurred but not paid for, either by the firm or the consumer (see Issues: Accountability, above):

> Over the past century, companies have been rewarded financially for maximizing externalities in order to minimize costs. . . . Not until we more broadly "price in" the external costs of investment decision across all sectors will we have a sustainable economy and society.[355]

In short, at present, our economy is founded on *waste*—the more the company and the consumer waste, the higher a country's GDP, and the stronger its economy. A question worth asking, therefore, is "Are we sinking under the weight of our disposable society?"[356]

According to the OECD, the average person creates 3.3lb (1.5kg) of rubbish a day in France, 2.7lb in Canada and no more than 2.3lb in Japan. By the OECD's reckoning, the average American produces 4.5lb a day, and more recent accounting puts the figure at over 7lb a day, less than a quarter of which is recycled.[357]

As economies across the world evolve, progress, and seek the lifestyle long-enjoyed by the developed economies, the total amount of trash continues to build:

China has surpassed the U.S. to become the world's largest trash producer, churning out more than 260 million tons a year. Beijing's 20 million residents generate about 18,000 tons a day, most of which goes to landfills.[358]

In terms of per capita trash, however, the U.S. is still far ahead: "At 7.1 pounds of trash a day, each of us is on track to produce a staggering 102 tons of waste in an average lifetime."[359] And this waste generates a significant drag on the economy as a whole:

American communities on average spend more money on waste management than on fire protection, parks and recreation, libraries or schoolbooks. . . . The Chief Executive of Waste Management, the world's largest trash company, estimates that there is at least $20 billion in valuable resources locked inside the materials buried in U.S. landfills each year, if only we had the technology to recover it cost effectively.[360]

CSR Newsletters: Waste

It will come as no surprise to many that a huge amount of the daily food consumption in the U.S. is wasted. An article in *The New York Times*,[361] however, reports research that attempts to quantify just how much food this wastage represents:

In 1997, in one of the few studies of food waste, the Department of Agriculture estimated that two years before, 96.4 billion pounds of the 356 billion pounds of edible food in the United States was never eaten.

This amounts to "an estimated 27 percent of the food available for consumption," "about 1 pound of waste per day for every adult and child in the nation at that time. That doesn't count food lost on farms and by processors and wholesalers." And, this is not only a U.S. phenomenon:

In England, a recent study revealed that Britons toss away a third of the food they purchase, including more than four million whole apples, 1.2 million sausages and 2.8 million tomatoes. In Sweden, families with small children threw out about a quarter of the food they bought, a recent study there found.

The article reports that a new study is being undertaken to update the figure, this time accounting for the recent growth in pre-prepared food produced

(Continued)

(Continued)

by supermarkets. Optimistically, Jonathan Bloom, the creator of the website WasteFood.com believes recent events suggest things might be improving. An article in the *Financial Times*,[362] however, shows that the amounts involved are truly staggering and depressing:

> The food wasted each day in the UK and the US alone would be enough to alleviate the hunger of 1.5bn people – more than the global number of malnourished.

More recent figures suggest that the amount of wasted food may be significantly higher—closer to 40% of all food in the U.S., worth an estimated $165 billion annually[363]:

The average U.S. family of four spends from $500 to $2,000 a year on food they never eat. . . . Food is the second-largest component in the U.S. solid waste stream, after paper and paperboard. Once paper and paperboard are removed for recycling, food ends up as the largest component in U.S. landfills and incinerators, weighing in at 33 million tons in 2010, according to the Environmental Protection Agency.[364]

What happens to our waste when we no longer need it? A lot of it is shipped overseas to countries with less strict environmental regulations. Even as we upgrade our industrial infrastructure and production processes in the West, our old factories and equipment are exported to the developing world to continue polluting:

The global market for hand-me-down industrial machinery and vehicles has been valued at an estimated $150 billion a year. . . . The U.S. feeds the market with products ranging from four-ton trucks to entire power plants. . . . A 1950s paper-making machine from Adams [Massachusetts], operates in Egypt; a rock-crushing machine from Vermont has been reassembled in Colombia; a five-story, coal-fired power plant in Turners Falls [Massachusetts], is being reassembled in Guatemala.[365]

In fact, waste is one of the developed economies' largest exports. While "China's No.1 export to the U.S. is computers. . . . The United States' No.1 export to China, by number of cargo containers, is scrap."[366] According to data compiled by the U.S. International Trade Commission, "Chinese imports of U.S. cast-offs (scrap metal, waste paper, and the like) surged by an eye-popping 916 percent over the 2000-2008 period, with most of that expansion occurring after 2004."[367] A large proportion of the scrap that is exported to China (and countries in Africa, such as Nigeria)[368] is electronic waste, or *e-waste*. E-waste is the waste associated with technology-related products, such as computers and cellphones.[369] In addition to the plastic casing that surrounds many of these products, various metals and soldering are used to make the electronic components inside. The amount of e-waste we produce as technology becomes an increasingly central component of our lives is a particular problem in terms of disposal or recycling because of these plastics and metals. Yet:

> Right now anyone can dump an old television [or any other consumer electronics product] into a trash can. But the average television is made of hundreds of chemical, some of which are toxic.[370]

Our consumer-oriented economic model dictates that we trade-in our fully-functioning old phone and buy a new model whenever one comes out, without thinking through the consequences of that purchase exchange. When Apple's new iPhone5 was released, for example, it was estimated it would replace "tens of millions of cell phones . . . in more than 100 countries."[371] As electronic consumer goods become obsolete, they are often stored (it is estimated that "the average American has at least three expired cellphones stockpiled at home"[372] and that "99 million television sets sit unused in closets and basements across the [U.S.])."[373] When they are eventually discarded, however, there is a significant environmental cost because e-waste "contains metals like mercury that are extremely harmful if they end up in landfills, where they can leach into the ground and water."[374] As such, *e-waste* stands as a poster child for the ecological consequences of our twenty-first century consumption-based economic model, which treats all resources as infinite and fails to fully account for the externalities created during the manufacture processes. According to the Environmental Protection Agency's latest figures (2010), the problem is immense and getting worse. In the U.S. alone:

- 142,000 computers and over 416,000 mobile devices are thrown away every day.
- In total, 2.4 million tons (384 million units) of e-waste are discarded annually.
- Only 27% (of total weight) and 19% (of total units) of e-waste is recycled.[375]

Figure 8.7 presents the scale of discarded e-waste for different consumer electronics products in the U.S. in terms of both weight (tons) and total units.

Figure 8.7 Total e-Waste in the U.S. (2010)

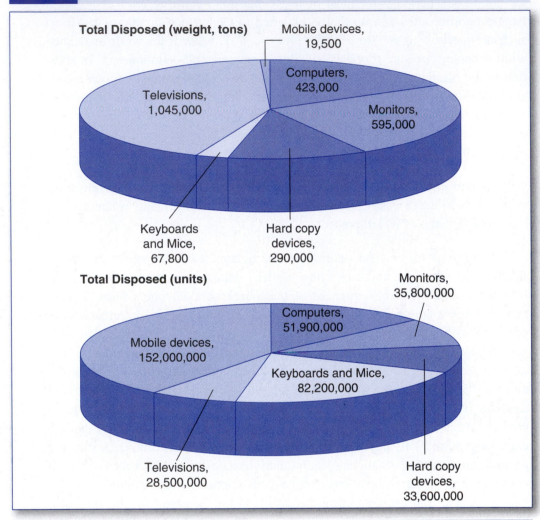

Total Disposed (weight, tons)
Mobile devices, 19,500
Computers, 423,000
Televisions, 1,045,000
Monitors, 595,000
Keyboards and Mice, 67,800
Hard copy devices, 290,000

Total Disposed (units)
Monitors, 35,800,000
Computers, 51,900,000
Mobile devices, 152,000,000
Keyboards and Mice, 82,200,000
Televisions, 28,500,000
Hard copy devices, 33,600,000

Source: EPA data, quoted in: 'Fact and Figures on E-Waste and Recycling,' *Electronics TakeBack Coalition*, February 21, 2012, p. 2.

As the technological revolution continues, the total amount of e-waste keeps piling up. As such, this is not just a problem for individual consumers, but companies, too. IBM, for example, has to process 38,000 electronic devices *a day* and maintains a staff of 250 people and "thousands of additional contractors" who are solely dedicated to e-waste disposal at the firm's 22 recycling plants worldwide.[376] And, because companies like IBM and Apple are global firms, and consumer appetite for their products is worldwide, the problem of e-waste is global, too, with "20 to 50 million metric tonnes of e-waste . . . generated worldwide every year, comprising more than 5% of all municipal solid waste."[377] The amount of heavy metals contained within all this waste adds up quickly and presents a serious problem that someone has to clean up:

> Discarded TVs and PCs can contain as much as eight pounds of lead, as well as mercury, cadmium and other substances that are harmless when part of a piece of equipment but a health risk when they reach a landfill.[378]

At present, much of the West's recycling is outsourced to China where it is often dismantled by hand by low paid women and children with little or no protective clothing or equipment. As such, consumers who want to dispose of products responsibly are left with few good options. In the case of plastics recycling, for example, "employees in Chinese recycling facilities are exposed to toxic fumes from the materials they are recycling. . . . Some choice: noxious chemicals in the soil versus the health of Chinese workers. It really isn't easy being green."[379] Specific areas in China, in particular, have become "wastelands"[380] as Chinese workers save us the cost and effort of recycling our own e-waste. With little more than hand tools, "they take apart old computers, monitors, printers, video and DVD players, photocopying machines, telephones and phone chargers, music speakers, car batteries and microwave ovens."[381] In Guiyu, China, where "100,000 people work in e-waste recycling":

> Standard practice is to separate the plastic by boiling circuit boards on stoves, and then leach the metals with acid. Workers risk burns, inhaling fumes and poisoning from lead and other carcinogens. A study by the nearby Shantou University found high miscarriage rates in local women.[382]

What is being done to regulate the movement of e-waste from country-to-country? The UN's Basel Convention and the EU legislation on Waste Electrical and Electronic Equipment are two important government-level initiatives to regulate e-waste. Although these international regulatory efforts are extensive and offer workers significant protection, however; in many developing countries, enforcement is problematic. In Guiyu, for example:

> . . . recycling e-waste is apparently free of any environmental or health and safety regulation. . . . Chinese law forbids the importation of electronic waste and Beijing is also a signatory to the Basel agreement, an international treaty banning the shipment of e-waste from the developed to the developing world. But so far, official prohibitions have been about as effective as the official banners urging environmental protection that flap in the breeze above the trash-congested streets of Guiyu.[383]

As a result of the difficulties with enforcement in different cultures and legal systems, some commentators have argued that a reduction in waste is a more realistic goal than better recycling at the current rate of consumption.[384] As landfills fill up and the dangers of e-waste become more apparent, local and state governments in the U.S. are pursuing innovative policies to try and change consumer behavior and limit the amount we throw away (or at least have it correctly recycled). In 2006, for example, Washington state passed a law "mandating that electronics and computer companies pay for the recycling of old equipment. . . . [As a result] no manufacturer can sell an electronic product in the state unless the manufacturer is participating in an approved electronic waste recycling plan."[385] And, by 2009, similar laws had been passed or were pending in 31 states.[386] Some innovative local governments are experimenting with a radical recycling program called *Pay-As-You-Throw* (PAYT):

> With PAYT, residents are charged based on how much garbage they generate, often by being required to buy special bags, tags or cans for their trash. Separated recyclables like glass and cardboard are usually hauled away free or at minimal cost. . . . The EPA said that about 7,100 cities and towns were using PAYT in 2006, up from 5,200 in 2001.[387]

The obvious incentive is to minimize disposed waste by maximizing the amount of waste each household recycles. Along these lines, in Nantucket MA, strict recycling rules mean that the island's residents send only 8% of household waste to the landfill, compared to 66% for the average Massachusetts' resident.[388] Across the country, San Diego (68%), Los Angeles (65%), Chicago (45%), Houston (26%), New York (26%), San Antonio (18%), and Pheonix (17%) are reporting similar decreases in total waste sent to landfills.[389] Equally impressive, Portland OR, has moved to a "biweekly garbage pickup program," which has allowed the city to reduce "the amount of garbage that [it] is shipping to landfills by 44 percent":

> Pioneers like Portland, Seattle and San Francisco have become so good at waste diversion that it is becoming harder to get much better. San Francisco reuses a whopping 78 percent of what enters its waste stream, compared with the national average of 34 percent.[390]

In spite of these plans' apparent common sense, however, implementation can be problematic. In particular, there is debate over whether pollution costs should be borne by the individual (based on the amount disposed) or society (based on the idea that comprehensive and efficient waste disposal is a public good):

About three-quarters of the nation's households still have unlimited disposal service. In some communities, they pay a flat annual fee. In others, local property taxes cover the tab so residents aren't aware of the cost, making the service seem free.[391]

So, what is the solution to the abundance of waste we generate? Those who advocate change tend to fall into one of two camps. People in the first camp tend to be more idealistic. They argue that we should be striving for a particular lifestyle, given the state of current knowledge. Above all, they demand *sacrifice*:

> In this mindset saving the planet demands that people give up their foreign holidays, abandon their cars, turn down the heating and clean their teeth in the dark. Through this prism, pain is a virtue and the halting global warming metamorphoses into a much broader attack on consumerism, materialism and, at the extreme, anything that smacks of the market.[392]

People in the second camp, however, tend to be more pragmatic. They think it is fruitless to try and get people in the developed world to consume less and ask people in the developing world to grow at slower rates. There is some truth to this position, as even the most progressive firms that are committed to sustainable business, such as Tesco in the UK, find it difficult to grow their business and reduce their overall carbon footprint simultaneously.[393] As a result, in this view, the only solution is through technological innovation and the issue is:

> . . . an opportunity rather than a burden. Technological innovation—in automobile design, energy efficiency, renewable energy and the rest—is more than a useful adjunct to an austere low carbon lifestyle. It is a vital pillar of any plan to reduce the build-up of CO_2. Bluntly stated, unless we find a way to capture emissions from coal-fired power stations, the game will be lost.[394]

Strategic CSR argues for a compromise position between the two extremes. Such a position recognizes that the status quo is unstable, but also recognizes the power of the market to innovate and overcome the most intractable human problems. In short, we need a comprehensive reassessment of our capitalist model, but one in which we retain what is most effective about market forces to mobilize and allocate valuable and scarce resources in ways that encourage innovation and, therefore, maximize social value. Firms like TerraCycle, through its pledge to "eliminate the idea of waste," demonstrate the power of innovation and entrepreneurial spirit to generate change along these lines.[395] TerraCycle is successful because it adopts a stakeholder perspective and implements it comprehensively throughout all aspects of operations and strategic planning. It is the inclusion of all aspects of firm operations that maximizes the strategic advantages of CSR. In terms of regulating waste disposal and recycling, it is important that firms work in tandem with government agencies and NGOs to incentivize efforts and identify best-practice solutions where the market is insufficient alone.[396] It is this concept of *system-wide* sustainability that is essential—maintaining a focus on CSR in its broadest interpretation. It is only by focusing on the system as a whole that meaningful and *sustainable* change can occur.

CEO Perspective

Lee Scott (Walmart)

Meeting social and environmental standards is not optional. I firmly believe that a company that cheats on overtime and on the age of its labor, that dumps its scraps and its chemicals in our rivers, that does not pay its taxes or honor its contracts, will ultimately cheat on the quality of its products. And cheating on the quality of products is the same as cheating on customers. We will not tolerate that at Walmart. Strengthening our relationship with customers—today and in the future—is tied hand-in-hand with improving the quality of our supplier factories and their products.[397]

Online Resources

- C40 Cities, http://www.c40cities.org/
- Carbon Price Communique, http://www.climatecommuniques.com/
- Carbon Principles, http://www.carbonprinciples.com/
- Ceres, http://www.ceres.org/
- Climate Policy Initiative, http://climatepolicyinitiative.org/
- Cool Earth, http://www.coolearth.org/
- Earth911.com, http://earth911.com/
- Electronic Industry Citizenship Coalition, http://www.eicc.info/
- Electronics TakeBack Coalition, http://www.electronicstakeback.com/
- EU Waste Electrical and Electronic Equipment (WEEE) Directive, http://ec.europa.eu/environment/waste/weee/index_en.htm
- Forest Stewardship Council, http://www.fsc.org/
- Freecycle, http://www.freecycle.org/
- GreenBiz.com, http://www.greenbiz.com/

- International Standards Organization (ISO), http://www.iso.org/iso/iso14000
- Marks & Spencer's Plan A, http://plana.marksandspencer.com/
- Rainforest Alliance, http://www.rainforest-alliance.org/
- SustainAbility, http://www.sustainability.com/
- TerraCycle, http://www.terracycle.com/
- United Nation's Basel Convention, http://www.basel.int/
- World Business Council for Sustainable Development, http://www.wbcsd.org/

Pro/Con Debate

Pro/Con Debate: Unsustainable resource exploitation (i.e., waste) is the most serious issue facing the planet today.

Questions for Discussion and Review

1. Is sustainability an issue you consider in your purchase decisions? Why or why not?

2. Have a look at this 20 minute video: http://www.storyofstuff.org/movies-all/story-of-stuff/. Does it change your answer to Question 1? How do you answer the main question posed in the video: How can we make a linear economic system more sustainable?

3. What is your image of the NGO Greenpeace? Do you trust the organization to provide accurate and objective assessments of the environmental impact of business? Visit the organization's website (http://www.greenpeace.org/). Is environmental sustainability given a high enough priority in business, politics, and society today? Why, or why not?

4. Look at Marks and Spencer's Plan A website (http://plana.marksandspencer.com/). What are your impressions? Do you get the sense that this is a genuine effort, or is it window dressing? More importantly, is it enough?

5. Have a look at this 60 Minutes report on e-waste in China titled 'The Wasteland': http://www.cbsnews.com/video/watch/?id=5274959n[398] What can you do to minimize your carbon footprint and the amount of e-waste you produce? How often do you change your cellphone? What about your computer? Is it *fair* that poor workers in India or China (often including children) have to clean up our e-waste?

VALUES

CSR Connection:	This issue explores the role of *values* in building an ethical company. It does so by looking at firms with strong *ethical* cultures, those with weak ethical cultures, and also considers whether values and ethics can be taught to the business leaders of the future.
Stakeholders:	All stakeholders.

Issue

CSR, in various forms, has been around for a long time:

> . . . even prior to Thomas Clarkson kicking off the first major boycott over the UK slave trade in 1787. Continuing through the Quakers and Marx in 19th century capitalism, early 20th century anti-trust and booms and busts, into 1950s American theory, the movement was resurgent in the late 1960s and throughout the social and economic unrest of the 1970s. The 1980s, with its junk bond-fuelled takeover frenzy and resulting scandals brought ethics sharply into focus once again. Soon after, in the midst of the 1990s boom, the Body Shop issued its first values report. And then . . . came Shell's planned disposal of the Brent Spar storage platform and the execution of Ken Saro-Wiwa in Nigeria. In 1995 these seminal events . . . can be said to be the beginning of the most recent stage in the evolution of stakeholder expectations of multi-national business.[399]

This historical framework, together with the arguments presented throughout this book, presents a compelling argument for firms to include CSR as an integral component of their day-to-day operations and strategic perspective. An important part of this process is to be open to collaborative relationships with the wide variety of groups that constitute an organization's primary constituents in today's globalizing world. In other words, a stakeholder perspective is part of a comprehensive, strategic approach to CSR. Firms will differ on which of their stakeholders are the most important and these priorities will also shift from issue-to-issue. What is important, however, is that firms are aware of their stakeholders' concerns so they can take them into account in making decisions. By implementing an effective stakeholder relations policy, firms counter the prevailing perception (enhanced by the turn-of-the-century corporate scandals and more recent Financial Crisis) that *business* is as much a force for bad as well as good. As the extent to which stakeholders are being considered and consulted before making significant company decisions increases, so the benefits of such policies gain wider recognition.

The importance of adopting a stakeholder perspective, however, is something that is easy to say and difficult to do. By definition, the interests and demands of different stakeholders will conflict. As such, firms will not be able to please all of their stakeholders all of the time—a pragmatic approach should be to please enough stakeholders enough of the time. Installing a process that allows the firm to take stakeholder concerns into account in its strategic decision making, therefore, will help it make better decisions, while insulating it from potential threats to its societal legitimacy. The goal should be to partner with stakeholders in order to maximize value added and minimize the danger of stakeholder disillusionment. But, there are not many companies that are able to do this effectively. What is common to all that are effective, however, is a genuine commitment to the process. Defining characteristics of such firms include a core culture and set of values that is inclusive more than it is exclusive, and that sees profit as a means to an end, rather than an end in itself; in short, a firm that is ethical in its approach to business.

Business Ethics vs. CSR

Business ethics differs from the related concept of corporate social responsibility (CSR) in two important ways. First, while *CSR* tends to include more of a macro perspective and evaluates the extent to which firm behavior affects society as a whole, *business ethics* focuses on more micro issues, such as individual behavior and decision making. And, second, while *CSR* is often externally focused and tied more closely to functions such as marketing, *business ethics* focuses internally on creating an ethical environment and has its roots in legal compliance.[400]

Morality vs. Ethics

"When we teach children not to steal, we are teaching them morality. When you have a conflict between two or more things that morality requires, that's when ethics steps up to the plate."[401]

An important question, therefore, is: What drives a company to be *ethical*, to be a good *corporate citizen* and implement CSR throughout operations? How should external stakeholders discern the difference between a firm that implements CSR substantively and genuinely, and a firm that implements it superficially and symbolically? After all, many of the observable components of an ethical or CSR corporate structure (a CSR/ethics officer, a code of conduct, a CSR report, ethics training, etc.) ostensibly can look and sound the same in both cases. When stakeholders read that "95% of consumer products [labels contain] at least one offense of 'greenwashing,'"[402] or that the firm's CEO has been fired for dishonesty,[403] or any number of other transgressions that create news every day, therefore, how can they tell whether that is representative of a firm's business practices, or the exception to the rule in an otherwise well-run organization? In general, should we assume that firms are ethical and that transgressions are the exception, or assume that firms will try and get away with what they can unless restrained by vigilant stakeholders?

CSR Newsletters: Human Nature

An article in *The Wall Street Journal*[404] is interesting because it reflects on a fundamental aspect of human nature – Are we essentially flawed beings who have to struggle against our innate tendencies in order to exist in a civilized society, or is 'evil' (immoral, unethical) behavior the exception and humans are preordained to be 'good'?

There are reflections of this debate within the CSR community in relation to the fundamental role of for-profit firms (and all organizations) in society. Are firms (and the executives who work in them) essentially powers for good that occasionally commit transgressions, or are they essentially negative elements of society—freeing the individuals that work there to pursue short-term, self-centered gain under the cloak of group anonymity?

The article, which is an interview with the psychiatrist Theodore Dalrymple, focuses on the horrific mass-shooting that occurred in Norway in the summer of 2011, but the discussion reflects on the motivations underlying human behavior more broadly:

First, it says something about us that we feel compelled to explain evil in a way that we don't feel about people's good actions. The discrepancy arises, he says, "because [Jean-Jacques] Rousseau has triumphed," by which he means that "we believe ourselves to be good, and that evil, or bad, is the deviation from what is natural." For most of human history, the prevailing view was different. Our intrinsic nature was something to be overcome, restrained and civilized. But Rousseau's view, famously, was that society corrupted man's pristine nature. This is not only wrong, Dr. Dalrymple argues, but it has had profound and baleful effects on society and our attitude toward crime and punishment. For one thing, it has alienated us from responsibility for our own actions. For another, it has reduced our willingness to hold others responsible for theirs.

The idea that we have divorced behavior from responsibility has many applications in the CSR debate (both for firms and stakeholders). It is connected to the belief that, as a society, we have moved away from valuing strong institutions that bind us and constrain our behavior within normative rules constructed over decades of civilization (a broad, long-term focus), towards a society that is focused on the pursuit of individual happiness and self-indulgence (a narrow, short-term focus) and any attempt to limit that pursuit is resisted.

This shift against society and in favor of the individual is a significant barrier to meaningful progress in the CSR debate. Without the idea that society is more important than the individual, rather than the other way around, we lose what Dalrymple describes as our "transcendent purpose," which governs our daily actions and, ultimately, guides our willingness to make personal sacrifice in the name of something larger than ourselves:

"After all," Dr. Dalrymple says, "having a very consistent worldview, particularly if it gives you a transcendent purpose, answers the most difficult question: What is the purpose of life?"

Take a look at this list of corporate values: Communication. Respect. Integrity. Excellence. They sound pretty good don't they? Strong, concise, meaningful. Maybe they even resemble your own company's values, the ones you spent so much time writing, debating, and revising. If so, you should be nervous. These are the corporate values of Enron, as stated in the company's 2000 annual report. And as events have shown, they're not meaningful; they're meaningless.[405]

Enron is a good example of a company that, on the surface, had excellent CSR credentials. It is also a good example of the danger presented by a firm's CSR policy that is ill-defined and superficially championed. Without genuine leadership, a company's CSR policy merely presents the organization with sufficient rope to hang itself (see Chapter 5):

The underlying reasons for Enron's collapse can be traced to characteristics common to all corporations: obsession with profits and share prices, greed, lack of concern for others and a penchant for breaking legal rules. [It shows] what can happen when the characteristics we take for granted in a corporation are pushed to the extreme.[406]

To what extent are a company's efforts at social responsibility window dressing? To what extent is there a genuine intention to recognize and reflect the shifting consumer market globalization is producing, as well as a company's larger responsibility to all its stakeholders and the wider social context in which it operates? CSR advocates understand that it is very easy for a company to say one thing while intending to do another. To what extent is the CSR movement a façade, therefore, providing cover to firms that are resistant to adopting a broader perspective?

Enron rang all the bells of CSR. It won a spot for three years on the list of the 100 Best Companies to Work for in America. In 2000 it received six environmental awards. It issued a triple bottom line report. It had great policies on climate change, human rights and (yes indeed) anti-corruption. Its CEO gave speeches at ethics conferences and put together a statement of values emphasizing communication, respect, and integrity. The company's stock was in many social investing mutual funds when it went down. Enron fooled us.[407]

How can stakeholders trust a company's actions if its CSR pronouncements are designed to mislead them into believing the firm is something that it is not? As Ken Lay wrote in a memo to all employees attached to Enron's Code of Ethics, "As officers and employees of Enron Corp., its subsidiaries, and its affiliated companies . . . we are responsible for conducting the business affairs of the Company in accordance with all applicable laws and in a moral and honest manner."[408]

Excerpts from Enron's Code of Ethics

Enron stands on the foundation of its Vision and Values. Every employee is educated about the Company's Vision and Values and is expected to conduct business with other employees, partners, contractors, suppliers, vendors and customers keeping in mind respect, integrity, communication and excellence.[409]

Everything we do evolves from Enron's Vision and Values statements. . . . We are dedicated to conducting business according to all applicable local and international laws and regulations . . . and with the highest professional and ethical standards.[410]

Employees of Enron Corp., its subsidiaries, and its affiliated companies (collectively the "Company") are charged with conducting their business affairs in accordance with the highest ethical standards. An employee shall not conduct himself or herself in a manner which directly or indirectly would be detrimental to the best interests of the Company or in a manner which would bring to the employee financial gain separately derived as a direct consequence of his or her employment with the Company. Moral as well as legal obligations will be fulfilled openly, promptly, and in a manner which will reflect pride on the Company's name.[411]

At the time of Enron's collapse, much was made of Jeffrey Skilling (former President of Enron and currently serving a 24-year jail term for his crimes at the firm)[412] being a Harvard MBA graduate. The implication was that business schools had failed in their responsibility to teach ethics and that individual ethics failings are responsible for corporate irresponsibility, an accusation that seems to raise its head every time an MBA commits a crime or ethics transgression. It is debatable, however, how much responsibility lies with business school professors, who are teaching adults with fully-formed ideas, values, and sets of beliefs.[413]

In other words, it is not clear how receptive students are to significantly challenging ingrained norms and patterns of behavior. The evidence that exists is mixed. On the one hand, "in a survey of American graduate students, 56% of those pursuing an MBA admitted to having cheated in the previous year, compared with 47% of other students."[414] On the other hand, there is clearly a constituency among business students that wants to channel the power of the market and business for good—"to foment social good and not just financial success. . . . to be a service to society."[415] Evidence for this lies with projects such as the MBA Oath, a movement which was started in 2009 by a group of Harvard business school students with the goal of developing a professional oath similar to the Hippocratic Oath taken by medical professionals:

We are now a broad coalition of MBA students, graduates and advisors, representing over 250 schools from around the world. . . . We want our degree to mean something more than it currently does. This oath is our way of laying out the principles of what we think an MBA ought to stand for.[416]

The MBA Oath[417]

As a business leader I recognize my role in society.

- My purpose is to lead people and manage resources to create value that no single individual can create alone.
- My decisions affect the well-being of individuals inside and outside my enterprise, today and tomorrow.

Therefore, I promise that:

- I will manage my enterprise with loyalty and care, and will not advance my personal interests at the expense of my enterprise or society.
- I will understand and uphold, in letter and spirit, the laws and contracts governing my conduct and that of my enterprise.
- I will refrain from corruption, unfair competition, or business practices harmful to society.
- I will protect the human rights and dignity of all people affected by my enterprise, and I will oppose discrimination and exploitation.
- I will protect the right of future generations to advance their standard of living and enjoy a healthy planet.
- I will report the performance and risks of my enterprise accurately and honestly.
- I will invest in developing myself and others, helping the management profession continue to advance and create sustainable and inclusive prosperity.

In exercising my professional duties according to these principles, I recognize that my behavior must set an example of integrity, eliciting trust and esteem from those I serve. I will remain accountable to my peers and to society for my actions and for upholding these standards.

This oath I make freely, and upon my honor.

Irrespective of an individual's values, morals, and ethical standards, however, it is also not clear how these characteristics translate to behavior in the workplace. There is plenty of evidence to suggest, for example, that many people who consider themselves to be ethical are also highly capable of unethical behavior: "As much as we would like to think that, put on the spot, we would do the right—and perhaps even heroic—thing, research has shown that that usually isn't true."[418] And what is true generally is particularly true in the workplace:

> When we are busy focused on common organizational goals, like quarterly earnings or sales quotas, the ethical implications of important decision can fade from our minds. Through the ethical fading, we end up engaging in or condoning behavior that we would condemn if we were consciously aware of it. The underlying psychology helps explain why ethical lapses in the corporate world seem so pervasive and intractable.[419]

This is important because there is evidence that students understand the conundrum that awaits them and expect to be challenged by it:

> Fifty-two percent of MBA students say they expect to have to make decisions [at work] that conflict with their values.[420]

Increasingly, firms are being held accountable for all aspects of operations by the societies in which they are located. Those firms that do not appreciate this, or attempt to circumvent responsibility with superficial commitments to CSR, run the risk of exposure in our always-on, media-driven world. Different firms and different industries have different CSR thresholds (see Chapter 5). Firms that avoid crossing their threshold by adopting an effective CSR perspective stand a much better chance of long term survival. Those firms that ignore the threshold, like Enron, eventually are held accountable for their actions. Those firms that embrace stakeholder relations and act with ethical integrity via employees devoted to pro-social change, however, will be rewarded in the marketplace.

Case Study: Ben & Jerry's

One of the earliest corporate pioneers in the area of values-based business was Ben & Jerry's, which opened its first shop in Vermont in 1981 and went public in 1984.[421] In building Ben & Jerry's into a global brand, the company's cofounders, Ben Cohen and Jerry Greenfield, set new standards in defining the concept of a concerned and responsive employer. Although the importance of addressing stakeholder needs and concerns were values on which the firm was established, it also felt it necessary to codify these values as part of its groundbreaking *Social Audit*— first commissioned in 1989. Ben & Jerry's was the first major corporation to allow an independent social audit of their business operations:

This social auditor recommended that the report be called a "Stakeholders Report" (the concept of stakeholders existed but this was possibly the first-ever report to stakeholders) and that it be divided into the major stakeholder categories: Communities (Community Outreach, Philanthropic Giving, Environmental Awareness, Global Awareness), Employees, Customers, Suppliers, Investors. After this first social audit in 1989, B&J continued to issue annual social reports, rotating to different social auditors as they sought to develop the concept.[422]

Ben & Jerry's has continued developing the concept of a business that places its stakeholder concerns at the core of its business model ever since, a stance that is reflected in the firm's Mission Statement.

Ben & Jerry's Mission Statement

Ben & Jerry's is founded on and dedicated to a sustainable corporate concept of linked prosperity. Our mission consists of 3 interrelated parts:

Social Mission: To operate the Company in a way that actively recognizes the central role that business plays in society by initiating innovative ways to improve the quality of life locally, nationally, and internationally.

Product Mission: To make, distribute and sell the finest quality all natural ice cream and euphoric concoctions with a continued commitment to incorporating wholesome, natural ingredients and promoting business practices that respect the Earth and the Environment.

Economic Mission: To operate the Company on a sustainable financial basis of profitable growth, increasing value for our stakeholders and expanding opportunities for development and career growth for our employees.

Underlying the mission of Ben & Jerry's is the determination to seek new and creative ways of addressing all three parts, while holding a deep respect for individuals inside and outside the company and for the communities of which they are a part.[423]

One practical example of Ben & Jerry's approach to business is the issue of executive pay, which was important to Ben and Jerry when they founded the firm. Specifically, no employee could earn more than seven times the salary of the lowest paid worker in the company:

The gap between CEO salaries and those on the factory floor is widening. In 1973, for example, the typical CEO made 45 times the wage of the average worker. Today, it's as much as 500 times [in the US]. . . . Japanese executives earn 20 to 30 times the lowest-paid worker while, in Europe, the ratio is about 40 times. Ben Cohen and Jerry Greenfield, the quirky entrepreneurs behind Ben & Jerry's ice cream, kept the [salary] ratio of top to bottom earners at 7:1— though that did not last after the two stepped down in 1995.[424]

As noted earlier, stakeholder interests often conflict and resolving these conflicts on this issue (and all issues) is not easy:

Costco Wholesale Corp. often is held up as a retailer that does it right, paying well and offering generous benefits. But Costco's kind-hearted philosophy toward its 100,000 cashiers, shelf-stockers and other workers is drawing criticism from Wall Street. Some analysts and investors contend that the Issaquah, Wash., warehouse-club operator actually is too good to employees, with Costco shareholders suffering as a result.[425]

In addition to the top-to-bottom pay ratio, other aspects of working for Ben & Jerry's, such as the firm's benefits (including an onsite day-care center) and its "no-layoff policy," ensured the commitment and loyalty of one of the firm's key stakeholder groups—its employees:

If a position required revamping or removal, the employee holding the position would be transferred to another position, with attention given to matching responsibilities and qualifications.[426]

As Ben & Jerry's became more successful, it began to attract the attention of other firms. As people began to worry about the prospect of a merger or acquisition, calls increased to protect the firm's independence and its stakeholder-centric approach to business. The Vermont state government responded by passing legislation "allowing a company's directors to reject a bid if 'they deem it to be not in the best interests of employees, suppliers, and the economy of the state.'"[427] In Vermont, the law became known as the "Ben & Jerry's law":

Thus, even when a company was offered a financial premium in a buyout situation, its directors where permitted to reject the offer based on the best interests of the State of Vermont.[428]

In spite of this legislation, Ben & Jerry's board agreed to a $326m takeover by the corporate giant Unilever in August 2000.[429] Although Unilever's management gave assurances that Ben & Jerry's unique approach to business would be maintained, the firm's cult status was tarnished by the takeover. One example: *Business Ethics* dropped Ben & Jerry's out of its list of 100 Best Corporate Citizens in 2001 because of its unfavorable evaluation of Unilever, the new parent company. A second example: The top-to-bottom compensation ratio, referred to above, (including benefits and bonuses) jumped to an average of 16:1 in 1999, 2000, and 2001.[430]

Today, at several points on the company's website, the firm's managers continue to reaffirm a strong activist message, while claiming to run Ben & Jerry's by "leading with progressive values across our business."[431] In addition, the following message is relayed by Ben & Jerry's CEO to visitors at "the world-famous Ben & Jerry's ice-cream factory" in Vermont:

> . . . our commitment to social and economic justice and the environment is as important to us as profitability. It's our heritage. . . . this isn't a short-term strategy to drive up sales. These are issues that are important for our society to address.[432]

Still, the suspicion remains that things have changed and the firm's commitment to its cofounders' original values is not as strong as it once was. This accusation is voiced by critics who say that the firm's activist message has become "just a slick Madison Avenue advertising gimmick to hike profits."[433] But, this position is becoming less and less easy to defend given the firm's recent actions that have emerged as Unilever's position regarding CSR has also evolved. For example, on its website today, the firm prominently claims that "We have a progressive, nonpartisan social mission that seeks to meet human needs and eliminate injustices in our local, national and international communities by integrating these concerns into our day-to-day business activities."[434] And the firm's commitment to social justice and progressive political platforms appears to be as strong as ever:

> Capitalism and the wealth it produces do not create opportunity for everyone equally. . . . We strive to create economic opportunities for those who have been denied them and to advance new models of economic justice that are sustainable and replicable. . . . We strive to minimize our negative impact on the environment. We seek and support nonviolent ways to achieve peace and justice. We believe government resources are more productively used in meeting human needs than in building and maintaining weapons systems. . . . We strive to show a deep respect for human beings inside and outside our company and for the communities in which they live.[435]

While, today, Ben & Jerry's is clearly a subsidiary of a corporate umbrella as a result of Unilever's steps to match Ben & Jerry's operating policies more closely with the corporate brand (such as the emphasis immediately after the acquisition of Ben & Jerry's being "Unilever legal"),[436] there is evidence that this discipline is paying off in that Ben & Jerry's is now a more stable organization that has continued to expand and build on its initial success. But, there is also evidence to suggest that the influence is not all one-way and that Unilever has also learned some lessons from Ben & Jerry's. For example, "Ben & Jerry's was the first ice-cream company in the world to use Fairtrade-certified ingredients in 2005; Unilever has a broader target of sourcing all agricultural raw materials sustainably by 2020."[437]

Today, Unilever is recognized as being one of the most proactive large companies with respect to CSR (see Issues: Profit, Chapter 7). And it appears that, as Unilever continues to push the boundaries in relation to CSR,[438] it is also seeing the value in allowing Ben & Jerry's to retain its broad stakeholder-focused, values-based business model. This is evident in Ben Cohen's involvement with the financing of Occupy Wall Street[439] and also when the firm "decided to celebrate the legalization of gay marriage in the US by rechristening its Chubby Hubby ice-cream Hubby Hubby in 2009."[440] It is also evident in the October 2012 press statement that Ben & Jerry's released, announcing the firm had received Benefit Corporation certification (see Issue: Corporate Responsibilities, above):

> A quarter-century after pioneering the socially responsible business movement, Ben & Jerry's is throwing its support behind the growing B Corporation (B Corp) movement, a network of companies that meet what Inc. magazine has called "the highest standard for socially responsible businesses." Ben & Jerry's is the first wholly-owned subsidiary to gain B Corp certification. The move was supported by Unilever, Ben & Jerry's parent company, as consistent with Ben & Jerry's core values and mission and fully aligned with Unilever's own ambitious sustainability agenda.[441]

CEO Perspective

Gandhi

Gandhi's Seven Social Sins[442] are the seven things that he believed would destroy us as a civilized society:

- Wealth without Work
- Pleasure without Conscience

(Continued)

(Continued)

- Knowledge without Character
- Commerce (Business) without Morality (Ethics)
- Science without Humanity
- Religion without Sacrifice
- Politics without Principle

Some of these are more pertinent today than others, but it is hard not to conclude that we are failing Gandhi's test on multiple levels. Many of the sins are, of course, directly relevant to the CSR debate. What is most striking about the list is Gandhi's emphasis on process, rather than outcome. Today, in contrast, we worry more about where we are, rather than how we got here (let alone where we are going). Just thinking through the implications of the first sin (wealth without work), for example, speaks volumes about the extent to which our values have shifted.

Online Resources

- Association for Integrity in Accounting (Citizen Works), http://www.citizen-works.org/actions/aia.php
- Ben & Jerry's, http://www.benjerry.com/
- Business Civic Leadership Center, http://bclc.uschamber.com/
- Corporate Responsibility Officers Association (CROA), http://www.croas-sociation.org/
- *CRO Magazine (formerly Business Ethics Magazine)*, http://www.thecro.com/
- *Ethics & Enron* (ethics online bookstore) has a collection of books, papers, SEC filings, and other documents about Enron, http://www.ethicsweb.ca/books/enron.htm
- Ethical Leadership Group, http://www.ethicalleadershipgroup.com/
- Ethics and Compliance Officers Association (ECOA), http://www.theecoa.org/
- Ethics Resource Center (ERC), http://www.ethics.org/
- Graduation Pledge Alliance, http://www.graduationpledge.org/
- Society of Corporate Compliance and Ethics (SCCE), http://corporatecompliance.org/
- The Ethics Classroom, http://www.ethicsclassroom.info/
- *The Smoking Gun* (TSG, Web site) presents a copy of Enron's in-house *Code of Ethics* at http://www.thesmokinggun.com/enron/enronethics1.shtml
- United Nations Principles of Responsible Management Education (PRME), 443 http://www.unprme.org/

Pro/Con Debate

> **Pro/Con Debate:**   It is not the responsibility of business schools to teach ethics to students (either undergraduate or graduate). By the time they arrive in the classroom, they are adults with fully-formed values and beliefs.

QUESTIONS FOR DISCUSSION AND REVIEW

1. What makes one person more or less ethical than another? Where does that component of an individual's character come from?

2. What does it mean for an organization to be *ethical*? What is the difference between an *unethical* and an *illegal* act?

3. What do you imagine the day-to-day work of an Ethics and Compliance Officer (ECO) entails? Do you think it is viewed as a position of importance within companies today?

4. An important component of implementing an ethical or CSR perspective company-wide is consistency across departments. Do you feel that the lessons you are learning in this class are supported by classes you take from other departments in the business school?

5. Look at some of the causes supported by Ben & Jerry's (http://www .benjerry.com/activism/inside-the-pint/). Do you agree with the stances they take? Do their positions make you more or less likely to buy their ice-cream? Is this what a for-profit company should be doing?

STUDENT STUDY SITE

Visit the Student Study Site at **www.sagepub.com/chandler3e** for additional learning tools.

NOTES AND REFERENCES

1. 'Patagonia Takes Next Step in Corporate Transparency and Accountability,' *CSRwire.com*, March 25, 2008, http://www.csrwire.com/News/11480.html
2. Paul Hohnen, 'What sustainability reports say about the state of business,' *Ethical Corporation Magazine*, July 12, 2011, http://www.ethicalcorp.com/communica tions-reporting/what-sustainability-reports-say-about-state-business-0

3. Paul Hohnen, 'What sustainability reports say about the state of business,' *Ethical Corporation Magazine*, July 12, 2011, http://www.ethicalcorp.com/communications-reporting/what-sustainability-reports-say-about-state-business-0

4. The Carbon Disclosure Project website, January 2013, https://www.cdproject.net/

5. Ceres Principles website, January 2013, http://www.ceres.org/about-us/our-history/ceres-principles

6. http://www.globalreporting.org/AboutGRI/

7. GMI Ratings website, January 2013, http://www3.gmiratings.com/home/history/

8. Greenhouse Gas Protocol website, January 2013, http://www.ghgprotocol.org/

9. ILO Labour Standards website, January 2013, http://www.ilo.org/global/standards/introduction-to-international-labour-standards/lang--en/index.htm

10. ILO Labour Standards website, January 2013, http://www.ilo.org/global/standards/lang--en/index.htm

11. Jason Perks, 'Reporting – Ensuring true assurance,' *Ethical Corporation Magazine*, August 31, 2011, http://www.ethicalcorp.com/communications-reporting/what-sustainability-reports-say-about-state-business-0

12. Paul Hohnen, 'ISO moves towards a social responsibility standard,' *Ethical Corporation,* October 5, 2005, http://www.ethicalcorp.com/content.asp?ContentID=3914

13. OECD website (Guidelines for Multinational Enterprises), January 2013, http://www.oecd.org/daf/internationalinvestment/guidelinesformultinationalenterprises/

14. Deborah Leipziger, 'Codes of conduct and standards: The pick of the bunch,' *Ethical Corporation Magazine*, February 21, 2011, http://www.ethicalcorp.com/governance-regulation/codes-conduct-and-standards-pick-bunch

15. See: http://www.unglobalcompact.org/AboutTheGC/TheTenPrinciples/index.html

16. UN Global Compact website, January 2013, http://www.unglobalcompact.org/ParticipantsAndStakeholders/index.html

17. 'New Guiding Principles on Business and Human Rights endorsed by the UN Human Rights Council,' *UN Human Rights Council*, June 2011, http://www.ohchr.org/en/NewsEvents/Pages/DisplayNews.aspx?NewsID=11164

18. Deborah Leipziger, 'Codes of conduct and standards: The top ten, part II,' *Ethical Corporation Magazine*, February 21, 2011, http://www.ethicalcorp.com/governance-regulation/codes-conduct-and-standards-pick-bunch

19. Mallen Baker, 'The Global Reporting Initiative (GRI),' January 2013, http://www.mallenbaker.net/csr/gri.php

20. Paul Hohnen, 'The Global Compact and GRI: Nightmare of 'dream team'?' *Ethical Corporation Magazine*, July 21, 2010, http://www.ethicalcorp.com/communications-reporting/global-compact-and-gri-nightmare-or-%E2%80%9Cdream-team%E2%80%99%E2%80%99

21. Paul Hohnen, 'What sustainability reports say about the state of business,' *Ethical Corporation Magazine*, July 12, 2011, http://www.ethicalcorp.com/communications-reporting/what-sustainability-reports-say-about-state-business-0

22. Michael Skapinker, 'Responsible companies need more than words,' *Financial Times*, May 26, 2011, p. 14.

23. For a full consideration of the GRI, as well as detailed insight into the G4 consultation document, see: Mallen Baker, 'The Global Reporting initiative is growing up,' *mallenbaker.net*, July 25, 2012, http://www.mallenbaker.net/csr/page.php?Story_ID=2739

24. 'Beyond petroleum: Why the CSR community collaborated in creating the BP oil disaster,' *Ethical Corporation Magazine*, August 2, 2010, http://www.ethicalcorp.com/communications-reporting/beyond-petroleum-why-csr-community-collaborated-creating-bp-oil-disaster

25. Heather Mak, 'Eco-labels: Radical rethink required,' *Ethical Corporation Magazine*, January 17, 2012, http://www.ethicalcorp.com/environment/eco-labels-radical-rethink-required

26. See Chapter 5, Figure 5.3.

27. 'Wood for the Trees,' *The Economist,* November 6, 2004, http://www.cfo.com/article.cfm/3372352

28. David Jolly, 'An Ecolabel for McDonald's Fish Fare,' *The New York Times*, January 27, 2013, http://green.blogs.nytimes.com/2013/01/27/an-ecolabel-for-mcdonalds-fish-fare/

29. Rebecca Smithers, 'Britons want to buy sustainable fish but labels leave us baffled,' *The Guardian*, May 24, 2010, http://www.guardian.co.uk/environment/2010/may/24/sustainable-fish-seafood-supermarkets-labels

30. Additional detail about the ISO 26000 can be found at: http://www.iso.org/iso/iso26000

31. Mallen Baker, 'Labelling the good company,' *Ethical Corporation,* July 5, 2005, http://www.ethicalcorp.com/content.asp?ContentID=3772

32. 'ISO 26000: Social responsibility talks tread on government toes,' *Ethical Corporation*, May 15, 2009, http://www.ethicalcorp.com/content.asp?ContentID=6474

33. Jon Entine, 'ISO 26000: Sustainability as standard?' *Ethical Corporation Magazine*, July 11, 2012, http://www.ethicalcorp.com/business-strategy/iso-26000-sustainability-standard

34. Mallen Baker, 'Why CSR reporting is broken—and how it should be fixed,' *Ethical Corporation Magazine,* November 28, 2008, http://www.ethicalcorp.com/content.asp?ContentID=6224

35. Mallen Baker, 'PUMA plucks numbers out of the CO_2,' *mallenbaker.net*, May 17, 2011, http://www.mallenbaker.net/csr/post.php?id=394

36. Richard Anderson, 'Puma first to publish environmental impact costs,' *BBC News*, May 16, 2011, http://www.bbc.co.uk/news/business-13410397

37. Sarah Skidmore, 'Whole Foods to label seafood's sustainability,' *msnbc.com*, September 17, 2010, http://www.msnbc.msn.com/id/39156472/ns/business-consumer_news

38. Heather Mak, 'Eco-labels: Radical rethink required,' *Ethical Corporation Magazine*, January 17, 2012, http://www.ethicalcorp.com/environment/eco-labels-radical-rethink-required

39. Tanzina Vega, 'Agency Seeks to Tighten Rules for 'Green' Labeling,' *The New York Times*, October 7, 2010, p. B4.

40. Tanzina Vega, 'Agency Seeks to Tighten Rules for 'Green' Labeling,' *The New York Times*, October 7, 2010, p. B4.

41. Peter Marsh, 'Clothing companies in push for eco-impact labelling,' *Financial Times*, March 1, 2011, p. 15.

42. See: http://www.ecoindexbeta.org/ and http://earth911.com/news/2011/03/01/nike-walmart-target-other-brands-launch-eco-clothing-index/

43. Kate Rockwood, 'Attention, Walmart Shoppers: Clean-up in Aisle Nine,' *Fast Company Magazine*, February 2010, p. 30.

44. Jeni Bauser, 'Eco Index: How green are your clothes?' *Ethical Corporation Magazine*, October 15, 2010, http://www.ethicalcorp.com/content.asp?ContentID=7110

45. Tom Zeller Jr., 'Clothes Makers Join To Set 'Green Score,'' *The New York Times*, March 1, 2011, p. B1.

46. Tom Zeller Jr., 'Clothes Makers Join To Set 'Green Score,'' *The New York Times*, March 1, 2011, p. B4.

47. OED website, January 2013, http://www.oed.com/view/Entry/66996?redirectedFrom=externality#eid

48. Usman Hayat, 'Future challenges for sustainable investing,' *Financial Times (FTfm)*, February 7, 2011, p. 12.

49. David Leonhardt, 'The Battle Over Taxing Soda,' *The New York Times*, May 19, 2010, p. B1. For more information about Pigovian taxes, see: R.H. Coase, 'The Problem of Social Cost,' *The Journal of Law & Economics*, Vol. III, October 1960, pp.1–44 & William J. Baumol, 'On Taxation and the Control of Externalities,' *The American Economic Review*, Vol. 62, June 1972, pp. 307-322.

50. Robert H. Frank, 'Of Individual Liberty And Cap and Trade,' *The New York Times*, January 10, 2010, p. BU7.

51. See: Walkers (http://www.walkerscarbonfootprint.co.uk/) and PepsiCo (Andrew Martin, 'How Green Is My Orange?' *The New York Times*, January 21, 2009, http://www.nytimes.com/2009/01/22/business/22pepsi.html)

52. See: http://www.nikebiz.com/crreport/content/environment/4-4-0-case-study-greenxchange.php

53. Natalya Sverjensky, 'A sustainable future: Why Al Gore is wrong,' *Ethical Corporation Magazine*, August 24, 2011, http://www.ethicalcorp.com/environment/sustainable-future-why-al-gore-wrong

54. See: http://www.youtube.com/watch?v=l_P_V0jk3Ig

55. http://www.ted.com/talks/ray_anderson_on_the_business_logic_of_sustainability.html

56. For a discussion about the limits of our current economic model based around growth and consumption, see: Tim Jackson, 'New economic model needed not relentless consumer demand,' *Guardian Sustainable Business*, January 18, 2013, http://www.guardian.co.uk/sustainable-business/blog/new-economic-model-not-consumer-demand-capitalism

57. Rob Walker, 'Wasted Data,' *The New York Times Magazine*, December 5, 2010, p. 20.

58. Joe Flower, 'Sustainable Goes Strategic,' *strategy+business*, Issue 54, Spring 2009, pp. 7–8.

59. Michael J. Ybarra, 'Free to Choose, And Conserve,' *The Wall Street Journal*, June 11, 2012, p. A11.

60. Adam Smith published *The Wealth of Nations* in 1776, but it is his book, *The Theory of Moral Sentiments* (first published in 1759), that leads many observers to describe Smith as a moral philosopher, rather than an economist. For example, see: James R. Otteson, 'Adam Smith: Moral Philosopher,' The Freeman Ideas on Liberty, Vol. 50, Issue 11, November, 2000, http://www.thefreemanonline.org/features/adam-smith-moral-philosopher/

61. 'The Corporate Welfare State,' Editorial, *The Wall Street Journal*, November 7, 2011, p. A18.

62. Paul Krugman, 'Here Comes the Sun,' *The New York Times*, November 7, 2011, p. A21.

63. Paul Krugman, 'Here Comes the Sun,' *The New York Times*, November 7, 2011, p. A21.

64. Gernot Wagner, 'Going Green but Getting Nowhere,' *The New York Times*, September 8, 2011, p. A25.

65. Howard Schultz, quoted in: '10 Conversations That Changed Our World: Starbucks Saves the Modern Organization,' *Fast Company Magazine,* February 2013, p. 7.

66. Sharon Begley, 'On the 40th Anniversary of Earth Day, Let's . . . Go Shopping,' *Newsweek,* April 21, 2010, http://www.thedailybeast.com/ncwsweek/2010/04/20/on-the-40th-anniversary-of-earth-day-let-s-go-shopping.html

67. Joe Nocera, 'How To Prevent Oil Spills,' *The New York Times,* April 14, 2012, p. A17.

68. David Vogel, 'The limits of the market for virtue,' *Ethical Corporation,* August 25, 2005, http://www.ethicalcorp.com/content.asp?ContentID=3855

69. 'Over-regulated America,' *The Economist,* February 18, 2012, p. 9. In the current U.S. healthcare code, there are also "21 separate categories for 'spacecraft accidents' and 12 for bee stings. There are over 140 million words of binding federal statutes and regulations, and states and municipalities add several billion more." In: Philip K. Howard, 'Starting Over With Regulation,' *The Wall Street Journal*, December 3-4, 2011, p. C2.

70. Peter S. Goodman, 'Rule No.1: Make Money by Avoiding Rules,' *The New York Times*, May 23, 2010, p. WK3.

71. Mallen Baker, 'Time to move on from the endless regulation debate,' *Ethical Corporation,* March 27, 2006, http://www.ethicalcorp.com/content.asp?ContentID=4170

72. Greg Ip, 'A Less-Visible Role for the Fed Chief: Freeing Up Markets,' *The Wall Street Journal,* November 19, 2004, pp. A1 & A8.

73. Greg Ip, 'A Less-Visible Role for the Fed Chief: Freeing Up Markets,' *The Wall Street Journal,* November 19, 2004, pp. A1 & A8.

74. Chris Lester, 'Alan, like Atlas, shrugged,' *The Kansas City Star*, November 3, 2008, http://www.kansascity.com/business/columnists/chris_lester/story/873110.html

75. Alex Blyth, 'EU Multi-Stakeholder Forum Presents Final Report,' *Ethical Corporation,* July 5, 2004, http://www.ethicalcorp.com/content.asp?ContentID=2327

76. *The Observer,* November 24, 2002, op. cit.

77. Deborah Doane, 'Mandated Risk Reporting Begins in UK,' *Business Ethics Magazine,* Spring 2005, p. 13.

78. Robert Cole & Reynolds Holding, 'Sarbanes-Oxley Test,' *The New York Times,* November 16, 2011, p. B2.

79. 'The endangered public company,' *The Economist,* May 19, 2012, p. 13.

80. *The Observer,* November 24, 2002, op. cit.

81. Carola Hoyos, 'Emissions disclosure study puts Shell bottom of the big oil class,' *Financial Times*, March 16, 2009, http://www.ft.com/cms/s/0/d02d7252-11a1-11de-87b1-0000779fd2ac.html

82. Lisa Roner, 'Anheuser-Busch Reports Recycling 97% of Solid Waste,' *Ethical Corporation Magazine,* June 21, 2004, http://www.ethicalcorp.com/content.asp?ContentID=2228

83. Anheuser-Busch website, January 2013, http://anheuser-busch.com/index.php/our-responsibility/environment-our-earth-our-natural-resources/reduce-reuse-and-recycle/

84. Mike Esterl, 'Plastic Recycling Falls Short as Too Few Do It,' *The Wall Street Journal*, August 19, 2011, p. B1.

85. Susan Freinkel, 'Plastic: Too Good to Throw Away,' *The New York Times*, March 18, 2011, p. A27.

86. Ann Monroe, 'Wal-Mart: Jolly 'green' giant?' *MSN Money*, January 18, 2008, http://articles.moneycentral.msn.com/Investing/StockInvestingTrading/Wal-MartJollyGreenGiant.aspx

87. Melanie Warner, 'Green Business: Plastic Potion No. 9,' *Fast Company*, Issue 128, September 2008, p. 103.

88. Elizabeth Royte, 'Moneybags: Citywide plastic-bag bans are gaining momentum. But will companies be the ones that force us to change?,' *Fast Company*, Issue 119, October 2007, p. 64.

89. Brenna Maloney & Laura Stanton, 'More than Meets the Eye: Paper or Plastic?' *The Washington Post*, October 4, 2007, http://www.washingtonpost.com/wp-dyn/content/graphic/2007/10/03/GR2007100301385.html

90. 'Paper or Plastic?' *The Washington Post*, July 6, 2007, http://www.washingtonpost.com/wp-dyn/content/article/2007/07/05/AR2007070501806.html

91. See: Carl Bialik, 'A Sack Standoff in the Checkout Aisle,' *The Wall Street Journal*, September 24-25, 2011, p. A2.

92. Elizabeth Royte, 'Moneybags: Citywide plastic-bag bans are gaining momentum. But will companies be the ones that force us to change?' *Fast Company*, Issue 119, October 2007, p. 64 and 'Banned: Plastic bags on way out in parts of L.A. County,' *msnbc.com*, November 16, 2010, http://today.msnbc.msn.com/id/40221169/ns/today-today_news/t/banned-plastic-bags-way-out-parts-la-county/

93. Erica Meltzer, 'Boulder's 10-cent fee on disposable grocery bags becomes law in July,' *The Denver Post*, November 15, 2012, http://www.denverpost.com/breakingnews/ci_22006596/boulders-10-cent-fee-grocery-bags-becomes-law

94. Kate Galbraith, 'Plastic bags: Ban, tax or let them be?' *The New York Times*, February 9, 2012, p. 18.

95. Lornet Turnbull, 'Plastic-bag ban catches some Seattle shoppers by surprise,' *The Seattle Times*, July 1, 2012, http://seattletimes.com/html/localnews/2018578859_plasticbags02m.html

96. Matt Richtel & Kate Galbraith, 'Back at Junk Value, Recyclables Are Piling Up,' *The New York Times*, December 8, 2008, http://www.nytimes.com/2008/12/08/business/08recycle.html

97. Frederik Balfour, 'China's Recycler: Is a Rebound Ahead?, *BusinessWeek*, January 26, 2009, http://www.businessweek.com/globalbiz/content/jan2009/gb20090126_576842.htm

98. For other perspectives on this debate, see: Jeffrey Ball, 'Paper or Plastic? A New Look a the Bag Scourge,' *The Wall Street Journal*, June 12, 2009, p. A11 and Jon Entine, 'Battle of the Bags: Are Plastic Bags an Environmental Threat?' *Global Governance Watch*, September 2, 2009, http://www.globalgovernancewatch.org/in_the_spotlight/battle-of-the-bags-are-plastic-bags-an-environmental-threat

99. Elizabeth Royte, 'Moneybags: Citywide plastic-bag bans are gaining momentum. But will companies be the ones that force us to change?,' *Fast Company*, Issue 119, October 2007, p. 64.

100. 'The Results are in...Over 92% of IKEA Customers Bagged the Plastic Bag! As of October 2008, IKEA will no longer offer plastic or paper bags,' IKEA press release, *CSRwire.com*, April 2, 2008, http://www.csrwire.com/News/11588.html For additional results, see: 'The 'No More Plastic Bag' Movement Continues,' IKEA press release, *CSRwire.com*, April 28, 2009, http://www.csrwire.com/press/press_release/16628

101. 'The Results are in...Over 92% of IKEA Customers Bagged the Plastic Bag! As of October 2008, IKEA will no longer offer plastic or paper bags,' IKEA press release, *CSRwire.com*, April 2, 2008, http://www.csrwire.com/News/11588.html

102. Elisabeth Rosenthal, 'With Irish Tax, Plastic Bags Go the Way of the Snakes,' *New York Times*, February 2, 2008, http://www.nytimes.com/2008/02/02/world/europe/02bags.html

103. Elisabeth Rosenthal, 'With Irish Tax, Plastic Bags Go the Way of the Snakes,' *New York Times*, February 2, 2008, http://www.nytimes.com/2008/02/02/world/europe/02bags.html

104. Jon Entine, 'Battle of the Bags: Are Plastic Bags an Environmental Threat?' *Global Governance Watch*, September 2, 2009, http://www.globalgovernancewatch.org/in_the_news/battle-of-the-bags-are-plastic-bags-an-environmental-threat

105. Mireya Navarro, 'Seeing a Pitched Battle for Plastic Bags,' *New York Times*, November 18, 2008, p. A20.

106. Heather Timmons, 'Paper or Plastic? At a Trade Show, the Latter Wins Easily,' *New York Times*, February 17, 2009, p. B3.

107. 'Tax plastic bags, says Lib Dem peer,' *The Daily Telegraph*, May 29, 2012, p. 2.

108. Elisabeth Rosenthal, 'With Irish Tax, Plastic Bags Go the Way of the Snakes,' *The New York Times*, February 2, 2008, http://www.nytimes.com/2008/02/02/world/

europe/02bags.html. See also: Elisabeth Rosenthal, 'Carbon Taxes Make Ireland Even Greener,' *The New York Times*, December 28, 2012, p. A1.

109. Greg Davies, 'Is it rational to listen to the Sirens?' *The Daily Telegraph*, June 2, 2012, p. R25.

110. James S. Duesenberry, 'Comment on 'An Economic Analysis of Fertility,'' in *Demographic and Economic Change in Developed Countries*, Princeton University Press, 1960, p. 233.

111. Nudge, nudge, think, think,' *The Economist*, March 24, 2012, p. 78.

112. Nudge, nudge, think, think,' *The Economist*, March 24, 2012, p. 78.

113. Cliff Kuang, 'The Google Diet,' *Fast Company Magazine*, April 2012, p. 48.

114. 'Nudge, nudge, think, think,' *The Economist*, March 24, 2012, p. 78.

115. Beth Terry, 'Will a NYC Ban on Large Sugary Sodas Decrease Obesity or Increase Plastic Waste?' *My Plastic-free Life*, June 19, 2012, http://myplasticfreelife.com/2012/06/will-a-nyc-ban-on-large-sugary-sodas-decrease-obesity-or-increase-plastic-waste/

116. Daniel E. Lieberman, 'Evolution's Sweet Tooth,' *The New York Times*, June 6, 2012, p. A23.

117. Betsy McKay, 'Dramatic Drop in Trans Fat in U.S. Adults,' *The Wall Street Journal*, February 14, 2012, p. D5.

118. Brian Wansink, David R. Just & Joe McKendry, 'Lunch Line Redesign,' *The New York Times*, October 22, 2010, p. A25.

119. Sean Poulter & Susie Taylor, 'Supermarkets are still tempting us with sweets at the checkouts as they claim to be helping shoppers make healthy choices,' *The Daily Mail*, October 24, 2012, http://www.dailymail.co.uk/news/article-2222785/Supermarkets-tempting-sweets-checkouts.html

120. David Brooks, 'The Unexamined Society,' *The New York Times*, July 8, 2011, p. A21.

121. Stephanie Simon, 'The Secret to Turning Consumers Green,' *The Wall Street Journal Report: Environment*, October 18, 2010, p. R1.

122. Milton Friedman, quoted in: 'The Chicago question,' *The Economist*, July 28, 2012, p. 68.

123. Richard Milne, 'Skirting the boards,' *Financial Times*, June 15, 2009, p. 2.

124. Richard Milne, 'Skirting the boards,' *Financial Times*, June 15, 2009, p. 2.

125. Business Ethics Magazine, Spring 2004, op. cit.

126. *Dodge v. Ford Motor Company*, 204 Mich. 459, 170 N.W. 668 (1919).

127. Joel Bakan, *The Corporation: The Pathalogical Pursuit of Profit and Power*, Free Press, 2004, p. 36.

128. Lynn Stout, *The Shareholder Value Myth: How Putting Shareholders First Harms Investors, Corporations, and the Public*, Berrett-Koehler Publishers, Inc., San Francisco, CA, 2012, pp. 3–4.

129. Lynn Stout, 'Why We Should Stop Teaching *Dodge v. Ford*,' UCLA School of Law, Law & Econ Research Paper Series, Research Paper No. 07-11, 2008, p. 3.

130. John Micklethwait & Adrian Wooldridge, *The Company: A Short History of a Revolutionary Idea*, Modern Library, 2003, p. 43 and p. 46.

131. Thomas K. McCraw, 'Mr. Hamilton's Growth Strategy,' *The New York Times*, November 12, 2012, p. A29.

132. Peter Kinder, 'Public purpose—Corporate history's lesson for companies now,' *Ethical Corporation*, October 3, 2007, http://www.ethicalcorp.com/content.asp?ContentID=5406

133. Peter Kinder, 'Public purpose—Corporate history's lesson for companies now,' *Ethical Corporation*, October 3, 2007, http://www.ethicalcorp.com/content.asp?ContentID=5406

134. *The Economist* describes limited liability ("one of the greatest wealth-creating inventions of all time") as "a privilege" and "a concession—something granted by society because it as a clear purpose." In: 'Light and wrong,' *The Economist*, January 21, 2012, p. 16.

135. Because the firm has been deemed by the Courts to be an autonomous legal person, shareholders do not own it (they simply can lay a claim to a share of future earnings. "What's more, when directors go against shareholder wishes—even when a loss in value is documented—courts side with directors the vast majority of the time. Shareholders seem to get this. They've tried to unseat directors through lawsuits just 24 times in large corporations over the past 20 years; they've succeeded only eight times. In short, directors are to a great extent autonomous." Loizos Heracleous & Luh Luh Lan, 'The Myth of Shareholder Capitalism,' *Harvard Business Review*, April, 2010, http://hbr.org/2010/04/the-myth-of-shareholder-capitalism/

136. President Bill Clinton, interviewed by John Stewart on *The Daily Show*, November 8, 2011 (Minutes: 19.38 to 20.55), http://www.thedailyshow.com/full-episodes/tue-november-8-2011-bill-clinton

137. James E. Austin & James Quinn, 'Ben & Jerry's: Preserving Mission and Brand within Unilever,' *Harvard Business School* [Case # 9-306-037], December 8, 2005, p5. See also: 'Ben & Jerry's takes a licking,' *Eurofood*, February 3, 2000, http://findarticles.com/p/articles/mi_m0DQA/is_2000_Feb_3/ai_59544165/ and John Tozzi, 'New Legal Protections for Social Entrepreneurs,' *BusinessWeek*, April 22, 2010, http://www.businessweek.com/smallbiz/content/apr2010/sb20100421_414362.htm

138. Mallen Baker, 'Remuneration – Value society, Mr President,' *Ethical Corporation*, March 11, 2009, http://www.ethicalcorp.com/content.asp?ContentID=6391

139. Charles Handy, 'The Unintended Consequences of Good Ideas,' *Harvard Business Review*, October 2012, http://hbr.org/2012/10/the-unintended-consequences-of-good-ideas/

140. Kent Greenfield, 'It's Time to Federalize Corporate Charters,' *Business Ethics Magazine*, Fall 2002, p. 6.

141. October 15, 2012, http://corp.delaware.gov/aboutagency.shtml

142. Kent Greenfield, 'It's Time to Federalize Corporate Charters,' *Business Ethics Magazine*, Fall 2002, p. 6.

143. Leslie Wayne, 'To Delaware, With Love,' *The New York Times*, July 1, 2012, p. 4.

144. Kent Greenfield, 'It's Time to Federalize Corporate Charters,' *Business Ethics Magazine*, Fall 2002, p. 6.

145. Leslie Wayne, 'To Delaware, With Love,' *The New York Times*, July 1, 2012, p. 4.

146. Kent Greenfield, 'It's Time to Federalize Corporate Charters,' *Business Ethics Magazine*, Fall 2002, p. 6.

147. Alex Marshall, 'How to Get Business to Pay Its Share,' *The New York Times*, May 4, 2012, p. A23.

148. Note: Of course, with federal oversight of corporate law, the risk would be that firms would incorporate overseas, in search of those places with the most favorable tax treatments. Even with the current favorable regulatory environment, this is happening. See, for example: Vanessa Houlder, 'The tax avoidance story as a morality tale,' *Financial Times*, November 22, 2004, p. 7; Roger Cowe, 'Special Report: Corporate Responsibility and tax,' *Ethical Corporation*, January 3, 2005, http://www.ethical corp.com/content.asp?ContentID=3341; and Mallen Baker, 'In search of the business case for responsible tax,' *Ethical Corporation*, March 27, 2006, http://www .ethicalcorp.com/content.asp?ContentID=4168

149. 'Shells and shelves,' *The Economist*, April 7, 2012, p. 70.

150. Note: *Tax avoidance* refers to the reduction in tax liability via legal means, while *tax evasion* refers to the criminal non-payment of tax that is owed.

151. Pratap Chatterjee, 'Starbucks: Espresso for Investors, Watery Americano in UK Taxes,' *CorpWatch*, October 26, 2012, http://www.corpwatch.org/article .php?id=15791. See also: Reuters, 'U.K. committees to examine Starbucks tax strategies,' *The Washington Post* in *The Daily Yomiuri*, October 23, 2012, p. 9.

152. http://www.citizenworks.org/corp/fact/code.pdf

153. Senate File 0510, https://www.revisor.leg.state.mn.us/bills/bill.php?b=Senate&f=SF 0510&ssn=0&y=2009

154. House File 0398, https://www.revisor.mn.gov/bills/bill.php?b=House&f=HF0398& ssn=0&y=2013

155. https://www.revisor.leg.state.mn.us/bin/bldbill.php?bill=S1267.0.html&session=ls87

156. Susan Wennemyr, 'Code for Corporate Responsibility Considered by Two State Legislatures,' *BizEthics Buzz*, March 2004, http://groups.yahoo.com/group/Babel/ message/7873?var=1

157. Robert Hinkley, 'How Corporate Law Inhibits Social Responsibility,' *Business Ethics Magazine,* Spring 2002, http://www.commondreams.org/views02/0119-04.htm

158. http://benefitcorp.net/

159. 'Patagonia Pioneers Sustainability Legal Status,' *Environmental Leader*, January 5, 2012, http://www.environmentalleader.com/2012/01/05/patagonia-pioneers-sustainability-legal-status/

160. http://www.bcorporation.net/

161. 'From Fringe to Mainstream: Companies Integrate CSR Initiatives into Everyday Business,' *Knowledge@Wharton*, May 23, 2010, http://knowledge.wharton.upenn .edu/article.cfm?articleid=3004

162. Danielle Sacks, "The Miracle Worker,' *Fast Company Magazine*, December 2009/ January 2010, p. 122.

163. Danielle Sacks, "The Miracle Worker,' *Fast Company Magazine*, December 2009/ January 2010, pp. 122-123.

164. Craig Sams, 'Why Kraft Must Keep Organic Cacao Farmers Sweet,' *The Guardian*, January 20, 2005, http://www.guardian.co.uk/environment/2010/jan/20/kraft-green-black-cadbury-ethical

165. David Teather, 'Roddick Nets £130m from Body Shop Sale,' *The Guardian*, March 17, 2006, http://www.guardian.co.uk/business/2006/mar/18/highstreetretailers.retail

166. 'Firms with benefits,' *The Economist*, January 7, 2012, http://www.economist.com/node/21542432

167. Angus Loten, 'With New Law, Profits Take a Back Seat,' *The Wall Street Journal*, January 19, 2012, http://online.wsj.com/article/SB100014240529702037353045771 68591470161630.html

168. Jo Confino, 'Ben & Jerry's: Parent Companies Don't Always Know Best,' *The Guardian*, October 22, 2012, http://www.guardian.co.uk/sustainable-business/ben-jerrys-b-corporation-social-responsibilities

169. 'Firms with benefits,' *The Economist*, January 7, 2012, http://www.economist.com/node/21542432

170. 'A Legal Framework for the Integration of Environmental, Social, and Governance Issues into Institutional Investment,' *UNEP Finance Initiative*, October 2005, http://www.unepfi.org/fileadmin/documents/freshfields_legal_resp_20051123.pdf

171. Toby Webb, 'Alternative capitalism: What's the big idea?' *Ethical Corporation Magazine*, June 4, 2012, http://www.ethicalcorp.com/business-strategy/alternative-capitalism-what%E2%80%99s-big-idea

172. Bart King, 'Patagonia Is First to Register for 'Benefit Corporation' Status in California,' *Sustainable Brands*, January 4, 2012, http://www.sustainablebrands.com/news_and_views/articles/patagonia-first-register-%E2%80%98benefit-corporation%E2%80%99-status-california

173. For example, see: Kaevan Gazdar, 'Special Report: Media responsibility – Making ethics headline news,' *Ethical Corporation*, October 14, 2007, http://www.ethical-corp.com/content.asp?ContentID=5433

174. Daniel Henninger, 'Perils of the Modern Presidency,' *The Wall Street Journal*, June 24, 2010, p. A19.

175. Michel Rocard, 'Entente *cordiale?*' *Kent Bulletin,* The University of Kent at Canterbury, No. 35, Autumn 2000, pp. 10–11, http://www.kent.ac.uk/alumni/pdf/kent35.pdf

176. See: Andrew Edgecliffe-Johnson, 'When papers fold,' *Financial Times*, March 17, 2009, p. 7 and Leonard Pitts Jr., 'As newspapers die, expect no mourning from the crooks,' *Chicago Tribune*, in *The Daily Yomiuri*, March 31, 2009, p. 17.

177. Tom Hayes & Michael S. Malone, 'The Ten-Year Century,' *Wall Street Journal*, August 11, 2009, p. A17.

178. http://twitter.com/jkrums/status/1121915133

179. Mark Laity, 'The Media: Part of the Problem or Part of the Solution?' *Kent Bulletin,* The University of Kent at Canterbury, No. 42, Spring 2004, pp. 8-10, http://www.kent.ac.uk/alumni/pdf/kent42.pdf

180. Al Jazeera's English channel was launched in November, 2006 (William Wallis, 'Al-Jazeera launches news channel in English,' *Financial Times*, November 15, 2006, p. 8 and Alessandra Stanley, 'Not Coming Soon to a Channel Near You,' *New York*

Times, November 16, 2006, p. A22) and on YouTube in April, 2007 (Sara Ivry, 'Now on YouTube: The Latest News From Al Jazeera, in English,' *New York Times*, April 16, 2007, p. C5).

181. Al Jazeera, *New York Times*, January 9, 2009, p. A7.

182. "According to a study published [in June, 2006] by the Business & Media Institute, in the world of TV entertainment, "businessmen [are] a greater threat to society than terrorists, gangs, or the mob." In: Review & Outlook, 'TV's Killer Capitalists,' *Wall Street Journal*, July 14, 2006, p. W9.

183. For an additional dimension to this issue, see: Mallen Baker, 'Corporate culture – Crisis management with extra cheese,' *Ethical Corporation*, May 11, 2009, http://www.ethicalcorp.com/content.asp?ContentID=6464

184. Stephanie Clifford, 'Video Prank at Domino's Goes Sour,' *New York Times*, April 16, 2009, p. B5.

185. Quoted in Mark Laity, 'The Media: Part of the Problem or Part of the Solution?' *Kent Bulletin,* The University of Kent at Canterbury, No. 42, Spring 2004, pp. 8–10, http://www.kent.ac.uk/alumni/pdf/kent42.pdf

186. Nick Davies quoted in: John Mecklin, 'Over the Horizon,' *Miller-McCune*, June-July, 2008, p. 7.

187. 'Business ethics: Doing well by doing good,' *The Economist,* April 22, 2000, pp 65–68.

188. Noah Oppenheim, 'Bookshelf: From Network to Nowhere,' *Wall Street Journal,* October 21, 2004, p. D8.

189. Steven Komarow, 'U.S. Attorneys Dispatched to Advise Military,' *USA Today,* March 10, 2003, http://www.usatoday.com/news/world/iraq/2003-03-10-jags_x.htm

190. National Public Radio, March 15, 2003.

191. *USA Today,* March 10, 2003, op. cit.

192. 'CNN Effect,' *Investopedia*, http://www.investopedia.com/terms/c/cnneffect.asp

193. U.S. Army General Tom Metz (quoted in *Flat Earth News* by Nick Davies) quoted in: John Mecklin, 'Over the Horizon,' *Miller-McCune*, June-July, 2008, p. 7.

194. Website: http://www.aljazeera.net/english and live online at: http://www.livestation.com/aje

195. Bill Carter, 'With Rivals Ahead, Doubts for CNN's Middle Road,' *New York Times*, April 27, 2009, p. B1.

196. Brian Stelter & Tim Arango, 'Business News With Attitude,' *New York Times*, March 9, 2009, p. B6.

197. Bill Carter, 'A Matrix of News Winners Buoys NBC,' *New York Times*, March 9, 2009, pp. B1 & B6.

198. Andrew Edgecliffe-Johnson, 'CNBC finds profit from a crisis,' *Financial Times*, January 28, 2010, p. 10.

199. Nik Deogun, quoted in: Brian Stelter, 'Market Ills Give CNBC A Bounce,' *The New York Times*, August 15, 2011, p. B1.

200. Andrew Edgecliffe-Johnson, 'Wall St riveted by comedy clash,' *Financial Times*, March 14/15, 2009, p. 1.

201. Clarence Page, 'A mad comic vs. 'Mad Money,'' *Chicago Tribune*, in *The Daily Yomiuri*, March 24, 2009, p. 17.

202. Jon Stewart interview with Charlie Rose, September 29, 2004, http://www.charlierose.com/view/interview/1252

203. Lionel Barber, 'A flawed first draft of history,' *Financial Times*, April 22, 2009, p. 11.

204. Rushworth M. Kidder, 'Second-Hand TV,' *Ethics Newsline*, October 24, 2011, http://www.globalethics.org/newsline/2011/10/24/second-hand-tv/

205. 'Unbiased and unloved,' *The Economist*, September 22, 2012, p. 72.

206. Stefan Stern, 'Snap out of it and smile: Four reasons to be cheerful,' *Financial Times*, April 14, 2009, p. 12.

207. John Lloyd, 'Has satire lost its sting?' *Financial Times*, September 11/12, 2010, Life & Arts, p. 19.

208. Rupert Murdoch, quoted in: Boyd Farrow, 'Control Freakonomics,' *CNBC Business*, March 2012, http://www.cnbcmagazine.com/story/control-freakonomics/1573/1/

209. Robert Jackall, *Moral Mazes*, Oxford University Press, 1988, p. 173.

210. January, 2013, http://www.census.gov/prod/www/religion.htm

211. Carl Bialik, 'Estimates of Religious Populations Require a Bit of Faith,' *The Wall Street Journal*, August 14-15, 2010, p. A2.

212. Bill Symonds, 'The Media Hears the Sermon,' *BusinessWeek*, December 14, 2005, http://www.businessweek.com/bwdaily/dnflash/dec2005/nf20051214_8338_db016.htm

213. Jon Meacham, 'The End of Christian America,' *Newsweek*, April 4, 2009, http://www.newsweek.com/id/192583

214. 'Lift every voice,' *The Economist*, May 4, 2012, p. 29.

215. Daniel Stone, 'One Nation Under God,' *Newsweek*, 2009, http://www.newsweek.com/id/192915

216. 'While shepherds watched,' *The Economist*, December 22, 2012, p. 100.

217. Daniel Stone, 'One Nation Under God,' *Newsweek*, 2009, http://www.newsweek.com/id/192915

218. 'Speak low if you speak God,' *The Economist*, August 4, 2012, p. 59. See also: Hanna Rosin, 'Religious Revival,' *New York Times Book Review*, April 26, 2009, p. 14; Laurie Goodstein, 'More Atheists Are Shouting It From Rooftops,' *New York Times*, April 27, 2009, p. A1; and Charles M. Blow, 'Defecting to Faith,' *New York Times*, May 2, 2009, p. A14.

219. 'God in austerity Britain,' *The Economist*, December 10, 2011, p. 63. See also the book by the British journalist Christopher Hitchins: *God Is Not Great: How Religion Poisons Everything*, Twelve Books, 2007.

220. 'Growing disbelief,' *The Economist*, August 25, 2012, p. 23.

221. David Leonhardt, Alicia Parlapiano & Lisa Waananen, 'A Historical Benchmark,' *The New York Times*, August 14, 2012, p. A9.

222. James Blitz, 'BA under fire over ban on employee's crucifix,' *Financial Times*, October 16, 2006, p. 3.

223. James Blitz, 'BA under fire over ban on employee's crucifix,' *Financial Times*, October 16, 2006, p. 3.

224. 'Veils harm equal rights – Harman,' *BBC News*, October 11, 2006, http://news.bbc .co.uk/2/hi/uk_news/politics/6040016.stm

225. Richard Dawkins, *The God Delusion*, Houghton Mifflin Harcourt, 2006.

226. Sarah Lyall, 'Atheists Decide to Send Their Own Message, on 800 Buses,' *New York Times*, January 7, 2009, p. A6.

227. Images of the bus ads can be seen at: http://www.atheistbus.org.uk/bus-photos/

228. Bill Symonds, 'The Media Hears the Sermon,' *BusinessWeek*, December 14, 2005, http://www.businessweek.com/bwdaily/dnflash/dec2005/nf20051214_8338_db016 .htm

229. Sandeep Kaushik, 'Microsoft Caves on Gay Rights,' *The Stranger*, April 21-April 27, 2005, http://www.thestranger.com/seattle/Content?oid=21105

230. Andrea James, 'Conservative pastor urges buying Microsoft stock to fight its gay rights efforts,' *Seattle Post-Intelligencer*, January 8, 2008, http://www.seattlepi.com/ business/346431_antiochmsft08.html

231. James C. McKinley Jr., 'For Atheist Ads on Buses, Equally Mobile Reaction,' *The New York Times*, December 14, 2010, p. A19.

232. Kevin Maher, 'Ridiculous, ridiculous, don't be so religulous!' *The Times*, in *The Daily Yomiuri*, April 5, 2009, p. 15.

233. Molly Worthen, 'One Nation Under God?' *The New York Times*, December 23, 2012, p. SR1.

234. Molly Worthen, 'One Nation Under God?' *The New York Times*, December 23, 2012, p. SR1.

235. 'Growing disbelief,' *The Economist*, August 25, 2012, p. 23.

236. Laurie Goodstein, 'Study Finds One in 6 Follows No Religion,' *The New York Times*, December 18, 2012, p. A6.

237. Editorial, 'Religion at work,' *Financial Times*, October 17, 2006, p. 12.

238. Devin Stewart, 'Is Ethical Capitalism Possible?' *CSRwire.com*, January 29, 2009, http://www.csrwire.com/PressRelease.php?id=14446

239. The full Charter will be announced in "late 2009," March, 2009, http://charter-forcompassion.com/

240. Craig Sams, 'Sweet industry,' *Financial Times*, November 13/14, 2010, Life & Arts p. 16.

241. Rob Moll, 'Outer Office, Inner Life,' *The Wall Street Journal*, January 20, 2010, p. A15.

242. For additional advice on how to accommodate the religious interests of stakeholders, both internally and externally, see: Simon Webley, 'Multiculturalism: Is your work-place faith-friendly?' *Ethical Corporation Magazine*, April 4, 2011 and 'Speak low if you speak God,' *The Economist*, August 4, 2012, p. 59.

243. Linda Tischler, 'God and Mammon at Harvard,' *Fast Company*, May, 2005, p. 81.

244. Ken Costa, *God at Work: Living Every Day with Purpose*, Continuum Books, 2007.

245. Stefan Stern, 'In the market for a messiah,' *Financial Times*, September 6, 2007, p. 10.

246. Max Colchester, 'British Banks Face Heat From on High,' *The Wall Street Journal*, October 1, 2012, p. C1.

247. Stefan Stern, 'In the market for a messiah,' *Financial Times*, September 6, 2007, p. 10.

248. Rob Moll, 'Doing God's Work—At the Office,' *The Wall Street Journal*, February 11, 2011, p. A11.

249. Rob Wherry, 'Putting Faith in Mutual Funds—Religious Investing Sometimes Offers Saintly Returns,' *The Wall Street Journal*, March 20, 2007, p. D2.

250. Gillian Tett, 'Islamic bonds recruited for purchase of 007's favourite car,' *Financial Times*, March 17, 2007, p. 1.

251. Aryeh Spero, 'What the Bible Teaches About Capitalism,' *The Wall Street Journal*, January 30, 2012, p. A15.

252. 'Prayers and playthings,' *The Economist*, July 14, 2012, p. 54.

253. As a result of this ban, Christians turned to Jews for moneylending services "since they were presumed to be already excommunicated." Gillian Tett, 'Make money, not war,' *Financial Times*, September 23/24, 2006, p. WK2.

254. 'Gold, God and forgiveness,' *The Economist*, December 17, 2011, p. 147.

255. 'Circle 7, cantos 12-17,' *University of Texas at Austin*, http://danteworlds.laits .utexas.edu/circle7.html

256. 'Circle 7, cantos 12-17,' *University of Texas at Austin*, http://danteworlds.laits .utexas.edu/circle7.html

257. 'On the origin of specie,' *The Economist*, August 18, 2012, p. 68.

258. 'On the origin of specie,' *The Economist*, August 18, 2012, p. 68.

259. 'The dangers of demonology,' *The Economist*, January 7, 2012, p. 60.

260. 'Circle 7, cantos 12-17,' *University of Texas at Austin*, http://danteworlds.laits.utexas .edu/circle7.html

261. John Micklethwait & Adrian Wooldridge, 'The Company: A Short History of a Revolutionary Idea,' Modern Library, 2003, p. 8.

262. Niall Ferguson, 'The Ascent of Money,' *BBC*, 2008.

263. Online Etymology Dictionary, January 2013, http://www.etymonline.com/index .php?term=money

264. 'Gold, God and forgiveness,' *The Economist*, December 17, 2011, p. 147.

265. Robyn Blumner, 'Road to ruin: Usury, greed and the paper economy,' *Chicago Tribune*, in *The Daily Yomiuri*, March 31, 2009, p. 16.

266. U.S. Supreme Court, Marquette National Bank of Minneapolis v. First of Omaha Service Corp., 439 U.S. 299 (1978).

267. Robyn Blumner, 'Road to ruin: Usury, greed and the paper economy,' *Chicago Tribune*, in *The Daily Yomiuri*, March 31, 2009, p. 16.

268. See also: Thomas Geoghegan, 'How unlimited interest rates destroyed the economy,' *Harper's Magazine*, April, 2009, http://www.harpers.org/archive/2009/04/0082450

269. Amy Goodman, 'Thomas Geoghegan on "Infinite Debt: How Unlimited Interest Rates Destroyed the Economy"' *Democracy Now*, March 24, 2009, http://www.democracynow.org/2009/3/24/thomas_geoghegan_on_infinite_debt_how

270. January, 2013, http://www.investopedia.com/terms/s/shariah.asp

271. Frederik Balfour, 'Islamic Finance May Be On to Something,' *BusinessWeek*, November 24, 2008, p. 88.

272. Jonathan Schanzer, 'A Nasty Neologism,' *The Wall Street Journal*, January 10, 2013, p. A15.

273. Liz Gooch, 'Malaysia Seeks to Gain Bigger Role in Halal Food,' *The New York Times*, January 1, 2011, p. B6.

274. Yaroslav Trofimov, 'Malaysia Transforms Rules for Finance Under Islam,' *Wall Street Journal*, April 4, 2007, p. A1.

275. For examples of the range of issues covered under the umbrella term "Islamic finance" and get a sense of how the industry has evolved, see the *Financial Times'* series of *Special Report: Islamic Finance*: http://www.ft.com/reports/islamicfinance2008 and http://www.ft.com/reports/islamic-finance-2009

276. Yaroslav Trofimov, 'Malaysia Transforms Rules for Finance Under Islam,' *Wall Street Journal*, April 4, 2007, p. A1.

277. Gillian Tett, 'Banks seek Islamic scholars versed in world of finance,' *Financial Times*, May 20/21, 2006, p. 1.

278. Joanna Slater, 'When Hedge Funds Meet Islamic Finance,' *Wall Street Journal*, August 9, 2007, p. A1.

279. For a detailed explanation of *sukuk*, see: Usman Hayat, 'Islamic finance's sukuk explained,' *Financial Times: FT Monthly Review of the Fund Management Industry*, April 12, 2010, http://www.ft.com/cms/s/0/cec38bf2-440b-11df-9235-00144fe ab49a.html

280. Gillian Tett, 'Secondary trading in Islamic bonds promises earthly riches,' *Financial Times*, July 14, 2006, p. 20.

281. Frederik Balfour, 'Islamic Finance May Be On to Something,' *BusinessWeek*, November 24, 2008, p. 88.

282. January, 2013, http://www.investopedia.com/terms/s/shariah-compliant-funds.asp

283. David Oakley, 'Growth survives the storms,' *Financial Times Special Report: The Future of Islamic Finance*, December 14, 2010, p. 1.

284. Robin Wigglesworth, 'Islamic banks caught between two worlds,' *Financial Times*, April 20, 2010, p. 15.

285. Roula Khalaf & Gillian Tett, 'Backwater sector moves into global mainstream,' *Financial Times, Special Report: Islamic Finance*, May 23, 2007, p. 1.

286. David Oakley, 'Growth survives the storms,' *Financial Times Special Report: The Future of Islamic Finance*, December 14, 2010, p. 2.

287. Farhan Bokhari, Roula Khalaf, & Gillian Tett, 'Booming Gulf gives fillip to Islamic bonds,' *Financial Times*, July 11, 2006, p. 17.

288. Gillian Tett, 'Make money, not war,' *Financial Times*, September 23/24, 2006, p. WK2.

289. Chris Prystay, 'Malaysia Seeks Role as Global Player After Nurturing Islamic Bond Market,' *Wall Street Journal*, August 9, 2006, p. C1.

290. Yaroslav Trofimov, 'Malaysia Transforms Rules for Finance Under Islam,' *The Wall Street Journal*, April 4, 2007, p. A1.

291. 'Banking on the ummah,' *The Economist*, January 5, 2013, p. 60.

292. See: David Oakley, 'Sharia-compliant institutions buck trend,' *Financial Times, Special Report: Middle East Banking & Finance*, November 25, 2008, p. 6; David Oakley, 'Britain leads secondary market for Islamic bonds,' *Financial Times*, February 6, 2007, p. 4; and Gillian Tett, 'UK aims to be global centre of Islamic finance,' *Financial Times*, June 13, 2006, p. 3.

293. 'Finding a Home for Islamic Finance in France,' *Knowledge@Wharton*, November 2, 2010, http://knowledge.wharton.upenn.edu/arabic/article.cfm?articleId=2557

294. 'Finding a Home for Islamic Finance in France,' *Knowledge@Wharton*, November 2, 2010, http://knowledge.wharton.upenn.edu/arabic/article.cfm?articleId=2557

295. 'Finding a Home for Islamic Finance in France,' *Knowledge@Wharton*, November 2, 2010, http://knowledge.wharton.upenn.edu/arabic/article.cfm?articleId=2557

296. Shyamantha Asokan, 'France and the US vie for the UK's crown,' *Financial Times Special Report: Islamic Finance*, May 6, 2009, p. 5.

297. Marc Chandler, 'An Islamic bond would be a golden opportunity for the US,' *Financial Times*, November 20, 2006, p. 13.

298. Gillian Tett, 'Make money, not war,' *Financial Times*, September 23/24, 2006, pp. WK1-2.

299. Hugh Pope, 'Islamic Banking Grows, With All Sorts of Rules,' *Wall Street Journal*, May 3, 2005, p. C1.

300. http://www.ftse.com/shariah

301. April, 2009, http://www.ftse.com/shariah

302. Samuel G. Freedman, 'A Hometown Bank Heeds a Call to Serve Its Islamic Clients,' *New York Times*, March 7, 2009, p. A9.

303. Farhan Bokhari, 'Dubai's facility keeps the faith,' *Financial Times*, April 16, 2007, p. 7.

304. Shyamantha Asokan, 'New class for Islamic finance,' *Financial Times*, January 19, 2009, p. 9.

305. Farhan Bokhari, 'Oil wealth paves way for Islamic MBA,' *Financial Times*, December 18, 2006, p. 10.

306. See: Faiza Saleh Ambah, 'Islamic Banking: Steady in Shaky Times,' *The Washington Post*, October 31, 2008, p. A16 and John Aglionby, 'Islamic banks urged to show west the sharia was forward,' *Financial Times*, March 3, 2009, p. 3.

307. Robin Wigglesworth, 'Islamic banks caught between two worlds,' *Financial Times*, April 20, 2010, p. 15.

308. For an example of how Islamic finance seeks to extend the range of *Sharia*-compliant instruments, see: Sophia Grene, 'Moves afoot to plug gap in Islamic finance,' *Financial Times FTfm*, August 3, 2009, p. 3.

309. Tarek El Diwany, 'How the banks are subverting Islam's ban on usury,' *Financial Times*, July 14, 2006, p. 11.

310. Andrew Ross Sorkin, 'A Financial Mirage In the Desert,' *The New York Times*, December 1, 2009, p. B1.

311. Tarek El Diwany, 'How the banks are subverting Islam's ban on usury,' *Financial Times*, July 14, 2006, p. 11.

312. For more information on Dan Cathy's controversial statements about his operating principles at Chick-fil-A, see: 'In Chick-fil-A, Parties Feast on Fast Feud,' *The Wall Street Journal*, August 4-5, 2012, p. A4; William McGurn, 'The Chick-fil-A War Is Back On,' *The Wall Street Journal*, September 25, 2012, p. A17; and W.W., 'Feathers flying,' *The Economist*, August 7, 2012, http://www.economist.com/blogs/democracy inamerica/2012/08/conscientious-consumption-and-culture-war

313. Dan Cathy. Quoted in: K. Allan Blume, "Guilty as charged,' Cathy says of Chick-fil-A's stand on biblical & family values,' *Baptist Press*, July 16, 2012, http://www .bpnews.net/bpnews.asp?id=38271

314. Bill Baue, 'Brundtland Report celebrates 20th anniversary since coining sustainable development, *Ethical Corporation*, June 18, 2007, http://www.ethicalcorp.com/ content.asp?ContentID=5175

315. Michael Hopkins, 'Sustainable development: From word to policy,' *openDemocracy*, April 11, 2007, http://www.opendemocracy.net/globalization-institutions_ government/sustainable_word_4515.jsp

316. *BizEthics Buzz,* December 2002. *BizEthics Buzz* is an online news report from *Business Ethics Magazine*.

317. *BizEthics Buzz,* December 2002. *BizEthics Buzz* is an online news report from *Business Ethics Magazine*.

318. For an in-depth discussion of this issue, see: Oliver Balch, 'Carbon accounting – Emissions disclosure stacking up,' *Ethical Corporation*, July 21, 2009, http://www .ethicalcorp.com/content.asp?ContentID=6540

319. 'PepsiCo and Carbon Trust Announce Groundbreaking Agreement and Certify Carbon Footprint of Tropicana,' *CSRwire.com*, PepsiCo Press Release, January 22, 2009, http://www.csrwire.com/News/14362.html

320. Andrew Martin, 'How Green Is My Orange?' *New York Times*, January 22, 2009, p. B1.

321. Fiona Harvey, 'Food footprints coming soon to a label near you,' *Financial Times*, *Special Report: Sustainable Business*, October 12, 2007, p. 4.

322. 'Environmental Leaders: Green beacons burning bright,' *Ethical Corporation*, September 3, 2009, http://www.ethicalcorp.com/content.asp?ContentID=6576

323. Marc Gunther, 'Money and Morals at GE,' *Fortune Magazine*, November 15, 2004, p. 178.

324. Sarah Murray, 'The products that never say die,' *Financial Times*, September 18, 2007, p. 12.

325. Carleen Hawn, 'Can't Buy Me Love,' *Fast Company*, December 2007/January 2008, pp. 60-62 and Mark Landler, 'Garden Is a Seedbed For Green Cosmetics,' *New York Times*, June 28, 2008, p. B3.

326. See Chapter 3.

327. Alan G. Robinson & Dean M. Schroeder, 'Greener and Cheaper,' *Wall Street Journal*, March 23, 2009, p. R4.

328. Daniel Vermeer & Robert Clemen, 'Why sustainability is still going strong,' *Financial Times, Managing in a Downturn Part IV: Sustainable Business*, February 13, 2009, p. 4.

329. John Bradburn, '10 things General Motors learned about going landfill-free,' *GreenBiz.com*, November 16, 2012, http://www.greenbiz.com/blog/2012/11/16/10-things-general-motors-learned-about-going-landfill-free

330. 'The next big bet,' *The Economist*, October 1, 2011, p. 75.

331. Mallen Baker, 'World's largest companies taking action on climate change,' *mallenbaker.net*, October 2011, http://www.mallenbaker.net/csr/page.php?Story_ID=2696

332. 'Environmental Reporting More than Doubles,' *Environmental Leader*, December 18, 2012, http://www.environmentalleader.com/2012/12/18/environmental-reporting-more-than-doubles/

333. 'Beyond The Green Corporation,' *BusinessWeek*, Cover Story, January 29, 2007, http://www.businessweek.com/magazine/content/07_05/b4019001.htm

334. Ram Nidumolu, C.K. Prahalad, & M.R. Rangaswami, 'Why Sustainability is Now the Key Driver of Innovation,' *Harvard Business Review*, September, 2009, p. 57.

335. Padma Nagappan, 'Carpet giant Interface shares pointers on being a green innovator,' *GreenBiz.com*, September 6, 2012, http://www.greenbiz.com/blog/2012/09/06/interface-shares-pointers-green-innovator

336. 'Interface Pioneers Plant-Based Carpeting,' *SustainableBusiness.com*, September 18, 2012, http://www.sustainablebusiness.com/index.cfm/go/news.display/id/24088

337. 'Ray Anderson,' *The Economist*, September 10, 2011, p. 99.

338. Paul Vitello, 'Ray Anderson, a Carpet Innovator, Dies at 77,' *The New York Times*, August 11, 2011, p. B17.

339. 'No sweat,' *The Economist*, January 5, 2013, p. 45.

340. David Leonhardt, 'There's Still Hope for the Planet,' *The New York Times*, July 22, 2012, p. SR1.

341. Justin Gillis, 'Global Temperatures Highest in 4,000 Years,' *The New York Times*, March 8, 2013, p. A15.

342. 'Boundary conditions,' *The Economist*, June 16, 2012, p. 87.

343. Thomas L. Friedman, 'The Earth Is Full,' *The New York Times*, June 8, 2011, p. A21.

344. For more detail about Marks & Spencer's Plan A and its value for the firm, see David E. Bell, Nitin Sanghavi, & Laura Winig, 'Marks and Spencer: Plan A, *Harvard Business School* [Case # 9-509-029], January 5, 2009.

345. http://plana.marksandspencer.com/about/

346. Simon Bowers, 'M&S promises radical change with £200m environmental action plan,' *The Guardian*, January 15, 2007, http://www.guardian.co.uk/business/2007/jan/15/marksspencer.retail

347. Simon Bowers, 'M&S promises radical change with £200m environmental action plan,' *The Guardian*, January 15, 2007, http://www.guardian.co.uk/business/2007/jan/15/marksspencer.retail

348. Michael Skapinker, 'Why corporate responsibility is a survivor,' *Financial Times*, April 21, 2009, p. 11.

349. EC Newsdesk, 'Marks and Spencer – A-grade progress,' *Ethical Corporation,* March 2, 2009, http://www.ethicalcorp.com/content.asp?ContentID=6363

350. Rob Bailes, 'Sustainability Commercialized: Marks & Spencer – Helping Suppliers Get With The Plan,' *Ethical Corporation Magazine,* September 5, 2012, http://www.ethicalcorp.com/business-strategy/sustainability-commercialised-marks-spencer-helping-suppliers-get-plan

351. Rob Bailes, 'Sustainability Commercialized: Marks & Spencer – Helping Suppliers Get With The Plan,' *Ethical Corporation Magazine,* September 5, 2012, http://www.ethicalcorp.com/business-strategy/sustainability-commercialised-marks-spencer-helping-suppliers-get-plan

352. Rob Bailes, 'Sustainability Commercialized: Marks & Spencer – Helping Suppliers Get With The Plan,' *Ethical Corporation Magazine,* September 5, 2012, http://www.ethicalcorp.com/business-strategy/sustainability-commercialised-marks-spencer-helping-suppliers-get-plan

353. Knut Haanaes, David Michael, Jeremy Jurgens & Subramanian Rangan, 'Making Sustainability Profitable,' *Harvard Business Review*, March 2013, p. 115.

354. James Hansen, 'Game Over for the Climate,' *The New York Times*, May 9, 2013, p. A25.

355. Al Gore & David Blood, 'For People and Planet,' *The Wall Street Journal*, March 28, 2006, p. A20.

356. 'Made to Break: Are we Sinking under the Weight of our Disposable Society?' *Knowledge@Wharton*, August 9, 2006, http://knowledge.wharton.upenn.edu/article.cfm?articleid=1536

357. 'Talking trash,' *The Economist Technology Quarterly*, June 2, 2012, p. 12.

358. Julie Makinen, 'Moooncakes' unwelcome hangover,' *Los Angeles Times* in *The Daily Yomiuri*, October 16, 2012, p. 12.

359. Edward Humes, 'Grappling With a Garbage Glut,' *The Wall Street Journal*, April 14-15, 2012, p. C3.

360. Edward Humes, 'Grappling With a Garbage Glut,' *The Wall Street Journal*, April 14-15, 2012, p. C3.

361. Andrew Martin, 'One Country's Table Scraps, Another Country's Meal,' *The New York Times*, May 18, 2008, p. A3.

362. Fiona Harvey, ''Our guilty secret,' *Financial Times*, July 18/19, 2009, Life & Arts, p14.

363. Bill Briggs, 'Americans throw away 40 percent of their food: Study,' *NBC News*, August 23, 2012, http://www.nbcnews.com/business/americans-throw-away-40-percent-their-food-study-959078

364. Sarah Nassauer, 'Leftovers: Tasty or Trash?' *The Wall Street Journal*, March 21, 2012, p. D1.

365. Beth Daley, 'Old Equipment Gets New Chance to Pollute,' *The Boston Globe*, August 19, 2007; reported in the *Wall Street Journal*, August 20, 2007, p. B7.

366. Edward Humes, 'Grappling With a Garbage Glut,' *The Wall Street Journal*, April 14-15, 2012, p. C3.

367. Jodie Allen, 'America's Biggest Trade Export to China? Trash,' *U.S. News*, March 3, 2010, http://www.usnews.com/opinion/blogs/jodie-allen/2010/03/03/americas-biggest-trade-export-to-china-trash

368. See: 'A cadmium lining,' *The Economist*, January 26, 2013, p56 and 'What to Do With All Those Old PCs,' *Bloomberg Businessweek*, January 2, 2013, http://www.bloomberg.com/video/ceo-tech-what-to-do-with-all-those-old-pc-s-4nG80QnOS1Kh9HBvUg9ElA.html

369. See: http://www.greenpeace.org/international/en/campaigns/toxics/electronics/

370. William McDonough & Michael Braungart, 'The NEXT Industrial Revolution,' *The Atlantic Monthly*, October 1998, p. 88.

371. Sarah Finnie Robinson, 'Got iPhone5 Fever? Here's how to recycle your old phone,' *practicallygreen*, September 13, 2012, http://blog.practicallygreen.com/2012/09/got-iphone5-fever-heres-how-to-recycle-your-old-phone/

372. Sarah Finnie Robinson, 'Got iPhone5 Fever? Here's how to recycle your old phone,' *practicallygreen*, September 13, 2012, http://blog.practicallygreen.com/2012/09/got-iphone5-fever-heres-how-to-recycle-your-old-phone/

373. Leslie Kaufman, 'New Laws Offer a Green Way To Dump Low-Tech Electronics,' *The New York Times*, June 30, 2009, p. A1.

374. Sarah Finnie Robinson, 'Got iPhone5 Fever? Here's how to recycle your old phone,' *practicallygreen*, September 13, 2012, http://blog.practicallygreen.com/2012/09/got-iphone5-fever-heres-how-to-recycle-your-old-phone/

375. EPA data, quoted in: 'Fact and Figures on E-Waste and Recycling,' *Electronics TakeBack Coalition*, February 21, 2012, pp. 2-3.

376. 'What to Do With All Those Old PCs,' *Bloomberg Businessweek*, January 2, 2013, http://www.bloomberg.com/video/ceo-tech-what-to-do-with-all-those-old-pc-s-4nG80QnOS1Kh9HBvUg9ElA.html

377. Press Release, 'Basel Conference Addresses Electronic Wastes Challenge,' *United Nations Environment Programme (UNEP)*, November 27, 2006, http://www.unep.org/Documents.Multilingual/Default.asp?DocumentID=485&ArticleID=5431&l=en

378. Laurie J. Flynn, 'A State Says Makers Must Pay for Recycling PCs and TVs,' *The New York Times*, March 25, 2006, p. B2.

379. Melanie Warner, 'Green Business: Plastic Potion No. 9,' *Fast Company*, Issue 128, September 2008, p. 103.

380. 'The Wasteland,' *CBS News: 60 Minutes*, August 30, 2009.

381. David Murphy, 'Toxic town,' *South China Morning Post*, June 7, 2005, p. A16.

382. 'A cadmium lining,' *The Economist*, January 26, 2013, p56.

383. David Murphy, 'Toxic town,' *South China Morning Post*, June 7, 2005, p. A16.

384. Fiona Harvey, 'Reduction should be the target,' *Financial Times*, *Special Report: Waste and the Environment*, April 18, 2007, p. 1.

385. Laurie J. Flynn, 'A State Says Makers Must Pay for Recycling PCs and TVs,' *The New York Times*, March 25, 2006, p. B2.

386. Leslie Kaufman, 'New Laws Offer a Green Way To Dump Low-Tech Electronics,' *The New York Times*, June 30, 2009, p. A1.

387. Robert Tomsho, 'Currents: Kicking the Cans: Plymouth, Mass., Wrestles With 'Pay-As-You-Throw' Trash Fees,' *The Wall Street Journal*, July 29, 2008, p. A12.

388. Leslie Kaufman, 'Nudging Recycling From Less Waste to None,' *The New York Times*, October 20, 2009, p. A1.

389. David Ferry, 'The Urban Quest for 'Zero' Waste,' *The Wall Street Journal Report: Environment*, September 12, 2011, p. R7.

390. William Yardley, 'Cities Get So Close To Recycling Ideal, They Can Smell It,' *The New York Times*, June 28, 2012, p. A14.

391. Robert Tomsho, 'Currents: Kicking the Cans: Plymouth, Mass., Wrestles With 'Pay-As-You-Throw' Trash Fees,' *The Wall Street Journal*, July 29, 2008, p. A12.

392. Philip Stevens, 'Global warming: The way not to mobilize the masses,' *Financial Times*, December 12, 2008, p. 9.

393. Zara Maung, 'Tesco's low carbon supermarket: A new way forward?' *Ethical Corporation*, January 21, 2009, http://www.ethicalcorp.com/content.asp?ContentID=6296

394. Philip Stevens, 'Global warming: The way not to mobilize the masses,' *Financial Times*, December 12, 2008, p. 9.

395. For an overview of the scope of TerraCycle's work and an indication of why their business model is successful, see: Tom Szaky (founder and CEO of TerraCycle), 'Eliminating the Idea of Waste,' 2012, http://blog.lohas.com/blog/lohas-trends/eliminating-the-idea-of-waste

396. See Issue: CSR Compliance.

397. Stephanie Rosenbloom, 'Wal-Mart to Toughen Standards,' *The New York Times*, October 22, 2008, http://www.nytimes.com/2008/10/22/business/22walmart.html

398. 'The Wasteland,' *CBS News: 60 Minutes*, August 30, 2009.

399. Editorial, 'Corporate responsibility in modern times,' *Ethical Corporation Magazine*, December, 2005, p. 8.

400. See also: http://strategiccsr-sage.blogspot.com/2012/01/strategic-csr-csr-vs-ethics.html

401. Ken Goodman, 'The ethics of right and wrong,' *The Miami Herald*, March 14, 2004, p. 3L.

402. Gwendolyn Bounds, 'Misleading Claims On 'Green' Labeling,' *The Wall Street Journal*, October 26, 2010, p. D4.

403. Michael J. de la Merced & Evelyn M. Rusli, 'Again Yahoo Loses Chief, This Time In a Scandal,' *The New York Times*, May 14, 2012, pB1 and Amir Efrati & Joann S. Lublin, 'Resume Trips Up Yahoo's Chief,' *The Wall Street Journal*, May 5-6, 2012, p. A1.

404. Brian M. Carney, 'Unraveling the Mystery of Murderous Minds,' *The Wall Street Journal*, 2 August 2011, p. A11.

405. Patrick M. Lencioni, 'Make Your Values Mean Something,' *Harvard Business Review*, Vol. 80, No. 7, July 2002, pp. 113–117.

406. Joel Bakan, 'The Corporation: The Pathological Pursuit of Profit and Power,' Free Press, 2004. Quoted in *Business Ethics Magazine,* Spring 2004, p. 6.

407. 'The Next Step for CSR: Economic Democracy,' *Business Ethics Magazine,* Cover Story, Summer 2002, p. 10.

408. Memorandum from Kenneth Lay to all employees, Subject: Code of Ethics, July 1, 2000.

409. Enron Corp.'s 'Code of Ethics,' p. 5.

410. Enron Corp.'s 'Code of Ethics,' p. 5.

411. Enron Corp.'s 'Code of Ethics,' p. 12.

412. Steven M. Davidoff, 'In Insider and Enron Cases, Balancing Lies and Thievery,' *The New York Times*, June 20, 2012, p. B7.

413. See: Martin Sandbu, 'Business ethics courses skirt main question,' *Financial Times,* May 2, 2011, p. 10 and 'Is it possible to teach ethics to business school students?' *Financial Times*, October 28, 2009, p. 10.

414. 'A tissue of lies,' *The Economist*, June 9, 2012, p. 75.

415. Melissa Korn, 'B-School Mixes Faith, Finance,' *The Wall Street Journal*, January 8, 2013, p. B9.

416. MBA Oath website, January 2013, http://mbaoath.org/

417. http://mbaoath.org/take-the-oath/

418. Alina Tugend, 'Doing the Ethical Thing May Be Right, But It Isn't Automatic,' *The New York Times*, November 19, 2011, p. B5.

419. Max H. Bazerman & Ann E. Tenbrunsel, 'Stumbling Into Bad Behavior,' *The New York Times*, April 21, 2011, p. A21.

420. Judith Samuelson & Bill Birchard, 'The Voice of the Stakeholder,' *strategy+society*, Issue 32, p. 8.

421. For a detailed history of Ben & Jerry's, see: James E. Austin & James Quinn, 'Ben & Jerry's: Preserving Mission and Brand within Unilever,' *Harvard Business School* [Case # 9-306-037], December 8, 2005.

422. Alice & John Tepper Marlin, 'A Brief History of Social Reporting,' *Ethical Corporation,* March 10, 2003, http://www.ethicalcorp.com/content.asp?ContentID=430

423. Ben & Jerry's website, January 2013, http://www.benjerry.com/activism/mission-statement/

424. Axtman & Scherer, op. cit., http://www.csmonitor.com/2002/0204/p01s01-ussc.html

425. Ann Zimmerman, 'Costco's Dilemma: Be Kind to Its Workers, or Wall Street?' *Wall Street Journal,* March 26, 2004, p. B1.

426. James E. Austin & James Quinn, 'Ben & Jerry's: Preserving Mission and Brand within Unilever,' *Harvard Business School* [Case # 9-306-037], December 8, 2005, p. 2.

427. 'Ben & Jerry's takes a licking,' *Eurofood*, February 3, 2000, http://findarticles.com/p/articles/mi_m0DQA/is_2000_Feb_3/ai_59544165/

428. James E. Austin & James Quinn, 'Ben & Jerry's: Preserving Mission and Brand within Unilever,' *Harvard Business School* [Case # 9-306-037], December 8, 2005, p. 5.

429. 'Unilever Scoops Up Ben & Jerry's,' BBC News, April 12, 2000, http://news.bbc
.co.uk/1/hi/business/710694.stm

430. Today, other firms have similar total compensation ratio limits in place, such as
Whole Foods Market, which has a 19:1 ratio between its *highest* and *average* paid
employees (Leslie Kwoh, 'Firms Resist New Pay-Equity Rules,' *The Wall Street
Journal*, June 27, 2012, p. B8) and the Swiss knife company, Victorinox, which as a
ratio of 5:1 between its *highest* and *average* paid employees ('How to cope with a
slump in demand,' *Financial Times*, December 23, 2010, p. 10).

431. September, 2009, http://www.benjerry.com/activism/mission-statement/

432. Stephen Moore, 'Ice Cream Hangover,' *Wall Street Journal*, October 20, 2005,
p. A15.

433. Stephen Moore, 'Ice Cream Hangover,' *Wall Street Journal*, October 20, 2005,
p. A15.

434. Ben & Jerry's website, January 2013, http://www.benjerry.com/activism/mission-
statement/

435. Ben & Jerry's website, January 2013, http://www.benjerry.com/activism/mission-
statement/

436. James E. Austin & James Quinn, 'Ben & Jerry's: Preserving Mission and Brand
within Unilever,' *Harvard Business School* [Case # 9-306-037], December 8, 2005,
p. 9.

437. Louise Lucas, 'Preserve your unique flavor,' *Financial Times*, February 8, 2011,
p. 12.

438. See: http://strategiccsr-sage.blogspot.com/2011/03/strategic-csr-unilever.html

439. Venessa Wong, 'Ben & Jerry's Cohen Repos Occupy Wall Street's 'Batmobile','
Bloomberg Businessweek, October 2, 2012, http://www.businessweek.com/
articles/2012-10-02/ben-and-jerry-repo-their-occupy-wall-street-batmobile

440. Louise Lucas, 'Preserve your unique flavor,' *Financial Times*, February 8, 2011,
p. 12.

441. 'Ben & Jerry's Joins the Growing B Corporation Movement,' *CSRWire.com*,
October 22, 2012, http://www.csrwire.com/press_releases/34773-Ben-Jerry-s-Joins-
the-Growing-B-Corporation-Movement-

442. For additional insight and commentary on each of the social sins, see this extract
from Steven Covey's book *Principle Centered Leadership*: http://www.mkgandhi
.org/mgmnt.htm

443. See also: 'The Rio Declaration on the Contribution of Higher Education Institutions and
Management Schools to *The Future We Want*: A Roadmap for Management Education
to 2020,' http://www.unprme.org/resource-docs/3rdPRMEGFRioDeclaration.pdf

COMPANY INDEX

SUBJECT INDEX

Page references followed by (figure) indicate an illustrated figure.

ABOUT THE AUTHORS

David Chandler is Assistant Professor of Management and Co-Director of the Managing for Sustainability Program at the University of Colorado Denver (david.chandler@ucdenver.edu). His broad area of research interest lies at the dynamic interface between the organization and its institutional environment. He is also interested in the relationship between institutions and values, and how firm actions reflect values that sustain meaningful institutions. Empirically, he focuses on studying organizations within the context of corporate social responsibility, business ethics, and firm/stakeholder relations. He received his Ph.D. in Management from the University of Texas at Austin.

Since graduating in 1991 with an undergraduate degree in 'American Studies: Politics and Government' (University of Kent, UK), David has divided his time between the United States, the UK, and Japan, working in the fields of business, politics, and education. In addition to his Ph.D., David has an M.Sc. in East Asian Business from the University of Sheffield, UK, an MBA from the University of Miami, FL, and an M.S. in Management from the University of Texas at Austin.

William B. Werther Jr. is Professor of Management at the University of Miami's School of Business Administration (werther@miami.edu). Additionally, he is a Fellow and former Chair of the International Society for Productivity and Quality Research, a Fellow in the World Academy of Productivity Science, and former Chair for the Managerial Consultation Division of the Academy of Management. His teaching and research focus on strategy with its implications for human performance and corporate social responsibility.

He is an award-winning author and teacher. In addition to more than 100 professional articles, his publications include *Third Sector Management* (Georgetown University Press, 2001), *Human Resources and Personnel Management 5/E*

(McGraw-Hill, 1996), and other books translated into more than a half-dozen languages. He earned a Ph.D. (University of Florida, 1971) in Economics and Business Administration (Phi Beta Kappa). Prior to joining the faculty at the University of Miami in 1985, he was a Professor of Management at Arizona State University for 14 years.

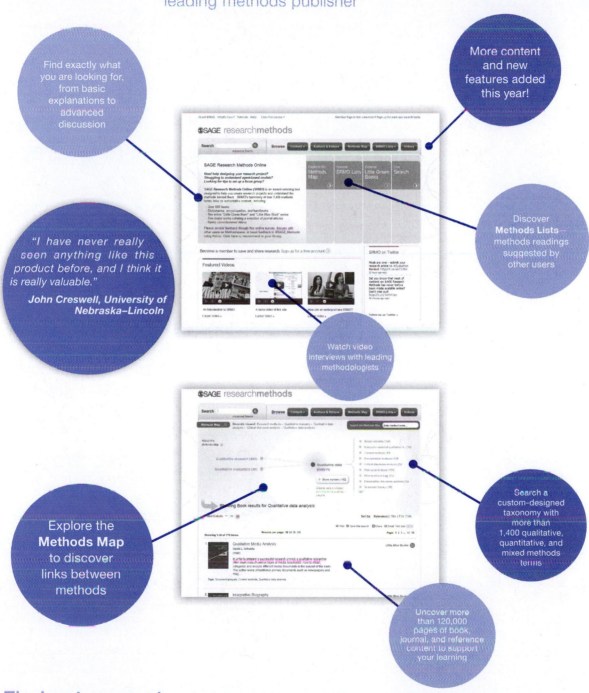

⑨SAGE researchmethods

The essential online tool for researchers from the world's leading methods publisher

Find exactly what you are looking for, from basic explanations to advanced discussion

More content and new features added this year!

"I have never really seen anything like this product before, and I think it is really valuable."

John Creswell, University of Nebraska–Lincoln

Discover **Methods Lists**—methods readings suggested by other users

Watch video interviews with leading methodologists

Explore the **Methods Map** to discover links between methods

Search a custom-designed taxonomy with more than 1,400 qualitative, quantitative, and mixed methods terms

Uncover more than 120,000 pages of book, journal, and reference content to support your learning

Find out more at
www.sageresearchmethods.com